January 17–20, 2015
Aberystwyth, UK

Association for
Computing Machinery

Advancing Computing as a Science & Profession

FOGA'15

Proceedings of the 2015 ACM Conference on
Foundations of Genetic Algorithms XIII

Sponsored by:
ACM SIGEVO

Supported by:
Aberystwyth University

Association for
Computing Machinery

Advancing Computing as a Science & Profession

The Association for Computing Machinery
2 Penn Plaza, Suite 701
New York, New York 10121-0701

ISBN: 978-1-4503-3434-1

Additional copies may be ordered prepaid from:

ACM Order Department
PO Box 30777
New York, NY 10087-0777, USA

Phone: 1-800-342-6626 (USA and Canada)
+1-212-626-0500 (Global)
Fax: +1-212-944-1318
E-mail: acmhelp@acm.org
Hours of Operation: 8:30 am – 4:30 pm ET

ACM Order No: 910154

Printed in the USA

Foreword

FOGA, the ACM SIGEVO Workshop on Foundations of Genetic Algorithms, started in 1990 and has, in the past 25 years, established itself as the premier event in the theory of all kinds of randomized search heuristics. Its latest installment, the 13th of its kind, is no exception.

FOGA 2015 is special not only because of the quarter of a century anniversary but also because it is the first FOGA to take place in the United Kingdom. Four organizers from all parts of Great Britain joined forces to bring the event to Aberystwyth in Wales. We had 27 participants from seven countries from four continents of the world. They brought with them 16 presentations for accepted papers, carefully selected from 26 submissions. An hour was allocated for each of the presentations to allow ample time to discuss ideas and inspect details. Following the FOGA tradition all papers have undergone another round of reviewing and rewriting after being presented and passionately discussed at the workshop. This ensures that what you find in these post-proceedings is the best and best polished current research in the field.

The presented papers cover many topics of current research in theory of evolutionary algorithms and other randomized search heuristics. This includes discussion of their limits and potentials, either from the perspective of black-box complexity (Golnaz Badkobeh, Per Kristian Lehre, Dirk Sudholt: *Black-box complexity of parallel search with distributed populations*; Thomas Jansen: *On the black-box complexity of example functions: the real jump function*) or from the perspective of adversarial optimization (Alan Lockett: *Insights from adversarial fitness functions*). A very important aspect of current research are investigations of the performance of specific evolutionary algorithms on specific problems or problem classes. Such work includes further investigations of the very well-known and simple (1+1) evolutionary algorithm (Timo Kötzing, Andrei Lissovoi, Carsten Witt: *(1+1) EA on generalized dynamic OneMax*; Johannes Lengler, Nick Spooner: *Fixed budget performance of the (1+1) EA on linear functions*), studies of the performance of evolutionary algorithms when confronted with noisy problems (Duc-Cuong Dang, Per-Kristian Lehre: *Efficient optimization of noisy fitness functions with population-based evolutionary algorithms*; Adam Prügel-Bennett, Jonathan Rowe, Jonathan Shapiro: *Run-time analysis of population-based algorithms in noisy environments*; Sandra Astete-Morales, Marie-Liesse Cauwet, Olivier Teytaud: *Evolution strategies with additive noise: a convergence rate lower bound*), studies of parallel evolutionary algorithms (Eric Scott, Kenneth De Jong: *Understanding simple asynchronous evolutionary algorithms*; Marie-Liesse Cauwet, Shih-Yuan Chiu, Kuo-Min Lin, David Saint-Pierre, Fabien Teytaud, Olivier Teytaud, Shi-Jim Yen: *Parallel evolutionary algorithms performing pairwise comparisons*) and studies concerned with improving the performance of evolutionary algorithms in applications (Mathys C. Du Plessis, Andries Engelbrecht, Andre Calitz: *Self-adapting the Brownian radius in a differential evolution algorithm for dynamic environments*; Oswin Krause, Christian Igel: *A more efficient rank-one covariance matrix update for evolution strategies*; Renato Tinos, Darrell Whitley, Francisco Chicano: *Partition crossover for pseudo-Boolean optimization*). FOGA also remains the best place to present fundamental observations about the way evolutionary algorithms work (Luigi Malagò, Giovanni Pistone: *Information geometry of the Gaussian distribution in view of stochastic optimization*; Keki Burjorjee: *Hypomixability elimination in evolutionary systems*) as well as studies of other complex systems like co-adapting agents (Richard Mealing, Jonathan Shapiro: *Convergence of strategies in simple co-adapting games*). We are confident that every reader with an interest in theory of randomized search heuristics will find something that he or she finds interesting, challenging and inspiring.

The National Library of Wales in Aberystwyth provided a splendid setting not only for the talks presenting the accepted submissions but also for our invited talk, presented by Professor Leslie Ann Goldberg from the University of Oxford, who gave an inspiring overview of evolutionary dynamics in graphs in the form of the Moran process. On Sunday, when the National Library is closed, the Department of Computer Science of Aberystwyth University kindly donated a seminar room and we are thankful for the support.

We are thankful to be given the opportunity of being the hosts of FOGA 2015. We owe thanks to all people who helped us "behind the scenes" in so many different ways at SIGEVO, ACM, Sheridan and the Department of Computer Science at Aberystwyth University. Most importantly, we are tremendously thankful to all the participants who helped make FOGA 2015 a success by engaging in scientific discourse. We hope to see you again at FOGA 2017!

Jun He
Aberystwyth University
Wales, UK

Thomas Jansen
Aberystwyth University
Wales, UK

Gabriela Ochoa
University of Stirling
Scotland, UK

Christine Zarges
University of Birmingham
England, UK

Table of Contents

ACM SIGEVO 2015 Foundations of Genetic Algorithms XIII (FOGA 2015)

Organizers: Jun He *(Aberystwyth University, UK)*
Thomas Jansen *(Aberystwyth University, UK)*
Gabriela Ochoa *(University of Stirling, UK)*
Christine Zarges *(University of Birmingham, UK)*

Program Committee: Youhei Akimoto *(Shinshu University, Japan)*
Anne Auger *(Inria Saclay, France)*
Hans-Georg Beyer *(Vorarlberg University of Applied Sciences, Austria)*
Juergen Branke *(University of Warwick, UK)*
Dimo Brockhoff *(Inria Lille, France)*
Keki Burjorjee *(Pandora Media Inc., USA)*
Duc-Cuong Dang *(University of Nottingham, UK)*
Kenneth De Jong *(George Mason University, USA)*
Benjamin Doerr *(École Polytechnique de Paris, France)*
Carola Doerr *(Université Pierre et Marie Curie, France)*
Christian Giessen *(Technical University of Denmark, Denmark)*
Tobias Glasmachers *(Ruhr-Universität Bochum, Germany)*
Walter Gutjahr *(University of Vienna, Austria)*
Jeffrey Horn *(Northern Michigan University, USA)*
Bin Hu *(Vienna University of Technology, Austria)*
Timo Kötzing *(Friedrich-Schiller-Universität Jena, Germany)*
Per Kristian Lehre *(University of Nottingham, UK)*
Andrei Lissovoi *(Technical University of Denmark, Denmark)*
Alan Locket *(Dalle Molle Institute for Artificial Intelligence Studies, Switzerland)*
Andrea Mambrini *(University of Birmingham, UK)*
Alberto Moraglio *(University of Exeter, UK)*
Frank Neumann *(University of Adelaide, Australia)*
Pietro S. Oliveto *(University of Sheffield, UK)*
Elena Popovici *(Icosystem Corp., USA)*
Mike Preuss *(Universität Münster, Germany)*
Jonathan Rowe *(University of Birmingham, UK)*
Günter Rudolph *(TU Dortmund, Germany)*
Manuel Schmitt *(University of Erlangen-Nuremberg, Germany)*
Dirk Sudholt *(University of Sheffield, UK)*
Andrew Sutton *(Friedrich-Schiller-Universität Jena, Germany)*
Olivier Teytaud *(Inria Saclay, France)*

Program Committee (continued):

Markus Wagner *(University of Adelaide, Australia)*
Karsten Weicker *(Leipzig University of Applied Sciences, Germany)*
R. Paul Wiegand *(University of Central Florida, USA)*
Carsten Witt *(Technical University of Denmark, Denmark)*
Yang Yu *(Nanjing University, China)*
Daniela Zaharie *(West University of Timisoara, Romania)*
Zhi-Hua Zhou *(Nanjing University, China)*

Additional Reviewer: Chao Qian *(Nanjing University, China)*

Sponsor:

sigevo

ACM Special Interest Group for
Genetic and Evolutionary Computation

Supporters:

PRIFYSGOL
ABERYSTWYTH
UNIVERSITY

Department of Computer Science

Evolutionary Dynamics on Graphs *

[Invited Talk]

Leslie Ann Goldberg
Department of Computer Science
University of Oxford
Wolfson Building, Parks Road, Oxford, OX1 3QD, UK

Categories and Subject Descriptors

F.2 [**Theory of Computation**]: Analysis of Algorithms and Problem Complexity; G.3 [**Mathematics of Computing**]: Probability and Statistics

General Terms

Moran process, fixation probability, absorption time

1. ABSTRACT

The Moran process [5], as adapted by Lieberman, Hauert and Nowak [4], is a discrete-time random process which models the spread of genetic mutations through populations. Individuals are modelled as the vertices of a graph. Each vertex is either *infected* or *uninfected*. The model has a parameter $r > 0$. Infected vertices have fitness r and uninfected vertices have fitness 1. At each step, an individual is selected to reproduce with probability proportional to its fitness. This vertex chooses one of its neighbours uniformly at random and updates the state of that neighbour (infected or not) to match its own. In the initial state, one vertex is chosen uniformly at random to be infected and the other vertices are uninfected. If the graph is strongly connected then the process will terminate with probability 1, either in the state where every vertex is infected (known as *fixation*) or in the state where no vertex is infected (known as *extinction*).

The principal quantities of interest are the *fixation probability* (the probability of reaching fixation) and the expected *absorption time* (the expected number of steps before fixation or extinction is reached). In general, these depend on both the graph topology and the parameter r. We study three questions.

1. What is the fixation probability of a graph? (We are interested in exact calculations, and on upper and lower bounds for classes of graphs.)
2. What is the expected absorption time?
3. What is the complexity of computing (or approximately computing) the fixation probability, given a graph. (The fixation probability can be computed exactly by solving a system of 2^n linear equations, but we are interested in more efficient solutions.)

This talk is a survey, describing what is known about these questions. The talk is based on the papers [1], [2] and [3] which are joint work with Díaz, Mertzios, Richerby, Serna and Spirakis, and on the words cited in these papers.

FOGA'15, January 17–20, 2015, Aberystwyth, UK.

ACM 978-1-4503-3434-1/15/01 ...$15.00.
http://dx.doi.org/10.1145/2725494.2725495.

2. BIOGRAPHY

Leslie Ann Goldberg is a Professor of Computer Science at the *University of Oxford* and a Fellow of St Edmund Hall, a college of the University of Oxford. Prior to this, she was a Professor in the Department of Computer Science, *University of Liverpool*, a Lecturer, Warwick Research Fellow, Senior Lecturer and Reader in the Department of Computer Science, *University of Warwick*, and a Research Fellow and Senior Member of Technical Staff in the Algorithms and Discrete Mathematics Department at *Sandia Labs* in New Mexico, USA.

Leslie holds a BA from *Rice University* and a PhD from the *University of Edinburgh* (winning the UK Distinguished Dissertations in Computer Science prize). Leslie is a member of *Academia Europaea*, and has several best-paper prizes from *ICALP*. She has served as PC chair of *ICALP 2008* and *RANDOM 2011* and has served on the Executive Committee of *STOC 2013*. She is an Editor-in-Chief of the *Journal of Discrete Algorithms*, and an Associate Editor of *SIAM Journal on Computing*. She has also served on the editorial board of the *ACM Transactions on Algorithms*, the *Journal of Algorithms*, and the *LMS Journal of Computation and Mathematics*. She is a member of the Council of the *EATCS*. Leslie's research has been funded by the *US DOE Office of Scientific Computing*, the *EU*, the *EPSRC*, and the *ERC*, including the prestigious ERC Advanced Grant *Mapping the Complexity of Counting* (MCC).

3. ACKNOWLEDGMENTS

The research leading to these results has received funding from the European Research Council under the European Union's Seventh Framework Programme (FP7/2007-2013) ERC grant agreement no. 334828. The paper reflects only the authors' views and not the views of the ERC or the European Commission. The European Union is not liable for any use that may be made of the information contained therein.

4. REFERENCES

[1] J. Díaz, L.A. Goldberg, G.B. Mertzios, D. Richerby, M. Serna, and P.G. Spirakis. On the fixation probability of superstars. *Proceedings of the Royal Society A : Mathematical, Physical and Engineering Sciences.*, 469:20130193, 2013.

[2] Josep Díaz, Leslie Ann Goldberg, George B. Mertzios, David Richerby, Maria J. Serna, and Paul G. Spirakis. Approximating fixation probabilities in the generalized moran process. *Algorithmica*, 69(1):78–91, 2014.

[3] Josep Díaz, Leslie Ann Goldberg, David Richerby, and Maria J. Serna. Absorption time of the moran process. In *Approximation, Randomization, and Combinatorial Optimization. Algorithms and Techniques, APPROX/RANDOM 2014, September 4-6, 2014, Barcelona, Spain*, pages 630–642, 2014.

[4] Erez Lieberman, Christoph Hauert, and Martin A. Nowak. Evolutionary dynamics on graphs. *Nature*, 433(7023):312–316, 2005.

[5] P. A. P. Moran. Random processes in genetics. *Proceedings of the Cambridge Philosophical Society*, 54(1):60–71, 1958.

Black-box Complexity of Parallel Search with Distributed Populations

Golnaz Badkobeh
University of Sheffield
Sheffield, S1 4DP,
United Kingdom

Per Kristian Lehre
University of Nottingham
Nottingham, NG8 1BB,
United Kingdom

Dirk Sudholt
University of Sheffield
Sheffield, S1 4DP,
United Kingdom

ABSTRACT

Many metaheuristics such as island models and cellular evolutionary algorithms use a network of distributed populations that communicate search points along a spatial communication topology. The idea is to slow down the spread of information, reducing the risk of "premature convergence", and sacrificing exploitation for an increased exploration.

We introduce the distributed black-box complexity as the minimum number of function evaluations *every* distributed black-box algorithm needs to optimise a given problem. It depends on the topology, the number of populations λ, and the problem size n. We give upper and lower bounds on the distributed black-box complexity for unary unbiased black-box algorithms on a class of unimodal functions in order to study the impact of communication topologies on performance. Our results confirm that rings and torus graphs can lead to higher black-box complexities, compared to unrestricted communication. We further determine cut-off points for the number of populations λ, above which no distributed black-box algorithm can achieve linear speedups.

Categories and Subject Descriptors

F.2.2 [**Analysis of Algorithms and Problem Complexity**]: Nonnumerical Algorithms and Problems

Keywords

Black-box complexity, query complexity, structured populations, island models, cellular evolutionary algorithms, runtime analysis, theory

1. INTRODUCTION

1.1 Parallel Evolutionary Algorithms

Evolutionary computation has a long history of using distributed or structured populations [13, 3]: instead of evolving one population where all individuals are mating and competing with one another, evolution is spread across a network of distributed populations. These populations evolve on their own, and they communicate or interact with other populations to coordinate their searches and to exchange promising solutions.

The best known examples of distributed evolutionary algorithms are island models and cellular evolutionary algorithms. In island models populations or *islands* evolve independently for a period of time and migrate selected solutions between them. Migration is performed according to a migration topology, a graph that connects the islands. Cellular evolutionary algorithms also use such a topology, most commonly rings or toroids. Each island represents a *cell* that evolves a single individual by applying variation and selection to individuals within its neighbourhood.

In cellular evolutionary algorithms new solutions are created by mating individuals from different cells, whereas in island models each island applies variation operators to its own population. Often island models use periodic migration: migration is only performed every τ generations, where τ is called *migration interval*. Island models are therefore also called *coarse-grained* evolutionary algorithms and cellular evolutionary algorithms are examples of *fine-grained* evolutionary algorithms.

Countless successful applications have demonstrated the usefulness of distributed populations, mostly, but not restricted to, the domain of parallel implementations. We refer the interested reader to the survey by Alba and Troya [3, Table 5] for an overview of seminal parallel implementations of evolutionary algorithms, dedicated monographs by Tomassini [25] as well as Luque and Alba [17], edited books by Alba [2], Nedjah, de Macedo Mourelle and Alba [19] as well as the most recent survey by Alba, Luque, and Nesmachnow [1] that lists more than 130 recent successful applications to problems from a multitude of disciplines.

One benefit of using distributed populations is that they are suitable for implementations on parallel hardware such as distributed memory MIMD computers like a cluster or multicore systems. Cellular evolutionary algorithms can even be run on SIMD computers such as GPUs. Given the rapidly increasing number of cores, this feature is becoming more and more relevant.

The other benefit is that distributed populations act like an implicit diversity-preserving mechanism. In contrast to a large panmictic population[1] of the same size, good solutions are spread more slowly. This increases exploration of the search space at the expense of exploitation. This makes

[1]Panmixia is the absence of a population structure.

FOGA '15, January 17 - 20, 2015, Aberystwyth, United Kingdom.
Copyright © 2015 ACM 978-1-4503-3434-1/15/01 ...$15.00.
http://dx.doi.org/10.1145/2725494.2725504 .

distributed populations attractive even for non-parallel implementations. Many empirical studies report that parallel evolutionary algorithms with distributed populations find a better solution quality in a shorter amount of time [17, 1].

One challenge for designing effective parallel evolutionary algorithms is that the impact of fundamental parameters on the dynamic behaviour and the performance of parallel evolutionary algorithms is not well understood [17]. This includes the choice of topology, the number of distributed populations, and parameters of migration governing the way how distributed populations communicate. These parameters are important as they can be used to tune the balance between exploration and exploitation.

One line of research, the consideration of so-called *takeover times*, asks how long it takes for a single high-fitness individual to spread throughout all distributed populations, given that only selection and migration are being used (see, e. g. Rudolph [22, 23] and Giacobini *et al.* [11, 12]). The resulting takeover times and growth curves, showing the number of high-fitness individuals over time, can be used to gauge the speed at which information is spread. For more detailed surveys we refer to [17]. The downside of this research is that an abstract setting is studied, where no variation takes place.

Recently, another line of research emerged: the runtime analysis of parallel evolutionary algorithms as surveyed in [24]. Lässig and Sudholt [14, 15] presented a method for proving general upper bounds on the parallel running time of island models based on the classic fitness level method. The basic observation is that in elitist evolutionary algorithms search points from the current best fitness level will be propagated through the topology by migration. Once the number of islands on the best fitness level reaches a certain threshold, there is a good probability that one of these will find an improvement from there. The authors gave upper bounds for different topologies, including rings, toroids, hypercubes and complete graphs. Applications to selected unimodal functions revealed a hierarchy of upper bounds: denser topologies were generally better at exploitation and showed smaller runtimes on simple functions such as LeadingOnes. However, their approach generally does not give any indication whether upper bounds resulting from their method are asymptotically tight.

Obtaining tight runtime bounds is important for determining the number of distributed populations or islands that lead to a *linear speedup* [14]: a realm where the parallel time, or number of rounds, decreases proportionally to the number of islands, but the sequential time, the total number of function evaluations across all islands, does not increase by more than a constant factor.

1.2 Black-Box Complexity

Black-box complexity (also widely known as *query complexity*) is one popular and powerful tool for obtaining lower bounds on the performance of search heuristics. It describes the difficulty of a problem class for all black-box algorithms, that is, all algorithms that rely solely on evaluations of candidate solutions. The black-box complexity of a function class describes the minimum number of function evaluations that *every* black-box algorithm needs to make to optimise the hardest problem from that class. More formally, black-box complexity can be defined as follows:

Definition 1. *The black-box complexity of a class of functions $\mathcal{F}$ for a class of algorithms $\mathcal{A}$ is*

$$\mathrm{T}(\mathcal{A};\mathcal{F}) := \inf_{A\in\mathcal{A}} \sup_{f\in\mathcal{F}} \mathrm{T}(A;f),$$

where $\mathrm{T}(A;f)$ is the expected number of queries made by algorithm A before algorithm A queries an optimal search point for f.

The benefits of black-box complexity are:

- it provides an insight into the working principles of optimal black-box algorithms which ultimately can lead to better EAs [5],
- it provides a rigorous theoretical foundation through capturing limits to the efficiency of black-box search algorithms,
- it provides a baseline for performance comparisons across *all* metaheuristics, including tailored black-box algorithms as well as algorithms that have yet to be invented, and
- it prevents algorithm designers from wasting effort on trying to achieve impossible performance.

The basic, unrestricted black-box complexity model by Droste, Jansen, and Wegener [10] does not make any restrictions on the way a black-box algorithm can query new search points. In particular, since only queries are counted and the computational effort to determine a new query is disregarded, this model allows to solve NP-hard problems with polynomial black-box complexity [10]. Subsequently, refined models were proposed that impose restrictions on how new queries can be made, aiming at excluding unrealistic algorithms from consideration [7, 8].

Lehre and Witt [16] introduced *unbiased black-box complexity*, where new queries can only be made through applying unbiased variation operators to previously queried search points. Unbiased means that operators cannot have an inherent bias towards particular regions of the search space (see Section 2.2 for details).

The unary unbiased black-box complexity allows only unary unbiased operators such as mutation or local search [16], whereas the binary or, more generally, the k-ary unbiased black-box complexity allows an algorithm to make a query based on multiple search points, like recombination [6, 9].

The present authors very recently introduced a parallel black-box complexity model [4]. It extends the unary unbiased black-box complexity model by forcing the algorithm to bundle queries in rounds making λ queries each. This corresponds to the total number of queries made in algorithms that evaluate λ search points at the same time. This model captures island models, cellular evolutionary algorithms as well as offspring populations creating λ offspring at a time. The black-box complexity is non-decreasing in λ as the parallel black-box complexity does not allow an algorithm to use knowledge gained from queries made earlier in the same batch. The authors showed how the black-box complexity increases with increasing problem size n and increasing degree of parallelism λ for LeadingOnes, OneMax, and all functions with a unique global optimum.

1.3 Our Contribution

In this work we propose a distributed black-box complexity model that additionally captures the way distributed populations communicate across topologies as found in many parallel metaheuristics. The distributed black-box complexity considers an ensemble of λ black-box algorithms, called *islands* in reference to the island model, that exchange information about queried search points along a communication topology.

The speed at which information is communicated depends on the communication topology and the communication policy, the strategy of how and when to communicate solutions. Denser topologies generally lead to a faster spread of information and to a faster exploitation. For function classes where exploitation is beneficial, we expect the distributed black-box complexity to be higher for sparse topologies and to decrease with the density of the topology. This intuition is supported by upper bounds on the running time of parallel evolutionary algorithms from [14]; these upper bounds become stronger for denser topologies.

In the following, we confirm this intuition for unary unbiased black-box algorithms and the class of unimodal functions with a small number ($\Theta(n)$) of function values[2]. For a reasonable value of λ, the number of islands, our lower bound on the distributed black-box complexity of a ring topology is higher than that of torus graphs, and this, in turn, is higher than that of a complete graph, where communication is not restricted (see Table 1 in Section 4).

While sparse communication topologies in practice often lead to better diversity and better exploration, our results suggest that they can inhibit exploitation and lead to worse performance on problems where exploitation is crucial.

Results in black-box complexity can provide insights into how given algorithmic characteristics [6, 9] impact performance. For example, it is known that the unbiased black-box complexity with higher-arity variation operators can be strictly lower than the unbiased black-box complexity with unary variation operators [6, 9]. Hence, allowing variation operators that combine more than one previously seen search point can lead to more efficient search. This insight about the impact of the arity of variation operators on performance is difficult to obtain without black-box complexity.

Our results allow for fundamental conclusions about the impact of communication topologies on performance. Furthermore, for the considered problem class our results enable us to locate a *cut-off point* for the choice of λ, above which the benefit of using distributed populations deteriorates and no linear speedup can be obtained by any distributed black-box algorithm. The amount of communication is restricted by the density of the communication topology. Hence, our results also give some insight into how performance degrades when communication between nodes becomes restricted.

The following Section 2 formally introduces distributed black-box models for unrestricted and unary unbiased black-box complexities, respectively. In Section 3 we present an approach for proving lower bounds on the distributed black-box complexity. This approach is then applied to a class of unimodal functions in Section 4.

[2] Unlike previous work [4], we do not consider ONEMAX as a starting point as all topologies led to the same upper bounds on the expected time for the parallel (1+1) EA in [14].

2. PRELIMINARIES

2.1 A Black-Box Model for Distributed Search Algorithms

Distributed black-box algorithms consist of multiple black-box algorithms communicating via a topology, represented by a digraph $G = (V, E)$. Individual black-box algorithms are also referred to as *islands* in reference to the island model.

Distributed black-box algorithms are formalised in Algorithm 1. Each island i keeps a record of its search history $I^i(t)$ in round t that contains all search points evaluated so far. In every round, every island generates one new search point based on its current history, evaluates it, and picks a (possibly empty) set of *emigrants*: search points whose details will be shared with neighbouring islands. After all islands have completed these steps, details of emigrants are communicated to all neighbouring islands. This is done by extending the search history of receiving islands. Note that the sending islands keep information about emigrants; we may imagine that copies of emigrants remain on the sending island.

Algorithm 1 Distributed black-box algorithm with topology $G = (V, E)$ where $|V| = \lambda$

1: Let $t := 1$ and $I^i(0) := \emptyset$ for all $1 \le i \le \lambda$.
2: **repeat**
3:   **for** $1 \le i \le \lambda$ **do**
4:     Sample $x^i(t)$ from a probability distribution that may depend on $I^i(t)$.
5:     Compute $f(x^i(t))$ and let $I^i(t) := I^i(t-1) \cup \{x^i(t), f(x^i(t))\}$.
6:     Select $M^i(t) \subseteq I^i(t)$ according to $I^i(t)$ and t.
7:   **end for**
8:   **for** $1 \le i \le \lambda$ **do**
9:     Let $I^i(t) := I^i(t) \bigcup \{M^j(t) \mid (j, i) \in E\}$.
10:   **end for**
11:   Let $t := t + 1$.
12: **until** termination condition met

The topology is hereinafter called *communication topology* and the choice of emigrants, that is, the definition of $M^i(t)$, is called *communication policy*.

Algorithm 1 stores all previously seen search points, whereas common search heuristics like evolutionary algorithms only keep track of a subset of search points (population) on each island and discard unwanted solutions. This is no contradiction as population-based algorithms naturally fit into the framework of Algorithm 1: in Step 4 $x^i(t)$ is sampled from the island's current population in round t, which is a subset of $I^i(t)$. We assume that given the current search history, the algorithm can infer the parent-child relation of the search points in the history. Likewise, the algorithm can infer the parent-child relation of received search points.

A special case of Algorithm 1 is obtained by setting $G = K_\lambda$, K_λ denoting the *complete graph* with undirected edges between all pairs of nodes, and using $M^i(t) := I^i(t)$ throughout. Then all black-box algorithms share the same history, so equivalently we can regard the process of one black-box algorithm that makes λ queries in parallel in one round. This model equals the *λ-parallel black-box complexity* model from [4] when considering no restrictions on how to generate new queries. The model contains offspring populations in evolutionary algorithms, for example (μ+λ) EAs or (μ,λ) EAs.

Another special case is the class of island models with periodic migration. Every τ rounds, selected individuals (or copies thereof) are being sent to neighbouring islands. Periodic migration can be implemented in Algorithm 1 by setting $M^i(t) = \emptyset$ if $t \neq 0 \bmod \tau$ in the communication policy and selecting migrants otherwise, according to a given *migration policy*. The framework of Algorithm 1 also includes adaptive migration intervals as used in [20, 18].

The *λ-distributed black-box complexity* of a function class $\mathcal{F}$, with regard to an ensemble of λ individual black-box algorithms, a communication topology G, and a communication policy, is defined as the minimum worst-case number of function evaluations until the optimal solution is queried for the first time. This is minimal among all such algorithms satisfying the framework of Algorithm 1.

DEFINITION 2. *The λ-distributed black-box complexity of a class of functions $\mathcal{F}$ for a class of algorithms $\mathcal{A}$, with respect to a communication topology $G = (V, E), |V| = \lambda$, is*

$$\mathrm{T}(\mathcal{A}; \mathcal{F}) \;:=\; \inf_{A \in \mathcal{A}} \sup_{f \in \mathcal{F}} \mathrm{T}(A; f),$$

where $\mathcal{A}$ is the set of all algorithms satisfying the framework of Algorithm 1 for topology G and $\mathrm{T}(A; f)$ is the expected number of queries made by algorithm A in all rounds up to the first round where A queries an optimal search point for f.

Note that the distributed black-box complexity accounts for all queries made in the first round where an optimum is queried. In particular, since there is at least one round, the λ-distributed black-box complexity of every function class is at least λ.

As in traditional black-box complexity, a black-box algorithm is free to ignore any parts of the search history when making its decisions. Therefore, extending a black-box model by making more information available in the search history can never increase the black-box complexity. A black-box algorithm can simply choose to ignore this new information. In particular, in distributed black-box complexity, increasing the information available in the search history by adding more edges to the communication topology, or increasing the frequency and amount of information communicated can never increase the black-box complexity.

In the following, we will therefore consider the most liberal communication policy $M^i(t) := I^i(t)$, i. e., islands communicate their entire search histories. Most distributed evolutionary algorithms communicate less information per round. Note that as explained above, any lower bound on the distributed black-box complexity where the entire search history is communicated also constitutes a lower bound for all distributed black-box algorithms that communicate less information.

2.2 Distributed Unary Unbiased Black-Box Complexity

In the following we consider a more restricted black-box model that models common properties of randomised search heuristics and gives rise to powerful lower bounds. It is based on the unary unbiased black-box complexity introduced by Lehre and Witt [16], where all algorithms use unary variation operators, i. e., variation operators creating a new search point out of one specific search point. This includes local search operators, mutation in evolutionary algorithms, but it does not include recombination.

Unbiasedness means that there is no bias towards particular regions of the search space; in brief, for $\{0,1\}^n$, unbiased operators must treat all bit values $0,1$ and all bit positions $1,\ldots,n$ symmetrically. In the following definition, $\{1,\ldots,n\}$ is denoted by $[n]$.

DEFINITION 3 (UNBIASED VARIATION OPERATOR [16]). *A randomised operator $\phi : \{0,1\}^n \to \{0,1\}^n$ is called* unary unbiased *if the following unbiasedness-conditions hold for all bitstrings $x, y, z \in \{0,1\}^n$ and permutations $\sigma : [n] \to [n]$*

1) $\Pr(\phi(x) = y) = \Pr(\phi(x \oplus z) = y \oplus z)$,
2) $\Pr(\phi(x) = y) = \Pr(\phi(\sigma_b(x)) = \sigma_b(y))$

where $\sigma_b(x_1 x_2 \cdots x_n) := x_{\sigma(1)} x_{\sigma(2)} \cdots x_{\sigma(n)}$.

It can be shown that any unary unbiased variation operator is Hamming-invariant [16]. This means that if two search points y and z have the same Hamming distance r to x, then the two events $\phi(x) = y$ and $\phi(x) = z$ have the same probability. Thus, the application of any unbiased variation operator ϕ to a search point x, can be described as first choosing a radius r, then sampling uniformly at random among all search points in Hamming distance r to x.

Rowe and Vose show unbiasedness-conditions can be generalised to arbitrary search spaces [21]. An important difference from the unrestricted black-box model is that unbiased black-box algorithms can only observe the history of function values, and not of the search points themselves.

Algorithm 2 shows an adaptation of our general distributed black-box model to unary unbiased algorithms, referred to as *distributed unary unbiased black-box complexity*. It is defined analogously to Definition 2, referring to the framework of Algorithm 2.

As in the classical unbiased black-box model, when making its decisions, the algorithm is not allowed to inspect the search points $x^i(t)$ in the search history, only their function values $f(x^i(t))$. However, the variation operator uses a previous search point $x^i(t)$ to generate a new search point. Communication of search histories between islands therefore includes the actual search points.

The special case of $G = K_\lambda$ and $M^i(t) := I^i(t)$ yields one black-box algorithm that makes λ queries in parallel in one round. This model equals the *λ-parallel unary unbiased black-box complexity* model from [4]. By specialising further, setting $\lambda = 1$ yields the *unary unbiased black-box* model from [16].

The *λ-distributed unbiased black-box complexity* λ-duBBC$_G(\mathcal{F})$ of a function class $\mathcal{F}$, with regard to an ensemble of λ individual black-box algorithms, a communication topology G, and a communication policy, is defined as the minimum worst-case number of function evaluations among all unbiased such algorithms satisfying the framework of Algorithm 2. The classical *unary unbiased black-box complexity* now becomes the special case uBBC$(\mathcal{F}_n) =$ 1-duBBC$_{K_\lambda}(\mathcal{F}_n)$.

The following lemma shows that the distributed black-box complexity increases with the degree of parallelism, modulo possible rounding issues.

LEMMA 4. *For any $\alpha, \beta \in \mathbb{N}$, if $\alpha \leq \beta$ then* α-duBBC$(\mathcal{F}_n) \leq \frac{\alpha}{\beta}\lceil\frac{\beta}{\alpha}\rceil \cdot \beta$-duBBC$(\mathcal{F}_n)$

Algorithm 2 Distributed unary unbiased black-box algorithm with topology $G = (V, E)$ where $|V| = \lambda$

Let $t := 1$. For all $1 \le i \le \lambda$ choose $x^i(t)$ uniformly at random and let $I^i(0) := \emptyset$.
repeat
  for $1 \le i \le \lambda$ **do**
    Compute $f(x^i(t))$ and let $I^i(t) := I^i(t-1) \cup \{f(x^i(t))\}$.
    Choose an index $0 \le j \le t$ according to $I^i(t)$.
    Choose an unbiased variation operator $\phi(\cdot \mid x^i(j))$ according to $I^i(t)$.
    Generate $x^i(t+1)$ according to ϕ.
    Select $M^i(t) \subseteq I^i(t)$ according to $I^i(t)$ and t.
  end for
  for $1 \le i \le \lambda$ **do**
    Let $I^i(t) := I^i(t) \cup \{M^j(t) \mid (j, i) \in E\}$.
  end for
  Let $t := t + 1$.
until termination condition met

Proof. Let A be an optimal β-distributed black-box algorithm for $\mathcal{F}_n$ and $\mathrm{T}(A; \mathcal{F}_n)$ denote the number of function evaluations A needs to find optimal of $\mathcal{F}_n$. One can construct an α-parallel black-box algorithm, A^*, which can simulate one round of A by making $\lceil \beta/\alpha \rceil$ batches of α queries. The number of generations for A to find the optimal is $\frac{1}{\beta} \cdot \mathrm{T}(A; \mathcal{F}_n) = \frac{1}{\beta} \cdot \beta\text{-duBBC}(\mathcal{F}_n)$. The number of rounds for A^* is thus $\lceil \beta/\alpha \rceil \cdot \frac{1}{\beta} \cdot \beta\text{-duBBC}(\mathcal{F}_n)$. Multiplying by α, A^* uses $\lceil \beta/\alpha \rceil \cdot \frac{\alpha}{\beta} \cdot \beta\text{-duBBC}(\mathcal{F}_n)$ queries. Since $\alpha\text{-duBBC}(\mathcal{F}_n) \le \mathrm{T}(A^*, \mathcal{F}_n;)$, this concludes the lemma. □

Lemma 4 implies the following for all function classes $\mathcal{F}_n$ (we omit $\mathcal{F}_n$ for brevity): First, if $\frac{\beta}{\alpha} \in \mathbb{N}$ then $\alpha\text{-duBBC} \le \beta\text{-duBBC}$. Otherwise, $\alpha\text{-duBBC} \le (1 + \frac{\alpha}{\beta}) \cdot \beta\text{-duBBC} \le 2 \cdot \beta\text{-duBBC}$ because $\lceil \frac{\beta}{\alpha} \rceil \le 1 + \frac{\beta}{\alpha}$ and $1 + \frac{\alpha}{\beta} \le 2$. In particular, this implies that for all $\alpha < \beta \in \mathbb{N}$,

$$\beta\text{-duBBC} = \Omega(\alpha\text{-duBBC}). \tag{1}$$

We conclude that the λ-distributed black-box complexity does not asymptotically decrease with the degree of parallelism, $\lambda = \lambda(n)$. This implies that there is a *cut-off point* such that for all $\lambda = O(\lambda^*)$ the λ-distributed unbiased black-box complexity of $\mathcal{F}_n$ is asymptotically equal to the regular unbiased black-box complexity.[3]

Definition 5. *A value λ^* is a cut-off point if*

- *for all $\lambda = O(\lambda^*)$, λ-duBBC $= O(\text{uBBC})$ and*
- *for all $\lambda = \omega(\lambda^*)$, λ-duBBC $= \omega(\text{uBBC})$.*

Such a cut-off point always exists because due to (1) the distributed black-box complexity cannot decrease asymptotically, and values of $O(\text{uBBC})$ can always be attained for suitable λ^*, e.g. for $\lambda^* := 1$. Furthermore, the λ-distributed black-box eventually diverges for very large λ (e.g. $\lambda = \omega(\text{uBBC})$) as trivially $\lambda\text{-duBBC} \ge \lambda$.

Note that cut-off points are not unique: if λ^* is a cut-off point, then every $\lambda' = \Theta(\lambda^*)$ is also a cut-off point.

[3]Strictly speaking, we should be writing $\lambda(n) = O(\lambda^*(n))$ as the degree of parallelism may depend on n. We omit this parameter for ease of presentation. Asymptotic statements always refer to n.

A cut-off point determines the realm of linear speedups [14], where parallelisation is most effective. Below the cut-off, for an optimal distributed black-box algorithm the number of function evaluations does not increase (beyond constant factors), but the number of rounds decreases by a factor of $\Theta(\lambda)$. The number of rounds corresponds to the parallel time if all λ evaluations are performed on parallel processors. Hence, below the cut-off it is possible to reduce the parallel time proportionally to the number of processors, without increasing the total computational effort (by more than a constant factor).

2.3 Common Communication Topologies

In this article we consider the following topologies as sketched in Figure 1: a *unidirectional ring* is a graph consisting of a single directed cycle.

A *grid* is a graph whose vertices are arranged on a two-dimensional grid using the von-Neumann neighbourhood (see Figure 1). We speak of a *torus* if the graph additionally contains undirected edges wrapping around (vertices in the top row are neighboured to the ones in the bottom row and vice versa, similarly for the leftmost and rightmost columns). Each vertex in a torus thus has 4 distinct neighbours, provided that the torus has at least 3 rows and at least 3 columns. Note that an undirected edge can be regarded as two directed edges.

Recall that the *complete graph* K_λ contains undirected edges between all pairs of nodes.

3. LOWER BOUNDS ON THE UNBIASED DISTRIBUTED BLACK-BOX COMPLEXITY

3.1 On Red and White Islands

In the following we consider a *potential* that describes the distance of an island to finding the optimum. The potential is defined for search points and islands: the potential of a search point x reflects its "distance" to the optimum and in the remainder is defined as the difference between the optimal fitness and the fitness of x. All global optima have a potential of 0. The potential of an island is the minimum potential of all search points in its history. Finally, the potential of a distributed black-box algorithm is defined as the minimum potential of any of its islands.

We call an island *red* if it has a minimum potential amongst all islands; otherwise the island is called *white*. In the remainder, for proving lower bounds on the black-box complexity we assume the following. After each round, all red islands receive knowledge about the histories of all white islands for free, at no expense of queries. Formally, their search histories are unified with the histories of all white islands.

As a consequence, under these assumptions red islands are never worse off than white islands, as they have access to a superset of search points that can be subjected to variation. And since they have the lowest potential, they have access to additional search points that are, loosely speaking, closest to global optima among all search points queried so far.

This allows us to define the following probabilities that reflect the progress of individual islands during one variation:

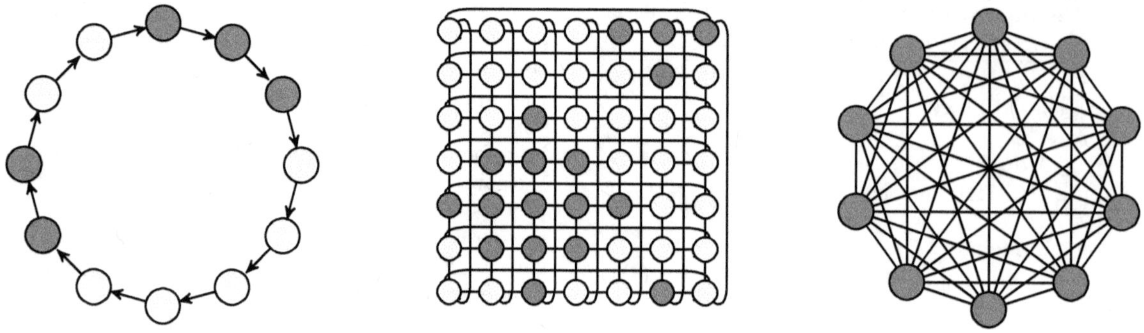

Figure 1: Examples of common topologies used in distributed evolutionary algorithms: a unidirectional ring, a toroid, and a complete graph. The colour of nodes shows red and white islands (see Section 3.1). Ring and torus each show two clusters of red islands of different sizes. In the complete graph, all islands form a single cluster.

Definition 6. *Referring to red islands as having a potential of k, let*

- *r_k be (an upper bound on) the probability that a red island decreases its current potential k in one variation.*
- *w_k be (an upper bound on) the probability that a white island decreases its current potential to a value smaller than k in one variation.*
- *γ_k be (an upper bound on) the probability that a white island reaches potential k in one variation.*

As discussed above, we can assume $r_k \geq w_k$, and in typical applications of this analytical framework we have $r_k \gg w_k$. Furthermore, we can assume that $\gamma_k + w_k < 1$, the rationale is that these two events are disjoint and the probability that a white island stays with its current best potential k is positive.

Remark 1. These three kinds of variables are necessary for proving lower bounds. The upper bound method from [14] relies on red islands spreading through migration, and probabilities for finding improvements are estimated by considering only red islands. For proving lower bounds we need to take into account that white islands can also find improvements. Moreover, white islands may become red, hence the number of red islands can grow faster than through migration alone. These effects can be pessimistically ignored when proving upper bounds, but proving lower bounds requires a more careful analysis.

In the following, we will derive lower bounds on the time it takes to decrease the potential from a value larger than k to a value less than k. This time depends on the probabilities r_k, w_k, γ_k as well as λ and the communication topology. Since we consider a transition from a value *larger* than k to a value *smaller* than k, unless the algorithm skips potential values of k altogether, the time is determined by the time a potential value of k is reached for the first time, and the time it then takes to find a smaller potential value from there. The latter time depends on the topology as information about potential values of k may spread to other islands.

Definition 7. *Let T_k^G be the random number of rounds needed to decrease the current potential of a given distributed black-box algorithm from a value larger than k to a value smaller than k.*

If we were looking for an *upper bound* on the number of queries needed by an algorithm, we could take $\sum_k T_k^G$ as such an upper bound. However, the following issue arise when proving *lower bounds.* If the potential decreased from, say, $k+2$ to $k-2$, the variables T_{k+1}^G, T_k^G, and T_{k-1}^G would all refer to the same time period. In other words, potential levels may be skipped, in which case the naive approach of summing up all T_k^G would give an incorrect result.

In our applications we will divide the potential scale into intervals and argue that jumps skipping a whole interval are unlikely. Assuming that no such jumps occur allows us to count one T_k^G value from each interval.

The differences between red and white islands are likely to impact performance only in a suitable range of λ. If the topology G and its size λ are such that the time needed to communicate a solution of minimum potential k to all other islands is relatively small in comparison to the expected waiting time for finding improvements from potential k, then white islands will quickly become red and the algorithm will behave similarly to a system with λ red islands, or topology K_λ.

On the other hand, if λ is very large, even white islands might have a good chance of finding improvements. Then the distinction between red and white islands becomes obsolete as well. The following theorem gives a general lower bound on T_k^G that covers these two extreme cases.

Theorem 8. *Consider T_k^G and r_k, w_k, γ_k as defined above, for any topology G of size λ. Every distributed black-box algorithm with topology G, starting with an arbitrary number of red islands, needs at least an expected number*

$$\lambda \cdot \mathbf{E}\left[T_k^G\right] = \Omega\left(\frac{1}{r_k} + \lambda\right)$$

of queries to find a solution with potential less than k.

Proof. Since $r_k \geq w_k$ the number of queries is minimal if all islands are red from the beginning. The expected number of queries to success is then $1/r_k$. The bound $\Omega(\lambda)$ is trivial as at least one round is needed: $T_k^G \geq 1$. □

The most interesting domain is the case of intermediate λ, where increasing the number of red islands noticeably increases the chance of the algorithm to find improvements.

The growth in the number of red islands is captured in the following definition.

DEFINITION 9. *For a topology $G = (V, E)$ the growth rate $F(t)$ for $t \in \mathbb{N}$ is defined as follows. $F(t) := \max_{v \in V} F_v(t)$, where $F_v(t)$ is the number of islands that can be reached from island v via at most $t-1$ arcs.*

The growth rate reflects the maximum size of a connected component, hereinafter referred to as a *cluster*, of red islands that has grown for $t-1$ rounds, starting from a single red island (assuming no other red islands emerge).

The following lemma gives tight bounds on the probability of having at least one success in λ independent Bernoulli trials, each of which is successful with probability p.

LEMMA 10. *For $0 \le p \le 1$ and $\lambda \in \mathbb{N}$ we have*

$$\frac{p\lambda}{1+p\lambda} \le 1-(1-p)^{\lambda} \le \min\{1,\ p\lambda\} \le \frac{2p\lambda}{1+p\lambda}.$$

PROOF. For the lower bound we have

$$1-(1-p)^{\lambda} \ge 1-e^{-p\lambda} = 1-\frac{1}{e^{p\lambda}} \ge 1-\frac{1}{1+p\lambda} = \frac{p\lambda}{1+p\lambda}.$$

For the upper bound observe that

$$1-(1-p)^{\lambda} \le \min\{1,\ p\lambda\}$$

follows from Bernoulli's inequality. If $p\lambda \ge 1$ then $1 = 2p\lambda/(2p\lambda) \le 2p\lambda/(1+p\lambda)$. Otherwise, $p\lambda = 2p\lambda/2 \le 2p\lambda/(1+p\lambda)$. □

Using Lemma 10, we now give a lower bound for $\mathbf{E}\left[T_k^G\right]$ that depends on the growth rate $F(t)$.

LEMMA 11. *Consider T_k^G and r_k, w_k, γ_k as defined above, for any topology G of size λ with growth rate $F(t)$. Every distributed black-box algorithm with topology G, starting with a potential larger than k, needs at least an expected number*

$$\mathbf{E}\left[T_k^G\right] \ge \sum_{t=0}^{\infty}\left[(1-w_k)\left(1-\gamma_k \min\left\{1, r_k \sum_{i=1}^{t} F(i)\right\}\right)\right]^{t\lambda}$$

of rounds to find a solution with potential less than k.

PROOF. In this proof we call islands k-red if they have potential k, and k-white otherwise. This coincides with our usual notation of "red" and "white" islands if and only if the current potential is k. This is initially not the case as we start with a potential larger than k.

Let the random variable R_t be the number of k-red islands in round t (possibly $R_t = 0$). Whenever there are R_t k-red islands, the probability of decreasing the potential in the next round is at most

$$1-(1-w_k)^{\lambda-R_t}(1-r_k)^{R_t} \le 1-(1-w_k)^{\lambda}(1-r_k)^{R_t}.$$

Let the random variable $S_t = \sum_{i=1}^{t} R_t$ describe the sum of all k-red islands over time, up to round t; this corresponds to the number of trials k-red islands have had in t rounds to find a solution with potential less than k. Given any event E, let I_E be the indicator function for the event, i.e., $I_E(\omega) = 1$ for all sample points $\omega \in E$, and $I_E(\omega) = 0$ for all complementary sample points $\omega \notin E$. It follows that $\mathbf{E}[I_E] = \Pr(E)$. The expected time to complete one potential level can now be lower bounded as

$$\begin{aligned}
\mathbf{E}\left[T_k^G\right] &= \sum_{t=0}^{\infty} \Pr\left(T_k^G \ge t\right) = \sum_{t=0}^{\infty} \mathbf{E}\left[I_{T_k^G \ge t}\right] \\
&= \sum_{t=0}^{\infty} \mathbf{E}\left[\mathbf{E}\left[I_{T_k^G \ge t} \mid R_1, \dots, R_t\right]\right] \\
&\ge \sum_{t=0}^{\infty} \mathbf{E}\left[\mathbf{E}\left[\prod_{i=1}^{t}(1-w_k)^{\lambda}(1-r_k)^{R_i} \mid R_1, \dots, R_t\right]\right] \\
&= \sum_{t=0}^{\infty} \mathbf{E}\left[\mathbf{E}\left[(1-w_k)^{t\lambda}(1-r_k)^{S_t} \mid R_1, \dots, R_t\right]\right] \\
&= \sum_{t=0}^{\infty} (1-w_k)^{t\lambda}\mathbf{E}\left[(1-r_k)^{S_t}\right].
\end{aligned}$$

To complete the proof, it remains to lower bound the moment-generating function of S_t. We start by estimating an upper bound on the number R_t of k-red islands in round t. A connected component of k-red islands is called a *cluster*. The number of k-red islands depends on the creation and growth of such clusters.

A new cluster is created when a k-white island discovers a search point with potential k through variation, and all the neighbouring islands are k-white. The number of new clusters that are created in any given round t is therefore stochastically dominated by the random variable $N_t \sim \mathrm{Bin}(\lambda, \gamma_k)$.

A cluster grows when islands at the periphery of the cluster inform neighbouring k-white islands about the current best solution. We pessimistically assume that clusters never overlap (otherwise we would overestimate the number of k-red islands), and that all emerging clusters have grown to the size they would have if they were created in round 0. This simplifying assumption implies that the size of a cluster in round t is at most $F(t)$. From these assumptions, it follows that

$$S_t = \sum_{i=1}^{t} R_t \le \sum_{i=1}^{t} F(i) \sum_{j=1}^{i} N_i < \left(\sum_{i=1}^{t} F(i)\right)\left(\sum_{j=1}^{t} N_i\right).$$

The random variables N_i are independent and binomially distributed, hence for $\eta = \ln(1-r_k)\sum_{i=1}^{t} F(i)$

$$\begin{aligned}
\mathbf{E}\left[(1-r_k)^{S_t}\right] &\ge \prod_{i=1}^{t} \mathbf{E}\left[e^{\eta N_i}\right] \\
&= (1-\gamma_k(1-e^{\eta}))^{t\lambda} \\
&= \left(1-\gamma_k\left(1-(1-r_k)^{\sum_{i=1}^{t} F(i)}\right)\right)^{t\lambda}
\end{aligned}$$

which by Lemma 10 is lower bounded by

$$\ge \left(1-\gamma_k \min\left\{1, r_k \sum_{i=1}^{t} F(i)\right\}\right)^{t\lambda}. \quad \square$$

In the following subsections, we use Lemma 11 to obtain tailored bounds for ring and torus graphs.

3.2 Analysis of Ring Topologies

On unidirectional rings every cluster will grow by at most one island in each round, hence $F(t) \le t$. The following theorem uses this observation and the probability estimates

r_k, γ_k, and w_k to derive a lower bound on $\lambda \cdot \mathbf{E}\left[T_k^{\text{ring}}\right]$, the expected number of queries needed to decrease the current potential below a value of k.

THEOREM 12. *Given probability estimates r_k, w_k, γ_k, if $r_k = O(\gamma_k)$, $w_k = O(r_k\gamma_k)$, and $w_k + \gamma_k < 1$ then for a unidirectional ring with λ vertices we have*

$$\lambda \cdot \mathbf{E}\left[T_k^{\text{ring}}\right] = \Omega\left(r_k^{-1} + \lambda^{2/3} r_k^{-1/3} \gamma_k^{-1/3} + \lambda\right).$$

PROOF. The summands r_k^{-1} and λ follow from Theorem 8, hence we only need to prove a lower bound of $\Omega(\lambda^{2/3} r_k^{-1/3} \gamma_k^{-1/3})$, and only in settings when this term dominates the overall bound.

Let $c \geq 1$ be a constant such that $r_k \leq c \cdot \gamma_k$ and $c' \geq 1$ be a constant such that $w_k \leq c' \cdot r_k\gamma_k$. We show that it is sufficient to consider λ in the following range:

$$r_k^{1/2} \gamma_k^{-1} \leq \lambda \leq c'^{-3/2} \cdot r_k^{-1} \gamma_k^{-1} \leq r_k^{-1} \gamma_k^{-1}. \quad (2)$$

If $\lambda < r_k^{1/2}\gamma_k^{-1}$, then $\lambda^{2/3} r_k^{-1/3} \gamma_k^{-1/3} < \gamma_k^{-1} \leq c \cdot r_k^{-1}$ and $\Omega(r_k^{-1})$ dominates the running time.

Likewise, if $\lambda > c'^{-3/2} r_k^{-1} \gamma_k^{-1}$ then $\lambda^{2/3} r_k^{-1/3} \gamma_k^{-1/3} < c'^{1/2}\lambda$ and the $\Omega(\lambda)$ term dominates the running time.

The size of a cluster in round t for the special case of unidirectional ring is $F(t) \leq t$, so $\sum_{i=1}^{t} F(i) \leq \frac{t(t+1)}{2}$.

Using Lemma 11 and $\frac{t(t+1)}{2} \leq t^2$ for all $t \geq 0$, we derive the following lower bound

$$\mathbf{E}\left[T_k^{\text{ring}}\right] \geq \sum_{t=0}^{\infty} (1 - w_k)^{t\lambda} \left(1 - \gamma_k \cdot \min\{1, r_k \cdot t^2\}\right)^{t\lambda}.$$

We truncate the sum at $r_k^{-1/2}/\alpha$ (assumed to be integral) for a variable $\alpha = \alpha(\lambda, n) \geq 1$ and $\alpha \leq r_k^{-1/2}$, such that the minimum is attained for $r_k \cdot t^2$. We get a lower bound of

$$\mathbf{E}\left[T_k^{\text{ring}}\right] \geq \sum_{t=0}^{r_k^{-1/2}/\alpha} (1 - w_k)^{t\lambda} \left(1 - \gamma_k \cdot r_k \cdot t^2\right)^{t\lambda}$$

(replacing t with its maximum value)

$$\geq \sum_{t=0}^{r_k^{-1/2}/\alpha} \left((1 - w_k)(1 - \gamma_k/\alpha^2)\right)^{t\lambda}$$

$$= \sum_{t=0}^{r_k^{-1/2}/\alpha} \left(1 - w_k - \gamma_k/\alpha^2 + w_k \cdot \gamma_k/\alpha^2\right)^{t\lambda}$$

$$\geq \sum_{t=0}^{r_k^{-1/2}/\alpha} \left(1 - w_k - \gamma_k/\alpha^2\right)^{t\lambda}$$

(using properties of the geometric series with base $(1 - w_k - \gamma_k/\alpha^2)^{\lambda}$, this base is positive because of the assumption $w_k + \gamma_k < 1$ and the fact that α is at least 1)

$$\geq \frac{1 - \left(1 - w_k - \gamma_k/\alpha^2\right)^{\lambda \cdot r_k^{-1/2}/\alpha}}{1 - (1 - w_k - \gamma_k/\alpha^2)^{\lambda}}$$

Now, for $0 < p \leq 1$ and integers a, b we have, using both inequalities of Lemma 10,

$$\frac{1 - (1-p)^a}{1 - (1-p)^b} \geq \frac{ap}{1 + ap} \cdot \frac{1 + bp}{2bp} \geq \frac{a}{2b \cdot (1 + ap)}.$$

Combining this with the above, we get a lower bound of

$$\mathbf{E}\left[T_k^{\text{ring}}\right] \geq \frac{r_k^{-1/2}}{2\alpha \cdot (1 + \lambda r_k^{-1/2}/\alpha \cdot (w_k + \gamma_k/\alpha^2))}$$

$$= \frac{r_k^{-1/2}}{2\alpha \cdot (1 + \lambda r_k^{-1/2} w_k/\alpha + \lambda r_k^{-1/2} \gamma_k/\alpha^3)}.$$

We now put $\alpha := \lambda^{1/3} \gamma_k^{1/3} r_k^{-1/6}$ and verify $1 \leq \alpha \leq r_k^{-1/2}$: the bounds in (2) imply $r_k^{1/2} \leq \lambda\gamma_k \leq r_k^{-1}$, hence $r_k^{1/6} \leq \lambda^{1/3}\gamma_k^{1/3} \leq r_k^{-1/3}$ and multiplying by $r_k^{-1/6}$ yields $1 \leq \alpha \leq r_k^{-1/2}$.

With this choice of α we simplify the denominator using

$$\lambda r_k^{-1/2} \gamma_k / \alpha^3 = 1$$

and, along with $w_k \leq c' r_k \gamma_k$ and (2),

$$\frac{\lambda r_k^{-1/2} w_k}{\alpha} = \lambda^{2/3} r_k^{-1/3} \gamma_k^{-1/3} w_k \leq \lambda^{2/3} \cdot c' r_k^{2/3} \gamma_k^{2/3} \leq 1.$$

Together, we get a lower bound of

$$\mathbf{E}\left[T_k^{\text{ring}}\right] \geq \frac{r_k^{-1/2}}{2\alpha \cdot (1 + 1 + 1)} = \frac{r_k^{-1/3} \gamma_k^{-1/3}}{6\lambda^{1/3}}.$$

Multiplying by λ yields the claimed bound. □

Remark 2. The lower bound from Theorem 12 also holds for bidirectional rings, i. e. a ring with undirected edges, as the growth rate there is at most twice as large as for a unidirectional ring. This only changes the above calculations by constant factors.

3.3 Analysis of Grid and Torus Topologies

For grid or torus graphs red islands grow in two dimensions, leading to a more rapid growth. That is, unless the torus has a very unbalanced aspect ratio; in an extreme case, a torus with one row or one column degenerates to a bidirectional ring. The following bound on the growth rate holds regardless of the aspect ratio, and regardless of whether the graph contains edges wrapping around or not.

LEMMA 13. *The growth rate of any grid or torus graph is $F(t) \leq 1 + 2t(t-1)$.*

PROOF. First, we assume that at $t = 1$ the cluster emerged, so $F(1) = 1$. At time t the cluster grows by $4t - 4$: for $t \geq 2$ we have $F(t) - F(t-1) \leq 4t - 4$. The reason is as follows. Unless the cluster has reached the end of the grid or run into itself after wrapping around on either side, at time t the cluster has neighbours in a shape of a diamond with side lengths t (4 sides each containing t vertices, see Figure 1). Thus the perimeter of this diamond contains $4t - 4$ vertices because the 4 vertices located the corners of the diamond are shared between two sides. If the cluster has wrapped around and run into itself, we use the same arguments, noting that nodes may be counted multiple times. Therefore,

$$F(t) \leq 1 + \sum_{i=2}^{t} 4(i-1)$$

$$= 1 + 4 \cdot \sum_{i=2}^{t} (i-1)$$

$$= 1 + 2t(t-1). \quad \square$$

THEOREM 14. *Given probability estimates r_k, w_k, γ_k, if $r_k = O(\gamma_k)$, $w_k = O(r_k\gamma_k)$, and $w_k + \gamma_k < 1$ then for a torus with λ vertices we have*

$$\lambda \cdot \mathbf{E}\left[T_k^{\text{torus}}\right] = \Omega\left(r_k^{-1} + \lambda^{3/4} r_k^{-1/4}\gamma_k^{-1/4} + \lambda\right).$$

PROOF. The proof is similar to the proof of Theorem 12. We show that it is sufficient to consider λ in the following range:

$$r_k^{1/3}\gamma_k^{-1} \le \lambda \le r_k^{-1}\gamma_k^{-1}/256. \qquad (3)$$

If $\lambda < r_k^{1/3}\gamma_k^{-1}$, then $\lambda^{3/4}r_k^{-1/4}\gamma_k^{-1/4} < \gamma_k^{-1} \le c \cdot r_k^{-1}$ and $\Omega(r_k^{-1})$ dominates the running time.

Likewise, if $\lambda > r_k^{-1}\gamma_k^{-1}/256$ then $\lambda^{3/4}r_k^{-1/4}\gamma_k^{-1/4} < \lambda/4$ and the $\Omega(\lambda)$ term dominates the running time.

Using Lemma 11, Lemma 13, and the fact that $\sum_{i=1}^{t} F(i) \le \frac{2t^3+3t^2+t}{3} \le 2t^3$ for all $t \ge 0$, we obtain the following bound:

$$\mathbf{E}\left[T_k^{\text{torus}}\right] \ge \sum_{t=0}^{\infty}(1-w_k)^{t\lambda}\left(1-\gamma_k \cdot \min\{1, r_k \cdot 2t^3\}\right)^{t\lambda}$$

We truncate the sum at $r_k^{-1/3}/\alpha$ (assumed to be integral) for a variable $\alpha = \alpha(\lambda, n) \ge 2$ and $\alpha \le \frac{r_k^{-1/3}}{2}$, such that the minimum is attained for $r_k \cdot 2t^3$. We get a lower bound of

$$\mathbf{E}\left[T_k^{\text{torus}}\right] \ge \sum_{t=0}^{r_k^{-1/3}/\alpha}(1-w_k)^{t\lambda}\left(1-\gamma_k \cdot r_k \cdot 2t^3\right)^{t\lambda}$$

(replacing t with its maximum value)

$$\ge \sum_{t=0}^{r_k^{-1/3}/\alpha}\left((1-w_k)(1-2\gamma_k/\alpha^3)\right)^{t\lambda}$$

$$= \sum_{t=0}^{r_k^{-1/3}/\alpha}\left(1-w_k-2\gamma_k/\alpha^3+2w_k\cdot\gamma_k/\alpha^3\right)^{t\lambda}$$

$$\ge \sum_{t=0}^{r_k^{-1/3}/\alpha}\left(1-w_k-2\gamma_k/\alpha^3\right)^{t\lambda}$$

(using properties of the geometric series with base $\left(1-w_k-2\gamma_k/\alpha^3\right)^{\lambda}$, this base is positive because of the assumption $w_k+\gamma_k<1$ and the fact that α^3 is at least 2)

$$= \frac{1-\left(1-w_k-2\gamma_k/\alpha^3\right)^{\lambda \cdot r_k^{-1/3}/\alpha}}{1-(1-w_k-2\gamma_k/\alpha^3)^{\lambda}}$$

Combining this with the direct consequence of Lemma 10 yields the lower bound of

$$\mathbf{E}\left[T_k^{\text{torus}}\right] \ge \frac{r_k^{-1/3}}{2\alpha\cdot(1+\lambda r_k{}^{-1/3}/\alpha\cdot(w_k+2\gamma_k/\alpha^3))}$$

$$= \frac{r_k^{-1/3}}{2\alpha\cdot(1+\lambda r_k{}^{-1/3}\cdot w_k/\alpha + 2\lambda r_k{}^{-1/3}\gamma_k/\alpha^4)}.$$

Now we choose $\alpha := 2\lambda^{1/4}\gamma_k^{1/4}r_k^{-1/12}$ and since by (3) $r_k^{1/3}\gamma_k^{-1} \le \lambda \le r_k{}^{-1}\gamma_k^{-1}/256$, we verify that $2 \le \alpha \le \frac{r_k^{-1/3}}{2}$. With this choice of α we can simplify the denominator using

$$2\lambda r_k{}^{-1/3}\gamma_k/\alpha^4 = 1/8$$

along with $w_k \le c' r_k \gamma_k$ and (3),

$$\frac{\lambda r_k{}^{-1/3} w_k}{\alpha} \le \lambda^{3/4} r_k^{-1/4}\gamma_k^{-1/4} w_k \le \lambda^{3/4}\cdot c' r_k^{3/4}\gamma_k^{3/4} \le c'/64.$$

Therefore, we derive the following bound

$$\mathbf{E}\left[T_k^{\text{torus}}\right] \ge \frac{r_k{}^{-1/3}}{2\alpha\cdot(1+c'/64+1/8)}$$

$$\ge \frac{r_k^{-1/3}}{(5+c')\lambda^{1/4}\gamma_k^{1/4}r_k^{-1/12}}$$

$$\ge \frac{1}{(5+c')\lambda^{1/4}\gamma_k^{1/4}r_k^{1/4}}$$

which implies the claim. □

4. THE DISTRIBUTED BLACK-BOX COMPLEXITY OF RANDOM PATHS

In this section we now apply our approach to bound the distributed black-box complexity of a class of unimodal functions with $\Theta(n)$ function values. A function is called *unimodal* if every non-optimal search point has at least one Hamming neighbour with strictly larger function value.

Previous work on parallel black-box complexity [4] as well as parallel evolutionary algorithms [14] considered the function LEADINGONES$(x) := \sum_{i=1}^{n}\prod_{j=1}^{i} x_i$ as a classic example, which counts the number of leading ones in the bit string. It is an example of a unimodal function, and its main characteristic is that one particular bit, the first 0-bit, must be flipped in order to increase the function value. This property makes it a difficult function among all unimodal functions with the same range, and a seemingly obvious choice for proving lower bounds on the black-box complexity of unimodal functions.

However, analysing LEADINGONES in our framework is problematic as in certain cases the distinction between red islands and white islands can break down, when taking the fitness difference to the optimum as potential. For example, the search points 111110 and 110111 both have the same chance to create the optimum by flipping the right bit, even though the former search point has a higher fitness. The latter search point contains a large number of so-called "free riders", i. e. bits following the first 0-bit that happen to be set to 1. In such a setting, red islands do not have an advantage over white islands.

In order to establish a lower bound on the black-box complexity of unimodal functions, we therefore consider another unimodal function with a similar range, where free riders do not exist. We follow an idea from Droste, Jansen, and Wegener [10, page 541]: a short random path. The path starts at 1^n and the next point is obtained by flipping a random 1-bit to 0. The path ends at a global optimum with $n/2$ 1-bits. All other search points give hints towards reaching 1^n, the start of the path.

DEFINITION 15. *Let π be a permutation of $[n]$ chosen uniformly at random. Define a path $\mathcal{P} = (p_0, p_1, \ldots, p_{n/2})$ such that $p_0 := 1^n$ and $p_i := p_{i-1} \oplus 0^{\pi_i - 1}10^{n-\pi_i}$. The function* RSP *(random short path) is then defined as*

$$\text{RSP}(x) := \begin{cases} n+i & \text{if } x = p_i \\ |x|_1 & \text{otherwise.} \end{cases}$$

	Ring	Grid/Torus	Complete/K_λ
Upper bounds	$O\left(\lambda n^{3/2}+n^2\right)$	$O\left(\lambda n^{4/3}+n^2\right)$	$O(\lambda n+n^2)$
Lower bounds	$\Omega\left(\lambda n+\lambda^{2/3}n^{5/3}+n^2\right)$	$\Omega\left(\lambda n+\lambda^{3/4}n^{3/2}+n^2\right)$	$\Omega\left(\lambda n+n^2\right)$
Cut-off point	$\lambda^*=\Theta(n^{1/2})$	$\lambda^*=\Theta(n^{2/3})$	$\lambda^*=\Theta(n)$

Table 1: Asymptotic bounds on the λ-distributed unary unbiased black-box complexity for various topologies on RSP and, more generally, the class $U(\Theta(n))$ of all unimodal functions with $\Theta(n)$ function values. The bounds reflect the number of function evaluations (sequential time); the corresponding number of rounds (parallel time) is obtained by dividing the former by λ. The upper bound on grid/torus topologies requires a torus with side lengths $\sqrt{\lambda}\times\sqrt{\lambda}$; the lower bound holds for all side lengths. The cut-off point λ^* determines the realm of possible linear speedups for each topology: below the cut-off the parallel (1+1) EA [14] has a linear speedup, while for $\lambda=\omega(\lambda^*)$ no distributed black-box algorithm can achieve a linear speedup.

Note that RSP is a unimodal function, that is, for every non-optimal search point there is a Hamming neighbour with strictly higher fitness.

Because of the randomness in the construction, black-box algorithms can only be efficient if they follow the path. Droste, Jansen, and Wegener [10] conjecture that the (unrestricted) black-box complexity of the class containing all possible RSP functions is $\Theta(n^2)$.

Remark 3. For the unbiased black-box complexity the randomness of RSP is not essential. This black-box complexity model does not allow algorithms to inspect search points; it can only act on their fitness values. This implies that even if an algorithm was to know the permutation π, it would be generally unable to judge how far a bit string is from the path point with the same number of ones. Hence the behaviour of unbiased black-box algorithms is identical for every permutation π used in the construction of RSP. We present RSP as a random instance to enable future studies of the unrestricted black-box complexity using for instance Yao's minimax principle as in [10, Theorem 8].

The fitness-level method for parallel evolutionary algorithms gives upper bounds on the parallel black-box complexities. As in [14, 15], we consider the parallel (1+1) EA: an island model running the (1+1) EA on every island and migrating in every round (see [14] for a formal definition). Note that the (1+1) EA with the standard mutation rate of $1/n$ always finds a better search point on RSP with probability at least $1/n\cdot(1-1/n)^{n-1}\geq 1/(en)$ due to its unimodality. Using Theorem 1 in [15] yields the results shown in the first row of Table 1.

In order to prove lower bounds on the distributed black-box complexity, we need to look more closely into the magnitude and probability of fitness improvements.

By construction, for any path point p_i and any $1\leq r\leq n/2-i$ there is just one further path point with Hamming distance r to p_i. This implies the following lemma.

LEMMA 16. *Consider an unbiased variation of a path point p_i with radius r. The probability that an improvement, that is, path point p_{i+r}, will be found is*

$$\binom{n}{r}^{-1}\leq\left(\frac{r}{n}\right)^r$$

for $1\leq r\leq n/2-i$ and 0 otherwise.

It follows directly from Lemma 16 that probabilities decrease monotonously on the path, i. e., for all $1\leq j\leq k$ with the best possible variation operators it is more likely to jump from p_i to p_{i+j} than to p_{i+k}:

$$\max_{\phi}\{\Pr\left(\phi(p_i)=p_{i+j}\right)\}\geq\max_{\phi}\{\Pr\left(\phi(p_i)=p_{i+k}\right)\},$$

where the maxima are taken with respect to the choice of unbiased variation operator ϕ.

LEMMA 17. *Let $\lambda=\text{poly}(n)$, then there exists a constant $\delta=\delta(\lambda)$ such that the probability of any variation of a path point p_i leads to a progress of at least δ is $o(1/(\lambda n^2))$.*

A probability this small implies that even within λn^2 queries the probability of making a progress of at least δ is just $o(1)$.

PROOF OF LEMMA 17. Define $\delta(\lambda):=k+2+\varepsilon$ where k is any constant such that $\lambda\leq n^k$, and $\varepsilon>0$ is any constant. By Lemma 16, the probability of progressing from point p_i by at least δ is no more than

$$\sum_{r=\delta}^{n/2-i}\left(\frac{r}{n}\right)^r\leq\left(\frac{\delta}{n}\right)^\delta\sum_{r=0}^{n/2-i-\delta}\left(\frac{r}{n}\right)^r<\left(\frac{\delta}{n}\right)^\delta\sum_{r=0}^{\infty}\left(\frac{1}{2}\right)^r$$
$$=2\delta^\delta n^{-k-2-\varepsilon}=o(1/(\lambda n^2))\quad\square$$

Finally, the following lemma shows that applying unary variation to a search point with i zeros is never better than choosing the path point p_i.

LEMMA 18. *For every i,r with $i+r\leq n/2$ and every x with i zeros, the probability of reaching p_{i+r} from x with the best possible unary unbiased variation operator is never larger than the probability of reaching p_{i+r} from p_i with the best possible unary unbiased variation operator.*

PROOF. The probability of reaching p_{i+r} from p_i with a variation of radius r is $\binom{n}{r}^{-1}$. The probability of reaching p_{i+r} from x is maximised when the radius equals the Hamming distance $H(x,p_{i+r})$, yielding a probability of $\binom{n}{H(x,p_{i+r})}^{-1}$. The latter probability is never larger than the former as $r\leq H(x,p_{i+r})\leq H(x,1^n)+H(1^n,p_{i+r})=2i+r=2i+2r-r\leq n-r$ as $i+r\leq n/2$. $\square$

LEMMA 19. *For every search point x, the probability that an unbiased variation of x with radius r hits a path point is at most*

$$\frac{1+\min\{r,n-r\}}{\binom{n}{r}}.$$

PROOF. First assume $r \leq n/2$ and let $0 \leq i \leq r$ be the number of 0-bits flipped in the variation. Each of $r+1$ choices of i leads to an increase in the number of ones by $i-(r-i)=2i-r$. Hence the number of ones in the mutant will have one out of $r+1$ possible values. Amongst all search points with the same number of ones, there exists at most one path point. Hence out of $\binom{n}{r}$ possible mutants, only $r+1$ can be on the path.

The case $r > n/2$ is symmetric; then $0 \leq i \leq n-r$ refers to the number of non-flipping 0-bits. □

As in Droste, Jansen, and Wegener [10], we consider $U(b)$ as the class of unimodal functions which take at most b different function values. Moreover, let $U(\Theta(n))$ be the union of $U(b)$ for all $b \in \Theta(n)$. Since RSP $\in U(\Theta(n))$, any lower bound on the black-box complexity of RSP extends to the larger class $U(\Theta(n))$. We now state the main results of this section.

THEOREM 20. *The λ-distributed unary unbiased black-box complexity of* RSP *and* $U(\Theta(n))$ *for* $\lambda = \text{poly}(n)$ *is*

- $\Omega(\lambda n + \lambda^{2/3} \cdot n^{5/3} + n^2)$ *for a unidirectional ring,*
- $\Omega(\lambda n + \lambda^{3/4} \cdot n^{3/2} + n^2)$ *for any grid or torus, and*
- $\Omega(\lambda n + n^2)$ *for the complete graph.*

The number of rounds (parallel time) for any of the above topologies is by a factor of λ smaller and does not increase with growing λ.

Note that the bound $\Omega(\lambda n + n^2)$ for the complete graph, along with the upper bound $O(\lambda n + n^2)$ from Table 1, shows that the λ-*parallel* black box complexity of RSP and $U(\Theta(n))$ is $\Theta(\lambda n + n^2)$.

The λ-*distributed* black-box complexity for ring and torus topologies is therefore larger than the λ-parallel one when the middle terms $\lambda^{2/3} \cdot n^{5/2}$ and $\lambda^{3/4} \cdot n^{3/2}$, respectively, dominate the lower bounds. For the ring, this realm is $\lambda \in \omega(n^{1/2}) \cap o(n^2)$, and for torus graphs it is $\lambda \in \omega(n^{2/3}) \cap o(n^2)$.

COROLLARY 21. *The λ-distributed unary unbiased black-box complexity of* RSP *and* $U(\Theta(n))$ *is asymptotically larger then the λ-parallel black-box complexity*

- *for a unidirectional ring if* $\lambda \in \omega(n^{1/2}) \cap o(n^2)$ *and*
- *for any grid or torus if* $\lambda \in \omega(n^{2/3}) \cap o(n^2)$.

These results also allow for conclusions about the cut-off point and the realm of linear speedups, i. e. values of λ where the number of function evaluations does not asymptotically increase above the non-parallel unary unbiased black-box complexity. The latter is given by the special case of $\lambda = 1$, where our upper and lower bounds yield a tight bound of $\Theta(n^2)$. Checking the upper bounds from Table 1 as well as lower bounds from Theorem 20 for values of λ leading to bounds of $O(n^2)$ and $\Omega(n^2)$, respectively, leads to the following cut-offs.

COROLLARY 22. *The cut-off point for* RSP *is*

- $\lambda^* = \Theta(n^{1/2})$ *for a unidirectional ring and*
- $\lambda^* = \Theta(n^{2/3})$ *for a torus with side lengths* $\sqrt{\lambda} \times \sqrt{\lambda}$.

For $\lambda \leq \lambda^*$ the parallel (1+1) EA shows a linear speedup on RSP, *while for $\lambda = \omega(\lambda^*)$ no distributed black-box algorithm can achieve a linear speedup.*

Previously, only lower bounds on the cut-off points were known. Note that the above also implies that the parallel (1+1) EA is an "optimal" distributed black-box algorithm for RSP in a sense that no distributed algorithm can have a larger range of linear speedups than the parallel (1+1) EA.

PROOF OF THEOREM 20. We consider the function RSP as a difficult subclass of the function class $U(\Theta(n))$. Let $\mathcal{A}$ be any black-box algorithm as stated in the theorem. With probability $1-o(1)$ the λ initial individuals chosen uniformly at random do not contain any path points. We assume in the following that this is the case.

We can only make $\mathcal{A}$ faster by granting additional knowledge to some or all islands (at no expense of queries). We assume that all islands initially know 1^n as well as all search points with less than $n/2$ ones; the fitness of these points is obvious from the definition of RSP and independent from the choice of path points $p_1, \dots, p_{n/2}$. For all islands, we assume that whenever the island evaluates a path point p_i, then that island receives knowledge about all points with at most i zeros.

Further, we partition the path into level sets for an integer $\delta \geq 2$ chosen as in Lemma 17. For $0 \leq i \leq n/(2\delta) - 1$ the level set L_i is defined as:

$$L_i := \{p_j \mid i \cdot \delta \leq j < (i+1) \cdot \delta\}.$$

If the current best search point is in L_i, as soon as an island finds a better search point in L_i, we grant all islands knowledge of all search points in L_i. We then say that $\mathcal{A}$ has completed the level set L_i. Islands that subsequently discover a point in L_{i+1} become red islands on the new potential level.

Combining Lemma 17 and Lemma 18, the probability of ever skipping a level set (i. e. completing a level set L_j for $j > i$ while the current best point is in L_i) within λn^2 rounds is $o(1)$. If this happens, we assume that $\mathcal{A}$ found the optimum within 0 queries. In the following, we consider the conditional expectation, working under the condition that this does not happen within λn^2 rounds. Compared to the unconditional expectation, this affects our lower bound only by a factor of $1 - o(1)$.

Now the lower bound follows from summing up all expected times spend on all level sets. If $\mathbf{E}[T_k]$ is the expected number of rounds spent to complete one potential level k in the described setting, then the black-box complexity is hence at least

$$(1-o(1)) \cdot \left\lfloor \frac{n}{2\delta} \right\rfloor \cdot \lambda \cdot \mathbf{E}[T_k] = \Omega(n) \cdot \lambda \cdot \mathbf{E}[T_k].$$

By Lemma 19, the probability of completing the current potential level from a variation of any search point in the history of a red island is maximised when choosing the smallest possible radius $r = 1$ with probability 1, hence $r_k := 2/n$. A white island only becomes red when discovering the best-so-far path point, which happens with probability at most $\gamma_k := 2/n$ for the same reasons.

Now consider a white island trying to find an improvement, that is, a new best-so-far fitness value. Any variation with radius $2 \leq r \leq n-2$ has a probability of completing the potential level of at most

$$\frac{1 + \min\{r, n-r\}}{\binom{n}{r}} \leq \frac{2}{\binom{n}{2}} = \frac{4}{n(n-1)} := w_k.$$

We show that a white island cannot do better by using a radius of $r = 1$. Let p_j be the best path point that a white island has found. The island cannot decrease the current potential by flipping a single bit of p_j, or any other solution with at most j zeros, as it has to discover p_{j+2} or a further path point. So the only case left is flipping one bit of a point which is not on the path and has at least $j+1$ zeros. However, points off the path with the same number of ones are indistinguishable to the algorithm as they have the same fitness, and only very few such points are Hamming neighbours of path points.

To illustrate this effect, consider all Hamming neighbours of p_j with $j+1$ zeros. The number of these search points, excluding p_{j+1}, is $n-j-1 \geq n/2$ (as $j+1 \leq n/2$), and only one of them is a Hamming neighbor of p_{j+2}. The probability of choosing the right parent out of at least $n/2$ indistinguishable ones, and reaching p_{j+2} by flipping the right bit, is $2/n \cdot 1/n < w_k$. The same holds for a trajectory starting at another point with at most j zeros instead of starting at p_j. For search points with more than $j+1$ zeros we can iterate this argument, and conclude that no such operation has a probability of completing the current potential level higher than w_k.

Note that the values r_k, γ_k, and w_k comply with the conditions of Theorems 12 and 14, i.e., $r_k = O(\gamma_k)$ and $w_k = O(r_k\gamma_k)$.

Therefore, substituting these values for the ring topology leads to the following lower bound:

$$\begin{aligned}\lambda \cdot \mathbf{E}\left[T_k^{\text{ring}}\right] &= \Omega(r_k{}^{-1} + \lambda^{2/3}\gamma_k^{-1/3}r_k^{-1/3} + \lambda)\\ &= \Omega(n + \lambda^{2/3}(1/n)^{-1/3}(1/n)^{-1/3} + \lambda)\\ &= \Omega(n + \lambda^{2/3}n^{2/3} + \lambda).\end{aligned}$$

Now, multiplying this by $\Omega(n)$ leads to a lower bound of

$$\Omega(n^2 + \lambda^{2/3} \cdot n^{5/3} + \lambda n).$$

Similarly, we calculate the lower bound when the structure is a torus

$$\begin{aligned}\lambda \cdot \mathbf{E}\left[T_k^{\text{torus}}\right] &= \Omega(r_k{}^{-1} + \lambda^{3/4}\gamma_k^{-1/4}r_k^{-1/4} + \lambda)\\ &= \Omega(n + \lambda^{3/4}(1/n)^{-1/4}(1/n)^{-1/4} + \lambda)\\ &= \Omega(n + \lambda^{3/4}n^{1/2} + \lambda).\end{aligned}$$

Now, multiplying this by $\Omega(n)$ leads to a lower bound of

$$\Omega(n^2 + \lambda^{3/4} \cdot n^{3/2} + \lambda n).$$

For the complete graph we have by Theorem 8

$$\lambda \cdot \mathbf{E}\left[T_k^{\text{complete}}\right] = \Omega(r_k^{-1} + \lambda) = \Omega(n + \lambda)$$

and multiplying by $\Omega(n)$ leads to a lower bound of

$$\Omega(n^2 + \lambda n). \quad \square$$

5. CONCLUSIONS AND FUTURE WORK

We have introduced a distributed black-box complexity model for distributed black-box algorithms that communicate through a given communication topology as commonly used in island models and cellular evolutionary algorithms. Lower bounds for the distributed black-box complexity of random short paths, or, equivalently, unimodal functions with $\Theta(n)$ search points, have confirmed that sparse topologies can asymptotically increase the distributed black-box complexity, compared to the parallel black-box complexity with unrestricted communication.

For unidirectional rings we showed that when $\lambda \in \omega(n^{1/2}) \cap o(n^2)$ the λ-distributed black-box complexity on RSP is asymptotically larger than the λ-parallel black-box complexity not restricted by a topology. For torus or grid graphs, the same holds for $\lambda \in \omega(n^{2/3}) \cap o(n^2)$. In the latter realm, the lower bound for ring graphs, $\Omega(\lambda^{2/3}n^{5/3})$, was larger than the lower bound for torus graphs, $\Omega(\lambda^{3/4}n^{3/2})$.

One application of these results is to determine the cut-off point λ^*, which describes the realm where linear speedups for parallel metaheuristics are possible. There is a linear speedup for the parallel (1+1) EA on RSP if and only if $\lambda \leq \lambda^* = \Theta(n^{1/2})$ for a unidirectional ring and $\lambda \leq \lambda^* = \Theta(n^{2/3})$ for a torus with side lengths $\sqrt{\lambda} \times \sqrt{\lambda}$. More importantly, for $\lambda = \omega(\lambda^*)$ no distributed black-box algorithm can achieve a linear speedup.

There are several possible avenues for future work. One idea is to extend our results on the distributed unary unbiased black-box complexity of RSP to the distributed unrestricted black-box complexity. This seems possible as random paths are difficult for every black-box algorithm [10], but it would require different arguments.

Another open question is how the choice of the communication policy affects the black-box complexity, particularly in the context of periodic and/or probabilistic communication. Finally, it would be interesting to study the amount of communication between islands and whether there is a trade-off between the amount of information communicated and the distributed black-box complexity.

Acknowledgments

The research leading to these results has received funding from the European Union Seventh Framework Programme (FP7/2007-2013) under grant agreement no 618091 (SAGE). The authors thank the anonymous FOGA reviewers as well as Timo Kötzing, Andrei Lissovoi, and Carsten Witt for many constructive comments that helped to improve the manuscript.

6. REFERENCES

[1] E. Alba, G. Luque, and S. Nesmachnow. Parallel metaheuristics: Recent advances and new trends. *International Transactions in Operational Research*, 20(1):1–48, 2013.

[2] Enrique Alba. *Parallel Metaheuristics: A New Class of Algorithms*. Wiley-Interscience, 2005.

[3] Enrique Alba and José M. Troya. A survey of parallel distributed genetic algorithms. *Complex.*, 4(4):31–52, 1999.

[4] Golnaz Badkobeh, Per Kristian Lehre, and Dirk Sudholt. Unbiased black-box complexity of parallel search. In *13th International Conference on Parallel Problem Solving from Nature (PPSN 2014)*, volume 8672 of *LNCS*, pages 892–901. Springer, 2014.

[5] Benjamin Doerr, Carola Doerr, and Franziska Ebel. From Black-Box Complexity to Designing New

Genetic Algorithms. *Theoretical Computer Science*, 567(0):87–104, 2015.

[6] Benjamin Doerr, Daniel Johannsen, Timo Kötzing, Per Kristian Lehre, Markus Wagner, and Carola Winzen. Faster black-box algorithms through higher arity operators. In *Proceedings of the 11th Workshop Proceedings on Foundations of Genetic Algorithms*, FOGA 2011, pages 163–172. ACM, 2011.

[7] Benjamin Doerr and Carola Winzen. Towards a complexity theory of randomized search heuristics: Ranking-based black-box complexity. *Computer Science-Theory and Applications*, pages 15–28, 2011.

[8] Benjamin Doerr and Carola Winzen. Playing Mastermind with Constant-Size Memory. *Theory of Computing Systems*, 2012.

[9] Benjamin Doerr and Carola Winzen. Reducing the arity in unbiased black-box complexity. *Theor. Comput. Sci.*, 545:108–121, 2014.

[10] Stefan Droste, Thomas Jansen, and Ingo Wegener. Upper and lower bounds for randomized search heuristics in black-box optimization. *Theory of Computing Systems*, 39(4):525–544, 2006.

[11] Mario Giacobini, Enrique Alba, Andrea Tettamanzi, and Marco Tomassini. Modeling selection intensity for toroidal cellular evolutionary algorithms. In *Proceedings of the Genetic and Evolutionary Computation conference (GECCO 2004)*, pages 1138–1149. Springer, 2004.

[12] Mario Giacobini, Marco Tomassini, and Andrea Tettamanzi. Takeover time curves in random and small-world structured populations. In *Proceedings of the Genetic and Evolutionary Computation Conference (GECCO 2005)*, pages 1333–1340. ACM Press, 2005.

[13] V. Scott Gordon and L. Darrell Whitley. Serial and parallel genetic algorithms as function optimizers. In *ICGA 1993*, pages 177–183. Morgan Kaufmann Publishers Inc., 1993.

[14] Jörg Lässig and Dirk Sudholt. General upper bounds on the runtime of parallel evolutionary algorithms. *Evolutionary Computation*, 22(3):405–437, November 2013.

[15] Jörg Lässig and Dirk Sudholt. Analysis of speedups in parallel evolutionary algorithms and (1+λ) EAs for combinatorial optimization. *Theoretical Computer Science*, 551:66–83, 2014.

[16] Per Kristian Lehre and Carsten Witt. Black-box search by unbiased variation. *Algorithmica*, 64(4):623–642, 2012.

[17] Gabriel Luque and Enrique Alba. *Parallel Genetic Algorithms–Theory and Real World Applications.* Springer, 2011.

[18] Andrea Mambrini and Dirk Sudholt. Design and analysis of adaptive migration intervals in parallel evolutionary algorithms. In *Proceedings of the Genetic and Evolutionary Computation Conference (GECCO 2014)*, pages 1047–1054. ACM Press, 2014.

[19] Nadia Nedjah, Luiza de Macedo Mourelle, and Enrique Alba. *Parallel Evolutionary Computations.* Springer, 2006.

[20] Karel Osorio, Enrique Alba, and Gabriel Luque. Using theory to self-tune migration periods in distributed genetic algorithms. In *IEEE Congress on Evolutionary Computation*, pages 2595–2601, 2013.

[21] Jonathan E. Rowe and Michael D. Vose. Unbiased black box search algorithms. In *Proceedings of the Genetic and Evolutionary Computation Conference (GECCO 2011)*, pages 2035–2042. ACM, July 2011.

[22] Günter Rudolph. On takeover times in spatially structured populations: Array and ring. In *Proceedings of the 2nd Asia-Pacific Conference on Genetic Algorithms and Applications*, pages 144–151. Global-Link Publishing Company, 2000.

[23] Günter Rudolph. Takeover time in parallel populations with migration. In *Proceedings of the Second International Conference on Bioinspired Optimization Methods and their Applications (BIOMA 2006)*, pages 63–72, 2006.

[24] Dirk Sudholt. Parallel evolutionary algorithms. In *Handbook of Computational Intelligence*. Springer. To appear. Preprint available from `staffwww.dcs.shef.ac.uk/~dirk/parallel-eas.pdf`.

[25] Marco Tomassini. *Spatially Structured Evolutionary Algorithms: Artificial Evolution in Space and Time.* Springer, 2005.

On the Black-Box Complexity of Example Functions: The Real Jump Function

Thomas Jansen
Department of Computer Science
Aberystwyth University
Aberystywyth SY23 3DB, UK
t.jansen@aber.ac.uk

ABSTRACT

Black-box complexity measures the difficulty of classes of functions with respect to optimisation by black-box algorithms. Comparing the black-box complexity with the worst case performance of a best know randomised search heuristic can help to assess if the randomised search heuristic is efficient or if there is room for improvement. When considering an example function it is necessary to extend it to a class of functions since single functions always have black-box complexity 1. Different kinds of extensions of single functions to function classes have been considered. In cases where the gap between the performance of the best randomised search heuristic and the black-box complexity is still large it can help to consider more restricted black-box complexity notions like unbiased black-box complexity. For the well-known Jump function neither considering different extensions nor considering more restricted notions of black-box complexity have been successful so far. We argue that the problem is not with the notion of black-box complexity but with the extension to a function class. We propose a different extension and show that for this extension there is a much better agreement even between the performance of an extremely simple evolutionary algorithm and the most general notion of black-box complexity.

Categories and Subject Descriptors

F.2.2 [**Analysis of Algorithms and Problem Complexity**]: Nonnumerical Algorithms and Problems

General Terms

Theory; Performance

Keywords

Black-Box Complexity; Run Time Analysis; Jump Function; (1+1) EA

FOGA'15, January 17–20, 2015, Aberystwyth, UK.

ACM 978-1-4503-3434-1/15/01 ...$15.00.
http://dx.doi.org/10.1145/2725494.2725507.

1. INTRODUCTION

Randomised search heuristics are a huge class of algorithms that are often used as general optimisers. They are attractive in practice because they are usually easy to implement and apply, and often yield good performance in acceptable time. To assess their performance it makes little sense to compare them with problem-specific algorithms since those are designed specifically for the problem at hand, make full use of its properties and cannot be applied to other problems. These fundamental differences make a comparison unfair and sometimes meaningless. A more appropriate way of assessing the performance of randomised search heuristics is black-box complexity, a complexity theory that matches optimisation in the black-box scenario (see [10] for a more in-depth discussion).

In black-box optimisation, we consider a scenario where an algorithm A is supposed to optimise an unknown objective function $f\colon S \to \mathbb{R}$ that comes from a known set of potential objective functions $\mathcal{F}$. The only way A can gather knowledge about f (apart from the knowledge that $f \in \mathcal{F}$) is by sampling f, i. e., by computing the function value $f(x)$ for $x \in S$. We call the number of function evaluations A makes to optimise f its optimisation time, $T_{A,f}$. For randomised algorithms we consider the expectation $\mathrm{E}(T_{A,f})$. We describe the performance of A on $\mathcal{F}$ by means of its worst case performance, $\sup\limits_{f\in\mathcal{F}} \mathrm{E}(T_{A,f})$. The black-box complexity is the performance of a best black-box algorithm for $\mathcal{F}$, i. e. $\inf\limits_{A} \sup\limits_{f\in\mathcal{F}} \mathrm{E}(T_{A,f})$.

If this expected number of function evaluations of a specific randomised search heuristic for some class of functions is asymptotically equal to the black-box complexity of this class of functions we know that it is very efficient for this class of functions. No algorithm can be significantly faster (as long as it is restricted to optimisation in the black-box scenario).

If the expected number of function evaluations of a specific randomised search heuristic for some class of functions is significantly larger than the black-box complexity of this class of functions (and the meaning of 'significant' may vary depending on the problem and the person considering the situation) this can have two very different causes and it is important to distinguish between the two. It may be the case that the randomised search heuristic is not very efficient and there is room for improvement. In this case one will try to come up with a more efficient heuristic and the design may be helped by an understanding of the shortcomings of the poorly performing randomised search heuristic.

But it may also be the case that black-box complexity is misleadingly small. In some sense this is an annoying case because we as algorithm designers feel unfairly punished by the result that our randomised search heuristics performs poorly where in reality the expectations that the black-box complexity raised are unrealistic. In these cases it can be much more constructive and useful to come up with a better suited notion of black-box complexity.

Black-box complexity was introduced by Droste et al. [5, 8]. Already in this first description the authors note that black-box complexity can yield misleadingly small values since it may allow for too powerful algorithms. In particular, there are many NP-hard problems that have a polynomially small black-box complexity. Clearly, this cannot be taken as indication that randomised search heuristics exist that have expected polynomial run time on these problems. Usually proofs for this polynomially small black-box complexity are constructive, i. e., one explicitly constructs a black-box algorithm that optimises any instance of the given NP-hard optimisation problem making only a polynomially small number of function evaluations. The idea of such algorithms tends to be simple. Using a polynomially small number of carefully selected function evaluations the algorithm determines the concrete input instance. In this phase it is not the goal of the algorithm to find an optimal solution but only to determine the concrete instance it is dealing with. In a second phase when this instance is now known the algorithm can compute an optimal solution easily without any further function evaluations. The reason is that once the instance is known the algorithm can compute the function value itself without the need to query for function values. Computing an optimal solution in a trivial manner is sufficient in this phase, e. g., by complete enumeration of all possible solutions. Finally, a last function evaluation is made with this optimal solution. Clearly, one would like to rule out such unrealistic algorithms that are very different from how 'real' randomised search heuristics actually function. That black-box complexity allows such algorithms may be seen as a shortcoming.

This obvious shortcoming of black-box complexity motivates the introduction of more restricted black-box models (and, consequently, the original notion of black-box complexity is today often referred to as unrestricted black-box complexity). Restricted black-box models can rule out algorithms that we consider to be unrealistic and give us a much more realistic understanding of the performance of our randomised search heuristics as well as the difficulty of a specific problem. It allows us to develop a better understanding of the power of certain mechanisms used in some randomised search heuristics by defining restricted black-box complexity notions that exclude the use of such a mechanism and by subsequently studying the impact on the black-box complexity.

It is not at all obvious how to restrict the notion of black-box complexity. Already Droste et al. [5, 8] discuss restricting the memory a black-box algorithm may use, hinting at memory-restricted black-box complexity. They do not present any results but Doerr and Winzen [3] prove that this memory-restricted black-box complexity can lead to larger lower bounds on the black-box complexity. Another possible restriction leads to ranking-based black-box complexity [4] where the black-box algorithm is not allowed to see the result of a function evaluation $f(x)$ but it is only informed about the rank of $f(x)$ in the sorted list of all search points it has sampled so far. Another and the arguably most important and so far most successful notion of restricted black-box complexity is that of unbiased black-box complexity (first presented 2010 [14], see also [15]). It restricts the way a black-box algorithm is allowed to generate the next search point. Creation is restricted to variation of existing search points and the variation operators are not allowed to have a bias with respect to 0- and 1-bits and neither with respect to bit positions.

While these restricted notions of black-box complexity have lead to many important and very satisfying results where the black-box complexity in these restricted notions matches the typical performances of many randomised search heuristics much better they are not able to solve every problem that still exists. For example, Doerr et al. [2] prove that the NP-hard PARTITION problem [9] has polynomial black-box complexity not only in the unrestricted black-box model but also in unbiased black-box complexity.

For a well-known family of example functions, Jump_k [7], it is known that a very simply evolutionary algorithm has expected optimisation time $\Theta(n^k + n \log n)$ (where $k \in \{1, 2, \ldots, n\}$ is a parameter of the function) and all mutation-based evolutionary algorithms have expected optimisation time $\Omega(n^{k-\varepsilon})$ for $k \ll n/2$ and any constant $\varepsilon > 0$ [12]. Doerr et al. [1] prove that for all values of k the unbiased black-box complexity is $O(n)$ and even for mutation-based algorithms, i. e., the unbiased black-box complexity with only unary variation operators, it is at most $O\left(n^{9/2}\right)$. This is a huge gap between the black-box complexity which is polynomial in all cases and the performance of evolutionary algorithms which becomes super-polynomial already for $k = \omega(1)$. Note that in complexity theory the difference between polynomial and super-polynomial performance is fundamental. The fundamental complexity classes P and NP (and many more) allow only a polynomial number of computational steps to be taken, i. e., only $n^{O(1)}$ steps. It is therefore of significance that for any k which is not constant but grows with increasing n (i. e., $\lim_{n\to\infty} 1/k = 0$) the number of function evaluations of all mutation-based evolutionary algorithms is no longer polynomial whereas the unbiased black-box complexity is only $O(n)$. Even when restricting the class of algorithms to mutation-based algorithms the black-box complexity is only $O\left(n^{9/2}\right)$, i. e., a polynomial of small degree.

One may be tempted to believe that this discrepancy between the performance of mutation-based evolutionary algorithms on Jump_k and its unary unbiased black-box complexity is another indicator that a more restricted form of black-box complexity is needed. However, in this case, we argue that the problem is not with the notion of black-box complexity but with the way the example function Jump_k is extended to a larger class of functions that allows for meaningful black-box complexity results. We discuss this issue in some detail in the following section. In Section 3 we provide the reader with formal definitions to make things precise. This includes not only the definition of the two known example functions that are relevant in our context and the definition of the very simple evolutionary algorithm we consider, the (1+1) EA. This section also contains the formal definition of the extension of the Jump_k function we propose. We analyse the performance of an extremely simple evolutionary algorithm for this extension in Section 4. When analysing the black-box complexity of this extension in Section 5 we see that even the unrestricted black-box complexity is close to this performance for small values of k. We conclude and discuss possible future research in Section 6.

2. EXTENDING THE JUMP FUNCTION

The example function Jump_k was first defined by Droste et al. [6] as follows (we will be using an equivalent definition in the next section).

$$\text{Jump}_k(x) = \begin{cases} k + \sum_{i=1}^{n} x[i] & \text{if } \sum_{i=1}^{n} x[i] \leq n-k \\ & \text{or } \sum_{i=1}^{n} x[i] = n \\ n - \sum_{i=1}^{n} x[i] & \text{otherwise} \end{cases}$$

It was presented as an example where a very simple evolutionary algorithm has an expected optimisation time of $\Theta(n^k + n\log n)$ [6] demonstrating that when one defines F_i as the set of functions that this algorithm can optimise in expected time $O(n^i)$ the sets F_i form a proper hierarchy $F_0 \subsetneq F_1 \subsetneq F_2 \subsetneq \cdots \subsetneq F_n$ (see also [7] which is the much better journal version; we cite [6] to make the order of events explicit). It was later used as a first example where evolutionary algorithms with crossover significantly outperform mutation-based evolutionary algorithms [12, 13] (we again cite [12] to make explicit the order of events and refer the reader to [13] where the presentation is better). In both cases the idea is that the function consists of one easy to optimise part (which is OneMax-like) that leads to a place where a significant 'jump' is needed to reach the unknown unique global optimum that is to be found at an unknown location in some distance from that place.

In this paper we discuss how one can extend the Jump function to a class of functions so that analysing its black-box complexity becomes a meaningful task and yields useful information about the difficulty of Jump for black-box algorithms. The black-box complexity $B_\mathcal{F}$ of a problem class $\mathcal{F}$ is determined by the worst case performance of an optimal black-box algorithm for this problem class. If a problem class $\mathcal{F}$ is finite one way of optimising an unknown function $f \in \mathcal{F}$ is to enumerate the optima of all functions in $\mathcal{F}$. This proves that $B_\mathcal{F} \leq |\mathcal{F}|$ holds. Using a random order instead of a fixed one improves this bound to $B_\mathcal{F} \leq (|\mathcal{F}|+1)/2$ (Lemma 4.4 in [10]). This implies that the black-box complexity of Jump_k is only 1 for any value of k. Clearly, one needs to extend a single example function to a class of functions to be able to obtain meaningful results on its black-box complexity. This extension should be done in a way that on the one hand it captures how common randomised search heuristics work on the function. Ideally, a randomised search heuristic should perform equal or at least similar on all functions that are member of this extension. On the other hand this extension should also capture the spirit of the example function.

Note that the problem that the black-box complexity of a single function is always 1 and one therefore needs to consider extensions of single functions to function classes is specific to unrestricted black-box complexity. This is different in unbiased black-box complexity where the unbiased black-box complexity of a single function with unique global optimum is $\Omega(n \log n)$ [15]. Thus, it makes sense to consider the unbiased black-box complexity of Jump_k without considering any extension to a class of functions. However, the result is $\Theta(n \log n)$ like it is for OneMax [15] since if we obtain $\text{Jump}_k(x)$ and know k we can calculate $\text{OneMax}(x)$ and behave as we do on OneMax. Thus, some form of extension is needed for meaningful results in unbiased black-box complexity, too.

Already in the first paper on black-box complexity there was a definition of three generic ways of extending a single example function to a class of example functions [5]. The first way implies that the roles of 0-bits and 1-bits can be exchanged arbitrarily. This makes sense since most randomised search heuristics treat 0-bits and 1-bits completely symmetrically. Having a bias towards one type of bit makes sense only if one knows that such a bias is useful for a specific problem [11]. Formally, for a function $f\colon \{0,1\}^n \to \mathbb{R}$ one defines another function $f_a\colon \{0,1\}^n \to \mathbb{R}$ by means of $f_a(x) = f(x \oplus a)$ where $a \in \{0,1\}^n$ is fixed and $x \oplus a$ denotes the bit-wise exclusive or of x and a. Unbiased black-box complexity [15] contains exactly the same kind of unbiasedness with respect to bit values as this notion expresses. For an example function f Droste et al. [5] call this extension $f^* = \{f_a \mid a \in \{0,1\}^n\}$ and we adopt this notation here.

The second way implies that the concrete function values should not be important. This makes sense since many randomised search heuristics react only to the order of search points defined by their function values but not to the exact function values themselves. Droste et al. [5] define this extension by considering $f^{**} = \{h \circ f \mid h\colon \mathbb{R} \to \mathbb{R} \text{ strictly increasing}\}$. While this is similar in spirit to ranking-based black-box complexity it is not the same [4].

The third way implies that the order of the bits should not be important. This makes sense for mutation-based randomised search heuristics (and, e. g., for those with mutation and uniform crossover) since those are oblivious to the ordering of the bits. Formally, this can be defined as $f^{***} = \{f_\pi \mid \text{permutation } \pi\}$ where we define f_π via $f_\pi(x) = f(x[\pi(1)]x[\pi(2)]\cdots x[\pi(n)])$ for a fixed permutation π. Unbiased black-box complexity [15] contains exactly the same kind of unbiasedness with respect to bit order as this notion expresses.

Depending on the example function at hand these extensions may also capture the spirit of the example function (which, admittedly, is a vague notion). For example, a well-known example function OneMax yields as its function value the number of 1-bits in the bit string. The extension OneMax^* yields the number of bits that coincide with the bits of an unknown target string. Thus, this extension expresses that OneMax is not really the search for the all 1-bits string (which is a trivial task) but the search for an unknown target string. Another example is the well-known example function LeadingOnes which yields as its function value the number of 1-bits in the bit string counted from left to right and stopping at the first 0-bit. Combining the first and third extension yields a function that gives as function value the number of bits that coincide with a hidden target string counted in an unknown order and stopping at the first mismatch, something that expresses the spirit of LeadingOnes.

For Jump, Doerr et al. [1] define Jump_k as OneMax for all points with a number of 1-bits that is either equal to n or larger than k and less than $n-k$. For all other points the function value is 0. Considering the unbiased black-box complexity means they consider the combination of the first and third extension. This turns Jump_k into a kind of OneMax (i. e., the search for an unknown target string) where large parts of the search space do not yield useful function values. The key observation is that the direct one-to-one correspondence between the number of correct bits and the function value is kept so that clever algorithms can infer the exact position of the hidden target string without the need to sample points in its vicinity. This is the basis for the surprisingly low black-box complexity that Doerr et al. [1] prove.

We argue that this does not capture the spirit of Jump_k that is more about locating an unknown target string that is hidden in some distance to points a search heuristic can find easily.

We present the formal definition of this extension in the following section, calling a specific function $\text{RealJump}_{k,x^*}$ and the class of functions that is the extension RealJump_k. The original function Jump_k is a member of RealJump_k which makes sense if we want to claim that RealJump_k is a generalisation of Jump_k since the notion of generalisation includes that the less general entity is a special case. (Note that this is not the case for the version defined by Doerr et al. [1].) For this extension we prove (for $k = \Theta(1)$) that the same very simple evolutionary algorithm, the (1+1) EA, has the same expected optimisation time $\Theta(n^k + n \log n)$ on RealJump_k in the worst case where the worst case is taken over the class of functions as usual (Section 4). Moreover, we prove that the black-box complexity of RealJump_k is $\Theta(n^{k-1})$ for $k = O(1)$. This shows that for small values of k (where the evolutionary algorithm at least has polynomial performance, i. e., where k is some constant and does not grow with growing n) the black-box complexity is only by a factor of $\Theta(n)$ smaller than the expected worst case optimisation time of the (1+1) EA. On the one hand this is a much better agreement between algorithm performance and black-box complexity. On the other hand it hints at the likely existence of better randomised search heuristics (as already indicated by the crossover result by Jansen and Wegener [12, 13]).

For larger values of k the agreement is less convincing. For $k = 1 + \ln n$ the algorithm's performance of $\Theta(n^{1+\ln n})$ has to be compared with a black-box complexity of only $O(n^{1+\ln n}/n^{\ln \ln n})$ which is by at least a super-polynomial factor of $\Omega(n^{\ln \ln n})$ smaller. For $k = n/2$ we have an algorithm performance of $\Theta\left(n^{n/2}\right)$. When we compare this with the black-box complexity of $\Theta(2^n)$ we see a factor of $2^{\Theta(n \log n)}$ between them. We conjecture that other randomised search heuristics perform significantly better than the simple (1+1) EA and that the black-box complexity is not too far off what can be achieved by realistic randomised search heuristics. Note that for $k = n/2$ pure random sampling of the search space (using the uniform distribution in each step) trivially yields a performance of $\Theta(2^n)$, matching the black-box complexity. However, since the performance of pure random sampling is $\Theta(2^n)$ for all values of k it cannot be considered a useful general random search heuristic for RealJump_k.

3. DEFINITIONS

For the sake of completeness we begin with the formal definition of ONEMAX and Jump. To enhance readability by saving some space we use OM instead of ONEMAX, J_k instead of JUMP_k and RJ_k instead of REALJUMP_k. Note that the definition of J_k is equivalent to the definition given at the beginning of Section 2.

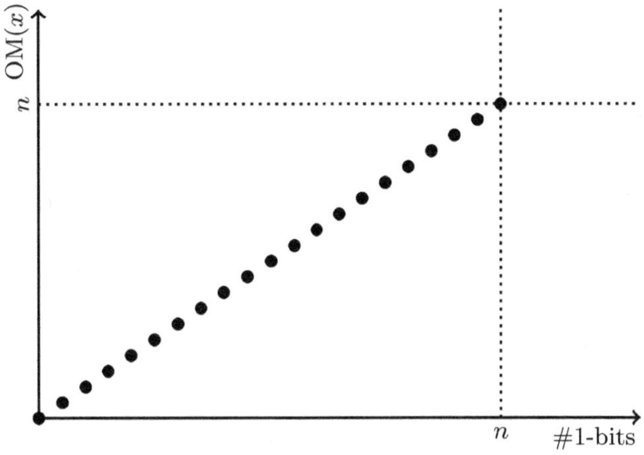

Figure 1: The function OM for $n = 20$. The plot shows the function values on the y-axis plotted over the number of 1-bits on the x-axis.

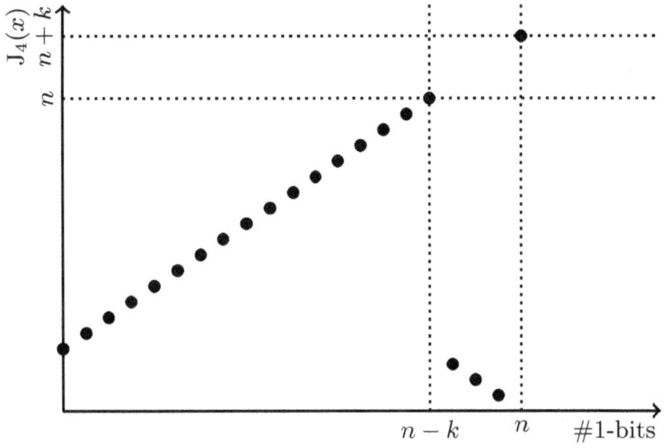

Figure 2: The function J_k for $n = 20$ and $k = 4$. The plot shows the function values on the y-axis plotted over the number of 1-bits on the x-axis.

DEFINITION 1. *Let $n \in \mathbb{N}$ and $k \in \{1, 2, \ldots, n\}$. We define the function OM: $\{0,1\}^n \to \mathbb{N}$ by $OM(x) = \sum_{i=1}^{n} x[i]$. We define the function J_k: $\{0,1\}^n \to \mathbb{N}$ by*

$$J_k(x) = \begin{cases} n - OM(x) & \text{if } n - k < OM(x) < n, \\ k + OM(x) & \text{otherwise.} \end{cases}$$

Since both functions, OM and J_k are symmetric (i. e., the function value depends only on the number of 1-bits and not on the specific bit string) we can easily given a visual impression of both functions by plotting the function value over the number of 1-bits. We do this for both functions for $n = 20$, in Figure 1 for OM and with $k = 4$ for J_k in Figure 2.

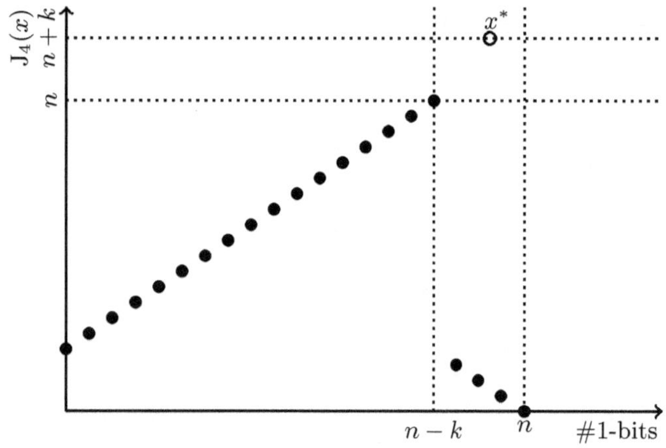

Figure 3: A visual impression of the function RJ_{k,x^*} for $n = 20$ and $k = 4$. The plot shows the function values on the y-axis plotted over the number of 1-bits on the x-axis. Note that the point marked with the circle drawn at height $n + k$ does not follow this pattern but represents a single point in the search space, the unique global optimum x^*.

DEFINITION 2. *Let $n \in \mathbb{N}$, $k \in \{1, 2, \ldots, n\}$, and $x^* \in \{0,1\}^n$ with $OM(x^*) > n - k$. We define the function $RJ_{k,x^*}\colon \{0,1\}^n \to \mathbb{N}$ by*

$$RJ_{k,x^*}(x) = \begin{cases} n - OM(x) & \text{if } n - k < OM(x) \leq n,\ x \neq x^*, \\ n + k & \text{if } x = x^*, \\ k + OM(x) & \text{otherwise.} \end{cases}$$

We define the class of functions RJ_k by $RJ_k = \{RJ_{k,x^*} \mid x^* \in \{0,1\}^n \text{ with } OM(x^*) > n - k\}$.

The two functions J_k and RJ_{k,x^*} differ in the function values of at most two points, their unique global optima, the all 1-bits string 1^n for J_k and x^* for RJ_{k,x^*}. If $x^* = 1^n$ the two functions are actually identical. Due to this change the function RJ_{k,x^*} is not symmetric in general. (It is for $x^* = 1^n$, obviously.) Therefore, it cannot really be visualised in the same way as OM in Figure 1 and J_k in Figure 2. We still give an impression in this spirit in Figure 3.

The expected optimisation time on OM and J_k has been determined for many different randomised search heuristics, and their black-box complexity has been determined for different notions of black-box complexity. While it makes sense to do the same for RJ_k, we restrict ourselves to the unrestricted black-box complexity and the expected optimisation time for the (1+1) EA with standard mutation probability $1/n$. For the sake of completeness we give a formal definition for this very simple EA as Algorithm 1.

As usual we measure the performance of the (1+1) EA by counting the number of function evaluations until a global optimum is reached. This is by 1 larger than the smallest t such that $f(x_t) = \max_{z \in \{0,1\}^n} f(z)$ holds. We denote this number of function evaluations as the optimisation time, $T_{(1+1)\ \mathrm{EA},f}$. We are interested in the expected optimisation time, $\mathrm{E}\big(T_{(1+1)\ \mathrm{EA},f}\big)$. For a class of functions $F \subset \{f\colon \{0,1\}^n \to \mathbb{R}\}$ we define the expected optimisation time of the (1+1) EA on F as the worst case expected optimisation time, i.e., $\mathrm{E}\big(T_{(1+1)\ \mathrm{EA},F}\big) = \sup_{f \in F} \mathrm{E}\big(T_{(1+1)\ \mathrm{EA},f}\big)$. This worst case perspective coincides with the usual perspective, in particular with the perspective of black-box complexity.

Algorithm 1: The (1+1) EA

Set $t := 0$;
Select $x_t \in \{0,1\}^n$;
while *termination criterion not fulfilled* **do**
  $y := x_t$;
  for $i \in \{1, 2, \ldots, n\}$ **do**
    With probability $1/n$ set $y[i] := 1 - y[i]$;
  end
  if $f(y) \geq f(x_t)$ **then**
    $x_{t+1} := y$;
  else
    $x_{t+1} := x_t$;
  end
  $t := t + 1$;
end

4. (1+1) EA ON RJ_K

The function class RJ_k is deliberately designed to be similar to the original function J_k. It comes therefore as no surprise that the expected optimisation time of the (1+1) EA on RJ_k is asymptotically equal to the expected optimisation time of the (1+1) EA on J_k. Note that RJ_k is a class of functions and we adopt a worst case perspective. This means that we prove two things. There is at least one function in RJ_k where the expected optimisation time of the (1+1) EA is asymptotically the same as on J_k. Moreover, no function in RJ_k is significantly more difficult for the (1+1) EA. It does not mean that RJ_k may not contain many functions where the (1+1) EA is more efficient. But since this is not relevant here we do not explore this aspect since it would only distract us from our goal.

Theorem 3 makes a statement only for constant k. Having $k = \Theta(1)$ simplifies things considerably because it implies $\binom{n}{k} = \Theta(n^k)$ and $n - k = \Theta(n)$. The proof of Theorem 3 makes use of this in several places.

THEOREM 3. *For each constant k, $\mathrm{E}\big(T_{(1+1)\ EA,RJ_k}\big) = \Theta\big(n^k + n \log n\big)$ holds.*

PROOF. The case $k = 1$ is particularly simple. Note that for $k = 1$ we have $x^* = 1^n$ as only valid choice for x^* since we need $\mathrm{OM}(x^*) > n - 1$ which implies $\mathrm{OM}(x^*) = n$ and $x^* = 1^n$ follows. Consequently, we have $\mathrm{RJ}_{1,1^n}(x) = 1 + \mathrm{OM}(x)$ for all $x \in \{0,1\}^n$ and $\mathrm{E}\Big(T_{(1+1)\ \mathrm{EA},\mathrm{RJ}_{1,1^n}}\Big) = \Theta(n \log n)$ is a direct consequence [7].

For $k > 1$ we partition the search space $\{0,1\}^n$ into two large areas A and B. The set A contains all search points where the function is essentially equal to OM (essentially equal meaning equal up to addition of one fixed value, k in this case). The set B contains the rest of the search space where the function is essentially equal to $-\mathrm{OM}$ and where the unique global optimum x^* is hidden. Since the definition of both sets depends on k we define $A(k) := \{x \in \{0,1\}^n \mid \mathrm{OM}(x) \leq n - k\}$ and $B(k) := \{0,1\}^n \setminus A(k)$. Note that $x^* \in B(k)$ holds. Also note that $\mathrm{RJ}_{k,x^*}(x) = k + \mathrm{OM}(x)$

holds iff $x \in A(k)$. Furthermore, $\mathrm{RJ}_{k,x^*}(x) = n+k$ iff $x = x^*$ and $\mathrm{RJ}_{k,x^*}(x) < n+k$ for all $x \neq x^*$.

We consider a run of the (1+1) EA on $\mathrm{RJ}_{k,1^n}$ and begin with the case $x_0 \in B(k)$. Note that this case is very unlikely since $k = O(1)$ implies that $\Pr(x_0 \in B_k) = 2^{-\Omega(n)}$ holds. As long as $x_0 \in B(k) \cup \{x^*\}$ holds the situation is essentially the same as on $-\mathrm{OM}$. We conclude that in expectation we have $x \in A(k) \cup \{x^*\}$ after $O(n \log n)$ steps and the contribution of this case to $\mathrm{E}(T_{(1+1)\text{ EA},\mathrm{RJ}_k})$ is $o(1)$. By the law of total expectation we have

$$\begin{aligned}&\mathrm{E}(T_{(1+1)\text{ EA},\mathrm{RJ}_k})\\ &\quad = \Pr(x_0 \in B(k)) \cdot \mathrm{E}(T_{(1+1)\text{ EA},\mathrm{RJ}_k} \mid x_0 \in B(k))\\ &\qquad + \Pr(x_0 \in A(k)) \cdot \mathrm{E}(T_{(1+1)\text{ EA},\mathrm{RJ}_k} \mid x_0 \in A(k)).\end{aligned}$$

We have just argued that for the first summand we have $\mathrm{E}(T_{(1+1)\text{ EA},\mathrm{RJ}_k} \mid x_0 \in B(k)) \cdot \Pr(x_0 \in B(k)) = o(1)$. Moreover, $\Pr(x_0 \in A(k)) = 1 - \Pr(x_0 \in B(k)) = 1 - 2^{-\Omega(n)}$ holds. We conclude that together this yields $\mathrm{E}(T_{(1+1)\text{ EA},\mathrm{RJ}_k}) = \Theta(\mathrm{E}(T_{(1+1)\text{ EA},\mathrm{RJ}_k} \mid x_0 \in A(k)))$ and it suffices to consider $\mathrm{E}(T_{(1+1)\text{ EA},\mathrm{RJ}_k} \mid x_0 \in A(k))$.

Consider the situation for $x_0 \in A(k)$. Note that in this situation for any $t' > 0$ we have that $x_{t'} \in B(k)$ implies that $x_{t'} = 1^n$ holds since for all other $x \in B(k)$ we have $\mathrm{RJ}_{k,x^*}(x) = n - \mathrm{OM}(x) \leq k - 1 < \mathrm{RJ}_{k,x^*}(x_t)$ and the (1+1) EA does not move to search points with smaller fitness value.

We now make a case distinction with respect to $\mathrm{OM}(x^*)$. We have $n - k + 1 \leq \mathrm{OM}(x^*) \leq n$ by definition of RJ_{k,x^*}.

For the case $\mathrm{OM}(x^*) = n$ things are the same as for J_k and we know that $\mathrm{E}\left(T_{(1+1)\text{ EA},\mathrm{RJ}_{k,1^n}}\right) = \Theta(n^k + n \log n)$ follows. Note that this already establishes $\mathrm{E}(T_{(1+1)\text{ EA},\mathrm{RJ}_k}) = \Omega(n^k + n \log n)$ since it suffices to identify at least one function where the expected run time is that large. Thus, we only have to prove an upper bound for the remaining case $n - k < \mathrm{OM}(x^*) < n$.

We begin by considering the case $\mathrm{OM}(x^*) = n - k + 1$. We consider a level of strings with l 1-bits in $A(k)$, i. e., $L(l) = \{x \in \{0,1\}^n \mid \mathrm{OM}(x) = l\}$ for $l \leq n - k$. For each $x \in L(l)$ the Hamming distance to x^* is at least $n-k+1-l = n - l - (k-1)$ because x^* contains $n - k + 1 - l$ more 1-bits than x. Note that the Hamming distance may significantly larger than this. Depending on the value of l it can get as large as $n - l + (k - 1)$.

We know that the expected time to reach x^* from some x is strictly increasing with increasing Hamming distance. However, we first concentrate on level $L(n-k)$ where the Hamming distance is minimal. We will carry out our reasoning a bit more general than is strictly needed on level $L(n-k)$ because we want to reuse the same line of reasoning for other levels $L(l)$, too. We will argue that it is the time spent on level $L(n-k)$ that dominates the expected run time.

On this level $L(n-k)$ the Hamming distance equals 1 for those bit strings that agree with x^* on all $k-1$ positions for 0-bits in x^*. For the remaining 0-bits in x there are $n - k + 1$ positions so that there are $n - k + 1 = \Theta(n)$ such bit strings. There cannot be any bit strings with Hamming distance 2. Assuming otherwise we see that such a bit string can be created by changing exactly 1 bit in a bit string that has Hamming distance 1. Clearly, this changes the number of 1-bits so that such a bit string cannot belong to level $L(n-k)$. The same way we see that no bit string on level $L(n-k)$ can have even Hamming distance to x^*. Thus, we only have to discuss bit strings with odd Hamming distance to the optimal bit string x^*.

We obtain all bit strings with Hamming distance 3 by taking each of the bit strings with Hamming distance 1 and changing one of $k-1$ 0-bits and one of the $n-k+1$ 1-bits. Note that this counts each bit string twice because we are considering each possible bit string with Hamming distance 1 as starting point. Thus, their number equals $(n-k)(k-1)(n-k+1)/2 = \Theta(n^2)$. Alternatively, we can obtain all bit strings with Hamming distance 3 by using x^* as starting point. We need to increase the number of 0-bits by 1 to obtain a bit string on level $L(n-k)$ and we need to change 3 bits to create a Hamming distance of 3. Thus, we have to choose two 1-bits ($\binom{n-k-1}{2}$ possibilities) and one 0-bit ($\binom{k-1}{1}$ possibilities). Clearly, this also yields $\binom{n-k-1}{2} \cdot \binom{k-1}{1} = (n-k)(k-1)(n-k+1)/2 = \Theta(n^2)$. We can extend both lines of reasoning to bit strings with Hamming distance $2i - 1$ to x^* in $L(n-k)$ and see that their number is $\Theta(n^i)$.

When reaching level $L(n-k)$, the probability to be in one of these bit strings equals $\Theta(n^i/n^k)$ for symmetry reasons since there $\binom{n}{k} = \Theta(n^k)$ bit strings on level $n - k$. The probability to have a mutation that changes the current bit string and stays in $L(n-k)$ equals $\Theta(1/n)$ since its necessary and sufficient to flip one of $\Theta(1)$ 0-bits and one of the $\Theta(n)$ 1-bits. Let us consider a graph $G = (V, E)$ that contains for each bit string $x \in L(n-k)$ one node and an edge between $x, x' \in L(n-k)$ if and only if the Hamming distance between x and x' equals 2. Note that we have an edge between two nodes $x, x' \in L(n-k)$ if and only if a direct mutation from x to x' has probability $\Theta(1/n)$.

The graph G has $|V| = \binom{n}{k} = \Theta(n^k)$ nodes and $|E| = (|V| \cdot (n-k)k)/2 = \Theta(n^{k+1})$ edges. Consider a random walk on this $(n-k)k$-regular graph G. It is obvious how this random walk corresponds to the random walk the (1+1) EA performs on $L(n-k)$. We claim that for any two nodes $x, x' \in V$ the expected time to get from x to x' and back (the so-called commute time) is $\Theta(n^{k+1})$. If this is the case we can conclude that we can expect to be in any of the $\Theta(n^i)$ bit strings in $L(n-k)$ with Hamming distance $2i-1$ to x^* every $\Theta(n^{k+1-i})$ steps. Note that i cannot become arbitrarily large since we assume that a Hamming distance of $2i - 1$ is possible and this imposes an upper limit on i. It is well known (see, e. g., Theorem 6.6 in [16]) that the commute time between two nodes x, x' is given by $2\,|E|\,R_{x,x'}$ where $R_{x,x'}$ denotes the effective resistance between x and x'. The Hamming distance between any two $x, x' \in L(n-k)$ by $2k = O(1)$ so that the Hamming distance is $\Theta(1)$ in any case. By traversing an edge in G we can decrease or increase the Hamming distance to our destination (assuming we want to reach x' from x) by at most 2 and there is always an edge that decreases it by 2. Together this implies that $R_{x,x'} = \Theta(1)$ holds. Thus the commute time is $\Theta(|E|) = \Theta(n^{k+1})$ as claimed.

If $\mathrm{H}(x_t, x^*) = 2i - 1$ holds the probability to reach x^* equals $\Theta(1/n^{2i-1})$. Since the probability not to change x_t equals $1 - O(1/n)$ we are able to make this jump to x^* with probability $\Theta(1/n^{2i-2})$ before we change x_t. Since the expected time to reach an appropriate x_t equals $\Theta(n^{k+1-i})$ the expected optimisation time once we have reached this level is $\Theta\left(n^{k+1-i} \cdot n^{2i-2}\right) = \Theta\left(n^{k+i-1}\right)$. This bound is true for each feasible value of i, in particular for $i = 1$. We see that we obtain $\Theta\left(n^k\right)$ as expected time to reach x^* from level $L(n-k)$.

Most of this argumentation carries over to other levels $L(l)$ with $l < n-k$. The only difference is that on level $L(l)$ with $l < n-k$ there is the possibility of leaving $L(l)$ for some level $L(l')$ with $l' > l$. Since this happens with probability $\Omega(1/n)$ we see that it is much more likely to reach x^* from $L(n-k)$ than from any other $L(l)$ with $l < n-k$. We see that this does not change the expected optimisation time and $\mathrm{E}\left(T_{(1+1)\ \mathrm{EA},\mathrm{RJ}_{k,x^*}}\right) = \Theta\left(n^k + n \log n\right)$ holds for this case, too. Thus, this concludes the proof for $\mathrm{OM}(x^*) = n-k+1$.

For $\mathrm{OM}(x^*) = n-k+i$ with $i > 1$ (but $i < k$ since we have already dealt with $\mathrm{OM}(x^*) = n$) not much changes. We can see this by comparing the case $i = 2$ with the case $i = 1$. The same comparison can be made for $i = 3$ with $i = 2$, $i = 4$ with $i = 3$ and so on. For $i = 2$ the minimal Hamming distance from a bit string $x \in L(n-k)$ increases by 1 in comparison to the case $i = 1$. This increases the expected waiting time for an appropriate mutation by a factor of $\Theta(n)$. On the other hand, the number of bit strings that have this minimal Hamming distance increases by a factor of $\Theta(n)$ which in turn decreases the expected waiting time for an appropriate mutation by a factor of $\Theta(1/n)$. We see that in summary, asymptotically speaking, nothing changes and we have $\mathrm{E}\left(T_{(1+1)\ \mathrm{EA},\mathrm{RJ}_k}\right) = \Theta\left(n^k + n \log n\right)$ as claimed. □

As pointed out above, the proof of Theorem 3 makes use of the fact that $k = \Theta(1)$ holds in many places. Extending the results to non-constant values of k is not completely trivial.

To illustrate the bounds from Theorem 3 we present the results of experiments. Since for $x^* = 1^n$ we have the original Jump function which has been studied in detail before we do not consider this case but instead concentrate on another extreme case, $x^* = 1^{n-k+1}0^{k-1}$ for RJ_{k,x^*}. We perform 100 independent runs for each value $n \in \{10, 20, 30, \ldots, 100\}$ and each value $k \in \{2, 3, 4\}$. We plot the average number of function evaluations on the y-axis over n on the x-axis together with the observed standard deviation to give an impression of the variance in the process. Together with these empirical values we plot the function $c_k n^k$ where the multiplicative constant c_k is obtained by using the nonlinear least-squares Marquardt-Levenberg algorithm (as implemented in gnuplot version 5.0). The results can be seen in Figures 4, 5 and 6 for $k = 2$, $k = 3$ and $k = 4$, respectively.

We see that in all three case there is an excellent agreement between the average run times and the theoretical bound of order $\Theta\left(n^k\right)$ when one allows the multiplicative factor to be determined numerically. The observed standard deviation is very large which was to be expected since the run time is determined by a random walk on a plateau of points of equal fitness n. We also see that the multiplicative factor c_k is clearly decreasing with k. While any dependency on k is lost in our results since we make the assumption that $k = \Theta(1)$ and present asymptotic results only it was to be expected that there is a dependency on k. It remains subject of future research to determine this dependency and to extend the results to non-constant values of k. Both aspects would distract us from our goal here and are therefore beyond the scope of this paper.

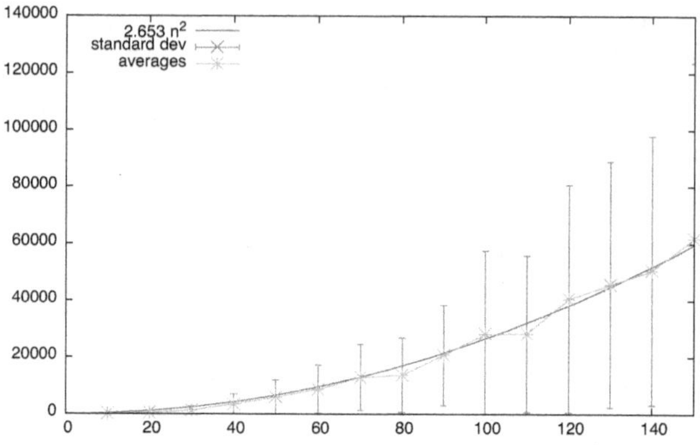

Figure 4: Results of 100 independent runs of the (1+1) EA on $\mathbf{RJ}_{2,1^{n-1}0}$. Shown are the average optimisation times together with the observed standard deviation and the theoretical curve $\mathbf{2.653}n^2$ where the factor 2.653 is the result of applying the nonlinear least-squares Marquardt-Levenberg algorithm.

5. BLACK-BOX COMPLEXITY OF RJ_K

In the black-box scenario an algorithm is free to make use of the knowledge that it is supposed to optimise some unknown function $f \in \mathcal{F}$ taken from some known set of functions $\mathcal{F}$. For $\mathcal{F} = \mathrm{RJ}_k$ this implies that an optimal black-box algorithm will not evaluate any search point where the function value is known simply from the fact that the unknown objective function is member of RJ_k. Recall the definition of $A(k)$ and $B(k)$ from the proof of Theorem 3. For $A(k) = \{x \in \{0,1\}^n \mid \mathrm{OM}(x) \leq n-k\}$ we know that $f(x) = k + \mathrm{OM}(x)$ holds. Thus, an optimal black-box algorithm will never sample points $x \in A(k)$. For points in $B(k)$ the function values are 'almost known', i. e., we know for $x \in B(k)$ that $\mathrm{RJ}_{k,x^*}(x) \in \{n-\mathrm{OM}(x), n+1\}$ holds. We have $\mathrm{RJ}_{k,x^*}(x) = n+1$ if $x = x^*$ and $\mathrm{RJ}_{k,x^*}(x) = n-\mathrm{OM}(x)$ otherwise. However, there is no way of knowing which is the case before sampling x. Thus, optimal black-box algorithms will sample points from $B(k)$ but each function evaluation will only reveal if $x = x^*$ holds or not, in spite of yielding one of k different function values. In this sense that each function evaluation only allows to distinguish one of two cases ($x = x^*$ or $x \neq x^*$) it yields only 1 bit of information. This is the same as it is for a function that has function value 0 for each point in the search space except for the unique global optimum (known as Needle function since it behaves like a needle in the haystack [10]). We can conclude that the black-box complexity of RJ_k equals $(|B(k)| + 1)/2$. We prove this in the following and spend some time proving bounds on $|B(k)|$. One main observation is that the expected optimisation time of the (1+1) EA on RJ_{k*} differs from the black-box complexity of RJ_k only by a factor of $\Theta(n)$ for constant $k > 1$. This indicates that the (1+1) EA is rather efficient on these functions, only a factor of $\Theta(n)$ away from optimal performance.

THEOREM 4. *Let $n \in \mathbb{N}$ and $k \in \{1, 2, \ldots, n\}$. Let $b(k) = \sum\limits_{i=0}^{k-1} \binom{n}{i}$.*

The black-box complexity of RJ_k equals $B_{RJ_k} = (b(k) + 1)/2$. For $k = O(1)$ it is $B_{RJ_k} = \Theta\left(n^{k-1}\right)$. For $k = 1 + \ln n$

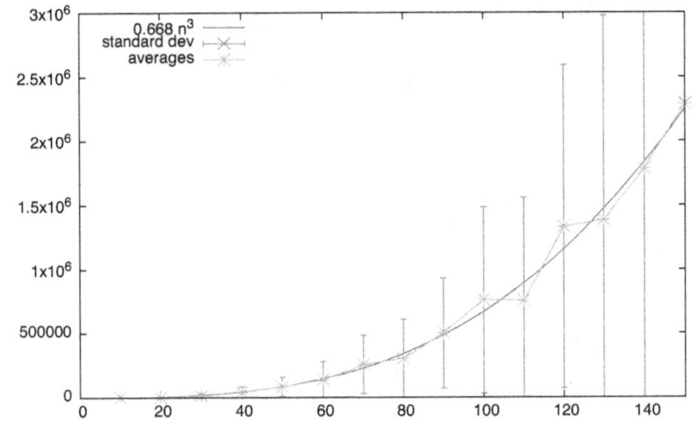

Figure 5: Results of 100 independent runs of the (1+1) EA on $\mathrm{RJ}_{3,1^{n-200}}$. Shown are the average optimisation times together with the observed standard deviation and the theoretical curve $0.668n^3$ where the factor 0.668 is the result of applying the nonlinear least-squares Marquardt-Levenberg algorithm.

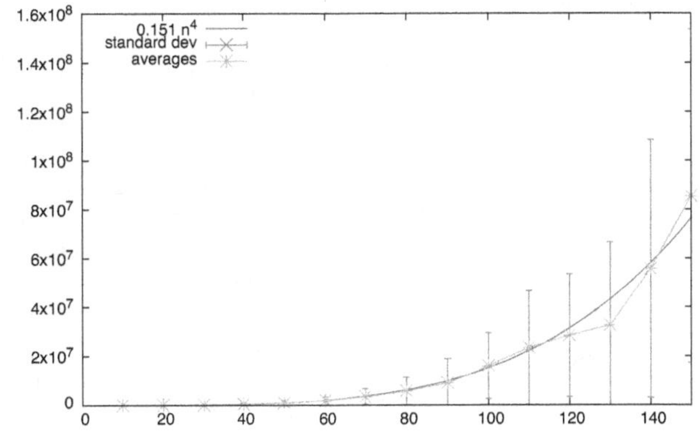

Figure 6: Results of 100 independent runs of the (1+1) EA on $\mathrm{RJ}_{4,1^{n-3000}}$. Shown are the average optimisation times together with the observed standard deviation and the theoretical curve $0.151n^4$ where the factor 0.151 is the result of applying the nonlinear least-squares Marquardt-Levenberg algorithm.

we have

$$\frac{n^{\ln n}}{n^{\ln\ln n}} \le B_{RJ_k} \le \frac{2n}{\sqrt{\ln n}} \cdot \frac{n^{\ln n}}{n^{\ln\ln n}}.$$

For $k = n/2$ we have $B_{RJ_k} = 2^{n-2} + 1/2$.

Proof. We know [10] that it suffices to prove a lower bound for an optimal deterministic black-box algorithm using an arbitrary fixed probability distribution over RJ_k to establish a lower bound on B_{RJ_k} since by application of Yao's minimax principle [17] this yields a lower bound for the worst case optimisation time of randomised black-box algorithms.

Consider some $f \in \mathrm{RJ}_k$. We know there is $x^* \in \{0,1\}^n$ such that $f = \mathrm{RJ}_{k,x^*}$ holds.

Consider an optimal deterministic black-box algorithm for RJ_k and consider its expected performance under the uniform distribution on RJ_k. Since it knows the function value for every $x \in A(k) = \{x \in \{0,1\}^n \mid \mathrm{OM}(x) \le n-k\}$ it only samples point in $B(k) = \{0,1\}^n \setminus A(k)$. Since sampling any point $x \in B(k) \setminus \{x^*\}$ only reveals that $x \ne x^*$ (because it was known that for $x \in B(k) \setminus \{x^*\}$ the function value equals $n - \mathrm{OM}(x)$) the algorithm can be described by a permutation of $B(k)$. The number of function evaluations it takes to optimise the function equals the position of x^* in this permutation. Therefore, the expected number of function evaluations equals

$$\sum_{t=1}^{|B(k)|} \frac{1}{|B(k)|} \cdot t = \frac{|B(k)|+1}{2}$$

and we obtain the lower bound $B_{\mathrm{RJ}_k} \ge (|B(k)|+1)/2$ as immediate consequence. For an upper bound on the black-box complexity B_{RJ_k} it suffices to analyse the performance of any (randomised or deterministic) black-box algorithm for RJ_k. Since a deterministic algorithm that enumerates $B(k)$ in a fixed order achieves exactly this performance in expectation we have $B_{\mathrm{RJ}_k} = (|B(k)|+1)/2$.

The set $B(k)$ contains all bit strings with less than k 0-bits, thus

$$|B(k)| = \sum_{i=0}^{k-1} \binom{n}{i} = b(k)$$

holds and the first claim follows.

For the second claim we observe that

$$\binom{n}{k-1} \le b(k) \le k \cdot \binom{n}{k-1}$$

holds. For $k = O(1)$ we obtain $b(k) = \Theta(n^{k-1})$ and $B_{\mathrm{RJ}_k} = \Theta(n^{k-1})$ is immediate.

For the lower bound in third claim it suffice to observe that

$$b(k) = \sum_{i=0}^{k-1} \binom{n}{i} \ge \binom{n}{k-1}$$

holds and use

$$\binom{n}{k-1} \ge \left(\frac{n}{k-1}\right)^{k-1}$$

(see Proposition B.2 in [16]). Using $k = 1 + \ln n$ yields the result. For the upper bound in the third claim it suffices to observe that

$$b(k) = \sum_{i=0}^{k-1} \binom{n}{i} \le k \cdot \binom{n}{k-1}$$

and use

$$\binom{n}{k-1} \le n^n/((k-1)!)$$

together with

$$(k-1)! > \frac{(k-1)^{k-1/2}}{e^{k-1}}.$$

Using $k = 1 + \ln n$ again yields the result.

For the fourth claim it suffices to note that $b(n) = 2^n$ and $b(n/2) = 2^{n-1}$ since the terms for i and $n-i$ are equal. □

6. CONCLUSIONS

Black-box complexity helps to assess the performance of randomised search heuristics in the context of optimisation. In cases where there is a huge gap between the black-box complexity of a problem and the performance of a randomised search heuristics there can be several different reasons for this. It can be the case that the randomised search heuristics actually performs poorly so that the black-box complexity accurately measures the problem difficulty and hints at the existence of better search heuristics. It can be the case that the applied notion of black-box complexity is not sufficiently restricted to appropriately mirror the optimisation scenario and that using a more restricted black-box complexity model yields result where one observes a better match between the black-box complexity in this restricted model and the performance of the randomised search heuristic. Finally, it can also be the case that the definition of the problem class does not actually match the problem one has in mind. For the well-known example function Jump_k we have argued that the surprisingly small black-box complexity that has been reported even for unbiased black-box complexity is caused by an extension of the example function to a class of function that does not capture the spirit of the example function.

We have presented a different extension of Jump_k, called RJ_k that better captures the main ideas of the original Jump_k function. We have proven for the simple (1+1) EA that the performance on the original function Jump_k and on RJ_k is asymptotically equal for any constant k. Moreover, we have shown that the black-box complexity of RJ_k is much closer to the performance of the (1+1) EA. This holds even for the unrestricted black-box complexity. For the most relevant case where the (1+1) EA has polynomial expected optimisation time the performance gap between its expected optimisation time and the black-box complexity is $\Theta(n)$. We conjecture that other, more sophisticated evolutionary algorithms may be able to close this gap, not only for small values of k but also for larger values of k where the gap between the performance of the (1+1) EA and the black-box complexity is much larger. The analysis of other existing randomised search heuristics and, if needed, the design of better suited randomised search heuristic remains subject of future research.

We also leave as subject of future research to determine the expected optimisation of the (1+1) EA on RJ_{k,x^*} for non-constant values of k and, in particular, to determine how the expected optimisation time depends on k. The latter is also a worthwhile research goal in the case of constant k.

Finally, we remember that the original Jump function was the first where it was rigorously proven that evolutionary algorithms with crossover can significantly outperform the (1+1) EA. This was done with a standard steady-state genetic algorithm that as the only measure to increase diversity in the population always removes a worst member of the population that has the largest number of copies. For this algorithm the expected optimisation time is polynomial on Jump_k for all $k = O(\log n)$. It is clear from Theorem 4 that this cannot be the case for all $f \in \text{RJ}_{k,x^*}$ with $k = O(\log n)$. Determining how the performance of this steady-state GA deteriorates as the optimum x^* is moved away from 1^n is also subject of future research.

7. REFERENCES

[1] B. Doerr, C. Doerr, and T. Kötzing. Unbiased black-box complexities of jump functions: how to cross large plateaus. In D. Arnold, editor, *Genetic and Evolutionary Computation Conference (GECCO 2014)*, pages 769–776. ACM Press, 2014.

[2] B. Doerr, C. Doerr, and T. Kötzing. The unbiased black-box complexity of partition is polynomial. *Artificial Intelligence*, 216:275–286, 2014.

[3] B. Doerr and C. Winzen. Memory-restricted black-box complexity of OneMax. *Information Processing Letters*, 112:32–34, 2012.

[4] B. Doerr and C. Winzen. Ranking-based black-box complexity. *Algorithmica*, 68:571–609, 2014.

[5] S. Droste, T. Jansen, K. Tinnefeld, and I. Wegener. A new framework for the valuation of algorithms for black-box optimization. In K. A. De Jong, R. Poli, and J. E. Rowe, editors, *Foundations of Genetic Algorithms 7 (FOGA)*, pages 253–270. Morgan Kaufmann, 2003.

[6] S. Droste, T. Jansen, and I. Wegener. On the analysis of the (1+1) evolutionary algorithm. Technical Report SFB CI-21/98, Universität Dortmund, Germany, 1998.

[7] S. Droste, T. Jansen, and I. Wegener. On the analysis of the (1+1) evolutionary algorithm. *Theoretical Computer Science*, 276:51–81, 2002.

[8] S. Droste, T. Jansen, and I. Wegener. Upper and lower bounds for randomized search heuristics in black-box optimization. *Theory of Computing Systems*, 39:525–544, 2006.

[9] M. R. Garey and D. S. Johnson. *Computers and Intractability. A Guide to the Theory of NP-Completeness.* Freeman, 1979.

[10] T. Jansen. *Analyzing Evolutionary Algorithms. The Computer Science Perspective.* Springer, 2013.

[11] T. Jansen and D. Sudholt. Analysis of an asymmetric mutation operator. *Evolutionary Computation*, 18:1–26, 2010.

[12] T. Jansen and I. Wegener. The analysis of evolutionary algorithms—A proof that crossover really can help. In J. Něsetřil, editor, *Proceedings of the European Symposium on Algorithms (ESA '99)*, pages 184–193. Springer, 1999.

[13] T. Jansen and I. Wegener. The analysis of evolutionary algorithms—A proof that crossover really can help. *Algorithmica*, 34:47–66, 2002.

[14] P. K. Lehre and C. Witt. Black-box search by unbiased variation. In *Genetic and Evolutionary Computation Conference (GECCO 2014)*, pages 1441–1448. ACM Press, 2010.

[15] P. K. Lehre and C. Witt. Black-box search by unbiased variation. *Algorithmica*, 64:623–642, 2012.

[16] R. Motwani and P. Raghavan. *Randomized Algorithms.* Cambridge University Press, 1995.

[17] A. C.-C. Yao. Probabilistic computations: Towards a unified measure of complexity. In *Proceedings of the 17th Annual IEEE Symposium on the Foundations of Computer Science (FOCS '77)*, pages 222–227. IEEE Press, 1977.

Insights From Adversarial Fitness Functions

Alan J. Lockett
Dalle Molle Institute for Artificial Intelligence Studies
Galleria 2, 6928 Manno-Lugano, Switzerland
alan.lockett@gmail.com

ABSTRACT

The performance of optimization is usually studied in specific settings where the fitness functions are highly constrained with static, stochastic or dynamic properties. This work examines what happens when the fitness function is a player engaged with the optimizer in an optimization game. Although the advantage of the fitness function is known through the No Free Lunch theorems, several deep insights about the space of possible performance measurements arise as a consequence of studying these adversarial fitness function, including: 1) Every continuous and linear method of measuring performance can be identified with the optimization game for some adversarial fitness; 2) For any convex continuous performance criterion, there is some deterministic optimizer that performs best, even when the fitness function is stochastic or dynamic; 3) Every stochastic optimization method can be viewed as a probabilistic choice over countably many deterministic methods. All of these statements hold in both finite and infinite search domains.

Categories and Subject Descriptors

H.4 [**Information Systems Applications**]: Miscellaneous; D.2.8 [**Software Engineering**]: Metrics—*complexity measures, performance measures*

General Terms

Theory

Keywords

Optimization Theory; Stochastic Optimization; Adversarial Fitness; Optimization Game; Functional Analysis; Optimizer-Fitness Duality

1. INTRODUCTION

The performance of black-box optimizers generally and evolutionary algorithms specifically has been studied theoretically in order to determine the advantages and limits of existing methods and to propose new methods based on theoretical observations. Usually, the optimization setting involves a static fitness function. Dynamic and stochastic fitness functions have also been considered, but are more difficult to analyze. In this study, we consider the even broader case of *adversarial optimization*, in which the optimization problem is viewed as a game between an optimizer and an adversarial fitness function whose behavior can adapt to the decisions of the optimizer.

It is known that an adversarial fitness function can frustrate the efforts of any optimizer by playing a No Free Lunch strategy, so the actual performance of an optimizer is not of interest here. Nonetheless, the flexibility of the setting makes it possible to draw broad conclusions about the structure of the space of optimization methods, including that the space is spanned by *deterministic optimizers* (Theorem 5.3) and that for any convex continuous function that measures the performance of an optimizer, the best performance is achieved by some deterministic optimizer in any setting. Most surprising, however, is the fact that every continuous linear measure of performance that is based on averaging scored optimization histories corresponds to a game with some adversarial fitness (Theorem 4.3).

The results are first developed for finite search spaces and fitness domains. Section 2 introduces the adversarial setting. Section 3 introduces a normed vector space arising from this setting, and performance in this space is studied in Section 4. Infinite spaces are discussed in Section 5.

2. ADVERSARIAL OPTIMIZATION

To begin, suppose that the search and fitness space are both finite, and imagine optimization to be a two-player zero-sum game between an optimizer and a fitness function.

2.1 Optimization as a Zero-Sum Game

In game theory [12], each player chooses a strategy, say, σ_X for the optimizer and σ_Y for the fitness, and each player receives a value based on both choices, e.g. $V_X(\sigma_X, \sigma_Y)$ for the first player and $V_Y(\sigma_X, \sigma_Y)$ for the second. For a zero-sum game, V_Y is defined so that $V_Y(\sigma_X, \sigma_Y) = -V_X(\sigma_X, \sigma_Y)$, i.e., the two values sum to zero.

For turn-based games, one distinguishes between the *normal form* and the *extended form* of a game. In the extended form, each player makes a series of choices that can depend on the choices made by the other player. This form is often represented as a *game tree*, in which alternating levels of the tree indicate the alternating turns of each player. From the perspective of the extended form, each player makes a

FOGA'15, January 17–20, 2015, Aberystwyth, UK.

http://dx.doi.org/10.1145/2725494.2725501.

sequence of choices that are dependent on the choices of the other player. By contrast, in the normal form, each player chooses a complete strategy in a single decision at the outset of the game; these are the strategies σ_X and σ_Y mentioned above. The normal form and extended form are generally equivalent for turn-based games. Under this equivalence, the strategy σ_X can be thought of as a function or a program that determines the first player's decisions at each step, conditioned on the opponent's responses.

Now consider the process of optimizing a fitness function as a game between an optimization method and a fitness function. In each turn of the optimization game, the optimization player first chooses a search point, and then the fitness player chooses a fitness value to assign to that search point. The turns continue on indefinitely, although an external observer might terminate the game if certain stopping criteria are met. For a fixed static fitness function, the responses of the fitness player are determined by the choice of search points. However, if the fitness player is allowed to take arbitrary actions, a more complex situation arises in which the fitness values can even be chosen to frustrate the optimization process. This type of fitness player will be called *adversarial.* An adversarial fitness subsumes a wide variety of optimization settings including static, stochastic, dynamic, and adaptive fitness functions.

2.2 Game Histories and Generators

Consider the extended form of the optimization game, which corresponds to how one thinks about iterative optimization methods. An optimizer proposes a search point that is scored by the fitness, and the previous points and their scores are used to determine the next search point.

Suppose the search domain is a finite space X, and the fitness domain Y is also finite. After i turns of the optimization game, the game history contains a sequence of i search points and a corresponding sequence of i fitness values assigned to those search points. Such a history will be written as $(z, v) \in X^i \times Y^i$, where z indicates i previously chosen search points and v the corresponding fitness observations. The superscripts X^i and Y^i indicate i copies of the search and fitness spaces, respectively.

An iterative optimization method is customarily thought of as a mechanism that examines the game history (z, v) and proposes one or more search points whose fitness is to be examined next. It is sufficient to consider the situation in which only one point is proposed, because many points can be generated in succession by the same mechanism.

A *generator* for histories of length i is a function $\mathcal{G}_i$ that tells how to generate the $(i+1)^{th}$ search point from the history (z, v) of length i. Specifically, $\mathcal{G}_i : X^i \times Y^i \to \mathcal{P}_X$ is such that $p = \mathcal{G}_i(z, v)$ is a probability vector over X. If the search space X has N elements, a *probability vector* over X is a real-valued vector of length N all of whose entries are positive such that $\sum_{k=1}^{N} p_k = 1$. Each entry of p indicates the probability of observing one particular search point. Therefore, we will index p to show this relationship. For each search point $x \in X$, p_x will indicate the p-probability of x. The notation $\mathcal{P}_X$ will refer to the set of probability vectors over X. In general, for any finite set F, $\mathcal{P}_F$ will likewise refer to the set of probability vectors over F, which forms the simplex in the Euclidean space $\mathbb{R}^{|F|}$. For a full development of this relationship, see Vose's book [13].

Suppose that optimization is allowed to continue for a fixed, finite number of steps T. A *generator set* is an indexed collection of generators $\mathcal{G} = \{\mathcal{G}_i \mid 0 \leq i < T\}$, such that $\mathcal{G}$ specifies how to extend histories of any length. The element $\mathcal{G}_0$ gives the initial distribution over search points; it has input space $X^0 \times Y^0$, which is just a single element space consisting of the empty history. The generator set $\mathcal{G}$ corresponds to what was called an *optimizer* by Lockett and Miikkulainen [10], except that the generator set obeys a *black-box* property in that it can only observe fitness values assigned to previous search points. The term *optimizer* is reserved to refer to the multi-step behavior of optimization methods below. Lockett and Miikkulainen showed how to embed genetic algorithms, evolution strategies, simulated annealing, differential evolution, and other evolutionary methods into these generator sets. It will be assumed from here that such an embedding is possible, that is, that the vast majority of evolutionary methods on finite spaces can be represented by some generator set.

The generator set can be thought of as the extended form of an optimization player. It specifies how the optimizer responds to each game history without depending on future moves. The next subsection extends these generators to recover the normal form of the optimization player.

2.3 Normal Form Optimization Players

Generator sets can be extended to form probability distributions over complete game histories. If the game is run for $T < \infty$ steps, a complete game history $(z, v) \in X^T \times Y^T$ pairs a search history of length T with a fitness history of length T. This complete history has also been called a *trace* of the optimization procedure [11]. The extension of a generator set will be called an *optimizer.* In an abstract sense, this optimizer represents a normal form player in the optimization game. That is, for each strategy of a fitness player (i.e., for each fitness history v of length T), it has a response that is a probability vector over X^T. This probability can be sampled to determine the optimization player's strategy, which is a sequence of length T in the search space.

Proceeding with this plan, a *preoptimizer from* X *to* Y is defined as a function $\mathcal{A} : Y^T \to \mathcal{P}_{X^T}$, where $\mathcal{P}_{X^T}$ is the set of probability vectors over X^T, which is finite. For each fitness history v of length T, $p = \mathcal{A}(v)$ is a probability vector over X^T. For each search history z of length T, p_z gives the probability that z is the history of search points chosen by the preoptimizer.

One can construct preoptimizers that choose search points dependent on future fitness values, violating the black-box assumption. So a preoptimizer is not an optimizer in the desired sense. A *black-box property* is defined below, and preoptimizers that have this property will be called *optimizers.* First, it will be seen how to convert generator sets into preoptimizers. Take any fitness history v of length T. For $i \leq T$, let $v_{[i]}$ be the fitness history of length i formed by taking the first i elements of v. The set $v_{[0]}$ is the empty history. For each search history z, $z_{[i]}$ is defined similarly. Suppose $\mathcal{G}$ is a generator set. Define a preoptimizer $\mathcal{A}$ by

$$\mathcal{A}(v)(z) = \prod_{i=1}^{T} \mathcal{G}_{i-1}(z_{[i-1]}, v_{[i-1]})(z_i), \tag{1}$$

so that the probability of search history z given preoptimizer $\mathcal{A}$ and fitness history v is just the running product of the probability of choosing each search point z_i using the generator set given the history so far. It is elementary that $\sum_{z \in X^T} \mathcal{A}(v)(z) = 1$, i.e., that $\mathcal{A}(v)$ is indeed a probability vector over the space of search histories X^T.

To move in the other direction, Suppose that we choose a number of steps $S < T$ and wish to look at what a preoptimizer does only in the first S steps. For each search history $z \in X^T$, let E_z be the subset of search histories in X^T that agree with z up to time S,

$$E_z = \{t \in X^t \mid t_{[S]} = z_{[S]}\}. \tag{2}$$

Let v be a fitness history. Marginalizing out extra steps, set

$$\mathcal{A}^{[S]}(v)(z_{[S]}) = \sum_{t \in E_z} \mathcal{A}(v)(t). \tag{3}$$

This $\mathcal{A}^{[S]}$ represents the probability distribution over the search history for the first $S < T$ steps. Note that $\mathcal{A}^{[S]}$ is not a preoptimizer because the parameter v has $v \in Y^T \neq Y^S$. That is, $\mathcal{A}^{[S]}$ may depend on future fitness values *beyond* S. Let $S = i$. The conditional probability of z_i given $z_{[i-1]}$ is

$$d\mathcal{A}_i(z_{[i-1]}, v)(z_i) = \frac{\mathcal{A}^{[i]}(v)(z_{[i]})}{\mathcal{A}^{[i-1]}(v)(z_{[i-1]})}. \tag{4}$$

The object $d\mathcal{A}_i : X^i \times Y^T \to \mathcal{P}_X$ represents the transition of the preoptimizer from time $i-1$ to time i. For the base case, observe that $d\mathcal{A}_1(z_{[0]}, v)(z_1) = \mathcal{A}^{[1]}(v)(z_{[1]})$. Notice that $d\mathcal{A}_i$ is only well-defined if the denominator is nonzero. If the denominator is zero, then $\mathcal{A}(v)(z) = 0$, and $d\mathcal{A}_i(z_{[i-1]}, v)(z_i)$ may take any value; it is unique *with* $\mathcal{A}^{[i]}$*-probability one.*

Observe that the generator $\mathcal{G}_i$ depends on the fitness history only up to time i, whereas $d\mathcal{A}_i$ depends on the complete fitness history. The black-box property is defined to represent the situation when $d\mathcal{A}_i$ depends on the fitness history only up to time i, so that it can be treated as a generator.

DEFINITION 1 (BLACK-BOX PROPERTY). *A preoptimizer* $\mathcal{A}$ *has the black-box property if for any search history prefix* $t \in X^{i-1}$*, all complete fitness histories* $v, w \in Y^T$*, and any search point* $x \in X$*,*

$$d\mathcal{A}_i(t, v)(x) = d\mathcal{A}_i(t, w)(x) \tag{5}$$

whenever $v_{[i-1]} = w_{[i-1]}$.

DEFINITION 2 (OPTIMIZER). *A preoptimizer from* X *to* Y *with the black-box property is called an optimizer with search domain* X *and fitness domain* Y.

That is, the black-box property says that the transition from step $i-1$ to step i can only depend on the fitness values and search points prior to step i. If this black-box property holds, then generators for $\mathcal{A}$ may be defined by $\mathcal{G}_i(t, v_{[i-1]})(x) = d\mathcal{A}_i(t, v)(x)$. As mentioned, the term *optimizer* is used here for preoptimizers with the black-box property. The following conclusion has been demonstrated.

PROPOSITION 2.1. *In finite spaces, every optimizer is generated by some generator set through Equation 1, and each generator set corresponds to a unique optimizer.*

Proposition 2.1 states that optimization methods defined one step at a time through generators (the extended form) are equivalent to preoptimizers with the black-box property holds (the normal form). Although the optimizer generated by a generator set is unique, there may be many generator sets for a given optimizer due to search histories that have probability zero. From this point on, we will work with the normal form, which is more amenable to analysis. The next subsection introduces fitness players as the complement of optimization players.

2.4 Adversarial Fitness Players

In the normal form of the optimization game, the optimization player proposes a search history in X^T and the fitness player responds with a fitness history in Y^T. For example, suppose that the fitness player is a single static objective function $u : X \to Y$. The optimization player proposes search historyz and the fitness player responds with a fitness history v such that for all $i \leq T$, $v_i = u(z_i)$. The following text develops a concept of fitness players that covers static, stochastic, dynamic, and adaptive fitness functions.

The optimization player plays an offensive role and the fitness player a defensive one. In subsequent games, the roles could be switched. So if Y were the search space and X the fitness space, the fitness player would become an optimization player. For this reason, a similar sequence of steps is followed as for optimizers, but the fitness player is allowed to observe the current search point before assigning it a fitness, whereas the optimizer cannot observe the current fitness value before choosing a search point for it.

Beginning as was done for optimizers, we first establish a mechanism whereby a fitness player assigns a fitness to the current search point given the search history and the history of previous fitness values. A *jagged generator* for histories of length i is a function $\mathcal{G}_i^* : Y^i \times X^{i+1} \to \mathcal{P}_Y$ that takes a partial fitness history v of length i and a partial search history z of length $i+1$ and assigns to them a probability vector over fitness values. Thus the probability of assigning fitness $y \in Y$ to the search point z_{i+1} is $\mathcal{G}_i^*(v, z)(y)$. A *jagged generator set* is an indexed collection of jagged generators $\mathcal{G}^* = \{\mathcal{G}_i^* \mid 0 \leq i < T\}$. The initial element $\mathcal{G}_0^* : X \to \mathcal{P}_Y$ describes how to assign the first fitness value to the first search point. Subsequent jagged generators describe how to transition from i fitness values to $i+1$ fitness values given $i+1$ search points. The jagged generator set is the extended form of the fitness player.

To develop the normal form of the fitness player, there is no need to define a *pre-fitness*, because the fitness player is just a preoptimizer from Y to X with the search space and the fitness space reversed. To indicate the fitness player, the notation $\mathcal{F} : X^T \to \mathcal{P}_{Y^T}$ will be used for these preoptimizers in place of $\mathcal{A}$, so that $\mathcal{F}(z)(v)$ is the probability of assigning fitness history v to search history z. As in Equation 1, a jagged generator set produces

$$\mathcal{F}(z)(v) = \prod_{i=1}^{T} \mathcal{G}_{i-1}^*(v_{[i-1]}, z_{[i]})(v_i). \tag{6}$$

In order to extract a jagged generator set form a normal form fitness player, the object $d\mathcal{F}_i$ may be defined for $\mathcal{F}$ exactly as in Equation 4, but with $\mathcal{A}$ replaced by $\mathcal{F}$ and argument labels reversed (i.e. $d\mathcal{F}_i(v_{[i-1]}, z)(v_i)$). It represents how to sample the fitness at time i given the previous fitness values and the entire search history. The *jagged black-box property* is defined to represent the case where $d\mathcal{F}_i$ may be treated as a jagged generator.

DEFINITION 3 (JAGGED BLACK-BOX PROPERTY). *A preoptimizer $\mathcal{F}$ from Y to X has the jagged black-box property if for any partial fitness history $v \in Y^i$, all complete search histories $z, t \in X^T$, and any fitness value $y \in Y$,*

$$d\mathcal{F}_i(v, z)(x) = d\mathcal{F}_i(v, t)(x) \quad (7)$$

whenever $z_{[i+1]} = t_{[i+1]}$.

DEFINITION 4 (ADVERSARIAL FITNESS). *A preoptimizer from Y to X with the jagged black-box property is an adversarial fitness with search domain X and fitness domain Y.*

In contrast to the black-box property, the jagged black-box property allows a preoptimizer to look at the opponent's current search point as well as the prior game history. Comparing with Equation 5 gives the following.

PROPOSITION 2.2. *Every optimizer with search domain Y and fitness domain X is an adversarial fitness with search domain X and fitness domain Y.*

PROPOSITION 2.3. *In finite spaces, every adversarial fitness is generated by some jagged generator set through Equation 1, and each jagged generator set corresponds to a unique adversarial fitness.*

This proposition states that adversarial fitnesses can be defined from jagged generator sets, and that a jagged generator set can always be obtained from an adversarial fitness. The next subsection considers the interaction between optimizers and adversarial fitnesses.

2.5 The Optimization Game

Together, an optimizer and an adversarial fitness play a game whose history is randomized. At each turn, the optimizer proposes a search point in X and the adversarial fitness responds with a fitness value in Y. The history of the entire game includes a sequence of T search points and a sequence of T fitness values assigned to them. The probability measure governing these random game histories is called the *optimization game*; it will be derived in this subsection.

For an optimizer $\mathcal{A}$ and an adversarial fitness $\mathcal{F}$, the optimization game is denoted $\mathcal{A} \times \mathcal{F}$. It is a probability vector over the space $X^T \times Y^T$, which contains all possible game histories and is a finite space. Suppose $\mathcal{G}$ is a generator set that yields $\mathcal{A}$ (so that $d\mathcal{A}_i = \mathcal{G}_i$) and $\mathcal{G}^*$ is a jagged generator set that extends to $\mathcal{F}$ (so that $d\mathcal{F}_i = \mathcal{G}^*_i$). The game $\mathcal{A} \times \mathcal{F}$ assigns probability

$$\begin{aligned}\mathcal{A} \times \mathcal{F}(z, v) &= \mathcal{A}(z)(v) \times \mathcal{F}(v)(z) \\ &= \prod_{i=1}^{T} \mathcal{G}_i(z_{[i-1]}, v_{[i-1]})(z_i)\ \mathcal{G}^*_i(v_{[i-1]}, z_{[i]})(v_i) \quad (8)\end{aligned}$$

to the search history z and the fitness sequence v. It is necessarily the case that $\sum_{z,v} \mathcal{A} \times \mathcal{F}(z, v) = 1$. Equation 8 simply says that the optimizer chooses the points, and the adversarial fitness then assigns fitness values.

THEOREM 2.4. *If $\mathcal{A}$ is an optimizer and $\mathcal{F}$ is an adversarial fitness, then there is a unique optimization game $\mathcal{A} \times \mathcal{F}$ on $X^T \times Y^T$, constructed above.*

Thus each pair $(\mathcal{A}, \mathcal{F})$ of an optimizer and an adversarial fitness yields a unique optimization game $\mathcal{A} \times \mathcal{F}$. The product in Equation 8 may be interpreted as the process of playing the optimization game by viewing $\mathcal{G}_i$ as a move of the optimizer and $\mathcal{G}^*_i$ as a move of the adversarial fitness.

This game is unique in the sense that there is no other game that may be generated from $\mathcal{A}$ and $\mathcal{F}$ in the same way. There may still be some other pair $(\mathcal{A}', \mathcal{F}')$ such that $\mathcal{A} \times \mathcal{F} = \mathcal{A}' \times \mathcal{F}'$. Some special cases are now considered and several examples are given to clarify the meaning of the optimizer, adversarial fitness, and optimization game.

2.6 Determinism and Agnosticism

Determinism and agnosticism are critical to the development of the duality theory below, and are introduced now.

DEFINITION 5. *A preoptimizer $\mathcal{A}$ is deterministic if there is a function $d : Y^T \to X^T$ such that for all search histories $z \in X^T$ and fitness sequences $v \in Y^T$, $\mathcal{A}(v)(d(v)) = 1$. The function d is called the deterministic core of $\mathcal{A}$.*

This definition says that a deterministic preoptimizer places all probability on a particular search history that is determined by the observed fitness history. A deterministic preoptimizer can have the black-box property or not have it; it depends on the nature of the deterministic core. In general, a deterministic preoptimizer has the black-box property if any pair of fitness histories that equal up to time i yield search histories that are also equal up to time i, i.e., $d(v)_{[i]} = d(w)_{[i]}$ whenever $v_{[i]} = w_{[i]}$. A deterministic preoptimizer has the jagged black-box property if $d(v)_{[i]} = d(w)_{[i]}$ whenever $v_{[i+1]} = w_{[i+1]}$. For a deterministic preoptimizer, its generator is also deterministic in the following sense.

DEFINITION 6. *The object $d\mathcal{A}_{i+1}$ from Equation 4 for a preoptimizer $\mathcal{A}$ is deterministic if there exists a function $d_{i+1} : Y^T \to X$ such that for all fitness histories $v \in Y^T$ and all i-length search histories $z \in X^i$ with $\mathcal{A}^{[i]}(v)(z) > 0$, $d\mathcal{A}_{i+1}(z, v)(d_{i+1}(v)) = 1$. The function d_{i+1} is called the deterministic generator of $\mathcal{A}$.*

PROPOSITION 2.5. *The generator of a deterministic preoptimizer is deterministic.*

PROOF. The deterministic generator is $d_i(v) = d(v)_i$, where d is the deterministic core. ☐

The above definitions should make it clear what is intended by the use of the adjective deterministic in this paper. In general, it means that the probability vectors are degenerate, i.e., that there is exactly one point that has non-zero probability. Deterministic optimizers and adversarial fitnesses play an important role in the development of the theory below, since they span the optimizers and the adversarial fitnesses, respectively.

2.7 Special Cases of the Fitness Player

Thus far, an adversarial fitness may not seem particularly useful. After all, if the fitness can make any decision whatsoever about the values sent to the optimizer, then successful optimization is impossible. The fitness can always confound the optimizer; the No Free Lunch theorems prove as much [7, 11]. However, the idea of an adversarial fitness is useful because it makes possible a high-level duality theory that is explored in Section 4. This duality is applies *a fortiori* to any of the following special cases, each of which represents a common practical optimization setting.

Static Fitness. Static optimization is the case where there is a single fitness function $u : X \to Y$. The goal of the optimizer is to find the minimum or maximum of u. This situation is represented by a deterministic adversarial fitness whose deterministic core is given by $d(z) = (u(z_i))_{i \le T}$.

Randomized Static Fitness. Static optimization can be performed with a randomly selected fitness function. In finite spaces, there are finitely many static fitness functions $u \in Y^X$. Suppose $q \in \mathcal{P}_{Y^X}$ is a probability vector over fitness functions. For each search history z, consider the projection $\pi_z : Y^X \to Y^T$ given by $\pi_z(u) = (u(z_i))_{i \le T}$. The function π_z induces a probability vector $p^z \in \mathcal{P}_{Y^T}$ on the fitness sequence space Y^T, with the probability of a fitness history $v \in Y^T$ given by

$$p^z(v) = \sum_{\{u \mid \pi_z(u) = v\}} q(u), \tag{9}$$

which is just the sum of the probability of all fitness functions that produce fitness sequence v given search history z. Then the map $z \mapsto p^z$ defines a preoptimizer from Y to X. This preoptimizer has the jagged black-box property because its response to search point z_i does not depend on future search points. It is therefore an adversarial fitness.

Stochastic Fitness. A randomized static fitness function randomly selects the fitness function, but once the fitness function is selected, the same response must be given to successive search queries at the same search point. A stochastic fitness removes this restriction but requires that the fitness at a point have the same distribution at all times.

A stochastic fitness can be defined by including multiple sources of randomness. Suppose Ω is some finite space and consider the space of extended fitness functions $Y^{X \times \Omega}$. If $u \in Y^{X \times \Omega}$, then it can happen that $u(x, \omega) \neq u(x, \omega')$ for $\omega, \omega' \in \Omega$. By randomly selecting ω independently of the search point, u can be thought of as a stochastic fitness function; the optimizer chooses x, but ω is chosen at random when the fitness value is queried. If Ω is large enough (say, at least as big as Y^X), then a single parameter can be shared over all search points without a loss of flexibility.

So suppose that q is a probability vector over $\Omega \times Y^{X \times \Omega}$, which is large but still finite. We will write $q(\omega, u)$ for the probability of choosing $\omega \in \Omega$ and $u \in Y^{X \times \Omega}$. Now for each search history $z \in X^T$, consider the expanded projection $\tilde{\pi}_z : \Omega \times Y^{X \times \Omega} \to Y^T$ given by $\tilde{\pi}_z(\omega, u) = (u(z_i, \omega))_{i \le T}$. As with randomized static objectives, $\tilde{\pi}_z$ induces a probability vector p^z over Y^T such that the probability $p^z(v)$ of observing fitness history v on search history z is given by

$$p^z(v) = \sum_{\{(\omega,u) \mid \tilde{\pi}_z(\omega,u) = v\}} q(\omega, u). \tag{10}$$

An adversarial fitness is again defined by the map $z \mapsto p^z$.

Dynamic Fitness. A dynamic fitness function is allowed to change over time. There are many possible definitions of dynamism. Some of these definitions correspond to proper subsets of the adversarial fitnesses, others comprise the entire set. We give a brief example that generalizes a stochastic fitness by defining a probability vector q over $\Omega \times Y^{[T] \times X \times \Omega}$, where the fitness function has been expanded again to take an index parameter (here $[T]$ represents the set of numbers from 1 to T). For each search history $z \in X^T$, the expanded projection $\tilde{\pi}_z(\omega, u) = (u(i, z_i, \omega))_{i \le T}$ again induces a probability vector p^z over Y^T for each search history z. The map $z \mapsto p^z$ is again an adversarial fitness.

A randomized static fitness is a subcase of a stochastic fitness, which is a subcase of a dynamic fitness. An potentially larger category is that of adaptive fitness functions that respond dynamically to the selected search points.

Now that it has been shown how an adversarial fitness function corresponds to a number of important optimization scenarios, an abstract generalization of optimizers and adversarial fitnesses will be introduced that embeds each of them inside a vector space.

3. THE GENERALIZED FINITE GAME

In the previous section, the choices of the optimizer and the adversarial fitness were modeled as probability vectors. In this section, the probability restriction is removed. That is, for a preoptimizer $\mathcal{A}$ and a fitness history v, $\mathcal{A}(v)$ is a real-valued vector in $\mathbb{R}^{|X|}$, the Euclidean space whose dimension equals the size of X. The components of this vector need not sum to one. Reviewing Equations 1, 3, and 4, it is evident that the definitions of $\mathcal{A}^{[i]}$ and $d\mathcal{A}_i$ did not depend on the fact that $\mathcal{A}(v)$ was a probability vector. Thus the black-box property remains well defined without the probability restriction, as does as the jagged black-box property. So if $\mathcal{A}$ has the black-box property in this generalized sense, we will continue to call it an optimizer. Similarly, for an adversarial fitness $\mathcal{F}$ and search history z, we now allow $\mathcal{F}(z)$ to be a real-valued vector in $\mathbb{R}^{|Y|}$. The meaning of sampling is lost along with the direct connection to stochastic optimization methods. However, this generalization will prove mathematically useful. Its implications are explored next.

3.1 Vector Spaces of Optimizers and Fitnesses

Given a preoptimizer $\mathcal{A}$, if $\mathcal{A}(v)$ is a real-valued vector for each fitness history v, then $\mathcal{A}$ is simply a function from the space of fitness histories Y^T to the $|X|$-dimensional Euclidean space, $\mathbb{R}^{|X|}$. Such functions can be added and multiplied by scalars. For preoptimizers $\mathcal{A}_1$ and $\mathcal{A}_2$ and any real number α, addition and multiplication are defined by

$$(\alpha\mathcal{A}_1 + \mathcal{A}_2)(v) = \alpha(\mathcal{A}_1(v)) + \mathcal{A}_2(v), \tag{11}$$

and these addition and multiplication operations follow the usual distributive, associative, commutative properties. The addition and multiplication operations also guarantee the existence of a zero preoptimizer ($\mathcal{A}(v) = 0$) as well as additive inverses. That is, the space of optimizers is a *vector space.* This structure implies that the properties of the space are *translation-invariant.* Given any optimizer in the space, the region of the space around it has the same topological structure as does the region around the zero optimizer.

Even further, the space of preoptimizers is a *normed vector space* under the norm

$$||\mathcal{A}|| = \max_v \sum_z |\mathcal{A}(v)(z)|, \tag{12}$$

where $\mathcal{A}(z)(v)$ is the arbitrary real number assigned to search history z given fitness history v. This norm provides a homogeneous notion of distance between any two preoptimizers $\mathcal{A}_1$ and $\mathcal{A}_2$ given by $d(\mathcal{A}_1, \mathcal{A}_2) = ||\mathcal{A}_1 - \mathcal{A}_2||$. It also implies an entire spectrum of preoptimizers between any two given preoptimizers. The space of preoptimizers is also *complete,* which intuitively that there are no "holes" in the space. The complete, normed vector space of preoptimizers from X to Y run for T steps will be denoted by $\mathcal{MF}^{[T]}_{X,Y}$.

The optimizers and adversarial fitnesses are vector subspaces of this space. First of all, it is clear that Equations 1, 3, and 4 do not depend on the fact $\mathcal{A}(v)$ was a probability vector. Thus all of these equations and hence the black-box property as well as the jagged black-box property remain well-defined when $\mathcal{A}(v)$ becomes a real vector. The terms *optimizer* and *adversarial fitness* will now be used for real-valued preoptimizers that have the required black-box and jagged black-box properties, respectively.

To obtain vector spaces of optimizers and adversarial fitnesses, it needs to be shown that the black-box property and the jagged black-box property are both linear. That is, if two optimizers are added, the result should have the black-box property. We begin with a simple lemma.

LEMMA 3.1. *Suppose $\mathcal{A}$ is a preoptimizer. Then the black-box property is equivalent to the claim that for all time steps i and all fitness histories v, w such that $v_{[i]} = w_{[i]}$,*

$$\mathcal{A}^{[i]}(v) = \mathcal{A}^{[i]}(w), \tag{13}$$

where $\mathcal{A}^{[i]}$ is defined according to Equation 3. The jagged black-box property is equivalent to the same claim, but with $v_{[i+1]} = w_{[i+1]}$.

PROOF. Suppose $\mathcal{A}$ has the black-box property. For any search history z, expand Equation 4 to obtain

$$\mathcal{A}^{[i]}(v)(z_{[i]}) = \prod_{j=1}^{i} d\mathcal{A}_j(z_{[j-1]}, v)(z_j). \tag{14}$$

The black-box property implies that each term on the right can replace v with w. Therefore, v can be replaced with w on the left as well. The converse follows from the same equation by induction on i since $d\mathcal{A}_1(z_{[0]}, v)(z_1) = \mathcal{A}^{[1]}(v)(z_{[1]})$. □

PROPOSITION 3.2. *The black-box property and the jagged black-box property are both closed under addition and multiplication. That is, addition and multiplication of optimizers result in a new optimizer, and addition and multiplication of adversarial fitnesses result in a new adversarial fitness.*

PROOF. The definition and Equation 3 imply that for each time step i, search history z, and fitness history v,

$$(\alpha\mathcal{A}_1+\mathcal{A}_2)^{[i]}(v)(z_{[i]}) = \alpha\left(\mathcal{A}_1^{[i]}(v)(z_{[i]})\right)+\mathcal{A}_2^{[i]}(v)(z_{[i]}). \tag{15}$$

Lemma 3.1 implies that for any fitness history w such that $v_{[i]} = w_{[i]}$, each term in this equation can replace v with w. Therefore $\alpha\mathcal{A}_1 + \mathcal{A}_2$ has the black-box property. The proof for the jagged black-box property is nearly identical. □

Proposition 3.2 implies that the set of all preoptimizers from X to Y with the black-box property forms a vector subspace of $\mathcal{MF}_{X,Y}^{[T]}$, and likewise for those preoptimizers with the jagged black-box property. The next subsection discusses the smallest vector subspace that contains all of the probability-valued optimizers and adversarial fitnesses.

3.2 Proper Optimizers and Fitnesses

A real-vector-valued optimizer $\mathcal{A}$ is proper if for every fitness history v, $\mathcal{A}(v)$ is a probability vector. Similarly, an adversarial fitness is *proper* if it assigns a probability vector to every fitness history.

Because our goal is to analyze the proper optimizers and adversarial fitnesses, we want to consider the smallest vector subspace of $\mathcal{MF}_{X,Y}^{[T]}$ that contains them. In addition the black-box and jagged black-box property, one more restriction is needed in order to obtain this space.

DEFINITION 7 (CONSISTENT SUMS). *A generalized preoptimizer $\mathcal{A}$ has consistent sums if there exists a constant c such that for each fitness history v, $\sum_z \mathcal{A}(v)(z) = c$.*

Consistent sums are needed because generalized preoptimizers can have different sums for different fitness histories. Every proper optimizer and every proper adversarial fitness has consistent sums with $c = 1$. As proven below, having consistent sums is preserved by addition and multiplication, and so proper optimizers can never be added or multiplied to produce a preoptimizer with inconsistent sums, even if that preoptimizer has the black-box property (which it may).

PROPOSITION 3.3. *The set of preoptimizers from X to Y with consistent sums is closed under vector addition and scalar multiplication and forms a vector subspace of $\mathcal{MF}_{X,Y}^{[T]}$.*

PROOF. If $\mathcal{A}_1$ and $\mathcal{A}_2$ each have consistent sums with constants c_1 and c_2, respectively, then for any real numbers α, β, it is evident from the definitions that $\alpha\mathcal{A}_1 + \beta\mathcal{A}_2$ has consistent sums with constant $\alpha c_1 + \beta c_2$. □

The space of optimizers that have consistent sums and run for T time steps with search domain X and fitness domain Y will be denoted by $\mathcal{BB}_{X,Y}^{[T]}$. The space of adversarial fitnesses with search domain X and fitness domain Y that have consistent sums is also a complete normed vector space, denoted $\mathcal{AF}_{Y,X}^{[T]}$ with the order of the subscripts reversed. The following theorem shows that these spaces are the smallest vector spaces containing the proper optimizers and adversarial fitness functions, respectively.

LEMMA 3.4. *Every optimizer $\mathcal{A}$ with consistent sums can be rewritten as a weighted difference between two proper optimizers, i.e., $\mathcal{A} = \alpha\mathcal{A}_1 - \beta\mathcal{A}_2$, where α and β are nonnegative real numbers and $\mathcal{A}_1, \mathcal{A}_2$ are proper optimizers.*

PROOF. The proof is by construction and works by first making the optimizer nonnegative, then normalizing. Suppose $\mathcal{A}$ is nonzero and non-constant and has consistent sum c. This proof only works for finite spaces. Define

$$\mu = \min_{z,v} \mathcal{A}(v)(z) \tag{16}$$

to be the minimum value of $\mathcal{A}$ across all search and fitness histories. If μ is nonnegative, the proof is complete with $\alpha = c$, $\mathcal{A}_1 = \frac{1}{c}\mathcal{A}$, $\beta = 0$, and $\mathcal{A}_2$ arbitrary. Otherwise define $\mathcal{A}_\circ$ and $\mathcal{A}_\mu$ for search history z and fitness history v by

$$\begin{aligned} \mathcal{A}_\circ(v)(z) &= \mathcal{A}(v)(z) - \mu & (17)\\ \mathcal{A}_\mu(v)(z) &= -\mu. & (18) \end{aligned}$$

Then $\mathcal{A}_\circ$ is nonnegative everywhere and has consistent sum $c - \mu|X|$. $\mathcal{A}_\mu$ is nonnegative with consistent sum $\mu|X|$. Both have the black-box property, since $\mathcal{A}_\mu^{[i]}(v)(z) = -\mu|X|^{T-i}$ independent of v and z and $\mathcal{A}_\circ^{[i]}(v)(z) = \mathcal{A}^{[i]}(v)(z) - \mu|X|^{T-i}$. Furthermore, $\mathcal{A} = \mathcal{A}_\circ - \mathcal{A}_\mu$. Since both components are nonnegative, they may be normalized to $\mathcal{A}_1 = \frac{1}{c-\mu|X|}\mathcal{A}_\circ$ and $\mathcal{A}_2 = \frac{1}{-\mu|X|}\mathcal{A}_\mu$, both of which are proper optimizers as long as the denominators are positive. The proof is complete with $\alpha = c - \mu|X|$ and $\beta = \mu|X|$. If either $\mathcal{A}_1$ or $\mathcal{A}_2$ is not proper, it can be replaced with any proper optimizer since the corresponding coefficient (α or β) is zero, which can happen if $\mathcal{A}$ is zero (whence $c = \mu = 0$) or constant (whence $c = \mu|X|$). $\square$

THEOREM 3.5. *The space of optimizers with consistent sums $\mathcal{BB}^{[T]}_{X,Y}$ is the smallest vector subspace of $\mathcal{MF}^{[T]}_{X,Y}$ containing all the proper optimizers.*

PROOF. On the one hand, it is clear that every proper optimizer lies in $\mathcal{BB}^{[T]}_{X,Y}$. Furthermore, Lemma 3.4 shows that the proper optimizers span this space. $\square$

LEMMA 3.6. *Every adversarial fitness can be rewritten as a weighted difference between two proper adversarial fitnesses.*

PROOF. The proof is exactly as for Lemma 3.4. $\square$

THEOREM 3.7. *The space of adversarial fitnesses with consistent sums $\mathcal{AF}^{[T]}_{X,Y}$ is the smallest subspace of $\mathcal{MF}^{[T]}_{X,Y}$ containing all the proper adversarial fitnesses.*

PROOF. The proof is as Theorem 3.5 using Lemma 3.6 $\square$

Because the black-box property implies the jagged black-box property with the search domain and fitness domain interchanged, every optimizer is the mirror image of an adversarial fitness function that assigns a fitness value without looking at the current search point. That is, the space of optimizers $\mathcal{BB}^{[T]}_{X,Y}$ is a closed vector subspace of the space of adversarial fitness functions $\mathcal{AF}^{[T]}_{X,Y}$ with reversed search and fitness domains. Finally, both spaces are subspaces of the complete normed vector space of preoptimizers, $\mathcal{MF}^{[T]}_{X,Y}$.

Although the vector space of optimizers is abstract, the set of proper optimizers has several nice properties. Within the vector space, the proper optimizers form a closed, convex subset that spans the space. *Convexity* means that for any real number $\alpha \in [0, 1]$ and any two proper optimizers $\mathcal{A}_1$ and $\mathcal{A}_2$, the optimizer $\mathcal{A} = \alpha\mathcal{A}_1 + (1-\alpha)\mathcal{A}_2$ is also proper. *Closed* means that the limit of any sequence of proper optimizers remains proper. These properties are important because alongside one further property (compactness) they will imply that deterministic optimizer span the proper optimizers and attain the best values on many measures of performance. These issues are discussed in Section 4.

Similarly, the set of proper adversarial fitnesses is also a closed, convex subset that spans the space of adversarial fitnesses. The next two subsections introduce tools to study this space, and then Section 4 examines performance abstractly within this space.

3.3 The Generalized Optimization Game

Suppose that $(\mathcal{A}, \mathcal{F})$ pairs an optimizer with an adversarial fitness, one of which is not proper. In Section 2.5, such pairs were used to define the optimization game as a probability distribution over game histories for proper optimizers. In the finite case, a generalized version of the optimization game $\mathcal{A} \times \mathcal{F}$ is obtained for $(\mathcal{A}, \mathcal{F})$ by simply repeating the first part of Equation 8. In the finite case, the second part of Equation 8 is equally valid. None of Equations 1, 3, and 4 require $\mathcal{A}$ to be a proper optimizer. Note that in the infinite case (when $T = \infty$), by contrast, the product in the second part of Equation 8 could go to infinity, so that the relationship between normal and extended form is completely preserved only in the finite case.

Rather than assigning probability to particular game histories, the generalized optimization game assigns a *measure* to these histories. One can compute the overall measure of the generalized optimization game by

$$\sum_{z,v} \mathcal{A} \times \mathcal{F}(z, v) = \sum_{z,v} \mathcal{A}(v)(z)\, \mathcal{F}(z)(v). \tag{19}$$

In subsequent sections, it will be shown that by appropriately choosing a non-proper adversarial fitness, every linear measure of performance for a proper optimizer corresponds the the overall measure of the generalized optimization game with some non-proper adversarial fitness.

3.4 A Basis For preoptimizer Space

When the search space, fitness domain, and the number of search steps are all finite, the preoptimizer space is a finite-dimensional vector space over the real numbers. Every such space can be identified with the Euclidean space $\mathbb{R}^K$ for some K. In the case of $\mathcal{MF}^{[T]}_{X,Y}$, $K = (|X||Y|)^T$. To construct a basis for preoptimizer space, fix the search history z and the fitness history v. Then define $\mathcal{B}_{z,v}$ such that for each search history t and fitness history w,

$$\mathcal{B}_{z,v}(w)(t) = \begin{cases} 1 & \text{if } z = t \text{ and } v = w, \\ 0 & \text{otherwise.} \end{cases} \tag{20}$$

The basis vector $\mathcal{B}_{z,v}$ is a generalized preoptimizer that is not proper. With slight revision of Definition 5, it is deterministic with deterministic core $d(w) = z$. Generalized to real-valued optimizers, the definition reads that $|\mathcal{A}(v)(d(v))| = \sum_{z\in X^T} |\mathcal{A}(v)(z)|$ in place of $\mathcal{A}(v)(d(v)) = 1$, that is, the deterministic core carries all mass (positive or negative). On the other hand, $\mathcal{B}_{z,v}$ does it have the black-box property, since for search history $w \neq v$ identical to v in the first i steps, i.e., $w_{[i]} = v_{[i]}$, one has that $\mathcal{B}^{[i]}_{z,v}(v)(z) = 1$ whereas $\mathcal{B}^{[i]}_{z,v}(w)(z) = 0$. The collection

$$\mathcal{B} = \left\{\mathcal{B}_{z,v} \mid z \in X^T, v \in Y^T\right\} \tag{21}$$

clearly spans $\mathcal{MF}^{[T]}_{X,Y}$, since for any preoptimizer $\mathcal{A}$ and real numbers $\alpha_{z,v} = \mathcal{A}(v)(z)$, it holds that

$$\mathcal{A} = \sum_{z\in X^T} \sum_{v\in Y^T} \alpha_{z,v}\, \mathcal{B}_{z,v}, \quad \text{i.e.,} \tag{22}$$

$$\mathcal{A}(w)(t) = \sum_{z\in X^T} \sum_{v\in Y^T} \alpha_{z,v}\, \mathcal{B}_{z,v}(w)(t) = \alpha_{t,w}. \tag{23}$$

It is critical that $\mathcal{B}_{z,v}$ does not have the black-box property. Otherwise every preoptimizer would be an optimizer, which is absurd since in an abstract sense there exist preoptimizers that do depend on future fitness values.

Since the preoptimizers have a finite basis, the adversarial fitnesses and the optimizers have such a basis as well, each with fewer elements than the basis above. This basis for preoptimizer space can be used to analyze mathematical operations on optimizers, such as measuring their performance. This subject will be taken up again in Section 4. First, some geometric facts about the proper optimizers and adversarial fitnesses are introduced.

3.5 Extreme Points and An Optimizer Basis

In this subsection, it is shown that the deterministic proper optimizers are the extreme points of among the proper optimizers. One consequence of this fact is that the deterministic optimizers span the space of optimizers with consistent sums, $\mathcal{BB}^{[T]}_{X,Y}$. Although this fact has been known in finite spaces for some time [14], the following facts also apply to infinite spaces, where this fact has not been previously proven. Similar facts also hold true for the proper adversarial fitnesses.

The term *extreme point* is used to denote the points that are on the edge of a set in a vector space. Our interest in extreme points comes from the Krein-Milman theorem, which asserts that extreme points generate compact convex sets in normed vector spaces, such as $\mathcal{BB}^{[T]}_{X,Y}$. *Compactness* is a property of sets. A set K is compact if any collection of open sets (including uncountable collections) whose union contains the set K can be thinned to a finite subcollection whose union still contains K. Compactness allows one to replace infinities with finitude.

The condition of compactness permits a set to be viewed as a union of finitely many small regions, so that convex combinations starting at the extreme points can "reach" any point inside the set in finitely many steps. It is possible to have a Krein-Milman-like theorem without compactness, but in this case the vector space is required to have the Radon-Nikodym property [5]; this topic is briefly discussed further in Section 6. A formal definition for extreme points is now given.

DEFINITION 8. *Given a convex set C in a real vector space, a point $x \in C$ is an extreme point if for any $\alpha \in (0,1)$ and any $y, z \in C$, $x = (1-\alpha)y + \alpha z$ implies that $y = z$.*

THEOREM 3.8. *Every deterministic proper optimizer is an extreme point of the set of proper optimizers.*

PROOF. It has been shown elsewhere that the set of proper optimizers is convex [8]. Let $\mathcal{A}$ be a deterministic proper optimizer. For all fitness histories v and search histories z, $\mathcal{A}(v)(z)$ is either 0 or 1. Suppose $\overline{\mathcal{A}}, \underline{\mathcal{A}}$ are proper optimizers distinct from each other and from $\mathcal{A}$ and that there is some $\alpha \in (0,1)$ with $\mathcal{A} = (1-\alpha)\underline{\mathcal{A}} + \alpha\overline{\mathcal{A}}$. Then because all three optimizers are distinct, there must be some fitness history v and search history z such that one of the four cases holds:

1. $\mathcal{A}(v)(z) = 1$ and $\overline{\mathcal{A}}(v)(z) > 1$.
2. $\mathcal{A}(v)(z) = 1$ and $\underline{\mathcal{A}}(v)(z) > 1$.
3. $\mathcal{A}(v)(z) = 0$ and $\overline{\mathcal{A}}(v)(z) < 0$.
4. $\mathcal{A}(v)(z) = 0$ and $\underline{\mathcal{A}}(v)(z) < 0$.

In all cases, one of $\underline{\mathcal{A}}$ and $\overline{\mathcal{A}}$ is not proper, which contradicts the assumptions and completes the proof. □

THEOREM 3.9. *Every extreme point of the set of proper optimizers is deterministic.*

PROOF. Suppose that $\mathcal{A}$ is a non-deterministic extreme point. Then there is a fitness history v and a subset E of the search histories such that $\sum_{z \in E} \mathcal{A}(v)(z) = p$ with $p \in (0,1)$. Let $\overline{E}$ be the complement of E, i.e. $\overline{E} = \{z \mid z \notin E\}$.

We will define $\underline{\mathcal{A}}$ and $\overline{\mathcal{A}}$ on either side of $\mathcal{A}$ to show that the non-deterministic proper optimizer $\mathcal{A}$ is not extreme. For fitness history w with $w \neq v$, let $\underline{\mathcal{A}}(w) = \overline{\mathcal{A}}(w) = \mathcal{A}(w)$. Pick $\epsilon > 0$ so that

$$0 < (1-\epsilon)p < p < (1+\epsilon)p < 1.$$

For all search histories $z \in E$, let

$$\underline{\mathcal{A}}(v)(z) = (1-\epsilon)\mathcal{A}(v)(z) \text{ and } \overline{\mathcal{A}}(v)(z) = (1+\epsilon)\mathcal{A}(v)(z).$$

For all search histories $z \notin E$, let

$$\begin{aligned} \underline{\mathcal{A}}(v)(z) &= \frac{1-p+p\epsilon}{1-p}\mathcal{A}(v)(z) \text{ and} \\ \overline{\mathcal{A}}(v)(z) &= \frac{1-p-p\epsilon}{1-p}\mathcal{A}(v)(z). \end{aligned}$$

Now $\underline{\mathcal{A}}(v)$ has probability $p\epsilon$ taken away from E and given to $\overline{E}$, and vice versa for $\overline{\mathcal{A}}(v)$. Both are clearly proper optimizers since ϵ is sufficiently small. It can be verified that

$$\mathcal{A} = \frac{1}{2}\left(\underline{\mathcal{A}} + \overline{\mathcal{A}}\right). \tag{24}$$

Therefore $\mathcal{A}$ is not an extreme point. □

It has been proven that, in an intuitive sense, the deterministic proper optimizers are at the edge of the set of the proper optimizers. The following theorem provides a new proof of the fact that the proper optimizers are spanned by the deterministic optimizers, i.e., that the deterministic optimizers form a basis for $\mathcal{BB}^{[T]}_{X,Y}$.

THEOREM 3.10. *For search space X and fitness domain Y, the deterministic proper optimizers form a minimal basis for the space of optimizers with consistent sums run for T time steps, $\mathcal{BB}^{[T]}_{X,Y}$, where X, Y, and T are all finite.*

PROOF. Theorem 3.9 has already shown that the deterministic proper optimizers are extreme points among the proper optimizers. Lemma 3.4 showed that every optimizer with consistent sum can be decomposed into a weighted difference of proper optimizers. Thus it suffices to show that every proper optimizer can be written as a convex combination of the deterministic proper optimizers. The Krein-Milman Theorem states that in a normed vector space, every compact, convex set is the closed convex hull of its extreme points. It has already been stated that the proper optimizers form a convex set, so it remains to show that this set is compact.

Compactness is achieved by a result known as *Riesz's Lemma*. This lemma implies that in a finite-dimensional normed vector space, the unit ball is compact. The *unit ball* consists of all elements with norm less than or equal to one, and contains the proper optimizers as a closed subset. Every closed subset of a compact space is also compact, so the set of proper optimizers is compact. Therefore, the Krein-Milman Theorem applies, and the proper optimizers are the closed, convex hull of the deterministic proper optimizers.

Consequently, every proper optimizer can be written as a weighted sum over the deterministic proper optimizers, and thus every optimizer with consistent sum can also be written in this way. Therefore the deterministic proper optimizers form a basis of $\mathcal{MF}^{[T]}_{X,Y}$. Since no deterministic proper optimizer can be realized as a weighted sum of distinct deterministic proper optimizers, this basis is minimal. □

Theorem 3.10 proves the case for finite spaces. The same is true for infinite spaces as well, but a more complex proof of compactness is required.

Notice that nothing in Theorem 3.9 depends on the black-box property. Thus its claim is also true for adversarial fitnesses: the deterministic proper adversarial fitnesses are the extreme points among the proper adversarial fitnesses. By the same reasoning as for Theorem 3.10, the following theorem can be proven.

THEOREM 3.11. *For search space X and fitness domain Y, the deterministic proper adversarial fitnesses form a minimal basis for the space of adversarial fitnesses with consistent sums run for T time steps, $\mathcal{AF}^{[T]}_{Y,X}$, where X, Y, and T are all finite.*

This basis for optimizer space can be used to analyze mathematical operations on optimizers, such as measuring their performance. The next section uses the vector spaces developed in this section in order to study the performance of optimizers.

4. FINITE PERFORMANCE ANALYSIS

One of the key goals for the theory of optimization is to analyze how optimization methods perform on a variety of problems. In this section, linear functionals are used to measure the performance of optimizers. As discussed below and in Lockett [9], such functionals include commonly used metrics such as the average runtime, the success rate, and the final error. It will be shown in this section that every linear measure of optimizer performance corresponds to an optimization game against a (non-proper) adversarial fitness. This fact is proven using concepts of *duality* from the study of vector spaces.

4.1 Linear Functionals and Duality

Before considering how to measure the performance of an optimizer, we will first consider linear functionals over preoptimizers from X to Y. It will be found that these functionals are in one-to-one correspondence with the class of preoptimizers from Y to X. That is, the set of linear functionals on $\mathcal{MF}^{[T]}_{X,Y}$ is topologically equivalent to $\mathcal{MF}^{[T]}_{Y,X}$.

In finite spaces, the linear functionals can be written explicitly. A *functional* is map from a vector space to its scalar field, in this case, a real-valued function $\ell : \mathcal{MF}^{[T]}_{X,Y} \to \mathbb{R}$. Such a function is *linear* if for all preoptimizers $\mathcal{A}_1, \mathcal{A}_2$ and all real numbers α, β, it holds that $\ell(\alpha\mathcal{A}_1 + \beta\mathcal{A}_2) = \alpha\ell(\mathcal{A}_1) + \beta\ell(\mathcal{A}_2)$. Using the basis from Section 3.4, linearity implies that

$$\ell(\mathcal{A}) = \sum_{z,v} \mathcal{A}(v)(z)\, \ell(\mathcal{B}_{z,v}), \tag{25}$$

so that the linear functional ℓ is determined by a set of coefficients $\eta_{z,v}$ such that $\ell(\mathcal{B}_{z,v}) = \eta_{z,v}$. There are $(|X||Y|)^T$ such coefficients, which is clearly the dimension of $\mathcal{MF}^{[T]}_{X,Y}$. One can even identify ℓ with a preoptimizer $\mathcal{F}_\ell$ from Y to X such that for each search history z and fitness history v, $\mathcal{F}_\ell(z)(v) = \eta_{z,v} = \ell(\mathcal{B}_{z,v})$. Rewriting Equation 25,

$$\ell(\mathcal{A}) = \sum_{z,v} \mathcal{A}(v)(z)\, \mathcal{F}_\ell(z)(v). \tag{26}$$

If $\mathcal{A}$ were an optimizer and $\mathcal{F}_\ell$ were an adversarial fitness, then $\ell(\mathcal{A})$ would be the overall measure of the generalized optimization game $\mathcal{A} \times \mathcal{F}$, as given in Equation 19.

In functional analysis, the collection of linear functionals on a finite-dimensional space is called the *topological dual* of the space. It is denoted by adding an asterisk to the space name, so that $\mathcal{MF}^{[T],*}_{X,Y}$ is the topological dual of $\mathcal{MF}^{[T]}_{X,Y}$. The topic of duality is important in vector space analysis because it enables many geometric and algebraic theorems about the properties of the space.

The above text has just shown that for every linear functional $\ell \in \mathcal{MF}^{[T],*}_{X,Y}$ there is a preoptimizer $\mathcal{F}_\ell \in \mathcal{MF}^{[T]}_{Y,X}$ that corresponds to it uniquely, where uniqueness comes from the fact that the coefficients $\eta_{z,v}$ are independent of the parameter $\mathcal{A}$. Thus there is an isomorphism between $\mathcal{MF}^{[T],*}_{X,Y}$ and $\mathcal{MF}^{[T]}_{Y,X}$ given by the map $\ell \mapsto \mathcal{F}_\ell$. We want to show further that these two spaces are actually topologically identical, that is, that they are the same vector space.

The topological dual of a normed vector space is itself a normed vector space, with the standard *operator norm*

$$||\ell|| = \sup_{\substack{\mathcal{A}\in\mathcal{MF}^T_{X,Y}\\ ||\mathcal{A}||\leq 1}} |\ell(\mathcal{A})| = \sum_v \max_z |\mathcal{F}_\ell(z)(v)|, \tag{27}$$

where sup is the *supremum*, i.e., the least upper bound of an arbitrary ordered set, and where the upper bound is taken over all preoptimizers with norm at most one. The last equality follows from Equation 26, since the upper bound is obtained by focusing all mass of $\mathcal{A}$ for each fitness history v on the search history z that has the largest coefficient.

Comparing Equation 27 with Equation 12, we see that $||\mathcal{F}_\ell||$ and $||\ell||$ are similar, but with the maximum and the sum in reverse order. Two norms $||\cdot||_1$ and $||\cdot||_2$ are *equivalent* if there is some constant C such that

$$\frac{1}{C}||\cdot||_2 \;\leq\; ||\cdot||_1 \;\leq\; C||\cdot||_2. \tag{28}$$

The operator norm and the preoptimizer norm are equivalent, and consequently, the space of linear functionals $\mathcal{MF}^{T,*}_{X,Y}$ and the space of preoptimizers $\mathcal{MF}^T_{X,Y}$ have the same topology. That is, with respect to their neighborhood structure, the two spaces are the same. The intuitive meaning of this fact is explained below, after the following proof.

LEMMA 4.1. *For a linear functional ℓ over preoptimizers from X to Y, the corresponding preoptimizer $\mathcal{F}_\ell$ has a norm equivalent to that of ℓ.*

PROOF. To begin, note that

$$\sum_v |\mathcal{F}_\ell(z)(v)| \leq \sum_v \max_{z'} |\mathcal{F}_\ell(z')(v)|, \tag{29}$$

where we have simply replaced each term under the sum with the maximum possible summand varying z. Maximizing z on each side yields that $||\mathcal{F}_\ell|| \leq ||\ell||$. Also, it is evident that

$$\max_z |\mathcal{F}_\ell(z)(v)| \leq \max_z \sum_{v'} |\mathcal{F}_\ell(z)(v')|, \tag{30}$$

and it follows that $||\ell|| =$

$$\sum_v \max_z |\mathcal{F}_\ell(z)(v)| \leq \sum_v \max_z \sum_{v'} |\mathcal{F}_\ell(z)(v')| = |Y|^T ||\mathcal{F}_\ell||. \tag{31}$$

Thus $||\ell||$ and $||\mathcal{F}_\ell||$ are equivalent norms with $C = |Y|^T$. □

THEOREM 4.2. *The space of preoptimizers from Y to X is isomorphic and topologically equivalent to the topological dual of the space of preoptimizers from X to Y.*

PROOF. The invertible map $\ell \mapsto \mathcal{F}_\ell$ described in the text provides the isomorphism. Lemma 4.1 proves that the two spaces have the same norm topology and are thus topologically equivalent, which completes proof. □

Theorem 4.2 says that every linear functional that assigns a real number to a preoptimizer from X to Y is identical to a preoptimizer from Y to X. In addition, the real number assigned is just the overall measure of an abstract optimization game. Although the dual $\mathcal{MF}^{[T],*}_{X,Y}$ and $\mathcal{MF}^{[T]}_{Y,X}$ are not *isometric* due to their different norms, they have the same elements and the same topology.

The statements in this subsection pertain to preoptimizers. We now ask what happens when linear functionals are applied to optimizers in order to measure their performance.

4.2 V-Performance

As in Lockett [9], the performance of an optimizer is regarded as a functional on the space of optimizers, $\mathcal{BB}^{[T]}_{X,Y}$, where X is the search space, Y the fitness domain, and T the number of time steps allowed. Essentially, a performance criterion must assign a real number to each optimizer so that they can be ranked.

Most of the performance criteria used to analyze black-box optimizers can be expressed in a more concrete way. Suppose that there is a value function $V : X^T \times Y^T \to \mathbb{R} \cup \{\pm\infty\}$ that scores game histories, including the search history and the fitness history. The average value of V is found by summing over all search histories z and fitness sequences v, with each history weighted according to its mass in the generalized optimization game. For an optimizer $\mathcal{A}$ and an adversarial fitness $\mathcal{F}$, the *V-performance* of $\mathcal{A}$ on $\mathcal{F}$ is

$$\begin{aligned} \langle \mathcal{A}, \mathcal{F} \rangle_V &= \sum_{z,v} V(z,v)\, \mathcal{A} \times \mathcal{F}(z,v) \\ &= \sum_{z,v} V(z,v)\, \mathcal{A}(v)(z)\, \mathcal{F}(z)(v). \end{aligned} \tag{32}$$

The V-performance is a linear functional on both $\mathcal{BB}^{[T]}_{X,Y}$ and $\mathcal{AF}^{[T]}_{Y,X}$ due to the definition of the generalized optimization game. If V is bounded, that is, if $\max_{z,v} |V(z,v)| < \infty$, then the V-performance is finite.

The value function V could be any function of the search history and fitness history. This value function is subtly weaker than that of Lockett [9] because it depends on a fitness history rather than a static fitness function. Thus there are certain properties that this value function cannot observe, such as the true minimum or maximum of a randomly chosen fitness function. However, it is acceptable for V to depend on the true minimum in some cases, for example, if an optimizer is being evaluated on a single fitness function or on a bank of fitness functions all of which have been normalized to have the same global minimum value.

The average runtime is a common metric for evaluating optimizers in static optimization. It is given for some $\epsilon \geq 0$ by $V(z,v) = \min\{i \leq T \mid |v - v^*| < \epsilon\}$, where v^* is the true minimum of a static fitness function or bank of fitness functions as in the last paragraph and $V(z,v) = \infty$ if there is no index satisfying the condition. Other value functions could represent the final error after some stopping criterion, the average error, or the probability of hitting some threshold around some minimal value. For details, see Lockett [8, 9].

In this paper, specific value functions are not studied. Instead, we are interested in the linear functionals that arise from bounded value functions and the theoretical results that come from this study. Examining the form of Equation 32, notice that

$$\langle \mathcal{A}, \mathcal{F} \rangle_V = \sum_{z,v} \mathcal{A}(v)(z)\ \mathcal{F}_\ell(z)(v) = \ell(\mathcal{A}) \tag{33}$$

where $\mathcal{F}_\ell$ is a preoptimizer from Y to X such that for search history z and all fitness history v, $\mathcal{F}_\ell(v)(z) = V(z,v)\, \mathcal{F}(v)(z)$. If $\mathcal{F}$ and V are fixed, then the V-performance with respect to $\mathcal{F}$ corresponds to the evaluation of the linear functional ℓ that is identified with $\mathcal{F}_\ell$ as described in Section 4.1.

The question now is whether $\mathcal{F}_\ell$ is an adversarial fitness. If so, then evaluation of the V-performance corresponds to playing the optimization game between $\mathcal{A}$ and $\mathcal{F}_\ell$ in extended form. Otherwise, the evaluation of $\mathcal{F}_\ell$ requires the observation of future search points and does not correspond to any possible game tree.

In fact, $\mathcal{F}_\ell$ is always an adversarial fitness. The absorption of the bounded value function V into adversarial fitness $\mathcal{F}$ preserves the jagged black-box property. This absorption process is an operation on adversarial fitnesses. It will be denoted as an operator $T^*_V : \mathcal{AF}^{[T]}_{Y,X} \to \mathcal{MF}^{[T]}_{Y,X}$ that maps adversarial fitnesses to preoptimizers from Y to X. For bounded value V, define T^*_V by

$$T^*_V \mathcal{F}(z)(v) = V(z,v)\, \mathcal{F}(z)(v). \tag{34}$$

It is obvious from the definition that T^*_V is a continuous linear operator on $\mathcal{AF}^{[T]}_{Y,X}$, and as such it preserves convex sets. It will be shown that the range of T^*_V is actually just $\mathcal{AF}^{[T]}_{Y,X}$, the space of adversarial fitnesses.

The proof of this fact constructs $T^*_V \mathcal{F}$ from generators using a progressive overestimate of the value. For $1 \leq i \leq T$, define sequences $\overline{V_i}$ and $\underline{V_i}$ that map $X^i \times Y^i$ to $\mathbb{R}$ by

$$\overline{V_i}(z,v) = \sup\left\{V(t,w) \,\middle|\, (t_{[i]}, w_{[i]}) = (v,z)\right\}, \tag{35}$$

$$\underline{V_i}(z,v) = \inf\left\{V(t,w) \,\middle|\, (t_{[i]}, w_{[i]}) = (v,z)\right\}. \tag{36}$$

Here $\overline{V_i}(z,v)$ is an upper bound on the value that can be obtained at the end of the game given partial search history z and partial fitness history v, each of length i. The lower bound on the final value is $\underline{V_i}(z,v)$. The sequences $\overline{V_i}$ and $\underline{V_i}$ approximate V from above and below.

Now consider a game history $(z,v) \in X^T \times Y^T$. Since (z,v) can occur under both the upper and lower bound,

$$\underline{V_i}(z_{[i]}, v_{[i]}) \leq V(z,v) \leq \overline{V_i}(z_{[i]}, v_{[i]}). \tag{37}$$

Additionally, since the set over which the upper and lower bounds are taken decreases in size as i increases,

$$\underline{V_i}(z_{[i]}, v_{[i]}) \leq \underline{V_{i+1}}(z_{[i+1]}, v_{[i+1]}) \tag{38}$$

$$\overline{V_i}(z_{[i]}, v_{[i]}) \geq \overline{V_{i+1}}(z_{[i+1]}, v_{[i+1]}). \tag{39}$$

Thus over time the upper and lower approximations of V approach each other monotonically. In the final step,

$$\underline{V_T}(z,v) = V(z,v) = \overline{V_T}(z,v). \tag{40}$$

These facts are sufficient to prove the following theorem.

THEOREM 4.3. *The operator T^*_V preserves the jagged black-box property, so that $\mathcal{F} \in \mathcal{AF}^{[T]}_{Y,X}$ implies $T^*_V \mathcal{F} \in \mathcal{AF}^{[T]}_{Y,X}$.*

PROOF. The theorem is first proven for any nonnegative value function V and any adversarial fitness $\mathcal{F}$. A jagged generator set as introduced in Section 2.4 is exhibited that extends to $T^*_V \mathcal{F}$. This jagged generator set thus corresponds to Radon-Nikodym derivatives $d[T^*_V\mathcal{F}]$, which therefore possesses the jagged black-box property. Define

$$V_1(z_{[1]}, v_{[1]}) = \overline{V_1}(z_{[1]}, v_{[1]})$$

$$V_{i+1}(z_{[i+1]}, v_{[i]}) = \begin{cases} 0 & \text{if } V_i(z_{[i]}, v_{[i]}) = 0 \quad \text{else} \\ \overline{V_{i+1}}(z_{[i+1]}, v_{[i+1]}) \,/\, V_i(z_{[i]}, v_{[i]}), \end{cases} \quad (41)$$

Now consider the product $\prod_{i=1}^T V_i^*(z_{[i]}, v_{[i]})$, which is either zero when $V(z,w) = 0$, or else

$$\prod_{i=1}^T V_i(z_{[i]}, v_{[i]}) = \overline{V_1}(z_{[1]}, v_{[1]}) \prod_{i=2}^T \frac{\overline{V_i}(z_{[i]}, v_{[i]})}{\overline{V_{i-1}}(z_{[i-1]}, v_{[i-1]})}$$

$$= \overline{V_T}(z,v) = V(z,v). \quad (42)$$

Let $d\mathcal{F}_i$ be as in Equation 4. Define $\mathcal{G}*_i$ to be a jagged generator such that for each search history z of length i, each fitness history v of length $i-1$, and each fitness $y \in Y$,

$$\mathcal{G}^*_i(v,z)(y) = V_i(z, v \cup y)\; d\mathcal{F}_i(v,t)(y), \quad (43)$$

where t is any complete search history equal to z in the first i steps, i.e., $t_{[i]} = z$, and $v \cup y$ indicates the fitness history obtained by appending y to v. Since $\mathcal{F}$ has the jagged black-box property, the choice of t does not change $\mathcal{G}^*_i(v,z)(y)$.

Proposition 2.3 implies that the jagged generator set $\mathcal{G}^* = (\mathcal{G}_i)_{i=1}^T$ extends to a unique adversarial fitness $\mathcal{F}^*$ such that for each search history z and fitness history v, Equations 42, 43, and 6 together imply

$$\mathcal{F}^*(z)(v) = \prod_{i=1}^T \mathcal{G}^*_i(z_{[i]}, v_{[i-1]})(v_i)$$

$$= \left(\prod_{i=1}^T V_i(z_{[i]}, v_{[i]})\right)\left(\prod_{i=1}^T d\mathcal{F}_i(v_{[i-1]}, z)(v_i)\right)$$

$$= V(z,v)\,\mathcal{F}(z)(v) = T^*_V\mathcal{F}(z)(v). \quad (44)$$

Therefore $T^*_V\mathcal{F}$ is an adversarial fitness.

If V is not nonnegative, it can be separated in to positive and negative parts, $V = V_+ - V_-$. The above proof shows $T^*_{V_+}\mathcal{F}$ and $T^*_{V_-}\mathcal{F}$ are both adversarial fitnesses, and so by linearity $T^*_V\mathcal{F} = T^*_{V_+}\mathcal{F} - T^*_{V_-}\mathcal{F}$ is an adversarial fitness. □

Theorem 4.3 means that different value functions do not create different measures of performance. Instead, changing the value function only shuffles the adversarial fitnesses that produce each performance measurement. All possible linear performance criteria are produced by the 1-performance, that is, by the V-performance with $V(z,v) = 1$. In particular, for any optimizer $\mathcal{A}$ and any adversarial fitness $\mathcal{F}$,

$$\langle \mathcal{A}, \mathcal{F}\rangle_V = \langle \mathcal{A}, T^*_V\mathcal{F}\rangle_1 . \quad (45)$$

It is possible for the value function to eliminate some linear functionals if the value function is not strictly positive; consider the 0-performance as an extreme example. But the number of linear functionals on the optimizers that can be produced by the V-performance is bounded above by the number of adversarial fitnesses, and this bound is attained for the 1-performance.

The 1-performance in turn corresponds to the overall measure of the generalized optimization game. Thus in every case, the V-performance reduces to some generalized optimization game. Even more is true: To study the set of linear performance criteria over optimizers, it suffices to study the generalized optimization game. Before proving this, some facts about deterministic optimizers are needed.

4.3 Optimizer-Fitness Duality

Returning to the subject of duality, we now consider the set of all linear functionals over the space of optimizers, $\mathcal{BB}^{[T]}_{X,Y}$. This set is the topological dual $\mathcal{BB}^{[T],*}_{X,Y}$. It may be considered as a source of linear performance measurements over optimizers. It has already been seen that each adversarial fitness function is isomorphic to a linear functional over optimizers through the optimization game. That is, for optimizer $\mathcal{A} \in \mathcal{BB}^{[T]}_{X,Y}$ and $\mathcal{F} \in \mathcal{AF}^{[T]}_{Y,X}$, the overall measure of the optimization game

$$\langle \mathcal{A}, \mathcal{F}\rangle_1 = \sum_{z,v} \mathcal{A}(v)(z)\mathcal{F}(z)(v) \quad (46)$$

is a linear functional over optimizers. This subsection establishes the relationship between $\mathcal{AF}^{[T]}_{Y,X}$ and $\mathcal{BB}^{[T],*}_{X,Y}$, which depends on the size of the search and fitness domain.

Consider the basis for $\mathcal{BB}^{[T]}_{X,Y}$ given by the deterministic proper optimizers as in Theorem 3.10, and suppose that $\mathcal{D}^{\text{opt}}_i$ is any element of this basis, indexed by i. Additionallly, let $\mathcal{D}^{\text{fit}}_j$ be a deterministic proper adversarial fitness that is an element of the basis for $\mathcal{AF}^{[T]}_{X,Y}$ from Theorem 3.11, indexed by j. For an arbitrary optimizer $\mathcal{A}$ and arbitrary adversarial fitness $\mathcal{F}$, we have the basis expansion

$$\mathcal{A} = \sum_i \alpha_i \mathcal{D}^{\text{opt}}_i \quad \text{and} \quad \mathcal{F} = \sum_j \beta_j \mathcal{D}^{\text{fit}}_j,$$

which yields by linearity that

$$\langle \mathcal{A}, \mathcal{F}\rangle_1 = \sum_{i,j} \alpha_i\beta_j \left\langle \mathcal{D}^{\text{opt}}_i, \mathcal{D}^{\text{fit}}_j\right\rangle_1 = \sum_i \alpha_i \sum_j \beta_j\, \eta_{i,j}, \quad (47)$$

where $\eta_{i,j}$ is the 1-performance of $\mathcal{D}^{\text{opt}}_i$ against $\mathcal{D}^{\text{fit}}_j$.

The matrix of games $\left\langle \mathcal{D}^{\text{opt}}_i, \mathcal{D}^{\text{fit}}_j\right\rangle_1$ thus determines the outcome of every generalized optimization game. Because both are deterministic, all values under the sum in Equation 46 are either one or zero for this game, and hence $\eta_{i,j}$ takes on nonnegative integer values. It can take on value zero if for all game histories (z,v), $\mathcal{D}^{\text{opt}}_i(v)(z) = 1$ implies that $\mathcal{D}^{\text{fit}}_j(z)(v) = 0$. This situation is, in fact, the most common one. The maximum value for $\eta_{i,j}$ is either $|X|^T$ or $|Y|^T$, whichever is smaller. This case occurs when for all game histories (z,v), $\mathcal{D}^{\text{opt}}_i(v)(z) = 1$ implies that $\mathcal{D}^{\text{fit}}_j(z)(v) = 1$.

Suppose that $\ell \in \mathcal{BB}^{[T],*}_{X,Y}$ is a linear functional over optimizers, and then basis decomposition gives

$$\ell(\mathcal{A}) = \sum_i \alpha_i\, \ell(\mathcal{D}^{\text{opt}}_i), \quad (48)$$

and therefore ℓ is determined by the real vector $\left(\ell(\mathcal{D}^{\text{opt}}_i)\right)_{i \le T}$. Each adversarial fitness $\mathcal{F}$ in $\mathcal{AF}^{[T]}_{Y,X}$ is associated with a linear functional ℓ that has

$$\ell(\mathcal{D}^{\text{opt}}_i) = \sum_j \beta_j\, \eta_{i,j}. \quad (49)$$

One can thus create a map from $\mathcal{AF}^{[T]}_{Y,X}$ into the dual space of the optimizers $\mathcal{BB}^{[T],*}_{X,Y}$. Equation 49 is just a matrix multiplication. Suppose there are I deterministic proper optimizers and J deterministic proper adversarial fitness functions.

Then let $\hat{\ell} \in \mathbb{R}^I$ be the vector that determines ℓ, and let $\beta \in \mathbb{R}^J$ be a vector with the β_j as components. If $H = [\eta_{i,j}]$ is the $I \times J$ matrix whose entries are given by the $\eta_{i,j}$, then

$$\hat{\ell} = H\beta^T \tag{50}$$

is equivalent to Equation 49. Each deterministic proper optimizer can be represented as a tree with branching factor $|Y|$, for which each node may take $|X|$ values. Similarly, a deterministic proper adversarial fitness corresponds to $|X|$ trees with branching factor $|X|$, for which each node may take $|Y|$ values. Therefore,

$$I = |X|^{\left(\sum_{i=0}^{T-1} |Y|^i\right)} \quad \text{and} \quad J = |Y|^{\left(\sum_{i=1}^{T} |X|^i\right)}, \tag{51}$$

where the difference in indexing reflects the fact that the optimizer moves first. Equation 50 is a system of equations that is either overdetermined or underdetermined depending on the relationship between I and J. The next set of theorems express these relationships. The proofs are self-evident given the above text.

THEOREM 4.4. *If $I = J$, then Equation 50 has a unique solution and $\mathcal{AF}^{[T]}_{Y,X}$ is topologically equivalent to $\mathcal{BB}^{[T],*}_{X,Y}$.*

THEOREM 4.5. *If $I < J$, then Equation 50 is underdetermined and $\mathcal{BB}^{[T],*}_{Y,X}$ is topologically equivalent to a proper vector subspace of $\mathcal{AF}^{[T]}_{Y,X}$.*

THEOREM 4.6. *If $I > J$, then Equation 50 is overdetermined and $\mathcal{AF}^{[T]}_{Y,X}$ is topologically equivalent to a proper vector subspace of $\mathcal{BB}^{[T]}_{X,Y}$.*

The topological equivalence in each of these theorems refers to the equivalent norms demonstrated in Lemma 4.1. If the search space and the fitness domain are the same, $X = Y$, then $I < J$ holds, and the adversarial fitnesses properly contain the linear functionals. In each case, the size of the search space X and the fitness domain Y determines whether there are more adversarial fitnesses or linear performance criteria. However, there is always a close relationship between the two in that one is a vector subspace of the other.

Based on the relationship between the V-performance of Section 4.2 and overall measure of the optimization game, Theorems 4.4 to 4.6 demonstrate that when $I \leq J$, every linear measure of performance corresponds to the V-performance for some value function, which in turn corresponds to the optimization game with a potentially transformed adversarial fitness through the operator T^*_V. If $J > I$, then there are infinitely many additional measures of performance.

4.4 Deterministic Performs Best

This section has considered performance as measured by linear functionals, typified by the V-performance of Section 4.2. For each performance criterion, it is natural to ask which optimizers perform best. In answer, if all of the proper optimizers are considered, then for linear functional measuring performance, there is one or more deterministic proper optimizer that equals or outperforms every nondeterministic proper optimizer. Leveraging the generality of the optimization game, this fact remains true irrespective of whether performance is measured against a static, stochastic, dynamic, or adaptive fitness function. It is also true not just for linear performance measurements, but for convex, continuous performance metrics as well.

THEOREM 4.7. *Suppose the search domain X, the fitness domain Y, and the number of time steps T are all finite. Let $\phi : \mathcal{BB}^{[T]}_{X,Y} \to \mathbb{R}$ be any convex continuous functional that assigns a real number to each optimizer with consistent sums. Then there is some deterministic proper optimizer that attains the extremal value (minimum or maximum) of ϕ over all proper optimizers. In addition, if C is any closed, convex subset of the proper optimizers, then the extremal value of ϕ is attained on the extreme points of C.*

PROOF. The latter statement is the more general one. The set of proper optimizers is a closed, convex subset of $\mathcal{BB}^{[T]}_{X,Y}$ that is also compact, as discussed in the proof of Theorem 3.10. The second claim is merely a restatement of the Bauer minimum principle, which states that any convex continuous functional attains its extreme values over a compact, convex set at the extreme points. Every closed subset of a compact set is also compact, and so if C is a closed and convex subset of the proper optimizers, it follows that C is also compact, and the Bauer minimum principle applies. The first statement is the case where C includes all proper optimizers, whose only extreme points are the deterministic proper optimizers by Theorem 3.8. □

A functional ϕ is *convex* if $\phi(\alpha\mathcal{A}_1 + \beta\mathcal{A}_2) \leq \alpha\phi(\mathcal{A}_1) + \beta\phi(\mathcal{A}_2)$, that is, if it is sublinear. Clearly, linear functionals such as the V-performance are convex.

Theorem 4.7 comes with two caveats. First, there exist performance measures that are non-convex; the black-box complexity discussed below is an example. Secondly, there are cases in which a class of optimizers considered that does not include all of the deterministic proper optimizers. If the class is still convex, then Theorem 4.7 says that the extreme values will be on the boundary of the class. But if the class is also non-convex, then even convex functionals can have extreme values in the interior of the set.

As mentioned above, for finite spaces this fact has already been known for some time as Yao's minimax priciple [14], which is itself a direct consequence of von Neumann's original minimax theorem for games [12]. As will be seen in Section 5, the same reasoning with some modifications also proves Theorem 4.7 for infinite spaces as well.

Having studied several aspects of performance in the vector space of optimizers, we now briefly generalize these findings to infinite spaces, for which the tools developed up to this point are well adapted.

5. INFINITE SPACES

The preceding results were presented for finite spaces to simplify some of the technical machinery. In this section, it is shown how to extend these results to infinite spaces. It is important for a theory of optimization to address infinite spaces, since common search domains and fitness domains are infinite. Examples include the real numbers, Euclidean space, and function spaces such as neural networks. It is true digital computers can only process finite objects, but there is no reason why a theory of optimization should be limited to the capabilities of digital computers. The main effect of infinite search and fitness domains is that the space of optimizers becomes infinite-dimensional. The results of this change are discussed in two steps below, first for countably infinite spaces and then for general topological spaces.

5.1 Countably Infinite Spaces

Suppose that the search space X and the fitness domain Y are countably infinite, and that the optimizer may be allowed to run for $T < \infty$ steps. For countably infinite spaces, the characterization of optimizers and adversarial fitnesses using probability vectors still works. Thus much of the theory above remains intact verbatim. However, the space of preoptimizers $\mathcal{MF}^{[T]}_{X,Y}$ becomes isomorphic to $\mathbb{R}^{\mathbb{N}}$, the space of real-valued infinite sequences. That is, for each fitness history $v \in Y^T$, a preoptimizer $\mathcal{A}$ from X to Y produces an infinite real-valued sequence $\mathcal{A}(v)$. For a proper preoptimizers, the infinite sum over search histories is equal to one for every fitness history, $\sum_z \mathcal{A}(v)(z) = 1$. The preoptimizer has consistent sums if this sum is equal to some constant c independent of v.

The first problem encountered is with the proposed norm from Equation 12, in which the maximum needs to be replaced with an upper bound (sup). This bound may not be finite for a pre-optimzer $\mathcal{A}$, even if it does have consistent sums. This issue is resolved by stipulating that membership in $\mathcal{MF}^{[T]}_{X,Y}$ is conditioned on the finiteness of the norm. That is, if $\mathcal{A} \in \mathcal{MF}^{[T]}_{X,Y}$, then $||\mathcal{A}|| < \infty$. Since addition and multiplication of preoptimizers with finite norm yield a preoptimizer with finite norm, $\mathcal{MF}^{[T]}_{X,Y}$ with the finiteness restriction still forms a complete normed vector space, that is, a *Banach space*. The space of optimizers with consistent sum and finite norm, $\mathcal{BB}^{[T]}_{X,Y}$, and the space of adversarial fitnesses with consistent sum and finite norm, $\mathcal{AF}^{[T]}_{X,Y}$ are both Banach spaces and subspaces of $\mathcal{MF}^{[T]}_{X,Y}$.

The basis from Section 3.4 still works, but is infinite in size, so that $\mathcal{MF}^{[T]}_{X,Y}$ is infinite-dimensional. Theorems 3.8 and 3.9 are both valid for infinite spaces, so that the deterministic proper optimizers are still the extreme points among the proper optimizers.

There is an issue, however, with Theorem 3.10, whose proof relies on the claim that the proper optimizers are compact by Riesz's Lemma. This lemma implies that the unit ball of a normed vector space is compact *if and only if* the space is finite-dimensional. Thus the unit ball in $\mathcal{MF}^{[T]}_{X,Y}$ is not compact when X and Y are infinite.

The issue of compactness is resolved by an appeal to duality, specifically, to the *Alaoglu Theorem* (also known as the *Banach-Alaoglu Theorem*), which states that the unit ball of every dual space is *weak-* compact*; that is, the unit ball is compact with an alternate topology, the *weak-* topology* [1]. We do not introduce this topology further here, except to say that it preserves the vector structure (and hence convexity) from the norm topology that has been used heretofore in this paper.

In order to apply the Alaoglu Theorem for this purpose, the space of optimizers $\mathcal{BB}^{[T]}_{X,Y}$ must be cast as a dual space. But this was already done in Section 4.1, where it was shown that the dual $\mathcal{MF}^{[T],*}_{Y,X}$ consisting of continuous linear functionals over preoptimizers from Y to X is isomorphic to the space of preoptimizers from X to Y, $\mathcal{MF}^{[T]}_{X,Y}$. Lemma 4.1 and Theorem 4.2 both hold for countably infinite spaces by replacing the maximums with upper bounds, so that the isomorphism is a topological equivalence. That is, in terms of structure, $\mathcal{MF}^{[T]}_{X,Y}$ and $\mathcal{MF}^{[T],*}_{Y,X}$ are the same space. Therefore, the unit ball of $\mathcal{MF}^{[T]}_{X,Y}$ is weak-* compact, and the following theorems are a result.

THEOREM 5.1. *The deterministic proper optimizers span the proper optimizers when the search space X and fitness domain Y are countably infinite and T is finite.*

PROOF. The unit ball of $\mathcal{MF}^{[T]}_{X,Y}$ is weak-* compact by the Alaoglu Theorem, so the set of proper optimizers is also weak-* compact since it is a weak-* closed subset. Since the deterministic proper optimizers are the extreme points among the proper optimizers by Theorems 3.8 and 3.9, the Krein-Milman Theorem implies that the proper optimizers are the weak-* closed convex hull of the deterministic proper optimizers, which completes the proof. □

THEOREM 5.2. *The statements of Theorem 4.7 apply to weak-* continuous convex functionals if the search domain X and the fitness domain Y are countably infinite.*

PROOF. The proof is identical to that of Theorem 4.7, but with compactness replaced by weak-* compactness. □

Theorem 5.2 yields that deterministic proper optimizers obtain optimal performance in countably infinite spaces, but with the requirement that performance be measured by convex functionals that are weak-* continuous. Not all continuous convex functionals are also weak-* continuous, but all continuous linear functionals (such as the V-performance for bounded V) are weak-* continuous due to the fact that a linear functional on an infinite-dimensional space is continuous if and only if it is bounded.

Completing the modifications for countably infinite spaces, the linear operator T^*_V still maps adversarial fitnesses to adversarial fitnesses (Theorem 4.3), and thus the 1-performance still induces all continuous linear measures of performance. That is, every performance measure that is produced by averaging a value function can be produced by a generalized optimization game with some adversarial fitness function, potentially non-proper. Theorems 4.4 to 4.6, however, cannot be easily restated for infinite spaces.

Thus most of the results developed for finite spaces also apply to countably infinite spaces with some alterations in the proofs and notation.

5.2 Topological Spaces

To apply this theory to search spaces and fitness domains that are uncountable, considerably more terminology and technical machinery is required. It will not be possible to give a full treatment of the subject here, but the basic ideas for a theory of the optimization game in arbitrary topological spaces are sketched in this subsection.

The fundamental problem is that probability vectors do not suffice to describe randomness in large spaces, where each point may have probability zero. Thus for each fitness history v, the optimizer $\mathcal{A}(v)$ must be represented as a *probability measure*, a set function that assigns probability to sets of search histories rather than to individual search histories. Further complicating matters, it is not always possible to assign consistent probabilities to all sets of search histories due to issues such as the Banach-Tarski paradox. Thus one introduces a σ-algebra that indicates which sets can be consistently measured. Such sets are called *measurable*, and the space that is measured is called a *measure space*. One simple way to get a σ-algebra is by generating the *Borel σ-algebra* from a topology, which consists of a set of subsets of a space that are declared to be *open*. The Borel σ-algebra is the smallest σ-algebra that makes all open, closed, and compact sets measurable. A probability measure is a nonnegative, subadditive set function $\mathbb{P}$ defined on a σ-algebra such that the measure of the whole space is one, e.g. $\mathbb{P}(X) = 1$. A *finite measure* requires only that the measure of the whole space be finite, and a *finite signed measure* is the difference of two finite measures [6].

If the search space is a topological space (X, τ_X) and the fitness domain is a topological space (Y, τ_Y), each equipped with their Borel σ-algebras, then a preoptimizer $\mathcal{A}$ from X to Y run for times steps indexed by $\mathcal{I}$ is such that for any fitness history $v \in Y^{\mathcal{I}}$, $\mathcal{A}(v)$ is a finite signed measure. The space of such preoptimizers from is $\mathcal{MF}^{\mathcal{I}}_{X,Y}$. Here $\mathcal{I}$ may be finite (e.g. $\mathcal{I} = [T]$, the numbers from 1 to T) or infinite (e.g. $\mathcal{I} = \mathbb{N}$). As with countably infinite spaces, membership in $\mathcal{MF}^{\mathcal{I}}_{X,Y}$ is conditioned on having a finite norm, i.e.,

$$||\mathcal{A}|| = \sup_v ||\mathcal{A}(v)|| < \infty, \qquad (52)$$

where $||\mathcal{A}(v)||$ is the *total variation norm* on measures.

To obtain optimizers and adversarial fitnesses, one defines

$$\mathcal{A}^{[i]}(v)(B) = \mathcal{A}(v)(\{z \mid (z_1, \ldots, z_i) \in B\}) \qquad (53)$$

for measurable subsets B of X^i and forms the generators by

$$\mathcal{A}^{[i+1]}(v)(B \times C) = \int_B d\mathcal{A}_i(z, v)(C)\, d\mathcal{A}^{[i]}(dz), \qquad (54)$$

where B is as before and C is a measurable subset of X. The generator $d\mathcal{A}_i : X^i \times Y^{\mathcal{I}} \to ca(X)$ maps partial search histories and complete fitness histories to the space of finite signed measures on X. It is well defined as a Radon-Nikodym derivative and is unique $\mathcal{A}^{[i]}$-almost everywhere. As before, the black-box property is the situation where the second argument v of $d\mathcal{A}_i$ can be replaced by $v_{[i]}$, the fitness history up to time i. The jagged black-box property is when it can be replaced by $v_{[i+1]}$.

The space of optimizers $\mathcal{BB}^{\mathcal{I}}_{X,Y}$ is the set of preoptimizers from X to Y that have the black-box property, finite norm, and consistent sums, which in this context means that $\mathcal{A} \in \mathcal{BB}^{\mathcal{I}}_{X,Y}$ has $\mathcal{A}(v)(X) = c$ for some constant c indepedent of v. The space of adversarial fitnesses $\mathcal{AF}^{\mathcal{I}}_{X,Y}$ relaxes the black-box property to the jagged black-box property. Both are Banach subspaces of $\mathcal{MF}^{\mathcal{I}}_{X,Y}$.

Using the Kolmogorov Extension Theorem, analogues of Proposition 2.1 and 2.3 are possible, but extra requirements of tightness and measurability must be placed on the generator sets to do so. Under the same conditions, the optimization game can be constructed as in Theorem 2.4, but with the extension theorem used to generalize a process similar to the second equality of Equation 8. The overall measure of the optimization game is written as $\mathcal{A} \times \mathcal{F}(X)$, and it is equivalent to the 1-performance $\langle \mathcal{A}, \mathcal{F} \rangle_1$.

The basis of Section 3.4 can no longer be used to prove that the dual of $\mathcal{MF}^{\mathcal{I}}_{X,Y}$ is $\mathcal{MF}^{\mathcal{I}}_{Y,X}$. However, the V-performance can be defined as an integral with respect to the optimization game, and it is a continuous linear functional of both arguments if and only if V is *essentially* bounded. The linear operator T^*_V maps $\mathcal{AF}^{\mathcal{I}}_{Y,X}$ to itself as in Theorem 4.3 with virtually the same proof, and there is a similar operator T_V that maps $\mathcal{BB}^{\mathcal{I}}_{X,Y}$ to itself.

To get the weak-* compactness of the unit ball in $\mathcal{BB}^{\mathcal{I}}_{X,Y}$, a duality argument is again used. The space of linear functionals over adversarial fitnesses generated by the V-performance is a vector space that is topologically equivalent to $\mathcal{BB}^{\mathcal{I}}_{X,Y}$ by an analogue of Lemma 4.1 and Theorem 4.2. Thus similar to Theorems 4.4-4.6, the space of optimizers $\mathcal{BB}^{\mathcal{I}}_{X,Y}$ is either a vector subspace of the dual of the adversarial fitnesses $\mathcal{AF}^{\mathcal{I},*}_{Y,X}$ or vice versa. In either case, the Alaoglu theorem implies that the unit ball of $\mathcal{BB}^{\mathcal{I}}_{X,Y}$ is weak-* compact, yielding the final two theorems, proven as were Theorems 5.1 and 5.2.

THEOREM 5.3. *The deterministic proper optimizers span the proper optimizers when the search space X and fitness domain Y are arbitrary topological spaces with $\mathcal{I}$ at most countable.*

THEOREM 5.4. *The statements of Theorem 4.7 apply to weak-* continuous convex functionals if the search domain X and the fitness domain Y are topological spaces.*

As mentioned in Section 5.1, every continuous linear functional is also weak-* continuous. Thus some deterministic proper optimizer attains optimal performance for any linear measure of performance, even in infinite spaces and even if the optimizer is evaluated with respect to stochastic, dynamic, or adaptive fitnesses. The results from earlier sections with respect to finite spaces are thus nicely complemented by similar results in infinite spaces.

6. DISCUSSION AND FUTURE WORK

The previous sections have developed the basic features of a study of adversarial optimization, in which both the optimizer and the fitness are given the freedom to deceive and outwit each other. Special cases have been pointed out in Section 2.7. The result is an analysis of performance that leads to general statements about the geometric nature and performance potential of optimizers within this framework.

6.1 Geometric Results

One of the most interesting results in this paper is Theorem 4.3, because it establishes that for any performance measure obtained by averaging a value function depending only on the optimization history, there is a generalized adversarial fitness such that the optimization game with that adversarial fitness corresponds to measuring the performance of an optimizer. This result yields the duality in Section 5.2 needed to prove compactness of the proper optimizers when either the search space or the fitness space is large. This duality is a potential source of future results.

Theorem 5.3 means that stochastic optimizers spanned by deterministic optimizers even in large search domains. This surprising fact suggests that the space of black-box optimizers is "small" in the sense that every optimizer $\mathcal{A}$ may be written as a countably infinite sum

$$\mathcal{A} = \sum_{n=1}^{\infty} w_n \mathcal{D}_n, \qquad (55)$$

where $\mathcal{D}_n$ is a deterministic and proper and $\sum_n w_n = 1$, even if the search space has uncountable cardinality or larger. These results depend implicitly on the Axiom of Choice.

Turning now to the question of performance, the expression of each proper optimizer as a countable sum of deterministic optimizers means that the performance of any nondeterministic proper optimizer can be improved by adjusting the weights $(w_n)_{n\in\mathbb{N}}$ to set $w_{n_0} = 1$ for the best deterministic optimizer $\mathcal{D}_{n_0}$ under the sum. This is the essence of Theorem 5.4: Any non-deterministic proper optimizer can always be improved to a deterministic version.

Theorem 5.4 says both more and less than it seems to. On the one hand, the statement applies to *any* convex (weak-*) continuous functional. A convex functional need not be defined by an integral, and there are strictly more such functionals than there are continuous linear functionals. On any of these, there is a deterministic proper optimizer that attains the best performance. The important case of the average runtime is a discontinuous value function to which this theory applies only if a maximal query budget is enforced.

Further, Theorem 5.4 only implies that deterministic optimizers perform best when the set of proper optimizers under consideration is spanned by deterministic optimizers, which is not always the case [3]. Since the proper optimizers form a simplex, a set of proper optimizers not spanned by the deterministic optimizers can be thought of as cutting off some corners. If the resulting set is convex, Theorem 5.4 says that the best optimizers still lie "on the cut".

6.2 Complexity of Optimization

A fascinating aspect of Theorem 5.4 is that it applies to every one of the special cases outlined in Section 2.7, including general stochastic optimization and general dynamic optimization. As long as the performance of an optimizer is a single number, a deterministic optimizer gets the highest score. But what is the complexity of the deterministic optimizer that attains this performance? The best optimizer makes optimal use of the information gleaned from fitness evaluations averaged over the randomness of the adversarial fitness [9], which requires an internal optimization and suggests that optimal optimization is computationally hard. There is a unavoidable tradeoff between the fitness evaluations and the time taken to compute search points.

The theory of black-box complexity bears on the question of how few fitness evaluations are needed to solve the hardest static fitness function drawn from fixed set [4, 2]. Take any (Baire measurable) set $\mathcal{U} \subseteq Y^X$ of static fitness functions. Let μ be any fitness probability measure (see Section 2.7) that places probability one on $\mathcal{U}$, and let $\mathcal{F}_\mu$ be the adversarial fitness $z \mapsto \mu \circ \pi_z$. The black-box complexity is

$$BlackBox(\mathcal{U}, \mathfrak{A}) = \inf_{\mathcal{A}\in\mathfrak{A}} \sup_{\mu} \langle \mathcal{A}, \mathcal{F}_\mu \rangle_V , \tag{56}$$

where the infimum ranges over a subset $\mathfrak{A}$ of the proper optimizers and V is the runtime. The black-box complexity is not subject to Theorem 5.4, because the inner supremum is non-convex. Future work should examine applications of duality theory to the black-box complexity.

7. CONCLUSION

By expanding the set of possible fitness functions to an extraordinarily general class of adversarial fitnesses, several insights into the nature of the space of optimization methods have been obtained. In particular, every optimization method is a weighted average of countably many deterministic methods, and for every convex continuous performance criterion, the best performance is attained on some deterministic optimizer. These results were made possible through the discovery that the adversarial fitnesses can be identified with the space of linear continuous performance measurements. Many other insights of this kind may yet be achieved by pursuing this framework to its logical extent.

Acknowledgements

This work was supported in part by US National Science Foundation grant OISE-1159008.

References

[1] C. C. Aliprantis and K. D. Border. *Infinite Dimensional Analysis: A Hitchhiker's Guide, 3rd Edition.* Springer, New York, New York, 2006.

[2] B. Doerr and C. Winzen. Towards a complexity theory of randomized search heuristics: Ranking-based black-box complexity. *CoRR*, abs/1102.1140, 2011.

[3] C. Doerr. Personal communication.

[4] S. Droste, T. Jansen, and I. Wegener. Upper and lower bounds for randomized search heuristics in black-box optimization. *Theoretical Computer Science*, 39, 2006.

[5] G. Edgar. A non-compact choquet theorem. *Proceedings of the American Mathematical Society*, 49:354–358, 1975.

[6] P. Halmos. *Measure Theory.* Springer-Verlag, New York, NY, 1974.

[7] C. Igel. No free lunch theorems: Limitations and perspectives of metaheuristics. In Y. Borenstein and A. Moraglio, editors, *Theory and Principled Methods for the Design of Metaheuristics.* Springer-Verlag, 2014.

[8] A. Lockett. Measure-theoretic analysis of performance in evolutionary algorithms. In *Proceedings of the 2013 IEEE Conference on Evolutionary Computation (CEC-2013).* IEEE Pres, 2013.

[9] A. Lockett. Model-optimal optimization by solving bellman equations. In *Proceedings of the 2014 Genetic and Evolutionary Computation Conference (GECCO-2014).* ACM Press, 2014.

[10] A. Lockett and R. Miikkulainen. A measure-theoretic analysis of stochastic optimization. In *Proceedings of the 12th Workshop on Foundations of Genetic Algorithms (FOGA-2013).* ACM, 2013.

[11] J. E. Rowe, M. D. Vose, and A. H. Wright. Reinterpreting no free lunch. *Evolutionary Computation*, 17(1):117–129, 2009.

[12] J. von Neumann and O. Morgenstern. *Theory of Games and Economic Behavior.* Princeton University Press, 1944.

[13] M. Vose. *The Simple Genetic Algorithm.* MIT Press, Cambridge, Massachusetts, 1999.

[14] A. Yao. Probabilistic computations: Toward a unified measure of complexity. In *Proceedings of the 18th IEEE Symposium on Foundations of Computer Science (FOCS)*, pages 222–227, 1977.

(1+1) EA on Generalized Dynamic OneMax

Timo Kötzing
Friedrich-Schiller-Universität
Jena, Germany

Andrei Lissovoi
DTU Compute, Technical
University of Denmark
Kongens Lyngby, Denmark

Carsten Witt
DTU Compute, Technical
University of Denmark
Kongens Lyngby, Denmark

ABSTRACT

Evolutionary algorithms (EAs) perform well in settings involving *uncertainty*, including settings with stochastic or dynamic fitness functions. In this paper, we analyze the (1+1) EA on dynamically changing OneMax, as introduced by Droste (2003). We re-prove the known results on first hitting times using the modern tool of drift analysis. We extend these results to search spaces which allow for more than two values per dimension.

Furthermore, we make an *anytime analysis* as suggested by Jansen and Zarges (2014), analyzing how closely the (1+1) EA can track the dynamically moving optimum over time. We get tight bounds both for the case of bit strings, as well as for the case of more than two values per position. Surprisingly, in the latter setting, the expected quality of the search point maintained by the (1+1) EA does not depend on the number of values per dimension.

Categories and Subject Descriptors

F.2 [**Theory of Computation**]: Analysis of Algorithms and Problem Complexity

General Terms

Theory, algorithms

Keywords

evolutionary computation, dynamic optimization, drift, theory

1. INTRODUCTION

Randomized search heuristics, such as evolutionary algorithms (EAs), are general purpose optimization algorithms applicable to virtually any (formal) optimization task. In particular, EAs (and other randomized search heuristics) have been applied very successfully in domains featuring *uncertainty*; for example, the objective functions (so-called fitness functions) can be *randomized* or *dynamically changing* (see Jin and Branke, 2005 for an excellent survey on evolutionary algorithms in settings featuring uncertainty). In this paper we focus on dynamically changing fitness functions.

We call a fitness function *dynamic* if the fitness values of search points depend on the iteration number (but might be *deterministic* for each iteration). For example, the shortest path between two cities might depend on whether it is rush hour or not. The classical task of an optimization algorithm is to find the best solution it can (in terms of fitness); for dynamic optimization, there need not be a single solution which is good at all times: solutions that are good now might be bad later. Thus, algorithms in this domain need to be able to find *and track* the optimal solution (or at least a good solution) over time as the problem changes.

With this paper we contribute to the *theoretical foundations* of randomized search heuristics, for the domain of dynamic fitness functions. While there has been a lot of work on the theory of randomized search heuristics in static settings (see Auger and Doerr, 2011; Neumann and Witt, 2010; Jansen, 2013), there are only a few works on dynamically changing fitness functions. The utility of a population for tracking problems was studied in evolutionary computation by Jansen and Schellbach (2005), while different mechanisms for ensuring population diversity have been considered by Oliveto and Zarges (2013). In particular, a mechanism called genotype diversity was proved to be inefficient on a particular dynamic problem. The papers by Kötzing and Molter (2012) and Lissovoi and Witt (2015) consider dynamic pseudo-Boolean functions where the optimum moves slowly from the all-ones to the all-zeros bit string; the papers show that, while the Max-Min Ant System is able to track the changes occurring in this fitness function, an evolutionary algorithm (in Lissovoi and Witt, 2015 using a population) loses track of the optimum. Jansen and Zarges (2014) analyzed the performance of a standard evolutionary algorithm on a dynamically changing fitness function, introducing "anytime analysis", the expected distance to the optimum at any given point in time.

The oldest theoretical running time analyses of evolutionary algorithms for dynamic fitness functions are probably due to Droste (2002, 2003). Here the fitness function is the (Hamming-) distance to a (dynamically changing) point in the hypercube (so-called *dynamic* OneMax). In each iteration, the current optimum is changed by flipping each bit with some fixed probability p; from Droste (2003) we know that the standard (1+1) EA is able to *find* the optimum in polynomial time if and only if $p = O(\log n/n^2)$.

FOGA'15, January 17–20, 2015, Aberystwyth, UK.

ACM 978-1-4503-3434-1/15/01 ...$15.00.
http://dx.doi.org/10.1145/2725494.2725502.

In this paper we build on the setting of dynamic OneMax from Droste (2003). We re-prove the classic results using the modern tools of drift theory and extend them as follows. First, we generalize the domain by allowing not only bit strings, but each position can take any of the values in $\{0,\ldots,r-1\}$. Fitness is again distance from the current optimum; we measure distances as the sum of the distances of each component, where in each component we measure distance "with wrap around" (giving each component the metric space of a ring, see Section 2 for a detailed definition). We extend the (1+1) EA by letting mutation change any position independently with probability $1/n$; any changed position is randomly increased or decreased by one (with probability $1/2$ each). Note that similar extensions of the OneMax function (without dynamic changes) have been studied by Doerr, Johannsen, and Schmidt (2011) and Doerr and Pohl (2012); they considered arbitrary linear functions over $\{0,\ldots,r\}$, and a mutation where changing a position means selecting a new value at this position uniformly at random (excluding the old value). We chose the ring topology, as we consider it more natural for a dynamically moving optimum, which can now never run into a boundary.

The second extension to Droste (2003) is that we do not only consider the first hitting time of the optimum but, as suggested by Jansen and Zarges (2014), we give an "anytime analysis", an analysis of the distance to the optimum at any time of the search process.

We state our setting more formally in Section 2. In Section 3 we give our anytime results, considering cases with $p = o(1/n)$. The first part is about the case of bit strings (i.e. $r = 2$), where we show that the distance to the optimum is (in the limit) strongly concentrated at $\Theta(pn^2)$. This gives an anytime result as suggested by Jansen and Zarges (2014). The second part shows that, for large r, the distance to the optimum in each dimension is strongly concentrated at $O(1)$, leading to an expected distance of $O(n)$ from the optimum (again an anytime result). Note that this shows that the distance is independent of r.

In Section 4 we consider the expected hitting times of the (randomly moving) optimum. Here we re-prove the result of Droste (2003) (who considered the case of $r = 2$) that the first hitting time is polynomial if $p = O(\log n/n^2)$. We use modern drift theory, leading to a much shorter and more elegant proof, resulting in a better bound. We extend this result to arbitrary r.

Droste (2003) also gave a lower bound, which shows that for $p = \omega(\log n/n^2)$ we do not get polynomial hitting times; in Section 5 we re-prove this result (again with modern drift theory) and extend them to arbitrary values of r.

As mentioned, we will use modern drift theory to derive our results. In Section 2 we restate known drift theorems, partly in more general form than before, and also present new variants. A new theorem regards variable drift, which allows for *negative* drift close the optimum and shows how stochastic processes can bridge such an area of headwind. For our anytime analysis, the crucial tool is a lemma by Lissovoi and Witt (2015), which we restate as Lemma 6 below, effectively turning expected drift into probabilities about deviating from the target of the drift after having reached that target.

2. PRELIMINARIES

In this section we first make our setting formal (see Section 2.1) and then give a number of helpful theorems, both from the literature and new theorems (see Section 2.2).

2.1 Setting

Droste (2003) proposes a dynamic version of OneMax and analyses the performance of (1+1) EA on this dynamic fitness function in terms of first hitting times of the optimum. We extend this dynamic version of OneMax as follows.

For all $r \in \mathbb{N}$, let $[r] = \{0,\ldots,r-1\}$; for two elements $x, y \in [r]$, we let $d(x,y) = \min((y-x) \bmod r, (x-y) \bmod r)$ (intuitively, d is the metric of $[r]$ with wrap-around). We consider the search space $[r]^n$ (note that $r = 2$ gives the standard setting of bit strings).

Given a current optimum a, we let

$$\textsc{OneMax}_a : [r]^n \to \mathbb{R}, x \mapsto \sum_{i=1}^{n} d(a_i, x_i).$$

The goal of the (1+1) EA is to evolve and *maintain* bit strings with as small as possible $\textsc{OneMax}_a$-value. In particular, in this setting optimization means *minimizing*.

We consider the following mutation operator on $[r]^n$, parametrized by $p \in [0,1]$. Given $x \in [r]^n$, create mutant x' by choosing, for each component $i \le n$ independently,

$$x'_i = \begin{cases} x_i + 1 \mod r, & \text{with probability } p/2; \\ x_i - 1 \mod r, & \text{with probability } p/2; \\ x_i, & \text{with probability } 1-p. \end{cases}$$

We use this operator with $p = 1/n$ for the (1+1) EA (see Algorithm 1).

Algorithm 1: (1+1)-EA

```
1 choose x ∈ [r]^n uniformly at random;
2 repeat
3     x' ← mutate(x);
4     if fitness(x') ≤ fitness(x) then
5         x ← x';
6 until forever;
```

In each iteration, we change the optimum by applying the mutation operator with some fixed p. This extends the setting of Droste (2003), where only the case of $r = 2$ was addressed.

2.2 Drift Theorems

In this section we first discuss drift theorems regarding first hitting times, and afterwards discuss how one can turn statements about the drift into statements about occupation probabilities (of a random process).

2.2.1 First Hitting Times

As mentioned in the introduction, almost all of our proofs use state-of-the-art drift statements, many of which were not available to Droste (2003). The simplest case is the one of additive drift, as described in the following theorem. It goes back to He and Yao (2001); however, is presented in a more general form here, which is proved in Lehre and Witt (2014).

Theorem 1 (Additive drift, expected time). *Let $(X^t)_{t\geq 0}$, be a stochastic process, adapted to some filtration $\mathcal{F}_t$, over a bounded state space $S \subseteq \mathbb{R}_0^+$. Let $T_0 := \min\{t \geq 0 \colon X^t = 0\}$ denote the first hitting time of 0 and assume that both $\mathrm{E}(X^0)$ and $\mathrm{E}(T_0 \mid X^0)$ are finite. Then:*

(i) If $\mathrm{E}(X^t - X^{t+1} \mid \mathcal{F}_t; X^t > 0) \geq \varepsilon$ then $\mathrm{E}(T_0 \mid X^0) \leq \frac{X^0}{\varepsilon}$.

(ii) If $\mathrm{E}(X^t - X^{t+1} \mid \mathcal{F}_t; X^t > 0) \leq \varepsilon$ then $\mathrm{E}(T_0 \mid X^0) \geq \frac{X^0}{\varepsilon}$.

Intuitively, the filtration $\mathcal{F}_t$ describes the history of the process up to time t. For Markov processes, it simplifies to the state at time t; for instance, the first drift condition would read $\mathrm{E}(X^t - X^{t+1} \mid X^t; X^t > 0) \geq \delta$ instead.

Often, the state space Z of the underlying stochastic process and the support S of the random variables X^t are not identical. Obviously, this is the case if the state space is not a subset of $\mathbb{R}$, e. g., if we are dealing with bit strings, where we have $Z := \{0,1\}^n$. In particular, even if the state space is the real numbers, it might be convenient to introduce a so-called potential function (also called Lyapunov function) $g \colon Z \mapsto S$, which leads to a new stochastic process $Y^t := g(X^t)$ on the new state space S. One reason might be that the drift of Y^t is easier to compute. We abstract away from this mapping by allowing the random variables X^t from Theorem 1 to represent a process obtained after any transformation of the original process using a potential function. Such a transformation might turn Markovian processes into non-Markovian ones.

Theorem 1 is only concerned with bounds on the expected value of the first hitting time of the target state 0. Recently, it has been shown in Kötzing (2014) that the first hitting time is sharply concentrated (exhibits so-called tail bounds) if additional assumptions are made on the step size. We restate this in the following theorem.

Theorem 2 (Additive Drift, Tail Bounds). *Let the prerequisites of Theorem 1 hold and assume additionally that $|X^t - X^{t+1}| < c$ for some $c > 0$ and all $t \geq 0$. Then:*

(i) If $\mathrm{E}(X^t - X^{t+1} \mid \mathcal{F}_t; X^t > 0) \geq \varepsilon$ then $\Pr(T_0 > s) \leq \exp(-s\varepsilon^2/(16c^2))$ for all $s \geq 2X^0/\varepsilon$.

(ii) If $\mathrm{E}(X^t - X^{t+1} \mid \mathcal{F}_t; X^t > 0) \leq \varepsilon$ then $\Pr(T_0 < s) \leq \exp(-(X^0)^2/(16c^2 s))$ for all $s \leq X^0/(2\varepsilon)$.

The previous two theorems dealt with a drift towards the target state 0. If the drift is directed away from the target, lower bounds on the hitting time can be proved. This is the realm of *negative drift theorems*, several variants of which exist (see Oliveto and Witt, 2011, 2012 for the original version). In this work we use the following version, adapted from Rowe and Sudholt (2014, Theorem 4), which takes into account the probabilities of staying at a state. For technical reasons, it is restricted to Markov processes and the use of a possible potential function is made explicit.

Theorem 3 (Negative drift with self-loops). *Let $(X^t)_{t\geq 0}$, be a Markov process over a state space S. Suppose there exist an interval $[a,b] \subseteq \mathbb{R}_0^+$, two constants $\delta, \varepsilon > 0$, a function $r(\ell)$ satisfying $1 \leq r(\ell) = o(\ell/\log(\ell))$, and a potential function $g \colon S \to \mathbb{R}_0^+$, such that for all $t \geq 0$, the following two conditions hold:*

(i) $\mathrm{E}(\Delta^t \mid X^t; a < g(X^t) < b) \geq \varepsilon(1 - p_{t,0})$,

(ii) $\Pr(|\Delta^t| \geq j \mid X^t; a < g(X^t)) \leq \frac{r(\ell)(1-p_{t,0})}{(1+\delta)^j}$ for $j \in \mathbb{N}_0$,

where $\Delta^t = g(X^{t+1}) - g(X^t)$ and $p_{t,0} := \Pr(\Delta^t = 0 \mid X^t)$.

Then there is a constant $c^* > 0$ such that for $T^* := \min\{t \geq 0 : g(X^t) \leq a \mid g(X^0) \geq b\}$ it holds

$$\Pr\left(T^* \leq 2^{c^*\ell/r(\ell)}\right) = 2^{-\Omega(\ell/r(\ell))}.$$

Intuitively, drift away from the target makes it difficult to reach the target. Nevertheless, if the drift is negative only for a few states and directed towards the target at the remaining states, the expected first hitting time of the target might still be small. Such a scenario of "headwind drift" on the way towards the target will appear in our analyses if the probability of flipping a bit of the optimum is small, e. g., $p = O((\log n)/n^2)$), resulting in only very few states close to the target having negative drift.

The following novel theorem proves upper bounds in the presence of possibly negative drift. The bounds $\delta(i)$ are lower bounds on the drift at state i, pessimistically assuming that all steps towards the target improve only by 1. The $p^-(i)$ and $p^+(i)$ are bounds on the probability of improving by at least 1 and worsening by at least 1, respectively. The theorem is general enough to analyze different scenarios, e. g., blind random walks on the hypercube. However, we will mostly apply Corollary 5, which is easier to use.

For notational convenience, we state the theorem only for Markov processes, however, it can easily be generalized to non-Markovian ones. Extensions to continuous search spaces seem also possible; however, these are not straightforward. Therefore, the state space is restricted to be non-negative integers.

Theorem 4 (Headwind drift, upper bound). *Let $(X^t)_{t\geq 0}$ be a Markov process on $\{0,\dots,N\}$. Let bounds*

$$p^-(i) \leq \Pr(X^{t+1} \leq i-1 \mid X^t = i)$$

and

$$p^+(i) \geq \Pr(X^{t+1} \geq i+1 \mid X^t = i),$$

where $0 \leq i \leq N$, be given, and define

$$\delta(i) := p^-(i) - \mathrm{E}((X^{t+1} - i) \cdot \mathbb{1}\{X^{t+1} > i\} \mid X^t = i).$$

Assume that $\delta(i)$ is monotone increasing w. r. t. i and let $\kappa \geq \max\{i \geq 0 \mid \delta(i) \leq 0\}$ (noting that $\delta(0) \leq 0$). The function $g \colon \{0,\dots,N+1\} \to \mathbb{R}^+$ is defined by

$$g(i) := \sum_{k=i+1}^{N} \frac{1}{\delta(k)}$$

for $i \geq \kappa$ (in particular, $g(N) = g(N+1) = 0$), and inductively by

$$g(i) := \frac{1 + (p^+(i+1) + p^-(i+1))g(i+1)}{p^-(i+1)}$$

for $i < \kappa$.

Then it holds for the first hitting time $T := \min\{t \geq 0 \mid X^t = 0\}$ of state 0 that

$$\mathrm{E}(T \mid X^0) \leq g(0) - g(X^0).$$

Remark. $\delta(i)$ respects the following simple lower bound:

$$\delta(i) \geq \mathrm{E}\big((i - X^{t+1}) \cdot \mathbb{1}\{X^{t+1} \geq i-1\} \mid X^t = i\big).$$

PROOF. We will prove that $g(i)$ is a monotone decreasing function and can be used as a potential function to satisfy the drift condition

$$\mathrm{E}\big(g(X^{t+1}) - g(i) \mid X^t = i \wedge i > 0\big) \geq 1.$$

Due to the monotonicity of $g(i)$, the first hitting time where $g(X^t) = g(0)$ equals the first hitting time where $X^t = 0$ for the original X^t-process. Then the theorem follows by the additive drift theorem (Theorem 1).

To prove the monotonicity of $g(i)$, we observe that $g(i) - g(i+1) \geq 0$ for $i \geq \kappa$ immediately by definition. For $i < \kappa$, we get

$$\begin{aligned}\frac{g(i)}{g(i+1)} &= \frac{\frac{1}{g(i+1)} + (p^+(i+1) + p^-(i+1))}{p^-(i+1)} \\ &\geq \frac{p^+(i+1) + p^-(i+1)}{p^-(i+1)} \geq 1,\end{aligned}$$

where we used $g(i+1) \geq 0$. This completes the proof of the monotonicity.

To prove the drift condition, we distinguish between two cases. Suppose $X^t = i > \kappa$. The monotonicity of the $\delta(i)$ implies the "concavity" condition $g(i-1) - g(i) \geq g(i) - g(i+1)$ for $i > \kappa$. We obtain

$$\begin{aligned}&\mathrm{E}\big(g(X^{t+1}) - g(i) \mid X^t = i\big) \\ &\geq p^-(i)(g(i-1) - g(i)) \\ &\quad - \left(\sum_{k=1}^{N} (g(i) - g(i+k))\Pr\big(X^{t+1} = i+k\big)\right) \\ &\geq p^-(i)(g(i-1) - g(i)) \\ &\quad - \left(\sum_{k=1}^{N} k(g(i-1) - g(i))\Pr\big(X^{t+1} = i+k\big)\right) \\ &= p^-(i)(g(i-1) - g(i)) \\ &\quad - (g(i-1) - g(i))\mathrm{E}\big((X^{t+1} - i)\mathbb{1}\{X^{t+1} > i\} \mid X^t = i\big) \\ &= (g(i-1) - g(i))\delta(i) = \frac{1}{\delta(i)} \cdot \delta(i),\end{aligned}$$

where the second inequality used the concavity repeatedly. If $X^t = i \leq \kappa$, we pessimistically assume all steps towards the target to reach $i-1$ and all away from it to reach N (resulting in zero g-value). Hence, using the definition of $g(i-1)$,

$$\begin{aligned}&\mathrm{E}\big(g(X^{t+1}) - g(i) \mid X^t = i\big) \\ &\geq p^-(i)(g(i-1) - g(i)) - p^+(i)g(i) \\ &= p^-(i)\left(\frac{1 + (p^+(i) + p^-(i))g(i)}{p^-(i)} - g(i)\right) - p^+(i)g(i) \\ &= 1,\end{aligned}$$

which proves the bound on the drift and, therefore, the theorem. □

We now state the announced corollary, which gives us a closed expression for the expected first hitting time $\mathrm{E}(T \mid X^0)$. This expression involves the factor $\sum_{k=\kappa+1}^{N} \frac{1}{\delta_k}$ that is reminiscent of the formula for the expected first hitting time of state κ under variable drift towards the target (see, e.g., Rowe and Sudholt, 2014 for a formulation of the variable drift theorem). For the states less than κ, where drift away from the target holds, the product $\prod_{k=1}^{\kappa} \frac{p^+(k)+p^-(k)}{p^-(k)}$ comes into play. Intuitively, it represents the waiting time for the event of taking κ consecutive steps against the drift. Since the product involves probabilities conditioned on leaving the states, which effectively removes self-loops, another sum of products must be added. This sum, represented by the second line of the expression for $\mathrm{E}(T \mid X^0)$, intuitively accounts for the self-loops.

COROLLARY 5. *Let the assumptions of Theorem 4 hold. Then*

$$\begin{aligned}\mathrm{E}(T \mid X^0) \leq &\left(\left(\sum_{k=\kappa+1}^{N} \frac{1}{\delta_k}\right)\left(\prod_{k=1}^{\kappa} \frac{p^+(k) + p^-(k)}{p^-(k)}\right)\right) \\ &+ \left(\sum_{k=1}^{\kappa} \frac{1}{p^-(k)} \prod_{j=1}^{k-1} \frac{p^+(j) + p^-(j)}{p^-(j)}\right).\end{aligned}$$

PROOF. It is sufficient to prove that the right hand side is an upper bound on the $g(0)$ defined in Theorem 4. We note that $\sum_{k=\kappa+1}^{N} \frac{1}{\delta_k} = g(\kappa)$. The inductive expression for $g(i)$ yields $g(i) \leq \frac{1+(p^+(i+1)+p^-(i+1))g(i+1)}{p^-(i+1)}$ for $i \leq \kappa - 1$. Inductively

$$\begin{aligned}g(0) \leq &\left(\prod_{j=0}^{\kappa-1} \frac{p^+(j+1) + p^-(j+1)}{p^-(j+1)}\right) g(\kappa) \\ &+ \left(\sum_{k=0}^{\kappa-1} \frac{1}{p^-(1)} \prod_{j=1}^{k} \frac{p^+(j) + p^-(j)}{p^-(j+1)}\right),\end{aligned}$$

and the corollary follows by index transformations and regrouping terms. □

2.2.2 *Occupation Probabilities*

In this section we move away from analyses of the first hitting time of a state and direct our attention to so-called occupation probabilities. For the anytime analysis in Section 3, we want to make statements about how far from the optimum the (1+1) EA will stray, and with what probability. In particular, we want to know the probability that the current search point is more than j away from the optimum in iteration t, for large t. The idea is that a stochastic process $(X^t)_{t\geq 0}$ on $\mathbb{R}$ which has a drift towards 0 will, after hitting 0 for the first time, likely stay in the proximity of 0 and stray off only with a low probability. This is what is meant by "occupation probabilities".

Hajek (1982), in his third section, already gives some general bounds on these probabilities. This is also the idea of another lemma regarding occupation probabilities given in Lissovoi and Witt (2015, Lemma 13) (restated below as Lemma 6), from which we will here derive a simple version (Theorem 7), tailored to the case of additive drift and Markov processes with self-loops.

LEMMA 6 (LISSOVOI AND WITT, 2015, LEMMA 13). *Let $(X^t)_{t\geq 0}$, be a stochastic process, adapted to a filtration $(\mathcal{F}_t)_{t\geq 0}$, over some state space $S \subseteq \{0\} \cup [x_{\min}, x_{\max}]$, where $x_{\min} \geq 0$. Let $a, b \in \{0\} \cup [x_{\min}, x_{\max}]$, $b > a$. Let $h\colon [x_{\min}, x_{\max}] \to \mathbb{R}^+$ be such that $1/h$ is integrable on $[x_{\min}, x_{\max}]$ and define $g\colon \{0\} \cup [x_{\min}, x_{\max}] \to \mathbb{R}^{\geq 0}$ by $g(x) := \frac{x_{\min}}{h(x_{\min})} + \int_{x_{\min}}^{x} \frac{1}{h(y)}\,\mathrm{d}y$ for $x \geq x_{\min}$ and $g(0) := 0$.*

If there exist $\lambda > 0$, $\beta < 1$ and $D > 0$ such that

$$\mathrm{E}\Big(e^{-\lambda(g(X^t)-g(X^{t+1}))} \cdot \mathbb{1}\{X^t > a\} \mid \mathcal{F}_t\Big) \le \beta$$

$$\text{and } \mathrm{E}\Big(e^{-\lambda(g(a)-g(X^{t+1}))} \cdot \mathbb{1}\{X^t \le a\} \mid \mathcal{F}_t\Big) \le D$$

then

$$\Pr(X^t \ge b \mid X^0) < \beta^t \cdot e^{\lambda(g(X^0)-g(b))} + \frac{1-\beta^t}{1-\beta} D e^{\lambda(g(a)-g(b))}$$

for $t > 0$.

We give two definitions regarding Markov processes before giving our theorem regarding occupation probabilities. Let a Markov process $(X^t)_{t\ge0}$ on $\mathbb{R}_0^+$ be given. We say that $(X^t)_{t\ge0}$ *has step size at most* $c \in \mathbb{R}$ if, for all t, $|X^t - X^{t+1}| \le c$. We say that $(X^t)_{t\ge0}$ *has self-loop probability at least* $p_0 \in \mathbb{R}$ iff, for all t such that $X^t > 0$ we have $\Pr(X^t = X^{t+1} \mid X^t) \ge p_0$. From Lemma 6 we derive the following statement on occupation probabilities for the case of bounded step sizes.

THEOREM 7 (OCCUPATION PROBABILITIES). *Let a Markov process $(X^t)_{t\ge0}$ on $\mathbb{R}_0^+$ with additive drift of at least d towards 0 be given, starting at 0 (i.e. $X_0 = 0$), with step size at most c and self-loop probability at least p_0. Then we have, for all $t \in \mathbb{N}$ and $b \in \mathbb{R}_0^+$,*

$$\Pr(X^t \ge b) \le 2e^{\frac{2d}{3c(1-p_0)}(1-b/c)}.$$

PROOF. First, we define a new Markov process $(Y^t)_{t\ge0}$ obtained from X^t by omitting all steps that do not change the current state; formally, since we consider Markov chains, we have $Y^t - Y^{t+1} = X^t - X^{t+1}$ in the conditional space where $X^{t+1} \ne X^t$. By definition of conditional probability and expectation, we obtain

$$\mathrm{E}(Y^t - Y^{t+1} \mid X^t) = \frac{\mathrm{E}(X^t - X^{t+1} \mid X^t)}{\Pr(X^{t+1} \ne X^t \mid X^t)} \ge \frac{\mathrm{E}(X^t - X^{t+1} \mid X^t)}{1-p_0}$$

since the probability of changing the state is at most $1 - p_0$.

The theorem makes a statement for all t, however, to prove it, it is enough to consider steps that actually change state. Hence, in the following, the aim is to analyze the Y-process using Lemma 6 with $a := x_{\min} := 0$ and the constant function $h(x) := 1$. From this we obtain the trivial potential function $g(x) = x$. From our prerequisites and the previous paragraph, we get

$$\begin{aligned}\mathrm{E}\big(g(Y^t) - g(Y^{t+1}) \mid Y_t; Y^t > 0\big) &= \mathrm{E}\big(Y^t - Y^{t+1} \mid Y_t; Y^t > 0\big)\\ &\ge \frac{\mathrm{E}(X^t - X^{t+1} \mid X^t; X^t > 0)}{1-p_0}\\ &\ge \frac{d}{1-p_0}.\end{aligned}$$

Let $d^* := d/(1-p_0)$. To bound the moment-generating function of the drift, we abbreviate $\Delta^t := Y^t - Y^{t+1}$. We already know that $\mathrm{E}(\Delta^t \mid Y^t; Y^t > 0) \ge d^*$ and argue

$$\mathrm{E}\Big(e^{-\lambda\Delta^t} \cdot \mathbb{1}\{Y^t > 0\} \mid Y^t\Big) \le \mathrm{E}\Big(e^{-\lambda\Delta^t} \mid Y^t; Y^t > 0\Big)$$

In the following, we condition on $Y^t; Y^t > 0$ everywhere but omit this from the formulas for the sake of readability. Using the Taylor expansion of the exponential function, we get

$$\mathrm{E}\Big(e^{-\lambda\Delta^t}\Big) \le 1 - \lambda\mathrm{E}(\Delta^t) + \sum_{k=2}^{\infty} \frac{\lambda^k \mathrm{E}(|\Delta^t|^k)}{k!},$$

which for any $\eta \ge \lambda$ is at most

$$1 - \lambda\mathrm{E}(\Delta^t) + \frac{\lambda^2}{\eta^2}\sum_{k=2}^{\infty} \frac{\eta^k \mathrm{E}(|\Delta^t|^k)}{k!}.$$

Now, by setting $\eta := 1/c$, $\lambda := 2d^*/(3c^2)$ and noting that $\Delta^t \le c$ (also for the Y-process), we get the bound

$$1 - \lambda\mathrm{E}(\Delta^t) + \lambda\frac{2d^*}{3c^2 \cdot (1/c^2)} \cdot \sum_{k=2}^{\infty} \frac{1}{k!} \le 1 - \lambda\mathrm{E}(\Delta^t) + \lambda\frac{d^*}{2}$$

where the last inequality used that $\sum_{k=2}^{\infty} \frac{1}{k!} = e - 2 \le 3/4$. Altogether, using $\mathrm{E}(\Delta^t) \ge d^*$, we get

$$\begin{aligned}\mathrm{E}\Big(e^{-\lambda\Delta^t} \cdot \mathbb{1}\{Y^t > 0\}\Big) &\le 1 - \frac{\lambda d^*}{2} \le e^{-\lambda d^*/2}\\ &= e^{-\frac{(d^*)^2}{3c^2}} =: \beta < 1.\end{aligned}$$

Moreover, in order to apply Lemma 6, we need to bound

$$\mathrm{E}\Big(e^{-\lambda(a-Y^{t+1})} \cdot \mathbb{1}\{Y^t = 0\} \mid Y_t\Big) \le e^{c\lambda} = e^{\frac{2d^*}{3c}} =: D > 1$$

using $a := 0$ and the bounded step size. Altogether, from the lemma we get

$$\begin{aligned}\Pr(Y^t \ge b) &\le \left(\beta^t + \frac{1-\beta^t}{1-\beta} D\right) e^{-\lambda b}\\ &\le (1 + D)e^{-\lambda b} \le 2e^{\frac{2d^*}{3c}} e^{-\frac{2bd^*}{3c^2}}\\ &= 2e^{\frac{2d}{3c(1-p_0)} - \frac{2bd}{3c^2(1-p_0)}},\end{aligned}$$

and the last expression is also a bound on $\Pr(X^t \ge b)$ as it does not depend on t. □

3. AN ANYTIME ANALYSIS

In this section we give our anytime analysis, separately for the cases of $r = 2$ and for large r. We will start in Section 3.1 with the classical case of $r = 2$, i. e., bit strings. In Section 3.2 we consider large r. We restrict ourselves to $p = o(1/n)$, i. e., in expectation less than one bit of the optimum is changed.

3.1 The Case of $r = 2$

We fix $r = 2$ and start by computing the expected change (drift) in the search point. We expect the (1+1) EA, starting from a random string, to make some progress towards the optimum until the number of incorrect bits is lower than the drift caused by the dynamically changing optimum.

More precisely, we consider the process X^t given by the current ONEMAX-value (i. e., the number of incorrect bits) and assume a current ONEMAX-value of $X^t = i < n/2$. We identify a forward drift

$$\Delta^-(i) := (i - X^{t+1}) \cdot \mathbb{1}\{X^{t+1} < i\}$$

caused by the selection mechanism of the (1+1) EA and a backward drift

$$\Delta^+(i) := (X^{t+1} - i) \cdot \mathbb{1}\{X^{t+1} > i\}$$

caused by the random movement of the optimum. The total drift $\Delta^t = (X^t - X^{t+1})$ under $X_t = i$ satisfies $\Delta^t = \Delta^-(i) - \Delta^+(i)$, and also $\mathrm{E}(\Delta^t) = \mathrm{E}(\Delta^-(i)) - \mathrm{E}(\Delta^+(i))$. We bound the forward and backward drift. Progress is made when one of the incorrect bits flips and neither the rest of the bits nor the optimum flips, and can only be made by flipping incorrect bits of the current string or the optimum. The total expected number of flipping bits among i bits is $i(p+1/n)$. We obtain

$$(1-p)^n\left(1-\frac{1}{n}\right)^{n-i}\frac{i}{n} \le \mathrm{E}(\Delta^-(i)) \le \frac{i}{n}+ip,$$

and, since $p = o(1/n)$,

$$\frac{i}{e^2 n} \le \mathrm{E}(\Delta^-(i)) \le \frac{2i}{n}.$$

Similarly, since the OneMax-value can only increase (move away from the optimum) by flipping bits of the optimum, we get

$$(1-1/n)^n(n-i)p(1-p)^i \le \mathrm{E}(\Delta^+(i)) \le np,$$

implying, since $i < n/2$

$$\frac{np}{4e^2} \le \mathrm{E}(\Delta^+(i)) \le np.$$

We solve $\mathrm{E}(\Delta^t) = 0$ to find an i^* where we have a drift of zero, and get from the inequalities above that

$$\frac{1}{8e^2}n^2 p \le i^* \le e^2 n^2 p.$$

If $i > e^2n^2p$, there is certainly a drift towards the optimum; and if $i < \frac{1}{8e}n^2p$, there is certainly a drift away from the optimum. In the region of $i^* = \Theta(n^2p)$ there is an equilibrium with zero drift, and we would expect the (1+1) EA to approach this region and not to move significantly away from it afterwards. This is made precise in the following theorem.

Theorem 8. *Let $r = 2$, $p = o(1/n)$ and $1/p = n^{O(1)}$. Let $(x^t, a^t)_{t\in\mathbb{N}}$ be the sequence of random variables denoting the pair of current search point and current optimum as given by running the (1+1) EA on dynamic OneMax. Then, for any $t \ge 0$ and any $\alpha = \omega(\ln n)$ there is $b_t := n - \frac{tpn}{7}$ such that*

$$\Pr\big(d(x^t, a^t) \ge \max\{\alpha b_t,\, 2e^2n^2p+\alpha\}\big) \le e^{-\Omega(\alpha)}.$$

Moreover, for all $t \ge \alpha/p$,

$$\Pr\big(d(x^t, a^t) \ge 2e^2n^2p+\alpha\big) \le e^{-\Omega(\alpha)}.$$

Proof. Still, $X^t := \mathrm{OneMax}_{a^t}(x^t) = d(x^t, a^t)$. We recall that there is a drift towards the target if $X^t > i^*$. More precisely, from the estimations presented before this theorem we obtain

$$\mathrm{E}(i - X^{t+1} \mid X^t = i) = \mathrm{E}(\Delta^-(i)) - \mathrm{E}(\Delta^+(i)) \ge \frac{i}{e^2 n} - np \ge np$$

for $i \ge 2e^2n^2p$. In the following, we analyze the X^t-process using Lemma 6 with $a := 2e^2n^2p$, $b = \max\{\alpha b_t, a+\alpha\}$, $x_{\min} := 0$ and the constant function $h(x) := 1$. From this we obtain the trivial potential function $g(x) = x$. To bound the moment-generating function of the drift if $X^t > a$, we use $\Delta := g(X^t) - g(X^{t+1}) = X^t - X^{t+1}$ and argue

$$\mathrm{E}\left(e^{-\lambda\Delta}\cdot \mathbb{1}\{X^t > a\} \mid X^t\right) \le \mathrm{E}\left(e^{-\lambda\Delta} \mid X^t; X^t > a\right).$$

In the following, we condition on $X^t; X^t > a$ in all expectations unless stated otherwise but omit this for the sake of readability. Using the tailor expansion of the exponential function, we get

$$\mathrm{E}\left(e^{-\lambda\Delta}\right) \le 1 - \lambda\mathrm{E}(\Delta) + \sum_{k=2}^{\infty}\frac{\lambda^k\mathrm{E}(|\Delta|^k)}{k!},$$

which for any $\eta \ge \lambda$ is at most

$$1 - \lambda\mathrm{E}(\Delta) + \frac{\lambda^2}{\eta^2}\sum_{k=2}^{\infty}\frac{\eta^k\mathrm{E}(|\Delta|^k)}{k!} = 1 - \lambda\mathrm{E}(\Delta) + \frac{\lambda^2}{\eta^2}\underbrace{\left(\mathrm{E}\left(e^{\eta|\Delta|}\right) - \eta\mathrm{E}(|\Delta|) - 1\right)}_{\Psi}.$$

The aim now is to bound the term in parentheses such that $\Psi = O(\eta^2(pn + i/n))$. To this end, note that $|\Delta|$ is stochastically dominated by a sum of two independent random variables

$$Z \sim \mathrm{Bin}(n,p) + \mathrm{Bin}(i, 1/n)$$

since it is necessary to flip a bit of the optimum or a wrong bit of the current state to change the state. The sum of the two random variables overestimates the change of distance since the two types of flips might cancel each other.

The moment-generating function of the binomial distribution is well known and, for our parameters, given by

$$\begin{aligned}\mathrm{E}\left(e^{\eta Z}\right) &= \mathrm{E}\left(e^{\eta\mathrm{Bin}(n,p)}\right)\cdot\mathrm{E}\left(e^{\eta\mathrm{Bin}(i,1/n)}\right)\\ &= (pe^\eta + 1 - p)^n\cdot\left(\frac{1}{n}e^\eta + \left(1-\frac{1}{n}\right)\right)^i\\ &\le \left(p\left(1+\eta+\eta^2\right)+1-p\right)^n\cdot\left(\frac{1}{n}\left(1+\eta+\eta^2\right)+1-\frac{1}{n}\right)^i\\ &= \left((\eta+\eta^2)p+1\right)^n\left(\frac{\eta+\eta^2}{n}+1\right)^i\end{aligned}$$

for $\eta \le 1$ as $e^x \le 1 + x + x^2$ for $x \le 1$. Using $1 + x \le e^x$, we obtain from this

$$\mathrm{E}\left(e^{\eta Z}\right) \le \left(e^{(\eta+\eta^2)p}\right)^n\left(e^{\eta/n+\eta^2/n}\right)^i = e^{(pn+i/n)\eta+(pn+i/n)\eta^2}$$

Introducing $q := pn + i/n \le 2$, we have

$$\begin{aligned}\mathrm{E}\left(e^{\eta Z}\right) &\le 1 + (q\eta + q\eta^2) + (q\eta+q\eta^2)^2\\ &= 1 + q\eta + q\eta^2 + q^2\eta^2 + 2q^2\eta^3 + q^2\eta^4\\ &\le 1 + q\eta + q\eta^2 + 2q\eta^2 + 2q\eta^3 + 2q\eta^4\\ &\le 1 + q\eta + 7q\eta^2,\end{aligned}$$

where we assumed $q\eta + q\eta^2 \le 1$, which holds for $\eta \le 1/4$. Since $\mathrm{E}(Z) = q$, we have established

$$\Psi = \sum_{k=2}^{\infty}\frac{\eta^k\mathrm{E}(|\Delta|^k)}{k!} \le \sum_{k=2}^{\infty}\frac{\eta^k\mathrm{E}(Z^k)}{k!} = \mathrm{E}\left(e^{\eta Z}\right) - \eta\mathrm{E}(Z) - 1 \le (1 + q\eta + 7q\eta^2) - q\eta - 1 = 7q\eta^2$$

since $\eta \le 1$.

Plugging this into the above bound on $\mathrm{E}(e^{-\lambda\Delta})$, we get

$$\mathrm{E}\left(e^{-\lambda\Delta}\right) \le 1 - \lambda\mathrm{E}(\Delta) + 7\lambda^2 q$$

for $\lambda \leq \eta \leq 1/4$. Since $\mathrm{E}(\Delta) \geq \frac{i}{e^2 n} - np$, we choose $\lambda = \frac{1}{21e^2}$ (and $\eta = 1/4$) to get

$$\begin{aligned}\mathrm{E}\left(e^{-\lambda\Delta}\right) &\leq 1 - \lambda\left(\frac{i}{e^2 n} - np\right) + 7\lambda\frac{1}{21e^2}q \\ &= 1 - \lambda\left(\frac{i}{e^2 n} - np\right) + \frac{\lambda}{3e^2}\left(\frac{i}{n} + pn\right) \\ &\leq 1 - \lambda\left(\frac{2i}{3e^2 n} - \frac{22pn}{21}\right) =: \beta \leq 1 - \frac{6pn}{441e^2}\end{aligned}$$

where the final inequality holds since $i \geq a = 2e^2 n^2 p$. In addition, we have then

$$\beta \leq e^{-6pn/(441e^2)}.$$

So far, we have bounded the moment-generating function of the drift by less than 1. We are left with a bound on

$$\mathrm{E}\left(e^{-\lambda(a - X^{t+1})} \cdot \mathbb{1}\left\{X^t \leq a\right\}\right).$$

Noting that the exponent is positive for $X^{t+1} \geq a \geq X^t$, we bound the expression by

$$\begin{aligned}\mathrm{E}\left(e^{\lambda|X^t - X^{t+1}|} \mid X^t \leq a\right) &\leq \mathrm{E}\left(e^{\lambda Z} \mid X_t \leq a\right) \\ &\leq 1 + 8\lambda q \leq 1 + 16\lambda =: D\end{aligned}$$

using the estimations that bounded $\mathrm{E}(e^{\eta Z})$ further above. Applying Lemma 6, we get

$$\begin{aligned}\Pr(X^t \geq b) &\leq \beta^t \cdot e^{\lambda(X^0 - b)} + \frac{1}{1-\beta} D e^{-\lambda\alpha} \\ &\leq e^{-\frac{6tpn}{441e^2}} e^{\frac{n-b}{21e^2}} + \frac{441e^2}{6pn}\left(1 + \frac{16}{21e^2}\right) e^{-\frac{\alpha}{21e^2}}.\end{aligned}$$

As $b \geq b_t = n - \frac{tpn}{7}$, the first term is $e^{-b/(882e^2)}$. Hence, if $b \geq \alpha(n - \frac{tpn}{7})$, it is $e^{-\Omega(\alpha)}$. Assuming $\alpha = \omega(\ln n)$, the second term is $e^{-\Omega(\alpha)} = n^{-\omega(1)}$, which makes the polynomial $\frac{441e^2}{6pn}$ negligible. This proves the first statement from the theorem. The second one follows for $t \geq n\alpha/(pn) = \alpha/p$ since then the first term is clearly $e^{-\Omega(\alpha)}$.

Altogether, for t large enough, we have

$$\Pr(X^t \geq b) \leq e^{-\Omega(\alpha)}. \quad \square$$

Theorem 8 shows that after a polynomial amount of time, the distance is very likely to be not by much above the equilibrium state. We can also show a somewhat symmetrical statement, showing that it is very likely to be not by much below the equilibrium state. This is proven in the following theorem.

THEOREM 9. *Let $r = 2$, $p = o(1/n)$ and $1/p = n^{O(1)}$. Let $(x^t, a^t)_{t\in\mathbb{N}}$ be the sequence of random variables denoting the pair of current search point and current optimum as given by running the (1+1) EA on dynamic* ONEMAX. *Then, for any $\alpha = \omega(\ln n)$ and all $t \geq 0$*

$$\Pr\left(d(x^t, a^t) \leq n^2 p/(16e^2) - \alpha\right) \leq e^{-\Omega(n)} + e^{-\Omega(\alpha)}.$$

PROOF. We essentially follow the analysis from the proof of Theorem 8, but focus on a region close to the target where the negative drift is stronger than the positive one. To match the drift theorem, we flip the orientation of the space and let $X^t = n - \mathrm{ONEMAX}_{a^t}(x^t)$. We recall that there is a drift away from the optimum if $n - X^t < i^*$. More precisely, from the estimations presented at the beginning of this subsection we obtain

$$\begin{aligned}&\mathrm{E}((n-i) - X^{t+1} \mid X^t = n - i) \\ &\qquad = \mathrm{E}(\Delta^+(i)) - \mathrm{E}(\Delta^-(i)) \\ &\qquad \geq \frac{np}{4e^2} - \frac{2i}{n} \geq \frac{np}{8e^2}\end{aligned}$$

for $i \leq n^2 \frac{p}{16e^2}$. This corresponds to $X^t \geq n - n^2 \frac{p}{16e^2}$. In the following, the aim is to analyze the X^t-process using Lemma 6 with $a := n - n^2 p/(16e^2)$, $b = a + \alpha$, $x_{\min} := 0$ and the constant function $h(x) := 1$. From this we obtain the trivial potential function $g(x) = x$. We define Δ and bound the moment-generating with the same procedure as in the proof of Theorem 8. Then (on $X^t; X^t > a$, which means $i < n^2 p/(16e^2)$)

$$\mathrm{E}\left(e^{-\lambda\Delta}\right) \leq 1 - \lambda\mathrm{E}(\Delta) + 7\lambda^2 q.$$

Since $\mathrm{E}(\Delta) \geq \frac{np}{8e^2}$, we choose $\lambda = \frac{1}{112e^2}$ to get

$$\mathrm{E}\left(e^{-\lambda\Delta}\right) \leq 1 - \lambda\left(\frac{np}{17e^2}\right) = 1 - \frac{np}{1904e^4} =: \beta < 1.$$

The bound

$$\mathrm{E}\left(e^{-\lambda(a - X^{t+1})} \cdot \mathbb{1}\left\{X^t \leq a\right\}\right) \leq 1 + 16\lambda =: D$$

is the same as in the proof of Theorem 8 since it only takes into account the worst-case distribution of Δ. Altogether,

$$\begin{aligned}&\Pr(X^t \geq b) \\ &\quad \leq e^{-\frac{tpn}{1904e^4}} e^{\frac{X^0 - b}{112e^2}} + \frac{1904e^4}{np}\left(1 + \frac{16}{112e^2}\right) e^{-\frac{\alpha}{112e^2}}.\end{aligned}$$

If $X^0 \leq 2n/3$, which happens with probability $1 - 2^{-\Omega(n)}$ according to Chernoff bounds, the first term is $e^{-\Omega(n)}$ since $b = n - O(n^2 p) = n - o(n)$. The second term is $e^{-\Omega(\alpha)}$ by the same arguments as in the proof of Theorem 8. Hence, turning back to the original state space,

$$\Pr\left(d(x^t, a^t) \leq n^2 p/(16e^2) - \alpha\right) \leq e^{-\Omega(n)} + e^{-\Omega(\alpha)}$$

as suggested. $\square$

3.2 The Case of Large r

In this section we consider large values of r. With the next theorem we show that, even for exponentially large r, the (1+1) EA maintains search points which differ from the optimum only by a constant in each dimension (in expectation)! This holds after an initial mixing phase, the length of which depends linearly on r.

THEOREM 10. *Let $p = o(1/n)$ and let $(x^t, a^t)_{t\in\mathbb{N}}$ be the sequence of random variables denoting the pair of current search point and current optimum as given by running the (1+1) EA on dynamic* ONEMAX. *Then there are $k_0, k_1 > 1$ such that, for all $t \geq k_0 rn^2$,*

$$\forall b \geq 4 : \Pr\left(\mathrm{ONEMAX}_{a^t}(x^t) \geq bn\right) \leq n2^{-k_1 b} \tag{1}$$

and

$$\mathrm{E}\left(\mathrm{ONEMAX}_{a^t}(x^t)\right) = O(n). \tag{2}$$

In particular, this bound is independent of r. In addition, for all $i \leq n$ and all $t \geq k_0 rn^2$,

$$\forall b \geq 4 : \Pr\left(d(a_i^t, x_i^t) \geq b\right) \leq 2^{-k_1 b}. \tag{3}$$

PROOF. We start by showing Equation (3). Fix a bit position $i \leq n$. We reason with drift on $d^t = d(a_i^t, x_i^t)$ and show that it leads towards 0. Note that this value can change by at most two per iteration (one movement step of the algorithm, one of the optimum). Let some time t be given and suppose $d^t \neq 0$.

Let E be the event that the (1+1) EA keeps all bits other than i unchanged. We bound the expectation of moving in the *wrong* direction conditional on $\overline{E}$ as

$$\mathrm{E}\left(d^{t+1} - d^t \mid \overline{E}\right) = o(1/n),$$

as the optimum might move away with probability $o(1/n)$ but, if the new solution is accepted at all, it is more likely to be accepted if the i was changed in the right direction than when it was changed in the wrong direction. We further bound expectation of moving in the *right* direction conditional on E as

$$\mathrm{E}\left(d^t - d^{t+1} \mid E\right) = \Omega(1/n),$$

as we will not accept a worsening, but do accept an improvement, which will happen with probability $\Omega(1/n)$. Using that $P(E)$ approaches $1/e$ as n approaches infinity, we get a drift of $\Omega(1/n)$ towards the optimum.

With the use of the additive drift theorem (Theorem 1), this shows that the first time we have $d^t = 0$ is expected to be at most $k_1 rn$ iterations, for some k_1 large enough. Let T be the random variable denoting the smallest t with $d^t = 0$. Using concentration bounds for additive drift (Theorem 2), we get

$$\forall s \geq 2k_1 rn : \Pr(T \geq s) \leq \exp\left(-\frac{s}{64n^2}\right).$$

Let $t_0 = 2k_1 rn^2$. Thus, we do not have $d^{t_0} = 0$ for the first time within the first t steps with probability $2^{-\Omega(r)}$.

We now set up to use Theorem 7 to derive bound for straying from the optimum after reaching it for the first time. In the notation of that lemma, our process has a drift of $d = O(1/n)$, a self-loop probability of $p_0 = 1 - O(1/n)$ and a step size of at most $c = 2$. Thus, Lemma 7 gives some k such that, for all t,

$$\forall b \geq 4 : \Pr\left(d(a_i^t, x_i^t) \geq b \mid t > T\right) \leq 2^{-kb}.$$

We have, for all $t \geq t_0$,

$$\begin{aligned}\Pr\left(X^t \geq b\right) &\leq \Pr\left(d(a_i^t, x_i^t) \geq b \mid t > T\right) + \Pr(t \leq T)\\ &\leq 2^{-kb} + 2^{-\Omega(r)}.\end{aligned}$$

This gives the existence of a k_1 as desired, which shows Equation (3). Equation (1) now follows from the union bound, while Equation (2) follows from linearity of expectation (and the trivial bound on the expectation of exponentially decaying random variables). □

4. UPPER BOUND ON HITTING TIME OF TARGET

In this section, we re-prove the upper bound given by Droste (2003) in Theorem 12 and then extend it to the case of arbitrary r in Theorem 14. We start with the case of $r = 2$. Let X^t, $t \geq 0$, be the Hamming distance of the current optimum string and the current search point of the (1+1) EA at time t. Hence, we get a process on $\{0, \ldots, n\}$ with target state 0. We lower bound the parameter $p^-(i)$ and the "drift" $\delta(i)$ in the sense of Theorem 4.

LEMMA 11. *For $i > 0$, $\Pr(X^{t+1} = i-1 \mid X^t = i) \geq (1-p)^n \frac{i}{en}$, $\Pr(X^{t+1} \geq i+1 \mid X^t = i) \leq pn$ and $\delta(i) \geq (1-p)^n \frac{i}{en} - pn$.*

PROOF. The distance to the optimum decreases if the optimum does not move (probability $(1-p)^n$) and exactly one wrong bit flips (probability $(1-1/n)^{n-1}\frac{i}{n} \geq \frac{i}{en}$), which proves the bound on $\Pr(X^{t+1} = i-1 \mid X^t = i)$. The distance to the optimum can only increase if the dynamic component flips a bit. By a union bound, the probability is at most pn, which proves the bound on $\Pr(X^{t+1} \geq i+1 \mid X^t = i)$.

To bound $\mathrm{E}\left((X^{t+1} - i) \cdot \mathbb{1}\{X^{t+1} > i\} \mid X^t = i\right)$, which appears in the definition of $\delta(i)$, we pessimistically assume that each change of the optimum string increases the distance to the current search point. The expected number of bits changed by the dynamic component equals pn, which altogether leads to the bound on $\delta(i)$. □

Hereinafter, we work with $p^-(i) = (1-p)^n \frac{i}{en}$ and $p^+(i) = pn$. We get the following polynomial upper bound in the case of bit strings.

THEOREM 12. *Let $r = 2$ and $p \leq c\frac{\ln n}{n^2}$ for some constant c. Then the expected optimization time of the (1+1) EA on the dynamic* ONEMAX *is $O(n^{4.8c+2} \ln^2 n)$.*

PROOF. By solving the equation $\delta(i) = 0$ with the bounds from Lemma 11, we are allowed to set $\kappa := \frac{pen^2}{(1-p)^n}$. Using the assumption on p, $\kappa = (1+o(1))ec\ln n \leq 3c\ln n$ for n large enough. Moreover, we have $p^+(i) + p^-(i) \leq \frac{c\ln n}{n} + \frac{c\ln n}{n} \leq \frac{2c\ln n}{n}$ for $i \leq \kappa$. Then

$$\begin{aligned}
&\mathrm{E}(T \mid X^0)\\
&\leq \left(\left(\sum_{k=3c\ln n+1}^{n} \frac{1}{\frac{k}{en} - (c\ln n)/n}\right) \prod_{k=1}^{3c\ln n} \frac{\frac{2c\ln n}{n}}{(1-p)^n \frac{k}{en}}\right)\\
&\quad + \left(\sum_{k=1}^{3c\ln n} \frac{1}{(1-p)^n \frac{k}{en}} \prod_{j=1}^{k-1} \frac{\frac{2c\ln n}{n}}{(1-p)^n \frac{j}{en}}\right)\\
&\leq \sum_{k=3c\ln n+1}^{n} \frac{1}{k/(10n\ln n)} \cdot P + 3c\ln n \cdot P,
\end{aligned}$$

where $P := en(1-p)^{-n} \prod_{k=2}^{3c\ln n} \frac{2ce\ln n}{k}$. If n is not too small, we have

$$\mathrm{E}(T \mid X^0) \leq (10n\ln^2 n) + 3c\ln n)P \leq (11n\ln^2 n)P.$$

Now,

$$\begin{aligned}
P &\leq en\left(1 - \frac{c\ln n}{n^2}\right)^{-n} \frac{(2ce\ln n)^{3c\ln n}}{(3c\ln n)!}\\
&\leq en(1+o(1))\left(\frac{2ce^2}{3c}\right)^{3c\ln n}\\
&\leq 2ene^{3c\ln(2e^2/3)\ln n} \leq 2en^{4.8c+1}
\end{aligned}$$

using $k! \geq (k/e)^k$. Altogether,

$$\mathrm{E}(T \mid X^0) \leq 22en^{4.8c+2} \ln^2 n$$

for n large enough. □

For comparison, Droste (2003) proves the upper bound $\mathrm{E}(T) = O(n^{4ce/\ln(2)+1} \ln n)$, i.e., the exponent is almost

12c. Hence, state-of-the-art drift analysis yields more precise results, is more versatile and leads to cleaner and shorter proofs than the previous analysis by Droste (2003).

It is not to difficult to generalize Theorem 12 to arbitrary r if we replace the prerequisite on p by $p \le c\frac{\ln n}{rn^2}$. Basically, a factor of r is lost if we work under the worst case assumption that wrong positions have distance r from the optimum, resulting in only $\textsc{OneMax}_{a^t}(x^t)/r$ wrong positions. To increase the regime of polynomial hitting times, we have to prove this worst case to be unlikely. Fortunately, the anytime analysis from Theorem 10 can be used here to show that we lose a factor of at most $O(\log n)$ regardless of r. To this end, we will use the following lemma, which immediately follows from Theorem 10.

LEMMA 13. *Let $p = o(1/n)$. Then there are constants $a > 0, b > 1$ such that for any $i \in [n]$, $j \in \mathbb{N}$ and all $t \ge rn^2 \ln n$ it holds $\Pr(d(a_i^t, x_i^t) \ge j) \le ab^{-j}$.*

We now state the theorem concerned with polynomial hitting times for large r. To ease the statement, we only consider polynomial-sized r.

THEOREM 14. *Let $r \le n^k$ for some constant k and $p \le \frac{c \ln n}{\min\{r, \ln n\} n^2}$ for some sufficiently small constant c (possibly depending on k). Then the expected optimization time of the (1+1) EA on the dynamic* ONEMAX *is polynomial in n.*

PROOF. Let $t^* = rn^2 \ln n$. Pessimistically ignoring the case that the optimum is hit in less than t^* steps, we apply Lemma 13. Choosing $j^* = \ln(an^2t^*)/(\ln b) = O(\log n)$, we obtain that $\Pr(d(a_i^t, x_i^t) \ge j^*) \le 1/(t^*n^2)$ for any j and $t \ge t^*$. By a union bound, the probability that for all $i \in [n]$ we have $d(a_i^t, x_i^t) \le j^*$ is $1 - O(1/(t^*n))$. From now on, we assume this to hold in a phase of length t^*, starting from time t^* up to time $2t^* - 1$. Again by a union bound, the probability that within t^* steps all positions have distance at most j^* from the target is still $1 - O(1/n) - n^{-\omega(1)} = 1 - o(1)$. If $j^* \ge r$, the assumption holds trivially, i. e., with probability 1.

Under our assumption, we conduct a drift analysis with respect to $X^t := \textsc{OneMax}_{a_t}(x_t)$. Similarly to Lemma 11, $\Pr(X^{t+1} \ge i+1 \mid X^t = i) \le pn$ since each changing position of the target increases the distance by at most 1 and also

$$\mathrm{E}\big((X^t - X^{t+1}) \cdot \mathbb{1}\{X^{t+1} > X^t\} \mid X^t = i\big) \le pn.$$

If $X^t = i$, then there are at least $\frac{i}{\min\{r, j^*\}}$ wrong positions, hence $p^-(i) = \Pr(X^{t+1} = i - 1 \mid X^t = i) \ge (1 - p)^n \frac{i}{\min\{r, j^*\} en}$ and

$$\begin{aligned}\delta(i) &\ge (1-p)^n \frac{i}{\min\{r, j^*\} en} - pn \\ &\ge (1-p)^n \frac{i}{\min\{r, j^*\} en} - \frac{c \ln n}{\min\{r, \ln n\} n}.\end{aligned}$$

By our assumptions, $j^* \le kc_1 \ln n$ for some constant c_1 (depending on a and b) for large enough n. Using our assumption on p, we get that $\delta(i) \ge 0$ for $i \ge c_3 \ln n$, where c_3 is a constant such that $c_3 = cc_1k + c_2$ for another constant c_2. Hence, we work with $\kappa := c_3 \ln n$. If c_2 is chosen appropriately, then we also have $p^+(i) + p^-(i) \le \frac{c_3 \ln n}{2n}$ for $i \le \kappa$. Similarly as in the proof of Theorem 12, we get for small enough c that

$$\mathrm{E}(T \mid X^0) \le \sum_{\ell = c_3 \ln n}^{j^* n} \frac{1}{\ell/(2ekc_1 n \ln n)} \cdot P + c_3 \ln n \cdot P,$$

where

$$P := en \min\{r, j^*\}(1-p)^{-n} \prod_{\ell=2}^{c_3 \ln n} \frac{(c_3/2) \ln n}{\ell}.$$

If n is not too small, $\mathrm{E}(T \mid X^0) \le 3ekc_1c_3n(\ln^2 n)P$, so we are left with an estimate for P. We get

$$P \le O(n \ln^2 n) \left(\frac{c_3 e \ln n}{2c_3 \ln n}\right)^{c_3 \ln n} \le n^{c_3}$$

for n large enough. Altogether,

$$\mathrm{E}(T \mid X^0) \le n^{cc_1k + c_2}.$$

If n is large enough and c is sufficiently small but still constant, then $n^{cc_1k+c_2} \le t^*/2$. Hence, by Markov's inequality, the probability that a phase of t^* steps is successful, i. e., the optimum is hit, is at least $1/2$; still conditioning on maximum distance j^* for all positions. By the considerations from above, the unconditional probability of a successful phase is at least $1/2 - o(1)$. In case of a failure, we consider the subsequent phase of t^* steps. The expected number of phases is at most $2 + o(1)$, hence the overall expected first hitting time of the target is at most $t^* + (2 + o(1))t^* = (3 + o(1))t^*$, i. e., polynomial. □

We conjecture that the assumption on p in Theorem 14 can be replaced by $p \le \frac{c \ln n}{n^2}$, i. e., that the same regime for polynomial first hitting time holds regardless of r. However, we cannot prove this at the moment since the processes describing the distance from the target for different positions are not independent.

5. LOWER BOUND ON HITTING TIME OF TARGET

When the mutation probability applied to the optimum is asymptotically larger than $\log n/n^2$, Droste (2003) shows that the first hitting time of (1+1) EA on ONEMAX for $r = 2$ is polynomial only with super-polynomially small probability. We re-prove this result for any $r \ge 2$ and $p \le 1/n$ using drift analysis.

THEOREM 15. *With $p \in \omega(\log n/n^2)$ and $p \le 1/n$, the first hitting time of the (1+1) EA on the dynamic* ONEMAX *for any $r \ge 2$ is polynomial only with super-polynomially small probability.*

PROOF. To prove the result, we let X^t be the current solution of the EA and apply Theorem 3 using potential function $g(X^t) = \sum_{i=1}^n [a_i^t \ne x_i^t]$, i. e., the number of characters the individual and the optimum differ by at time t.

Consider the effects of mutating the optimum and the mutation/selection step separately. When $g(X^t) \le n/2$, the effect of optimum mutation on $g(X^t)$ non-matching characters is countered by the effect of mutation on $g(X^t)$ matching characters, leaving $n - 2g(X^t)$ matching characters which cause a drift away from the optimum:

$$\mathrm{E}(g(X^{t+1}) - g(X^t) \mid S^t) \ge (n - 2g(X^t)) \cdot p,$$

where S^t is the event that no mutation occurs during the mutation/selection step of iteration t.

For the mutation/selection step, the expected increase in the number of matching characters is at most the number of mutated non-matching characters. We can consider the mutation/selection occurring after the optimum is mutated, so the number of non-matching characters is in expectation increased by at most 1 for $p \leq 1/n$, leading to a combined drift of:

$$\mathrm{E}(g(X^{t+1}) - g(X^t)) \geq (n - 2g(X^t)) \cdot p - (g(X^t) + 1) \cdot 1/n.$$

Let $p = \alpha(n) \cdot \log n/n^2 \leq 1/n$, where $\alpha(n) \in \omega(1) \leq n/\log n$; limiting $g(X^t) < b = \alpha(n)^c \log n$, where $c < 1$ is a constant, reveals a drift away from the optimum:

$$\begin{aligned}
&\mathrm{E}(g(X^{t+1}) - g(X^t) \mid g(X^t) < b)\\
&\quad \geq (n - 2g(X^t)) \cdot p - (g(X^t) + 1) \cdot 1/n\\
&\quad \geq \frac{\alpha(n) \log n}{n} - \frac{\alpha(n)^c \log n}{n}\left(\frac{2\alpha(n)\log n}{n} + 1\right) - \frac{1}{n}\\
&\quad \in \Omega\left(\frac{\alpha(n) \log n}{n}\right).
\end{aligned}$$

With low p and $g(X^t)$, a large number of iterations might not alter the value of $g(X^t)$ (causing a "self-loop"). The probability p_O of an iteration resulting in a self-loop can be bounded by considering the probability that none of the characters of the optimum mutate, and none of the non-matching characters in the current individual mutate:

$$\begin{aligned}
p_O &= \Pr(g(X^{t+1}) = g(X^t) \mid X^t)\\
&\geq (1-p)^n \cdot (1 - 1/n)^{g(X^t)}\\
&\geq 1 - \frac{n\alpha(n)\log n}{n^2} - \frac{\alpha(n)^c \log n}{n}\\
(1 - p_O) &\in O\left(\frac{\alpha(n)\log n}{n}\right).
\end{aligned}$$

Thus, there exists a constant $\varepsilon > 0$ satisfying the first requirement of Theorem 3. We then need to bound the probabilities of $g(X^t)$ changing significantly in a single iteration. Throughout the following, let M be the event that a self-loop does not occur, i. e., $g(X^{t+1}) \neq g(X^t)$.

Let $c_1 = n - g(X^t) \leq n$ be the number of matching characters in the optimum and the current individual (for which $d(a_i, x_i) = 0$). We note that mutating such a character in the optimum would increase $g(X^{t+1})$ unless it is also mutated in the current individual; let C_1 be the number of such mutations that occur:

$$\begin{aligned}
\Pr(M) &\geq c_1 \cdot p(1-p)^{n-1} \cdot (1 - 1/n)^n\\
&\geq c_1 p/4e\\
\Pr(C_1 \geq j) &\leq \binom{c_1}{j} p^j\\
\Pr(C_1 \geq j \mid M) &\leq \frac{(c_1 p)^{j-1} 4e}{2^{j-1}} \leq \frac{8e}{2^j}
\end{aligned}$$

for $n \geq 2$.

Let $c_2 \leq g(X^t) \leq n$ be the number of characters for which $d(a_i, x_i) \geq 2$, i. e., those that would not transform into matching characters even if improved by mutation; notably, $c_2 = 0$ if $r = 2$. When both, a matching character mutation, and a mutation improving such a character occurs in the current individual, $g(X^{t+1})$ increases without reducing fitness, allowing the mutated individual to be accepted; let C_2 be the number of such mutations that occur:

$$\begin{aligned}
\Pr(M) &\geq c_1 c_2/(8en^2)\\
\Pr(C_2 \geq j) &\leq \binom{c_1}{j}\binom{c_2}{j} n^{-2j}\\
\Pr(C_2 \geq j \mid M) &\leq \frac{(c_1 c_2)^j}{2^{2(j-1)} n^{2j}} \frac{8en^2}{c_1 c_2}\\
&\leq \frac{(c_1 c_2)^{j-1}}{n^{2(j-1)}} \frac{32e}{4^j} < \frac{32e}{4^j}
\end{aligned}$$

as $c_1 c_2 \leq n^2$.

The increase in potential value is at most the sum of these two effects, and hence:

$$\Pr(g(X^{t+1}) - g(X^t) \geq j \mid M) \leq \Pr(C_1 + C_2 \geq j \mid M).$$

By Lemma 16, there exists a choice of $r(\ell)$ and δ that satisfies the second condition of Theorem 3 for jumps away from the optimum.

For jumps toward the optimum, let k_1 be the number of characters for which $d(a_i, x_i) = 1$, i. e., those that can be corrected by a mutation in either the optimum or the current individual; let J_1 be the number of such characters corrected in a given iteration. Proceeding as before,

$$\begin{aligned}
\Pr(J_1 \geq j \mid M) &\leq \binom{2k_1}{j} \frac{1}{n^j} \frac{8en}{k_1}\\
&\leq \frac{(2k_1)^{j-1} 8e}{n^{j-1} 3^{j-2}} \leq \frac{36e}{1.5^j},
\end{aligned}$$

noting that if $r > 2$, a mutation in a specific direction is required while considering $P(M)$, while a mutation either direction is acceptable to upper-bound $P(J_1 \geq j)$.

Furthermore, let k_2 be the number of characters for which $d(a_i, x_i) = 2$, i. e., those that can match if they are mutated appropriately in both the optimum and the current individual; let J_2 be the number of such characters corrected in a given iteration. Similarly,

$$\begin{aligned}
\Pr(J_2 \geq j \mid M) &\leq \binom{k_2}{j} \left(\frac{p}{4n}\right)^j \frac{16en}{k_2 p}\\
&\leq \frac{{k_2}^{j-1} 4e}{8^{j-1}} \left(\frac{p}{n}\right)^{j-1} \leq \frac{32e}{8^j}
\end{aligned}$$

as $k_2 \leq n \leq 1/p$.

The reduction in potential value is at most the sum of these two effects, and so:

$$\Pr(g(X^{t+1}) - g(X^t) \leq -j \mid M) \leq \Pr(J_1 + J_2 \geq j \mid M).$$

Per Lemma 16, there exists a choice of $r(\ell)$ and δ that satisfies the second condition of Theorem 3 for jumps toward the optimum.

Thus, there exists a choice of $r(\ell)$ and δ that satisfies the second requirement of Theorem 3 both for jumps away from and jumps toward the optimum.

Finally, we note that the probability of a randomly initialized character matching the optimum is $1/r \leq 1/2$. Using Chernoff's inequality, the probability that more than $3n/4$ characters are initialized correctly is at most $e^{-n/12}$, and therefore $g(X^0) \geq n/4 > b$ with high probability.

By applying Theorem 3 with $g(X^t)$, $b = \alpha(n)^c \log n$ and $a = 0$, and hence $\ell = \omega(\log n)$, we can conclude that if

$p \in \omega(\log n/n^2) \leq 1/n$, the (1+1) EA finds the optimum in polynomial time with only super-polynomially small probability. □

While proving that large jumps are exponentially unlikely even after removing self-loops from the process, we used the following lemma to combine upper bounds for different kinds of jumps.

LEMMA 16. *Let $J = J_1 + J_2$; if there exist constants $r_1, r_2 \geq 1$, and $d_1, d_2 > 1$, s.t. for some event E,*

$$\Pr(J_1 \geq j \mid E) \leq r_1/{d_1}^j$$
$$\Pr(J_2 \geq j \mid E) \leq r_2/{d_2}^j$$

and it holds that $\Pr(J_2 \geq j_2 \mid E, J_1 \geq j_1) \leq \Pr(J_2 \geq j_2 \mid E)$, *then there also exist constants r, $d > 1$, s.t.*

$$\Pr(J \geq j \mid E) \leq r/d^j.$$

PROOF. Let $r_* = \max(r_1, r_2)$ and $d_* = \min(d_1, d_2)$; given the conditions, it is the case that:

$$\begin{aligned}
&\Pr(J \geq j \mid E) \\
&\leq \sum_{i=0}^{j} \Pr(J_1 \geq i \mid E)\Pr(J_2 \geq j - i \mid E, J_1 \geq j_1) \\
&\leq \sum_{i=0}^{j} \Pr(J_1 \geq i \mid E)\Pr(J_2 \geq j - i \mid E) \\
&\leq r_*^2 d_*^{-j}(j+1).
\end{aligned}$$

We note that $(j+1)d_*^{-j} \leq \sqrt{d_*}^{-j}$ for $j \geq 16/(\ln^2 d_*)$. It is possible to pick a constant $c = \sqrt{d_*}^{16/(\ln^2 d_*)}$, ensuring that $c/\sqrt{d_*}^j \geq 1$ for $j \leq 16/(\ln^2 d_*)$, which proves the lemma with $r = r_* c$ and $d = \sqrt{d_*}$. □

6. CONCLUSION

In this paper we revisited the setting of dynamic ONEMAX as introduced by Droste (2003), where the optimum moves by flipping the bit of each position with some fixed probability p.

We showed that his results, both the upper and the lower bound, extend to versions of dynamic ONEMAX where each dimension has r different possible values. By using modern drift analysis, the proof is shorter and more elegant.

Furthermore, we made an analysis of how far from the optimum the (1+1) EA strays after getting close for the first time. For the case of bit strings, this value is concentrated around $\Theta(pn^2)$ (for $p = o(1/n)$), which shows that the optimum is very elusive unless p is small. On the other hand, we showed that only the *dimension*, and not the *size*, of the search space has an impact on the ability of the (1+1) EA to track good solutions. We did this by considering search spaces with r possible values in each dimension, and saw that r does not influence the resulting bounds, i. e., the distance is bounded by a constant in expectation in each dimension if r is large (see Theorem 10).

We believe that the methods we used, especially the statements about the occupation probabilities as given in Lemma 13 of Lissovoi and Witt (2015) or in our Theorem 7, will be beneficial in many more settings, especially those aiming at an anytime analysis for dynamic problems.

Acknowledgments

The authors would like to thank Benjamin and Carola Doerr for interesting discussions on the topic of this paper. The anonymous reviewers of the pre-conference reviews made many valuable suggestions which improved the paper. Furthermore, Golnaz Badkobeh, Per Kristian Lehre and Dirk Sudholt gave many useful suggestions as part of the FOGA post-conference reviews. Financial support from the Danish Council for Independent Research (grant no. DFF–4002-00542) is gratefully acknowledged.

References

Auger, Anne and Doerr, Benjamin (2011). *Theory of Randomized Search Heuristics – Foundations and Recent Developments.* World Scientific Publishing.

Doerr, Benjamin, Johannsen, Daniel, and Schmidt, Martin (2011). Runtime analysis of the (1+1) evolutionary algorithm on strings over finite alphabets. In *Proc. of FOGA'11*, 119–126. ACM Press.

Doerr, Benjamin and Pohl, Sebastian (2012). Run-time analysis of the (1+1) evolutionary algorithm optimizing linear functions over a finite alphabet. In *Proc. of GECCO'12*, 1317–1324. ACM Press.

Droste, Stefan (2002). Analysis of the (1+1) EA for a dynamically changing OneMax-variant. In *Proc. of CEC'02*, 55–60. IEEE Press.

Droste, Stefan (2003). Analysis of the (1+1) EA for a dynamically bitwise changing OneMax. In *Proc. of GECCO'03*, 909–921. Springer.

Hajek, Bruce (1982). Hitting-time and occupation-time bounds implied by drift analysis with applications. *Advances in Applied Probability*, **13**, 502–525.

He, Jun and Yao, Xin (2001). Drift analysis and average time complexity of evolutionary algorithms. *Artificial Intelligence*, **127**, 57–85.

Jansen, Thomas (2013). *Analyzing Evolutionary Algorithms – The Computer Science Perspective.* Natural Computing Series. Springer.

Jansen, Thomas and Schellbach, Ulf (2005). Theoretical analysis of a mutation-based evolutionary algorithm for a tracking problem in the lattice. In *Proc. of GECCO'05*, 841–848. ACM Press.

Jansen, Thomas and Zarges, Christine (2014). Evolutionary algorithms and artificial immune systems on a bi-stable dynamic optimisation problem. In *Proc. of GECCO'14*, 975–982. ACM Press.

Jin, Yaochu and Branke, Jürgen (2005). Evolutionary optimization in uncertain environments—A survey. *IEEE Transactions on Evolutionary Computation*, **9**, 303–317.

Kötzing, Timo (2014). Concentration of first hitting times under additive drift. In *Proc. of GECCO'14*, 1391–1398. ACM Press.

Kötzing, Timo and Molter, Hendrik (2012). ACO beats EA on a dynamic pseudo-boolean function. In *Proc. of PPSN'12*, 113–122. Springer.

Lehre, Per Kristian and Witt, Carsten (2014). Concentrated hitting times of randomized search heuristics with variable drift. In *Proc. of ISAAC'14*, 686–697. Springer. Extended version at `http://arxiv.org/abs/1307.2559`.

Lissovoi, Andrei and Witt, Carsten (2015). MMAS versus population-based EA on a family of dynamic fitness functions. *Algorithmica*. In press, final version online at `http://dx.doi.org/10.1007/s00453-015-9975-z`.

Neumann, Frank and Witt, Carsten (2010). *Bioinspired Computation in Combinatorial Optimization – Algorithms and Their Computational Complexity*. Natural Computing Series. Springer.

Oliveto, Pietro Simone and Witt, Carsten (2011). Simplified drift analysis for proving lower bounds in evolutionary computation. *Algorithmica*, **59**, 369–386.

Oliveto, Pietro Simone and Witt, Carsten (2012). Erratum: Simplified drift analysis for proving lower bounds in evolutionary computation. Tech. rep., `http://arxiv.org/abs/1211.7184`.

Oliveto, Pietro Simone and Zarges, Christine (2013). Analysis of diversity mechanisms for optimisation in dynamic environments with low frequencies of change. In *Proc. of GECCO'13*, 837–844. ACM Press.

Rowe, Jonathan E. and Sudholt, Dirk (2014). The choice of the offspring population size in the (1,λ) evolutionary algorithm. *Theoretical Computer Science*, **545**, 20–38.

Fixed Budget Performance of the (1+1) EA on Linear Functions

Johannes Lengler
Institute for Theoretical Computer Science
ETH Zürich, Switzerland
johannes.lengler@inf.ethz.ch

Nick Spooner
ETH Zürich, Switzerland
spoonen@student.ethz.ch

ABSTRACT

We present a fixed budget analysis of the (1+1) evolutionary algorithm for general linear functions, considering both the quality of the solution after a predetermined 'budget' of fitness function evaluations (a priori) and the improvement in quality when the algorithm is given additional budget, given the quality of the current solution (a posteriori). Two methods are presented: one based on drift analysis, the other on the differential equation method and Chebyshev's inequality. While the first method is superior for general linear functions, the second can be more precise for specific functions and provides concentration guarantees. As an example, we provide tight a posteriori fixed budget results for the function OneMax.

General Terms

Theory

Keywords

fixed budget, (1+1) EA, evolutionary algorithm, linear functions, theory

1. INTRODUCTION

The theoretical analysis of randomised search heuristics for discrete optimization problems has typically focused on the question of expected running time, i.e. the number of steps required on average to reach an optimal solution. In their seminal paper, Jansen and Zarges [10, 11] introduce a different perspective: so-called 'fixed budget' analysis. To measure the quality of an (evolutionary) algorithm on a specific problem, Jansen and Zarges ask two related, but not identical, questions. Firstly, given an predetermined number of iterations, or 'budget', what is the quality of the best solution found within this budget? Secondly, if the algorithm has spent budget B, then how does the quality of the best solution found improve when the algorithm is allowed to continue searching for an additional budget ΔB? We will call answers to the two questions *a priori* and *a posteriori* fixed budget results, respectively.

Arguably, fixed budget analysis is a better approximation to how evolutionary algorithms are actually employed than classical models: often the problem is such that it is not possible to determine when the optimum, or a certain quality of approximation, is reached. Instead, we decide *a priori* on a budget, and run the algorithm for a fixed number of steps. This is also the way the quality of novel evolutionary algorithms is estimated: typically, some time budget is fixed, and several algorithms are run for this time budget on a benchmark function. The algorithm finding the best solution in this time is considered best for this problem.

Traditionally the runtime of an evolutionary algorithm is measured by the number of evaluations of the fitness function ("queries") until the optimum is found. We will adopt this notion throughout the paper. Moreover, we will restrict ourselves to discrete optimization functions, i.e., we have a fitness function $f : \{0,1\}^n \to \mathbb{R}$ on the hypercube that we want to minimize (or maximize). However, note that the tools that we develop in Section 2 do not depend on the search space being discrete.

In this paper we analyse the $(1+1)$ EA, a simple evolutionary algorithm (cf. Algorithm 1 below). In each round, the current solution $x^{(t)}$ produces an offspring by flipping each bit independently with probability $p = 1/n$. If the fitness of the offspring is at least as good as the fitness of $x^{(t)}$, then the offspring replaces the current solution. We note that in the literature other mutation rates besides $1/n$ are also studied (e.g., [3]), but we restrict ourselves to this case.

We will analyze the $(1+1)$ EA on *linear functions.* A linear function f on the hypercube can be described by 'weights' $w_1, \ldots, w_n$, and it is given by $f(x) = \sum_i w_i x_i$,

---

Algorithm 1: The $(1+1)$ evolutionary algorithm $(1+1)$ EA for minimizing an unknown function $f : \{0,1\}^n \to \mathbb{R}$. The operator MUT flips each bit of the input string independently with probability $1/n$.

Initialization: Sample $x^{(0)}$ uniformly at random.
Optimization: **for** $t = 1, 2, 3, \ldots$ **do**
  Set $y^{(t)} \leftarrow \mathrm{MUT}(x^{(t-1)})$.
  if $f(y^{(t)}) \leq f(x^{(t-1)})$ **then**
    $x^{(t)} \leftarrow y^{(t)}$
  else
    $x^{(t)} \leftarrow x^{(t-1)}$.

FOGA'15, January 17–20, 2015, Aberystwyth, UK.

ACM 978-1-4503-3434-1/15/01 ...$15.00.
http://dx.doi.org/10.1145/2725494.2725506.

where x_i denotes the ith bit value of x. By symmetry of the (1 + 1) EA, we may and will assume throughout the paper that $w_1 \geq w_2 \geq \ldots \geq w_n \geq 0$; furthermore we will ignore functions with zero weights, since they have more than one optimum and are thus fundamentally different from those with nonzero weights (and not particularly instructive here). A function of particular interest in the study of EAs is ONEMAX, defined by setting $w_1 = w_2 = \ldots = w_n = 1$; we will often refer to this function as OM.

The analysis of the (1 + 1) EA on linear functions, particularly ONEMAX, is quite mature. Droste, Jansen and Wegener [7] introduced the subject with their paper showing that the expected optimisation time of any linear function is $\Theta(n \log n)$. Successive improvements [5, 15] in the precision of this result have shown that this expectation is $(1 \pm o(1))en \log n$, where $\log n$ denotes the natural logarithm. For ONEMAX in particular it has been shown [13] that the expected optimisation time is at most $en \log n + O(n)$. Recently, a proof improving these bounds to $en \log n + c_1 n + e/2 \cdot \log n + c_2 + O(n^{-1} \log n)$ for explicit constants c_1 and c_2 has been uploaded to arXiv [8], which even gives a limiting distribution for the number of rounds needed.

Fixed budget analysis is comparatively young, introduced by Jansen and Zarges [10] with an analysis of the properties of randomised local search on the toy problems LEADINGONES and ONEMAX, and of the (1 + 1) EA on LEADINGONES. Fixed budget results are closely related to results on the hitting time of a fixed fitness level. In particular, Doerr et al. [4] show how to derive fixed-budget results from tail bounds on the optimisation time, and they apply their method to the (1 + 1) EA on LEADINGONES. We employ a more direct approach. We draw heavily on an analysis due to Jägersküpper [9] which establishes some fundamental properties of the distribution of the individual as a bitstring.

We seek to provide fixed-budget results for the (1+1) EA operating on linear functions including ONEMAX, which are as yet missing in the literature. For technical reasons we assume that the weights are all positive and sum up to n. We present a straightforward drift method and show that it can be applied to obtain relatively good bounds. To get more precise results, we take an indirect approach: we first show in Lemma 6 that the expected fitness is at most by a factor of $2 \log n$ larger than the expected OM potential, i.e., than the expected number of 1-bits. This allows us to focus on the OM potential, for which we can give *a posteriori* bounds that hold with high probability (Theorem 9). For the analysis of the OM potential we make use of the differential equation method [16], which to the best of our knowledge has not been applied in the theoretical study of EAs before. A shortcoming of our method is the rather weak link between the fitness and the OM potential, which only applies to expectations. If this link could be amended with tail bounds, then "with high probability" statements could also be obtained for the actual fitness.

For the (1+1) EA operating on ONEMAX, we obtain tight *a priori* and *a posteriori* bounds on the expected fitness after β iterations, where $\beta \leq (1-\varepsilon)en \log n$. The *a priori* bounds involve a numeric function given by some differential equation (Theorem 19), for which we present a numerical analysis in Section 5, but the *a posteriori* bound is very explicit: if at time t, we have reached fitness value $a = o(n/\log n)$, then with high probability $\mathrm{OM}(x^{(t+\beta)}) = ae^{-\beta/(en)}(1 \pm o(1))$ provided a is not too small or β too large, cf. Theorem 18.

The structure of the paper is as follows. In Section 2 we provide a simple multiplicative drift theorem for fixed budgets, and a more sophisticated version for lower bounds which can employ expected approximation time results. In Section 3 we give the main contribution, a detailed analysis of the behaviour of the (1 + 1) EA on linear functions with respect to the ONEMAX potential, giving *a posteriori* (and weak *a priori*) results. In Section 4 we apply the analysis to ONEMAX itself, yielding explicit *a posteriori* and numeric *a priori* results. In Section 5 we plot the a priori results for the ONEMAX potential of linear functions and for ONEMAX, and compare them with experimental results.

2. FIXED-BUDGET DRIFT

Drift techniques are widely used in the analysis of evolutionary algorithms [13]. They are particularly useful in deriving expected optimisation times, since they provide bounds on the expected time based on bounds on the expected progress in a single step, which is much easier to analyse. Drift analysis also naturally applies to the fixed-budget case, as the following theorem demonstrates.

THEOREM 1 (FIXED-BUDGET MULTIPLICATIVE DRIFT). *Let $(X_t)_{t \geq 0}$ be a stochastic process, and let $b \in \mathbb{N}$ and $0 < \delta < 1$.*

(i) If $\forall t \leq b$: $\mathrm{E}[X_t - X_{t+1} \mid X_t = x] \geq \delta x$ then

$$\mathrm{E}[X_b \mid X_0] \leq X_0(1-\delta)^b \leq X_0 e^{-\delta b};$$

(ii) If $\forall t \leq b$: $\mathrm{E}[X_t - X_{t+1} \mid X_t = x] \leq \delta x$ then

$$\mathrm{E}[X_b \mid X_0] \geq X_0(1-\delta)^b \geq X_0 e^{-2\delta b}$$

for $\delta \leq 0.797$.

PROOF. For (i), simply observe that $E[X_{t+1} | X_t = x] \leq (1-\delta)x$. Thus by the law of total expectation,

$$\mathrm{E}[X_{t+1}|X_0] \leq (1-\delta)\,\mathrm{E}[X_t|X_0].$$

The statement now follows from a trivial induction. The second statement is proven in the same way, where the second inequality holds only for $\delta \leq 0.797$. □

This allows us to directly apply existing drift bounds to obtain fixed-budget results. For example, the well-known drift lower bound for ONEMAX of $\mathrm{OM}(x)/en$ gives immediately that $\mathrm{E}[\mathrm{OM}(x^{(b)})] \leq \frac{1}{2}ne^{-b/(en)}$. In some cases, however, it is not clear how existing results can be employed; for example, if the drift refers to some potential function, or if the argument does not involve drift at all. The following theorem uses the expected approximation time as a 'black box' to give lower bounds on the expected fitness value. In the following, for a monotonically decreasing stochastic process $(X_t)_{t \geq 0}$, we define the expected approximation time for any $x \in \mathbb{R}$ as $T_x := \min\{t \in \mathbb{N} \mid X_t \leq x\}$, i.e. the first time t such that X_t drops below x.

THEOREM 2. *Let $(X_t)_{t \geq 0}$ be a monotonically decreasing stochastic process. Let $a \in \mathbb{R}$, let $b, c \geq 0$. If $\forall t \leq b$, $\mathrm{E}[X_t - X_{t+1} \mid X_t = x, X_t \geq a] \leq \delta x$, and $b \geq \mathrm{E}[T_a] \geq c$, then*

$$\mathrm{E}[X_b] \geq a(1-\delta)^{b-c} \geq ae^{-2\delta(b-c)}$$

for all $0 < \delta \leq 0.797$.

PROOF. We define $Y_t = (1-\delta)^{-t} X_t$ for $T_a \leq t \leq b$. Then Y_t is a submartingale, and hence by the optional stopping theorem [12] $\mathrm{E}[Y_b] \geq \mathrm{E}[Y_\tau]$ for all $T_a \leq \tau \leq b$. Then

$$\begin{aligned}
\mathrm{E}[Y_b] &= \mathrm{E}[Y_b \mid T_a \leq b] \Pr[T_a \leq b] + \mathrm{E}[Y_b \mid T_a > b] \Pr[T_a > b] \\
&\geq \mathrm{E}[Y_{T_a}] \Pr[T_a \leq b] + (1-\delta)^{-b} \mathrm{E}[X_b \mid T_a > b] \Pr[T_a > b] \\
&\geq \mathrm{E}[(1-\delta)^{-T_a}] \cdot a \cdot \Pr[T_a \leq b] + (1-\delta)^{-b} \cdot a \cdot \Pr[T_a > b] \\
&\geq (1-\delta)^{-\mathrm{E}[T_a]} \cdot a \cdot \Pr[T_a \leq b] + (1-\delta)^{-b} \cdot a \cdot \Pr[T_a > b] \\
&\geq a \cdot (1-\delta)^{-\mathrm{E}[T_a]} .
\end{aligned}$$

The second inequality follows since the value of $\mathrm{E}[X_t]$ is monotonically decreasing in t, so if $T_a > b$ then $\mathrm{E}[X_b] \geq \mathrm{E}[X_{T_a}] = a$. The third inequality follows from Jensen's inequality on the convex function $f(x) = (1-\delta)^{-x}$, and the fourth from the condition $b \geq \mathrm{E}[T_a]$.

By definition, $\mathrm{E}[Y_b] = (1-\delta)^{-b} \cdot \mathrm{E}[X_b]$, so $\mathrm{E}[X_b] \geq a \cdot (1-\delta)^{b-\mathrm{E}[T_a]}$. The bound then follows by the required properties of c and δ. □

To demonstrate the application of this theorem, we derive an *a priori* fixed-budget result for ONEMAX (weaker than the result we obtain in Section 4). Let T_a^{OM} be the expected approximation time of the (1+1) EA on ONEMAX, i.e., T_a^{OM} is the expected number of queries until the first search point of objective value at most a is found. For the lower bound we will employ Theorem 2, for which we require a lower bound on $\mathrm{E}[T_a^{\mathrm{OM}}]$ for some a. This we can obtain using the fitness level method for lower bounds due to Sudholt [14]. We present a modification to [14, Theorem 3], allowing us to extend its result about expected optimisation time to the expectation of T_a^{OM}.

COROLLARY 3 (OF [14, THEOREM 4]). *For $a \in \mathbb{N}$,*

$$\mathrm{E}[T_a^{\mathrm{OM}}] \geq en\log(n/a) - 2n\log\log n - 16n.$$

PROOF. The proof is a straightforward modification of the proofs given in [14], so we outline only the changes needed in these proofs. Let $\ell := \lfloor n - n/\log n \rfloor$, and let A_ℓ be the set of all search points of fitness at most ℓ. Further, for $\ell + 1 \leq i \leq n$ let A_i be the set of all search points of fitness i. Finally, let values $u_i, \gamma_{i,j}$ be as in [14, Theorem 4]. Note that the following considers a maximisation setting, so let $k := n - a$. Let $A'_k := A_k \cup A_{k+1} \cup \ldots \cup A_n$. We require values u_i and $\gamma_{i,j}$ which fulfil the conditions of [14, Theorem 2]. The values of u_i we employ as in [14]. For $\gamma_{i,j}$, we make a natural modification:

$$\gamma'_{i,j} = \begin{cases} \gamma_{i,j} & \text{if } j < k, \\ \sum_{j=a}^{n} \gamma_{i,j} & \text{if } j = k. \end{cases}$$

Now the probability of moving from level i to level j in one step is unchanged if $i, j < k$. For $j = k$, we have simply that

$$\begin{aligned}
&\Pr[\text{move from } A_i \text{ to } A'_k \text{ in one step}] \\
&= \sum_{j=k}^{n} \Pr[\text{move from } A_i \text{ to } A_j \text{ in one step}] \\
&\leq \sum_{j=k}^{n} u_i \cdot \gamma_{i,j} = u_i \sum_{j=k}^{n} \gamma_{i,j} = u_i \cdot \gamma'_{i,k}.
\end{aligned}$$

Furthermore, $\sum_{i=j}^{n} \gamma'_{i,j} = \sum_{i=j}^{n} \gamma_{i,j}$ for any $j \leq k$, and hence $u_i, \gamma'_{i,j}$ and $A_\ell, \ldots, A'_k$ satisfy [14, Theorem 2]. The expected time to reach some search point $x \in A'_k$ is then, by a small modification to the proof of [14, Theorem 4],

$$\begin{aligned}
\mathrm{E}[T_a^{\mathrm{OM}}] &\geq (1 - \frac{8}{\log n}) en \sum_{i=a+1}^{\lfloor n-\ell \rfloor} \frac{1}{i} \\
&\geq en\log(n/a) - 2n\log\log n - 16n. \quad \square
\end{aligned}$$

With this preparation, we are ready to state the following a priori fixed budget result for ONEMAX.

THEOREM 4. *Let $x^{(t)}$ be the individual at time t for (1+1) EA operating on* ONEMAX. *Then for any $\varepsilon > 0$,*

$$n^{1-\frac{3}{2}\varepsilon} \cdot \Omega(\log^{-2} n) \leq \mathrm{E}[\mathrm{OM}(x^{(\varepsilon e n \log n)})] \leq \frac{1}{2} n^{1-\varepsilon} .$$

PROOF. The upper bound follows directly from Theorem 1 and the drift lower bound of $\mathrm{OM}(x)/en$.

Let $a := n^{1-\varepsilon'}$ for $\varepsilon' > 0$. Then the drift at fitness value x is bounded above [1] by $\frac{x}{en}\left(1 + \frac{16x}{n}\right) = \frac{x}{en}(1 + O(n^{-\varepsilon'}))$ for $x \geq a$. Applying Theorem 2 with Corollary 3 and $\delta := \frac{1}{en}(1 + O(n^{-\varepsilon'}))$ yields

$$\begin{aligned}
\mathrm{E}[X_b] &\geq n^{1-\varepsilon'} e^{-\frac{2}{en}(1+O(n^{-\varepsilon'}))(b - \varepsilon' en\log n + 2n\log\log n + 16n)} \\
&\geq n^{1-\varepsilon'} e^{-\frac{2}{e}(b/n - \varepsilon' e\log n)} \log^{-2}(n) \cdot e^{-32/e - o(1)} \\
&\geq \frac{1}{\log^2(n) \cdot 1.3 \times 10^5} \cdot n^{1-\varepsilon'} e^{-\frac{2}{e}(b/n - \varepsilon' e \log n)} \\
&= n^{1-\varepsilon'} e^{-\frac{2}{e}(b/n - \varepsilon' e\log n)} \Omega(\log^{-2} n)
\end{aligned}$$

Setting $b := \varepsilon \cdot en\log n$, $\varepsilon = 2\varepsilon'$, yields the stated lower bound. □

3. LINEAR FUNCTIONS

In this section we consider a 'restricted' class of linear functions, where the weights $w_1 \geq w_2 \geq \ldots \geq w_n > 0$ sum to n, i.e. $\sum_{i=1}^{n} w_i = n$. This is the case for ONEMAX and hence allows us to directly compare these results with those obtained for ONEMAX. Note that since the behaviour of the (1+1) EA is invariant under uniform scaling of weights, the results obtained apply for any linear function when scaled appropriately.

3.1 Preliminary bounds

We begin with some bounds which arise from simple properties of the (1+1) EA.

THEOREM 5. *For the (1+1) EA minimising a linear function, the following holds for the expected fitness of the individual generated at time b:*

$$\frac{1}{2} n e^{-\frac{b}{n}} - O(b/n) \leq \mathrm{E}[f(x^{(b)})] \leq \frac{1}{2} n e^{-\frac{b}{en}} .$$

Note that the bounds differ by a factor of $e^{\frac{b}{n}(1-1/e)}$, which tends to 1 so long as b is $o(n)$. For larger budgets, we require a more precise analysis, which will follow in subsequent sections.

PROOF OF THEOREM 5. Clearly, a mutation in which only a single 1-bit is flipped, and no 0-bit, is guaranteed to be accepted. The probability that a particular bit is flipped in this way in a given round is $\frac{1}{n}(1 - \frac{1}{n})^{n-1} \geq \frac{1}{en}$.

Let $I = \{i \in \{1, \ldots, n\} \mid x_i^{(t)} = 1\}$. Since $f(x_t) - f(x_{t+1})$ is always nonnegative,

$$\begin{aligned}
&\mathrm{E}[f(x_t) - f(x_{t+1}) \mid f(x_t)] \\
&\geq \sum_{i=1}^{n} (\mathrm{E}[f(x_t) - f(x_{t+1}) \mid f(x_t), \text{ only bit } i \text{ flipped}] \\
&\qquad \cdot \Pr[\text{only bit } i \text{ flipped}]) \\
&\geq \frac{1}{en} \sum_{i \in I} \mathrm{E}[f(x_t) - f(x_{t+1}) \mid f(x_t), \text{ only bit } i \text{ flipped}] \\
&= \frac{1}{en} \sum_{i \in I} w_i = \frac{f(x_t)}{en} .
\end{aligned}$$

so by Theorem 1,

$$\mathrm{E}[f(x_b)] \leq \mathrm{E}[f(x_0)] e^{-\frac{b}{en}} = \frac{1}{2} n e^{-\frac{b}{en}} ,$$

since $\mathrm{E}[f(x_0)] = \sum_{i=1}^{n} \frac{1}{2} w_i = \frac{1}{2} n$.

For a lower bound, we use the simple observation that a 1-bit that has not been flipped at all cannot have been optimised. Since each round is independent,

$$\Pr[x_i^{(b)} = 1] \geq \frac{1}{2} \left(1 - \frac{1}{n}\right)^b \geq \frac{1}{2} e^{-\frac{b}{n}} - O(b/n^2).$$

Applying linearity of expectation yields the theorem. □

3.2 OneMax potential and fitness

In what follows, we aim to analyse the progress of the algorithm with reference to some potential function. This approach is commonly used to bound expected optimisation time, and is central to more sophisticated drift analysis techniques. Here our chosen potential is simply the number of 1-bits in the individual, $\mathrm{OM}(x)$. The following theorem relates the expected value of the potential to the expected fitness of the individual.

LEMMA 6. *For the* $(1+1)$ *EA minimising a linear function* f *on* n *bits, and any* $b \in \mathbb{N}$,

$$\mathrm{E}[f(x^{(b)})] \leq 2 \log n \cdot \mathrm{E}[\mathrm{OM}(x^{(b)})]$$

where $\mathrm{OM}(x)$ *is the number of 1-bits in* x.

PROOF. We make use of a theorem due to Jägersküpper [9, Theorem 1], which we modify slightly here to suit the current context.

THEOREM 7 (JÄGERSKÜPPER). *Let* $x^{(b)}$ *denote the random individual obtained after* b *iterations of the* $(1+1)$ *EA operating on a linear function. Then* $\Pr[x_1^{(b)} = 1] \leq \ldots \leq \Pr[x_n^{(b)} = 1]$ *for* $b \geq 0$.

The above theorem also holds when conditioned on the value of $\mathrm{OM}(x^{(b)})$. For a given $k \in [n]$, we are interested in the quantity $\mathrm{E}[f(x^{(b)}) \mid \mathrm{OM}(x^{(b)}) = k] = \sum_{i=1}^{n} w_i p_i$, where $p_i := \Pr[x_i^{(b)} = 1 \mid \mathrm{OM}(x^{(b)}) = k]$.

By the condition on $\mathrm{OM}(x^{(b)})$, the restriction on the weights and Theorem 7, we get the following constraints:

$$w_1 \geq w_2 \ldots \geq w_n \quad \text{and} \quad \sum_{i=1}^{n} w_i = n;$$

$$p_1 \leq p_2 \ldots \leq p_n \quad \text{and} \quad \sum_{i=1}^{n} p_i = k,$$

from which we can deduce that $w_i \leq \frac{n}{i}$ and $p_i \leq \frac{k}{n-(i-1)}$. Hence

$$\begin{aligned}
\mathrm{E}[f(x^{(b)}) \mid \mathrm{OM}(x^{(b)}) = k] &= \sum_{i=1}^{n} w_i p_i \leq \sum_{i=1}^{n} \frac{kn}{i(n-i+1)} \\
&= k \sum_{i=1}^{n} \left(\frac{1}{i} + \frac{1}{n-i+1}\right) \leq 2k \log n.
\end{aligned}$$

By the law of total expectation,

$$\begin{aligned}
\mathrm{E}[f(x^{(b)})] &= \sum_{k=0}^{n} \mathrm{E}[f(x^{(b)}) \mid \mathrm{OM}(x^{(b)}) = k] \Pr[\mathrm{OM}(x^{(b)}) = k] \\
&\leq 2 \log n \sum_{k=0}^{n} k \Pr[\mathrm{OM}(x^{(b)}) = k] \\
&= 2 \log n \cdot \mathrm{E}[\mathrm{OM}(x^{(b)})].
\end{aligned}$$

□

3.3 Bounds on the OneMax potential

We are now interested in predicting the ONEMAX potential. The main contribution of this section are the following theorems, and the remainder of the section is devoted to their proofs. We start with a theorem that gives both *a priori* and *a posteriori* bounds for the starting phase. For the remainder of the section, we fix $\kappa = 1/e - (3-e) \approx 0.08616$ and $\kappa' = (3-e) - 1/(2e) \approx 0.09778$.

THEOREM 8. *Let* $x^{(t)}$ *be the individual at time* t *for the* $(1+1)$ *EA operating on a linear function, and let* $t_0 \geq 0$. *For any* $0 < x < 1$, *let* $f_1(x) = -x/e - x(e^x - 1)$ *and* $f_2(x) = -\kappa x + \kappa' x^2$. *Let* z_1 *and* z_2 *be the solutions of the differential equations* $z_1'(t) = f(z_1(t))$ *and* $z_2'(t) = f(z_2(t))$, *respectively, with starting conditions* $z_1(0) = z_2(0) = \mathrm{OM}(x^{(t_0)})/n$. *Then for every* $T = O(n \log \log n)$, *with probability* $1 - o(1)$,

$$n z_1(T/n)(1 \pm o(1)) \leq \mathrm{OM}(x^{(t+T)}) \leq n z_2(T/n)(1 \pm o(1)).$$

The function z_2 can be computed explicitly. In particular, for $t_0 = 0$ we have $\mathrm{OM}(x^{(t_0)}) = n/2(1 + o(1))$ with high probability, in which case $z_2(t) = \frac{\kappa}{(2\kappa - \kappa')e^{\kappa t} + \kappa'}(1 \pm o(1))$. Note in particular that for $t = \omega(1)$, $z_2(t) = \frac{\kappa}{2\kappa - \kappa'} e^{-\kappa t}(1 - o(1))$. The differential equation for z_1 has no elementary solution, but note that $f_1(t) = -x/e - O(x^2)$. Therefore, if $z_1(t_0) = \varepsilon$ for some $t_0 > 0$, then $z_1(t_0 + t) = \varepsilon e^{-t/e}(1 - O(\varepsilon))$.

Note that for a suitable choice of $t = O(n \log \log n)$, $\mathrm{OM}(x^{(t)}) = o(n/\log n)$. From this point onwards, we may use the following *a posteriori* bound to track the progress.

THEOREM 9. *Let* $x^{(t)}$ *be the individual at time* t *for the* $(1+1)$ *EA operating on a linear function. Let* $0 < \gamma < \rho$ *be constants, and suppose that at time* t, $\mathrm{OM}(x^{(t)}) \in o(n/\log n)$ *and* $\mathrm{OM}(x^{(t)}) \in \Omega(n^\rho)$. *Then with probability* $1 - o(1)$,

$$e^{-\beta/(en)}(1 \pm o(1)) \leq \frac{\mathrm{OM}(x^{(t+\beta)})}{\mathrm{OM}(x^{(t)})} \leq e^{-\kappa\beta/n}(1 \pm o(1))$$

where the lower bound holds for all $\beta \leq (1-\gamma) en \log n$ *and the upper bound holds for all* $\beta \leq (1-\gamma)(1/\kappa) n \log n$.

We may combine both results. Applying Theorem 9 for $t_0 = 0$ and a suitable $T = O(n \log \log n)$, and applying afterwards Theorem 8 with $t = T$, we get the following *a priori* statement.

COROLLARY 10. *Let $x^{(t)}$ be the individual at time t for the (1+1) EA operating on a linear function, and let $\gamma > 0$. Then with probability $1 - o(1)$,*

$$ne^{-\frac{T}{en}}\operatorname{poly}(\log^{-1} n) \le \mathrm{OM}(x^{(T)}) \le ne^{-\frac{\kappa T}{n}}\operatorname{poly}(\log n),$$

where the lower bound holds for all $T \le (1-\gamma)en\log n$ and the upper bound holds for all $T \le (1-\gamma)(1/\kappa)n\log n$.

The reason why the exponent in the upper and lower bound of Theorem 9 do not coincide is that for general linear functions, it may happen that in a single step we decrease (= improve) the fitness, but increase the OM-value. We call such a mutation "bad" (with some additional conditions, cf. below). Bad mutations may occur even at later points in the optimization process; e.g., after $\varepsilon n \log n$ steps there is still a large number of bits that have never been flipped, including possibly some non-optimal bits of high weight. If one of these is flipped, then with constant probability two or more low-weight bits are also flipped. If the weight distribution is strongly skewed, then such a mutation will be accepted, and these bad mutations contribute substantially to the drift. For ONEMAX, bad mutations do not occur, and we get matching upper and lower bounds: see Section 4.

The strategy for the proof of Theorems 8 and 9 is as follows. For the upper bound, we couple $X_t := \mathrm{OM}(x^{(t)})$ with a random walk Y_t that stochastically dominates X_t, cf. Lemma 12. We show that Y_t has a negative multiplicative drift whenever $Y_t \le 0.8n$. Then we show that Y_t follows with high probability the trajectory that we would expect if we only consider the drift. This part may be viewed as a multiplicative drift result with two-sided tail bounds (opposed to the general drift theorems, which give only one-sided tail bounds, e.g. [2]). To this end, we proceed in two steps: while Y_t is still close to n, we employ the differential equation method to show that with high probability Y_t follows (after appropriate scaling) the solution of the differential equation $z'(t) = f(z)$, where $f(z) = \mathrm{E}[Y_{t+1} - Y_t \mid Y_T = zn]$ is the drift of Y_t. Once Y_t is $o(n/\log n)$, we use induction and Chebyshev's inequality to show that it still follows the same trajectory with high probability. For the lower bound, we take the same approach, only that we can couple it with a different (and simpler) random walk.

We start with some useful facts about transition probabilities.

LEMMA 11. *Let $X_{i,j}$ be the event that the algorithm flips i 1-bits and j 0-bits of the current individual, and accepts the mutation. Then if $\mathrm{OM}(x^{(t)}) = \varepsilon n$,*

(i) $\Pr[X_{i,j}] \le \frac{\varepsilon^i}{i!}\cdot\frac{1}{j!}$ *for* $0 \le i \le \varepsilon n, 0 \le j \le (1-\varepsilon)n$*;*

(ii) $\Pr[X_{1,j}] \le \frac{\varepsilon}{(j+1)!}$ *for* $0 \le j \le (1-\varepsilon)n$.

PROOF. For i, j as above we have

$$\Pr[X_{i,j}] \le \binom{x}{i}\binom{n-x}{j}\left(\frac{1}{n}\right)^{i+j}\left(1-\frac{1}{n}\right)^{n-(i+j)}\cdot p_{i,j}$$
$$\le \frac{\varepsilon^i}{i!}\cdot\frac{1}{j!}\,p_{i,j}$$

using the approximation $\binom{n}{k} \le \frac{n^k}{k}$ and that $\frac{x}{n} = \varepsilon$, where $p_{i,j}$ is an upper bound on the probability that an i 1-bit, j 0-bit mutation is accepted. We obtain (i) by the trivial bound $p_{i,j} \le 1$. For (ii), we have from [9, Lemma 4] that $p_{1,j} \le 1/(j+1)$, and the bound follows. □

Let $x = x^{(t)}$ denote the current individual, and let $\varepsilon = \varepsilon^{(t)} := \mathrm{OM}(x)/n$. We call a round 'irregular' if at least two 1-bits flip, and 'regular' otherwise. Let p_j be the probability that the next round is regular, *and* that it is accepted, *and* that the number of 1-bits increases by exactly $j \ge 1$. We refer to such a mutation as 'bad'. Note that this corresponds to the event $X_{1,j+1}$ in the terminology of Lemma 11. Then we have shown

$$p_j \le \frac{\varepsilon}{(j+2)!}.$$

Moreover, let q_j be the probability that the next round is *irregular*, is accepted, and increases the number of 1-bits by exactly $j \ge 1$. Then

$$q_j = \sum_{i=2}^{\mathrm{OM}(x)} \Pr[X_{i,i+j}] \le \sum_{i=2}^{\mathrm{OM}(x)} \frac{\varepsilon^i}{i!}\frac{1}{(j+i)!} \le \frac{\varepsilon^2}{(j+2)!}.$$

Let p_1^* be the probability that in the next round exactly one bit is flipped, and this bit is a 1-bit. Then

$$p_1^* = \binom{\varepsilon n}{1}\frac{1}{n}\left(1-\frac{1}{n}\right)^{n-1} \ge \frac{\varepsilon}{e}.$$

Finally, let p_2^* be the probability that in the next round exactly *two* bits are flipped and both of them are 1-bits. Such a mutation is also guaranteed to be accepted.

$$p_2^* = \binom{\varepsilon n}{2}\frac{1}{n^2}\left(1-\frac{1}{n}\right)^{n-2} \ge \frac{\varepsilon^2}{4e}.$$

So the probability that in the next round the number of 1-bits increases by $j \ge 1$ is at most $p_j + q_j \le (1+\varepsilon)\varepsilon/(j+2)!$, while the probability that it decreases by one is at least ε/e, and by two at least $\varepsilon^2/4e$. With this in mind, and for any fixed $t_0 > 0$ we can couple $(X_t)_{t\ge t_0}$ to a random walk $(Y_t)_{t\ge t_0}$, $Y_t \in \mathbb{N}$, defined as follows. Let $Y_{t_0} := \mathrm{OM}(X_{t_0})$, and for any $t \ge t_0$, let

$$Y_{t+1} := \begin{cases} Y_t + j & \text{with prob } \left(1+\frac{Y_t}{n}\right)\frac{Y_t}{n}\frac{1}{(j+2)!} \text{ for any } j \ge 1,\\ Y_t - 1 & \text{with prob } \frac{Y_t}{en},\\ Y_t - 2 & \text{with prob } \frac{1}{4e}\left(\frac{Y_t}{n}\right)^2,\\ Y_t & \text{otherwise.}\end{cases}$$

Note that the transition of Y_t is not always well-defined since Y_t could in principle become much larger than n, and then the probabilities add up to more than 1. However, as we will see later, Y_t remains smaller than n for all $t > t_0$ with very high probability. For the sake of exposition, we ignore the case of large Y_t. We frequently make use of the following facts, easily derived from the above definition.

LEMMA 12. *Let $\Delta_t := Y_{t+1} - Y_t$, and let $\varepsilon = Y_t/n$. Then*

$$\mathrm{E}[\Delta_t] = -\kappa\varepsilon + \kappa'\varepsilon^2 \text{ and}$$
$$\mathrm{E}[\Delta_t^2] = (2e - 5 + 1/e)(\varepsilon + \varepsilon^2),$$

where $\kappa = 1/e - (3-e) \approx 0.08616$ and $\kappa' = (3-e) - 1/(2e) \approx 0.09778$. For $\varepsilon \le 0.8$, $\mathrm{E}[\Delta_t]$ is negative.

The connection between X_t and Y_t is formalised in the following lemma.

LEMMA 13. *Y_t dominates $\mathrm{OM}(x^{(t)})$ stochastically. More precisely, for all $t \geq t_0$ and all $a \in \mathbb{N}$,*

$$\Pr[\mathrm{OM}(x^{(t)}) \geq a] \leq \Pr[Y_t \geq a].$$

PROOF. We proceed by induction on t. For $t = t_0$, there is nothing to show. For the inductive step, we first observe that by our definition of Y_t, for all $a, b \in \mathbb{N}$,

$$\Pr[\mathrm{OM}(x^{(t+1)}) \geq a \,|\, \mathrm{OM}(x^{(t)}) = b] \leq \Pr[Y_{t+1} \geq a \mid Y_t = b]. \tag{1}$$

Moreover, a straightforward calculation shows that for all $a, b, c \in \mathbb{N}$, $b < c$,

$$\Pr[Y_{t+1} \geq a \mid Y_t = b] \leq \Pr[Y_{t+1} \geq a \mid Y_t = c]. \tag{2}$$

Hence for all $a, b \in \mathbb{N}$,

$$\begin{aligned}
\Pr[Y_{t+1} \geq a] &= \sum_{b \in \mathbb{N}} \Pr[Y_{t+1} \geq a \mid Y_t = b] \Pr[Y_t = b] \\
&\geq \sum_{b \in \mathbb{N}} \Pr[Y_{t+1} \geq a \mid Y_t = b] \Pr[\mathrm{OM}(x^{(t)}) = b] \\
&\overset{(1)}{\geq} \sum_{b \in \mathbb{N}} \Pr[\mathrm{OM}(x^{(t)}) \geq a \mid \mathrm{OM}(x^{(t)}) = b] \Pr[\mathrm{OM}(x^{(t)}) = b] \\
&= \Pr[\mathrm{OM}(x^{(t)}) \geq a],
\end{aligned}$$

where the first inequality can be realised as follows. Consider the sum in the first line as weighted sum where $\Pr[Y_t = b]$ are the weights. The other factors $\Pr[Y_{t+1} \geq a \mid Y_t = b]$ are monotone in b by (2). Thus by the induction hypothesis, replacing the weights $\Pr[Y_t = b]$ by $\Pr[\mathrm{OM}(x^{(t)}) = b]$ corresponds to shifting weights from larger factors to smaller factors, thus decreasing the total weighted sum. This establishes the inductive step and the lemma. □

Proof of Theorem 8 (upper bound). Due to Lemma 12 we may investigate Y_t in order to get an estimate for $\mathrm{OM}(x^{(t)})$. To analyse Y_t we begin by employing inductively the differential equation method developed by Wormald [16]. The differential equation method allows us to track the quantity Y_t/n by the solution of some differential equation. For convenience, we give a simplified version of Wormald's theorem tailored to our situation.

THEOREM 14 (THEOREM 5.1. IN [16], SIMPLIFIED). *Let $T_2 > T_1$ and $a > 0$, and let $D = [T_1, T_2] \times [0, a] \subset \mathbb{R}^2$. Assume the following three conditions hold.*

(i) (Boundedness hypothesis.) For some functions $\beta = \beta(n) \geq 1$ and $\gamma = \gamma(n)$, the probability that

$$|Y_{t+1} - Y_t| \leq \beta$$

is at least $1 - \gamma$ whenever $(t/n, Y_t) \in D$.

(ii) (Drift hypothesis.) For some function $\lambda_1 = \lambda_1(n) = o(1)$ there is a function f such that

$$|\mathrm{E}[Y_{t+1} - Y_t | Y_t = xn] - f(x)| \leq \lambda_1$$

whenever $(t/n, x) \in D$.

(iii) (Lipschitz hypothesis.) The function f satisfies a Lipschitz condition on D, i.e., there exists a constant L such that $|f(x) - f(y)| \leq L||x - y||$ for all $x, y \in D$, where $||x - y||$ is the Euclidean distance of x and y.

Then the following are true.

(a) For every $z_0 \in (0, a)$ the differential equation

$$\frac{dz}{dt} = f(z)$$

has a unique solution in D for $z : \mathbb{R} \to \mathbb{R}$ passing through $z(0) = z_0$, which extends to points arbitrarily close to the boundary of D;

(b) Let $\lambda > \lambda_1 + n\gamma$ with $\lambda = o(1)$. For some $C > 0$, with probability $1 - O(n\gamma + \frac{\beta}{\lambda}\exp(-\frac{n\lambda^3}{\beta^3}))$,

$$Y_t = nz(t/n) + o(\lambda n) \tag{3}$$

uniformly for $T_1 n \leq t \leq \min\{T_2, \sigma\}n$, where $z(t)$ is the solution in (a) *with $z_0 = \frac{1}{n}Y(T_1 n)$, and $\sigma = \sigma(n)$ is the supremum of those x for which $C\lambda \leq z(x) \leq a - C\lambda$.*

Assume that $Y_{t_0} = \varepsilon n$ for some $0 < \varepsilon \leq 0.8$. To apply Theorem 14 we choose $z_0 = \varepsilon$, $T_1 = t_0/n$, and somewhat arbitrarily $a = 2\varepsilon$ and $T_2 = T_1 + 1$. Then we choose the function f as

$$\begin{aligned}
f(x) = f_1(x) &= -\frac{x}{e} + \sum_{j \geq 1} (1 + x)\frac{xj}{(j+2)!} \\
&= -\kappa x + \kappa' x^2.
\end{aligned}$$

where κ, κ' are as in Lemma 12, matching exactly the expected change of Y_t; note that this is negative for our choice of ε. Hence, the drift hypothesis holds with error term $\lambda_1 = 0$. (For the proof of the lower bound we will use $\lambda_1 = O(1/n)$, which is fine as well). Choosing $\beta := \log n$ the boundedness hypothesis is satisfied with $\gamma = O((\log n)!^{-1})$, which approaches 0 superpolynomially fast. Finally, the Lipschitz condition is trivially true as f is continuously differentiable. Let $\delta > 0$. Since z is easily seen to be monotonically decreasing, for any $n^{-1/3+\delta} < \varepsilon \leq 1$ we may choose $\sigma = \omega(1)$, and for $\lambda = n^{-1/3+\delta}$ we get with probability superpolynomially close to 1

$$Y_t = nz(t/n) + o(n^{2/3+\delta}) \qquad \text{for all } T_1 n \leq t \leq T_2 n. \tag{4}$$

Then we use T_2 as a new starting point and iterate the process $\rho := \rho(n) := C \log\log n$ times for a suitable constant $C > 0$ to be chosen below. Thereby we prove that Equation (4) does not only hold for all $t \in [T_1 n, T_2 n]$, but actually for all $t \in [T_1 n, \rho(n)n]$, with a slightly increased error term. Since the function f satisfies a Lipschitz condition with the same Lipschitz constant for all iterations, the constant in the error term of (4) can be chosen uniform over all iterations. Moreover, due to the Lipschitz condition, changing $z(t)$ by a factor of $(1 \pm x)$ changes $z(t+1)$ by at most a factor of $(1 \pm x)^{O(1)}$. So by iterating the process ρ times, and using $(1 + x)^\rho = 1 + O(\rho x)$ for $\rho x < 1$, we get with probability superpolynomially close to 1

$$Y_{tn} = nz(t/n) \pm o(\rho n^{2/3+\delta}) \qquad \text{for all } T_1 n \leq t \leq \rho n. \tag{5}$$

To estimate the relative size of the error term, observe that $f(x) = -\kappa x + \kappa' x^2 \in \Theta(x)$ for sufficiently small x. Thus, if $z_0 = z(T_1) = 1/nY(T_1 n)$ is sufficiently small (e.g., ≤ 0.8, see Lemma 12), then there are constants $\alpha, \beta > 0$ such that the function $z(t)$ can be sandwiched by

$$e^{-\alpha(t-T_1)} z_0 \leq z(t) \leq e^{-\beta(t-T_1)} z_0. \tag{6}$$

In particular, $z(T_1 + \rho) = z(T_1 + C \log\log n)$ is lower bounded by the reciprocal of a polylogarithmic function, and is thus much larger than the error term. Altogether we have proved that $Y_{T_1+Cn\log\log n}$ is concentrated around $nz(T_1 + C\log\log n)$. This proves the upper bound in Theorem 8.

Proof of Theorem 9 (upper bound). Again by Lemma 12 we may study Y_t instead of $\mathrm{OM}(x^{(t)})$. We first show that the probability that the process takes a step decreases with time.

LEMMA 15. *For $t \in \mathbb{N}$ s.t. $Y_t/n < 0.8$, $a = o(n/\log n)$, and for sufficiently large n,*

$$\Pr[Y_{t+a} - Y_{t+(a-1)} \neq 0] \leq \Pr[Y_{t+1} - Y_t \neq 0]$$

PROOF. Let Δ_i denote $Y_{i+1} - Y_i$. From the definition of Y_t,

$$\Pr[\Delta_i \neq 0 \mid Y_i] = \frac{Y_i}{n}\left(\frac{1}{e}\left(1 + \frac{Y_i}{4en}\right) + \sum_{j=1}^{\infty}\frac{1+Y_i/n}{(j+2)!}\right)$$
$$= \frac{Y_i}{n}\left(k + k'\frac{Y_i}{n}\right)$$

for constants $k = 1/e + e - 2.5$, $k' = e - 2.5 + 1/(4e)$. Hence

$$\Pr[\Delta_{i+1} \neq 0 \mid \Delta_i = j] = \frac{Y_i + j}{n}\left(k + k'\frac{Y_i+j}{n}\right)$$
$$= \Pr[\Delta_i \neq 0]\left(1 + \frac{j}{Y_i}\right) + \frac{k'j}{n^2}(Y_i + j).$$

Denoting $\Pr[\Delta_i \neq 0]$ by p, we compute

$$\Pr[\Delta_{i+1}{\neq}0 \,|\, \Delta_i{\neq}0] = \sum_{\substack{j=-2\\ j\neq 0}}^{\infty}\frac{\Pr[\Delta_{i+1}{\neq}0\,|\,\Delta_i{=}j]\Pr[\Delta_i{=}j]}{\Pr[\Delta_i \neq 0]}$$
$$= \sum_{j\neq 0}\Pr[\Delta_i = j]\left(1 + \frac{j}{Y_i}\right) + \frac{k'Y_i}{n^2 p}\sum_{j\geq -2} j\Pr[\Delta_i = j]$$
$$+ \frac{k'}{n^2}\sum_{j\geq -2} j^2\Pr[\Delta_i = j]$$
$$= \Pr[\Delta_i \neq 0] + \left(\frac{1}{Y_i} + \frac{k'Y_i}{n^2 p}\right)\mathrm{E}[\Delta_i] + \frac{k'}{n^2 p}\mathrm{E}[\Delta_i^2]$$
$$= \Pr[\Delta_i \neq 0] + \Theta(1/Y_i)(\mathrm{E}[\Delta_i] + O(1/n)\,\mathrm{E}[\Delta_i^2])$$
$$= \Pr[\Delta_i \neq 0] - \Omega(1/n),$$

for sufficiently large n, and provided $\mathrm{E}[\Delta_i]$ is negative, which is the case if $Y_t/n \leq 0.8$. With probability $1 - O(a/(\log n)!)$, which is superpolynomially close to 1, Y_t increases within a steps by less than $a\log n = o(n)$, so

$$\Pr[\Delta_{i+1} \neq 0] \leq \Pr[\Delta_i \neq 0] - \Omega(1/n) + o(1/n) \leq \Pr[\Delta_i \neq 0].$$

Clearly, $\Pr[\Delta_{i+1} \neq 0 \mid \Delta_i = 0] = \Pr[\Delta_i \neq 0]$. Hence by the law of total probability, $\Pr[\Delta_{i+1} \neq 0] \leq \Pr[\Delta_i \neq 0]$. □

We bound the probability that Y_t changes too fast. Let $\varepsilon_t := Y_t/n$. The number of times the walk takes a step in q rounds is, by the above lemma, stochastically dominated by $Z \sim \mathcal{B}(q, k\varepsilon)$, provided $q = o(n/\log n)$. By the Chernoff bound,

$$\Pr[Z \geq (1+\delta)qk\varepsilon] \leq e^{-qk\varepsilon\delta^2/2}.$$

Assume that $q = \varepsilon_t^{-1}n^\gamma$ where $0 < \gamma < 1$ is a constant to be fixed later. Then we see that with probability $1 - O(n^{-\gamma})$, the number of steps in q rounds is bounded by n^γ. As before, the probability that such a step is larger than $\log n$ is $O((\log n)!^{-1})$, so again with probability $1 - O(n^{-\gamma})$, $|Y_t - Y_{t+q}| \leq n^\gamma \log n$. The following lemma tells us that Y_{t+q} is concentrated.

LEMMA 16. *Let $\Delta_t := Y_{t+1} - Y_t$ and $\Delta_t^{(q)} := \sum_{i=1}^{q}\Delta_{t+i}$. Then for $Y_t = o(n/\log n)$, $q := n^{1+\gamma}/Y_t$, any constant $C > 0$, and any constant $0 < \gamma < 1$ such that $n^\gamma\log^2 n = o(Y_t)$, with probability at least $1 - O(n^{-\gamma}\log^4 n)$,*

$$\Delta_t^{(q)} = -n^\gamma\left(\kappa \pm o\left(\frac{1}{\log n}\right)\right).$$

PROOF. Let $\varepsilon_t := Y_t/n$. By Lemma 12 we can bound the variance of Δ_t by

$$\mathrm{Var}[\Delta_t] \leq \mathrm{E}[\Delta_t^2] = (2e - 5 + 1/e)(\varepsilon_t + \varepsilon_t^2) \leq D\varepsilon_t$$

for some constant D.

With probability $1 - O(n^{-\gamma})$, $|Y_t - Y_{t+q}| \leq n^\gamma\log n$ for $q = \varepsilon_t^{-1}n^\gamma$. Hence, when $n^\gamma\log^2 n = o(Y_t)$, by Lemma 12,

$$\mathrm{E}[\Delta_t^{(q)}] = -q\kappa(\varepsilon_t \pm n^{\gamma-1}\log n)(1 - O(\varepsilon_t))$$
$$= \kappa n^\gamma\left(1 \pm o\left(\frac{1}{\log n}\right)\right), \text{ and}$$
$$\mathrm{Var}[\Delta_t^{(q)}] \leq Dq(\varepsilon_t + n^{\gamma-1}\log n) = Dn^\gamma(1 + o(1)).$$

Now Chebyshev's inequality gives

$$\Pr\left[\left|\Delta_t^{(q)} - \mathrm{E}[\Delta_t^{(q)}]\right| \geq \frac{n^\gamma}{\log^2 n}\right] \leq \frac{Dn^\gamma\log^4 n}{n^{2\gamma}} + O(n^{-\gamma}),$$

which is $O(n^{-\gamma}\log^4 n)$. Therefore, with probability $1 - O(n^{-\gamma}\log^4 n)$,

$$\Delta_t^{(q)} = -\kappa n^\gamma\left(1 \pm o\left(\frac{1}{\log n}\right)\right) \pm \frac{n^\gamma}{\log^2 n},$$

which implies the lemma. □

We are now ready to conclude the proof of Theorem 9 by applying Lemma 16 inductively for several values of t. Let $q_{\tau+1} = n^{1+\gamma}/Y_{t+Q(\tau)}$, where $Q(\tau) = \sum_{i=1}^{\tau} q_i$. Then a simple induction shows that under the assumptions of Lemma 16, with probability $1 - O(\tau n^{-\gamma}\log^4 n)$,

$$\sum_{i=1}^{\tau}\Delta_t^{(q)} = \tau n^\gamma(\kappa \pm o(1/\log n)). \tag{7}$$

In particular, for $\alpha := Y_t/(n^\gamma\log^2 n)$ we have $\sum_{i=1}^{\tau}\Delta_t^{(q)} = O(Y_t/\log^2 n)$. Therefore, Equation (7) implies that with probability at least $1 - O(Y_t n^{-2\gamma}\log^2 n)$,

$$Y_{t+Q(\alpha)} = Y_t\left(1 - \frac{\kappa \pm o(1/\log n)}{\log^2 n}\right), \tag{8}$$

and that moreover $Y_{t+Q(\tau)} = Y_t(1 \pm O(1/\log^2 n))$ for all $1 \leq \tau \leq \alpha$. Therefore, using $1/(1-x) = 1 + O(x)$ for $x \to 0$, with probability at least $1 - O(Y_t n^{-2\gamma}\log^2 n)$,

$$Q(\alpha) = \sum_{i=1}^{\alpha}\frac{n^{1+\gamma}}{Y_t(1 - in^\gamma\kappa/Y_t \cdot (\kappa \pm o(1/\log n))}$$
$$= \frac{\alpha n^{1+\gamma}}{Y_t}\left(1 + O\left(\frac{n^\gamma}{\alpha Y_t}\sum_{i=1}^{\alpha} i\right)\right)$$
$$= \frac{n}{\log^2 n}\left(1 \pm O\left(\frac{1}{\log^2 n}\right)\right). \tag{9}$$

Recall that we get (8) and (9) only if $Y_t = \omega(n^\gamma \log^2 n)$, since otherwise we cannot apply Lemma 16. On the other hand, these equations hold with high probability if $Y_t = o(n^{2\gamma}/\log^2 n)$. We can find a γ that satisfies both conditions if $Y_t = \Omega(n^\rho)$ for some constant $0 < \rho \le 1$, and in this case (8) and (9) hold with probability $1 - o(1/\log^3 n)$.

We want to advance from Y_t to $Y_{t+\beta}$, where $\beta = O(n \log n)$ and $Y_{t+\beta} = \Omega(n^\rho)$ for some constant $0 < \rho \le 1$. In this case, we may apply (8) and (9) at most $O(\log^3 n)$ times. More precisely, we may write $t+\beta = t + Q(\alpha)\beta \log^2 n/n(1 \pm O(1/\log^2 n))$. Thus, using $1 - x = e^{-x-O(x^2)}$ for $x = o(1)$, we get for all $\beta \in O(n \log n)$,

$$\begin{aligned} Y_{t+\beta n} &= Y_t \left(1 - \frac{\kappa \pm o(1/\log n)}{\log^2 n}\right)^{(1 \pm O(1/\log^2 n))\beta \log^2 n/n} \\ &= Y_t e^{-\kappa\beta/n}(1 \pm o(1)) \end{aligned} \quad (10)$$

with probability $1 - o(1)$. Together with Lemma 13, this proves the upper bound in Theorem 9. The condition on β in Theorem 9 stems from the fact that we need $Y_{t+\beta}$ to be at least $\Omega(n^\rho)$ for some constant $0 < \rho \le 1$.

Proof of the Lower Bounds. To give a lower bound we consider the process Y'_t, defined by:

$$Y'_{t+1} := \begin{cases} Y'_t - j & \text{with prob } \left(\frac{Y'_t}{n}\right)^j/(j!) \text{ for any } j \ge 2, \\ Y'_t - 1 & \text{with prob } \frac{Y'_t}{en}(1 + 1/n), \\ Y'_t & \text{otherwise.} \end{cases}$$

The process Y'_t stochastically dominates the (1 + 1) *EA* process X_t, by a similar argument to Lemma 13. Note in particular that the probability that we flip i one-bits in a single step is by Lemma 11 (i) at most $(X_t/n)^i/(i!)$. We assume that if this occurs, for $i \le 2$, the number of one bits reduces by exactly i (it may be less). In the case of $i = 1$, note that for such a mutation to have a *negative* effect on X_t, no other bit may flip, which occurs with probability $(1 - 1/n)^{n-1} \le 1/e(1 + 1/n)$.

LEMMA 17. *Let* $\Delta'_t := Y'_{t+1} - Y'_t$, *and let* $\varepsilon = Y'_t/n$. *Then*

$$\mathrm{E}[\Delta'_t] = -\varepsilon/e - \varepsilon(e^\varepsilon - 1) - \varepsilon/(en) = -\varepsilon/e - O(\varepsilon^2) \text{ and}$$
$$\mathrm{E}[\Delta'^2_t] = -\varepsilon/e - O(\varepsilon^2).$$

The above results are analogous to Lemma 12, only with $1/e$ in place of κ. From there on, the rest of the proof follows exactly the lines for the upper bounds, except that we apply the differential equation method with error term $\lambda_1 = O(1/n)$ instead of $\lambda_1 = 0$; see the comment there. This concludes the proof of Theorems 8 and 9.

We could use the a priori result on the ONEMAX potential in conjunction with Lemma 6 to give an upper bound on $\mathrm{E}[f(x^{(b)})]$, but the bound that results is actually weaker than the bound obtained in Theorem 5. This suggests that the ONEMAX potential does not quite capture the behaviour of general linear functions. In particular, throughout the process, 'bad' mutations can occur with non-negligible probability, meaning that for a general linear function we cannot bound the drift any more strongly than $-\kappa\varepsilon + O(\varepsilon^2)$ with this method.

4. ONEMAX

The above analysis clearly applies to ONEMAX; indeed in this case the potential function is identical to the fitness. We can make an even stronger statement about ONEMAX, however, since the process by definition is not subject to 'bad' mutations, which means that we may use $1/e$ instead of κ for the upper bound. In this way, upper and lower bound match tightly. Analogously to Theorem 9, we thus obtain the following *a posteriori* result.

THEOREM 18. *Let* $x^{(t)}$ *be the individual at time* t *for the* (1 + 1) *EA operating on* ONEMAX. *Let* $0 < \gamma < \rho$ *be constants, and suppose that at time* t, $\mathrm{OM}(x^{(t)}) \in o(n/\log n)$ *and* $\mathrm{OM}(x^{(t)}) \in \Omega(n^\rho)$. *Then with probability* $1 - o(1)$,

$$\mathrm{OM}(x^{(t+\beta)}) = \mathrm{OM}(x^{(t)})e^{-\beta/(en)}(1 \pm o(1))$$

for $\beta \le (\rho - \gamma)en \log(n)$.

We can also formulate the analogue of Theorem 9. A Chernoff bound applied to the random initialisation shows that with high probability $\mathrm{OM}(x^{(0)}) = (1/2 + o(1))n$. Thus we obtain the following *a priori* result.

THEOREM 19. *Let* $x^{(t)}$ *be the individual at time* t *for the* (1 + 1) *EA operating on* ONEMAX, *and let* $t_0 \ge 0, t_0 = O(n \log\log n)$. *For any* $0 < x < 1$, *let* $f(x) = \mathrm{E}[\mathrm{OM}(x^{(t+1)}) - \mathrm{OM}(x^{(t)}) \mid \mathrm{OM}(x^{(t)}) = xn]$ *be the drift at point* xn, *and let* z *be the solution of the differential equation* $z'(t) = f(z(t))$ *with starting condition* $z(0) = \mathrm{OM}(x^{(t_0)})/n$ *(or* $z(0) = 1/2$ *if* $t_0 = 0$*). Then for every* $0 < T = O(n \log\log n)$, *with probability* $1 - o(1)$,

$$\mathrm{OM}(x^{(t_0+T)}) = nz(T/n).$$

In principle, Theorem 19 is tight; however, the statement is rather implicit. In order to turn it into a more explicit statement, it would be necessary to estimate the drift $\mathrm{E}[X_{t+1} - X_t \mid X_t = xn]$ precisely. While x is still large, this is rather difficult, although more and more accurate estimates for the drift (e.g., polynomials in x to which we add more and more terms) may be used to get arbitrarily good estimates for z. However, for small x note that $f(x) = -x/e \pm O(x^2)$. Therefore, if $z(t_0) = \varepsilon$ for some $0 < t_0 = O(n \log\log n)$, then $z(t_0 + T) = \varepsilon e^{-T/e}(1 \pm O(\varepsilon))$ for $T = O(n \log\log n)$. Combining this with Theorem 18, we obtain that in this case for every $\delta > 0$ with probability at least $1 - o(1)$,

$$\mathrm{OM}(x^{(t+\beta)}) = \mathrm{OM}(x^{(t)})e^{-\beta/(en)}(1 \pm O(\varepsilon) \pm o(1))$$

for $\beta \le (1 - \delta)en \log(n)$.

5. NUMERICAL COMPARISON

In Figure 1, we show upper and lower bounds for the ONEMAX potential for general linear functions (upper left), and for the fitness for ONEMAX itself. While for the linear functions the gap between upper and lower bounds grows rather quickly, for ONEMAX we obtain numerically small gaps. In the latter case, we bound the drift by more and more precise polynomial expressions: for the first plot, we consider only the contribution of the event that exactly one 1-bit is flipped and the search point is accepted, giving a value of $x^{(t)}/(en)$ (this is correct up to an $O(1/n)$ error term, which we may ignore due to Theorem 14). Then we bound the contribution of other events to the drift below by 0, and above by assuming that every time i 1-bits are flipped, $i \ge 1$, then the fitness decreases by i. This contributes at most $\frac{x^{(t)}}{en}(e^{x^{(t)}/n} - 1)$ to

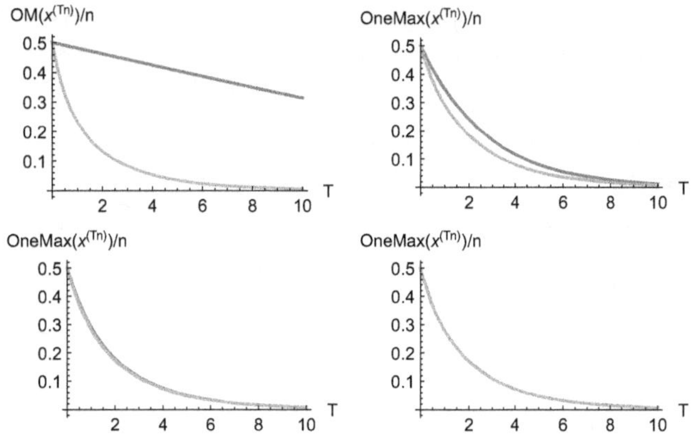

Figure 1: Upper bounds (blue) and lower bounds (purple) for the evolution of the OneMax potential for linear functions (upper left) and for OneMax (other panels). For OneMax, we compute exactly the contribution of the drift for events in which at most one (upper right), at most two (lower left), or at most three (lower right) 1-bits are flipped. The x-axis represents scaled time $T := t/n$, and the y-axis the scaled OneMax potential $\mathrm{OM}(x^{(Tn)})/n$.

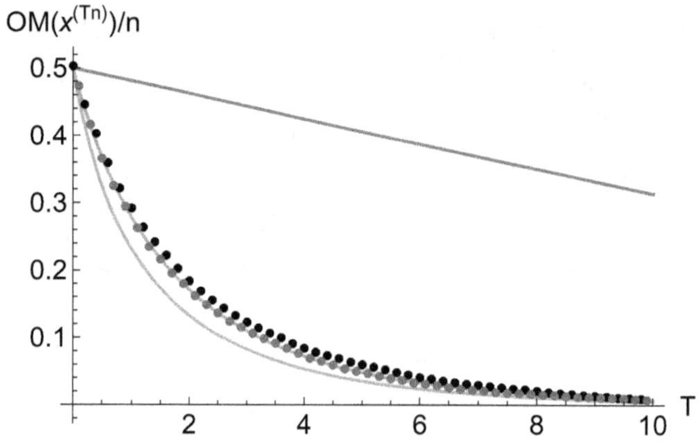

Figure 2: Experimental results ($n = 400$, average of 30 trials) for the trajectory of the OneMax potentials of OneMax (green points) and BinVal (black points), and upper (blue) and lower (orange) bounds. The green curve is the third-order upper/lower bound (visually indistinguishable) for OneMax, as in Figure 1. The x-axis represents scaled time $T := t/n$, and the y-axis the scaled OneMax potential $\mathrm{OM}(x^{(Tn)})/n$.

the drift. For the second (third) plot, we refine the bounds by computing exactly the contribution to the drift of events when at most two (at most three) 1-bits are flipped, obtaining similar formulas. We define the maximal relative error to be the difference of the upper and lower bounds, divided by the lower bound. Then the maximal relative error after $10n$ steps is 0.54, 0.034, and 0.0031 for the first, second, and third refinement, respectively, while the absolute OneMax value after $10n$ steps is $0.00718n$.

The experimental results (Figure 2) show clearly that the real ONEMAX potentials of ONEMAX and BINVAL ($w_i = 2^i$) follow the lower bound much more closely. Indeed, the two values remain very close together, and both show small variance. The experiment also corroborates the precise bounds obtained by considering third-order terms of the drift (i.e. rounds with at most three 1-bit flips). In the figure we see a small deviation from the theoretical trajectory, which is an effect hidden by the asymptotic analysis: the deviation becomes smaller with increasing n.

6. CONCLUSIONS

We have described in detail the progress of the $(1+1)$ EA operating on linear functions with respect to the ONEMAX potential, and given *a priori* and *a posteriori* bounds. We find that in expectation, the true fitness is bounded by the ONEMAX potential multiplied by a logarithmic factor. Our analysis of the potential does not provide a tighter bound on this expectation than a drift argument does; this would require a more precise account of 'bad' mutations. Nonetheless, the explicit analysis of the evolution of the process is of independent interest, and is moreover able to provide tail bounds which are presently not supplied by fixed-budget drift methods. For ONEMAX as a special case we give asymptotically precise results, along with an *a priori* upper bound.

Besides a detailed investigation of 'bad' mutations, it may also be fruitful to consider potential functions which follow the fitness value more closely but are still simple enough to analyse, such as those used in [6, 7]; we suppose that a relationship analogous to Lemma 6 holds for such potential functions also. A lower-bound version of Lemma 6, or even a result showing that ONEMAX is 'easiest' in a fixed-budget sense, would also be very enlightening.

For ONEMAX, a promising alternative approach may have been opened up by the new methods developed in [8]. Since the authors derive upper and lower tail bounds for the optimization time of the $(1+1)$ EA on ONEMAX, it seems feasible to obtain similar bounds for T_a^{OM}. From such tail bounds, fixed budget results can easily be derived [4]. In particular, it seems reasonable to believe that the *a priori* bound

$$\mathrm{OM}(x^{(\beta)}) = ne^{-(\beta - c_1 n)/(en) - \gamma}(1 \pm o(1))$$

holds for all $\beta = \omega(n), \beta \leq (1-\varepsilon)en\log n$, where $c_1 = 1.89...$ is the constant given in [8] and $\gamma = 0.577...$ is the Euler-Mascheroni constant. Since the drift of the $(1+1)$ EA operating on linear functions is multiplicative, upper tail bounds can also be obtained by classical drift analysis [2], but we are unaware of any lower-tail results for multiplicative drift.

Acknowledgements

This work was supported by an ETH Excellence Scholarship (NS).

7. REFERENCES

[1] B. Doerr, M. Fouz, and C. Witt. Sharp bounds by probability-generating functions and variable drift. In *Proc. of the 13th Annual Genetic and Evolutionary Computation Conference (GECCO'11)*, pages 2083–2090, 2011.

[2] B. Doerr and L. A. Goldberg. Adaptive Drift Analysis. *Algorithmica*, 65(1):224–250, Oct. 2011.

[3] B. Doerr, T. Jansen, D. Sudholt, C. Winzen, and C. Zarges. Mutation rate matters even when optimizing monotonic functions. *Evolutionary computation*, 21(1):1–27, 2013.

[4] B. Doerr, T. Jansen, C. Witt, and C. Zarges. A method to derive fixed budget results from expected optimisation times. In *Proc. of the 15th Annual Genetic and Evolutionary Computation Conference (GECCO'13)*, pages 1581–1588, 2013.

[5] B. Doerr, D. Johannsen, and C. Winzen. Multiplicative drift analysis. In *Proc. of the 12th Annual Genetic and Evolutionary Computation Conference (GECCO'10)*, pages 1449–1456, 2010.

[6] B. Doerr, D. Johannsen, and C. Winzen. Multiplicative drift analysis. *Algorithmica*, 64:673–697, 2012.

[7] S. Droste, T. Jansen, and I. Wegener. On the analysis of the (1+1) evolutionary algorithm. *Theoretical Computer Science*, 276:51–81, 2002.

[8] H.-K. Hwang, A. Panholzer, N. Rolin, T.-H. Tsai, and W.-M. Chen. Probabilistic analysis of the (1+1)-evolutionary algorithm. *ArXiv e-prints*, Sept. 2014.

[9] J. Jägersküpper. A blend of Markov-chain and drift analysis. In *Proc. of the 10th International Conference on Parallel Problem Solving from Nature (PPSN'08)*, LNCS 5199, pages 41–51. Springer, 2008.

[10] T. Jansen and C. Zarges. Fixed budget computations: A different perspective on run time analysis. In *Proc. of the 14th Annual Genetic and Evolutionary Computation Conference (GECCO'12)*, page 1325–1332, 2012.

[11] T. Jansen and C. Zarges. Performance analysis of randomised search heuristics operating with a fixed budget. *Theoretical Computer Science*, 2013.

[12] G. Lawler. *Introduction to Stochastic Processes, Second Edition.* Chapman & Hall/CRC Probability Series. Taylor & Francis, 2006.

[13] P. K. Lehre and C. Witt. General drift analysis with tail bounds. *CoRR*, abs/1307.2559, 2013. Available online at http://arxiv.org/abs/1307.2559.

[14] D. Sudholt. General lower bounds for the running time of evolutionary algorithms. In *Parallel Problem Solving from Nature (PPSN XI)*, volume 6238 of *Lecture Notes in Computer Science*, pages 124–133. Springer Berlin Heidelberg, 2010.

[15] C. Witt. Tight bounds on the optimization time of a randomized search heuristic on linear functions. *Combinatorics, Probability & Computing*, 22:294–318, 2013.

[16] N. C. Wormald. The differential equation method for random graph processes and greedy algorithms. *Lectures on approximation and randomized algorithms*, pages 73–155, 1999.

Efficient Optimisation of Noisy Fitness Functions with Population-based Evolutionary Algorithms

Duc-Cuong Dang
ASAP Research Group
School of Computer Science
University of Nottingham
duc-cuong.dang@nottingham.ac.uk

Per Kristian Lehre
ASAP Research Group
School of Computer Science
University of Nottingham
perkristian.lehre@nottingham.ac.uk

ABSTRACT

Population-based EAs can optimise pseudo-Boolean functions in expected polynomial time, even when only partial information about the problem is available [7]. In this paper, we show that the approach used to analyse optimisation with partial information extends naturally to optimisation under noise. We consider pseudo-Boolean problems with an additive noise term. Very general conditions on the noise term is derived, under which the EA optimises the noisy function in expected polynomial time. In the case of the OneMax and LeadingOnes problems, efficient optimisation is even possible when the variance of the noise distribution grows quickly with the problem size.

Categories and Subject Descriptors

F.2 [**Theory of Computation**]: Analysis of Algorithms and Problem Complexity

General Terms

Theory, Algorithms, Complexity

Keywords

Noisy optimisation, Runtime Analysis, Non-elitism

1. INTRODUCTION

Rigorous analyses of Evolutionary Algorithms (EA) over the past decade often concerned simple settings of EAs or Randomised Search Heuristics (RSH), such as the (1+1) EA or RLS (Randomised Local Search), on standard functions. These studies laid the foundations for the technical and methodological development of runtime analysis of EAs [12]. In this paper, we focus on the efficiency of population-based EAs in optimising noisy fitness functions.

Engineering and other application domains have to deal with large amounts of noisy and inaccurate data. Consequently, in real-world optimisation, accurate information about the quality of candidate solutions is rarely available, or expensive to obtain. It has been observed that zero-knowledge or derivative-free optimisation methods, such as Evolutionary Algorithms (EA) or Evolution Strategies (ES), are highly robust to noise or uncertainty, which make them favoured in practical applications [13]. However, most studies of EAs in noisy environments are experimental. There are fewer theoretical studies, especially in discrete optimisation. This in contrast with research in continuous optimisation, where there are several theoretical studies of the convergence rate of ES in noisy optimisation [4].

In discrete optimisation under uncertainty, the inefficiency of the (1+1) EA has been rigorously demonstrated for noisy and dynamic optimisation [9, 10] on the OneMax. Recently, the same negative behaviour of exponential expected runtime has been shown for the (1+1) EA in the positive additive noise model [11], and in an optimisation model under incomplete information [7]. We will discuss the relationship between the two models in the next section. The (1+1) EA is often inefficient in such environments because it too often makes the wrong decision by not choosing the truly better candidate solution, and hence moves away from the target. Therefore, modifications to the simple setting of the single-solution approach of the (1+1) EA are required.

A straight-forward modification to overcome the presence of noise is to reduce the noise magnitude by re-evaluating each solution many times and averaging the observed fitness values [5]. The number of re-evaluations needed for the (1+1) EA to behave as in a noise-free environment was quantified in [2, 3]. The result presented in [3] is very general and not restricted to any specific objective function. Another modification is to extend the population size of the algorithm from 1 to μ. It has been shown in [11] that polynomial runtime is guaranteed for (μ+1) EA in optimising OneMax and LeadingOnes under various noise models. The key feature is to have the population size μ sufficiently large.

Noisy optimisation has been rigorously investigated both for single-individual based EAs and population-based EAs. However, those studies were limited to elitist populations and the polynomial expected runtime only holds for noise models with constant variance. In this paper, we show that a similar result also holds for non-elitist populations. Furthermore, in our result the variance of the noise is allowed to grow polynomially in the problem size. Our analysis is based on the approach of [7] developed for models of incomplete information. The approach makes use of a recent fitness-level theorem for non-elitist populations [8]. The result is re-

FOGA'15, January 17–20, 2015, Aberystwyth, UK.
Copyright © 2015 ACM 978-1-4503-3434-1/15/01 ...$15.00.
http://dx.doi.org/10.1145/2725494.2725508.

ported for standard functions OneMax, LeadingOnes and for standard noise distributions such as uniform, Gaussian, and exponential distributions.

The remainder of the paper is organised as follows. The next section introduces notation and the basics of runtime analysis for non-elitist populations. Section 3 generalises the result of [7] to predict the runtime of non-elitist EAs on OneMax and LeadingOnes under general circumstances. A minimalist instance of the non-elitist EAs and an illustrative result for the noise model of [9] are presented in Section 4. The section that follows discusses the additive noise model, we show that polynomial runtime also holds for standard noise distribution with high variances. Finally, some conclusions are drawn and future work is discussed.

2. PRELIMINARIES

For any positive integer n, define $[n] := \{1, 2, \ldots, n\}$. The Hamming-distance is denoted by $H(\cdot,\cdot)$. The natural logarithm is denoted by $\ln(\cdot)$, and the logarithm to the base 2 is denoted by $\log(\cdot)$. For a bitstring x of length n, define $|x|_1 := \sum_{i=1}^{n} x_i$.

We consider the optimisation of a function $f : \mathcal{X} \to \mathbb{R}$ in which each evaluation of a solution returns a random value $F(x)$ instead of $f(x)$. The stochastic function F in this case is the noisy version of f. We will use two classical functions on $\{0,1\}^n$ as example for f: $\text{OneMax}(x) := |x|_1$ and $\text{LeadingOnes}(x) := \sum_{j\in[n]}\prod_{i\in[j]} x_i$. We consider the additive noise model defined as follows.

Definition 1. *Let $f : \{0,1\}^n \to \mathbb{R}$ be any function. In the additive noise model with noise distribution D, an evaluation of f on $x \in \{0,1\}^n$ returns $F(x) := f(x)+X$, where X is a random variable sampled independently from the noise distribution D.*

In the additive noise model, a new noise value X is sampled every time $F(x)$ is evaluated. Results can also be obtained straightforwardly for the so-called "prior" noise model of [10] on the Boolean hypercube $\{0,1\}^n$.

Definition 2. *Let $f : \{0,1\}^n \to \mathbb{R}$ be any function. In the prior noise model with a parameter $c \in (0,1)$, an evaluation of f on $x \in \{0,1\}^n$ returns*

$$F(x) = \begin{cases} f(x) & \text{with probability } c, \text{ and} \\ f(x') & \text{with probability } 1-c \end{cases}$$

$$\text{where } x' \sim \text{Unif}\left(\{y \mid H(x,y) = 1\}\right)$$

The term *prior* in this particular noise model was only introduced later in [11] to indicate the origin of noise. In the model, noise was introduced to the genotypic structure of the solution before the actual evaluation. Note that the model of *partial evaluation* [7] is related to the prior noise model, e.g. one can consider that noise has been introduced at a phenotypic level causing selection mechanism to only make use of a random subset of the features of a solution. With regards to runtime, we are only concerned with the time to discover a true optimal solution.

Definition 3. *The runtime $T(A, f, D)$ of an algorithm A on a problem $f : \{0,1\}^n \to \mathbb{R}$ with noise distribution D, is the number of times algorithm A queries $F(x) = f(x)+X$ with $X \sim D$ before algorithm A queries an optimal search point x^* w.r.t. f.*

Algorithm 1 Population Selection-Variation Algorithm

Require: Finite search space $\mathcal{X}$,
  and initial population $P_0 \sim \text{Unif}(\mathcal{X}^\lambda)$.

for $t = 0, 1, 2, \ldots$ until termination condition met **do**
  for $i = 1$ to λ **do**
    Sample $I_t(i) \in [\lambda]$ according to $p_{\text{sel}}(P_t)$.
    $x := P_t(I_t(i))$.
    Sample x' according to $p_{\text{mut}}(x)$.
    $P_{t+1}(i) := x'$.
  end for
end for

The population-based algorithm analysed in this paper belongs to the scheme of Algorithm 1. In each step t, the scheme generates a new population P_{t+1} based on the current one P_t. Each individual of P_{t+1} is generated independently by picking one parent from P_t using a selection mechanism, denoted by p_{sel}, then by mutating it using a variation operator, denoted by p_{mut}. Formally, the operators are represented by transition matrices: $p_{\text{sel}} : [\lambda] \to [0,1]$, where $p_{\text{sel}}(i \mid P)$ is the probability of selecting the i-th individual from population P; $p_{\text{mut}} : \mathcal{X} \times \mathcal{X} \to [0,1]$, where $p_{\text{mut}}(y|x)$ is the probability of mutating $x \in \mathcal{X}$ into $y \in \mathcal{X}$. For notational convenience, we let $p_{\text{mut}}(x)$ denote the distribution over $\mathcal{X}$ induced by applying the variation operator p_{mut} to search point $x \in \mathcal{X}$.

The scheme is non-elitist because of the non-overlapping populations. It is reasonable to assume that solutions with higher objective values have a better chance of being selected by p_{sel}. A selection mechanism satisfying this property is called *f-monotone.*

Definition 4 ([14]). *Let $p_{\text{sel}}(i \mid P)$ be the probability that a selection mechanism p_{sel} selects the i-th individual in population P. Then p_{sel} is called* f-monotone *if for all $P \in \mathcal{X}^\lambda$ and pairs $i, j \in [\lambda]$ it holds that,*

$$p_{\text{sel}}(i \mid P) \geq p_{\text{sel}}(j \mid P) \iff f(P(i)) \geq f(P(j)).$$

The *cumulative selection probability* of p_{sel} is the probability of selecting an individual with fitness at least as good as that of the γ-ranked individual in the population. Formally,

Definition 5 ([14]). *The* cumulative selection probability *function $\beta : (0,1] \times \mathcal{X}^\lambda \to [0,1]$ associated with a selection mechanism p_{sel} and fitness function $f : \mathcal{X} \to \mathbb{R}$ is defined for all $\gamma \in (0,1]$ and $P \in \mathcal{X}^\lambda$ by*

$$\beta(\gamma, P) := \sum_{i\in[\lambda]} p_{\text{sel}}(i \mid P) \cdot [f(P(i)) \geq f(P(I(\lceil\gamma\lambda\rceil)))],$$

where $I(\lceil\gamma\lambda\rceil)$ is the individual with rank $\lceil\gamma\lambda\rceil$ according to fitness function f in population P.

Often, it is possible to obtain a lower bound for $\beta(\gamma, P)$ that is independent of P. In these cases, we write $\beta(\gamma)$ instead of $\beta(\gamma, P)$. Rigorous runtime analysis of Algorithm 1 was initiated with the work of [14, 15, 16]. In short, the algorithm has exponential expected runtime when the selective pressure is low relative to the mutation rate [14, 16]. Conversely, when the cumulative selection probability is sufficiently high, it is possible to derive upper bounds on the expected runtime using a fitness-level technique [15].

Recently, a further improvement which provides tighter upper bounds than [15] was presented in [8]. It was shown in [6] that the approach can be generalised to algorithms beyond the scheme of Algorithm 1, e.g. to include crossover operators. In the next sections, we will show that the argument of [7] is indeed very general and can be applied to prove polynomial runtime for non-elitist populations in optimising noisy functions.

3. GENERAL CONDITION

The following theorem summarises Theorem 4 and its corollaries (5 and 6) of [7]. Note that Theorem 4 is also Theorem 8 in [8].

THEOREM 6 ([7]). *Given a function $f : \mathcal{X} \to \mathbb{R}$, and a fitness-based partition $(A_1, \ldots, A_{m+1})$ of $\mathcal{X}$, let T be the number of function evaluations until Algorithm 1 with an f-monotone selection mechanism p_{sel} obtains an element in A_{m+1} for the first time. If there exist parameters $s_1, \ldots, s_m$, s_*, $p_0 \in (0,1]$, δ with $1/\delta \in \text{poly}(m)$ and a constant $\gamma_0 \in (0,1)$ such that*

(C1) $p_{\text{mut}}\left(y \in A_j^+ \mid x \in A_j\right) \geq s_j \geq s_*$ *for all* $j \in [m]$
(C2) $p_{\text{mut}}\left(y \in A_j \cup A_j^+ \mid x \in A_j\right) \geq p_0$ *for all* $j \in [m]$
(C3) $\beta(\gamma, P)p_0 \geq (1+\delta)\gamma$ *for all* $P \in \mathcal{X}^\lambda$ *and* $\gamma \in (0, \gamma_0)$

then there exists a constant b such that any instance of the algorithm with $\lambda \geq (b/\delta^2)\ln m$ has,

$$\mathbf{E}[T] \leq \frac{1536}{\delta^5}\left(m\lambda\left(1 + \ln\left(1 + \frac{\delta^4\lambda}{384}\right)\right) + \frac{1}{\gamma_0}\sum_{j=1}^{m}\frac{1}{s_j}\right)$$

Similar to the standard fitness-level technique [18], the theorem assumes a fitness-based partition $(A_1, \ldots, A_{m+1})$, i.e. $\cup_{j\in[m+1]} = \mathcal{X}$, $A_i \cap A_j = \emptyset$ for $i \neq j$ and if $i > j$ then $f(x) \geq f(y)$ for all $x \in A_i$ and $y \in A_j$, then lower bounds on the probabilities of leaving each level to a better one in condition (C1). Here A_j^+ is a short notation for $\cup_{k>j} A_k$. Condition (C2) implies a certain lower bound p_0 on the probability for p_{mut} to not downgrade an input solution to a lower fitness-level. In the case of $\mathcal{X} = \{0,1\}^n$ and the bitwise mutation operator with mutation rate $\chi/n \in (0,1)$, one can choose $p_0 = (1 - \chi/n)^n$, i.e. the probability of not flipping any bits. Condition (C3) requires a certain selective pressure induced by p_{sel} which depends on p_0. When all the conditions are satisfied, the expected runtime can be computed for algorithms with sufficiently large populations.

Most of the results of [7] were proved using Theorem 6. The observation is that we will deal with some $\delta < 1$, hence conditions (C2) and (C3) can be simplified with the right choice for χ. We have the following general result for OneMax and LeadingOnes.

THEOREM 7. *Consider any $\delta < 1$ where $1/\delta \in \text{poly}(n)$. If Algorithm 1 uses bitwise mutation with mutation rate $\chi/n = \delta/(3n)$ and any f-monotone selection mechanism p_{sel} satisfying $\beta(\gamma) \geq (1+2\delta)\gamma$ for all $\gamma \in (0, \gamma_0]$, then there exists a constant b such that the algorithm with population size $\lambda = b\ln(n)/\delta^2$ optimises* OneMax *in expected time*

$$O\left(\frac{n\ln(n)\ln(\ln(n))}{\delta^7}\right).$$

and optimises LeadingOnes *in expected time*

$$O\left(\frac{n\ln(n)}{\delta^7} + \frac{n^2}{\delta^6}\right).$$

PROOF. For both functions, we use the canonical fitness-based partition $A_j := \{x \in \{0,1\}^n \mid f(x) = j\}$. For OneMax, the probability of improving a solution at fitness level j is lower bounded by the probability of flipping a single 0-bit and not flipping the other bits,

$$(n-j)\left(\frac{\chi}{n}\right)\left(1 - \frac{\chi}{n}\right)^{n-1} > \left(1 - \frac{j}{n}\right)\chi(1-\chi)$$

The inequality is due to $1 - \chi/n < 1$ and Theorem 15, i.e. $(1-\chi/n)^n > 1 - \chi$. In addition, because $\chi = \delta/3$ with $\delta < 1$, we have $\chi(1-\chi) > (\delta/3)(1-1/3) = 2\delta/9$. Therefore condition (C1) of Theorem 6 is satisfied for $s_j := (1-j/n)(\delta/9)$ and $s_* = \delta/(9n)$. Condition (C2) is satisfied with $p_0 := 1-\chi < (1-\chi/n)^n$, the probability of not flipping any bit and again using Theorem 15. It follows from the given condition $\beta(\gamma) \geq (1+2\delta)\gamma$ that

$$\begin{aligned}\beta(\gamma)p_0 &\geq \gamma(1+2\delta)(1-\chi) = \gamma(1+2\delta)(1-\delta/3)\\ &= \gamma(1 - \delta/3 + 2\delta - 2\delta^2/3) \geq \gamma(1 - \delta/3 + 2\delta - 2\delta/3)\\ &= \gamma(1+\delta)\end{aligned}$$

Therefore, condition (C3) is satisfied. The expected optimisation time according to Theorem 6 is,

$$\begin{aligned}\mathbf{E}[T] &= O\left(\frac{1}{\delta^5}\left(m\lambda(1+\ln(1+\delta^4\lambda)) + \sum_{j=1}^{m}\frac{1}{s_j}\right)\right)\\ &= O\left(\left(\frac{n\ln(n)}{\delta^7}\right)(1+\ln(1+\delta^2\ln(n))) + \frac{n}{\delta^6}\sum_{j=1}^{n}\frac{1}{j}\right)\\ &= O\left(\frac{n\ln(n)(1+\ln(1+\delta^2\ln(n)))}{\delta^7}\right)\\ &= O\left(\frac{n\ln(n)\ln(\ln(n))}{\delta^7}\right)\end{aligned}$$

For LeadingOnes, the approach is similar. The only exception is the choice of s_j and s_* for condition (C1) to hold. The probability of improving a solution at fitness level j is lower bounded by the probability flipping the leftmost 0-bit and not flipping the others,

$$\left(\frac{\chi}{n}\right)\left(1-\frac{\chi}{n}\right)^{n-1} > \left(\frac{1}{n}\right)(\chi(1-\chi)) \geq \frac{2\delta}{9n}$$

Hence, we can pick $s_j = s_* = \delta/(9n)$ and the expected optimisation time is

$$\begin{aligned}\mathbf{E}[T] &= O\left(\frac{1}{\delta^5}\left(\left(\frac{n\ln(n)}{\delta^2}\right)(1+\ln(1+\delta^2\ln(n))) + \frac{n^2}{\delta}\right)\right)\\ &= O\left(\frac{n\ln(n)}{\delta^7} + \frac{n^2}{\delta^6}\right) \quad \square\end{aligned}$$

The theorem is a general statement about the expected runtime of non-elitist EAs in optimising the two fitness functions under various circumstances. For example in noisy optimisation, the main task will be to show that for some constant $\gamma_0 \in (0,1]$ and parameter δ with $1/\delta \in \text{poly}(n)$, $\beta(\gamma) \geq (1+\delta)\gamma$ for all $\gamma \in (0,\gamma_0]$. In asymptotic notation, any constant factor in front of δ can be ignored, e.g. the factor 2 in the statement of the theorem. As mentioned before, we often deal with some $\delta < 1$, this fits the requirement on the parameter. Remark that in the case of OneMax, the theorem overestimates the optimisation time for small δ, in fact the term $\ln(\ln(n))$ can be ignored if $\delta^2 \ln(n) = O(1)$.

4. SIMPLE NON-ELITIST EA

Let us consider Algorithm 2 as a simple instance of the algorithmic scheme. The selection mechanism is tournament selection with tournament size 2, which is detailed from line 4 to line 12 below. The bitwise mutation operator p_{mut} is specified in line 13.

Algorithm 2 EAs (2-Tournament, Noisy function)

```
1: Sample P_0 ~ Unif(X^λ), where X = {0,1}^n.
2: for t = 0,1,2,... until termination condition met do
3:   for i = 1 to λ do
4:     Sample two parents x, y ~ Unif(P_t).
5:     f_x := F(x) and f_y := F(y).
6:     if f_x > f_y then
7:       z := x
8:     else if f_x < f_y then
9:       z := y
10:    else
11:      z ~ Unif({x, y})
12:    end if
13:    Flip each bit position in z with probability χ/n.
14:    P_{t+1}(i) := z.
15:  end for
16: end for
```

We are interested in the capability of the selection mechanism in Algorithm 2 to make the right decision while relying only on the noisy fitness F. Formally, we want to quantify a lower bound p such that $\Pr(z = x) \geq p$ for all pairs $\{x, y\}$ with $f(x) > f(y)$, where z is defined by Algorithm 2 above. Remark that if $F(x)$ does not provide any information about $f(x)$, $\Pr(z = x)$ should be equal to $1/2$. Otherwise, $\Pr(z = x)$ is strictly bigger than $1/2$, for example we should have $p = 1/2 + \delta$. We now show that this δ is indeed proportionate to the one required in Theorem 7.

Lemma 8. *For any constant $\gamma_0 \in (0,1)$, if there exists a parameter δ with $1/\delta \in \text{poly}(n)$ such that the selection mechanism of Algorithm 2 satisfies $\Pr(z = x) \geq 1/2 + \delta$ for all inputs $x, y \in \{0,1\}^n$ with $f(x) > f(y)$, then $\beta(\gamma) \geq (1 + 2(1 - \gamma_0)\delta)\gamma$ for all $\gamma \in (0, \gamma_0]$.*

Proof. Tournament selection of size two will return an individual from the γ-upper portion of the population when: (i) both x and y are picked from the upper γ-portion, the probability of this event is γ^2; or (ii) one of individual is picked from the upper γ-portion while the other individual is picked from the remaining part of the population, in the case we need the selection mechanism to make the right decision relying on F and the probability is then at least $2\gamma(1-\gamma)(1/2+\delta)$. Altogether, for all $\gamma \in (0, \gamma_0]$ it holds that

$$\begin{aligned}\beta(\gamma) &\geq \gamma^2 + 2\gamma(1-\gamma)(1/2+\delta)\\ &= \gamma(\gamma + (1-\gamma)(1+2\delta))\\ &= \gamma(1 + (1-\gamma)2\delta)\\ &\geq \gamma(1 + (1-\gamma_0)2\delta) \quad \square\end{aligned}$$

The constant factor in front of δ is $2(1-\gamma_0)$, for example one can pick $\gamma_0 = 1/2$ and obtain that $\beta(\gamma) \geq (1+\delta)\gamma$ for all $\gamma \in (0, 1/2]$. However, as mentioned earlier, this constant will be embedded in constant factor of Theorem 7 and its asymptotic notation. We illustrate the use of the lemma on the prior noise model.

Theorem 9. *Under the prior noise model for any $c \in [0,1]$, there exist constants χ and b such that Algorithm 2 with mutation rate χ/n and population size $\lambda = b\ln(n)$ optimises OneMax in expected time $O(n \ln(n) \ln(\ln(n)))$.*

Proof. The fitness $F(u)$ of a search point u in the prior model satisfies for any integer k

$$\Pr(F(u) = |u|_1 + k) = \begin{cases} (1-c)\left(1 - \frac{|u|_1}{n}\right) & \text{if } k = 1\\ c & \text{if } k = 0\\ (1-c)\left(\frac{|u|_1}{n}\right) & \text{if } k = -1, \text{ and}\\ 0 & \text{otherwise}\end{cases}$$

Given any pair of bitstrings x and y where $|x|_1 \geq |y|_1 + 1$, we need to lower bound the probability that the selection mechanism chooses the fitter search point x. In the prior model, it is clear that this probability is smallest when $|x|_1 = i+1$ and $|y|_1 = i$, for any integer $i \in [n-2]$. Hence, the probability of choosing the less fit search point y is upper bounded by

$$\begin{aligned}&\Pr(z = y)\\ &= \frac{1}{2}\Pr(F(x) = i+1)\Pr(F(y) = i+1)\\ &\quad + \Pr(F(x) = i)\left(\frac{1}{2}\Pr(F(y) = i) + \Pr(F(y) = i+1)\right)\\ &= \frac{c(1-c)}{2}\left(1 - \frac{i}{n}\right) + (1-c)\left(\frac{i+1}{n}\right)\left(\frac{c}{2} + (1-c)\left(1 - \frac{i}{n}\right)\right)\\ &= \frac{c(1-c)}{2}\left(1 + \frac{1}{n}\right) + (1-c)^2\left(\frac{i+1}{n}\right)\left(1 - \frac{i}{n}\right)\end{aligned}$$

which using $(1-c)^2 \leq 1$ simplifies to

$$< \frac{c(1-c)}{2}\left(1 + \frac{1}{n}\right) + \left(\frac{i}{n}\right)\left(1 - \frac{i}{n}\right) + \frac{1}{n}$$

and finally noting that $i \in [0, n]$ and $c \in [0,1]$ give

$$\leq \frac{1}{8}\left(1 + \frac{1}{n}\right) + \frac{1}{4} + \frac{1}{n} \leq \frac{1}{8} + \frac{1}{4} + \frac{9}{8 \cdot 18} = \frac{1}{2} - \frac{1}{16}.$$

where the last inequality holds for any $n \geq 18$. Therefore, $\Pr(z = x) \geq 1/2 + 1/16$ and it follows from Lemma 8 that for any constant $\gamma_0 \in (0,1)$, we have $\beta(\gamma) > (1 + (1-\gamma_0)/8)\gamma$ for all $\gamma \in (0, \gamma_0]$. The result follows by applying Theorem 7 for the OneMax function. $\square$

It is well-known that the elitist (1+1) EA cannot achieve polynomial runtime for too small constant c [10], while elitist population-based EAs like the $(\mu + 1)$ EA with sufficiently large parent population size μ can [11]. We have just shown in Theorem 9 that polynomial runtime can be achieved with non-elitist EAs for any c. In the next section, we extend the result to the additive noise model and derive results for several noise distributions.

5. ADDITIVE NOISE DISTRIBUTIONS

The following lemma in combination with Lemma 8 provides a mean to compute the selective pressure δ of Algorithm 2 under additive noise.

LEMMA 10. *Given any $\varepsilon > 0$, let $f : \mathcal{X} \to \mathbb{R}$ be any function such that for all $x, y \in \mathcal{X}$ either $f(x) = f(y)$ or $|f(x) - f(y)| \geq \varepsilon$. Let X and Y be independently sampled from some distribution D. If $\Pr(X - Y > -\varepsilon) \geq 1/2 + \delta$, then the selection mechanism of Algorithm 2 satisfies $\Pr(z = x) \geq 1/2 + \delta$ for all inputs $x, y \in \mathcal{X}$ with $f(x) > f(y)$.*

PROOF. Assume that for two solutions x and y, we have $F(x) = f(x) + X$ and $F(y) = f(y) + Y$ with $X, Y \sim D$. We have,

$$\begin{aligned}\Pr(z = x) &\geq \Pr(F(x) > F(y)) \\ &\geq \Pr(f(y) + \varepsilon + X > f(y) + Y) \\ &= \Pr(X - Y > -\varepsilon) \geq 1/2 + \delta \quad \square\end{aligned}$$

Note that the first inequality in the proof ignores the event $F(x) = F(y)$, hence it is tight for continuous distributions. The following corollary can also be used to compute δ.

COROLLARY 11. *The result of Lemma 10 also holds if $\Pr(0 < X - Y < \epsilon) \geq \delta$, or if D is a continuous distribution and $\Pr(|X - Y| < \epsilon) \geq 2\delta$.*

PROOF. Remark that $\Pr(X - Y \leq k) = \Pr(Y - X \leq k)$ or the distribution of the difference $Z = X - Y$ is symmetric around 0. This implies that $\Pr(Z \leq 0) \geq 1/2$, and

$$\begin{aligned}\Pr(z = x) &\geq \Pr(X - Y > -\varepsilon) \\ &= \Pr(X - Y \geq 0) + \Pr(0 > X - Y > -\varepsilon) \\ &= 1/2 + \Pr(\varepsilon > X - Y > 0) \geq 1/2 + \delta\end{aligned}$$

If D is continuous then so is the distribution of $(X - Y)$, therefore $\Pr(\varepsilon > X - Y > 0) = \Pr(|X - Y| < \varepsilon)/2$. $\square$

For ONEMAX and LEADINGONES, ε is 1. The lemma or its corollary implies a condition on the distribution D of the noise. Particularly for noise distributions D over the positive reals $\mathbb{R}^+$, [11] showed that polynomial runtime for $(\mu+1)$ EA can be achieved if $X \sim D$ has $\Pr(X < 1)$ equal to a constant. A similar result can be easily deduced for non-elitist EAs using Corollary 11, Lemma 8 and Theorem 7. Furthermore, the result can be extended D over $\mathbb{R}$, and to $\Pr(X < 1)$ being smaller than a constant, e.g. polynomially decreasing with n. This means that the distribution D can have a very heavy tail or a large variance.

We now show for many noise distributions, including the uniform distribution, the normal distribution, and the exponential distribution, that polynomial runtime can be achieved even if the variance of the noise grows polynomially in the problem size n.

THEOREM 12. *Under an additive noise model with normally distributed noise $\mathcal{N}(0, \sigma^2)$ where $\sigma \in \text{poly}(n)$, there exist constants a and b such that Algorithm 2 with $\chi = a/(3\sigma)$ and $\lambda = b\sigma^2 \ln(n)$ optimises* ONEMAX *in expected time*

$$O\left(\sigma^7 n \ln(n) \ln(\ln(n))\right)$$

and optimises LEADINGONES *in expected time*

$$O\left(\sigma^7 n \ln(n) + \sigma^6 n^2\right).$$

PROOF. Note that if $Y \sim \mathcal{N}(0, \sigma^2)$ then $-Y$ also follows the same distribution $\mathcal{N}(0, \sigma^2)$. Therefore, if we put $Z = X - Y$, then $Z \sim \mathcal{N}(0, \sigma^2) + \mathcal{N}(0, \sigma^2) = \mathcal{N}(0, 2\sigma^2)$. Let $F(z)$ be the cumulative density function of Z, by the symmetry of Z we have that $\Pr(X - Y > -1) = \Pr(Z > -1) = \Pr(Z < 1) = F(1)$. Applying Lemma 18 on Z (here with standard deviation $\sigma\sqrt{2}$) we get,

$$\begin{aligned}\Pr(X - Y > -1) = F(1) &> 1 - \frac{1}{\sqrt{\frac{\pi}{2\sigma}} + 4} \\ &= \left(1 - \left(\frac{1}{\sqrt{\frac{\pi}{2\sigma}} + 4}\right)^2\right) / \left(1 + \frac{1}{\sqrt{\frac{\pi}{2\sigma}} + 4}\right) \\ &> \left(\frac{\pi/(2\sigma) + 3}{\pi/(2\sigma) + 4}\right) / (3/2) \\ &= \left(\frac{1 + 6\sigma/\pi}{1 + 8\sigma/\pi}\right)\left(\frac{4}{3}\right)\left(\frac{1}{2}\right) \\ &= \frac{1}{2}\left(1 + \frac{1}{3 + 24\sigma/\pi}\right)\end{aligned}$$

So Lemmas 10 and 8 are satisfied for $\delta = 1/(6 + 48\sigma/\pi) = \Theta(1/\sigma)$. The result then follows by applying Theorem 7. $\square$

THEOREM 13. *Under an additive noise model in which the distribution of the noise is $\text{Unif}(-\rho, \rho)$ where $\rho \in \text{poly}(n)$, there exist constants a and b such that Algorithm 2 with $\chi = a/(3\rho)$ and $\lambda = b\rho^2 \ln(n)$ optimises* ONEMAX *in expected time*

$$O\left(\rho^7 n \ln(n) \ln(\ln(n))\right)$$

and optimises LEADINGONES *in expected time*

$$O\left(\rho^7 n \ln(n) + \rho^6 n^2\right)$$

PROOF. If $Y \sim \text{Unif}(-\rho, \rho)$ then $-Y \sim \text{Unif}(-\rho, \rho)$, therefore $Z = X - Y = X + Y$. Let F_X, F_Y and F_Z be the cumulative density functions of X, Y and Z respectively, recall that $F_X(x) = F_Y(x) = (x + \rho)/2\rho$ for $x \in [-\rho, \rho]$. By the symmetry of Z, we have

$$\begin{aligned}\Pr(X - Y > -1) &= \Pr(Z > -1) = \Pr(Z < 1) = F_Z(1) \\ &= \int_{-\rho}^{\rho} F_Y(1 - x) dF_X(x) \\ &= \int_{-\rho}^{\rho} \left(\frac{1 - x + \rho}{2\rho}\right)\left(\frac{dx}{2\rho}\right) \\ &= \frac{1}{4\rho^2}\left[(1 + \rho)x - \frac{x^2}{2}\right]_{-\rho}^{\rho} = \frac{1}{2} + \frac{1}{2\rho}\end{aligned}$$

Hence Lemmas 10 and 8 hold for $\delta = \Theta(1/\rho)$. The result follows by applying Theorem 7. $\square$

THEOREM 14. *Under an additive noise model in which the distribution of the noise is $\text{Exp}(\theta)$ where $1/\theta \in \text{poly}(n)$, there exist constants a and b such that Algorithm 2 with $\chi = a\theta/3$ and $\lambda = b\ln(n)/\theta^2$ optimises* ONEMAX *in expected time*

$$O\left(\frac{n \ln(n) \ln(\ln(n))}{\theta^7}\right)$$

and optimises LEADINGONES *in expected time*

$$O\left(\frac{n \ln(n)}{\theta^7} + \frac{n^2}{\theta^6}\right)$$

PROOF. Let $Z = X - Y$, and F_X, F_{-Y}, F_Z be the cumulative density functions of X, $-Y$, Z respectively. Recall that $F_X(x) = 1 - e^{-\theta x}$ for $x \in [0, \infty)$, $F_{-Y}(x) = 1 - F_X(-x) = e^{\theta x}$ for $x \in (-\infty, 0]$ and $F_{-Y}(x) = 1$ for $x > 0$. We have

$$\begin{aligned}\Pr(X - Y > -1) &= \Pr(Z > -1) = \Pr(Z < 1) = F_Z(1) \\ &= \int_0^\infty F_{-Y}(1-x)dF_X(x) \\ &= \int_0^1 \theta e^{-\theta x}dx + \int_1^\infty e^{\theta(1-x)}\theta e^{-\theta x}dx \\ &= \theta\left(\left[\frac{e^{-\theta x}}{-\theta}\right]_0^1 + \left[\frac{e^{\theta(1-2x)}}{-2\theta}\right]_1^\infty\right) \\ &= (-e^{-\theta} - (-1)) + (0 - (-e^{-\theta}/2)) \\ &= \frac{1}{2} + \left(\frac{1}{2} - \frac{e^{-\theta}}{2}\right) > \frac{1}{2} + \frac{1}{2}\left(1 - \frac{1}{\theta+1}\right) \\ &= \frac{1}{2} + \frac{1}{2}\left(\frac{1}{1+1/\theta}\right)\end{aligned}$$

Therefore, Lemmas 10 and 8 are satisfied for $\delta = \Theta(\theta)$. The result then follows by applying Theorem 7. □

Note that the variances of $\mathcal{N}(0, \sigma^2)$, $\text{Unif}(-\rho, \rho)$, $\text{Exp}(\theta)$ are σ^2, $\rho^2/3$ and $1/\theta^2$ respectively. In Theorems 12, 13 and 14, those quantities are allowed to grow polynomially with the length of the bitstring n, still the runtime of the non-elitist EAs on ONEMAX and LEADINGONES is polynomial.

6. CONCLUSIONS

We have analysed rigorously the runtime of non-elitist Evolutionary Algorithms (EA) in optimising pseudo-Boolean functions subject to noise. The results have been reported for the *prior* noise model of [10] and for the well-known *additive* noise model. A general condition based on the capability of the selection mechanism to make the right decision under noise is proposed to the computation of the runtime, the condition in turn implies a specific property on the distribution of the noise. On standard functions such as ONEMAX and LEADINGONES, polynomial runtime for non-elitist EAs is guaranteed, even when the noise distribution has variance growing polynomially with the problem size. A sufficient strategy to cope with noise in these cases is to have large enough population size and a moderate mutation rate.

Future work should investigate the relationship between population-based approaches and multiple re-evaluations in single-solution-based approach [2, 3]. Note that the reduction of mutation rate in non-elitist EAs is very similar to re-evaluations, nevertheless the population-based algorithms do not compute the average fitnesses explicitly.

Acknowledgements

The authors would like to thank the anonymous reviewers and Sandra Astete-Morales, Marie-Liesse Cauwet, and Olivier Teytaud for constructive comments. This research received funding from the European Union Seventh Framework Programme (FP7/2007-2013) under grant agreement no 618091 (SAGE).

7. REFERENCES

[1] Milton Abramowitz and Irene A. Stegun. *Handbook of Mathematical Functions, With Formulas, Graphs, and Mathematical Tables.* Dover Publications, Incorporated, 1974.

[2] Y. Akimoto, S. Astete, and O. Teytaud. Additive noise in discrete optimization. The 7th Workshop on Theory of Randomised Search Heuristics (ThRaSH'2013).

[3] Y. Akimoto, S. Astete, and O. Teytaud. Analysis of runtime of optimization algorithms for noisy functions over discrete codomains. Preprint, 2014.

[4] D. V. Arnold. *Noisy Optimization With Evolution Strategies.* Genetic algorithms and evolutionary computation. Kluwer Academic Publishers, 2002.

[5] D. V. Arnold and H. G. Beyer. A general noise model and its effects on evolution strategy performance. *IEEE Transactions on Evolutionary Computation,* 10(4):380–391, 2006.

[6] Dogan Corus, Duc-Cuong Dang, Anton V. Eremeev, and Per Kristian Lehre. Level-based analysis of genetic algorithms and other search processes. In *Proceedings of the 13th International Conference on Parallel Problem Solving from Nature,* PPSN'14, pages 912–921. Springer International Publishing, 2014.

[7] Duc-Cuong Dang and Per Kristian Lehre. Evolution under partial information. In *Proceedings of the 16th Annual Conference on Genetic and Evolutionary Computation,* GECCO'14, pages 1359–1366, New York, NY, USA, 2014. ACM.

[8] Duc-Cuong Dang and Per Kristian Lehre. Refined upper bounds on the expected runtime of non-elitist populations from fitness-levels. In *Proceedings of the 16th Annual Conference on Genetic and Evolutionary Computation,* GECCO'14, pages 1367–1374, New York, NY, USA, 2014. ACM.

[9] Stefan Droste. Analysis of the (1+1) EA for a dynamically bitwise changing OneMax. In *Proceedings of the 2003 International Conference on Genetic and Evolutionary Computation,* GECCO'03, pages 909–921, Berlin, Heidelberg, 2003. Springer-Verlag.

[10] Stefan Droste. Analysis of the (1+1) EA for a noisy OneMax. In *Proceedings of the 2004 International Conference on Genetic and Evolutionary Computation,* GECCO'04, pages 1088–1099, Berlin, Heidelberg, 2004. Springer-Verlag.

[11] Christian Gießen and Timo Kötzing. Robustness of populations in stochastic environments. In *Proceedings of the 16th Annual Conference on Genetic and Evolutionary Computation,* GECCO'14, pages 1383–1390, New York, NY, USA, 2014. ACM.

[12] Thomas Jansen. *Analyzing Evolutionary Algorithms - The Computer Science Perspective.* Natural Computing Series. Springer, 2013.

[13] Yaochu Jin and Jürgen Branke. Evolutionary optimization in uncertain environments - a survey. *IEEE Transactions on Evolutionary Computation,* 9(3):303–317, 2005.

[14] Per Kristian Lehre. Negative drift in populations. In *Proceedings of the 11th International Conference on Parallel Problem Solving from Nature,* PPSN'10, pages 244–253, Berlin, Heidelberg, 2010. Springer-Verlag.

[15] Per Kristian Lehre. Fitness-levels for non-elitist populations. In *Proceedings of the 13th Annual Conference on Genetic and Evolutionary*

Computation, GECCO'11, pages 2075–2082, New York, NY, USA, 2011. ACM.

[16] Per Kristian Lehre and Xin Yao. On the impact of mutation-selection balance on the runtime of evolutionary algorithms. *IEEE Transactions on Evolutionary Computation*, 16(2):225–241, 2012.

[17] Dragoslav S. Mitrinović. *Elementary Inequalities*. P. Noordhoff Ltd, Groningen, 1964.

[18] Ingo Wegener. Methods for the analysis of evolutionary algorithms on pseudo-boolean functions. In *Evolutionary Optimization*, volume 48, pages 349–369. Springer US, 2002.

APPENDIX

THEOREM 15 (BERNOULLI'S INEQUALITY [17]). *For any integer $n \geq 0$ and any real number $x \geq -1$, it holds that $(1+x)^n \geq 1+nx$.*

THEOREM 16 (ERROR FUNCTION RELATED [1], 7.1.13).

$$\int_x^\infty e^{-t^2}\,dt \leq \frac{e^{-x^2}}{x+\sqrt{x^2+\frac{4}{\pi}}}$$

LEMMA 17. *For all $x > 0$ and $a \geq 1/4$, it holds that $x + \sqrt{x^2+a} > \sqrt{x+a}$.*

PROOF. Given that $x > 0$ and $a \geq 1/4$, we get $\sqrt{x+a} > 1/2$. Multiplying both sides with $2x > 0$ gives $2x\sqrt{x+a} > x$. This can be written as,

$$\begin{aligned} 2x\sqrt{x+a} + a + x^2 &> x + a + x^2 \\ \text{or } a + x^2 &> x + a - 2x\sqrt{x+a} + x^2 \\ &= (\sqrt{x+a} - x)^2 \end{aligned}$$

Therefore, $\sqrt{x^2+a} > |\sqrt{x+a} - x| \geq \sqrt{x+a} - x$, or $x + \sqrt{x^2+a} > \sqrt{x+a}$. □

LEMMA 18. *Let $F(x)$ be the cumulative density function of normal distribution $\mathcal{N}(0,\sigma^2)$, for $x > 0$ we have*

$$F(x) > 1 - \frac{1}{\sqrt{\frac{x\pi}{\sigma\sqrt{2}} + 4}}$$

PROOF. Recall the error function is $\text{erf}(x) = \frac{2}{\sqrt{\pi}}\int_0^x e^{-t^2}\,dt$. The complementary error function is defined with identities $\text{erfc}(x) = 1 - \text{erf}(x) = \frac{2}{\sqrt{\pi}}\int_x^\infty e^{-t^2}\,dt$. The cumulative density function is then,

$$F(x) = \frac{1}{2}\left(1 + \text{erf}\left(\frac{x}{\sigma\sqrt{2}}\right)\right) = 1 - \frac{1}{2}\,\text{erfc}\left(\frac{x}{\sigma\sqrt{2}}\right)$$

It follows from Theorem 16 that

$$\text{erfc}(x) \leq \frac{2e^{-x^2}}{\sqrt{\pi}\left(x + \sqrt{x^2+\frac{4}{\pi}}\right)}$$

Note that for $x > 0$, we have $e^{-x^2} < 1$. It also follows from Lemma 17 with $a = 4/\pi > 1/4$ that x + $\sqrt{x^2+\frac{4}{\pi}} > \sqrt{x+\frac{4}{\pi}}$. Therefore,

$$\text{erfc}(x) < \frac{2}{\sqrt{\pi}\sqrt{x+\frac{4}{\pi}}} = \frac{2}{\sqrt{\pi x + 4}}$$

The lemma follows by applying this inequality to $F(x)$. □

Run-Time Analysis of Population-Based Evolutionary Algorithm in Noisy Environments

Adam Prügel-Bennett
Electronics and Computer Science
University of Southampton
Southampton SO17 1BJ, UK
apb@ecs.soton.ac.uk

Jonathan Rowe
Department of Computer Science
University of Birmingham
Birmingham, UK
J.E.Rowe@cs.bham.ac.uk

Jonathan Shapiro
Department of Computer Science
University of Manchester
Manchester, UK
jls@cs.man.ac.uk

ABSTRACT

This paper analyses a generational evolutionary algorithm using only selection and uniform crossover. With a probability arbitrarily close to one the evolutionary algorithm is shown to solve onemax in $O(n \log^2(n))$ function evaluations using a population of size $cn \log(n)$. We then show that this algorithm can solve onemax with noise variance n again in $O(n \log^2(n))$ function evaluations.

Categories and Subject Descriptors

F.2 [**Analysis Of Algorithms And Problem Complexity**]; G.1.6 [**Optimization**]: Global optimization

General Terms

Theory

Keywords

Run-time analysis; uniform crossover; noisy optimisation.

1. INTRODUCTION

This paper is aimed at clarifying the mechanisms whereby a population-based evolutionary algorithm (EA) might provide a substantial advantage over local search. In particular we focus on the ability of crossover to focus search and a population to not be mislead by high levels of noise. The run-time analysis reveals the scaling behaviour of the mechanisms being analysed. The run-time analyse for the noise problem builds on an analysis of an evolutionary algorithm that uses uniform crossover and selection to solve onemax (that is, to find a binary string of all ones, where the only heuristic information is the number of ones in the string).

In the last few years there has been a significant push on obtaining run-time results for EAs. Mechanisms where crossover is necessary were first investigated by Jansen and Wegner who introduced a problem in which the performance gap between mutation-based and mutation-crossover based algorithms is superpolynomial [8], and a class of Royal Road functions in which the performance gap is exponential [7]. Subsequently, investigators have discovered other problems in which the addition of crossover improves performance significantly. For example, Sudholt [11] showed that a $(\mu + \lambda)$ EA with a constant population size needs exponential time to solve the Ising model on a complete binary tree, whereas a $(2+2)$ EA with crossover, mutation, and fitness-sharing has polynomial runtime. Doerr et. al. [2] showed for the all-pairs shortest path problem a polynomial speedup by using forms of crossover appropriate to the problem. Recently, Corus et al. [1] developed a technique which extends the level-based approach to single-point and uniform crossover and applied it to the onemax and leading ones problem.

We believe our paper makes two contributions. First, we analyse an algorithm with crossover and selection alone. We believe that this brings into focus the role of crossover in solving problems. Other analyses of crossover of which we are aware contain mutation as well. Of course, real practical EAs *do* contain mutation, so it is natural to include it in the algorithms studied. We introduce it as a theoretical tool to allow us to compare crossover as a search operator to mutation as a search operator. We know that one role of mutation is to maintain diversity in the population, so using crossover alone will likely required larger population sizes.

The second contribution is the addition of a further problem which crossover is necessary, in the strongest sense. We consider the problem of onemax plus noise of order $\sqrt{n}$. We show that our selection plus crossover EA can solve the problem efficiently while a $(1 + 1)$ EA fails to make substantial progress towards the solution at all. This extends previous rigorous work on this problem to much higher amplitude noise. Droste [4] considered a $(1 + 1)$ EA to onemaxs in which one bit was flipped with probability p and the string was unchanged with probability $1 - p$, and showed that the run time was polynomial only if $p = O(\ln n/n)$. Gießen and Kötzing generalise the form of noise and show that the introduction of populations can allow the EA can increase the size of noise that the EA can handle. We increase this much further.

The paper is organised as follows. In the next section we introduce the techniques that we use and define the EA that we use through out the paper. In section 3, we derive run-times bound for solving onemax. Section 4 considers the problem of coping with noise on the fitness evaluation. We

FOGA'15, January 17–20, 2015, Aberystwyth, UK.

http://dx.doi.org/10.1145/2725494.2725498.

consider the problem of solving onemax plus noise of order $\sqrt{n}$. We conclude in section 5.

2. BACKGROUND MATERIAL

In this section we briefly recap on the main proof tools that we use throughout the paper and then describe the evolutionary algorithm that we use.

2.1 Proof Tools

The main proof tools we will use are the drift bounds. We use the multiplicative drift theorem which provides an upper bound on the expected time to achieve some goal in terms of the expected progress towards the goal. For completeness we state the theorem without a proof.

THEOREM 1. *Let $(X_t)_{t\geq 0}$ be a series of positive random variables describing a Markov chain. Define T to be the first time to reach a state with value less than $a > 0$*

$$T = \min\{t \geq 0 : X_t < a\}.$$

If there exists a $\delta > 0$ such that at any step $t \geq 0$, and at any state X_t with $X_t > a$

$$\mathbb{E}[X_{t+1} - X_t | X_t] \geq \delta\, X_t$$

then the expected time, T, for X_t to reach a value less than a is bounded by

$$\mathbb{E}[T] \leq \frac{1 + \log(\mathbb{E}[X_0]/a)}{\delta}.$$

◇

The theorem is proved in [3]. In fact we give a slightly modified version of the theorem in that we consider the expected time to reach a value less than (rather than equal to) some positive constant a and we take the expected initial position, but both extensions are trivial.

We also require a negative drift theorem. We could use the standard theorem of [9] [10], however, we can obtain a tighter bound using the following theorem.

THEOREM 2. *Let $(X_t)_{t\geq 0}$ be a series of random variables describing a Markov chain. We consider the points $a < b < c$ with $b - a = c - b = \ell$.*

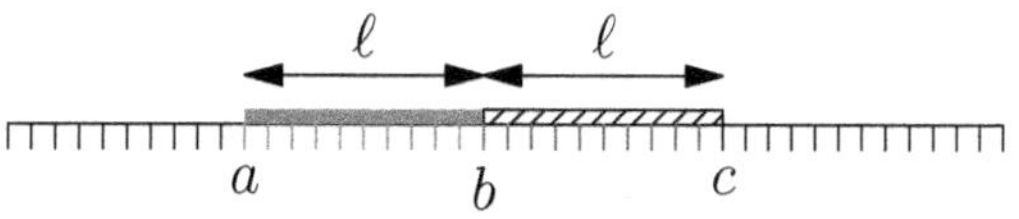

If $X_0 \geq b$ and the following two conditions apply

1. *For $X_{t-1} > c$ there exists a constant $\varepsilon > 0$ such that*
$$\mathbb{P}\big(X_t \leq b | X_{t-1}\big) \leq \mathrm{e}^{-\varepsilon\,\ell}$$
2. *For $a \leq X_{t-1} \leq c$ there exists constants Δ and $\nu > 0$ such that*
$$\log\Big(\mathbb{E}\Big[\mathrm{e}^{-\lambda(X_t - X_{t-1})} | X_{t-1}\Big]\Big) \leq -\lambda\,\Delta + \frac{\nu\lambda^2}{2}$$

then

$$\mathbb{P}\big(X_T \leq a\big) \leq T\max(\mathrm{e}^{-\varepsilon\,\ell}, \mathrm{e}^{-2\,\ell\,\Delta/\nu}).$$

◇

PROOF. The first condition states that the probability of making a jump from $X_{t-1} > c$ to $X_t < b$ is exponentially unlikely. Assuming no such jump happens then for $X_\tau \leq a$ for some τ the system must have made a series of steps across the interval $[a, b]$ where at each step the second condition holds. We show that such a series of steps is exponentially unlikely. Using the usual Chernoff-bound construction we have for $\lambda > 0$

$$\mathbb{P}\big(X_t - X_0 \leq -\ell\big) = \mathbb{P}\Big(\mathrm{e}^{-\lambda\,(X_t - X_0)} \geq \mathrm{e}^{\lambda\,\ell}\Big) \leq \frac{\mathbb{E}\Big[\mathrm{e}^{-\lambda\,(X_t - X_0)}\Big]}{\mathrm{e}^{\lambda\,\ell}}$$

using Markov's inequality. This is true for any $\lambda > 0$, thus

$$\mathbb{P}\big(X_t - X_0 \leq -\ell\big) \leq \mathrm{e}^{-\psi(\ell)},$$
$$\psi(\ell) = \max_{\lambda>0} \lambda\,\ell - \log\Big(\mathbb{E}\Big[\mathrm{e}^{-\lambda\,(X_t - X_0)}\Big]\Big).$$

However

$$\mathbb{E}\Big[\mathrm{e}^{-\lambda\,(X_t - X_0)}\Big] = \mathbb{E}\Big[\mathbb{E}\Big[\mathrm{e}^{-\lambda\,(X_t - X_{t-1})} | X_{t-1}\Big]\,\mathrm{e}^{-\lambda\,(X_{t-1} - X_0)}\Big]$$

but, by the assumption, $a \leq X_{t-1} \leq b$ and from condition 2

$$\mathbb{E}\Big[\mathrm{e}^{-\lambda\,(X_t - X_0)}\Big] \leq \mathrm{e}^{-\lambda\Delta + \frac{\nu\lambda^2}{2}}\,\mathbb{E}\Big[\mathrm{e}^{-\lambda\,(X_{t-1} - X_0)}\Big].$$

Iterating we have

$$\log\Big(\mathbb{E}\Big[\mathrm{e}^{-\lambda\,(X_t - X_0)}\Big]\Big) \leq -\lambda\,\Delta\,t + \frac{\nu\lambda^2 t}{2}$$

where $t + 1$ is the length of time since $X_t > b$.

$$\psi(\ell) \geq \max_{\lambda>0} \lambda\,(\ell + \Delta\,t) - \frac{\nu\lambda^2 t}{2} = \frac{(\ell + \Delta\,t)^2}{2\,\nu t}$$

giving

$$\mathbb{P}\big(X_t \leq a\big) \leq \mathrm{e}^{-(\ell + \Delta\,t)^2/(2\,\nu t)}.$$

The right-hand side reaches its maximum when $t = \ell/\Delta$ so that

$$\mathbb{P}\big(X_t \leq a\big) \leq \mathrm{e}^{-2\,\ell\,\Delta/\nu}$$

assuming that $a \leq X_\tau \leq b$ for $\tau < t$. The system may have reached the $X_t > c$ (possibly many time) and either made a very large jump or have jumped back into the interval $[b, c]$ and subsequently walked the interval $[a, b]$. Taking a union bound on the most likely way to reach a state with $X_\tau \leq a$ for all time steps T we obtained the result given in the theorem. □

The basic tool we use for obtaining concentration results are bounds for the cumulant generating function of a random variable $X - \mathbb{E}[X]$, defined by

$$\bar{G}_X(\lambda) = \log\Big(\mathbb{E}\Big[\mathrm{e}^{\lambda(X - \mathbb{E}[X])}\Big]\Big).$$

We use the following well known inequality associated with Bernstein and Chernoff.

THEOREM 3. *For a random variable X if $\bar{G}_X(\lambda) \leq c\,\lambda^2$ then*

$$\mathbb{P}\big(|X - \mathbb{E}[X]\,| \geq \varepsilon\big) \leq \mathrm{e}^{-\varepsilon^2/(4\,c)}.$$

◇

A useful result due to Hoeffding [6] is

THEOREM 4. *For a bounded random variable $a \le X \le b$ then*

$$\bar{G}_X(\lambda) \le \frac{(b-a)^2}{8}\lambda^2.$$

or

$$\log\Big(\mathbb{E}\Big[e^{\lambda X}\Big]\Big) \le \lambda \mathbb{E}[X] + \frac{(b-a)^2}{8}\lambda^2.$$

◇

Using theorems 3 and 4 on the sum, S_n, of n independent random variables bounded in an interval from a to b we obtain Hoeffding's inequality

$$\mathbb{P}(S_n - \mathbb{E}[S_n] \ge t) \le e^{-\frac{2t^2}{n\,(b-a)^2}}. \qquad (1)$$

Finally we need the following identity for the binomial sum

$$S_n = \frac{1}{2^n}\sum_{i=0}^{n}\left|i - \tfrac{n}{2}\right|\binom{n}{i} = \frac{1}{2^n}\left\lceil \tfrac{n}{2}\right\rceil \binom{n}{\lceil n/2\rceil} \ge \sqrt{\frac{n}{8}}. \quad (2)$$

To prove the equality we note

$$\begin{aligned}
2^n\, S_n &\overset{1}{=} 2\sum_{i=0}^{\lfloor n/2\rfloor}\left(\tfrac{n}{2} - i\right)\binom{n}{i} \\
&\overset{2}{=} \sum_{i=0}^{\lfloor n/2\rfloor}(n-i)\binom{n}{i} - \sum_{i=1}^{\lfloor n/2\rfloor} i\binom{n}{i} \\
&\overset{3}{=} \sum_{i=0}^{\lfloor n/2\rfloor} n\binom{n-1}{i} - \sum_{i=1}^{\lfloor n/2\rfloor} n\binom{n-1}{i-1} \\
&\overset{4}{=} n\binom{n-1}{\lfloor n/2\rfloor} \overset{5}{=} \left(n - \lfloor \tfrac{n}{2}\rfloor\right)\binom{n}{\lfloor n/2\rfloor} = \left\lceil \tfrac{n}{2}\right\rceil\binom{n}{\lceil n/2\rceil}
\end{aligned}$$

where equality 1 follows from the symmetry of the binomial, $\binom{n}{i} = \binom{n}{n-i}$; equality 2 splits the coefficient and throws out the $i = 0$ term in the second sum which vanishes, equality 3 follow from the binomial identities

$$(n-i)\binom{n}{i} = n\binom{n-1}{i}, \qquad i\binom{n}{i} = n\binom{n-1}{i-1},$$

equality 4 follows from cancelling terms in the two sum, finally equality 5 uses $n\binom{n-1}{i} = (n-i)\binom{n}{i}$. The inequality for S_n follows form using Stirling's bound for the factorial.

2.2 Paired-Crossover EA

The results presented in this paper are for an algorithm we call the *paired-crossover evolutionary algorithm* or PCEA. The algorithm consists of a population of P strings. It generates a new population of P strings by taking pairs of strings, $\boldsymbol{X}^\alpha$ and $\boldsymbol{X}^\beta$, and applying uniform crossover to generate two complementary children, $\boldsymbol{X}^\mu$ and $\bar{\boldsymbol{X}}^\mu$, such that the variables at the ith site of the children are

$$X_i^\mu = a_i\, X_i^\alpha + (1-a_i)\, X_i^\beta$$
$$\bar{X}_i^\mu = (1-a_i)\, X_i^\alpha + a_i\, X_i^\beta$$

where $a_i \in \{0,1\}$ are random independent variables with a probability of a half of being in either state. Having generated two complementary children, it chooses the fitter of the two, or chooses either with equal probability if they have the same fitness and puts it into the new population. This is repeated P times to generate the new population. Each pair of strings is selected independently from the parent population.

The initial population consists of strings drawn uniformly at random. Note that our algorithm has no mutation, this is because we wish to investigate crossover as a search operator. Although this means that the search can fail, it prevents the need either for elitism or to anneal the mutation rate to stop the population from reaching a mutation selection balance away from the optimum.

3. ONEMAX

We apply the PCEA to the onemax problem. We consider strings $\boldsymbol{X} = (X_1, X_2, \ldots, X_n)$, where each element of the string is binary (i.e. $X_i \in \{0,1\}$). We denote the number of ones in a string $\boldsymbol{X}$ by $\|\boldsymbol{X}\|$. The fitness of the string for onemax is equal to the number of ones in the string

$$F_{\text{onemax}}(\boldsymbol{X}) = \|\boldsymbol{X}\| = \sum_{i=1}^{n} X_i.$$

The only heuristic information we are given is the fitness of the strings. The optimum is the all ones string.

In uniform crossover, for a child μ produced from parents α and β,

$$\begin{aligned}
\|\boldsymbol{X}^\mu\| &= \sum_{i=1}^{n} X_i^\mu = \frac{1}{2}\sum_{i=1}^{n}\Big(X_i^\alpha + X_i^\beta + (2a_i - 1)(X_i^\alpha - X_i^\beta)\Big) \\
&= \frac{\|\boldsymbol{X}^\alpha\| + \|\boldsymbol{X}^\beta\|}{2} + \eta^{\alpha\beta} \qquad (3)
\end{aligned}$$

where

$$\eta^{\alpha\beta} = \frac{1}{2}\sum_{i=1}^{n}(2\,a_i - 1)(X_i^\alpha - X_i^\beta).$$

Since $(2\,a_i - 1)$ is equal to ± 1 with equal probability and $X_i^\alpha - X_i^\beta$ is equal to ± 1 at the sites where the two parents differ, and 0 otherwise,

$$\mathbb{P}\Big(\eta^{\alpha\beta} = k\Big) = 2^{-d^{\alpha\beta}}\binom{d^{\alpha\beta}}{(k + d^{\alpha\beta})/2}$$

where $d^{\alpha\beta}$ is the Hamming distance between the parents two (i.e. the number of sites where the parents differ). In the PCEA where we perform complementary crossover, the number of ones in the children will be

$$\|\boldsymbol{X}^\mu\| = \frac{1}{2}\Big(\|\boldsymbol{X}^\alpha\| + \|\boldsymbol{X}^\beta\|\Big) + \eta^{\alpha\beta}$$
$$\|\bar{\boldsymbol{X}}^\mu\| = \frac{1}{2}\Big(\|\boldsymbol{X}^\alpha\| + \|\boldsymbol{X}^\beta\|\Big) - \eta^{\alpha\beta}.$$

For the onemax problem we choose the child with the largest number of ones. Thus the number of ones for the selected child is

$$\frac{1}{2}\Big(\|\boldsymbol{X}^\alpha\| + \|\boldsymbol{X}^\beta\|\Big) + \Big|\eta^{\alpha\beta}\Big|.$$

Applying equation (2), we find the expected increase in the number of ones is

$$\mathbb{E}\Big[|\eta^{\alpha\beta}|\Big] = 2^{-d^{\alpha\beta}}\left\lceil\frac{d^{\alpha\beta}}{2}\right\rceil\binom{d^{\alpha\beta}}{\lceil d^{\alpha\beta}/2\rceil} \ge \sqrt{\frac{d^{\alpha\beta}}{8}}. \qquad (4)$$

We denote the average number of zeros per string by

$$\bar{z} = n - \frac{1}{P}\sum_{\alpha=1}^{P} \|\boldsymbol{X}^\alpha\| = \frac{1}{P}\sum_{\alpha=1}^{P}\sum_{i=1}^{n}(1 - X_i^\alpha).$$

Since in the PCEA we use a crossover where every member of the population is used twice to create the next population, the expected number of zeros in the population at the next generation is

$$\mathbb{E}\left[\bar{z}'\right] = \bar{z} - \mathbb{E}\left[|\eta^{\alpha\beta}|\right]$$

where the expectation is with respect to all possible pairings of the string and all possible values of $\eta^{\alpha\beta}$. Using equation (4), the expected number of zeros at the next generation is thus

$$\mathbb{E}\left[\bar{z}'\right] \le \bar{z} - \mathbb{E}\left[\sqrt{\frac{d^{\alpha\beta}}{8}}\right] \tag{5}$$

where the expectation is over Hamming distances produced by all pairings.

We see that there is a drift towards reducing the number of zeros in the population. However, for an EA using only crossover and selection it is possible to reach a state where, at a particular site, the allele values of all the strings equals 0. This is known as fixation[1] as it is no longer possible to obtain a 1 at this site. When fixation occurs the EA is no longer able to solve onemax. We will show that, for a population of size $P = c\sqrt{n}\,\log(n)$ we can always choose a c such that the probability of fixation to all 0's occurs with arbitrarily small probability.

To establish this and to obtain a run time bound for solving onemax we consider the evolution of the number of ones in the population at each site

$$M_i = \sum_{\alpha=1}^{P} X_i^\alpha.$$

Crossover can yield a 1 at site i, either if both parents had 1 at site i or one parent had a 1 at site i and the other had a 0. The probability of choosing two different parents who both have a 1 at site i, is $M_i\,(M_i-1)/(P\,(P-1))$. The probability that the two parents have different allele values at site i is $2\,M_i(P - M_i)/(P\,(P-1))$. In this case, there is a slight bias towards choosing the child with the 1 at site i over that with 0, because, in expectation over all crossovers, it will be fitter than the complementary child. As we have seen in crossing two strings $\boldsymbol{X}^\alpha$ and $\boldsymbol{X}^\beta$ the expected increase in the number of ones of the selected child is at least $\sqrt{d^{\alpha\beta}/8}$. As we are using an unbiased uniform crossover the probability of obtaining a 1 at each site where the strings differ is at least

$$\frac{1}{2} + \frac{1}{\sqrt{8\,d^{\alpha\beta}}} \ge \frac{1}{2} + \frac{1}{\sqrt{8\,n}}.$$

[1]Fixation also occurs when all the values at a site are equal to 1, although our current interest is in preventing fixation to all 0's.

It follows that the expected number of ones at site i is bounded by

$$\begin{aligned}\mathbb{E}\left[M_i'\right] &\ge P\left(\frac{M_i\,(M_i-1)}{P\,(P-1)} + \frac{2\,M_i(P-M_i)}{P\,(P-1)}\left(\frac{1}{2} + \frac{b}{\sqrt{n}}\right)\right)\\ &= M_i + 2\,M_i\left(\frac{P-M_i}{P-1}\right)\frac{b}{\sqrt{n}}\end{aligned} \tag{6}$$

where $b = 1/\sqrt{8}$. We use this result both to prove that we never get near to fixation at any site and to obtain a run-time bound on solving onemax. Later on we consider modified problems where we obtain a similar equation as equation (6), but with different numerical values of b. In the following theorems we therefore take b to be an arbitrary constant.

The next theorem shows that with high probability we do not get near to fixation during the run time of our algorithm. We consider this for an arbitrary site. Using a union bound we can then show that the probability of fixation at any site can be arbitrarily small by choosing a sufficiently large population.

THEOREM 5. *For the PCEA, with a population of size $P = c\sqrt{n}\,\log(n)$, the probability that the number of ones, $M_i(t)$, in the population at site i and time t is bounded by*

$$\mathbb{P}\left(M_i(t) < \frac{P}{4}\right) \le t\,n^{-c\,b/8},$$

where for onemax $b = 1/\sqrt{8}$. For sufficiently large c this can be made arbitrarily small. ◇

PROOF. This theorems follows from theorem 2 applied to the $M_i(t)$, the number of ones in the population at site i at generation t. Consider the random variable

$$M_i(t) - M_i(t-1) = \sum_{\mu=1}^{P}\left(X_i^\mu(t) - X_i^\mu(t-1)\right)$$

where $X_i^\mu(t) - X_i^\mu(t-1) \in \{-1, 0, 1\}$. As this is a sum of variables that differ by at most 2 and are independent we can apply Hoeffding's inequality. Note that each child is independent of any other child since the parents are chosen independently and the crossover between each pair of parents is independent (of course, the probability of $X_i^\mu(t)$ and $X_j^\mu(t)$ are not independent, but we use a union bound to show that fixation does not occur at any of the sites). Using Hoeffding's inequality for the cumulant generating function (theorem 4)

$$\log\left(\mathbb{E}\left[e^{-\lambda\,\Delta M_i(t)}\right]\right) \le -\,\mathbb{E}[\Delta M(t)]\;\lambda + \frac{P\,\lambda^2}{2}$$

where $\Delta M_i(t) = M_i(t) - M_i(t-1)$. But, from equation (6), for $P/4 \le M_i(t-1) \le 3P/4$

$$\mathbb{E}[M_i(t)] - \mathbb{E}[M_i(t-1)] > \frac{P\,b}{4\sqrt{n}}$$

thus

$$\log\left(\mathbb{E}\left[e^{-\lambda\,\Delta M_i(t)}\right]\right) \le -\frac{P\,b\,\lambda}{4\sqrt{n}} + \frac{P\,\lambda^2}{2}.$$

This satisfies condition 2 of theorem 2 with $\Delta = P\,b/4\sqrt{n}$, $\sigma^2 = P$ and $\ell = P/4$. To obtain a bound on the probability of jumping to $M_i(t) \le P/2$ given $M_i(t-1) > 3P/4$, we can ignore any drift and using a simple Hoeffding's inequality, equation (1),

$$\mathbb{P}\left(M_i(t) \leq \frac{P}{2} \middle| M_i(t-1) \geq \frac{3P}{4} \right) \leq \mathrm{e}^{-(P/4)^2/(4P)} = \mathrm{e}^{-P/64}.$$

Thus, condition 1 of theorem 2 is also satisfied so we have the bound

$$\mathbb{P}\left(M(t) \leq \frac{P}{4} \right) \leq t\, \mathrm{e}^{-P\,b/(8\sqrt{n})}.$$

Choosing $P = c\sqrt{n}\log(n)$ then

$$\mathbb{P}\left(M(t) \leq \frac{P}{4} \right) \leq t\, n^{-c\,b/8}$$

□

The theorems above show that provided we make the population sufficiently large (through choosing the constant c) then we can make the probability of fixation at a single site arbitrarily small. By using a union bound we can also choose a constant c so that fixation at any site is arbitrarily small. Thus, in all but a very small number of runs we can assume that $M_i \geq P/4$, through out the run. Using this result we can now establish our main run-time theorem.

THEOREM 6. *The PCEA with a population of size $P = c\sqrt{n}\log(n)$ will solve onemax in $O(\sqrt{n}\log(n))$ generation in expectation, in a proportion of, at least, $1 - n^{-\Omega(c)}$ of its runs.* ◇

PROOF. We can use equation (6) together with the multiplicative drift theorem to obtain a bound on the run time to solve onemax. Using the result of theorem 5, we can assume $M_i \geq P/4$, substituting this into equation (6) we find

$$\mathbb{E}\left[M_i'\right] \geq M_i + \frac{b\,P}{2\sqrt{n}} \left(\frac{P - M_i}{P-1} \right).$$

To use the standard drift theorem, we consider the total number of zeros in the whole population

$$Z = n\,P - \sum_{i=1}^{n} M_i = \sum_{i=1}^{n} \sum_{\alpha=1}^{P} (1 - X_i^{\alpha}).$$

Summing the inequality for the expected number of ones over all sites and subtracting from $n\,P$ we find

$$\mathbb{E}\left[Z'\right] \leq Z - \frac{b\,P}{2\sqrt{n}} \left(\frac{Z}{P-1} \right) \leq Z \left(1 - \frac{b}{2\sqrt{n}} \right).$$

This shows we have a multiplicative drift towards states with a smaller number of zeros. We are guaranteed that the first member of the population will have found the optimal solution when $Z < P$. Using the multiplicative drift theorem (theorem 1) with $\delta = b/(2\sqrt{n})$ then the expected time for $Z < P$ is

$$\mathbb{E}\left[T\right] \leq \frac{2\sqrt{n}}{b} \left(1 + \log(n)\right).$$

For onemax, $b = 1/\sqrt{8}$ and $\mathbb{E}\left[T\right] < 12\sqrt{n}(1 + \log(n))$.

By theorem 5, the probability of failure due to fixation is less than $t\,n^{-c\,b/8}$. □

4. COPING WITH NOISE

Clearly solving onemax using this algorithm is of little practical interest. However, we can, with small modifications, obtain much more interesting results where we can show an evolutionary algorithm using crossover can substantially out-perform many common search algorithms that do not use crossover. We illustrate this by considering the problem of solving a problem with very large measurement noise.

4.1 PCEA Solving Onemax with Noise

We consider a onemax problem on binary strings of length n, but where we are returned an approximate fitness for string $\boldsymbol{X}$ of

$$F_{\text{o+noise}}(\boldsymbol{X}) = \|\boldsymbol{X}\| + \sqrt{n}\,\eta$$

where η is a normally distributed random variable with zero mean and unit variance (i.e. $\eta \sim \mathcal{N}(0,1)$). The noise is assumed to be independent every time the fitness of the string is evaluated. We summarise our run-time analysis in the following theorem.

THEOREM 7. *For the PCEA with a population of $P = c\sqrt{n}\log(n)$ the expected time to solve the onemax with noise problem is $O(\sqrt{n}\log(n))$ in all but a proportion of no more than $n^{-\Omega(c)}$ of the runs.* ◇

PROOF. The proof follows very closely the proof for onemax (theorem 6). We establish that there is a positive bias towards increasing the number of ones at each site. The only difference is the constant in the drift term. Everything else follows the proof of theorem 6.

As with the normal onemax problem we denote the number of ones at an arbitrary site i by M_i. A child will have a 1 at site i if either: (a) its two parents have a 1 at this site, which happens with a probability $M_i(M_i - 1)/(P(P-1))$; or (b) one of its parent has a 1 and the other has a 0 at this site and the child with the 1 is selected. Denoting the child with the extra 1 by $\boldsymbol{X}^{\mu}$ and its complement by $\bar{\boldsymbol{X}}^{\mu}$ then the child with the extra one is selected if

$$\sum_{\substack{j=1\\ j\neq i}}^{n} (X_j^{\mu} - \bar{X}_j^{\mu}) + \sqrt{n}\,(\eta^{\mu} - \bar{\eta}^{\mu}) > -1 \tag{7}$$

where η^{μ} is the noise added to child $\boldsymbol{X}^{\mu}$ and $\bar{\eta}^{\mu}$ is the noise added to the complementary child $\bar{\boldsymbol{X}}^{\mu}$. Child $\boldsymbol{X}^{\mu}$ will be selected in preference to child $\bar{\boldsymbol{X}}^{\mu}$ if $1 + S > 0$, where S is the term on the left-hand side of equation (7). We note that if $\boldsymbol{X}^{\mu}$ and $\bar{\boldsymbol{X}}^{\mu}$ differ at site j then $X_j^{\mu} - \bar{X}_j^{\mu} = \pm 1$ with equal probability. Furthermore, if we consider all possible crossovers then the value of $X_j^{\mu} - \bar{X}_j^{\mu}$, η^{μ} and $\bar{\eta}^{\mu}$ are independent of each other. To calculate the probability density of S, it is useful to consider the characteristic function (i.e. the Fourier transform of the probability density function) defined by

$$\tilde{f}_S(\omega) = \int_{-\infty}^{\infty} f_S(S)\,\mathrm{e}^{\mathrm{i}\,\omega\,S}\,\mathrm{d}S.$$

The characteristic function for a sum of random independent variables is just equal to the product of the characteristic function for the independent variables. Defining $D_j = X_j^{\mu} - X_j^{\nu}$, then assuming $\boldsymbol{X}^{\mu}$ and $\boldsymbol{X}^{\nu}$ differ at site j

the characteristic function for D_j is

$$P_{D_j}(\omega) = \sum_{D_j \in \{-1,1\}} \frac{1}{2} e^{i\,\omega\, D_j} = \cos(\omega).$$

The characteristic function for a normal deviate $\sqrt{n}\,\eta \sim \mathcal{N}(0, n)$ (note that we have absorbed the $\sqrt{n}$ factor into the variance) is $\exp(-n\,\omega^2/2)$. Thus the characteristic function for S is

$$\tilde{f}_S(\omega) = \cos^{d-1}(\omega)\, e^{-n\,\omega^2}$$

where d is the number of sites on which $\boldsymbol{X}^\mu$ and $\bar{\boldsymbol{X}}^\mu$ differ (i.e. the Hamming distance between these two strings). Similarly to the onemax case there is a small bias towards choosing the child with the one in the ith position. We compute a bound for this bias below.

The probability of choosing a one on site i (averaging over all crossovers and possible noise) is

$$\int_{-1}^{\infty} f(S)\,\mathrm{d}\,S = \frac{1}{2} + \frac{1}{2}\int_{-1}^{1} f(S)\,\mathrm{d}\,S$$

where we have used that fact that $f(S)$ is symmetric. Using the inverse Fourier transform

$$f(S) = \int_{-\infty}^{\infty} e^{-i\,\omega\, S}\,\tilde{f}_S(\omega)\frac{\mathrm{d}\omega}{2\,\pi}$$

and substituting this in and performing the integral over S we find the bias towards choosing the string with a one at site i is

$$\begin{aligned} b' &= \frac{1}{2}\int_{-1}^{1} f(S)\,\mathrm{d}\,S \\ &= \int_{-\infty}^{\infty} \frac{\sin(\omega)}{\omega}\,\tilde{f}_S(\omega)\frac{\mathrm{d}\omega}{2\,\pi} \\ &= \int_{-\infty}^{\infty} \mathrm{sinc}(\omega)\,\cos^{d-1}(\omega)\,e^{-n\,\omega^2}\frac{\mathrm{d}\omega}{2\,\pi} \end{aligned}$$

where we use the standard notation that $\mathrm{sinc}(\omega) = \sin(\omega)/\omega$. Using $\log(\mathrm{sinc}(x)) \geq \log(1 - x^2/6)$ and $\log(\cos(x)) \geq \log(1 - x^2/2)$ (which follows as the difference in the Taylor expansions involves purely positive terms) then

$$\log(\mathrm{sinc}(\omega)\cos^{d-1}(\omega)) \geq \log\left(1 - \left(\frac{3\,d-2}{6}\right)\omega^2\right) \qquad (8)$$

(where we have used that $n\,\log(1-a) \geq \log(1 - n\,a)$ and $\log(1-a) + \log(1-b) \geq \log(1-a-b)$). Exponentiating both sides

$$\mathrm{sinc}(\omega)\cos^{d-1}(\omega) \geq 1 - \left(\frac{3\,d-2}{6}\right)\omega^2 \geq 1 - \left(\frac{3\,n-2}{6}\right)\omega^2$$

so that

$$\begin{aligned} b' &\geq \int_{-\infty}^{\infty}\left(1 - \left(\frac{3\,n-2}{6}\right)\omega^2\right) e^{-n\,\omega^2}\frac{\mathrm{d}\omega}{2\,\pi} \\ &= \frac{1}{\sqrt{\pi\,n}}\left(\frac{3}{8} + \frac{1}{12\,n}\right) > \frac{0.211}{\sqrt{n}}. \end{aligned}$$

Thus the probability of choosing the child with a 1 at site i rather than 0 is at least $1/2 + b'/\sqrt{n}$. Just as in onemax we are left with a small drift towards fixation at all 1 of

$$\mathbb{E}\left[M_i'\right] \geq M_i\left(1 + \frac{2\,b'}{(P-1)\sqrt{n}}\right).$$

The only difference to the onemax case is that we replace b by b'. The rest of the proof follow theorem 6. □

5. CONCLUSION

This paper shows that a crossover only evolutionary algorithm is able to solve onemax with high probability provide $P = \Omega(\sqrt{n}\,\log(n))$ in an expected run time of $O(\sqrt{n}\,\log(n))$ generations. From some theoretical considerations we believe the true run time is more likely to be $\Theta(\sqrt{n})$ generations or $\Theta(n\,\log(n))$ function evaluations. This is also supported by empirical evidence, see Fig. 1.

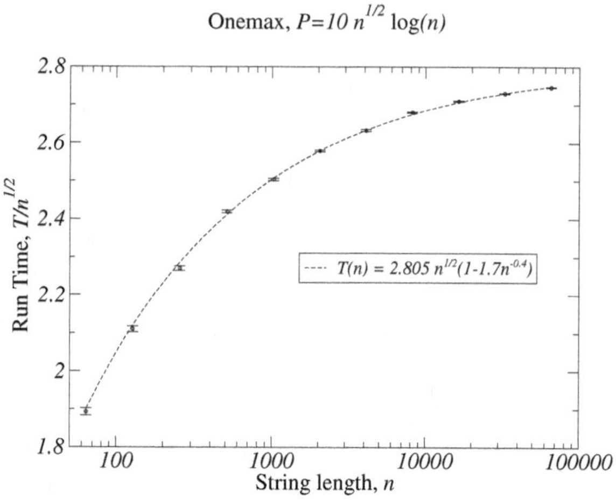

Figure 1: Empirically measured number of generations to solve onemax using a population of $P = 10\sqrt{n}\,\log(n)$. The data points show the mean from simulations with the error bars showing estimated errors in the mean. The dashed line is a fit showing the data is consistent with a run time of approximately $2.8\sqrt{n}(1 + o(1))$ generations.

We have further shown that using the same algorithm we can also solve onemax in the presence of noise of variance n. Gießen and Kötzing had previously shown in [5] that a $(\mu+1)$-EA was able to solve onemax in the presence of noise of variance $O(1)$. However, for an mutation-based search algorithm the variation in fitness of a child population will be dwarfed by our noise. As mutation has a natural tendency to explore the high-entropy part of the solution space the very small bias towards solutions with more ones will be dominated by larger number of solutions with less ones. In contrast, using crossover as a search operator the total number of ones in the children will be same as the parents. Furthermore the fluctuations in the number of ones also has variance of order n so there is considerably more gradient information available. It is the combined effect of focused search and the averaging effect of a population that allows our algorithm to solve onemax with a large degree of noise.

Of course, the problem could also be solved by a hill-climber by resampling the same points until the noise was of order 1. This would allow a hill-climber to solve the problem in around n^2 iterations. We conjecture, however, that our algorithm would be able to find high quality solutions for onemax plus a random function, where the random function has the same statistical properties as the noise (but does not vary each time the point is sampled). The reason for this is that we believe our algorithm rarely visits the same points of the search space, at least, until the algorithm is close to converging. Thus, our algorithm should behave very similarly on the two problems, at least, until it is only a small way from the all ones configuration. This is a problem we believe would be hard for algorithms not using crossover.

6. REFERENCES

[1] D. C., D.-C. Dang, A. V. Eremeev, and P. K. Lehre. Level-based analysis of genetic algorithms and other search processes. arXiv:1407.7663v1[cs.NE].

[2] B. Doerr, E. Happ, and C. Klein. Crossover can provably be useful in evolutionary computation. In *Proceedings of the 10th Annual Conference on Genetic and Evolutionary Computation*, GECCO '08, pages 539–546, New York, NY, USA, 2008. ACM.

[3] B. Doerr, D. Johannsen, and C. Winzen. Multiplicative drift analysis. *Algorithmica*, 64(4):673–697, 2012.

[4] S. Droste. Analysis of the (1 + 1) ea for a noisy onemax. In K. Deb, editor, *Genetic and Evolutionary Computation, GECCO 2004*, volume 3102 of *Lecture Notes in Computer Science*, pages 1088–1099. Springer Berlin Heidelberg, 2004.

[5] C. Gießen and T. Kötzing. Robustness of populations in stochastic environments. In *Proc. of GECCO (Genetic and evolutionary computation)*, 2014.

[6] W. Hoeffding. Probability inequalities for sums of bounded random variables. *Journal of the American Statistical Association*, 58(301):13–30, 1963.

[7] T. Jansen and I. Wegener. On the analysis of evolutionary algorithms — a proof that crossover can really help. In J. Nešetřil, editor, *Proceedings of the 7th Annual European Symposium on Algorithms (ESA'99)*, pages 184–193, Berlin, 1999. Springer.

[8] T. Jansen and I. Wegener. Real royal road functions: where crossover provably is essential. *Discrete Appl. Math.*, 149(1-3):111–125, 2005.

[9] P. S. Oliveto and C. Witt. Simplified drift anaalysis for proving lower bounds in evolutionary computation. *Algorithmica*, 59:369–386, 2011.

[10] P. S. Oliveto and C. Witt. Erratum: Simplified drift anaalysis for proving lower bounds in evolutionary computation. *arXiv*, page abs/1211.7184, 2012.

[11] D. Sudholt. Crossover is provably essential for the ising model on trees. In *Proceedings of the 7th Annual Conference on Genetic and Evolutionary Computation*, GECCO '05, pages 1161–1167, New York, NY, USA, 2005. ACM.

Evolution Strategies with Additive Noise: A Convergence Rate Lower Bound

Sandra Astete-Morales
TAO, Inria, Lri, Umr Cnrs 8623
Bat. 650, Univ. Paris-Sud
91405 Orsay Cedex, France
sandra-cecilia.astete-morales@inria.fr

Marie-Liesse Cauwet
TAO, Inria, Lri, Umr Cnrs 8623
Bat. 650, Univ. Paris-Sud
91405 Orsay Cedex, France
marie-liesse.cauwet@inria.fr

Olivier Teytaud
TAO, Inria, Lri, Umr Cnrs 8623
Bat. 650, Univ. Paris-Sud
91405 Orsay Cedex, France
olivier.teytaud@inria.fr

ABSTRACT

We consider the problem of optimizing functions corrupted with additive noise. It is known that Evolutionary Algorithms can reach a Simple Regret $O(1/\sqrt{n})$ within logarithmic factors, when n is the number of function evaluations. Here, Simple Regret at evaluation n is the difference between the evaluation of the function at the current recommendation point of the algorithm and at the real optimum. We show mathematically that this bound is tight, for any family of functions that includes sphere functions, at least for a wide set of Evolution Strategies without large mutations.

Categories and Subject Descriptors

G.1.6 [**Optimization**]: Unconstrained optimization

General Terms

Theory

Keywords

Evolution Strategies; Noisy Optimization; Additive Noise

1. INTRODUCTION

Evolutionary Algorithms (EAs) have received a significant amount of attention due to their wide applicability in optimization problems. In particular, they show robustness when confronted with rugged fitness landscapes. This robustness becomes a strong feature of EAs when facing objective functions corrupted by noise.

Black-Box Noisy Optimization. When we only have access to an *approximate* or *noisy* value of the objective function, the problem is termed a *Noisy Optimization Problem*. Additionally, we can consider that the values of the objective function are given by a *black-box* which receives as an input a feasible point and outputs the value of the (noisy) objective function at that point. This is the only information available regarding to the objective function. This will be termed a *Black-Box Noisy Optimization Problem* (BBNOP).

Noise models. To analyze the performance of an algorithm in front of a BBNOP, several *noise models* are considered in the literature. These models are appreciated for their simple and natural design. If we let $f(x)$ be the objective function, then the noisy version of it, $f(x,\omega)$ [1] can be define, as one of the following examples:

$$\begin{aligned} [\textbf{Additive noise}]\ f(x,\omega) &= f(x) + N(\omega), \\ [\textbf{Multiplicative noise}]\ f(x,\omega) &= f(x) \times (1 + N(\omega)) \\ [\textbf{Actuator noise}]\ f(x,\omega) &= f(x + N(\omega)) \end{aligned}$$

where $N(\omega)$ is some random variable with $\mathbb{E}_\omega[N(\omega)] = 0$.

Regardless of the noise model considered, EAs are commonly used to find the optimum of (noisy) objective functions. Nonetheless, their versatility comes with a disadvantage; EAs are slower than other methods used to solve BBNOP (more details on this in Section 1.2).

In the remaining of the Introduction we describe the characteristics of a special type of EAs, Evolution Strategies, and discuss the convergence rates reached by them both in noisy and noise-free environments. We compare these rates with the strictly better (or faster) convergence rates reached by algorithms that, opposite to Evolution Strategies, sample feasible points far away from the optimum.

1.1 Evolution Strategies

EAs are usually classified depending on certain specific characteristic in some of the stages that define them. For Evolution Strategies (ESs) in the continuous setting considered in the present paper[2], the traditional **mutation** operator creates an *offspring* by taking the *parent* of a generation and adding to it some random perturbation. This random perturbation is usually extracted from a Gaussian distribution. Therefore, the mutation operator favors "smaller mutations" by being more likely to create offsprings "close" to its parents. It is defined as follows:

$$\begin{aligned} \mathbb{R}^d &\to \mathbb{R}^d \\ x &\mapsto x + \sigma\mathcal{N}(0, C) \end{aligned}$$

[1]More formally, $f(x,\cdot)$ is a random variable on a probability space $(\Omega, \mathcal{A})$ and $\omega \in \Omega$ is an element of the sample space. So each time we draw a ω we have a new realization of the random variable $f(x,\cdot)$

[2]Some but not all authors consider that ESs are by definition working in the continuous case; anyway the present paper considers continuous domains only.

FOGA'15, January 17–20, 2015, Aberystwyth, UK.

ACM 978-1-4503-3434-1/15/01 ...$15.00.
http://dx.doi.org/10.1145/2725494.2725500.

The term σ is denominated *step-size* and the adaptation of it has been subject of study since the creation of ESs. The first achievement in that direction is the 1/5-success-rule [21] which is followed by the study of self-adaptation of the step-size using a variation process on it. The latter study gives birth to the so-called SA-ES: *Self-Adaptive Evolution Strategies* [8]. Additionally, the work on [17] develops a technique where the whole covariance matrix C is adapted, leading to the CMA-ES algorithm.

For the **selection** stage, ESs generally use *ranking-based* operators. Thus, when we consider BBNOP, the problem in the selection is the *misranking* of individuals. In other words, if we consider individuals x_1 and x_2 and an additive noise model, then due to the noise perturbation we might obtain $f(x_1, \omega_1) > f(x_2, \omega_2)$ whereas actually the real ordering between individuals is the opposite i.e. $f(x_1) < f(x_2)$. To deal with this problem, specific methods have been studied, including increasing the population size [1], using surrogate models [6, 19] and resampling many times per search point [16, 18]. In this context, resampling means that the query to the black-box is repeated several times for a given search point. Afterwards, some statistic of the repeated sample (usually the mean) is used as the objective function value of the point.

1.2 Typical Convergence behaviour

Calls to the black-box might be expensive, so the goal is to minimize the number of queries necessary to find a good approximation of the optimum of the function. In this paper, in order to measure the error between the approximated optimum given by the algorithm and the real optimum of the objective function, we use the *Simple Regret* criterion (definition in Eq. 3). We are interested in the relationship between the simple regret and the number of iterations/evaluations: the simple regret has to converge to 0 and with the least amount of iterations (or function evaluations) possible. To address this analysis we focus on the graph of both variables either in *log-linear* or *log-log* scale (for precise definitions see Eq. 5 and Eq. 6).

Convergence rate for ESs in the noise-free or small noise case. For ESs, in the case of noise-free optimization, the convergence typically occurs in *log-linear* scale: the logarithm of the simple regret decreases linearly when the number of iterations increases. Such results can be found in [4, 5, 21, 27]. In some cases, the same behavior can be achieved in the noisy case; typically in the case of variance decreasing faster than in the multiplicative model, and if fitness values are averaged over a constant ad-hoc number of resamplings [9].

Convergence rate for ESs in the noisy case. The convergence behaviour with additive noise occurs generally in *log-log* scale: the logarithm of the simple regret decreases linearly as a function of the logarithm of the number of evaluations [2, 3, 10, 11, 13].
The work presented on [3] shows mathematically that an exponential number of resamplings (w.r.t. number of iterations) or an adaptive number of resamplings (scaling as a polynomial function of the inverse step-size) can both lead to a *log-log* convergence scale in the case of the sphere function with additive noise when using Evolutionary Strategy.

However, in the previous cases, further information on the value of the convergence rate is not provided in most of these papers.

Convergence rate for algorithms sampling farther away from the optimum. Not only EAs are used in the resolution of BBNOP. Other techniques for the optimization of functions in noisy environments have been explored in the literature. They usually consist in the development of algorithms that sample far away from the optimum in order to approximate the shape of the objective function, using machine learning or finite differences. In this context, Fabian [14] and Shamir [24] approximate the tangent of the objective function through a gradient approximated by finite differences, and use it in the optimization process. They both obtain linear convergence in the *log-log* scale. More precisely, the work on [24] proves that the convergence occurs with a slope -1 in the case of strongly convex quadratic functions, as detailed later, whereas Fabian [14] proves similar rates (arbitrarily close to -1) asymptotically but on a wider family of functions. The tightness of rates in [14] is proved in [10]). A key feature which is common to all these algorithms is that they sample farther from the optimum than ESs.

1.3 Outline of this paper

Section (2) presents the notations used througout the article. Section (3) covers the formalization of algorithms and the main result of the paper. In Section (3.1) we define the optimization algorithms in a general framework. We also discuss the scope of the definition. The section includes as well a definition for the Evolution Strategies family considered in this paper. Section (3.2) is devoted to the enunciation and proof of the main result of this paper: we show a lower bound on the slope of the *log-log* graph, proving that Evolution Strategies family can not reach rates as fast as those reached by algorithms that approximate the shape of the function thanks to samplings far from the optimum. Section (4) shows the empirical verification of the proved results. We present experiments for Evolution Strategies ((1+1)-ES and UHCMAES) covered by the Theorem 1, and for the algorithm in [24], which is not covered by our results and presents convergence rates strictly faster than ESs. Finally in Section (5) we discuss the results both theoretically and empirically and we conclude the work.

2. PRELIMINARIES

Consider d a positive integer and a domain $\mathcal{D} \subset \mathbb{R}^d$. Given a function $f : \mathcal{D} \to \mathbb{R}$, the noisy version of it is a stochastic process, also denoted f but defined as $f : \mathcal{D} \times \Omega \to \mathbb{R}, (x, \omega) \mapsto f(x, \omega)$ where ω represents the realization of a random variable over some Ω. Henceforward, $f(x)$ will be the exact value of f in x whereas $f(x, \omega)$ denotes a noisy value of f in x. $f(x, \omega)$ is supposed to be unbiased, i.e. $\mathbb{E}_\omega f(x, \omega) = f(x)$. We assume that x^* is the unknown exact and unique optimum (minimum) of f.

In the present paper, the noise model corresponds to **additive noise**:

$$f(x, \omega) = f(x) + N(\omega), \tag{1}$$

with $\mathbb{E}_\omega[N] = 0$. The noise is then an additive term, independent of x and with *constant variance*, i.e $\forall x \in \mathcal{D}, \forall \omega$, $Var(f(x, \omega)) = Var(N)$ is constant.

In our analysis n denotes the number of function evaluations and x_n denotes the nth search point, which is the point that will be evaluated by the objective function. We define also $\tilde{x}_n$ denoting the approximation of the optimum that the algorithm proposes after $(n-1)$ function evaluations. The recommendation point can be the same as the search point, but not necessarily: the recommendation point can be computed without evaluating the objective function on it (as in [24, 14]). We denote y_n the evaluation of the noisy function in x_n. The sequence of search points and their evaluation on the noisy function is:

$$Z_n = ((x_0, y_0), \ldots, (x_{n-1}, y_{n-1})) \tag{2}$$

The Simple Regret and the Cumulative Regret, SR_n and CR_n respectively, are defined as follows:

$$SR_n = \mathbb{E}[f(\tilde{x}_n, \omega_n)] - \inf_x f(x); \tag{3}$$

$$CR_n = \left(\sum_{i=1}^{n} \mathbb{E}[f(x_i, \omega_i)]\right) - n \inf_x f(x) \tag{4}$$

We are interested in the linear relationship between the Regret and the number of function evaluations using scale *log-linear* or *log-log* graphs. Therefore, the rates of convergence are the *slopes* of the *log-linear* (Eq. 5) or *log-log graphs* (Eq. 6).

$$\textbf{Log-linear: } \limsup_n \frac{\log SR_n}{n} = -\alpha < 0. \tag{5}$$

$$\textbf{Log-log: } \limsup_n \frac{\log SR_n}{\log n} = -\alpha < 0, \tag{6}$$

In this paper we will use the the slope in *log-log* graph: $-\alpha$ on Eq. 6. Precisely, we say that the slope $-\alpha$ is *verified* on a family F of noisy objective functions if α is such that:

$$\forall f \in F,\ \exists C > 0,\ \forall n \in \mathbb{N},\ SR_n \le C/n^\alpha. \tag{7}$$

This means that several different slopes might be verified. Note that the important is the supremum of such α.

In the following the inner product in $\mathbb{R}^d$ is represented by $\cdot$ and *sgn*() refers to the sign function.

3. THEORETICAL ANALYSIS

This section consists of the formalization of the algorithms and the main result of the paper. We present on one side the formalization of the concept of *black-box noisy optimization algorithm* (Algorithm 1, section (3.1)) and on the other side a formalization of "classical" ES (Def. 1, Section (3.1)). Notably, the ESs covered by the formalization of ES in Definition 1 correspond to a wide family but not all of them. The condition on Eq. 10 refers to the evolution of the step-size and the approximation to the optimum. The latter condition holds provably for some ESs, and probably for much more, but not necessarily for e.g. ESs with surrogate models learnt with large mutations [15, 20, 28]. Also algorithms using several Gaussian distributions simultaneously or multimodal random variables for generating individuals are not covered. Thus, we mainly consider here ESs with one Gaussian distribution which scales roughly as the distance to the optimum.

In Section (3.2) we prove the theorem that states that the family of evolution strategies described by the formalization converges at best with rate $-1/2$ (tightness comes from [12]).

3.1 Formalization of Algorithms

General Optimization Framework

Basically, an optimization algorithm samples some search points, evaluates them and proposes a recommendation (i.e. an approximation of the optimum) from this information. We formalize a general optimization algorithm in Algorithm 1.

Algorithm 1 General Optimization Framework.

```
Input: s = random seed, p = parameter, I = initial internal state
  n ← 0
  loop
    r = rand(s)
    x̃_n = R(Z_n, r, n, p, I).                    ▷ Recommend
    x_n = SP(Z_n, r, n, p, I).                    ▷ Search
    y_n = f(x_n, ω_n)                ▷ Evaluate f in search point
    n ← n + 1.
  end loop
```

The procedures R and SP correspond to the *Recommendation* and *Search Point* stages of the algorithm. R outputs a feasible point that stands as the approximate optimum of the respective iteration and SP generates new search points to be evaluated. $\mathcal{I}$ represents the internal state of the algorithm, possibly modified inside SP. The sequence Z_n is as defined in Eq. 2.

When $n = 0$, Z_n is void and the points x_0 and $\tilde{x}_0$ are initialized depending on the parameters of the algorithm and on the random seed s. Starting from $n = 1$, both the R and the SP functions return values depending on the results of previous iterations.

The presented framework is in fact very general. First, if we consider algorithms that make use of populations for the optimization process, this characteristic can be simulated in the framework even when apparently the population size in Algorithm 1 is always 1. For example, let us say we want to check if an algorithm that uses a population of size λ (λ-population-based) can fit the framework. Then, an iteration on the λ-population-based algorithm can be "split" into several iterations in the framework, so that the λ individuals can be generated by λ iterations of a population size 1, just by adapting the R and SP functions.

Second, thanks to r, randomized algorithms are included. We propose different algorithms which match this framework in Section (4) [3].

The framework presented encodes black-box algorithms and therefore both evolution strategies and algorithms reaching fast rates as those presented in [14, 24]. Note that there is no restriction regarding the distance between x_n and $\tilde{x}_n$. In particular, in the case of [14, 24, 11] the search points and the recommendation points can be far from each other (it is even desirable). On the contrary, ESs have a search point procedure that dictates that x_n should not be very far from the $\tilde{x}_n$.

Perimeter covered by General Optimization Framework

We provide some observations to clarify the scope of Algorithm 1, and how it covers the usual definitions of black-box optimization algorithms.

In general, a black-box optimization algorithm uses the objective function as an oracle. Since we consider a black-

[3] In particular Algorithm 2 in section 4.1 is presented as an explicit example of an algorithm written to fit the framework described by Algorithm 1.

box setting, there is no access to any internal characteristic of the objective function.

On the other side, a black-box optimization algorithm has a state that is either its initial state (in case we are at the first time step) or a function of its internal state and of the results of requests to the oracle.

And since the algorithm is an algorithm for optimization, it must provide an approximation of the optimum. Such an approximation is termed "recommendation". We here decide that the approximation of the optimum should not change between two calls to the objective (i.e. oracle) function.

Therefore, an optimization algorithm is a sequence of internal computations, which modify an internal state. This sequence is sometimes interrupted by a call to the oracle function, or by a change in the recommendation.

We can then rewrite the algorithm, hiding all internal transformations of the internal state $\mathcal{I}$ between two calls to the oracle in some SP function. The algorithm then evaluates the objective function at x_n (call to the oracle). Next, it proposes a new approximation of the optimum; this computation is encoded in R. We have specified that this does not modify $\mathcal{I}$; but the procedure R can be duplicated inside SP, which is allowed to modify the internal state, if necessary, so this is not a loss of generality. The random seed is available for all functions so that there is no limitation around randomization.

We have assumed that the algorithm never spends infinite computation times between two calls to the oracle, and does not stop. We can just decide that in such a case we report the same output for R and the same output for SP.

All the elements discussed in this section allow us to use the general optimization framework described in Algorithm 1 to represent many of black-box optimization algorithms

Simple Evolution Strategies definition

ESs are black-box optimization algorithms and they fit the framework in Algorithm 1. Nonetheless, one important feature that characterizes them is the way to generate search points. Normally, the sampling of new search points is made "around" the recommendation point of the previous generation. This means that the SP procedure is defined by:

$$\mathtt{SP}(\mathfrak{Z}_n) = \mathtt{R}(\mathfrak{Z}_n) + \sigma(\mathfrak{Z}_n)\Psi(\mathfrak{Z}_n) \tag{8}$$

where, for short, $\mathfrak{Z}_n = (Z_n, r, n, p, \mathcal{I})$. The step-size $\sigma(\mathfrak{Z}_n)$ is usually updated at each generation. $\Psi(\mathfrak{Z}_n)$ is an independent d-dimensional zero-mean random variable, not necessarily Gaussian, with

$$\mathbb{E}\|\Psi(\mathfrak{Z}_n)\|^2 = d. \tag{9}$$

Also, we consider that the ESs should satisfy the following condition on the evolution of the step-size with regards to the recommendation points. In the following section we will explain with more details the reasons behind this condition:

$$\exists D > 0,\ \forall n \geq 0,\ \mathbb{E}[\sigma(\mathfrak{Z}_n)^2] \leq D\mathbb{E}[\|\tilde{x}_n - x^*\|^2]. \tag{10}$$

Now we can state the definition of ES covered by the theorem in Section (3.2).

DEFINITION 1. [**Simple Evolution Strategy**] *A Simple Evolution Strategy is an algorithm that matches framework of Alg. 1 and satisfies both Eq. 8 and Eq. 10.*

Perimeter covered by Simple Evolution Strategy definition

Let us discuss the assumptions in our Evolution Strategy framework above.
Eq. 9 is not a strong constraint, as one can always rephrase the algorithm for moving multiplicative factors from $\Psi(\mathfrak{Z}_n)$ to $\sigma(\mathfrak{Z}_n)$ so that $\mathbb{E}\|\Psi(\mathfrak{Z}_n)\|^2 = d$.

The assumption in Eq. 8 is easy to understand. It is verified for a classical EA with a single parent or a μ/μ recombination (i.e. parent equal to the average of selected offspring), including weighted recombinations.
The assumption in Eq. 10 is more difficult to grasp. It means that $\tilde{x}_n$ and $\sigma(\mathfrak{Z}_n)$ decrease at the same rate towards the optimum. The literature provides the following cases:

- The scale-invariant algorithm obviously verifies the assumption, by definition. The scale-invariant algorithm is however essentially a theoretical algorithm, used for theoretical proofs rather than for real applications.
- Related results are proved for some EAs in the noise-free case, as shown in [4]; $\sigma(\mathfrak{Z}_n)/\|\tilde{x}_n - x^*\|$ converges to some distribution. The work in [3] shows that it is also true for some provably convergent noisy optimization evolutionary algorithm with resamplings. However, it is not clear that these results imply Eq. 10.
- Beyond mathematical proofs (indeed there are many evolutionary algorithms for which we have no convergence proof at all), Eq. 10 is widely verified in experimental results when algorithms converge, in the $(1+1)$-ES [21], in self-adaptive algorithms [8], in Covariance Matrix Adaptations variants [17], and indeed most EAs [7].

What would be an EA which does *not* verify Eq. 10? A natural example is an Evolutionary Algorithm which samples far from the current estimate $\tilde{x}_n$ of the optimum, e.g. for building a surrogate model. Interestingly, all optimization algorithms which are fast in noisy optimization with constant noise variance in the vicinity of the optimum verify such a property, namely sampling far from the optimum [14, 24, 11]. This suggests that modified ESs which include samplings far from the optimum, might be faster.

3.2 Lower bound for Simple Evolution Strategies

We now state our main theorem, namely the proof that Evolution Strategies, in their usual setting without mutations far from the optimum, can not reach rate as good as algorithms without such restrictions.

THEOREM 1. *Let F be the set of quadratic functions $f : \mathcal{D} \to \mathbb{R}$ defined on $\mathcal{D} = \mathbb{R}^d$ by $f(x) = \frac{1}{2}\|x\|^2 - (x^* \cdot x)$ for some $\|x^*\| \leq \frac{1}{2}$. Consider a simple Evolution Strategy as in definition 1 and the noisy optimization of $f \in F$ corrupted by some additive noise with variance 1 in the unit ball: $f(x,\omega) = f(x) + N(\omega)$ such that $\mathbb{E}_\omega[f(x,\omega)] = f(x)$. Then, for all $\alpha > \frac{1}{2}$, the slope $-\alpha$ is not reached.*

REMARK 1. **(Tightness in the framework of evolution strategies.)** *The work in [12] shows that, within logarithmic factors, an evolution strategy with Bernstein races* *(with modified sampling in order to avoid huge numbers of resamplings due to individuals with almost equal fitness values) can reach a slope $-\alpha$ arbitrarily close to $-\alpha = -\frac{1}{2}$. To the best of our knowledge, it is not known whether we can reach $\alpha = \frac{1}{2}$.*

REMARK 2. **(Scope of the lower bound)** *Note that Theorem 1 considers a particular set of quadratic functions, but the result is valid for any family of functions that includes sphere functions.*

Proof: Let us assume, in order to get a contradiction, that a slope $\alpha > \frac{1}{2}$ is reached. Then, $SR_n \leq C/n^\alpha$ for some $\alpha > 1/2$ and $C > 0$.
Notations are similar to Section (3.1): for any $i \in \{1, \dots, n\}$, $x_i = \mathtt{SP}(\mathfrak{Z}_i)$, $\tilde{x}_i = \mathtt{R}(\mathfrak{Z}_i)$, $\sigma_i = \sigma(\mathfrak{Z}_i)$, $\Psi_i = \Psi(\mathfrak{Z}_i)$, where Ψ_i are centered independent random variables in $\mathbb{R}^d$ with $\mathbb{E}\|\Psi_i\|^2 = d$. Let us evaluate the cumulative regret:

$$
\begin{aligned}
2CR_n &= 2\sum_{i=1}^{n} (\mathbb{E}f(x_i, \omega_i) - f(x^*)) \text{ by definition in Eq. 4.} \\
&= \sum_{i=1}^{n} \mathbb{E}[\|x_i\|^2 - 2(x^* \cdot x_i) + \|x^*\|^2] \\
&= \sum_{i=1}^{n} \mathbb{E}[\|x_i - x^*\|^2] \\
&= \sum_{i=1}^{n} \mathbb{E}[\|\tilde{x}_i - x^* + \sigma_i \Psi_i\|^2] \text{ by Eq. 8} \\
&\leq \sum_{i=1}^{n} \left(\mathbb{E}\|\tilde{x}_i - x^*\|^2 + \mathbb{E}\sigma_i^2 \mathbb{E}\Psi_i^2\right) \text{ by independence} \\
&\leq \sum_{i=1}^{n} \left(\mathbb{E}\|\tilde{x}_i - x^*\|^2 + d\mathbb{E}\sigma_i^2\right) \text{ by Eq. 9} \\
&\leq 2(1 + dD)\sum_{i=1}^{n} \mathbb{E}[SR_i] \text{ by Eq. 10}
\end{aligned}
$$

The last equation leads to

$$CR_n \leq C(1 + dD)n^{1-\alpha} \qquad (11)$$

Shamir [24, Theorem 6] has shown that, for any optimization algorithm as defined in Section (3.1), there is at least one function in $f \in F$ for which the cumulative regret is $CR_n \geq 0.02\min(1, d\sqrt{n})$, which contradicts Eq. 11. □

4. EXPERIMENTAL VERIFICATION OF THE LOWER BOUND

This section is devoted to the verification of the lower bound on the convergence rate for ESs stated in Theorem 1 and the comparison with the convergence rate of a "fast" Algorithm: SHAMIR ALGORITHM [24].
We show experimentally that the rate -1 promised by the results in [24] is visible on experiments, even with moderate budgets in terms of numbers of function evaluations. We then show that, consistently with theory, we could not do better than slope $-1/2$ with ESs (Section (4.2)). The experimental results presented on this section use an approximation of the slope of simple regret (Eq. 6)[4]:

$$\log(SR_n/d)/\log(n)$$

4.1 Fast Convergence: Shamir Algorithm

Shamir [24] designed an optimization algorithm using stochastic approximation methods ([26, 25]). At each iteration, it computes a natural gradient and uses it to update the estimate of the optimum. This algorithm is described in Algorithm 2 and is named SHAMIR ALGORITHM in the following. Note that in procedure SP are defined the search points and thanks to the random direction r these search points can be far from the current approximation. This algorithm provably asymptotically reaches some slope arbitrarily close to $\alpha = 1$ in the quadratic case. Importantly, we present the algorithm in the framework of Section (3.1), however, neither Eq. 8, nor Eq. 10 are satisfied so that this cannot be considered a Simple Evolution Strategy as in Def. 1.

Algorithm 2 SHAMIR ALGORITHM. Written in the general optimization framework.

```
procedure R(x_0, ..., x_{n-1}, y_0, ..., y_{n-1}, r, n, p, I)
                        ▷ I is a vector of n elements in the domain.
    if ||I_n|| ≥ B then
        I_n = B I_n/||I_n||
    end if
    x̃_n = (2/n) Σ_{j=⌈n/2⌉,...,n}^{n} I_j
end procedure
procedure SP(x_0, ..., x_{n-1}, y_0, ..., y_{n-1}, r, n, p, I)
    if n = 0 then
        I = (0)
        Return x_0 = 0
    end if
    Compute x_n = x_{n-1} + (ε/√d) r
    Compute g̃ = (√d y_{n-1}/ε) r
    Compute I = (I, x_{n-1} - (1/(λn)) g̃)
end procedure

Input: : p = (λ, ε, B) ∈ ℝ_+ × (0,1] × R_+, s = random seed
  n ← 0
  loop
    Generate r ∈ {-1,1}^d, uniformly and randomly
    x̃_n = R(x_0, ..., x_{n-1}, y_0, ..., y_{n-1}, r, n, p, I)
    x_n = SP(x_0, ..., x_{n-1}, y_0, ..., y_{n-1}, r, n, p, I)
    y_n = f(x_n, ω)
    n ← n + 1
  end loop
```

We compare the performance of Shamir's Algorithm on the noisy sphere function: $x \mapsto \|x - 0.5\|^2 + \mathcal{N}(0, 1)$, where $\mathcal{N}(0, 1)$ is a standard Gaussian.
Results are presented in Figure 1. Experiments are performed in various dimensions: 2, 4, 8 and 16. We observe that independently of the dimension, the algorithm's slope is smaller than $-1/2$ and converges toward -1 (i.e. faster than the bound we have proved).

4.2 Slow Convergence: UHCMAES and (1+1) ES

UHCMAES (Uncertainty Handling Covariance Matrix Adaptation Evolution Strategy) was introduced in [16]. This algorithm is a specific variant of CMAES designed for dealing with noise. More specifically, it uses an adaptive number of resamplings in order to reduce the noise. It combines the

[4]Note that dividing by d does not matter asymptotically and both theory [24] and experiments show that it is a good normalization for convergence rates.

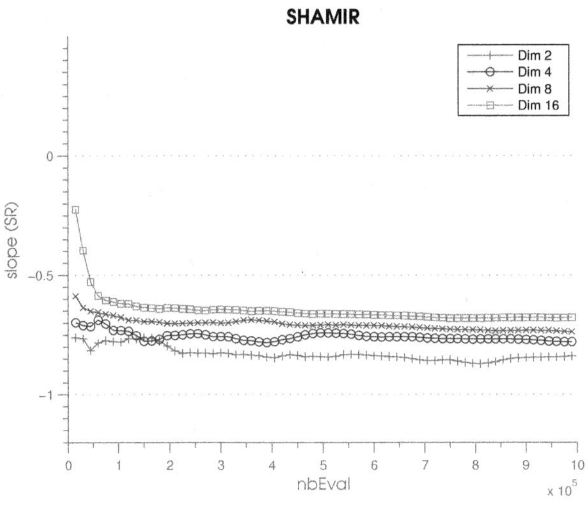

Figure 1: Shamir's algorithm [24] on the sphere function $x \mapsto \|x\|^2 + \mathcal{N}(0,1)$ where $\mathcal{N}(0,1)$ is an independent Gaussian standard random variable. X-axis: number of function evaluations. Y-axis: estimate of the slope (see Eq. 4). The maximum standard deviation for all averages presented here (experiments are averaged over 21 runs) is 10^{-3}.

traditional CMA-ES algorithm with an Uncertainty-Handling tool. The Uncertainty-Handling tool is made of two parts. The first part *measures* the uncertainty due to the noise and the second part *handles* the uncertainty. The treatment of the uncertainty is twofold. If the measurement of the uncertainty exceeds a given threshold, then *the computation time* (typically the number of resamplings) increases and/or the variance (the step-size) of the population increases. Whereas if the uncertainty is below the threshold, the *computation time* decreases. In the format presented on this paper, *computation time* refers to the number of resamplings.

We provide a high-level pseudo-code of UHCMAES in Algorithm 3. For the sake of clarity, the pseudo-code given in Algorithm 3 is not cast into the setting of Section (3.1). However, as any optimization algorithm, it could be rewritten so that it matches the general setting of Algorithm 1 (see Section (3.1)).

The CMAES part of the algorithm generates a new population at each iteration. The new population is obtained by mutating the old one thanks to a Gaussian random variable. The mean, the variance σ^2 and a (scaled) covariance C of this Gaussian random variable are adapted at each iteration, depending of the selection/ranking of the μ best offspring. Then, the center of the Gaussian is recommended as an approximation of the optimum. The so-called evolution path p_σ (resp. p_C) of σ (resp. C) is updated and used to update σ (resp. C). All these updates are grouped into Line 10 and are based on both the old and new population, parameters σ, p_σ, C, p_C and parameters which are not detailed. For brevity, these updates are not detailed in Algorithm 3, see [17] for extra information.

The "UH" part is based on the resamplings (Line 5), on the evaluation of the uncertainty (**Generate** λ' and **Compute** threshold $\bar{t}$) and consequently, on the adjustment of parameters σ and r. The two procedures **Generate** λ' and **Compute** threshold $\bar{t}$ are described in Subroutines 1 and 2 respectively.

Algorithm 3 UH-CMA-ES. $\mathcal{N}(a,b)$ stands for a normal random variable of mean a and covariance b. *hparam* stand for hidden parameters, it includes the parameters used in the update of σ, p_σ, C, p_C, in functions **Generate** λ' and **Compute threshold** $\bar{t}$.

Require: $\lambda \in \mathbb{N}$, $\alpha_r \in \mathbb{R}$, $\alpha_\sigma \in \mathbb{R}$, hparam
1: **Initialization:** $x_i = 0 \in \mathbb{R}^d$, $\forall i \in \{1,\dots,\lambda\}$, $m = 0$, $\sigma = 0.6$, $C = I$, p_σ, p_c, $r = 1$, $\epsilon = 10^{-7}$, $\bar{t} = 0$
2: **while** not terminate **do**
3:   **for** $i = 1$ *to* λ **do**
4:     $x_i \leftarrow \mathcal{N}(m, \sigma^2 C)$
5:     $y_i \leftarrow \frac{1}{r}\sum_{j=1}^{r} f(x_i, \omega)$
6:   **end for**
7:   Sort (y_i) such that $y_{s(1)} \le \dots \le y_{s(\lambda)}$
8:   $(x_1,\dots,x_\lambda) \leftarrow (x_{s(1)},\dots,x_{s(\lambda)})$
9:   $m \leftarrow \frac{1}{\lambda}\sum_{i=1}^{\lambda} x_i$
10:   Update parameters σ, C, p_σ, p_c
11:   **Generate** λ' ▷ possibly 0
12:   **for** $i = 1$ *to* λ' **do**
13:     $x_i' \leftarrow x_i + \epsilon\sigma\mathcal{N}(0, C)$
14:     $y_i' \leftarrow \frac{1}{r}\sum_{j=1}^{r} f(x_i', \omega)$
15:   **end for**
16:   **Compute threshold** $\bar{t}$.
17:   $y_i'' \leftarrow \frac{y_i + y_i'}{2}$ if $i \le \lambda'$ and $y_i'' \leftarrow y_i$ otherwise
18:   Sort (y_i'') such that $y''_{s''(1)} \le \dots \le y''_{s''(\lambda)}$
19:   $(x_1,\dots,x_\lambda) \leftarrow (x_{s(1)},\dots,x_{s(\lambda)})$
20:   **if** $\bar{t} > 0$ **then**
21:     $r \leftarrow \alpha_r r$, $\sigma \leftarrow \alpha_\sigma \sigma$
22:   **else**
23:     $r \leftarrow \frac{r}{\alpha_r^{0.25}}$
24:   **end if**
25: **end while**
26: **return:** x_1

Subroutine 1 Generate λ'

Input: $g_\lambda = \max(0.2, \frac{2}{\lambda})$
if $\lambda' = 0$ for more then $\frac{2}{g_\lambda \lambda}$ generations **then**
  $\lambda' \leftarrow 1$
else
  $\lambda' \leftarrow \lfloor g_\lambda \times \lambda \rfloor + 1$ with probability $g_\lambda \times \lambda - \lfloor g_\lambda \times \lambda \rfloor$
  $\lambda' \leftarrow \lfloor g_\lambda \times \lambda \rfloor$ otherwise
end if
    return λ'

We here experiment this algorithm on $f(x) = \|x - x^*\|^2 + 0.3\mathcal{N}(0,1)$, where $\mathcal{N}(0,1)$ is a standard Gaussian random variable and with $x^* = 0.5$. In these experiments, we use all the default parametrizations of UHCMAES[5].

Results are shown in Figure 2. Even though the rate of convergence to the optimum decreases as the dimension increases, we can observe rates of between −0.1 and −0.3, all of them greater than −0.5.

Now let us consider a Simple Evolution Strategy, namely the (1 + 1)ES with one-fifth rule [21, 23], with additional revaluations, implemented as shown in Algorithm 4.

A way to slightly improve Algorithm 4 is to improve the computation of the fitness value of the current best recommendation by averaging the current estimate with the previous estimates of the same search point, when the mutation

[5]See settings at URL `https://www.lri.fr/~hansen/cmaes.m`.

Subroutine 2 Compute threshold $\bar{t}$. $\Delta_\theta^{lim}(R)$ is the $\theta \times 50\%$-ile of the set $\{|1-R|, |2-R|, \ldots, |2\lambda-1-R|\}$.

Input: $\theta = 0.2$, $c_t = 1$, (y_i), $(y_i^{'})$
Rank $Y = (y_i) \cup (y_i^{'})$
for $i \in \{1, \ldots, \lambda^{'}\}$ **do**
    $\Delta_i \leftarrow \text{rank}(y_i^{'}) - \text{rank}(y_i) - sgn(\text{rank}(y_i^{'}) - \text{rank}(y_i))$
end for
Compute

$$t \leftarrow \frac{1}{\lambda'} \sum_{i=1}^{\lambda'} \left(2|\Delta_i| - \Delta_\theta^{lim}\left(\text{rank}(y_i^{'}) - \mathbf{1}_{y_i^{'} > y_i}\right) - \Delta_\theta^{lim}\left(\text{rank}(y_i) - \mathbf{1}_{y_i > y_i^{'}}\right)\right)$$

$\bar{t} \leftarrow (1 - c_t)\bar{t} + c_t t$
    return $\bar{t}$

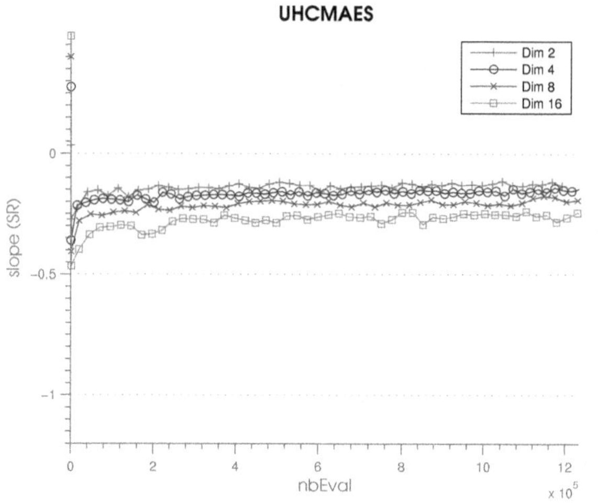

Figure 2: UHCMAES algorithm [16] on the sphere function $x \mapsto ||x||^2 + 0.3\mathcal{N}(0,1)$ where $\mathcal{N}(0,1)$ is an independent Gaussian standard random variable. The maximum standard deviation for all averages presented here (experiments are averaged over 21 runs) is 1.

has not been accepted and $x_n = x_{n-1}$. We propose such a modification in Algorithm 5 by using a weighted average in the estimate fitness value of the current best search point.

Experiments on the noisy sphere function $||x - x^*||^2 + \mathcal{N}(0,1)$, where $\mathcal{N}(0,1)$ is a standard Gaussian, are provided, using Algorithm 5. Results are presented in Figure 3 in various dimensions (2, 4, 8, 16 respectively). Seemingly both exponential and polynomial resamplings lead to a slope $-1/2$.

5. CONCLUSIONS

We have shown that Evolution Strategies, at least under their most common form, can not reach the same rate as noisy optimization algorithms which use evaluations of the objective function farther from the approximate optimum in order to obtain extra information on the function. On the contrary, ESs use evaluations of objective functions only in the neighborhood of the optimum. Therefore, usual ESs cannot reach rates as the ones in [14, 24] (Shamir [24] in the quadratic case non-asymptotically, Fabian [14] in the general case but asymptotically). The latter type of algorithms reach a slope -1, whereas we have a limit at $-1/2$ with evolution strategies. This solves the conjecture proposed in [24] just after theorem 1. This also shows the optimality of the rate $-1/2$ obtained by R-EDA [22], in the framework of local sampling only.

Algorithm 4 $(1+1)-ES$ for noisy optimization with resamplings. $\mathcal{N}(0,1)$ is a standard Gaussian. The function *number_of_revaluations* depends on the current iteration and on a parameter p. Typically the number of revaluations is polynomial: n^p or exponential: p^n.

Initialization: $n = 0$, $\sigma = 1$, $x = (0, \ldots, 0)$, p
while not terminate **do**
    $x' \leftarrow x + \sigma\mathcal{N}(0,1)$
    $n \leftarrow n + 1$
    $r \leftarrow$ number_of_revaluations(n, p)
    $y \leftarrow \frac{1}{r}\sum_{i=1}^{r}(f(x), \omega))$
    $y' \leftarrow \frac{1}{r}\sum_{i=1}^{r}(f(x', \omega))$
    if $y' < y$ **then**
        $x \leftarrow x'$ and $\sigma \leftarrow 2\sigma$
    else
        $\sigma \leftarrow .84\sigma$
    end if
end while
    return x

Algorithm 5 Slightly improved $(1+1)-ES$ for noisy optimization with resamplings.

Initialization: $n = 0$, $\sigma = 1$, $k = 0$, $x = (0, \ldots, 0)$, $y = 0$
while not terminate **do**
    $x' \leftarrow x + \sigma\mathcal{N}$ ▷ Gaussian mutation
    $n \leftarrow n + 1$
    $r \leftarrow$ number_of_revaluations(n)
    $y \leftarrow k \times y + r \times \frac{1}{r}\sum_{i=1}^{r} f(x, \omega)$
    $k \leftarrow k + r$
    $y \leftarrow y/k$
    $y' \leftarrow \frac{1}{r}\sum_{i=1}^{r} f(x', \omega)$
    if $y' < y$ **then**
        $x \leftarrow x'$
        $\sigma \leftarrow 2\sigma$
        $y \leftarrow 0$
        $k \leftarrow 0$
    else
        $\sigma \leftarrow .84\sigma$
    end if
end while

It is important to note that the result in this paper indeed covers not only Evolutionary Algorithms, but also, for example, many pattern search methods. We proved the results for algorithms which perform sampling within some distance of the approximate optimum, this distance scaling roughly as the distance to the optimum. This property is known to be satisfied by most ESs (see Section (3.1)). However, for many algorithms it is verified only experimentally and not formally proved.

ESs with surrogate models are not concerned by our lower bound. More precisely, if we include strong surrogate modelling with large mutations (and so contradicting Eq. 10), then we can recover fast rates with slope -1. An extreme example of this situation is the case in which the sampling/ surrogate model is exactly the algorithm in [14], [24] or [11]. Using them as to obtain surrogate models within an ES will ensure a fast convergence rate for the ES. Obviously, it is desirable to verify if such result can also be obtained with more "evolutionary" approaches.

The bound presented in this paper does not cover evolutionary algorithms that would use very large mutations.

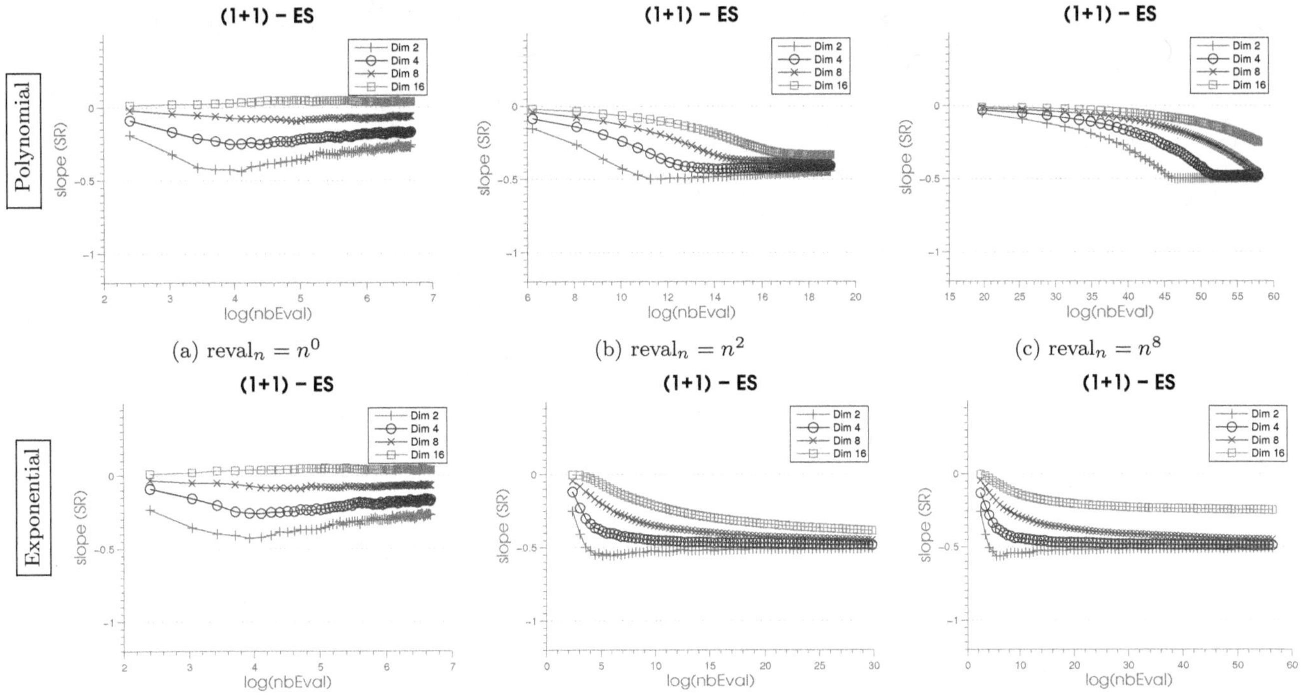

(a) $\text{reval}_n = n^0$ (b) $\text{reval}_n = n^2$ (c) $\text{reval}_n = n^8$

(d) $\text{reval}_n = 1^n$ (e) $\text{reval}_n = 1.03^n$ (f) $\text{reval}_n = 1.07^n$

Figure 3: Results (1+1) ES for dimension 2, 4, 8 and 16. First row of plots presents Polynomial resampling and the second row Exponential resampling. The maximum standard deviation for all averages presented here (experiments are averaged over 400 runs) is 0.025. Note that (nbEval) is the number of evaluations, n.

Maybe this is a good path to follow for designing fast evolutionary noisy optimization algorithms.

For all experiments we check convergence rates on the sphere function with additive noise.

We consider an algorithm with theoretical fast rate, the SHAMIR ALGORITHM, and two ESs: UHCMAES and (1+1) ES. For SHAMIR ALGORITHM we have achieved a successful implementation of the algorithm [6] and confirmed empirically the fast convergence rate proved in [14, 24] (i.e. slope of SR $= -1$). For UHCMAES and (1+1) ES we have shown that ESs can approximate slope of SR -0.5 using $(1+1)$ES. UHCMAES also reaches linear convergence in the log-log scale but with a slower rate (slope of SR around -0.2).

Further work

A first further work consists in proving the result in a wider setting, this is, weakening the assumption in Eq. 10. We might also check other criteria than non-asymptotic expected simple regret, e.g. almost sure convergence. Another further work is investigating which optimization algorithms, other than Evolution Strategies, are concerned by our result or by similar results. In the case of strongly convex functions with a lower bound on eigenvalues of the Hessian, we conjecture that the asymptotic rate -1 can also not be reached by the considered family of evolutionary algorithms.

[6]Shamir [24] delivers only the theoretical analysis of his algorithm and an implemented version.

Acknowledgements

We are grateful to the Ademe Post project for making this work possible (`post.artelys.com`).

Possibilities of algorithms using huge mutations were discussed in the noisy optimization working group at Dagstuhl's seminar 2014; we are grateful to N. Hansen, Y. Akimoto, J. Shapiro, A. Prügel-Benett for fruitful discussions there.

6. REFERENCES

[1] D. Arnold and H.-G. Beyer. Investigation of the (μ, λ)-ES in the presence of noise. In *Proceedings of the IEEE Conference on Evolutionary Computation (CEC 2001)*, pages 332–339. IEEE, 2001.

[2] D. Arnold and H.-G. Beyer. Local performance of the (1 + 1)-ES in a noisy environment. *Evolutionary Computation, IEEE Transactions on*, 6(1):30–41, Feb 2002.

[3] S. Astete-Morales, J. Liu, and O. Teytaud. Log-log convergence for noisy optimization. In *Artificial Evolution*, Lecture Notes in Computer Science, pages 16–28. Springer International Publishing, 2014.

[4] A. Auger. Convergence results for (1,λ)-SA-ES using the theory of φ-irreducible Markov chains. *Theoretical Computer Science*, 334(1-3):35–69, 2005.

[5] A. Auger, M. Jebalia, and O. Teytaud. Algorithms (x, sigma, eta): Quasi-random mutations for evolution strategies. In *Artificial Evolution*, Lecture Notes in Computer Science, pages 296–307. Springer Berlin Heidelberg, 2006.

[6] A. Auger, M. Schoenauer, and O. Teytaud. Local and global order 3/2 convergence of a surrogate evolutionary algorithm. In *Proceedings of the 7th Annual Conference on Genetic and Evolutionary Computation*, GECCO '05, pages 857–864, New York, NY, USA, 2005. ACM.

[7] H.-G. Beyer. *The Theory of Evolution Strategies*. Natural Computing Series. Springer Berlin Heideberg, 2001.

[8] H.-G. Beyer and H.-P. Schwefel. Evolution strategies — A comprehensive introduction. *Natural Computing*, 1(1):3–52, 2002.

[9] M.-L. Cauwet. Noisy optimization: Convergence with a fixed number of resamplings. In *Applications of Evolutionary Computation*, Lecture Notes in Computer Science, pages 603–614. Springer Berlin Heidelberg, 2014.

[10] H. Chen. Lower rate of convergence for locating a maximum of a function. *The Annals of Statistics*, 16(3):1330–1334, Sep 1988.

[11] R. Coulom. Clop: Confident local optimization for noisy black-box parameter tuning. In *Advances in Computer Games*, Lecture Notes in Computer Science, pages 146–157. Springer Berlin Heidelberg, 2012.

[12] R. Coulom, P. Rolet, N. Sokolovska, and O. Teytaud. Handling expensive optimization with large noise. In *Proceedings of the 11th Workshop Proceedings on Foundations of Genetic Algorithms*, FOGA '11, pages 61–68, New York, NY, USA, 2011. ACM.

[13] J. Decock and O. Teytaud. Noisy optimization complexity under locality assumption. In *Proceedings of the 12th workshop on Foundations of genetic algorithms*, FOGA '13, pages 183–190, New York, NY, USA, 2013. ACM.

[14] V. Fabian. Stochastic approximation of minima with improved asymptotic speed. *The Annals of Mathematical Statistics*, 38(1):191–200, Feb 1967.

[15] B. Grossman. Surrogate models in aircraft design. In *Proc. of the 1st Int. Work. on Surrogate Modelling and Space Mapping for Engineering Optimization*, 2000.

[16] N. Hansen, A. Niederberger, L. Guzzella, and P. Koumoutsakos. A method for handling uncertainty in evolutionary optimization with an application to feedback control of combustion. *Evolutionary Computation, IEEE Transactions on*, 13(1):180–197, Feb 2009.

[17] N. Hansen and A. Ostermeier. Completely derandomized self-adaptation in evolution strategies. *Evolutionary Compututation*, 9(2):159–195, June 2001.

[18] V. Heidrich-Meisner and C. Igel. Hoeffding and bernstein races for selecting policies in evolutionary direct policy search. In *Proceedings of the 26th Annual International Conference on Machine Learning*, ICML '09, pages 401–408, New York, NY, USA, 2009. ACM.

[19] Y. Jin and J. Branke. Evolutionary optimization in uncertain environments-a survey. *IEEE Transactions on Evolutionary Computation*, 9(3):303–317, June 2005.

[20] Y. Ong, K.-Y. Lum, P. Nair, D. Shi, and Z. Zhang. Global convergence unconstrained and bound constrained surrogate-assisted evolutionary search in aerodynamic shape design. In *Proceedings of the IEEE Congress on Evolutionary Computation (CEC 2003)*, pages 1856–1863. IEEE, 2003.

[21] I. Rechenberg. *Evolutionsstrategie: Optimierung technischer Systeme nach Prinzipien der biologischen Evolution*. Problemata, 15. Frommann-Holzboog, 1973.

[22] P. Rolet and O. Teytaud. Adaptive noisy optimization. In *Applications of Evolutionary Computation*, Lecture Notes in Computer Science, pages 592–601. Springer Berlin Heidelberg, 2010.

[23] H.-P. Schwefel. Adaptive Mechanismen in der biologischen Evolution und ihr Einfluss auf die Evolutionsgeschwindigkeit. Technical Report of the Working Group of Bionics and Evolution Techniques at the Institute for Measurement and Control Technology Re 215/3, Technical University of Berlin, July 1974.

[24] O. Shamir. On the complexity of bandit and derivative-free stochastic convex optimization. *CoRR*, abs/1209.2388, 2012.

[25] J. Spall. Adaptive stochastic approximation by the simultaneous perturbation method. *Automatic Control, IEEE Transactions on*, 45(10):1839–1853, Oct 2000.

[26] J. Spall. Feedback and weighting mechanisms for improving jacobian estimates in the adaptive simultaneous perturbation algorithm. *Automatic Control, IEEE Transactions on*, 54(6):1216–1229, June 2009.

[27] O. Teytaud and H. Fournier. Lower bounds for evolution strategies using VC-dimension. In *Parallel Problem Solving from Nature, PPSN X*, Lecture Notes in Computer Science, pages 102–111. Springer Berlin Heidelberg, 2008.

[28] Z. Zhou, Y.-S. Ong, and P. Nair. Hierarchical surrogate-assisted evolutionary optimization framework. In *Proceedings of the IEEE Conference on Evolutionary Computation (CEC 2004)*, pages 1586–1593. IEEE, 2004.

Understanding Simple Asynchronous Evolutionary Algorithms

Eric O. Scott
Computer Science Department
George Mason University
Fairfax, Virginia USA
escott8@gmu.edu

Kenneth A. De Jong
Computer Science Department
George Mason University
Fairfax, Virginia USA
kdejong@gmu.edu

ABSTRACT

In many applications of evolutionary algorithms, the time required to evaluate the fitness of individuals is long and variable. When the variance in individual evaluation times is non-negligible, traditional, synchronous master-slave EAs incur idle time in CPU resources. An asynchronous approach to parallelization of EAs promises to eliminate idle time and thereby to reduce the amount of wall-clock time it takes to solve a problem. However, the behavior of asynchronous evolutionary algorithms is not well understood. In particular, it is not clear exactly how much faster the asynchronous algorithm will tend to run, or whether its evolutionary trajectory may follow a sub-optimal search path that cancels out the promised benefits. This paper presents a preliminary analysis of simple asynchronous EA performance in terms of speed and problem-solving ability.

Categories and Subject Descriptors

I.2 [**Computing Methdologies**]: ARTIFICIAL INTELLIGENCE—*Problem Solving, Control Methods, and Search*

Keywords

Evolutionary Algorithms, Parallel Algorithms, Asynchronous Algorithms

1. INTRODUCTION

Evolutionary algorithms are increasingly being used to tune the parameters of large, complex and stochastic simulation models in various domains of science and engineering. In these applications, evaluating the fitness of an individual may take on the order of minutes or hours of CPU time. Parallel evaluation is thus essential to obtaining EA results from these models in a tolerable amount of "wall-clock" time.

In the neuroscience and agent-based modeling applications we are involved with, we observe a non-negligible amount of parameter-dependent variance in the evaluation times of the simulation models being tuned. At any

FOGA '15 January 17 - 20, 2015, Aberystwyth, United Kingdom
ACM Copyright 2015 ACM 978-1-4503-3434-1/15/01 ... $15.00.
http://dx.doi.org/10.1145/2725494.2725509

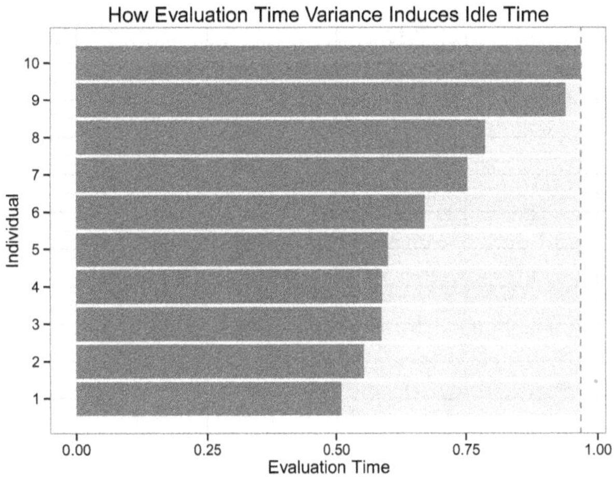

Figure 1: When there is variance in individual evaluation times, a parallelized generational EA suffers idle time.

given generation, the slowest individual in the population may take several times longer to evaluate than the fastest-evaluating individuals.

This poses a problem for the 'generational' master-slave EAs which practitioners often use to parallelize the solution of optimization and design problems. Traditional master-slave EAs synchronize their threads at each generation, in imitation of the sequential EAs they are derived from. As all the CPUs must wait for the individual with the longest evaluation time to complete before moving to the next generation, a significant amount of CPU idle time may result. Figure 1 illustrates this with 10 simulated evaluation times sampled uniformly from $[0.5, 1.0]$. The lightly shaded region shows the idle CPU time induced as 9 of the 10 nodes wait for the next generation.

A natural alternative, which we analyze in this paper, is to abandon the (μ, λ) generational scheme and turn to a $(\mu + 1)$-style EA with asynchronous evaluation. Here, new individuals are generated one-at-a-time by the selection and reproduction operators as CPUs become available, and are integrated into the population immediately when they finish having their fitness evaluated. As the processing nodes never wait for a generation boundary, idle time is virtually eliminated. We refer to algorithms that follow this approach as *simple asynchronous evolutionary algorithms* (the details of which will be given in Section 1.2).

Simple asynchronous EAs promise to eliminate the performance impediment that eval-time variance induces in generational master-slave EAs, thereby increasing *throughput* in terms of the number of individuals evaluated per unit time. One contribution we offer in this paper is a model (under simplified assumptions) of just how much extra throughput a simple asynchronous EA gains over a generational EA. This increase in computational efficiency is purchased, however, at the cost of a significant change in EA behavior. It could be that, on some problems, the increased throughput in fitness evaluations is offset by slower evolutionary convergence.

The aim of this paper is to further our understanding of that potential trade-off. The practitioner would like to know whether she can reliably expect beneficial results from a simple asynchronous EA, as compared to a parallel (μ, λ)-style EA. Little to no such guidance currently exists in the literature.

The remainder of this section gives some background on parallel and asynchronous EAs that have been studied, introduces the simple asynchronous evolutionary algorithm up close, and details concerns that may arise about its performance. Sections 2, 3 and 4 proceed with theoretical and empirical analysis of the algorithm's speed and behavior, and we conclude with a summary in Section 5.

1.1 Background

In general, evolutionary algorithms use either a *global* population model (*panmixia*), in which selection and reproduction operators apply to a single monolithic population, or they use a *structured population* model that decomposes the population into components that interact locally. Structured models can be further divided into the 'course-grained' island models and 'fine-grained' cellular EAs, respectively, yielding three broad families of EA (four if you count hybrid approaches separately). Parallelization of all three families has been studied extensively (cf. surveys in [1, 4, 17]).

Asynchronous communication appears only occasionally in the parallel EA literature. Island models have been created that permit asynchronous migrations between subpopulations [2, 13], and asynchronous cell updating has been studied in cellular EAs [10], but in general asynchronous mechanisms have not been advertised as promising major performance advantages for structured population models. Recent work on 'pool-based' EAs allows subsets of a centralized population to be farmed out asynchronously to slave processors for evolution, as a sort of intermediate between panmictic and structured population models (ex. [15]). The purely panmictic (global) population model, however, is by far the easiest kind of EA to parallelize, and is thus the most widely used parallel EA in practice.

Panmictic parallel EAs typically take the form of a (μ, λ)-style generational EA, in which fitness evaluation is performed in parallel, either on a shared-memory machine or over a distributed cluster [5]. Selection and reproduction operators typically operate sequentially on the master processor (though these can sometimes be parallelized as well). These master-slave EAs are especially effective when the execution time of fitness evaluation dwarfs the cost of selection and reproduction. Thanks to its synchronization at each generation (cf. Figure 2), the generational master-slave EA

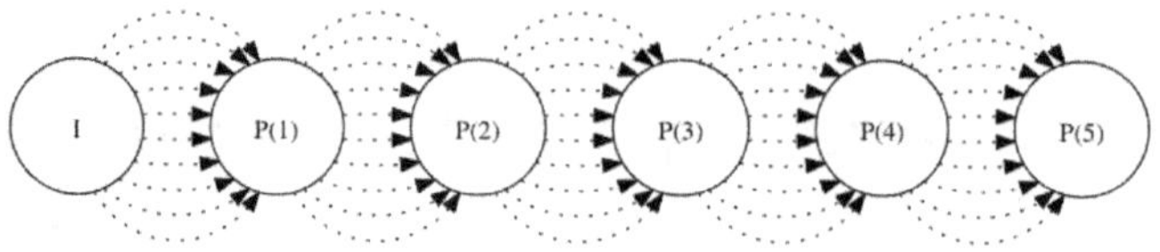

Figure 2: A generational master-slave EA synchronizes after each population has been evaluated in parallel.

is also well-understood: its evolutionary behavior is identical to its slower, sequential counterpart. The potential drawback of synchronization, and the primary motivation for turning to an asynchronous approach, is the idle time already pointed out by Figure 1.

Asynchronous algorithms based on the $(\mu + 1)$-style steady-state EA have been used intermittently by practitioners for decades as an easy-to-implement means of reducing idle CPU resources (e.g. [5, 20]). First used in genetic algorithms [32], asynchronous evaluation was introduced into multi-objective EA (MOEA) applications as early as 1995 (ex. [24, 26]), and similar approaches have been used in master-slave implementations of ant colony optimization [25], differential evolution [18], and particle swarm optimization [12, 16, 27].

Interest in the asynchronous master-slave scheme (which we describe in more detail below) has grown in recent years as EA applications involving computationally expensive simulations become more common. For instance, Churchhill et al. apply an asynchronous MOEA to a tool-sequence optimization problem for automatic milling machine simulations, finding that both the synchronous and asynchronous methods achieve solutions that are comparable in quality after a fixed number of evaluations, but that the asynchronous method completes those evaluations in 30-50% less wall-clock time [6]. Yagoubi et al. similarly apply an asynchronous MOEA to the design of an engine part in a simulation of diesel combustion, with favorable results after a fixed number of evaluations [29].

While several successful applications of asynchronous master-slave EAs are attested in the literature, few studies have attempted to tease out a theoretical or empirical understanding of what kinds of problems they may be poorly- or well-suited for. As we will see below, the performance of the asynchronous EA depends in a readily evident but poorly understood way on the number of slave processors and the distribution of individual evaluation times.

Zeigler and Kim were among the first to suggest the benefits of asynchrony in master-slave EAs and to perform preliminary analysis of their throughput and problem solving capacity [11, 32]. They observed that, with an asynchronous EA, an unlimited number of threads may be used to keep a cluster fully utilized, even when the number of available processors is greater than the population size. Runarsson has shown empirically, however, that as the number of slave processors is increased, more function evaluations are needed for his asynchronous evolution strategy to make progress on unimodal functions [21]. The extra throughput is thus apparently purchased at the cost of making the algorithm less greedy than a non-parallelized steady-state EA.

This is caused by what Depolli et al. call the *selection lag*, defined as "the number of solutions created while an observed solution is being evaluated" [8]. The selection lag describes the key behavioral difference between the asynchronous EA and the steady-state EA.

While our focus in this paper is on single-objective problems, most recent analysis of the asynchronous master-slave model has taken place in the context of multi-objective optimization, using MOEA approaches that are inspired by the steady-state EA. In empirical studies on small test suites, Durillo et al. and Zăvoianu et al. each find that the asynchronous approach performs well at finding good Pareto fronts in less time than other approaches [9, 31]. Zăvoianu et al. also use an argument based on Amdahl's law to put a lower bound on the speedup in evaluations-per-unit-time that the asynchronous approach provides as compared to a generational approach. They suggest that the asynchronous EA can provide some improvement in computational capacity even when evaluation times are very short and have negligible variance. When evaluation times are much longer than the EA's sequential operations (i.e. reproduction, selection), negligible speedup is predicted unless there is variation in evaluation times. Their analysis applies unmodified to single-objective EAs.

A concern that we give considerable attention to in this paper is how the distribution of evaluation times changes over the course of an evolutionary run, and how this may impact performance. In particular, in some applications, solutions that lie close to the optimum may take much longer (or shorter) to evaluate than poor solutions. It's not clear how the relationship between the fitness landscape and heritable evaluation time traits may affect EA performance. The only prior work we know that has raised this question is Yagoubi et al.'s empirical analysis of a multi-objective test suite in [30], which found that an asynchronous MOEA had a harder time finding good solutions when they were located in a region of the search space that was artificially configured to have slower evaluation times. This raises the concern that asynchronous EAs may in general have a bias toward fast-evaluating individuals.

1.2 The Simple Asynchronous EA

The key notion behind asynchronous master-slave EAs is that we integrate an individual into the population as soon as it finishes evaluating, and immediately generate a new individual to take its place on the open CPU resource. There seems to be no way to accomplish this without abandoning the generational model, which is inherently synchronous, and instead introducing a generation gap (cf. [23]), so as to allow a continuous evolutionary process.[1] The simplest generation gap algorithm is the $(\mu+1)$-style steady-state EA, and almost all asynchronous master-slave EAs are based on the steady-state EA.

Figure 3 illustrates the difference between traditional steady-state evolution and the simple asynchronous EA. In the steady-state model, a single individual i is generated by selecting parents from the population $P(t)$ at step t. The new individual has its fitness evaluated, and then competes for a place in the population. How that competition takes place is a design decision, but a typical approach (and the one we take in this paper) is to choose a random individual in $P(t)$, and have i replace it in the population *iff* i has a fitness strictly better than the randomly chosen individual. The result of this replacement is the new population $P(t+1)$. By convention, we say that one 'generation' has passed in a steady-state or simple asynchronous EA when μ individuals have been generated, where μ is the population size.

[1]That said, we note that Durillo et al. have created a hybrid approach in [9] that they call 'asynchronous generational.'

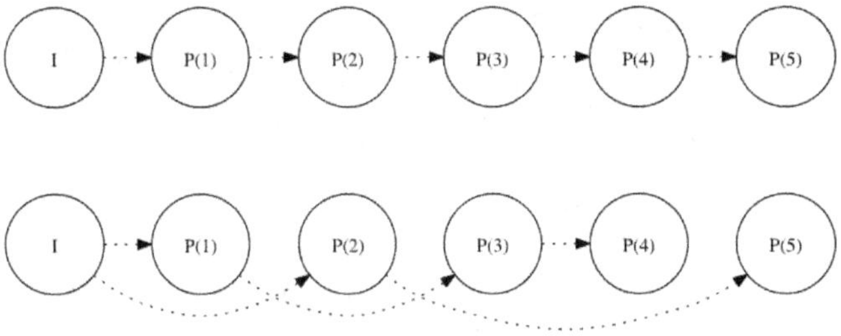

Figure 3: In steady-state evolution, individuals compete for a space in the population at the subsequent step (Top). In the simple asynchronous EA, several evolutionary steps may pass before an individual enters the population (Bottom).

In the asynchronous model, at any given time more than one individual is having its fitness evaluated. In the bottom of Figure 3, $T=2$ slave processors are in use. As the population is initialized, $T-1$ extra initial individuals are created to keep the slaves busy while the first evolutionary step executes. From that point on, individuals that are being evaluated on the slaves compete for a place in the population as soon as they finish evaluating. As a result, several evolutionary steps may take place while an individual evaluates.

The simple asynchronous EA we use in this work is detailed from the perspective of the master processor in Algorithm 1. The first loop initializes the population by sending randomly generated individuals to a free node for evaluation (`send()`). When this `while` loop terminates, there are n individuals in the population that have had their fitness evaluated, there are $T-1$ randomly generated individuals currently being evaluated on the T slaves, and there is one free slave node. We then breed one individual from the population and send it off for evaluation to fill the free node (`breedOne()` represents both parent selection and reproductive operators). Evolution then proceeds in the `for` loop, which waits for an individual to complete evaluating and thus free up a slave processor (`nextEvaluatedIndividual()`). Each newly evaluated individual competes against an individual chosen by `selectOne()` for a place in the population. Finally, a new individual is generated and sent off to fill the free slave node, and the cycle continues.

In our experiments below, we use tournament selection of size 2 to select parents in `breedOne()`, and we use random selection for survival selection (`selectOne()`), as parent selection already provides ample selection pressure. Practitioners (for instance, [19]) also sometimes choose to use a FIFO replacement strategy, amongst others, instead of random replacement, since Sarma and De Jong have shown in [22] that using a FIFO strategy in $(\mu+\lambda)$-style EAs leads to search behavior that is more like the (μ, λ)-style EA. See [28] for a study of survival selection strategies in a simple asynchronous EA.

Algorithm 1 The Simple Asynchronous EA

```
function AsynchronousEvolution(n, gens)
    P ← ∅
    while |P| < n do
        if ¬nodeAvailable() then
            wait()
        while nodeAvailable() do
            ind ← randomIndividual()
            send(ind)
        finishedInd ← nextEvaluatedIndividual()
        P ← P ∪ {finishedInd}
    newInd ← breedOne(P)
    send(newInd)
    for i ← 0 to (n · gens) do
        finishedInd ← nextEvaluatedIndividual()
        replaceInd ← selectOne(P)
        if betterThan(finishedInd, replaceInd) then
            P ← (P − replaceInd) ∪ finishedInd
        newInd ← breedOne(P)
        send(newInd)
```

Once the asynchronous dynamics depicted in Figure 3 are understood, several concerns about the algorithm's behavior become readily apparent.

As Rasheed and Davison observe with their application of a similar asynchronous EA, "the creation of a new individual may not be affected by individuals created one or two steps ago because they have not yet been placed into the population" [20]. That is, the parallelism introduces *selection lag*, which (as mentioned above) is the number of evolutionary steps that go by while an individual is being evaluated. Selection lag occurs whether or not there is variance in individual evaluation times. A sequential steady-state EA always has a selection lag of 0, but Depolli et al. prove that, even in the presence of evaluation-time variance, the average selection lag in $(\mu + 1)$-style asynchronous EAs is $T - 1$ steps, where T is the number of slave processors [8].

"Even worse," continue Rasheed and Davison, variance in evaluation times induces a *re-ordering effect*: the algorithm "may get back individuals in a different order than originally created, as some processors/processes may complete their evaluations faster than others (such as a result of heterogeneous processing environments, external loads, etc.)."

Variance in individual evaluation times may originate in a heritable component and/or a non-heritable component.

- **Non-Heritable** eval-time variance may arise from heterogenous CPU resources, load conditions, and process scheduling effects – but it can be especially pronounced in cases where fitness evaluation involves executing a stochastic simulation.
- **Heritable** eval-time variance arises where there is a dependency between the parameters of the simulation and the time it takes to execute. Heritable variance may be independent of fitness, or there may be a relationship between fitness and evaluation time.

We would like to understand how these sources of variance impact both an asynchronous EA's throughput (the number of individuals evaluated per unit time) and its ability to converge to an optimal solution to a problem. In particular, in the remainder of this paper we investigate three research questions, treated now below.

First, we are concerned about the role that the re-ordering effect described above may play in altering the EA's search trajectory. When evaluation time is a heritable trait, many fast-evaluating individuals may be born, evaluated, and compete for a place in the population in the time it takes for a single slower individual to evaluate. This raises the concern that simple asynchronous EAs may be biased away from slow-evaluating regions of the search space. As mentioned in Section 1.1, Yagoubi et al. observe evidence that this does in fact occur in a multi-objective context [30]. They found that on at least one test problem, an evaluation-time bias helped to prevent premature convergence. An evaluation-time bias could just as easily *cause* premature convergence in other problems, however, so if eval-time bias is a significant aspect of asynchronous EA behavior, then it is something practitioners ought to be made aware of.

> **RQ 1**: When individual evaluation times are a heritable trait, does the asynchronous EA give a reproductive advantage to faster-evaluating individuals? That is, is the EA biased toward individuals with lower evaluation times?

After studying evaluation-time bias, we turn to the more basic question of how much idle CPU resources a simple asynchronous EA can reclaim, compared to a generational EA.

> **RQ 2**: How great an increase in throughput does the simple asynchronous EA offer over a parallelized generational EA? How does it depend on the population size, number of processors, and the distribution of evaluation times? How does it depend on how the distribution of evaluation times changes over the course of the evolutionary run?

Doing more fitness evaluations in the same amount of time is only beneficial if those extra evaluations can be put to work to make progress toward the optimum. It's not obvious how the asynchronous and generational EAs differ in balancing exploration and exploitation, so we compare the two algorithms' performance on single- and multi-modal test functions.

> **RQ 3**: How does the convergence time of an asynchronous EA compare to what we would expect from the increase in throughput? Can we be both fast and smart? How does the asynchronous EA's performance depend on the relationship between evaluation time and fitness?

In the next three sections we address **RQ 1**, **RQ 2** and **RQ 3** in turn. The evolutionary behavior of the asynchronous EA is complex and difficult to describe in a purely analytical way. For instance, the replicator dynamics of the system are (perhaps not surprisingly) non-Markovian. As such, while we use some preliminary analytical results where possible, this paper relies heavily on empirical studies to begin improving our understanding of asynchronous EAs. All our experiments use the asynchronous EA implementation provided by the ECJ evolutionary computation toolkit [14], which closely follows Algorithm 1.

2. EVALUATION-TIME BIAS

The intuition depicted in Figure 3 would seem to indicate that when evaluation time is a heritable trait, fast-evaluating individuals may obtain a reproductive advantage in an asynchronous EA. This can be worrying in some applications, such as when scientific simulations are being tuned so that their results match some experimental data. The goal of such parameter tuning is to find the best-fitting model – not a model that runs faster than the alternatives!

The simplest way to study a possible bias toward fast-evaluating genotypes is in isolation from other evolutionary effects. We define a heritable runtime trait by a gene that can take on one of two alleles: `fast` and `slow`, where `slow` takes 10 times longer to evaluate. Further assume that there is no reproductive variation (offspring are generated only by cloning), and that the fitness landscape is flat – i.e. every individual has an equal chance of being selected as a parent. Each cloned offspring replaces a random individual in the population with 100% probability. In this scenario, any systematic change in genotype frequency can only be due to some implicit selection acting on the evaluation-time trait.

Now, given a number of evolutionary steps, will a disproportionate number of `fast`-type individuals be produced on average? We can approach this by letting the random variable X denote the number of `fast`-type individuals that complete evaluation during a fixed interval of m evolutionary steps. Then define X_i as the indicator random variable

$$X_i = I\{\text{The individual evaluated at step } i \text{ is } \texttt{fast}\text{-type}\}, \tag{1}$$

which evaluates to 1 if the proposition is true and 0 otherwise. Now, the linearity of expectation shows that we can answer our question by considering each X_i independently of any other part of the evolutionary trajectory:

$$\mathbb{E}[X] = \mathbb{E}\left[\sum_{i=1}^{m} X_i\right] \tag{2}$$

$$= \sum_{i=1}^{m} \mathbb{E}[X_i] \tag{3}$$

$$= \sum_{i=1}^{m} p(X_i = 1) \tag{4}$$

$$= \sum_{i=1}^{m} f_i, \tag{5}$$

where f_i is the probability that the processor that completed evaluation at step i contained a `fast`-type individual. But since individuals are cloned from a randomly selected parent, f_i is simply the expected frequency of `fast`-type alleles that existed when the individual was first cloned and sent off for evaluation.

For large populations we know that f_i will not change very quickly. Empirically, we find that, apart from a very short transient period at initialization, the expected value of the f_i's is roughly constant on a flat landscape with a population size of 100 (Figure 4). We seeded the initial population with random genotypes that were drawn with equal probability from both `fast` and `slow` alleles, so that the initial `fast`-type frequency averaged $f = 0.5$. We then ran the asynchronous EA with 10 slave processors for a total of 50 independent runs. This allows us to estimate the expected value of f_i at any step i. We find that in all but just the first few steps, f_i consistently hovers around $f = 0.5$ without any systematic trend up or down.

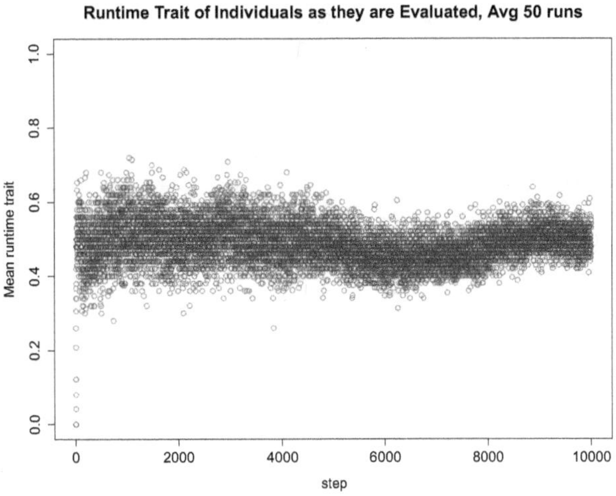

Figure 4: Each point represents the fraction of individuals out of 50 independent runs that finished evaluating with `slow` type at that step. Since the fraction hovers around 0.5, the frequency of each genotype does not change very much.

By Equation 5, then, $\mathbb{E}[X]$ reduces to mf for any value of m. That is, if $f = 0.5$ and $m = 10$ evolutionary steps, we expect to see 5 `fast`-type individuals and 5 `slow`-type individuals produced, for no net change in the population genotype. By this analysis, we do not anticipate any change in the expected genotype frequencies on flat landscapes outside the brief transient phase.

This is confirmed in our experiments (Figure 5). We measured the genotype frequency over time in 50 independent runs and found no evidence of selection pressure favoring either allele. At least on flat landscapes, we have a clear indication that there is no selective advantage for fast fitness evaluations. Similar results were obtained for the case where individual runtimes are allowed to vary continuously along an interval, and for population sizes of 10 and 500 (not shown).

Expected value models like the one we just derived are useful in characterizing the ensemble averages of a sufficiently large number of finite-population models, but not the behavior of individual runs. Notice that in Figure 5 the variance in genotype frequency over the 50 independent runs continues to increase over time. This is an indication that there are in fact significant changes in the `slow`/`fast` ratios on individual runs. This is due to the well-studied problem of genetic drift in finite populations (see, for example, [7]). Alleles are lost simply due to sampling variance occurring in the random parent and survival selection steps. This drift occurs even if the evaluation times of `fast` and `slow`-type individuals are set to be equal.

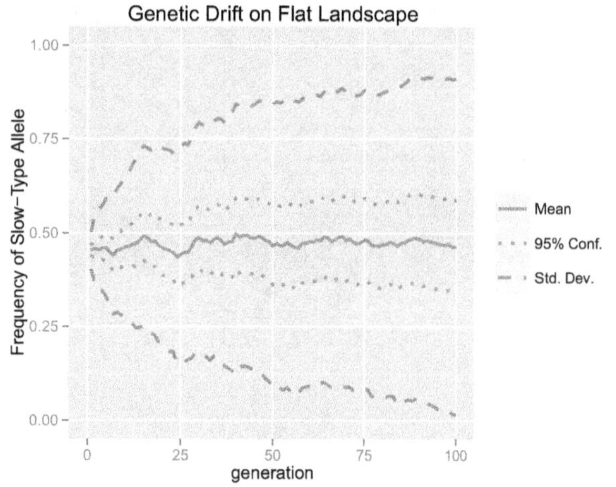

Figure 5: Frequency of `slow`-type individuals on a flat fitness landscape, averaged over 50 runs. No systematic drift toward `fast` alleles is observed.

We have thus answered **RQ 1** in the negative on flat fitness landscapes with cloning: there is no independent selection pressure that favors fast-evaluating individuals. This does not, however, rule out an evaluation-time bias that emerges from a combination of reproduction, variation and selection, so our results do not contradict the bias observed in practice by Yagoubi et al. [30].

3. SPEEDUP IN THROUGHPUT

Asynchronous EAs are interesting primarily because they promises to increase the total number of individuals that complete evaluation per unit of wall-clock time – i.e. *throughput*. We measure throughput by considering the time it takes for an EA to execute a fixed number of evaluations. We call the ratio between two algorithms' throughput the *improvement* in throughput, or the *throughput speedup*. It is important to distinguish throughput improvement from *true speedup*, which would take the quality of the resulting solution into account.[2] In this section we are concerned with the throughput improvement of the simple asynchronous EA over the parallel generational EA. We defer consideration of true speedup – i.e. convergence time – to Section 4.

3.1 A Model of Throughput Improvement

As we stated in the opening to this paper, we have assumed that the evaluation time of individuals dwarfs all other EA overhead, and thus that an asynchronous EA has near-zero idle time. Under this assumption, the speedup in throughput that the asynchronous EA offers is completely described by the amount of idle CPU resources it recovers. Algebraically, the throughput speedup is thus expressed as the ratio

$$S = \frac{1}{1-\hat{I}}, \tag{6}$$

where $\hat{I}$ is the fraction of CPU resources that the generational EA would have left idle.

[2]In [31], Zăvoianu et al. use the term 'structural improvement' for what we call 'throughput speedup.'

To get a quantitative handle on what actual values for the throughput speedup S might look like, consider the case where individual evaluation times are independent and identically distributed according to some distribution. Furthermore, assume for simplicity that the ratio of CPUs available to the population size $T/n = 1$, i.e. there is one CPU for each individual in the population. We will now analyze the expected value of S.

Let $P = \{Y_1, Y_2, \dots, Y_n\}$ be a set of values drawn i.i.d. from some distribution, where $Y_i \in \mathbb{R}^+$ represents the evaluation time of the ith individual in the population. Then, as illustrated in Figure 1, the absolute idle time suffered by the generational EA is the total number of CPU-seconds processors spend waiting for the longest-evaluating individual to complete:

$$I = \sum_{i=1}^{n} (\max[P] - Y_i). \tag{7}$$

To express idle time as a normalized value between 0 and 1, $\hat{I}$, we divide I by the total number of CPU-seconds available to the algorithm during the generation, which is $n \max[P]$.

$$\hat{I} = \frac{I}{n \max[P]}. \tag{8}$$

Computing the expected value of this ratio distribution is difficult for most distributions, in part because $\max[P]$ and I are not independent. We can derive a lower bound on the expectation, however, if we confine our attention to the case where the Y_i's are sampled from a uniform distribution over the interval $[a, b]$.

$$\begin{aligned}
\mathbb{E}[\hat{I}] &= \mathbb{E}\left[\frac{I}{n \max[P]}\right] && (9)\\
&\geq \mathbb{E}\left[\frac{I}{nb}\right] && (10)\\
&= \frac{1}{nb}\mathbb{E}\left[\sum_{i=1}^{n}(\max[P] - Y_i)\right] && (11)\\
&= \frac{1}{b}\left(\mathbb{E}[\max[P]] - \mathbb{E}[Y]\right), && (12)
\end{aligned}$$

where the last step follows by the linearity of expectation. Since $\max[P]$ quickly approaches b as $n \to \infty$, this lower bound on $\mathbb{E}[\hat{I}]$ will be tight for large n.

Finally, in Appendix A we show by some straightforward calculus that for the uniform distribution,

$$\mathbb{E}[\max[P]] = b - \frac{1}{n+1}(b-a). \tag{13}$$

Therefore, in the case where all runtimes are uniformly distributed between a and b, we have the following lower bound on the expected normalized idle time:

$$\begin{aligned}
\mathbb{E}[\hat{I}] &\geq \frac{1}{b}\left[b - \frac{1}{n+1}(b-a) - \left(a + \frac{b-a}{2}\right)\right] && (14)\\
&= \left(\frac{b-a}{b}\right)\left(\frac{1}{2} - \frac{1}{n+1}\right), && (15)
\end{aligned}$$

where n is population size, which we have assumed is equal to the number of processors.

We can see from Equation 15 that the expected idle time is determined entirely by the population size n and the ratio of the standard deviation (which is related to $(b-a)$ by a constant factor) to its maximum value b. Moreover, the

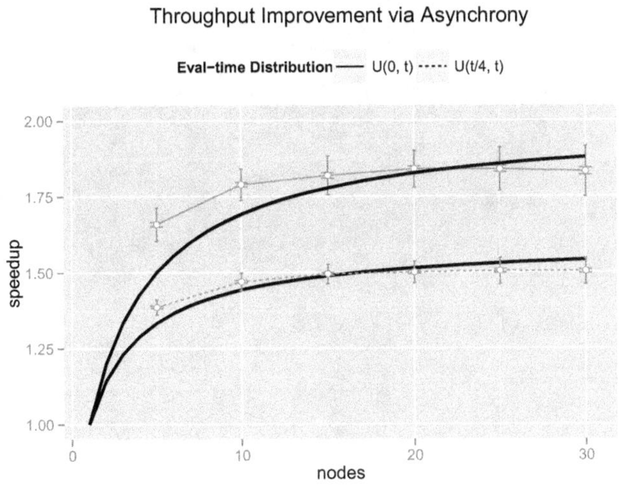

Figure 6: Observed throughput improvement, shown along with theoretical lower bounds predicted by Equation 15 (bold lines).

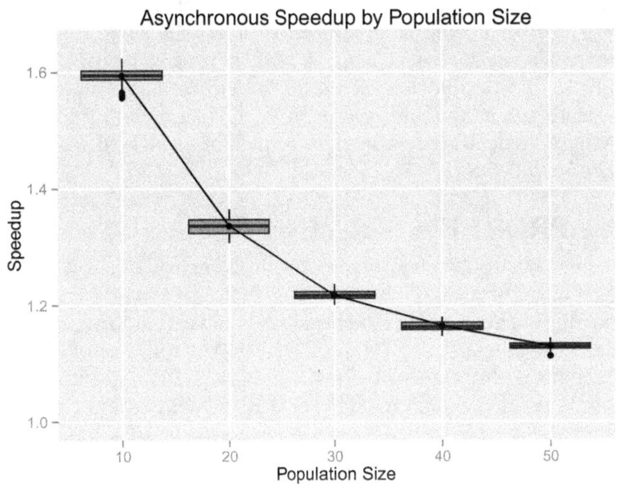

Figure 7: Observed throughput improvement when the number of slave processors is fixed at 10 and the population size varies.

maximum attainable speedup is determined by the limit of the idle time as n grows:

$$\lim_{n\to\infty} \mathbb{E}[\hat{I}] = \frac{1}{2}\left(\frac{b-a}{b}\right). \tag{16}$$

This result indicates that the generational EA will never incur an idleness greater than 50% when evaluation times follow a uniform distribution, and consequently an asynchronous EA can never provide a throughput improvement of greater than 2. We note in passing that for other distributions, such as the Gaussian, a speedup of much greater than 2 is possible.

3.2 Experimental Validation

We used Equation 15 to predict the idle time of the generational EA, and converted this into a prediction of speedup via Equation 6. Figure 6 compares the result against simulation experiments.

Each data point represents the speedup in throughput measured by pairing 50 independent runs of an asynchronous EA against 50 runs of a generational EA. Each algorithm was run for as close as possible to 500 fitness evaluations.[3] For the lower curve, individual evaluation times were non-heritable and sampled uniformly from the interval $[\frac{t}{4}, t]$, where t is a sufficiently long time that EA overhead is negligible. The upper curve is a similar experiment with a larger amount of variance – evaluation times were sampled from $[0, t]$. Since evaluation times were independent of fitness, the objective function is irrelevant to throughput. To simulate specific evaluation times, individuals were configured to simply wait a period of time. Since this was not resource intensive, we were able to simulate large numbers of processors on a shared-memory machine that had just a few cores. The thin error bars indicate the standard deviation in the speedup across the 50 runs. Tighter, wide error bars showing the 95% confident interval on the mean are barely visible in the figure, indicating that we obtained a precise estimate of the expected speedup.

The results confirm that Equation 15 provides a reasonably tight estimate of the throughput improvement. For large numbers of processors ($T = n > 20$), however, the prediction no longer serves as an accurate lower bound. We found that the degree to which the results conform to the prediction vary somewhat depending on the architecture of the computer we run the experiments on. We surmise that the deviation from the prediction at high n is an artifact of our experimental setup, which simulates more processors than we actually have available.

The assumption that $T = n$ simplified our analytical approach to throughput, but in practice our population size will typically be significantly greater than the number of processors. Figure 7 shows the effect of holding the number of processors fixed at $T = 10$, and varying the population size while individual evaluation times are sampled non-heritably from $[0, t]$ (50 independent runs of 250 generations each). As n increases, each processor becomes responsible for evaluating a larger share of the population, and the throughput improvement quickly decreases.

In the experiments shown so far, the variance in throughput improvement from run to run is very small. When evaluation time is a heritable trait, this is no longer the case, as genetic drift and/or selection can significantly alter the distribution of evaluation times as evolution progresses. The amount of throughput improvement we attain over the entire run depends heavily on how the magnitude and variation of evaluation times expands or shrinks over time. How that change occurs depends in turn on how the heritable component of evaluation time is related to an individual's fitness. We return to these nuances (which form the remainder of **RQ 1**) in Section 4, where we consider several scenarios in which the evaluation-time trait is heritable in some way (ex. Figure 9).

The specific results in this subsection are limited to evaluation times that are uniformly distributed and non-heritable. Qualitatively, however, we expect similar results for other

[3] We say "as close as possible" only because 500 does not divide evenly into an integral number of generations for some population sizes.

simple distributions: asynchronous parallelization is especially advantageous over the generational EA when the number of slave processors is large and the ratio T/n of processors to the population size is high. Decreasing returns appear to set in quickly, however, so it is important to have realistic expectations about how much of an advantage asynchrony will offer.

4. PROBLEM SOLVING

The throughput improvement an asynchronous EA offers over a generational alternative is an intuitively appealing metric, because we are inclined to believe that progress toward the solution can be measured by the number of fitness evaluations an algorithm has completed. In his early analysis of asynchronous master-slave EAs, Kim called this the *requisite sample set hypothesis*, and used it to express the importance of throughput [11]:

> "Given an [algorithm] for which the invariance of the requisite sample set size holds, search speed is determined by the throughput of fitness evaluation. The greater the number of processors dedicated to the evaluation of individuals, and the higher the utilization of these processors, the faster the global optimum will be located."

When the number of samples an asynchronous EA needs to find a high quality solution on the given problem is equal to the number of samples a generational EA requires, then throughput improvement is an accurate predictor of true speedup. This assumption is unlikely to hold in practice. In principle, on some problems the asynchronous EA could require so many more samples that it takes longer to converge than the generational EA, despite the increase in throughput.

In this section we continue our approach of simulating various kinds of evaluation-time distributions, but now on non-flat fitness landscapes. The aim is to gain a preliminary understanding of how gains in throughput combine with the evolutionary trajectory of the asynchronous EA to produce true speedup.

4.1 Methods

The performance of an asynchronous EA depends not only on the fitness landscape of the problem at hand, but also on the how an individual's location in the search space is related to its evaluation time. As such, we used four distinct simulated scenarios on each test function to see how the asynchronous EA performs on real-valued minimization problems. In all four scenarios, we represented individual genomes as vectors in $\mathbb{R}^l$, used a Gaussian mutation operator at a per-gene probability of 0.05, and used a 100% rate of two-point crossover. The population size was fixed at $n = 10$ in each case, and the number of slave processors was also $T = 10$.

1. In the **Non-Heritable** scenario, individual evaluation times are uniformly sampled from the interval $[0, t_{\max}]$.
2. In the **Heritable**, fitness-independent scenario, we define a special gene to represent the individual's evaluation-time trait. The trait is randomly initialized on $[0, t_{\max}]$, and undergoes Gaussian mutation within these bounds with a standard deviation of $0.05 \cdot t_{\max}$. This gene is ignored during the calculation of fitness.

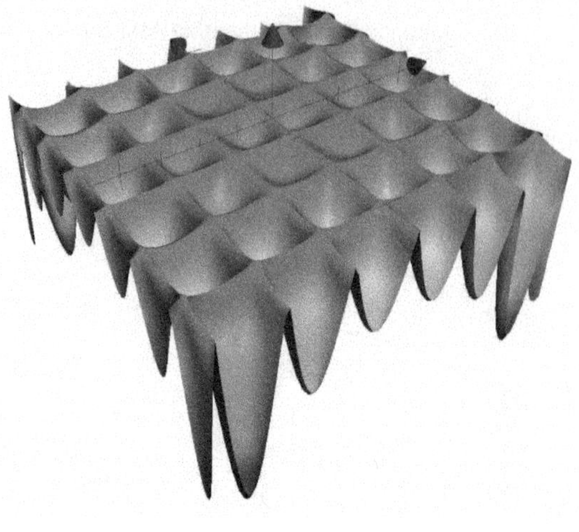

Figure 8: The Hölder table function.

3. In the **Positive** fitness-correlated scenario, the evaluation time $t(\vec{x})$ of an individual $\vec{x}$ is a linear function of fitness with a positive slope m and zero intercept:

$$t(\vec{x}) = mf(\vec{x}) \tag{17}$$

This simulates the case where evaluation becomes faster as we approach the optimum.

4. In the **Negative** fitness-correlated scenario, evaluation time is a linear function of fitness with a negative slope and a non-zero intercept:

$$t(\vec{x}) = \max\left(0, -mf(\vec{x}) + t_{\max}\right). \tag{18}$$

In this case, evaluation becomes slower as we approach the optimum (up to a maximum of $t_{\max}$ seconds).

We tested all four scenarios on the 2-dimensional Rastrigin function, the Hölder table function, and the venerable 10-dimensional sphere function. While the Rastrigin function has many local optima, it is linearly separable and has a quadratic macro-structure which makes the global optimum relatively easy to find:

$$f(\vec{x}) = 10l + \sum_{i=1}^{l}[x_i^2 - 10\cos(2\pi x_i)]. \tag{19}$$

The Hölder table function (Figure 8) is also highly multimodal:

$$f(\vec{x}) = -\left|\sin(x_1)\cos(x_2)\exp\left(\left|1 - \frac{\sqrt{x_1^2 + x_2^2}}{\pi}\right|\right)\right| + 19.2085, \tag{20}$$

where we have added the non-traditional constant 19.2085 so that the global optima have a fitness of approximately zero. We select the Hölder table because it is moderately difficult, in the sense that the EAs we are studying sometimes converge on a local optimum, and fail to converge on a global optimum after several hundred generations.

During both initialization and the application of reproductive operators, we bound each gene between -10 and 10 on all three objectives, and we set the standard deviation of the Gaussian mutation operator to 0.5. For the fitness-correlated scenarios, we set the parameter m to 1 for the sphere function and 5 on the Rastrigin and Hölder table. We ran each EA for 250 generations on the sphere function, 500 on the Hölder function, and 1000 on the Rastrigin function.

4.2 Results

4.2.1 *Sphere and Rastrigin Functions*

Our first observation on non-flat fitness landscapes relates back to Section 2, where we found no evidence of a selective bias toward fast-evaluating individuals on flat landscapes. That result does not preclude the possibility that a special kind of bias could still exist on non-flat landscapes.

In particular, we might anticipate that in the positively correlated scenario, where evaluation time decreases as fitness improves, a preference for fast-evaluating individuals may cause the population to be "accelerated" toward the optimum. Conversely, we might also expect the population to be more reluctant to move into areas of better fitness when evaluation time is negatively correlated with fitness. In fact, however, we observe no statistically significant ($p < 0.05$) difference among the four scenarios in the number of fitness evaluations it takes for the asynchronous EA to converge on the sphere function (not shown). This indicates that as Gaussian mutation leads the population to exploit a unimodal function, the effect of evaluation-time bias is negligible.

Secondly, we would like to know how well the naïve promises of throughput improvement serve as a predictor of true speedup on these simple objectives. Figures 9 and 10 show the true speedup and throughput improvement for each of the four scenarios on the sphere and Rastrigin functions, respectively. The true speedup is measured by considering the amount of wall-clock time it takes each algorithm to reach a fitness value of less than the threshold value $\eta = 2$. Each scenario was tested by pairing 50 independent runs of each algorithm and measuring the resulting speedup distribution.

The asynchronous EA converges in less time than the generational EA in all four scenarios on both functions. On the Rastrigin, but not the sphere, the true speedups are remarkably high. All of them average over 2.0, which is the maximum attainable expected value for throughput improvement as determined by Equation 16, and outliers are visible in Figure 10 with true speedup values in excess of 20 or 30. This is possible because the asynchronous EA requires fewer fitness evaluations to solve the Rastrigin function than the generational EA.

On the sphere function, most of the true speedup is more readily explained by an increase in throughput: We find at $p < 0.05$ with the Bonferroni correction for testing four simultaneous hypotheses that there is no statistically significant difference between the means of the throughput speedup and true speedup in the non-heritable, heritable, and positive scenarios. We reject the hypothesis, however, that the mean true speedup in the negative scenario is equal to the mean of its throughput improvement: the true speedup is higher on average.

When evaluation time is negatively correlated with fitness on a minimization problem, the majority of the processing time is spent in the later stages of the run, where the population consists primarily of high-quality individuals with long evaluation times. The late stages of the run are also where

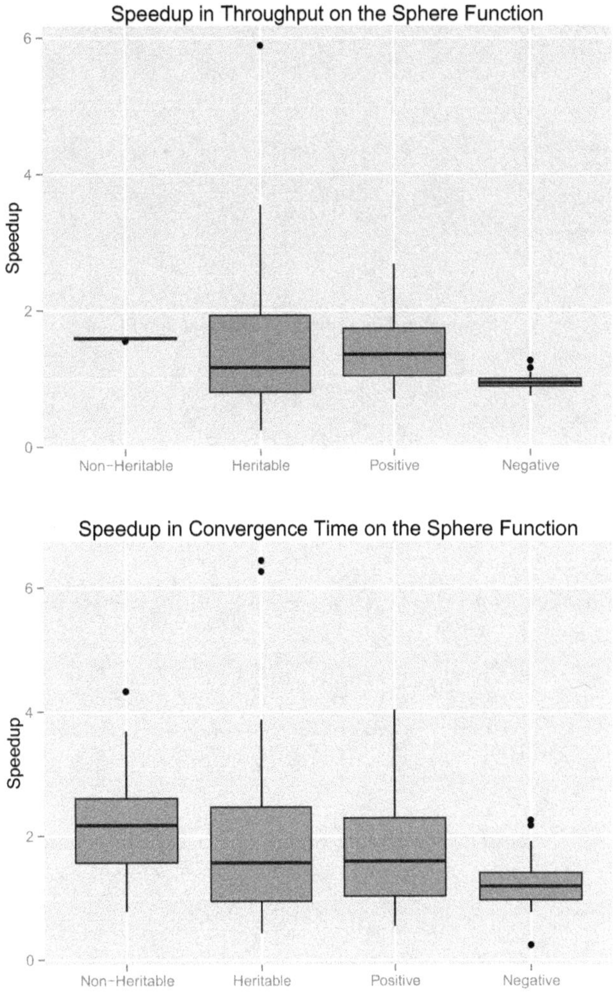

Figure 9: Speedup in throughput (Top) and convergence time (Bottom) of the asynchronous EA on the sphere function.

genetic variation is low in the population, so there is very little evaluation-time variance. As we saw in Section 3, low evaluation-time variance translates to very little difference in throughput between the two algorithms – when there is no eval-time variance, there is no idle time to eliminate. As such, we predict that the throughput improvement in the negative scenario will be very close to 1 on any objective function, provided that the algorithm is run for a sufficiently long period of time.

The true speedup in the negative scenario is observed at an average of 1.23 +/- 0.05 (95% confidence interval) for the sphere function and 3.09 +/- 0.58 for the Rastrigin. The fact that the true speedup is greater than 1 for both functions indicates that it is the evolutionary trajectory of the asynchronous EA, not the elimination of idle time, that is producing the true speedup.

In fact, the asynchronous EA is fundamentally greedier than the generational EA. This can be seen in Figure 11, which depicts average best-so-far trajectories on the sphere function for the non-heritable scenario. $(\mu + \lambda)$-style EAs

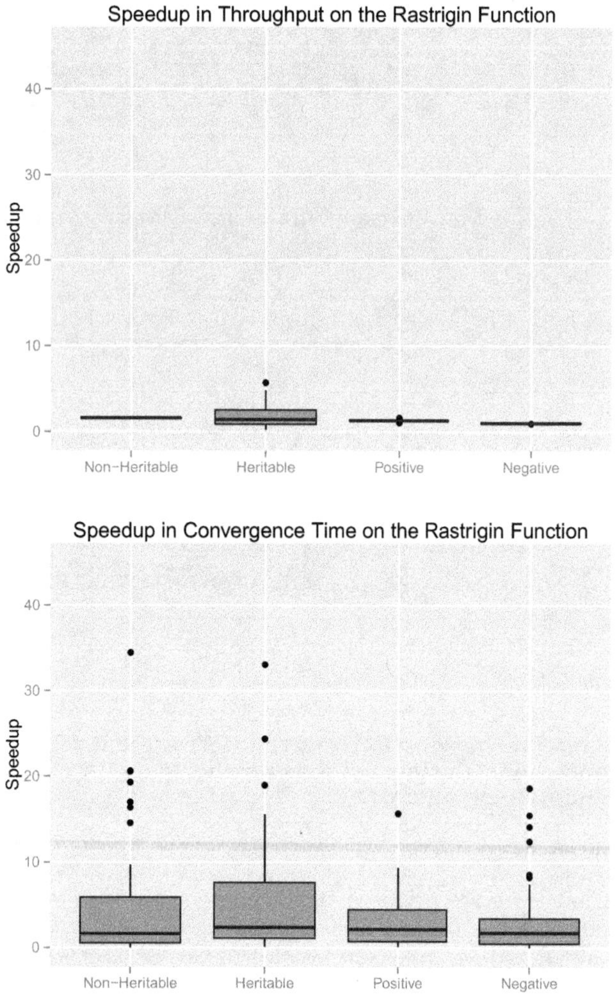

Figure 10: Speedup in throughput (Top) and convergence time (Bottom) of the asynchronous EA on the Rastrigin function.

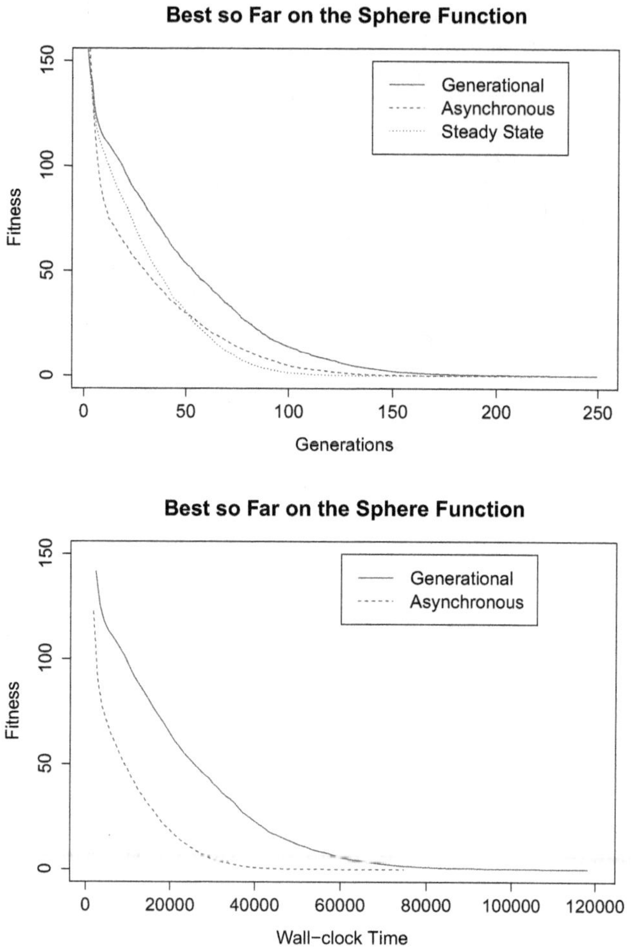

Figure 11: On the sphere function, the simple asynchronous EA consistently takes fewer fitness evaluations on average to reach the optimum (Top). This contributes to its ability to find the solution in less wall-clock time than the generational EA (Bottom).

are known to be greedier than (μ, λ)-style EAs in general, and the simple asynchronous EA is no exception. In all four scenarios on both the sphere and Rastrigin functions, the asynchronous EA converges in fewer fitness evaluations than the generational EA, not just fewer seconds. Part of the true speedup in Figures 9 and 10, then, is attributable to an increase in throughput (working "faster"), but a major component is due to the fact that the asynchronous EA takes a different search trajectory than the generational EA. Because the asynchronous EA requires fewer fitness evaluations to reach the optimum, in these cases we can say it works both faster and "smarter."

4.2.2 *Hölder Table Function*

Both algorithms frequently fail to converge to a global minimum on the Hölder table function. Since many of our runs fail to converge, we cannot fully describe the run-length distribution, which we used to compute the distribution of speedups on the other objectives. Instead, we characterize just part of the run-length distribution by measuring the *success ratio* of each algorithm after a fixed amount of resources have been expended (such as wall-clock time). We define the success ratio as the fraction of 50 independent runs that achieved a fitness of less than $\eta = 2$. Cf. [3] for a discussion of run-length distributions, success ratios and related measures.

In all four scenarios, the asynchronous EA is able to find a global optimum on the Hölder table function much more frequently than the generational EA does. When both algorithms do find a solution, the asynchronous EA finds it at least as quickly as the generational EA does. This can be seen for the heritable and negative scenarios in Figure 12 (the results for the other two scenarios are qualitatively similar).

On all three test functions, then, we have found that the asynchronous EA does not exhibit any particularly adverse performance. To the contrary, it does a good job of delivering the promised speedup in time-to-convergence on the two more tractable problems, and it allows us a much smaller risk of premature convergence on the more difficult Hölder table problem. These results are, of course, problem-dependent, and performance may vary on other objective functions. What this preliminary study has confirmed is that, on a few simple functions, the idiosyncrasies of the asynchronous EA's behavior did not undermine it's ability to improve EA performance. We have learned something about where asynchronous EAs can succeed, even if we do not yet understand how they might fail.

5. DISCUSSION

The potential benefits of asynchronous master-slave EAs were first recognized at least twenty years ago [32]. The growing prevalence of evolutionary computation applications that involve resource-intensive simulations, however, pushes evaluation time to a higher position on the list of pertinent concerns in the EA community than it was in the 1990's. This makes the throughput-enhancing advantages of asynchronous master-slave EAs especially relevant.

In this paper, we have made a number of observations that we hope can save practitioners some confusion as they turn to asynchrony to improve their EA performance. Using the assumption of uniformly distributed evaluation-time

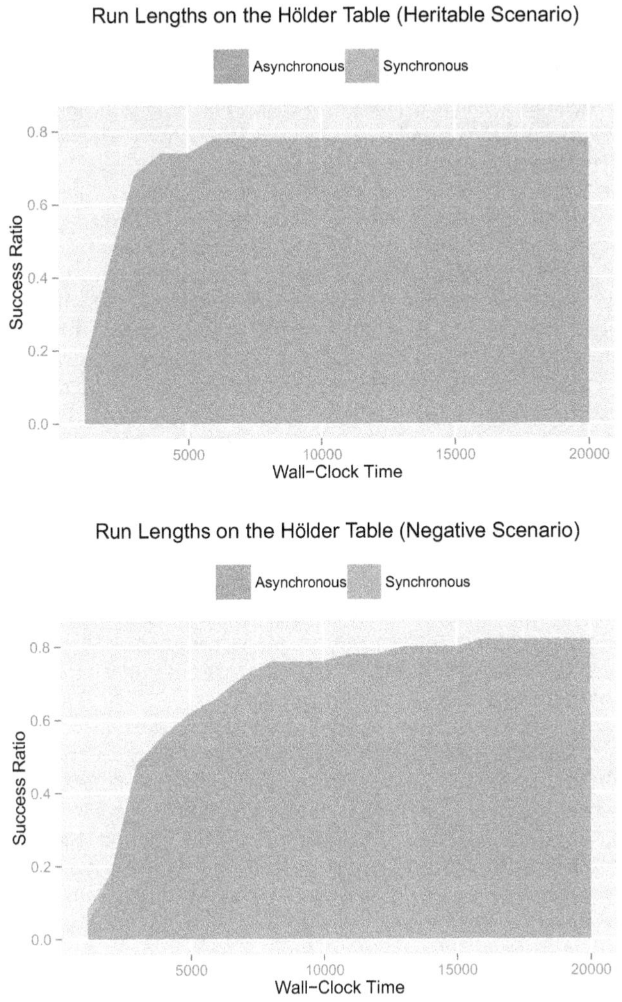

Figure 12: The asynchronous EA is able to find a global optimum on the Hölder table function more often than the generational EA.

variance as an example, we have quantitatively explained how the amount of throughput you gain by choosing a simple asynchronous EA over a generational one depends on the number of slave processors, the size of the population, and the variance of the eval-time distribution.

Throughput improvement merely quantifies how much "faster" the algorithm is working, though, not other implications of its evolutionary behavior, such as how much "smarter" (or not) it is at traversing the search space. We were concerned that asynchronous EAs may have a pernicious bias toward fast-evaluating individuals. The evidence we have presented, however, has ruled out evaluation-time bias that is independent of selection and reproductive variation, and further suggests that evaluation-time bias does not affect the EA's ability to exploit a basin of attraction.

We have clarified the distinction between non-heritable and heritable components of evaluation-time variance, and demonstrated that the latter has different implications on performance depending on whether it is negatively correlated with fitness, positively correlated with fitness, or independent. We also found that when individual evaluation times have a deterministic negative correlation with fitness, the variance in evaluation time quickly drops off, and the asynchronous EA ceases to provide an increase in throughput over the generational competition. Finally, we have emphasized the distinction between throughput improvement and true speedup, and in our experiments we found that the true speedup was often far greater than what the reduction in idle time can account for by itself.

5.1 Threats to Validity

This work isolates several interesting properties of asynchronous EA behavior, but was based entirely on simplifying assumptions about evaluation-time variance, its heritability and its relation to fitness. In our experience with tuning the parameters of spiking neural network simulations, it is not uncommon to observe evaluation times that follow a highly skewed or multi-modal distribution, even in just the non-heritable component that arises from changing the simulator's pseudo-random number seed. The relationship between fitness and heritable evaluation time is also much less straightforward than the linear models in Section 4 imply. Furthermore, most of our experiments in this paper used very small population sizes ($n = 10$), assumed a uniform distribution of evaluation times, and were limited to a real vector genetic representation and Gaussian mutation operator. All these are good reasons to question the extent to which our results will generalize to practical applications.

5.2 Future Work

We have ruled out some kinds of evaluation-time bias, but we know from [30] that evaluation-time bias does exist in some asynchronous EA applications. Further work is needed to understand what kinds of problems may exhibit a bias against slow-evaluating parts of the search space.

The model of throughput improvement we presented for the uniform distribution can be extended to produce similar predictions for evaluation-time distributions that are more likely to be encountered in practice. More challenging, the simple asynchronous EA is quite complex from a dynamical systems perspective. The question of whether and when an asynchronous EA might exhibit a selection effect on the evaluation-time trait could benefit from a better theoretical understanding of how evolution and evaluation times interact. We also may need a better understanding of asynchronous EA dynamics before we can competently describe what kinds of functions they are prone to fail on. What would an 'asynchronous-deceptive' function look like?

Our discrimination between the selection lag and the re-ordering caused by eval-time variance raises the possibility of constructing an *order-preserving* parallel EA, that allows a selection lag but does not allow re-ordering. Such an algorithm could preserve some of the throughput improvement offered by the asynchronous EA while eliminating its evaluation-time bias.

Acknowledgments

This work was funded by U.S. National Science Foundation Award IIS/RI-1302256.

6. REFERENCES

[1] E. Alba and M. Tomassini. Parallelism and evolutionary algorithms. *IEEE Transactions on Evolutionary Computation*, 6(5):443–462, 2002.

[2] E. Alba and J. M. Troya. Analyzing synchronous and asynchronous parallel distributed genetic algorithms. *Future Gener. Comput. Syst.*, 17(4):451–465, Jan. 2001.

[3] T. Bartz-Beielstein. *Experimental Research in Evolutionary Computation: The New Experimentalism.* Springer, 2006.

[4] E. Cantú-Paz. A survey of parallel genetic algorithms. *Calculateurs paralleles, reseaux et systems repartis*, 10(2):141–171, 1998.

[5] E. Cantu-Paz. *Efficient and accurate parallel genetic algorithms.* Springer, 2000.

[6] A. W. Churchill, P. Husbands, and A. Philippides. Tool sequence optimization using synchronous and asynchronous parallel multi-objective evolutionary algorithms with heterogeneous evaluations. In *IEEE Congress on Evolutionary Computation (CEC) 2013*, pages 2924–2931. IEEE, 2013.

[7] K. A. De Jong. *Evolutionary Computation: A Unified Approach.* MIT Press, Cambridge, MA, 2001.

[8] M. Depolli, R. Trobec, and B. Filipič. Asynchronous master-slave parallelization of differential evolution for multi-objective optimization. *Evolutionary Computation*, 21(2):261–291, 2013.

[9] J. J. Durillo, A. J. Nebro, F. Luna, and E. Alba. A study of master-slave approaches to parallelize nsga-ii. In *IEEE International Symposium on Parallel and Distributed Processing 2008*, pages 1–8. IEEE, 2008.

[10] M. Giacobini, E. Alba, and M. Tomassini. Selection intensity in asynchronous cellular evolutionary algorithms. In E. Cantú-Paz, J. Foster, K. Deb, L. Davis, R. Roy, U.-M. O'Reilly, H.-G. Beyer, R. Standish, G. Kendall, S. Wilson, M. Harman, J. Wegener, D. Dasgupta, M. Potter, A. Schultz, K. Dowsland, N. Jonoska, and J. Miller, editors, *Genetic and Evolutionary Computation — GECCO 2003*, volume 2723 of *Lecture Notes in Computer Science*, pages 955–966. Springer Berlin Heidelberg, 2003.

[11] J. Kim. *Hierarchical asynchronous genetic algorithms for parallel/distributed simulation-based optimization.* PhD thesis, The University of Arizona, 1994.

[12] B.-I. Koh, A. D. George, R. T. Haftka, and B. J. Fregly. Parallel asynchronous particle swarm optimization. *International Journal for Numerical Methods in Engineering*, 67(4):578–595, 2006.

[13] P. Liu, F. Lau, M. J. Lewis, and C.-l. Wang. A new asynchronous parallel evolutionary algorithm for function optimization. In *Parallel Problem Solving from Nature—PPSN VII*, pages 401–410. Springer, 2002.

[14] S. Luke. *The ECJ Owner's Manual.* `http://cs.gmu.edu/~eclab/projects/ecj/`, 22nd edition, August 2014.

[15] J. Merelo, A. M. Mora, C. M. Fernandes, and A. I. Esparcia-Alcázar. Designing and testing a pool-based evolutionary algorithm. *Natural Computing*, 12(2):149–162, 2013.

[16] L. Mussi, Y. S. Nashed, and S. Cagnoni. Gpu-based asynchronous particle swarm optimization. In *Proceedings of the 13th Annual Conference on Genetic and Evolutionary Computation (GECCO)*, pages 1555–1562. ACM, 2011.

[17] M. Nowostawski and R. Poli. Parallel genetic algorithm taxonomy. In *Third International Conference on Knowledge-Based Intelligent Information Engineering Systems*, pages 88–92. IEEE, 1999.

[18] J. Olenšek, T. Tuma, J. Puhan, and Á. Bűrmen. A new asynchronous parallel global optimization method based on simulated annealing and differential evolution. *Applied Soft Computing*, 11(1):1481–1489, 2011.

[19] M. Parker and G. B. Parker. Using a queue genetic algorithm to evolve xpilot control strategies on a distributed system. In *IEEE Congress on Evolutionary Computation (CEC) 2006*, pages 1202–1207. IEEE, 2006.

[20] K. Rasheed and B. D. Davison. Effect of global parallelism on the behavior of a steady state genetic algorithm for design optimization. In *IEEE Congress on Evolutionary Computation (CEC) 1999*, volume 1. IEEE, 1999.

[21] T. P. Runarsson. An asynchronous parallel evolution strategy. *International Journal of Computational Intelligence and Applications*, 3(04):381–394, 2003.

[22] J. Sarma and K. A. De Jong. Generation gaps revisited. *Foundations of Genetic Algorithms 1993*, 1993.

[23] J. Sarma and K. A. De Jong. Generation gap methods. In T. Bäck, D. B. Fogel, and Z. Michalewicz, editors, *Evolutionary Computation I*, pages 205–211. CRC Press, 2000.

[24] T. J. Stanley and T. N. Mudge. A parallel genetic algorithm for multiobjective microprocessor design. In *Proceedings of the 6th International Conference on Genetic Algorithms (ICGA)*, pages 597–604, San Francisco, CA, 1995. Morgan Kaufmann.

[25] T. Stützle. Parallelization strategies for ant colony optimization. In *Parallel Problem Solving from Nature—PPSN V*, pages 722–731. Springer, 1998.

[26] E.-G. Talbi and H. Meunier. Hierarchical parallel approach for gsm mobile network design. *Journal of Parallel and Distributed Computing*, 66(2):274–290, 2006.

[27] G. Venter and J. Sobieszczanski-Sobieski. Parallel particle swarm optimization algorithm accelerated by asynchronous evaluations. *Journal of Aerospace Computing, Information, and Communication*, 3(3):123–137, 2006.

[28] J. Wakunda and A. Zell. Median-selection for parallel steady-state evolution strategies. In *Parallel Problem Solving from Nature—PPSN VI*, pages 405–414. Springer, 2000.

[29] M. Yagoubi, L. Thobois, and M. Schoenauer. An asynchronous steady-state nsga-ii algorithm for multi-objective optimization of diesel combustion. In H. Rodrigues, editor, *Proceedings of the 2nd International Conference on Engineering Optimization*, volume 2010, page 77, 2010.

[30] M. Yagoubi, L. Thobois, and M. Schoenauer. Asynchronous evolutionary multi-objective algorithms with heterogeneous evaluation costs. In *IEEE Congress on Evolutionary Computation (CEC) 2011*, pages 21–28. IEEE, 2011.

[31] A.-C. Zăvoianu, E. Lughofer, W. Koppelstätter, G. Weidenholzer, W. Amrhein, and E. P. Klement. On the performance of master-slave parallelization methods for multi-objective evolutionary algorithms. In *Artificial Intelligence and Soft Computing*, pages 122–134. Springer, 2013.

[32] B. P. Zeigler and J. Kim. Asynchronous genetic algorithms on parallel computers. In *Proceedings of the 5th International Conference on Genetic Algorithms*, page 660. Morgan Kaufmann Publishers Inc., 1993.

APPENDIX

A. EXPECTED MAXIMUM OF UNIFORM SAMPLES

Let $P = \{Y_1, Y_2, \ldots, Y_n\}$ be a set of random variables, with the Y_i's i.i.d. from some distribution. Then, from the theory of order statistics, the probability that the maximum value in P obtains a given value is characterized by the cumulative distribution

$$p(\max[P] \leq x) = \prod_{i=1}^{n} p(Y_i \leq x). \tag{21}$$

Differentiating both sides yields the p.d.f.

$$p(\max[P] = x) = \frac{\mathrm{d}}{\mathrm{d}x} \prod_{i=1}^{n} p(Y_i \leq x). \tag{22}$$

We can combine this definition with integration by parts to express the expected value of the maximum value as a function of the c.d.f. of the Y_i's:

$$\mathbb{E}[\max[P]] = \int_{-\infty}^{\infty} x \cdot p(\max[P] = x)\mathrm{d}x \tag{23}$$

$$= \int_{-\infty}^{\infty} x \frac{\mathrm{d}}{\mathrm{d}x} \prod_{i=1}^{n} p(Y_i \leq x)\mathrm{d}x \tag{24}$$

$$= \left[x \prod_{i=1}^{n} p(Y_i \leq x) - \int \prod_{i=1}^{n} p(Y_i \leq x)\mathrm{d}x \right|_{-\infty}^{\infty} \tag{25}$$

This expression cannot be solved in closed form for most distributions. The c.d.f. of a uniform distribution over the interval $[a, b]$, however, is given by

$$p(Y_i \leq x) = \int_a^x \frac{1}{b-a}\mathrm{d}y = \frac{x-a}{b-a}. \tag{26}$$

Substituting into Equation 25, we have

$$\mathbb{E}[\max[P]] = \left[x \left(\frac{x-a}{b-a}\right)^n - \int \left(\frac{x-a}{b-a}\right)^n \mathrm{d}x \right|_a^b \tag{27}$$

$$= b - \frac{1}{n+1}(b-a). \tag{28}$$

Parallel Evolutionary Algorithms Performing Pairwise Comparisons

Marie-Liesse Cauwet,
Olivier Teytaud
TAO, Inria, Lri, Umr Cnrs 8623
Bat. 650, Univ. Paris-Sud
91405 Orsay Cedex, France
cauwet@lri.fr

Shih-Yuan Chiu,
Kuo-Min Lin,
Shi-Jim Yen
Computer Science
and Information Engineering
National Dong-Hwa University
Hualien, Taiwan

David L. St-Pierre
Industrial Engineering
Univ. du Québec at
Trois-Rivières
Québec, Canada

Fabien Teytaud
Univ. Lille Nord de France,
ULCO, LISIC, Calais, France
fabien.teytaud@lisic.univ-littoral.fr

ABSTRACT

We study mathematically and experimentally the convergence rate of differential evolution and particle swarm optimization for simple unimodal functions. Due to parallelization concerns, the focus is on lower bounds on the runtime, i.e. upper bounds on the speed-up, as a function of the population size. Two cases are particularly relevant: A population size of the same order of magnitude as the dimension and larger population sizes. We use the branching factor as a tool for proving bounds and get, as upper bounds, a linear speed-up for a population size similar to the dimension, and a logarithmic speed-up for larger population sizes. We then propose parametrizations for differential evolution and particle swarm optimization that reach these bounds.

Categories and Subject Descriptors

G.1.6 [**Optimization**]: Unconstrained optimization

General Terms

Theory

Keywords

Differential Evolution; Parallelism; Particle Swarm Optimization

1. INTRODUCTION

Evolutionary algorithms are population-based algorithms designed to solve black-box optimization problems. An evolutionary algorithm typically (i) generates a population of search points (ii) selects an approximate solution for the optimization problem. The selection is performed thanks to the ranking/comparisons between the search points. Parallelization is highly relevant when the population is large: each point can be evaluated on a single processor [36, 21].

We first introduce parallel black-box optimization in Section 1.1. We then present the convergence rate of an algorithm in Section 1.2 before explaining what is the branching factor in Section 1.3. We then focus on parallel black-box optimization algorithms which use only "paired" comparisons, as explained in Section 1.4. Section 2 applies branching factor analysis to these algorithms, and provides lower bounds on runtimes. Sections 3 and 4 confront bounds with experimental rates for differential evolution and particle swarm optimization respectively.

Throughout the paper, unless stated otherwise, log refers to the natural logarithm.

1.1 Parallel black-box optimization

Typical optimization problems consist in searching for the minimum x^* of some objective function $f : \mathbb{R}^D \to \mathbb{R}$, i.e. x^* is such that $\forall x,\ f(x^*) \leq f(x)$. f is also known as the fitness function and D represents the dimension of the problem. A black-box optimization consists in doing so by successive calls to f only. f is seen as an oracle; no internal property of f is used, and the goal of the optimization algorithm consists in finding a good approximation of x^*, within a moderate number of calls to the objective function.

Parallel synchronous black-box optimization is the setting in which p simultaneous calls to the objective function are possible. Therefore, p is the number of processors or cores, possibly on GPU architectures, which allow large numbers of cores. When measuring speed-up, i.e. the factor by which speed is improved when using p processors, there are several cases: (i) Cases in which the objective function is fast. In such cases, the internal cost of the optimization algorithm and possibly communication costs are not negligible. (ii) Cases in which the cost of the objective function is not approximately constant. Then, asynchronous algorithms might be more relevant. (iii) Cases in which the computational cost is mainly in the objective function, and

FOGA '15 January 17 - 20, 2015, Aberystwyth, UK

http://dx.doi.org/10.1145/2725494.2725499

the computational cost of the fitness function is constant. This makes synchronous algorithms relevant.

We focus on case (iii). Additionally, we consider that the structure of the optimization algorithm is not modified: we just use an increased population size, so that we can simultaneously evaluate one fitness value on each core or each processor. We will study the speed-up as a function of the population size, assuming that the population size is the number of cores. This does not cover all parallelism scenarios, but it is an important one.

[6] is an interesting related work; a key difference is that they focus on black-box complexity and unbiased mutations in discrete settings, rather than comparison-based methods.

1.2 Convergence Rate

We aim to study the effectiveness and limits of some evolutionary algorithms. As such, we define the *convergence rate* of an algorithm.

At each iteration n, the evolutionary algorithm provides an approximation x_n of the optimum x^*. We consider the following convergence measure:

$$\lim_{n\to\infty} \frac{1}{n} \log \|x_n - x^*\| = -C_{\lambda,D} \qquad (1)$$

where the equality holds almost surely. $C_{\lambda,D}$ is a positive constant, depending on the population size λ and the dimension D only. Both theoretical and empirical results ([4, 5, 9, 32]) show that a wide range of evolutionary algorithms may converge in the sense of Eq. 1 when the objective function is unimodal and reasonably smooth. Our purpose is to exhibit some bounds on this convergence rate $C_{\lambda,D}$ when it is well defined. We also get lower bounds on the corresponding limit inferior.

The definition of the convergence rate (Eq. 1) means that the speed-up associated to λ processors, with respect to a fixed λ_0, is proportional to the convergence rate. We use the speed-up term which is classical in parallelism; this is equivalent to studying the convergence rate as a function of λ. Hence, in the following, results on the convergence rate also hold for the speed-up.

The state of the art proposes other information on the convergence rate $C_{\lambda,D}$, as follows (see [16] for a more detailed writing).

(i) Convergence with a population size equal to the dimension. We know that some algorithms have the following property (and it is not possible to scale better, according to [16, Section 5]):

$$\textbf{Linear scalability: } \lim_{\lambda\to\infty} C_{\lambda,\lambda} = C_{linear}. \qquad (2)$$

Eq. 2 is written for $C_{\lambda,\lambda}$. Indeed, Eq. 2 also holds for $C_{\lambda,D(\lambda)}$ where $\lambda \to D(\lambda)$ verifies $D(\lambda)/\lambda = \Theta(1)$.

When we have linear scalability - i.e. when a constant C_{linear} verifies Eq. 2 - it means that we "cancel" out the curse of dimensionality thanks to

- A parallel implementation with one individual evaluated on each processor.
- A linear number of processors (linear in the dimension).

(ii) Convergence with a large population size: for some algorithms,

$$\textbf{Logarithmic speed-up: } \lim_{\lambda\to\infty} C_{\lambda,D} = C_{large,D} \log(\lambda) \qquad (3)$$

$$\text{with } \lim_{D\to\infty} D \times C_{large,D} = C_{large} \qquad (4)$$

For a wide class of comparison-based algorithms, including evolution strategies and pattern search methods, no algorithm can do better than this bound ([16, Fig. 2 and Prop. 8]).

We here show that these results also hold in the case of differential evolution and particle swarm optimization. Explicit bounds on C_{linear} and C_{large} are available thanks to the *branching factor* analysis sketched in Section 2.

The convergence rate above (Eq. 1) is a convergence rate in the search space; we can also consider the convergence rate in the fitness space:

$$\lim_{n\to\infty} \frac{1}{n} \log \left(f(x_n) - \inf_x f(x) \right) = -C'_{\lambda,D}. \qquad (5)$$

where inf denotes the infimum. On the sphere function, $C'_{\lambda,D} = 2C_{\lambda,D}$. We will use this convergence rate $C'_{\lambda,D}$ (in fitness space) in all our experiments.

1.3 Branching factor

Many comparison-based algorithms, after having evaluated the population, keep only a concise representation of the evaluations they have performed.

EXAMPLE 1.1 (ORDERED (μ,λ)-ES). *In the case of an ordered (μ,λ)-ES, this concise representation is the ordered list of the indices of the μ best among the λ generated individuals. There are $\binom{\lambda}{\mu} \times (\mu!)$ possibilities.*

EXAMPLE 1.2 (UNORDERED (μ,λ)-ES). *In the case of an unordered (μ,λ)-ES, this concise representation is the family (unordered) of the indices of the μ best among the λ generated individuals. There are $\binom{\lambda}{\mu}$ possible configurations.*

A crucial property of comparison-based algorithms is that the number of possible indices configurations is finite.

DEFINITION 1 (BRANCHING FACTOR). *Consider an algorithm which uses only a finite set of possible concise representations of fitness values at a given iteration for updating its internal state. Then, the* branching factor *of this algorithm is the cardinal of these possible concise representations.*

For evolution strategies, the branching factor can be strongly reduced, by assuming some regularity of the objective function (VC-dimension assumption on the objective function [40, 15, 16]).

The branching factor is then used to prove that comparison-based algorithms usually have convergence rate increasing at most logarithmically with the population size λ as in Eq. 3. This upper bound is proved for evolution strategies in [16, Fig. 2]. Moreover, this bound is tight: ad hoc variants of evolutionary algorithms match it up to multiplicative factors. Thanks to some specific tuning, [37] shows empirically that this logarithmic speed-up can be reached by some evolutionary algorithms, namely CMSA, EMNA and CMAES. Similarly, the branching factor leads to finding a lower bound on the convergence rate provided that the population size is limited. Here again, this bound is tight, hence Eq. 2 holds for comparison-based algorithms (see [16, Section 5]).

1.4 Differential evolution and particle swarm optimization

Two families of comparison-based algorithms are studied in the present paper, namely Particle Swarm Optimization (PSO) and Differential Evolution (DE). They share several common points. They both are population based optimization algorithms and do not require heavy calculations for gradient or Hessian updates. Furthermore, the run of these algorithms depends on "paired" comparisons only: instead of comparing or sorting most of the population, these two algorithms compare each individual to only one possible mutation. This leads to specific mathematical properties, discussed in Section 2.

Among evolutionary algorithms, Differential Evolution was, from the very beginning [36], presented as a tool with high relevance for parallel optimization in continuous domains. Particle Swarm Optimization [21, 35] is also a general purpose black-box optimization algorithm, aimed at quickly finding approximate solutions to optimization problems.

In the implementation of these algorithms (see Algorithms 1 and 2), we use two loops per generation: one loop for computing fitness values of candidate vectors; one loop for updating "best" points (best search point so far, and best point so far for each given particle for PSO). One can implement variants of PSO and DE in which this is done in one loop only. However, such variants are less parallel, because the mutations, which depend on "best" points, might change during the loop and therefore cannot be computed simultaneously.

Choosing the right parameters for these algorithms is a challenging task. In this paper, we define rules for choosing these parameters in a parallel black-box optimization setting. This experimental part of the study is restricted to the case of unimodal well conditioned fitness functions. Our empirically developed formula for the parameters is validated in front of both (i) standard values used for DE and PSO and (ii) theoretically known bounds.

Differential evolution. Differential evolution (DE) [36] is one of the main evolutionary algorithms for continuous optimization. It performs well on optimization testbeds [36, 3, 2, 29]. At each iteration, each point p_i of the population undergo mutations of some of its components, then comparisons are performed between the old point and its corresponding mutated version. The best of the two points is selected for the next iteration. Different parameters are involved in the mutation step. A classical version of DE is presented in Algorithm 1. Many variants exist, including self-adaptive parameters [11, 22, 42, 30] and meta-heuristics for choosing parameters [28]. In some variants [36] (DE/best/1, DE/best/2), we need to compute at each generation the best search point so far. When this property is required, we set parameter *best* to 1 in Algorithm 1, and to 0 otherwise. Henceforward, when *best* = 1, we denote this version of DE by DE/best, and when *best* = 0, this version of DE is named DE/rand.

On the technical side, the large scale parallelization of the evaluations is performed with CUDA in [31]. [26] focuses on the asynchronous parallelization, which is not considered in the present paper; they combine DE and simulated annealing. [41] considers a ring topology and focuses on avoiding premature convergence. [43] considers the problem of multiple populations from the point of view of global convergence and maintaining diversity, while we, in the present paper, consider mainly (at least for experimental rates - our lower bounds on runtime are for arbitrary functions with unique global optimum) local convergence. Consistently with [1], we consider the performance as a function of the population size; we also prove lower bounds and discuss the optimal parametrization of DE with large population size.

Algorithm 1 Pseudo-code of basic differential evolution. The first loop on the population contains the fitness evaluations, supposed to be the key part of the computational cost; it is fully parallel. For $j \in \{1, \ldots, D\}$, $x_{i,j}$ denotes the jth coordinate of a vector $x_i \in \mathbb{R}^D$. $\mathcal{U}(a,b)^D$ stands for an uniform random variable in the domain $(a,b)^D$.

```
Require: D: Dimension, N: Number of generations, F ∈ [0,2]: Differential weight, Cr ∈ [0,1]: Crossover probability, λ: Population size, best ∈ {0,1}
  for each i ∈ {1,...,λ} do
    Initialize p_i ~ U(−500,500)^D
    Compute f(p_i)
  end for
  if best = 1 then
    g ← argmin_{p_1,...,p_λ} f(p_i)
  end if
  n ← 1
  while n<N do
    for i ∈ {1,...,λ} parallel loop do
      Randomly draw a, b and c distinct
          in {1,...,i−1,i+1,...λ}
      if best = 1 then
        Define p'_i ← g + F(p_b − p_c)
      else
        Define p'_i ← p_a + F(p_b − p_c)
      end if
      Randomly draw R ∈ {1,...,D}
      for each j ∈ {1,...,D} do
        p''_{i,j} ← p'_{i,j} if rand < Cr or if j = R
        p''_{i,j} ← p_{i,j} otherwise
      end for
      Compute f(p''_i)
    end for
    for i ∈ {1,2,...,λ} do
      if f(p''_i) < f(p_i) then
        p_i ← p''_i
        if best = 1 & f(p_i) < f(g) then
          g ← p_i
        end if
      end if
    end for
    n ← n + 1
  end while
  if best = 0 then
    g ← argmin_{p_1,...,p_λ} f(p_i)
  end if
  Return g
```

Particle Swarm Optimization. Particle Swarm Optimization (PSO) is another classical comparison-based algorithm for continuous domain. Let $\mathcal{P}$ be a population of particles; for each $i \in \mathcal{P}$, $x_i \in \mathbb{R}^D$ is in the search space and the particle has a velocity $v_i \in \mathbb{R}^D$. Let p_i be the best known position of the particle i and g be the best found solution so far. Algorithm 2 presents a basic PSO following this notation.

Algorithm 2 Basic PSO. The first loop on the population contains the fitness evaluations, supposed to be the key part of the computational cost; it is fully parallel. Notations are the same as in Algorithm 1, ie. x_j (resp. $x_{i,j}$) is the jth component of vector x (resp. x_i).

```
Require: D: Dimension, N: Number of generations, P: Population, b_l: Lower bound of the search space, u_l: Upper bound of the search space, ω,φ_p,φ_g: Parameters
  for each particle i ∈ P do
    Initialize its position x_i from a uniform distribution: x_i ~ U(b_l, b_u)^D
    Initialize its best known position: p_i ← x_i
    Initialize its velocity: v_i ~ U(−|b_u − b_l|, |b_u − b_l|)^D
  end for
  Initialize best solution: g ← arg min_{x_i, i∈P} f(x_i)
  n ← 1
  while n < N do
    for each i ∈ P   parallel loop do
      Pick r_p, r_g ~ U(0, 1)
      for each j ∈ {1, ..., D} do
        v_{i,j} ← ω v_{i,j} + φ_p r_p (p_{i,j} − x_{i,j}) + φ_g r_g (g_j − x_{i,j})
      end for
      x_i ← x_i + v_i
      Compute f(x_i)
    end for
    for each i ∈ P do
      if f(x_i) < f(p_i) then
        p_i ← x_i
        if f(p_i) < f(g) then
          g ← p_i
        end if
      end if
    end for
    n ← n + 1
  end while
  Return g
```

It has several parameters leading to complicated dynamics; for example ω (see Algorithm 2) is often thought of as an inertia, but it can be negative or greater than 1. Therefore, many works are devoted to choosing optimally these parameters [27, 39, 14].

As explained before, PSO is relevant for parallelization. [17] uses speculative parallelization. Speculative parallelization is known to ensure an asymptotic logarithmic convergence rate (i.e. the optimal rate as described in Eq. 3), but it does not, in the general case, ensure optimality in large dimension (Eq. 2). They use the topology for defining a parallel variant of PSO, without necessarily increasing the population size. We will here consider the simple increasing of the population size. [25] focuses on the implementation part of a parallel PSO, in particular taking care of node failure and communication costs, using MapReduce - we will here assume that communication costs can be neglected, e.g. due to expensive fitness functions. [23] uses a fuzzy controller for a parallel PSO, applied to a power dispatch problem; the fuzzy part generates rules for the simulations. Other experimental works on parallel-PSO include [34] (focusing on parallel global optimization, whereas we focus on unimodal functions) and [12] (detailing communication strategies, which are beyond the scope of the present paper, because we focus on the case in which most of the cost is in the fitness evaluations).

Outline of this paper. The branching factor methodology has never been applied to differential evolution and particle swarm optimization. This is the purpose of the theoretical part of this paper. In this paper:

- We show mathematically that, whatever may be the parametrization, differential evolution and particle swarm optimization can not do better than a logarithmic speed-up (Eq. 3) and a linear scalability (Eq. 2).
- We estimate empirically the convergence rate, in the case of the sphere function. These convergence rates, in the easy considered setting, match the lower bounds.
- We propose some variants designed to reach a good convergence rate when the population size is large.

2. MATHEMATICAL ANALYSIS

In [16], the *branching factor* was identified as a crucial component of a comparison-based algorithm. We present a general framework of optimization in Alg. 3.

Algorithm 3 General framework of algorithms with bounded branching factor K.

```
Initialize some state S
while not finished do
  Generate (possibly randomly) a family E of individuals, using S only.
  Let I be the extracted information, which depends on (i) the fitness function (ii) S (iii) E; we assume that I has values in a finite set {1, ..., K}.
  Update: S ← update(S, I).
  Recommend: let x = recom(S) be the approximation of the optimum proposed by the algorithm.
end while
```

Define, for the theorem below, x_m the approximation of the optimum that it recommends after m iterations in Algorithm 3. It is known, by the following theorem [38] that the runtime necessary for hitting the optimum with probability $1-\delta$ and precision ϵ is lower bounded by a function of the branching factor.

THEOREM 1 (BRANCHING FACTOR THEOREM). *Assume that an optimization algorithm has branching factor K. Let $\mathcal{D}$ be the search domain. We define $\mathcal{F}$, $n_{\epsilon,\delta}$ and $N(\epsilon)$ as follow:*

- *We denote by $\mathcal{F}$ the set of objective functions on $\mathcal{D}$, i.e. functions from $\mathcal{D}$ to $\mathbb{R}$. Each function in $\mathcal{F}$ has a unique minimum $x^*(f)$ in $\mathcal{D}$. We assume that for each $x \in \mathcal{D}$, there is at least one objective function $f \in \mathcal{F}$ with optimum $x^*(f) = x$.*
- *Let $n_{\epsilon,\delta}$ be the minimum number of iterations in the While loop in Algorithm 3 such that, for any $f \in \mathcal{F}$, with probability $1-\delta$, $\|x_{n_{\epsilon,\delta}} - x^*(f)\| \leq \epsilon$.*
- *We define $N(\epsilon)$ the maximum integer n such that there exist n points $(x_1, \dots, x_n) \in \mathcal{D}^n$ satisfying $\|x_i - x_j\| \geq 2\epsilon$ for any $i \neq j$.*

Then, $n_{\epsilon,\delta} \geq \frac{\log(1-\delta)}{\log K} + \frac{\log N(\epsilon)}{\log K}$. (6)

$N(\epsilon)$ is the so-called packing number, which counts how many non-overlapping hyperspheres of radius ϵ can be fit in the space $\mathcal{D}$. In [16], bounds on the branching factor are computed for evolution strategies based either on a full ranking of the population or on a selection of the μ best individuals. The bounds are improved when the objective function is simple, e.g. has bounded VC-dimension. The purpose of this section is to show a bound on the branching factor in the case of differential evolution (Algorithm 1) and particle swarm optimization (Algorithm 2). Lemma 1 exhibits such a bound.

LEMMA 1. *If the objective function is* $f(x) = \|x - x^*\|^2$ *over* $\mathcal{D} = (0,1)^D$ *for some* $x^* \in \mathcal{D}$, *or any composition* $x \mapsto m(\|x - x^*\|^2)$ *with* m *increasing, then the branching factor of DE/rand (see Algorithm 1, best = 0) is at most:*

$$K \leq \min\{(\lambda+1)^D, 2^\lambda\}, \quad (7)$$

where λ *is the population size. With the same assumptions, the branching factor of DE/best (see Algorithm 1, best = 1) and PSO (see Algorithm 2) is at most:*

$$K \leq \min\{\lambda(\lambda+1)^D, \lambda 2^\lambda\}. \quad (8)$$

PROOF. First, let us give the proof when DE/rand is used. The right hand side of the min corresponds to the branching factor of λ comparisons; there are λ comparisons, hence 2^λ possible comparison results, hence the 2^λ bound. We just have to show the left hand side of the min. There are λ comparisons at each iteration, each of them between two points. This does not follow the scheme in [16] because, there, the branching was directly a ranking of the μ best among λ or a selection (without ranking) of the μ best among λ. Here, one of two points is selected, λ times. When p_1 and p_1'' are compared, p_1 is selected if $\|p_1 - x^*\| < \|p_1'' - x^*\|$. Similarly, the result of the comparison of p_i and p_i'' depends on the position of x^* w.r.t the median hyperplane of p_i and p_i''. Therefore, the final comparison result depends on in which cell, among the cells obtained by the arrangement of λ hyperplanes, contains x^*. The branching factor is therefore upper-bounded by the number of cells obtained by λ hyperplanes in $\mathbb{R}^D$. By Zaslavsky's Theorem (see e.g. [45] and [33, Th 4, p. 27]), this number of cells is upper bounded by $\sum_{i=0}^{D}\binom{\lambda}{i}$; this is upper bounded by $(\lambda+1)^D$, hence the expected result for DE/rand.

We now extend to DE/best and PSO, as follows:

- When DE/best is used, the best point is one of the λ selected points; hence the additional λ factor: beyond the 2^λ possible results of the pairwise comparisons, we have λ possibilities for the best of the λ selected points. Hence the expected result for DE/best.
- When PSO is used, the "global" best so far g is one of the λ "best so far per particle" p_i. Hence, there are λ possibilities; and the expected result for PSO with best particle.

□

Please note that if $\phi_g = 0$, then the branching factor of PSO verifies the same bound as DE without best (e.g. DE/rand).

LEMMA 2. *For an arbitrary family* F *of objective functions, the branching factor of DE/rand is at most*

$$K \leq 2^\lambda, \quad (9)$$

and the branching factor of PSO and of DE/best is at most

$$K \leq \lambda 2^\lambda.$$

PROOF. The 2^λ and $\lambda 2^\lambda$ parts of Lemma 1 do not use any property of F. □

PROPERTY 1 (RUNTIME OF DE/RAND). *If the objective function is* $f(x) = \|x - x^*\|^2$ *over* $\mathcal{D} = (0,1)^D$ *for some* $x^* \in \mathcal{D}$, *or any composition* $x \mapsto m(\|x - x^*\|^2)$ *with* m *increasing, for DE/rand, the runtime* $n_{\epsilon,\delta}$ *is lower bounded:*

$$n_{\epsilon,\delta} \geq \frac{\log(1-\delta)}{D\log(\lambda+1)} + \frac{\log(\lceil 1/(2\epsilon)\rceil)}{\log(\lambda+1)}. \quad (10)$$

Again when applying DE/rand, but with an arbitrary family F *of objective functions, if* $\lambda = D$, *the runtime* $n_{\epsilon,\delta}$ *is lower bounded:*

$$n_{\epsilon,\delta} \geq \frac{\log(1-\delta)}{\lambda\log(2)} + \frac{\log(\lceil 1/(2\epsilon)\rceil)}{\log 2}. \quad (11)$$

PROOF. Just plug the bound (Eq. 7, 8 and 9) on the branching factor above in Theorem 1, Eq. 6, and use $\log N(\epsilon) \geq D\log(\lceil 1/(2\epsilon)\rceil)$ when $\epsilon \to 0$ if the domain $\mathcal{D}$ is bounded with non-empty interior. □

PROPERTY 2 (RUNTIME OF PSO AND DE/BEST). *If the objective function is* $f(x) = \|x - x^*\|^2$ *over* $\mathcal{D} = (0,1)^D$ *for some* $x^* \in \mathcal{D}$, *or any composition* $x \mapsto m(\|x - x^*\|^2)$ *with* m *increasing, for PSO and DE /best, the runtime* $n_{\epsilon,\delta}$ *is lower bounded:*

$$n_{\epsilon,\delta} \geq \frac{\log(1-\delta)}{\log(\lambda) + D\log(\lambda+1)} + \frac{D\log(\lceil 1/(2\epsilon)\rceil)}{\log(\lambda) + D\log(\lambda+1)}. \quad (12)$$

Again when applying PSO or DE/best, but with an arbitrary family F *of objective functions, if* $\lambda = D$, *the runtime* $n_{\epsilon,\delta}$ *is lower bounded:*

$$n_{\epsilon,\delta} \geq \frac{\log(1-\delta)}{\log(\lambda) + \lambda\log(2)} + \frac{\log(\lceil 1/(2\epsilon)\rceil)}{1 + \log 2}. \quad (13)$$

PROOF. See proof of Property 1. □

Remarks (without detailed proof due to length constraints): Eq. 10, 11, 12, 13 imply that if DE and PSO algorithms converge in the sense of Eq. 1 then

$$\text{for any fixed } D, \text{ and for } \lambda \text{ large}, -C_{\lambda,D}/\log(\lambda) = O(1). \quad (14)$$

$$\text{for } \lambda \text{ large}, -C_{\lambda,\lambda} = O(1). \quad (15)$$

We have therefore proved that the differential evolution algorithm can not do better than $O(\log(\lambda))$ speed-up, when using λ fitness evaluations per iteration. Eq. 11 and 13 do not prevent a linear speed-up until $\lambda = D$ - i.e. when considering problems of variable dimension $D \to \infty$, we might have an excellent benefit (such as a λ/λ_0 ratio on the convergence rate) in using D processors, with a population size $\lambda = D$ evaluated on λ distinct processors, compared to a fixed $\lambda = \lambda_0$. In the case of evolution strategies, it is known that such a case is possible; for DE and PSO, no such result has been proved. We will investigate this empirically in Sections 3 and 4.

3. EXPERIMENTS: SPEED-UP AND SCALABILITY OF PARALLEL DIFFERENTIAL EVOLUTION

We have shown mathematical lower bounds on the runtime when using differential evolution; hence, if Eq. 1 holds, this implies bounds on $CR = -C'_{\lambda,D}$ (see Eqs. 5, 14 and 15). We now check if these bounds are reached or approximately reached; we will see that this is approximately the case, as far as we can tell on (necessarily finite) experiments.

In all this section, experiments are performed on the sphere function $x \mapsto \|x\|^2$. We use 1000 iterations for evaluating the convergence rate. So now on, the convergence rate CR is estimated as (see Eq. 5):

$$CR \simeq \frac{1}{1000} (\log(\text{best fitness at 1000 iterations}) \\ - \log(\text{initial best fitness}))\,.$$

This is an estimated of the slope on a log-log representation. Differential evolution depends on two parameters that take place in the mutation step of the algorithm: the differential weight F and the crossover probability Cr. We are interested in finding the parameters F and Cr which enable to reach these lower bounds. We first do experiments with the baseline differential evolution DE/rand (Algorithm 1 with $best = 0$) in Section 3.1. We then perform additional experiments with large population sizes and extreme values of the parameters (Section 3.2). Finally, we test adaptive variants of differential evolution (Section 3.3).

3.1 Experiments with standard differential evolution

3.1.1 *Testing* $D = 5$ *and large population size* λ.

The purpose of this section is to experimentally check Eq. 3 by considering a fixed dimension $D = 5$. We increase the population size λ, and check if the convergence rate reaches the optimal $C'_{\lambda,D} = \Theta(\log(\lambda))$ rate. Section 2 has shown that it can not be better (see Eq. 14) than this $\log(\lambda)$ rate. Results presented in Figure 1 are averaged over 15 runs and the number of generations N is fixed to 1000. The x-axis is the base-10 logarithm of the population size, and the y-axis shows the convergence rate CR, multiplied by D, as suggested in Eq. 4. Hence, if Eq. 3 holds, we should observe curves decreasing linearly with $log(\lambda)$.

We first experiment differential evolution with various constant parametrizations (i.e. parametrizations which are independent from the population size λ). Different parameters F and Cr are tested in Figure 1a. It appears that (i) the parameter Cr seems to have no impact on the convergence rate CR; (ii) when the population size increases, a smaller parameter F is better. For example, when $\log_{10}(\lambda) \in [1, 1.3]$, $F = 0.41$ is a good parameter choice. Then when $\log_{10}(\lambda) \in [1.3, 1.5]$, $F = 0.24$ becomes a better choice. Finally, when $\log_{10}(\lambda) \in [2.7, 4.4]$, $F = 0.07$ appears to be a better parametrization. That is why from now on we experiment some differential evolution parametrizations with F decreasing when the population size λ increases. In Figure 1b, we investigate the case of parameter F equal to $.5(\log\lambda)^{-A}$ for various parameters A. Parameter A fixed to 0.76 is seemingly a good choice, as the corresponding curve is linear for $\log_{10}(\lambda)$ large enough; whereas other choices of parametrizations lead to plateauing curves. Figure 1c displays results for various values of F when $F = .5\lambda^{-A}$. For several values of A ($A = 0.4$, $A = 0.11$), the curves have the expected behavior: quasi-linear, when $\log_{10}(\lambda)$ is large enough. The slopes seem also better than in the case of $F = .5(\log\lambda)^{-0.76}$. Specifically, $F = .5\lambda^{-0.4}$ reaches the best slope of these experiments. Hence, a detailed look at results shows that, for population sizes as in these experiments,

$$Cr = .44, F = .5\lambda^{-0.4} \tag{16}$$

is a reasonable tuning - though only mathematics could validate the (expected) logarithmic asymptotic convergence rate ($\simeq \log(\lambda)$) for λ large.

3.1.2 *Testing* $D = \lambda/2$*, large population size* λ.

The purpose of this section is to experimentally check, with DE, variants of Eq. 2. We set $D = \lambda/2$ (as an arbitrary choice with D linear in λ), and we observe what happens when λ gets arbitrarily large. Results are presented in Figure 2. Each experiment is launched 15 times and the number of generations N is set to 1000. The x-axis is the base-10 logarithm of the population size, and the y-axis shows the convergence rate CR. We expect a negative constant convergence rate if Eq. 2 holds in the case of differential evolution (see Eq. 15).

First, various constant parameters F and Cr are tested (see Figure 2a); in this case, none of the results are satisfactory as the curves converge toward 0: the algorithm does not converge. Figure 2b exhibit experiments when F is inversely proportional to an exponent of $\log(\lambda)$. All but one converge toward 0 and the last one decreases linearly as a function of $\log(\lambda)$, which is also not the expected behavior. Last, parameter F decreasing as an exponent of λ is investigated (see Figure 2c). A seemingly good behavior happened when $F = .5\lambda^{-0.4}$; with this value, the curve is close to -0.005 - though the asymptotic result, for λ large, is unclear. With other tunings, either the curves converge toward 0 or decrease linearly. Crossover probability Cr has seemingly no impact on the convergence rate CR. Experiments suggest that for λ large and 1000 iterations the best performing tested variant is Eq. 16 ($Cr = .44$ and $F = .5\lambda^{-0.4}$), independently of the dimension.

3.2 Extension: the case $F = 0$ and larger population sizes

Section 3.1 shows some surprisingly good results with F very small. We investigate then the specific case $F = 0$. With this parametrization, DE performs only some recombinations of a finite set of coordinates, in particular, the mutation step is removed. Goldberg, in [19] has shown that provided that the population size is large enough, GA with only crossover, i.e. without mutation (this is a situation analogous to $F = 0$ here) approximates reasonably well the optimum. The case of ES using only dominant recombination, no mutations, has also been studied in [18].

Similarly, DE with $F = 0$ and fixed budget can still provide an approximation of the optimum. This optimization does not converge asymptotically, because it is restricted to a finite set; yet, unless the number of iterations is huge, it works quite well empirically. This is shown in Figure 3, with a number of iterations N set to 1000. Each result is the average of 15 runs. We present here experiments with larger population size, including $F = 0$.

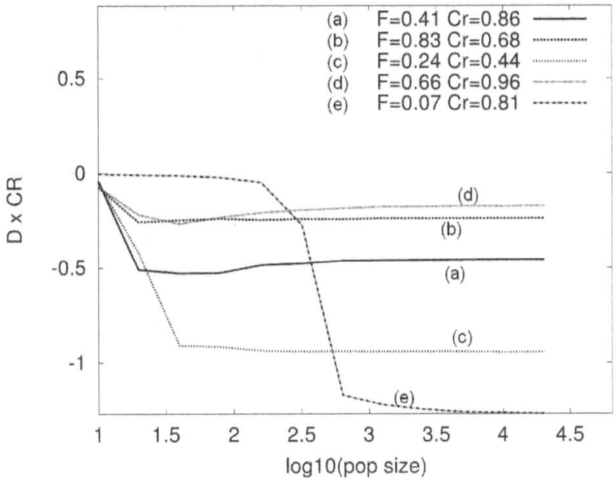

(a) F independent of λ. Seemingly, the convergence rate reaches a plateau.

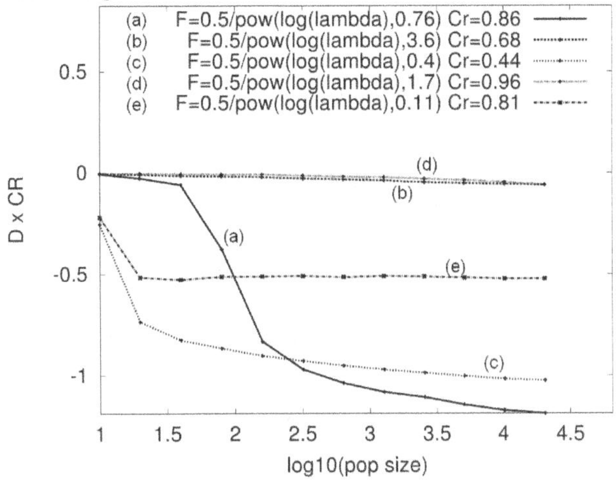

(b) F inversely proportional to an exponent of $\log(\lambda)$. Results are better than above.

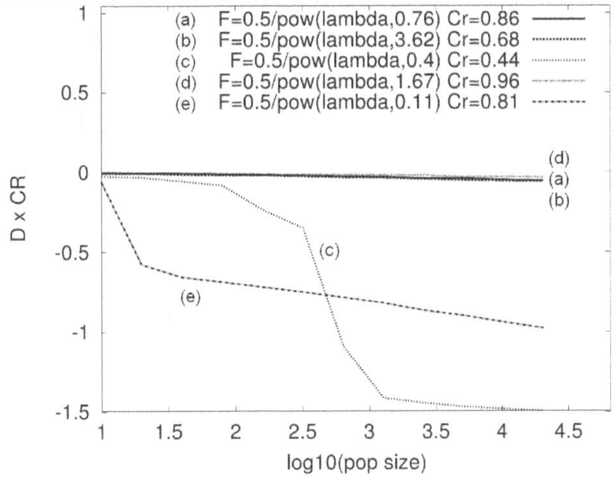

(c) F inversely proportional to an exponent of λ. Results are better, in particular with $Cr = .44$ and $F = \frac{1}{2}\lambda^{-0.4}$.

Figure 1: X-axis: logarithm of the population size. Y-axis: estimate of CR (large negative values mean fast convergence). Experiments in dimension 5 with various randomly chosen parameters. Here we plot the convergence rates CR (Eq. 5) of various parametrizations of differential evolution (estimated on 1000 iterations). All experiments are averaged over 15 runs. Standard deviations are very small and not presented. We essentially see that F should decrease when λ increases. Figure 3 will experiment with a few variants with larger population sizes.

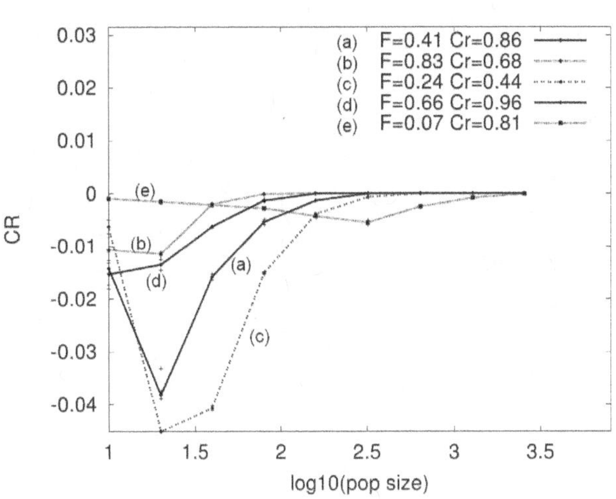

(a) F independent of λ

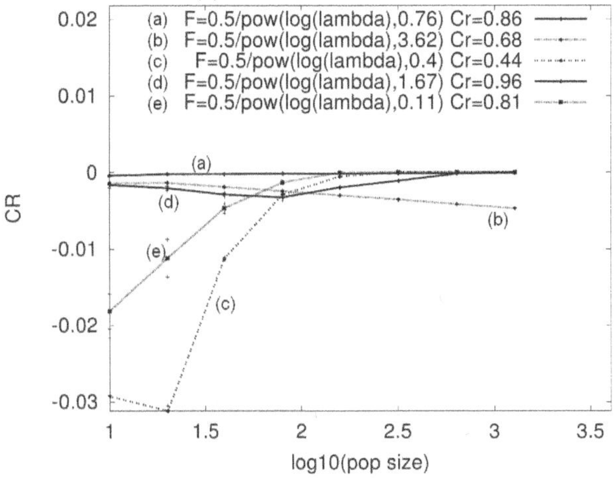

(b) F inversely proportional to an exponent of $\log(\lambda)$

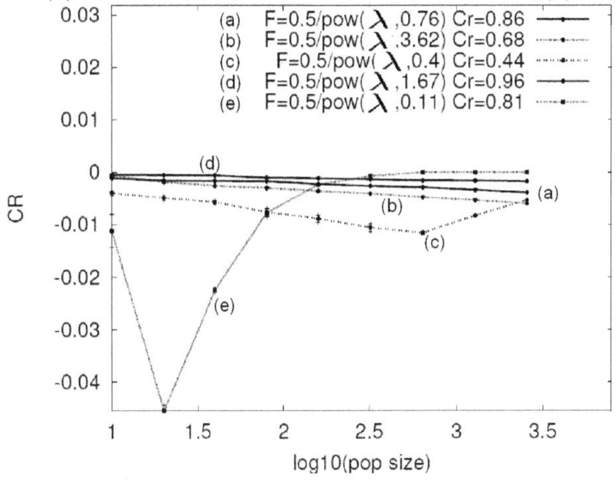

(c) F inversely proportional to an exponent of λ

Figure 2: Here we plot the convergence rates (Eq. 5) of various parametrizations of differential evolution in the case $D = \lambda/2$ with D the dimension. All experiments are averaged over 15 runs. Standard deviations are very small and not presented. Figure 3 presents experiments with a few selected variants with larger population sizes.

Figure 3a displays the Convergence Rate in y-axis and the population size λ in x-axis. Dimension D is fixed to 3. Figure 3b presents experiments of Figure 3a with the Convergence Rate divided by $\log(\lambda)$ in y-axis and the population size λ in x-axis. Thanks to this division by $\log(\lambda)$ on the y-axis, if Eq. 3 holds, we should observe a negative plateau if λ is large enough. We notice that $F = 0$ is a bad parameter choice - even with a moderate number of iterations (1000)- as the convergence rate remains in 0 (the algorithm does not converge). Two parametrizations appear to perform well when the population size is large: $(F = .1, Cr = .5)$ and $(F = .5\lambda^{-0.4}, Cr = 0.44)$. These experiments, for sure, do not prove that properties in Eq. 3 and 2 hold for such a parametrization; we just propose them as preliminary candidates for such a proof.

Figure 3c exhibits results when population size and dimension are linked. Dimension D is here $\lambda/2$. We see that $F = 0$ is very satisfactory in such a case, and $F = .5\lambda^{-0.4}$ (which is also satisfactory in Figures 3a and 3b with fixed dimension) has the same performance in this $D = \lambda/2$ setting.

As a result, these experiments show that (i) $F = 0$ is suitable in the important case λ proportional to the dimension and a fixed number of iterations. (ii) However, $F = 0$ is strongly suboptimal for a fixed dimension and λ goes to infinity. (iii) F decreasing such as $F = .5\lambda^{-0.4}$ independently of the dimension is seemingly a reasonably good idea in all cases. It is not clear whether it succeeds asymptotically for our two parallelization criteria (Eqs. 2 and 3 for $\lambda \to \infty$), but the behavior was better than other methods as far as we have seen on a simple sphere function problem.

We see on these experiments that for a fixed total budget, when the dimension and/or the population size increase, the effect of the F parameter is much more important than the Cr value.

3.3 Adaptive DE

We here test adaptive variants of DE, aimed at choosing adaptively the Cr and F parameters. Experiments are performed with $F = 0.5$, $Cr = 0.9$, for DE/rand/1, DE/rand/2, DE/best/1, DE/best/2. The variants JADE and MDE_pBX are adaptive and choose their parameters themselves. We refer to [46, 20, 24] for more on the parametrization of differential evolution and the adaptive variants. Experimental results are presented in Figure 4 with 50 iterations. For large population sizes for a given dimension, the adaptive variants of DE do not reach the same performance as our non-adaptive variants (see Figure 4a). For $D = \lambda/2$, JADE succeeds reasonably well (see Figure 4b).

4. EXPERIMENTS: SPEED-UP AND SCALABILITY OF PARALLEL PARTICLE SWARM OPTIMIZATION

We now try to reach the previous theoretical bounds in the case of PSO. The problem investigated in this section is the possibility to find parameters of PSO such that we get approximately these two good properties, namely linear scalability (Eq. 2) and logarithmic speed-up (Eq. 3). The theoretical results are asymptotic, but we only have a finite time to run the experiments. Hence we focus on the

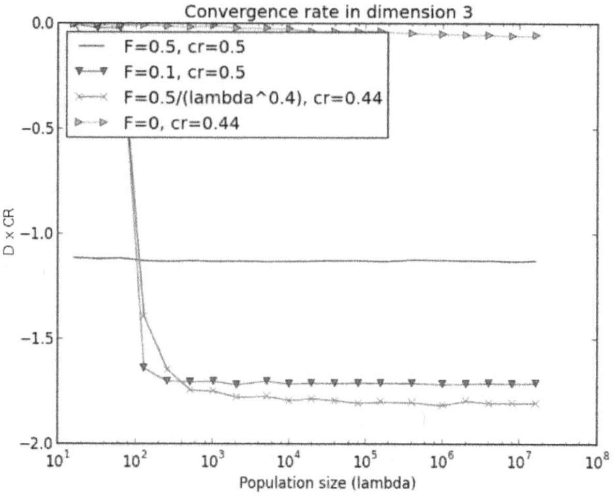

(a) Dimension $D = 3$, $D \times CR$ as a function of λ.

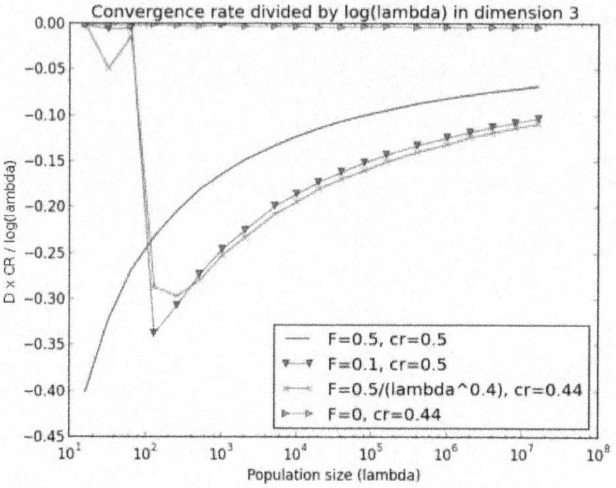

(b) Dimension $D = 3$, $D \times CR/\log(\lambda)$ as a function of λ.

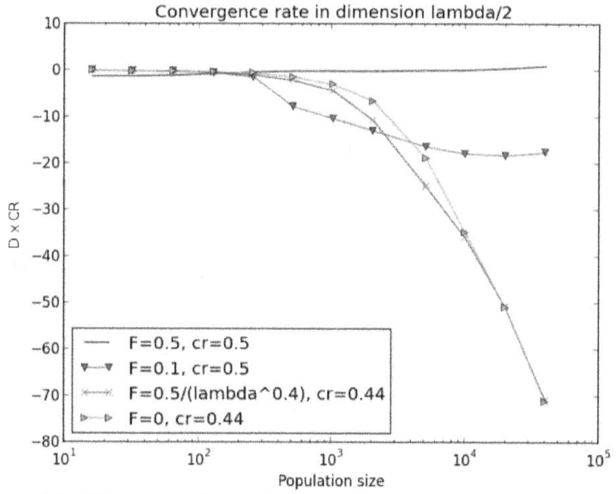

(c) Dimension $D = \lambda/2$, $D \times CR$ as a function of λ.

Figure 3: Convergence rate in the fitness space (Eq. 5) for large population sizes, including a parametrization with $F = 0$, some classical parametrizations, and our proposed formula $F = 0.5\lambda^{-0.4}$. Each point is averaged over 15 runs. These experiments performed in different settings are aimed at validating our proposed formula for large population sizes and checking that it is better than (i) some usual parametrizations (ii) the limit value $F = 0$. We see that $F = 0$ is not efficient for a fixed dimension: the algorithm does not converge. When the dimension is huge, then the case $F = 0$ performs well, whereas one can show mathematically that it does not converge. F prescribed by $.5\lambda^{-0.4}$ performs well.

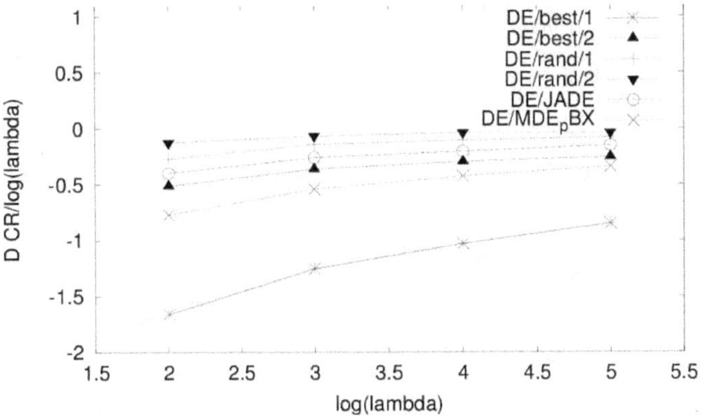

(a) Variants of DE with $D = 10$

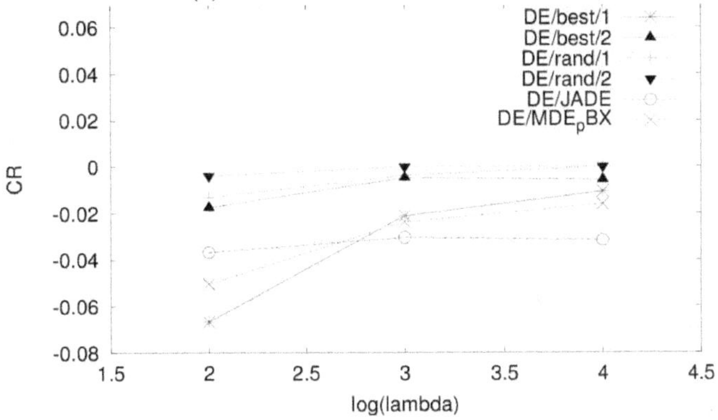

(b) Variants of DE with $D = \lambda/2$

Figure 4: Experiments aimed at comparing our proposed variants with small values for F as $\lambda \to \infty$ to adaptive variants of DE. In these experiments, variants of DE are tested with $D = 10$ and with $D = \lambda/2$ respectively, as the population size λ goes to infinity. These results are convergence rates in the fitness space. Figure 4a shows that adaptive variants of DE can not compete with the standard DE (e.g. DE/best/1), which could not compete with our variants with $F = \frac{1}{2}\lambda^{-0.4}$ in previous experiments. Figure 4b shows that JADE performs reasonably well when the population size is proportional to the dimension.

following non-asymptotic versions:

$$PR_D(\lambda) = \frac{D}{100}\,(\log(\text{best fitness at 100 iterations}) - \log(\text{initial best fitness})) \quad (17)$$

$$PR_{lin}(\lambda) = \frac{1}{100}\,(\log(\text{best fitness at 100 iterations}) - \log(\text{initial best fitness})) \text{ with } D = \lambda/2 \quad (18)$$

where PR stands for Progress Rate, and is directly adapted from [7, 8]. We here use progress rate, in terms of fitness values instead of convergence in the domain, just because we will use, for our PSO experiments, both the sphere function and the cigar function - for the cigar function convergence in the domain is not equivalent to convergence in fitness values. Implicitly, here, fitness values depend on λ, which is the population size.

We do experiments on simple unimodal functions, the sphere function $f(x) = \|x\|^2$, plus a validation on the cigar function.

The parameters of PSO are ω, ϕ_g and ϕ_p (see Algorithm 2). We evaluate the impact of each parameter. For the sake of comparison, we need a standard PSO [44, 13, 10] as a baseline. We choose $\omega = 1/(2\log(2)) \simeq 0.72$, $\phi_p = \phi_g = 0.5 + \log(2) \simeq 1.2$.

In Section 4.1, we investigate the case of large population size and logarithmic speed-up. Population size of the same order as the dimension and linear scalability are studied in Section 4.2.

4.1 Asymptotic scalability: large population size, fixed dimension

In this section we check if Eq. 3 holds. The fitness function used in these experiments shown in Figure 5 is $f(x) = \|x\|^2$. We limited the search space to an upper bound $b_u = 1$ and a lower bound $b_l = -1$. The number of generations N is fixed to 100 and the dimension D to 30. In Figure 5, the x-axis shows the natural log of the population size. Figure 5a displays $PR_{30}(\lambda)$ in order to show progress rate whereas Figure 5b displays $PR_{30}(\lambda)/\log(\lambda)$ to check if PSO reaches the optimal asymptotic behavior $PR_{30}(\lambda) = \Theta(\log(\lambda))$. If it is the case, the curves should show a plateau. Each experiment is repeated 10 times. Figure 5 seems to indicate that there exist different parameter values for which PSO reaches the optimal convergence rate (within a constant factor), at least as far as we can see in dimension 30. This comes a bit as a surprise as other algorithms struggle with such convergence rates (see [37] for efforts aimed at making some classical algorithms verify this optimal behavior) - standard PSO appears to be more naturally parallel than most existing evolutionary algorithms, from the point of view of the convergence rate as the population size grows to infinity, for simple unimodal functions. However, we will see below that for lower dimensions, things are not so nice for standard PSO.

Choosing ϕ_g and ϕ_p in PSO: Figures 6a, 6b and 6c look at the impact of ϕ_g and ϕ_p for different ω around these standard values. The x-axis still shows the population size expressed as $\log(\lambda)$ and the y-axis displays the progress rate. From Figure 6, it appears that ϕ_p and ϕ_g can only slightly change the convergence rate in our simple unimodal setting, which is in line with the current literature. From several empirical tests, in the following experiments we choose 0.9 instead of the recommended $0.5 + \log(2)$ as it seems to give better results regardless of the ω for the unimodal function under study in this paper.

Choosing ω in PSO: Figure 7 evaluates the impact of different ω for a given dimension $D = \{2, 3, 5, 10\}$, respectively Figures 7a, 7b, 7c , 7d, to see whether a dynamic ω could yield better results. As such, we are looking for curves that crosses one another. The x-axis still shows the population size expressed as $\log(\lambda)$ and the y-axis displays the progress rate. The first conclusion we can infer from Figure 7 is that the parameter ω clearly varies in relation to λ. Especially on lower dimensions (Figures 7a, 7b, 7c and 7d), we observe patterns that emerge. For instance, in dimension $D = 5$, when the population size $\log(\lambda)$ is between $[2, 3]$, the best ω is 0.7. As the population size increases to $\log(\lambda) \in [3, 4]$, the best ω is equal to 0.6. At $\log(\lambda) \in [4, 5]$, the best ω becomes 0.5, etc. The rate at which the different curves crosses one another gives an important indication that there is a dependency of ω over both λ and the dimension D.

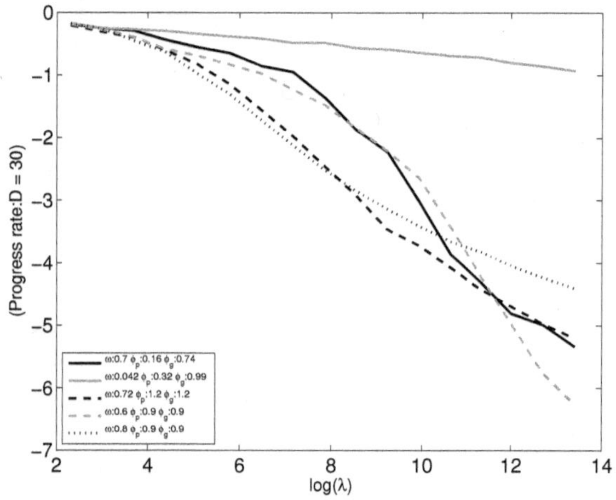

(a) Progress rate $PR_{30}(\lambda)$

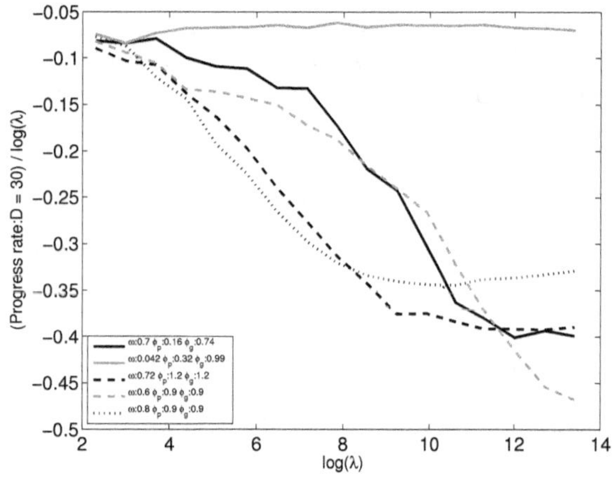

(b) Progress rate divided by $\log(\lambda)$, i.e. $PR_{30}(\lambda)/\log(\lambda)$

Figure 5: The progress rate, expressed as variants of Eq. (17), for different set of parameters ω, ϕ_p, ϕ_g, including the values of standard PSO (black dash line with values $\omega = 0.72$ and $\phi_p = \phi_g = 1.2$). We observe that standard PSO performs well and even seems to reach the optimal convergence rate as λ grows. For small λ a higher value of ω is slightly more appropriate and eventually (around a population $\lambda = 80k$) smaller values of ω outperform standard PSO. Standard deviations are of order 0.01.

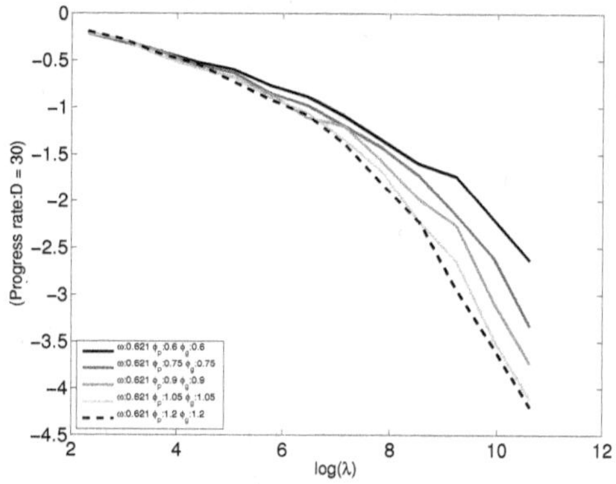

(a) $\omega = \frac{1}{2 \cdot \log(2)} - 0.1$

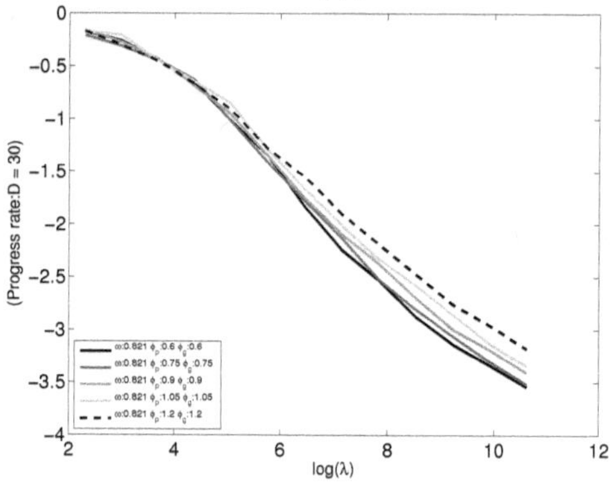

(b) $\omega = \frac{1}{2 \cdot \log(2)} + 0.1$

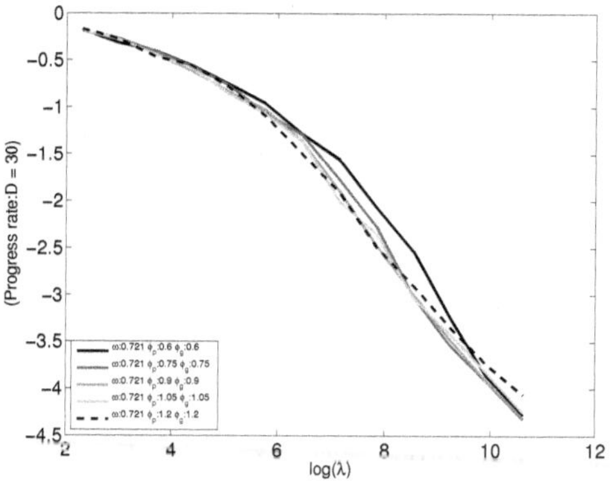

(c) $\omega = \frac{1}{2 \cdot \log(2)}$

Figure 6: $PR_{30}(\lambda)$ for different values of ω. In this figure, different values of ϕ_g and ϕ_p for values around those proposed in standard PSO are applied to the study of the (unimodal) sphere function $x \mapsto \|x\|^2$. We see that ω smaller (than standard PSO) is better for λ large and ω larger is better for λ small. The impact is, however, moderate in this case (dimension 30). Standard deviations are of order 0.01.

Figure 8 compares 3 different sets of parameters across dimensions $D = \{2, 3, 5, 50\}$, respectively Figures 8a, 8b, 8c, 8d. The first set of parameters are those provided by standard PSO. As we observe in Figure 7, as the population size λ grows, smaller ω yields better performance. Thus, we can suppose that when $\lambda \to \infty$, $\omega = 0$ could be the best parameter. This is the second set of parameters with $\phi_p = \phi_g = 0.9$. The third one ω_λ is a set of parameters that depends on both λ and the dimension D; this formula is extrapolated from the empirical results of Figure 7. It is given by:

$$\omega_\lambda = \max\left(0.025 + 4 \cdot \exp\left(-\frac{\lambda}{70}\right), 0.9 - \log\left(\frac{\lambda}{2.5 \cdot D}\right)\right). \tag{19}$$

From Figure 8, it appears that using ω_λ instead of standard PSO yields results more robust in relation to different dimensions. In lower dimensions $D = \{2, 3, 5, 10\}$, the factor of improvement oscillates between 7 and 8. This means that using ω_λ instead of standard PSO in a parallel environment is up to 8 times more efficient. The parameters of standard PSO are essentially optimal for a dimension $D = 30$. It is important to note that ω_λ performs at least as good as standard PSO. As the dimension increases $D = 50$, ω_λ becomes again more efficient than standard PSO by a small margin. The special case $\omega = 0$ gives very good results in small dimensions $\{2, 3, 5\}$, improving over standard PSO by

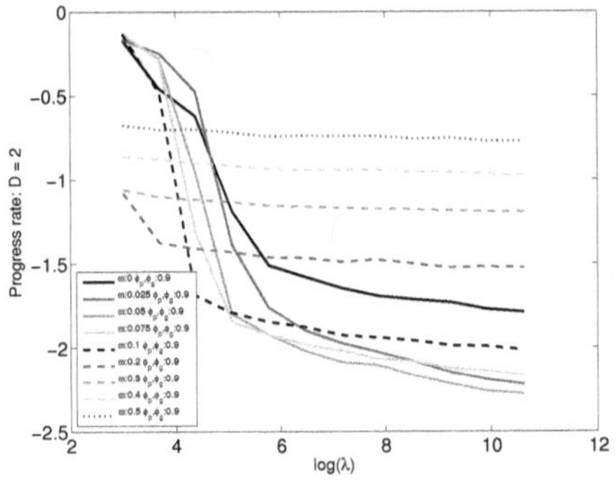

(a) Dimension 2, $\phi_g = \phi_p = 0.9$

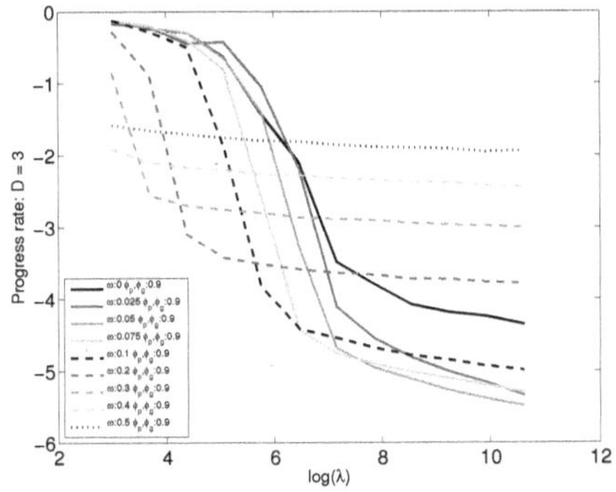

(b) Dimension 3, $\phi_g = \phi_p = 0.9$

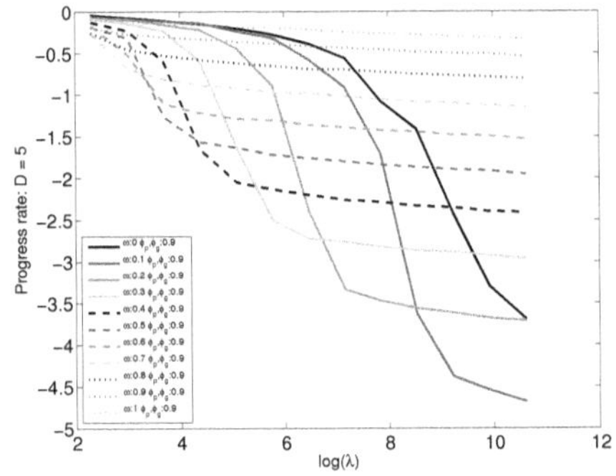

(c) Dimension 5, $\phi_g = \phi_p = 0.9$

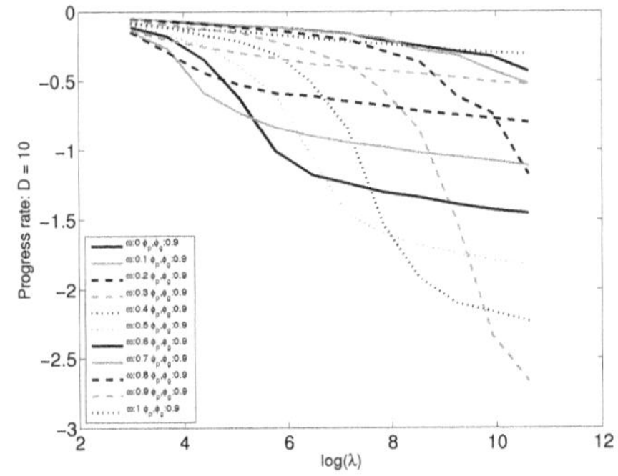

(d) Dimension 10, $\phi_g = \phi_p = 0.9$

Figure 7: In dimension $D = \{2, 3, 5, 10\}$ we check the progress rate $PR_D(\lambda)$ for different values of ω. In all cases, as λ becomes large, smaller ω yield better results. The effect is more exacerbate on lower dimensions $\{2, 3, 5, 10\}$. The different values of ω produce curves that cross one another which indicate that there is a dependency over the population size λ for the parameter ω. We use these curves for designing rules for choosing ω as a function of the population size and the dimension (Eq. 19). Standard deviations are of order 0.01.

an average factor of 5, but never equals to ω_λ and rapidly becomes irrelevant in higher dimension $D > 10$ for the tested population sizes λ.

Figure 9 presents the same study as Figure 8 but using another unimodal fitness function, the Cigar. This fitness is defined as $f(x_i) = x_{i,1}^2 + 10^6 \sum_{d=2}^{D} x_{i,d}^2$. The use of ω_λ also appears to yield better results in relation to different dimensions. We observe the same behavior for $\omega = 0$ as in Figure 8.

4.2 Linear scalability: population size linear in the dimension

In this section we check if we can observe on experiments the linear scalability as in Eq. 2 for different variants of PSO. As a reminder, the fitness function used in these experiments is still $f(x) = \|x\|^2$. We limit the search space to an upper bound $b_u = 1$ and a lower bound $b_l = -1$. The number of generations N is fixed to 100. The dimension D is given by $\lambda/2$. Each experiment is repeated 10 times. Figure 10 presents the results for different parametrizations of ω, ϕ_p and ϕ_g.

From Figure 10 it appears that again ω_λ yields the best progress rate. Standard PSO is following closely (in this setting; not in other settings as mentioned previously). The case where $\omega = 0$ is by far the worst setting of the 3 tested. Thus, we conclude that ω_λ seems to be a good parametrization for a parallel PSO environment, in terms of convergence rates.

5. CONCLUSION

We have studied the speed-up of PSO and DE, as a function of population size λ. λ is equal to the number of simultaneous fitness evaluations, in a model with a number of cores equal to the population size. Our results can also be used in the sequential case, though large values of λ are more likely in a parallel setting.

We have investigated (i) theoretically the lower bound on runtime for a large class of objective functions and (ii) empirically on the sphere function (i.e. a model of unimodal well conditioned function) the convergence rate of differential evolution and particle swarm optimization when the population size λ is large. Roughly speaking, the present paper extends [16] in the sense that it gives more precise bounds for DE and PSO, and it extends [37] in the sense that it provides (unproved) formulas for approximately optimal speed-ups for DE and PSO. The improvement compared to standard parametrizations grows seemingly indefinitely for DE, whereas it is rather limited for PSO where the standard parametrizations perform well even with huge values of λ.

We have identified a similarity between PSO and DE: both are based on pairwise comparisons. We have shown that DE and PSO:

- can not be faster than $-\frac{\log(\|x_n - x^*\|)}{n} = \Theta(\log(\lambda))$, with x_n the best individual at iteration n, a fixed dimension, and x^* the optimum;
- can not do better than $-\frac{\log(\|x_n - x^*\|)}{n} = \Theta(1)$ when the dimension is proportional to λ, e.g. $D \simeq \lambda/2$.

This mathematical lower bound on the runtime is for arbitrary families of fitness functions, provided that the optimum can be anywhere in the domain (i.e. for all x in the

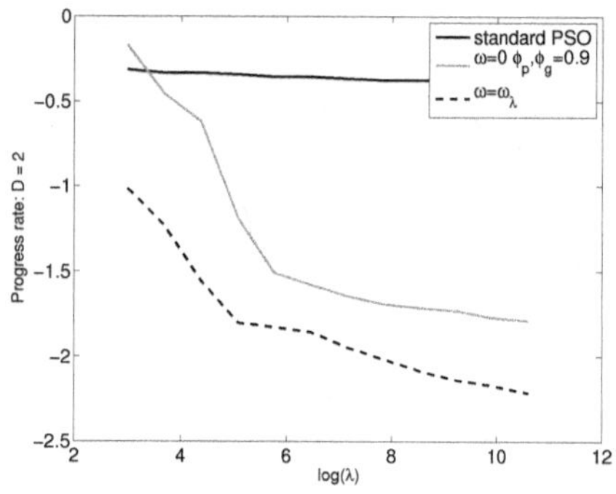

(a) Dimension 2

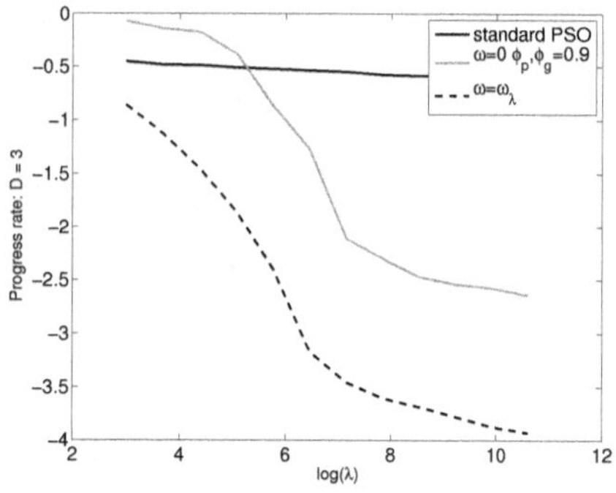

(b) Dimension 3

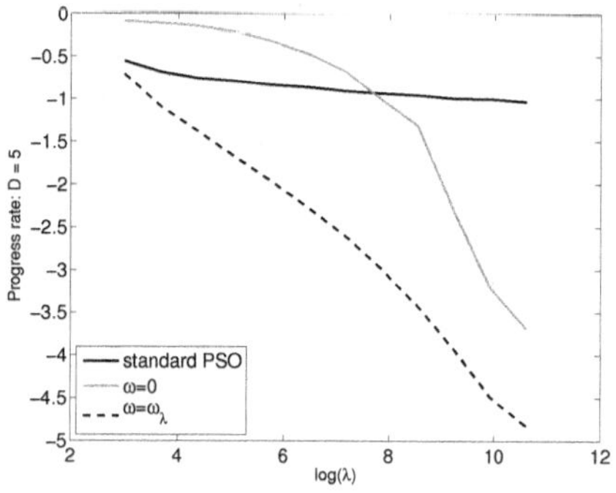

(c) Dimension 5

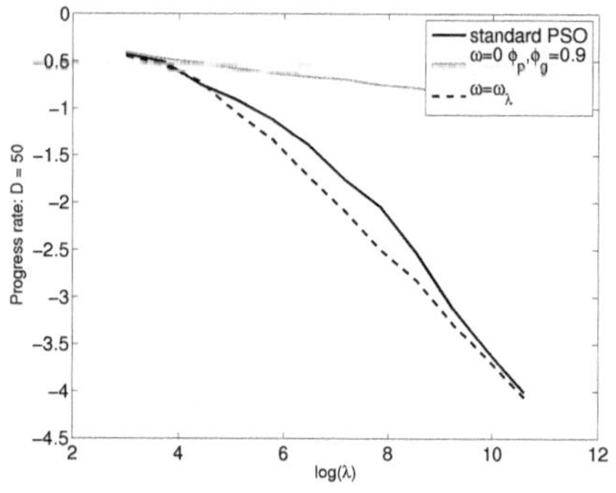

(d) Dimension 50

Figure 8: In dimension $D = \{2, 3, 5, 50\}$ respectively, we check the progress rate $PR_D(\lambda)$ for different values of ω. At dimension $D = 2$, the use of ω_λ over standard PSO for parallelization yield an improvement by a factor of 7. At dimension $D = 3$, ω_λ improves over standard PSO by a factor of 8. At dimension $D = 5$, the factor is also 8. At dimension $D = 10$ (unpresented), the factor is 7.5. The case of dimension $D = 30$ (unpresented) provides no improvement, standard PSO is equal to ω_λ. At dimension $D = 50$, there is a small advantage to use ω_λ over standard PSO. Standard deviations are of order 0.01.

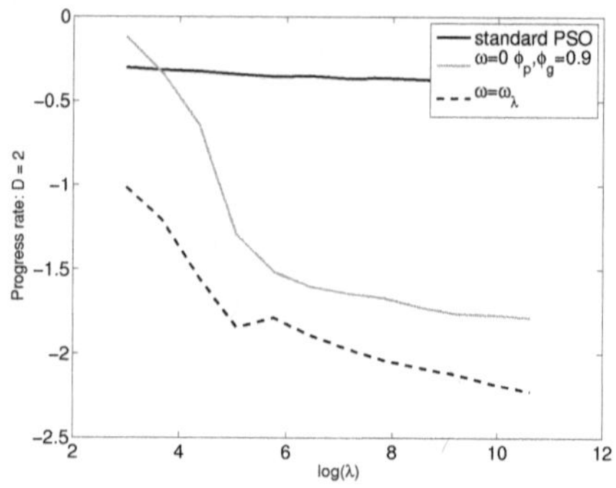

(a) Dimension 2

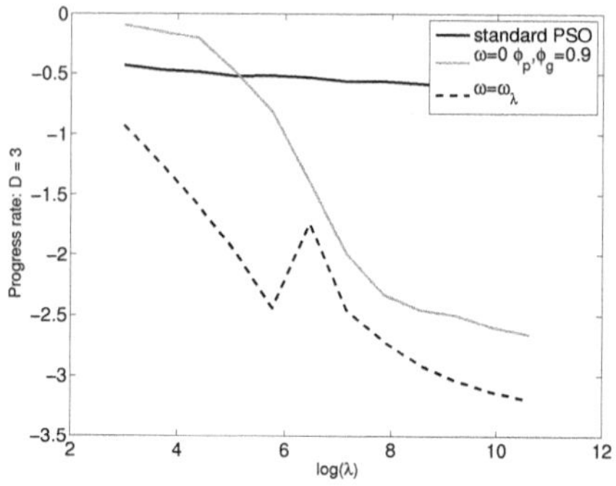

(b) Dimension 3

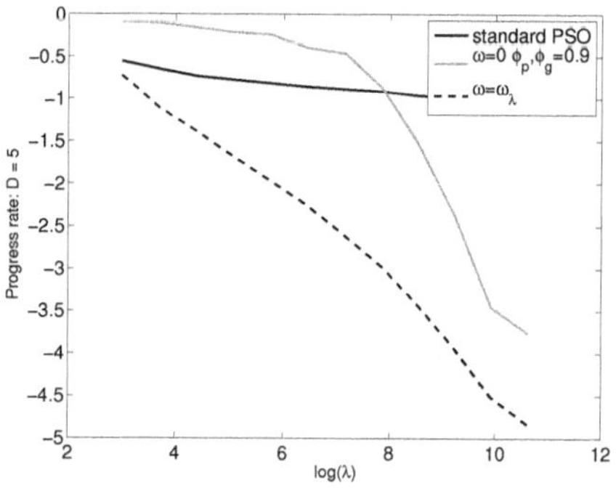

(c) Dimension 5

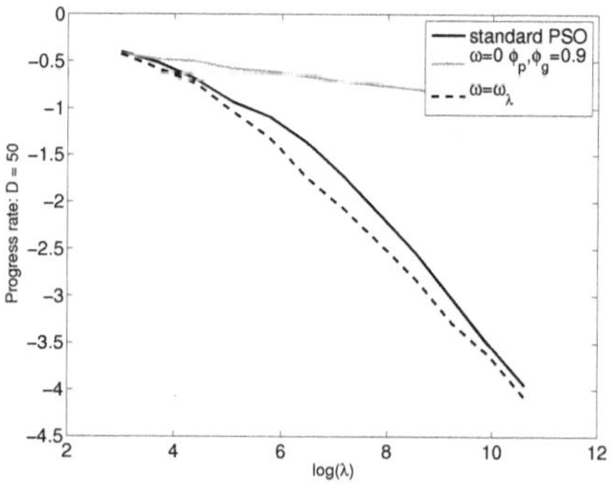

(d) Dimension 50

Figure 9: In dimension $D = \{2, 3, 5, 50\}$ respectively, we check the progress rate $PR_D(\lambda)$ for different values of ω. At dimension $D = 2$, the use of ω_λ over standard PSO for parallelization yield an improvement by a factor of more than 5. At dimension $D = 3$, ω_λ improves over standard PSO by a similar factor. At dimension $D = 5$, the factor is around 9. At dimension $D = 10$ (unpresented), the factor is 2.5. The case of dimension $D = 30$ (unpresented) provides no improvement, standard PSO is essentially equal to ω_λ. At dimension $D = 50$, there is a small advantage to use ω_λ over standard PSO. Standard deviations are of order 0.01.

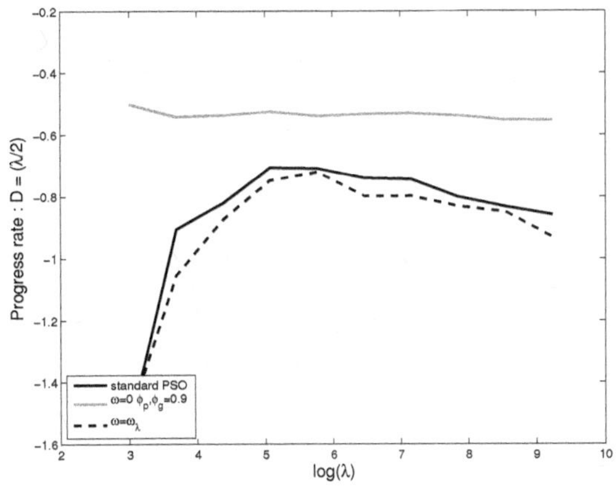

Figure 10: The performance (progress rate) for different population size λ where the dimension is given by $\lambda/2$. Three sets of parameters are tested. The first set is the values given by standard PSO. The second test is given by $\omega = 0$, ϕ_g,$\phi_p = 0.9$. The third and last set is the formula given by ω_λ, ϕ_g,$\phi_p = 0.9$. Again, we observe that ω_λ gives the best progress rate - though standard PSO is almost equivalent. Standard deviations are of order 0.01.

domain, the family of functions contains at least one function with optimum x). The detailed bounds are improved when we consider the sphere function.

Interestingly, these rates are exactly the known limits for evolution strategies [16]. In the case of DE or PSO, we have no mathematical proof that these limits are reached. We checked experimentally whether some parametrization can be as fast as allowed by the mathematical bounds. Runtimes are estimated experimentally.

Parametrization of differential evolution for large population sizes. Experimentally, for differential evolution, a good parametrization might be $F \simeq .5\lambda^{-0.4}$ and some fixed Cr (Eq. 16). Maybe such a parametrization reaches the bounds above. The improvement compared to standard parametrizations seemingly (on experiments) grows indefinitely as the population size goes to infinity.

Parametrization of particle swarm optimization for large population sizes. The ω parameter should decrease, whereas other parameters can be chosen close to those of standard PSO; for large population sizes, we get a factor 8 on the progress rate in dimension 5 thanks to the parametrization proposed in Eq. 19. Furthermore, standard PSO performs well on the important case λ proportional to the dimension D, as well as when the dimension is 30; we had only minor improvements in these cases. Overall, PSO, under its standard forms, except for moderate dimensions (roughly from 2 to 10), performs well in a parallel setting with a large population size.

We certainly do not claim that Eq. 19 (for PSO) and Eq. 16 (for DE) are universal solutions for choosing parameters in PSO and DE respectively. They are relevant formulas for a clearly defined setting, namely a unimodal well conditioned setting with λ large. Let us discuss limitations. First, this work is limited to unimodal well conditioned functions. Another limitation of this work is the choice of the number of iterations. We checked the convergence rates on limited numbers of iterations, which might be misleading. However, we believe that in a practical world, our population sizes (corresponding to parallelization on hundreds of thousands of cores - quite a big number even for clusters of machines equipped with GPU) and iteration numbers make sense.

Further work. We have shown runtime lower bounds for a class of algorithms including differential evolution and particle swarm optimization, for large population sizes. We have shown empirically some runtime results for simple problems. It is difficult to be sure, from the empirical results, whether the runtime lower bounds are tight or not. Proving a corresponding upper bound on the runtime, matching the lower bound, is the main further work.
Designing adaptive rules which provide good rates for a wide class of fitness functions, beyond the simple unimodal scenario in the present paper, is also part of the agenda. Parametrization of ω (resp. F) proposed for PSO (resp. DE) might be improved, using some information on the budget, or maybe parameters depending on the iteration index; mathematical analysis of these formulas and/or improved variants is an interesting challenge.
Another natural extension is to adapt the bound for differential evolution variants with topology (e.g. [41]).

Acknowledgement: We are grateful to the Ademe Post project for making this work possible (`www.artelys.com`).

6. REFERENCES

[1] J. Arabas, O. Maitre, and P. Collet. Parade: A massively parallel differential evolution template for easea. In L. Rutkowski, M. Korytkowski, R. Scherer, R. Tadeusiewicz, L. Zadeh, and J. Zurada, editors, *Swarm and Evolutionary Computation*, volume 7269 of *Lecture Notes in Computer Science*, pages 12–20. Springer Berlin Heidelberg, 2012.

[2] D. Ardia, J. O. Arango, and N. G. Gomez. Jump-diffusion calibration using Differential Evolution. *Wilmott Magazine*, 55:76–79, 2011.

[3] D. Ardia, K. Boudt, P. Carl, K. M. Mullen, and B. G. Peterson. Differential Evolution with DEoptim: An application to non-convex portfolio optimization. *The R Journal*, 3(1):27–34, 2011.

[4] A. Auger. Convergence results for (1,λ)-SA-ES using the theory of φ-irreducible Markov chains. *Theoretical Computer Science*, 334(1-3):35–69, 2005.

[5] A. Auger, M. Jebalia, and O. Teytaud. (x,sigma,eta) : quasi-random mutations for evolution strategies. In *EA*, page 12p., 2005.

[6] G. Badkobeh, P. K. Lehre, and D. Sudholt. Unbiased black-box complexity of parallel search. In *Proceedings of 13th International Conference on Parallel Problem Solving from Nature (PPSN 2014)*, pages 892–901, Ljubljana, Slovenia, 2014.

[7] H.-G. Beyer. Toward a theory of evolution strategies: Some asymptotical results for the $(1, +\lambda)$-theory. *Evolutionary Computation*, 1(2):165–188, 1993.

[8] H.-G. Beyer. Toward a theory of evolution strategies: The (μ, λ)-theory. *Evolutionary Computation*, 2(4):381–407, 1994.

[9] H.-G. Beyer. *The Theory of Evolution Strategies*. Natural Computing Series. Springer, Heidelberg, 2001.

[10] D. Bratton and J. Kennedy. Defining a standard for particle swarm optimization. In *IEEE Swarm Intelligence Symposium*, pages 120–127, 2007.

[11] J. Brest, S. Greiner, B. Boskovic, M. Mernik, and V. Zumer. Self-adapting control parameters in differential evolution: A comparative study on numerical benchmark problems. *Trans. Evol. Comp*, 10(6):646–657, Dec. 2006.

[12] J.-F. Chang, S.-C. Chu, J. F. Roddick, and J.-S. Pan. A parallel particle swarm optimization algorithm with communication strategies. *J. Inf. Sci. Eng.*, 21(4):809–818, 2005.

[13] M. Clerc. Beyond standard particle swarm optimisation. *IJSIR*, 1(4):46–61, 2010.

[14] M. Clerc and J. Kennedy. The particle swarm - explosion, stability, and convergence in a multidimensional complex space. *IEEE Transactions on Evolutionary Computation*, 6(1):58–73, 2002.

[15] L. Devroye, L. Györfi, and G. Lugosi. *A probabilistic Theory of Pattern Recognition.* Springer, 1997.

[16] H. Fournier and O. Teytaud. Lower Bounds for Comparison Based Evolution Strategies using VC-dimension and Sign Patterns. *Algorithmica*, 2010.

[17] M. Gardner, A. W. McNabb, and K. D. Seppi. A speculative approach to parallelization in particle swarm optimization. *Swarm Intelligence*, 6(2):77–116, 2012.

[18] H. georg Beyer. On the dynamics of eas without selection. In *Foundations of Genetic Algorithms*, pages 5–26. Morgan Kaufmann, 1999.

[19] D. E. Goldberg. *Genetic Algorithms in Search, Optimization and Machine Learning.* Addison-Wesley Longman Publishing Co., Inc., Boston, MA, USA, 1st edition, 1989.

[20] S. M. Islam, S. Das, S. Ghosh, S. Roy, and P. N. Suganthan. An adaptive differential evolution algorithm with novel mutation and crossover strategies for global numerical optimization. *IEEE Transactions on Systems, Man, and Cybernetics, Part B*, 42(2):482–500, 2012.

[21] J. Kennedy and R. C. Eberhart. Particle swarm optimization. In *Proceedings of the IEEE International Conference on Neural Networks*, pages 1942–1948, 1995.

[22] J. Liu and J. Lampinen. A fuzzy adaptive differential evolution algorithm. *Soft Comput.*, 9(6):448–462, June 2005.

[23] B. Mahdad, K. Srairi, T. Bouktir, and M. Benbouzid. Fuzzy Controlled Parallel PSO to Solving Large Practical Economic Dispatch. In IEEE, editor, *Proceedings of the 2010 IEEE International Conference of the IEEE Industrial Electronics Society*, pages 2695–2701, Phoenix, United States, Nov. 2010. IEEE.

[24] R. Mallipeddi, P. Suganthan, Q. Pan, and M. Tasgetiren. Differential evolution algorithm with ensemble of parameters and mutation strategies. *Applied Soft Computing*, 11(2):1679 – 1696, 2011.

[25] A. McNabb, C. Monson, and K. Seppi. Parallel PSO using MapReduce. In *Evolutionary Computation, 2007. CEC 2007. IEEE Congress on*, pages 7–14, 2007.

[26] J. Olensek, T. Tuma, J. Puhan, and Á. Bürmen. A new asynchronous parallel global optimization method based on simulated annealing and differential evolution. *Appl. Soft Comput.*, 11(1):1481–1489, 2011.

[27] K. E. Parsopoulos and M. N. Vrahatis. Parameter selection and adaptation in unified particle swarm optimization. *Mathematical and Computer Modelling*, 46(1-2):198–213, 2007.

[28] M. E. H. Pedersen. *Tuning & simplifying heuristical optimization.* PhD thesis, University of Southampton, January 2010.

[29] P. Pošík and V. Klemš. Jade, an adaptive differential evolution algorithm, benchmarked on the bbob noiseless testbed. In *Proceedings of the fourteenth international conference on Genetic and evolutionary computation conference companion*, GECCO Companion '12, pages 197–204, New York, NY, USA, 2012. ACM.

[30] K. V. Price, R. M. Storn, and J. A. Lampinen. *Differential Evolution - A Practical Approach to Global Optimization.* Natural Computing. Springer-Verlag, January 2006. ISBN 540209506.

[31] A. K. Qin, F. Raimondo, F. Forbes, and Y. S. Ong. An improved cuda-based implementation of differential evolution on gpu. In *Proceedings of the 14th Annual Conference on Genetic and Evolutionary Computation*, GECCO '12, pages 991–998, New York, NY, USA, 2012. ACM.

[32] I. Rechenberg. *Evolutionstrategie: Optimierung Technischer Systeme nach Prinzipien des Biologischen Evolution.* Fromman-Holzboog Verlag, Stuttgart, 1973.

[33] E. Samansky. Zaslavsky's theorem, 2002. http://www.math.rice.edu/ samans/ZaslavskyTheorem.pdf.

[34] J. F. Schutte, J. A. Reinbolt, B. J. Fregly, R. T. Haftka, and A. D. George. Parallel global optimization with the particle swarm algorithm. *Journal of numerical methods in engineering*, 61:2296–2315, 2003.

[35] Y. Shi and R. C. Eberhart. A Modified Particle Swarm Optimizer. In *Proceedings of IEEE International Conference on Evolutionary Computation*, pages 69–73, Washington, DC, USA, May 1998. IEEE Computer Society.

[36] R. Storn and K. Price. Differential evolution: A simple and efficient heuristic for global optimization over continuous spaces. *J. of Global Optimization*, 11(4):341–359, Dec. 1997.

[37] F. Teytaud and O. Teytaud. Log(lambda) Modifications for Optimal Parallelism. In *Parallel Problem Solving from Nature, PPSN XI*, pages 254–263, Krakow, Pologne, September 2010. Springer.

[38] O. Teytaud and S. Gelly. General lower bounds for evolutionary algorithms. In *Parallel Problem Solving from Nature, PPSN IX*, pages 21–31. Springer, 2006.

[39] I. C. Trelea. The particle swarm optimization algorithm: convergence analysis and parameter selection. *Information Processing Letters*, 85(6):317 – 325, 2003.

[40] V. N. Vapnik. *The Nature of Statistical Learning.* Springer Verlag, 1995.

[41] M. Weber, F. Neri, and V. Tirronen. Parallel random injection differential evolution. In C. Di Chio, S. Cagnoni, C. Cotta, M. Ebner, A. EkÃąrt, A. Esparcia-Alcazar, C.-K. Goh, J. Merelo, F. Neri, M. PreuÃY, J. Togelius, and G. Yannakakis, editors, *Applications of Evolutionary Computation*, volume

6024 of *Lecture Notes in Computer Science*, pages 471–480. Springer Berlin Heidelberg, 2010.

[42] M. Yang, J. Guan, Z. Cai, and L. Wang. Self-adapting differential evolution algorithm with chaos random for global numerical optimization. In Z. Cai, C. Hu, Z. Kang, and Y. Liu, editors, *Advances in Computation and Intelligence*, volume 6382 of *Lecture Notes in Computer Science*, pages 112–122. Springer Berlin Heidelberg, 2010.

[43] W.-J. Yu and J. Zhang. Multi-population differential evolution with adaptive parameter control for global optimization. In *Proceedings of the 13th Annual Conference on Genetic and Evolutionary Computation*, GECCO '11, pages 1093–1098, New York, NY, USA, 2011. ACM.

[44] M. Zambrano-Bigiarini, M. Clerc, and R. Rojas. Standard particle swarm optimisation 2011 at cec-2013: A baseline for future pso improvements. In *IEEE Congress on Evolutionary Computation*, pages 2337–2344. IEEE, 2013.

[45] T. Zaslavsky. Facing up to arrangements: Face-count formulas for partitions of space by hyperplanes. *Mem. Am. Math. Soc.*, 154:102, 1975.

[46] J. Zhang and A. C. Sanderson. Jade: adaptive differential evolution with optional external archive. *Trans. Evol. Comp*, 13(5):945–958, Oct. 2009.

Self-Adapting the Brownian Radius in a Differential Evolution Algorithm for Dynamic Environments

Mathys C. du Plessis
Department of CS
Nelson Mandela Metropolitan University
Port Elizabeth, South Africa
mc.duplessis@nmmu.ac.za

Andries P. Engelbrecht
Department of Computer Science
University of Pretoria
Pretoria, South Africa
engel@cs.up.ac.za

Andre Calitz
Department of CS
Nelson Mandela Metropolitan University
Port Elizabeth, South Africa
andre.calitz@nmmu.ac.za

ABSTRACT
Several algorithms aimed at dynamic optimisation problems have been developed. This paper reports on the incorporation of a self-adaptive Brownian radius into competitive differential evolution (CDE). Four variations of a novel technique to achieving the self-adaptation is suggested and motivated. An experimental investigation over a large number of benchmark instances is used to determine the most effective of the four variations. The new algorithm is compared to its base algorithm on an extensive set of benchmark problems and its performance analysed. Finally, the new algorithm is compared to other algorithms by means of reported results found in the literature. The results indicate that CDE is improved the the incorporation of the self-adaptive Brownian radius and that the new algorithm compares well with other algorithms.

General Terms
Dynamic Environments, Brownian radius, Self-Adaptation, Differential Evolution

1. INTRODUCTION
A dynamic optimisation problem refers to a search space that does not remain constant over time. Evolutionary algorithms aimed at static optimisation problems often fail to effectively optimise dynamic problems. The main reason for this is that the algorithms converge to a single optimum in the search space, and then lack the necessary diversity to locate new optima once the environment changes.

Various approaches have been developed to make optimisation algorithms more effective in dynamic environments. One of the approaches that is found in several algorithms is the use of Brownian individuals [33]. Random noise is injected into a portion of the individuals in the population to increase the diversity of the population, thus making the algorithm more effective at responding to changes in the environment. The magnitude of the random noise is controlled by a parameter (known as the Brownian radius) to the algorithm. This paper reports on the self-adaptation of this parameter in competitive differential evolution (CDE) [19].

The rest of the paper is structured as follows: Section 2 describes other algorithms aimed at dynamic environments. CDE, the base algorithm for this work, is discussed in Section 3. The proposed technique to self-adapting the Brownian radius is described in Section 4. The experimental procedure is described in Section 5 and results are discussed in Section 6. The performance of the new algorithm is analysed in Section 7. Section 8 compares the new algorithm to the published results from other algorithms. Conclusions are drawn in Section 9.

FOGA '15 January 17 - 20, 2015, Aberystwyth, United Kingdom

http://dx.doi.org/10.1145/2725494.2725505

2. RELATED WORK
A dynamic environment, in the context of optimisation problems, is a fitness landscape that varies over time. Formally, $\exists\ t, t' \in \mathcal{T}$, where $\mathcal{T}$ is the set of all time steps, and $\exists\ \vec{x} \in \mathcal{S}^{n_d} \subseteq \mathbb{R}^{n_d}$ such that

$$F(\vec{x}, t) \neq F(\vec{x}, t') \quad (1)$$

where F is a dynamic function. Consequently, the optima in the fitness landscape may vary in number, location, and function value over time. The objective of an algorithm applied to a dynamic optimisation problem (DOP) is to find the best solutions at all time steps during the optimisation process [49], i.e. for all $t \in \mathcal{T}$, assuming a minimisation problem, find

$$\vec{x}^*(t) : F(\vec{x}^*(t), t) \leq F(\vec{x}, t)\ \forall\ \vec{x} \in \mathcal{S}^{n_d} \quad (2)$$

where $\vec{x}^*(t) \in \mathcal{S}^{n_d}$ is the location of a global optimum at time step t.

Algorithms aimed at dynamic optimisation problems (DOPs) are discussed in the following sections in terms of their respective base algorithms. Section 2.1 describes algorithms based on genetic algorithms, Section 2.2 describes algorithms based on particle swarm optimisation, Section 2.3 describes algorithms based on differential evolution [42] [45], and Section 2.4 describes algorithms with hybrids or other bases.

2.1 Genetic Algorithm-Based Algorithms
Early GA approaches to solving DOPs endeavoured to increase population diversity after changes occurred in the dynamic environment by increasing the mutation rate. Cobb

[16] suggested temporarily dramatically increasing the mutation rate of a GA after a change occurred, while Vavak *et al.* [48] advocated a more gradual increase.

Later algorithms sustain high diversity throughout the optimisation process as opposed to only increasing diversity directly after changes in the environment. Approaches aimed at maintaining a high amount of diversity during the entire execution of the GA algorithm include Grefenstette's random immigrants algorithm [20], which introduces random individuals into a GA's population after each generation. Morrison [34] proposed an algorithm which, in contrast to introducing random individuals, makes use of sentinels that are uniformly distributed throughout the search space to increase diversity.

Utilising the search history is useful in dynamic optimisation problems where the shape of the fitness landscape is oscillating or cyclic. Ramsey and Grefenstette [43] made use of a knowledge base of individuals that performed well in previous generations. These individuals are inserted into the population when a change occurs that results in a previously seen environment. Yang [51] made use of a memory of individuals which are used as memory-based immigrants. Various approaches to maintaining the memory archive have also been explored [44][53].

Several algorithms employ multiple, independent populations to track the locations of optima in the environment before and after changes occur. Three of the seminal GA algorithms employing this strategy are self-organizing scouts (SOS) [12][10][13], shifting balance GA (SBGA) [40] and the multinational GA (MGA) [47]. All three of these approaches make use of a custom technique to intelligently distribute individuals among the populations.

2.2 Particle Swarm Optimisation-Based Algorithms

Considerable success has been achieved in applying modern optimisation algorithms, such as PSO, to dynamic optimisation problems. Hu and Eberhart [24] suggested that diversity should be increased by reinitialising the particles in the PSO algorithm when a change in the environment occurs. Blackwell and Bentley suggested charged particles [8], where each particle of a PSO is assigned a virtual charge and is then allowed to repel other particles based on the laws of electrostatics. Another proposed strategy is increasing diversity by reinitialising a portion of the swarm of particles within a hyper-sphere, centred around the best particle within the swarm [5, 6]. These particles are called *quantum particles.* The cloud radius determines how far from the best particle the quantum particles are dispersed.

Parrot and Li [41] suggested a multiple swarm PSO approach to solving DOPs, called speciation. Multiple swarms correspond to the idea of multiple populations in GAs, and have the same benefits: increased diversity and parallel discovery of optima. Blackwell and Branke [6] introduced a multiple swarm PSO-based algorithm (MPSO) that is based on three components: exclusion, anti-convergence and quantum individuals. Exclusion [5] is a technique meant to prevent sub-swarms from clustering around the same optimum by means of selective reinitialisation. Anti-convergence was incorporated to prevent stagnation by reinitialising the weakest sub-swarm if it is found that all sub-swarms have converged.

The MPSO algorithm was adapted and improved by Amo *et al.* [17] to reinitialise or pause sub-swarms that perform badly. A swarm is flagged as performing badly if, for five iterations, its improvement falls below 15% of its best improvement since the last change in the environment and if the swarm is in the set containing the 20% of swarms that have the lowest fitness value. Once a swarm is thus flagged, the algorithm, using a history of previous changes, then estimates the number of iterations before the next change in the environment. Should less than 20% of the estimated period between changes remain, the swarm is paused until the next change in the environment (hence preventing it from wasting function evaluations). Otherwise, the swarm is reinitialised to continue searching for new optima.

Blackwell [4] modified MPSO by self-adapting the number of swarms in the search space. This algorithm (referred to as MPSO2) is aimed at situations where the number of optima in the dynamic environment is unknown. MPSO2 can find an effective value for the number of sub-swarms by introducing and removing a sub-swarm when necessary. Blackwell *et al.* [7] adapted MPSO2 by converting all particles to quantum particles for one iteration after a change in the environment occured.

Li *et al.* [30] improved the speciation algorithm of Parrot and Li [41] by introducing quantum individuals [5] to increase diversity, and anti-convergence to detect stagnation and subsequently reinitialise the worst-performing populations. This algorithm is called Speciation-based PSO (SPSO).

Cellular PSO [21] incorporates ideas from cellular automata into a PSO algorithm aimed at DOPs. The search space is divided into equally-sized cells. The migration of particles from one cell to another is controlled based on the coverage of the search space. The motivation for partitioning particles into cells is similar to that for forming sub-swarms and also provides the benefits of parallel search and tracking multiple optima. Hashemi and Meybodi [22] adapted Cellular PSO by introducing quantum particles.

Kamosi *et al.* [26] proposed an algorithm that utilises a single parent swarm to locate promising areas in the search space and a dynamic number of child swarms to exploit the promising areas. This multi-swarm optimisation algorithm is referred to here as MSO. Exclusion is used to prevent child swarms from converging to the same optimum. The algorithm reacts to changes in the environment by re-evaluating all parent swarm particles. Kamosi *et al.* [25] improved MSO by introducing a hibernation metaphor to place child swarms into a "sleep" state when they become unproductive. This approach (referred to here as hibernating MSO (HMSO)) is motivated by the fact that function evaluations are wasted on a child swarm which has located the summit of the optimum that it tracks.

Novoa-Hernández *et al.* [39] removed the quantum particle component of the MPSO algorithm [6]. The authors introduced a diversity increasing scheme directly after a change in the environment by replacing the worst-performing particles within each sub-swarm by particles that are randomly created in a hypersphere centred at the best particle in the sub-swarm. A control rule was introduced which allows bad sub-swarms to "sleep" and consequently save function evaluations. This algorithm is referred to as MPSOD.

The clustering PSO (CPSO) algorithm [52] clusters the main swarm into independent sub-swarms after each change in the environment. CPSO transfers information from one environment to the next by means of a memory archive containing good solutions found before the change. Sub-swarms which search overlapping areas of the search space are detected by calculating the percentage of particles from one sub-swarm that fall within the search area of another. Two sub-swarms are merged if the percentage of overlap exceeds a threshold value.

2.3 Differential Evolution-Based Algorithms

The first application of the DE algorithm to DOPs occurred relatively recently. Consequently, researchers could apply earlier successful DOP approaches from GA and PSO-based algorithms when adapting DE for dynamic environments. An approach similar to quantum particles, called Brownian individuals, is utilised by DynDE, a DE-based algorithm for dynamic environments [33]. Use of Brownian individuals involves the creation of individuals close to the best individual by adding a small random value, sampled from a zero-mean normal distribution, to each component of the best individual. Mendes and Mohais [33] adapted the ideas from Blackwell and Branke [5] to create their multi-population algorithm, DynDE, which uses exclusion to prevent populations from converging to the same peak. Furthermore, it was determined that the DE/best/2/bin best scheme is the most effective for use by DynDE. More details regarding DynDE is given in later sections. The favoured populations DE (FPDE) [18] is an adaptation to DynDE. The adaptation aims to prevent wasting function evaluations on sub-populations with inferior performance.

Brest *et al.* [15] proposed a self-adaptive multi-population DE algorithm, called *jDE*, for optimising dynamic environments. This work focused on adapting the DE scale factor and crossover probability and is based on a previous algorithm [14] for optimising static environments. The motivation behind using self-adaptive control parameters is that the algorithm can change the scale factor and crossover probability during the optimisation process to appropriate values as the environment changes. Exclusion is used to prevent sub-populations from converging to the same optimum. An aging metaphor is used to reinitialise sub-populations that have stagnated on a local optimum. Sub-populations of which the best individual is too old are reinitialised so that the sub-population can discover other optima. The algorithm also utilises a form of memory called an archive. The best individual is added to the archive every time a change in the environment occurs.

Noroozi *et al.* [38] proposed a DE-based algorithm aimed at dynamic environments, referred to as Cellular DE. Cellular DE is a DE implementation of Cellular PSO which was discussed in the previous section. Cellular DE track multiple optima in the dynamic environment by allowing individuals to converge to cells representing the areas where optima occur.

2.4 Other Dynamic Environment Algorithms

This section describes algorithms for dynamic environments that are either hybrids of GA, PSO and DE algorithms, or those that are not based on these algorithms.

An algorithm that uses both a DE population and a PSO swarm was proposed by Lung and Dumitrescu [31]. This algorithm is called collaborative evolutionary-swarm optimisation (CESO). A swarm optimised by using PSO refines the best found optimum, while a DE variant, called crowding differential evolution, is used to maintain diversity and locate local optima. Crowding DE [46] is an algorithm aimed at locating multiple optima in static environments. Crowding DE changes the offspring operator of DE so that the most similar individual in the parent population, rather than the target vector, is replaced. Multiple optima are thus tracked simultaneously. CESO was improved by incorporating a second DE population [32]. The new algorithm is referred to as the evolutionary swarm cooperative algorithm (ESCA). The second DE population is used to maintain a search history and acts as a memory of previously found optima for the first DE population.

Several investigations have focused on the self-adaptation of control parameters. Angeline *et al.* [1] made use of a self-adaptive evolutionary programming (EP) algorithm to evolve finite machines to predict the next value of an input string. The string to be predicted was changed dynamically during the execution of the algorithm. Evolution strategies (ES) have been applied to DOPs by several researchers [2], [50], [3].

Moser and Hendtlass [37] proposed the multi-phase multi-individual extremal optimisation (MMEO) algorithm. Extremal optimisation (EO) [9] makes use of a single individual which is mutated. EO was adapted [37] to contain several individuals to locate and track multiple optima in the dynamic environment, each of which used five steps to find optima. Firstly, a stepwise sampling of the fitness landscape is performed to locate areas that potentially contain optima. From these potential points, an individual performs a local search to find a local optimum. If changes in the environment occur, individuals are optimised further using a local search. Finally, individuals are fine tuned using finer-grained hill climbing. Moser [35] refined the MMEO algorithm by making use of the Hooke-Jeeves search algorithm [23] to perform the local search (HJEO). Further improvements were found in Moser and Chiong [36] by tuning the step sizes to more problem appropriate values (LSEO).

3. COMPETITIVE DIFFERENTIAL EVOLUTION

The base algorithm used for the proposed adaptations presented in this paper is competitive differential evolution (CDE) [19]. CDE is an extension to DynDE, created by Mendes and Mohais [33]. The following sections describe the CDE algorithm. The components described in sections 3.1 to 3.4 are inherited from DynDE.

3.1 Multiple Populations

Algorithms aimed at optimising dynamic environments typically benefit from tracking not only the global optimum, but also local minima, as a local minimum may become the global optimum when a change in the environment occurs. An effective method of tracking all optima is to maintain several independent sub-populations of DE individuals, one sub-population on each optimum. DynDE [33] used 10 sub-populations, each containing six individuals.

3.2 Exclusion

In order to track all optima, it is necessary to ensure that all sub-populations converge to different optima. Exclusion [33] is used exclusion to prevent sub-populations from converging to the same optimum. Exclusion compares the locations of the best individuals from each sub-population. If the spatial difference between any two of these individuals becomes too small, the entire sub-population of the inferior individual is randomly reinitialised. A threshold is used to determine if two individuals are too close. This threshold, or exclusion radius, is calculated as

$$r_{excl} = \frac{V_{max,F} - V_{min,F}}{2 n_k^{\frac{1}{n_d}}} \quad (3)$$

where n_k is the number of sub-populations, and $V_{max,F}$ and $V_{min,F}$ are the upper and lower search range of function F in the n_d dimensions (assuming equal ranges for all dimensions). Note that this equation differs slightly from the original [33][6] in that the number of sub-populations is used rather than the number of optima (which is not generally known when faced with an optimisation problem).

The exclusion approach causes DynDE to reinitialise the weaker sub-population when two sub-populations are located within the exclusion radius of each other. This approach does not take into account the case when two optima are located extremely close to each other, i.e. within the exclusion threshold of one another. One of the sub-populations will be reinitialised in these situations, leaving one of the optima unpopulated. This problem be partially remedied by determining whether the midpoint between the best individuals in each sub-population constitutes a higher error value than the best individuals of both sub-populations. If this is the case, it implies that a trough exists between the two sub-populations and that neither should be reinitialised. Let $\vec{x}_{best,k}$ be the best individual in sub-population P_k, $k \in \{1, 2, \ldots, n_k\}$. Exclusion in CDE is thus performed as described in Algorithm 1 (assuming a minimisation function, F).

3.3 Brownian Individuals

In cases where a change in the environment results in the positional movement of some of the optima, it is unlikely that all of the sub-populations will still be clustered around the optimal point of their respective optima, even if the change is small. In order for the individuals in the sub-populations to track the moving optima more effectively, the diversity of each population should be increased. Mendes and Mohais [33] successfully used Brownian individuals for this purpose. In every generation, a predefined number of the weakest individuals are flagged as Brownian. These individuals are then replaced by new individuals created by adding a small random number, sampled from a zero centred Gaussian distribution, to each component of the best individual in the sub-population. A Brownian individual, $\vec{x}_{brown}$, is thus created from the best individual, $\vec{x}_{best}$, using

$$\vec{x}_{brown} = \vec{x}_{best} + \vec{r} \quad (4)$$

where $\vec{r}$ is a random vector with $r_j \sim N(0, r_{brown})$ and r_{brown}, the Brownian radius, is the standard deviation of the Gaussian distribution. Mendes and Mohais [33] showed that a suitable value to use for r_{brown} is 0.2.

The addition of the small random values to the components of the Brownian individuals ensures that the population never completely converges. This is especially important in a DE-based algorithm, since mutation step-sizes depend on the vector differences between individuals. Without the Brownian individuals, it is conceivable that the entire population could converge to a single point in the fitness landscape which would result in all vector differences being zero. The evolution process would cease and the algorithm would be unable to respond to changes in the environment. This paper made use of a single Brownian individual in each sub-population.

Algorithm 1: Exclusion

for $k_1 = 1, \ldots, n_k$ **do**
  for $k_2 = 1, \ldots, n_k$ **do**
    if $\|\vec{x}_{best,k_1} - \vec{x}_{best,k_2}\|_2 < r_{excl}$ **and** $k_1 \neq k_2$ **then**
      Let $\vec{x}_{mid} = (\vec{x}_{best,k_1} + \vec{x}_{best,k_2})/2$;
      if $F(\vec{x}_{mid}) > F(\vec{x}_{best,k_1})$ **and** $F(\vec{x}_{mid}) > F(\vec{x}_{best,k_2})$ **then**
        if $F(\vec{x}_{best,k_1}) < F(\vec{x}_{best,k_2})$ **then**
          Reinitialise population P_{k_2}
        else
          Reinitialise population P_{k_1}
        end
      end
    end
  end
end

3.4 DE Scheme

Mendes and Mohais [33] found that the most effective scheme to use in conjunction with DynDE is DE/best/2/bin, where each temporary individual is created using

$$\vec{v} = \vec{x}_{best} + \mathcal{F} \cdot (\vec{x}_1 + \vec{x}_2 - \vec{x}_3 - \vec{x}_4) \quad (5)$$

where $\mathcal{F}$ is the DE scale factor, $\vec{x}_1 \neq \vec{x}_2 \neq \vec{x}_3 \neq \vec{x}_4$ and $\vec{x}_{best}$ is the best individual in the sub-population.

3.5 Competitive Population Evaluation

The primary goal of competitive population evaluation (CPE) [19] is not to decrease the error value found by DynDE, but rather to make the algorithm reach the lowest error value in fewer function evaluations. The proposed algorithm aims to achieve this by initially allocating all function evaluations, after a change in the environment, to the sub-population that has the current best solution. Thereafter function evaluations are allocated to other sub-populations.

The mechanism used by CPE to allocate function evaluations is based on the performance of sub-populations. The best-performing sub-population is evolved on its own until its performance drops below that of another sub-population. The new best-performing sub-population then evolves on its own until its performance drops below that of another sub-population. This process is repeated until a change in the environment occurs. Ideally, CPE would locate the global optimum early, while locating local optima later. CPE thus differs from DynDE in that peaks are not located in parallel, but sequentially. The CPE process is detailed in Algorithm 2. Changes in the environment are always followed by the evolution of all sub-populations for two generations. These two generations are necessary in order to calculate the performance value, $\mathcal{P}_k$, for each of the P_k sub-populations. However, after the initial two generations, the CPE process evolves only one sub-population per generation.

Algorithm 2: Competitive population evaluation

```
while termination criterion not met do
    Allow the standard DynDE algorithm to run for two
    generations;
    repeat
        for k = 1, ..., n_k do
            Calculate the performance value, P_k(t)
        end
        Select sub-population P_a such that
        P_a(t) = min_{k=1,...,n_k} {P_k(t)};
        Evolve only sub-population P_a using DE for one
        generation;
        t = t + 1;
        Perform exclusion according to Algorithm 1;
        Create Brownian individuals;
    until a change in the environment occurs;
end
```

The performance value, $\mathcal{P}_k$, of sub-population P_k depends on two factors: The current fitness of the best individual in the sub-population and the error reduction of the best individual during the last evaluation of the sub-population. Let n_k be the number of sub-populations, $\vec{x}_{best,k}$ the best individual in sub-population P_k, and $F(\vec{x}_{best,k}, t)$ the fitness of the best individual in sub-population P_k during iteration t. The performance $\mathcal{P}_k(t)$ of population P_k, after iteration t, is given by:

$$\mathcal{P}_k(t) = (\Delta F(\vec{x}_{best,k}, t) + 1)(R_k(t) + 1) \tag{6}$$

where

$$\Delta F(\vec{x}_{best,k}, t) = |F(\vec{x}_{best,k}, t) - F(\vec{x}_{best,k}, t-1)| \tag{7}$$

For function minimisation problems, $R_k(t)$ is calculated as:

$$R_k(t) = |F(\vec{x}_{best,k}, t) - \max_{a=1,\ldots,n_k} \{F(\vec{x}_{best,a}, t)\}| \tag{8}$$

The best performing sub-population is, therefore, the sub-population with the highest product of fitness and improvement.

4. ADAPTING THE BROWNIAN RADIUS

The creation of Brownian individuals was discussed in Section 3.3. The purpose of the Brownian individuals is to increase the diversity within sub-populations, so that the DE process can respond effectively to changes in the environment. A secondary advantage of using Brownian individuals is that it acts as a random local search around the best individual in the sub-population, which helps to reduce the error. A self-adaptive approach is suggested in this section to eliminate the need for tuning the Brownian radius parameter. The new approach is presented in Section 4.1, while alternative implementations to the proposed approach are presented in Section 4.2.

4.1 Proposed Approach

Section 3.3 gave the equation used to create Brownian individuals and specified that a value for the Brownian radius of $r_{brown} = 0.2$ has been found to produce good results. Intuitively, it seems unlikely that a single value for r_{brown} would produce the best results at all stages of the optimisation process, for example, more diversity would likely be required after a change in the environment. Furthermore, the Brownian radius is likely to be function-dependent.

This section proposes a novel approach to self-adapting the Brownian radius to appropriate values for different functions and different stages of the optimisation process. The new approach relies on the assumption that the Brownian radius should initially be large, as new optima need to be discovered. Appropriate values for the Brownian radius, $r_{brown}(t)$, can later be deduced from radii used by successful Brownian individuals that resulted in lower error values. The Brownian radius, $r_{brown}(t)$, is set equal to the absolute value of a random number selected from a normal distribution:

$$r_{brown}(t) \sim |N(0, r_{dev}(t))| \tag{9}$$

where $r_{dev}(t)$ is the standard deviation of the normal distribution, and the actual value that is self-adapted.

The proposed self-adaptive approach commences with a Brownian radius proportional to the sub-population radius of the first sub-population that is evaluated. The population radius, $r_{pop,k}$, is calculated for sub-population P_k using:

$$r_{pop,k} = \frac{\max_{i_1,i_2 \in \{1,\ldots,n_{I,k}\}} \left\{ \|\vec{x}_{i_1} - \vec{x}_{i_2}\|_2 \right\}}{2} \tag{10}$$

The initial value of $r_{dev}(t)$ is thus half of the maximum Euclidian distance between any two individuals in the sub-population, i.e. $r_{dev}(0) = r_{pop,k}$, where P_k is the first sub-population that is evaluated. The algorithm keeps track of the $r_{brown}(t)$ values of all Brownian individuals that have a higher fitness than the best individual within the sub-population, $\vec{x}_{best,k}(t)$, that was used in their creation. An average of all successful r_{brown} values are used to calculate successive values for r_{dev}. Algorithm 3 formally describes the new approach (assuming a function minimisation problem).

The proposed algorithm uses the average of successful values

Algorithm 3: Self-adaptive Brownian radius algorithm

$t = 0$;
$DevSum = r_{pop,0}$ with P_0 being the first sub-population evaluated;
$DevCount = 1$;
foreach *Brownian individual to be created in sub-population* P_k **do**
  $r_{dev}(t) = DevSum/DevCount$;
  $r_{brown}(t) \sim| N(0, r_{dev}(t)) |$;
  $\vec{x}_{brown} = \vec{x}_{best,k} + \vec{r}$ with $r_j \sim N(0, r_{brown}(t))$;
  if $F(\vec{x}_{brown}) < F(\vec{x}_{best,k})$ **then**
    $DevSum = DevSum + r_{brown}(t)$;
    $DevCount = DevCount + 1$;
  end
  $t = t + 1$;
end

of r_{brown} as the standard deviation of the normal distribution to select the next r_{brown} value. Smaller values than the average r_{brown} value are thus more likely to be produced, but larger values will also be produced by the normal distribution.

4.2 Alternative Techniques

Two alternative techniques of implementing the self-adaptive Brownian radius algorithm are presented here. The first technique pertains to the distribution used to create the value of $r_{brown}(t)$. The second technique involves a response to changes in the environment.

Equation (9) selects the new value for $r_{brown}(t)$ from a normal distribution. About 68.27% of values selected from a normal distribution fall within one standard deviation from the mean value, and 99.73% of values fall within three standard deviations of the mean. This means, in the context of equation (9), that the next selected value of $r_{brown}(t)$ would likely be smaller than the current value of $r_{dev}(t)$, and cases where $r_{brown}(t) > 3r_{dev}(t)$ are extremely unlikely. The propensity for selecting small values for $r_{brown}(t)$ could potentially negatively affect the performance of the algorithm, as too little diversity may be introduced into the sub-populations by the Brownian individuals.

The Cauchy distribution is a distribution function with two parameters, the location of the median and a scale value. A random number from a Cauchy distribution, in contrast to a random number from a normal distribution, is more likely to be greater than the scale value. For example, only 50% of values selected from a Cauchy distribution fall within one scale value from the median, while less than 80% of values fall within three scale values from the median.

The use of a Cauchy distribution, rather than a normal distribution, to select new values for $r_{brown}(t)$, would thus result in larger values being selected more frequently. This could potentially avoid the problem of low sub-population diversity which could result from using a normal distribution. This section thus proposes to use a Cauchy distribution to calculate the values for $r_{brown}(t)$, as follows:

$$r_{brown}(t) \sim | C(0, r_{dev}(t)) | \quad (11)$$

The algorithm that utilises a normal distribution is referred to as SABrNor and the algorithm that uses a Cauchy distribution is referred to as SABrCau.

An issue that has not been addressed is how the adapted Brownian radius would transfer between changes in the environment. The value of $r_{dev}(t)$ may have been adapted to assist in exploitation by the time a change in the environment occurs, which would make it ineffective for the necessary exploration that must occur after a change in the environment. A resetting scheme is proposed here whereby the value of $r_{dev}(t)$ is reset to the original population radius, and the average over successful values is cleared. Algorithm 3 is consequently changed into Algorithm 4.

Algorithm 4: Self-adaptive Brownian radius algorithm with resetting

$t = 0$;
$DevSum = r_{pop,0}$ with P_0 being the first sub-population evaluated;
$DevCount = 1$;
foreach *Brownian individual that to be created in sub-population* P_k **do**
  if *A change in the environment occurred* **then**
    $DevSum = r_{pop,0}$;
    $DevCount = 1$;
  end
  $r_{dev}(t) = DevSum/DevCount$;
  $r_{brown}(t) \sim| N(0, r_{dev}(t)) |$;
  $\vec{x}_{brown} = \vec{x}_{best,k} + \vec{r}$ with $r_j \sim N(0, r_{brown}(t))$;
  if $F(\vec{x}_{brown}) < F(\vec{x}_{best,k})$ **then**
    $DevSum = DevSum + r_{dev}(t)$;
    $DevCount = DevCount + 1$;
  end
  $t = t + 1$;
end

Resetting of $r_{dev}(t)$ can also be used in conjunction with a Cauchy distribution. The algorithm that utilises a normal distribution with resetting is referred to as ABrCDE and the algorithm that uses a Cauchy distribution with resetting is referred to as SABrCauRes. Four basic variations of Brownian radius adaptation algorithm are thus investigated: SABrNor (This algorithm uses a normal distribution to select values for $r_{dev}(t)$), SABrCau (This algorithm uses a Cauchy distribution to select values for $r_{dev}(t)$), ABrCDE (This algorithm uses a normal distribution to select values for $r_{dev}(t)$, and resets $r_{dev}(t)$ to the original population radius when a change in the environment occurs) and SABrCauRes (This algorithm uses a Cauchy distribution to select values for $r_{dev}(t)$, and resets $r_{dev}(t)$ to the original population radius when a change in the environment occurs).

5. EXPERIMENTAL PROCEDURE

Two benchmarks have commonly been adopted within the DOP community to evaluate the performance of algorithms. The first is the moving peaks benchmark (MPB) [11]. The multi-dimensional problem space of the moving peaks function contains several peaks, or optima, of variable height, width, and shape. These peaks move around with height and width changing periodically. The second benchmark is generalised dynamic benchmark generator (GDBG) [28] [27]. This benchmark consists of six main functions that are moved in the environment using six different change types.

The simplicity of the MPB makes it ideal for investigating the effect of different change severities, while the GDBG provides functionality to investigate different change types and underlying functions. Accordingly, a *standard set* of experiments is defined here. Variations of the Scenario 2 settings on the MPB which are included in the standard set are given in Table 1. The settings include several values for change severity and both the cone and sphere peak functions. The combinations of change severity and peak function results in 12 MPB variations which are included in the standard set.

Table 1: MPB Scenario 2 Variations

Setting	Value
Number of dimensions (n_d)	5
Number of Peaks	10
Max and Min Peak height	[30,70]
Max and Min Peak width	[1.0,12.0]
Change period (Cp)	5000
Change severity (C_s)	1.0, 5.0, 10.0, 20.0, 40.0, 80.0
Height severity	7.0
Width severity	1.0
Function (F)	Cone, Sphere
Correlation	0.0

The GDBG problems considered here consist of six change types (T_1 to T_6) and six functions (F_1 to F_6). The creators of the GDBG suggested that two instances of F_1 be used: one containing 10 peaks and one containing 50 peaks. These instances are denoted by F_{1a} and F_{1b} respectively. The combinations of change types and functions thus yield a total of 42 GDBG environments that are included in the standard set. The GDBG variations are summarised in Table 2. The default values for the number of dimensions and change period are in accordance with the settings for the IEEE WCCI-2012 competition on evolutionary computation for dynamic optimisation problems [29].

Table 2: GDBG Variations

Setting	Value
Number of dimensions (n_d)	5
Change period (Cp)	50000
Function (F)	F_{1a}, F_{1b}, F_2, F_3, F_4, F_5, F_6
Change type (Ct)	T_1, T_2, T_3, T_4, T_5, T_6

The 54 environments in the standard set thus contain 12 environments from the MPB and 42 environments from the GDBG. The standard set is varied to investigate the effect of different numbers of dimensions and various values for the change period (number of function evaluations between changes in the environment), refer to Table 3.

A stopping criterion of 60 changes in the environment was used for all experiments as suggested in [28], [29]. This paper

Table 3: Standard Set Variations

Setting	Values
Number of dimensions (n_d)	5, 10, 25, 50, 100
Change period (Cp)	100, 500, 1000, 5000, 10000, 25000, 50000, 100000

uses the offline error as performance measure. The offline error is the running average of the lowest-so-far error found since the last change in the environment [10]:

$$H_{OE} = \frac{\sum_{t=1}^{n_t} E(\vec{x}_{best}(t), t)}{n_t} \tag{12}$$

where n_t is the total number of function evaluations and $E(\vec{x}_{best}(t), t)$ is the error of the best individual found since the last change in the environment (also known as the current error). Experiments were repeated 30 times to facilitate drawing statistically valid conclusions from the results. Mann-Whitney U tests were used to test statistical significance when comparing algorithms.

In cases where it is useful to consider the magnitude of improvements of one algorithm over the other (for example algorithm X over algorithm Y), the average percentage improvement (API) in offline error is used. The API is calculated using:

$$API = \frac{\sum_{a=1}^{n_{exp}} 100 \times PI_a}{n_{exp}} \tag{13}$$

with

$$PI_a = \begin{cases} \frac{H_{OE,a}(\mathrm{X})}{H_{OE,a}(\mathrm{Y})} - 1 \text{ if } H_{OE,a}(\mathrm{X}) < H_{OE,a}(\mathrm{Y}) \\ 1 - \frac{H_{OE,a}(\mathrm{Y})}{H_{OE,a}(\mathrm{X})} \text{ if } H_{OE,a}(\mathrm{X}) > H_{OE,a}(\mathrm{Y}) \end{cases} \tag{14}$$

where n_{exp} is the total number of experimental environments, and $H_{OE,a}(\mathrm{X})$ and $H_{OE,a}(\mathrm{Y})$ are the average offline errors of algorithm X and algorithm Y on experimental environment a, respectively. API is thus calculated by averaging the percentage improvement or deterioration over all experiments.

6. RESULTS

The purpose of the experimental work is two-fold. Firstly, the most effective approach to adapting the Brownian radius must be determined out of the four suggested variations (Section 6.1). Secondly, the identified approach must be evaluated to determine whether it does indeed constitute an improvement over CDE (Section 6.2).

6.1 Comparison of Variations

This section investigates the performance of each of the four self-adaptive Brownian radius algorithms in comparison with CDE. The standard set of environments was used to test each of the four possible approaches. The standard set was also varied for each of the change periods and numbers of dimensions listed in Table 3. Each approach was thus tested on a total of 648 environments.

Table 4 lists the results of the performance analysis comparing each of the four algorithms to CDE. The table gives the number of times that each of the algorithms performed statistically significantly better than CDE (**Nr Better**), the number of times that each algorithm performed significantly worse than CDE (**Nr Worse**), the difference between the number of times that each algorithm performed better and worse (**Diff**), and the average percentage improvement (**API**) over CDE.

Table 4: Performance of SA Brownian radius algorithms vs CDE

Algorithm	Nr Better	Nr Worse	Diff	API
SABrNor	241	283	-42	-4.41 %
SABrCau	241	269	-28	-4.20 %
ABrCDE	419	125	294	18.44 %
SABrCauRes	413	126	287	18.23 %

The analysis of the experimental results shows that SABrNor and SABrCau, the two algorithms that did not reset the $r_{dev}(t)$ value after changes in the environment, performed worse than CDE more often than they performed better. Furthermore, the average percentage improvement values for these algorithms were found to be negative. These two approaches thus degrade the performance of CDE.

Algorithms ABrCDE and SABrCauRes both yielded positive API values, indicating that, on average, their performances were superior to those of CDE. The number of times that these algorithms performed better than CDE was also more than the number of times that they performed worse. ABrCDE performed better than CDE slightly more often than SABrCauRes. The average percentage improvement of ABrCDE over CDE was also slightly higher than the average percentage improvement of SABrCauRes over CDE. The higher sup-population diversity offered by using the Cauchy distribution is thus not as beneficial as anticipated. The experimental results indicate that ABrCDE is the most effective of the four algorithms.

6.2 Comparison to CDE

ABrCDE was identified under the previous research question as the most effective of the algorithms that were investigated. The purpose of this section is to perform a comparative performance analysis of ABrCDE, with respect to CDE, on a wide range of experimental environments. The standard set of environments was varied over all combinations of change periods and dimensions given in Table 3. The standard set contains 54 environments which, multiplied by the five dimensional settings and the eight change period settings, gives a total of 2 160 environments on which each algorithm was evaluated.

The results were analysed by counting the number of times that ABrCDE was outperformed by CDE and the number of times that CDE outperformed ABrCDE. Only results that were statistically significantly different were considered. The performance analysis of ABrCDE compared to CDE is given in Tables 5 and 6. Each cell in the tables gives the number of cases in which ABrCDE performed better than CDE (indicated by $\uparrow$) and the number of cases in which CDE outperformed ABrCDE (indicated by $\downarrow$). The results were aggregated by function, change type and change severity for all the values of the change period and number of dimensions and totals are given to support the analysis of the data. The value in column **Max** indicates the maximum possible score that can be found in the cells in each row. Note that rows labelled **All**, which gives aggregated results per change period, do not give totals of values in each row as some results are duplicated in the stratifications of the different categories. For example, results for each function are summed over all change types, while the result for each change type is summed over all functions. Shaded cells indicate that ABrCDE performed better than CDE more often, while italics indicate that CDE performed better more often.

ABrCDE performed statistically significantly better than CDE on 1 076 environments and worse in 686 environments. ABrCDE performed better more often than CDE on change periods of more than 5 000 function evaluations. CDE performed better more often than ABrCDE in 100 dimensions.

The analysis indicates that the comparative performances of CDE and ABrCDE was dependent on the underlying function. ABrCDE was especially effective on the MPB functions, with the exception of experiments in 100 dimensions. The GDBG function F_5 proved particularly challenging to ABrCDE in dimensions below 50, where CDE performed better more often. Conversely, F_5 was one of only two GDBG functions in which ABrCDE performed better than CDE more often in 50 and 100 dimensions.

ABrCDE performed better than CDE more often than CDE performed better than ABrCDE. However, the CDE did perform better than ABrCDE in almost a third of all experimental environments. ABrCDE can therefore not definitively be described as better than CDE without considering the magnitude of the differences between the two algorithms.

The average percentage improvement (API), calculated as in equation (13), of ABrCDE over CDE was calculated to determine how much better, on average, ABrCDE is than CDE. The average percentage improvement of ABrCDE over CDE over all experiments was found to be 9.5%. The APIs per dimension were found to be 19.96%, 13.57%, 9.17%, 10.03% and -5.23% for 5, 10, 25, 50 and 100 dimensions respectively. ABrCDE thus consistently yielded substantial improvements with the exception of 100 dimensional environments. The APIs per change period were found to be 0.17%, 8.43%, 7.05%, 2.89%, 4.42%, 10.79%, 17.64% and 24.60% for change periods of 100, 500, 1 000, 5 000, 10 000, 25 000, 50 000 and 100 000 function evaluations, respectively. ABrCDE, on average, thus performed very similar to CDE at a change period of 100 function evaluations. The magnitude of the improvement over CDE increased to a considerable percentage as the change period was increased.

This research question investigated the comparative performance of ABrCDE and its predecessor algorithms. ABrCDE performed better more often than CDE on a large set of dynamic environments. This, and the fact that sizable percentage improvements of ABrCDE over CDE were found, leads to the conclusion that ABrCDE is a more effective algorithm for solving DOPs than CDE.

Table 5: ABrCDE vs CDE performance analysis - Part 1

Cp		100	500	1000	5000	10000	25000	50000	100000	Total
Set.	**Max**	**5 Dimensions**								
		MPB								
C_s 1	(2)	↑1 ↓0	↑1 ↓0	↑1 ↓0	↑1 ↓1	↑1 ↓0	↑1 ↓1	↑1 ↓0	↑1 ↓0	↑8 ↓2
5	(2)	↑2 ↓0	↑2 ↓0	↑2 ↓0	↑1 ↓0	↑1 ↓0	↑1 ↓0	↑1 ↓0	↑1 ↓0	↑11 ↓0
10	(2)	↑2 ↓0	↑2 ↓0	↑2 ↓0	↑2 ↓0	↑2 ↓0	↑2 ↓0	↑1 ↓0	↑1 ↓0	↑14 ↓0
20	(2)	↑2 ↓0	↑2 ↓0	↑2 ↓0	↑2 ↓0	↑2 ↓0	↑2 ↓0	↑2 ↓0	↑2 ↓0	↑16 ↓0
40	(2)	↑2 ↓0	↑2 ↓0	↑2 ↓0	↑2 ↓0	↑2 ↓0	↑2 ↓0	↑2 ↓0	↑2 ↓0	↑16 ↓0
80	(2)	↑2 ↓0	↑2 ↓0	↑2 ↓0	↑2 ↓0	↑2 ↓0	↑2 ↓0	↑2 ↓0	↑2 ↓0	↑16 ↓0
C	(6)	↑6 ↓0	↑5 ↓0	↑5 ↓0	↑4 ↓1	↑4 ↓0	↑4 ↓1	↑3 ↓0	↑3 ↓0	↑34 ↓2
S	(6)	↑5 ↓0	↑6 ↓0	↑6 ↓0	↑6 ↓0	↑6 ↓0	↑6 ↓0	↑6 ↓0	↑6 ↓0	↑47 ↓0
		GDBG								
F_{1a}	(6)	↑1 ↓1	*↑0 ↓3*	*↑0 ↓5*	↑2 ↓2	↑5 ↓0	↑6 ↓0	↑6 ↓0	↑6 ↓0	↑26 ↓11
F_{1b}	(6)	*↑2 ↓3*	*↑0 ↓4*	*↑0 ↓6*	↑3 ↓0	↑5 ↓0	↑6 ↓0	↑6 ↓0	↑6 ↓0	↑28 ↓13
F_2	(6)	↑0 ↓0	*↑0 ↓3*	*↑0 ↓6*	*↑0 ↓5*	↑4 ↓0	↑6 ↓0	↑6 ↓0	↑6 ↓0	↑22 ↓14
F_3	(6)	↑1 ↓1	↑5 ↓0	↑6 ↓0	↑6 ↓0	↑6 ↓0	↑6 ↓0	↑6 ↓0	↑6 ↓0	↑42 ↓1
F_4	(6)	*↑0 ↓2*	↑1 ↓1	*↑0 ↓4*	*↑0 ↓4*	*↑1 ↓3*	↑4 ↓0	↑6 ↓0	↑6 ↓0	↑18 ↓14
F_5	(6)	*↑0 ↓5*	*↑0 ↓6*	*↑0 ↓6*	*↑0 ↓6*	*↑0 ↓5*	↑3 ↓3	↑3 ↓2	↑3 ↓2	*↑9 ↓35*
F_6	(6)	↑3 ↓1	↑3 ↓1	↑2 ↓2	↑4 ↓1	↑5 ↓0	↑6 ↓0	↑6 ↓0	↑6 ↓0	↑35 ↓5
T_1	(7)	*↑0 ↓3*	*↑1 ↓6*	*↑1 ↓6*	*↑2 ↓5*	↑4 ↓1	↑7 ↓0	↑7 ↓0	↑7 ↓0	↑29 ↓21
T_2	(7)	↑3 ↓1	↑2 ↓2	*↑1 ↓6*	*↑2 ↓4*	↑4 ↓2	↑7 ↓0	↑7 ↓0	↑7 ↓0	↑33 ↓15
T_3	(7)	↑1 ↓1	↑3 ↓1	*↑2 ↓3*	*↑2 ↓3*	↑2 ↓2	↑5 ↓1	↑6 ↓1	↑6 ↓1	↑27 ↓13
T_4	(7)	*↑0 ↓6*	*↑1 ↓4*	*↑1 ↓5*	↑3 ↓2	↑6 ↓0	↑7 ↓0	↑7 ↓0	↑7 ↓0	↑32 ↓17
T_5	(7)	*↑0 ↓2*	*↑0 ↓2*	*↑1 ↓5*	*↑2 ↓3*	↑5 ↓2	↑5 ↓1	↑6 ↓1	↑6 ↓1	↑25 ↓17
T_6	(7)	↑3 ↓0	*↑2 ↓3*	*↑2 ↓4*	↑4 ↓1	↑5 ↓1	↑6 ↓1	↑6 ↓0	↑6 ↓0	↑34 ↓10
All	(54)	↑18 ↓13	↑20 ↓18	*↑19 ↓29*	↑25 ↓19	↑36 ↓8	↑47 ↓4	↑48 ↓2	↑48 ↓2	↑261 ↓95
Set.	**Max**	**10 Dimensions**								
		MPB								
C_s 1	(2)	↑2 ↓0	↑2 ↓0	↑2 ↓0	↑1 ↓0	↑1 ↓0	↑1 ↓0	↑1 ↓0	↑2 ↓0	↑12 ↓0
5	(2)	↑2 ↓0	↑2 ↓0	↑2 ↓0	↑1 ↓0	↑1 ↓0	↑1 ↓0	↑1 ↓0	↑1 ↓0	↑11 ↓0
10	(2)	↑2 ↓0	↑2 ↓0	↑2 ↓0	↑2 ↓0	↑1 ↓0	↑1 ↓0	↑1 ↓0	↑1 ↓0	↑12 ↓0
20	(2)	↑2 ↓0	↑2 ↓0	↑2 ↓0	↑2 ↓0	↑2 ↓0	↑2 ↓0	↑1 ↓0	↑1 ↓0	↑14 ↓0
40	(2)	↑2 ↓0	↑2 ↓0	↑2 ↓0	↑2 ↓0	↑2 ↓0	↑2 ↓0	↑2 ↓0	↑2 ↓0	↑16 ↓0
80	(2)	↑1 ↓0	↑2 ↓0	↑2 ↓0	↑2 ↓0	↑2 ↓0	↑2 ↓0	↑2 ↓0	↑2 ↓0	↑15 ↓0
C	(6)	↑5 ↓0	↑6 ↓0	↑6 ↓0	↑4 ↓0	↑3 ↓0	↑3 ↓0	↑2 ↓0	↑3 ↓0	↑32 ↓0
S	(6)	↑6 ↓0	↑6 ↓0	↑6 ↓0	↑6 ↓0	↑6 ↓0	↑6 ↓0	↑6 ↓0	↑6 ↓0	↑48 ↓0
		GDBG								
F_{1a}	(6)	↑1 ↓1	↑2 ↓2	*↑1 ↓2*	↑3 ↓2	↑6 ↓0	↑5 ↓0	↑6 ↓0	↑6 ↓0	↑30 ↓7
F_{1b}	(6)	↑1 ↓1	*↑1 ↓2*	*↑1 ↓3*	↑2 ↓0	↑5 ↓0	↑6 ↓0	↑6 ↓0	↑6 ↓0	↑28 ↓6
F_2	(6)	*↑0 ↓3*	↑2 ↓2	*↑0 ↓3*	*↑2 ↓3*	↑4 ↓1	↑6 ↓0	↑6 ↓0	↑6 ↓0	↑26 ↓12
F_3	(6)	*↑0 ↓2*	↑6 ↓0	↑3 ↓0	↑6 ↓0	↑6 ↓0	↑6 ↓0	↑6 ↓0	↑6 ↓0	↑39 ↓2
F_4	(6)	*↑0 ↓2*	*↑1 ↓2*	*↑0 ↓3*	*↑1 ↓3*	↑3 ↓2	↑6 ↓0	↑6 ↓0	↑6 ↓0	↑23 ↓12
F_5	(6)	*↑2 ↓3*	*↑0 ↓6*	*↑0 ↓6*	*↑0 ↓6*	*↑0 ↓6*	*↑0 ↓6*	*↑0 ↓6*	*↑0 ↓4*	*↑2 ↓43*
F_6	(6)	↑0 ↓0	↑3 ↓1	↑3 ↓2	↑4 ↓1	↑4 ↓1	↑6 ↓0	↑6 ↓0	↑6 ↓0	↑32 ↓5
T_1	(7)	*↑0 ↓2*	*↑1 ↓6*	*↑1 ↓6*	*↑1 ↓5*	*↑3 ↓4*	↑6 ↓1	↑6 ↓1	↑6 ↓0	*↑24 ↓25*
T_2	(7)	↑0 ↓0	↑2 ↓1	*↑1 ↓3*	*↑2 ↓4*	↑5 ↓1	↑6 ↓1	↑6 ↓1	↑6 ↓0	↑28 ↓11
T_3	(7)	↑1 ↓1	↑3 ↓1	↑1 ↓1	↑4 ↓1	↑5 ↓1	↑5 ↓1	↑6 ↓1	↑6 ↓1	↑31 ↓8
T_4	(7)	*↑0 ↓6*	*↑1 ↓5*	*↑1 ↓6*	*↑2 ↓3*	↑3 ↓2	↑6 ↓1	↑6 ↓1	↑6 ↓1	↑25 ↓25
T_5	(7)	*↑0 ↓3*	↑3 ↓1	↑3 ↓1	↑5 ↓1	↑6 ↓1	↑6 ↓1	↑6 ↓1	↑6 ↓1	↑35 ↓10
T_6	(7)	↑3 ↓0	↑5 ↓1	*↑1 ↓2*	↑4 ↓1	↑6 ↓1	↑6 ↓1	↑6 ↓1	↑6 ↓1	↑37 ↓8
All	(54)	↑15 ↓12	↑27 ↓15	↑20 ↓19	↑28 ↓15	↑37 ↓10	↑44 ↓6	↑44 ↓6	↑45 ↓4	↑260 ↓87
Set.	**Max**	**25 Dimensions**								
		MPB								
C_s 1	(2)	↑1 ↓0	↑2 ↓0	↑2 ↓0	↑2 ↓0	↑1 ↓0	↑1 ↓0	↑2 ↓0	↑1 ↓0	↑12 ↓0
5	(2)	↑1 ↓0	↑2 ↓0	↑2 ↓0	↑1 ↓0	↑1 ↓1	↑1 ↓1	↑1 ↓0	↑1 ↓0	↑10 ↓2
10	(2)	↑1 ↓0	↑2 ↓0	↑2 ↓0	↑1 ↓1	↑1 ↓1	↑1 ↓1	↑1 ↓0	↑1 ↓0	↑10 ↓3
20	(2)	↑1 ↓0	↑2 ↓0	↑2 ↓0	↑1 ↓0	↑1 ↓1	↑1 ↓1	↑1 ↓0	↑1 ↓0	↑10 ↓2
40	(2)	↑1 ↓0	↑2 ↓0	↑2 ↓0	↑2 ↓0	↑2 ↓0	↑1 ↓0	↑1 ↓0	↑1 ↓0	↑12 ↓0
80	(2)	*↑0 ↓2*	↑2 ↓0	↑2 ↓0	↑2 ↓0	↑2 ↓0	↑2 ↓0	↑2 ↓0	↑2 ↓0	↑14 ↓2
C	(6)	*↑0 ↓1*	↑6 ↓0	↑6 ↓0	↑3 ↓1	*↑2 ↓3*	*↑1 ↓3*	↑2 ↓0	↑1 ↓0	↑21 ↓8
S	(6)	↑5 ↓1	↑6 ↓0	↑6 ↓0	↑6 ↓0	↑6 ↓0	↑6 ↓0	↑6 ↓0	↑6 ↓0	↑47 ↓1
		GDBG								
F_{1a}	(6)	*↑0 ↓4*	*↑0 ↓3*	*↑0 ↓3*	*↑1 ↓2*	↑3 ↓0	↑5 ↓0	↑5 ↓0	↑6 ↓0	↑20 ↓12
F_{1b}	(6)	*↑0 ↓5*	*↑0 ↓3*	*↑1 ↓3*	*↑1 ↓2*	↑2 ↓0	↑5 ↓0	↑6 ↓0	↑6 ↓0	↑21 ↓13
F_2	(6)	*↑0 ↓6*	*↑0 ↓2*	*↑0 ↓3*	*↑0 ↓6*	*↑0 ↓1*	↑6 ↓0	↑6 ↓0	↑6 ↓0	↑18 ↓18
F_3	(6)	*↑0 ↓6*	↑5 ↓0	*↑1 ↓3*	↑3 ↓1	↑4 ↓0	↑4 ↓0	↑5 ↓0	↑4 ↓0	↑26 ↓10
F_4	(6)	*↑0 ↓6*	*↑0 ↓2*	*↑0 ↓2*	*↑0 ↓4*	*↑0 ↓2*	↑6 ↓0	↑6 ↓0	↑6 ↓0	↑18 ↓16
F_5	(6)	↑6 ↓0	↑4 ↓2	↑3 ↓3	*↑0 ↓6*	*↑0 ↓6*	*↑0 ↓6*	*↑0 ↓6*	*↑0 ↓6*	*↑13 ↓35*
F_6	(6)	*↑0 ↓4*	↑2 ↓0	↑3 ↓2	↑3 ↓1	↑3 ↓0	↑5 ↓1	↑5 ↓1	↑5 ↓1	↑26 ↓10
T_1	(7)	*↑1 ↓3*	*↑1 ↓5*	*↑1 ↓6*	*↑1 ↓6*	↑1 ↓1	↑6 ↓1	↑6 ↓1	↑6 ↓1	*↑23 ↓24*
T_2	(7)	*↑1 ↓6*	↑3 ↓0	*↑1 ↓5*	*↑0 ↓5*	*↑0 ↓2*	↑5 ↓2	↑5 ↓2	↑5 ↓2	*↑20 ↓24*
T_3	(7)	*↑1 ↓5*	↑3 ↓1	↑2 ↓1	*↑1 ↓4*	↑1 ↓1	↑3 ↓1	↑4 ↓1	↑6 ↓1	↑21 ↓15
T_4	(7)	*↑1 ↓5*	*↑1 ↓4*	*↑0 ↓5*	*↑1 ↓3*	↑3 ↓3	↑6 ↓1	↑6 ↓1	↑6 ↓1	↑24 ↓23
T_5	(7)	*↑1 ↓6*	↑2 ↓2	↑2 ↓1	↑4 ↓2	↑4 ↓1	↑6 ↓1	↑6 ↓1	↑5 ↓1	↑30 ↓15
T_6	(7)	*↑1 ↓6*	↑1 ↓0	↑2 ↓1	*↑1 ↓2*	↑3 ↓1	↑5 ↓1	↑6 ↓1	↑5 ↓1	↑24 ↓13
All	(54)	*↑11 ↓33*	↑23 ↓12	↑20 ↓19	*↑17 ↓23*	↑20 ↓12	↑38 ↓10	↑41 ↓7	↑40 ↓7	↑210 ↓123

Table 6: ABrCDE vs CDE performance analysis - Part 2

Cp		100	500	1000	5000	10000	25000	50000	100000	Total
Set.	Max	50 Dimensions								
		MPB								
C_s 1	(2)	↑1 ↓1	↑2 ↓0	↑2 ↓0	↑2 ↓0	↑1 ↓0	↑1 ↓0	↑2 ↓0	↑2 ↓0	↑13 ↓1
5	(2)	↑0 ↓1	↑2 ↓0	↑2 ↓0	↑1 ↓0	↑1 ↓1	↑1 ↓1	↑1 ↓0	↑1 ↓0	↑9 ↓3
10	(2)	↑0 ↓1	↑2 ↓0	↑2 ↓0	↑1 ↓1	↑1 ↓1	↑1 ↓1	↑1 ↓1	↑1 ↓0	↑9 ↓5
20	(2)	↑1 ↓1	↑2 ↓0	↑2 ↓0	↑1 ↓0	↑1 ↓1	↑1 ↓1	↑1 ↓1	↑1 ↓0	↑10 ↓4
40	(2)	↑0 ↓0	↑2 ↓0	↑2 ↓0	↑2 ↓0	↑1 ↓0	↑1 ↓1	↑1 ↓1	↑1 ↓0	↑10 ↓2
80	(2)	↑0 ↓2	↑2 ↓0	↑2 ↓0	↑2 ↓0	↑2 ↓0	↑1 ↓0	↑1 ↓1	↑2 ↓0	↑12 ↓3
C	(6)	↑0 ↓5	↑6 ↓0	↑6 ↓0	↑3 ↓1	↑1 ↓3	↑0 ↓4	↑1 ↓4	↑2 ↓0	↑19 ↓17
S	(6)	↑2 ↓1	↑6 ↓0	↑6 ↓0	↑6 ↓0	↑6 ↓0	↑6 ↓0	↑6 ↓0	↑6 ↓0	↑44 ↓1
		GDBG								
F_{1a}	(6)	↑0 ↓3	↑0 ↓5	↑0 ↓5	↑0 ↓4	↑2 ↓1	↑5 ↓0	↑6 ↓0	↑6 ↓0	↑19 ↓18
F_{1b}	(6)	↑0 ↓6	↑0 ↓5	↑0 ↓5	↑0 ↓6	↑2 ↓2	↑6 ↓0	↑6 ↓0	↑6 ↓0	↑20 ↓24
F_2	(6)	↑0 ↓6	↑0 ↓6	↑1 ↓3	↑0 ↓5	↑0 ↓6	↑4 ↓0	↑5 ↓0	↑5 ↓0	↑15 ↓26
F_3	(6)	↑0 ↓6	↑3 ↓0	↑0 ↓3	↑1 ↓4	↑1 ↓3	↑1 ↓0	↑2 ↓2	↑1 ↓2	↑9 ↓20
F_4	(6)	↑0 ↓6	↑0 ↓5	↑0 ↓4	↑0 ↓5	↑0 ↓5	↑4 ↓0	↑6 ↓0	↑5 ↓0	↑15 ↓25
F_5	(6)	↑6 ↓0	↑6 ↓0	↑6 ↓0	↑3 ↓3	↑1 ↓3	↑1 ↓4	↑1 ↓5	↑1 ↓5	↑25 ↓20
F_6	(6)	↑0 ↓6	↑2 ↓0	↑1 ↓1	↑4 ↓1	↑4 ↓0	↑5 ↓1	↑5 ↓1	↑4 ↓1	↑25 ↓11
T_1	(7)	↑1 ↓5	↑3 ↓4	↑1 ↓4	↑1 ↓6	↑1 ↓4	↑6 ↓1	↑6 ↓1	↑6 ↓1	↑25 ↓26
T_2	(7)	↑1 ↓5	↑2 ↓4	↑2 ↓3	↑1 ↓6	↑0 ↓6	↑4 ↓2	↑4 ↓2	↑4 ↓2	↑18 ↓30
T_3	(7)	↑1 ↓5	↑1 ↓2	↑1 ↓2	↑2 ↓3	↑1 ↓3	↑2 ↓1	↑5 ↓2	↑4 ↓2	↑17 ↓20
T_4	(7)	↑1 ↓6	↑2 ↓4	↑1 ↓5	↑1 ↓6	↑3 ↓3	↑5 ↓1	↑5 ↓2	↑5 ↓1	↑23 ↓28
T_5	(7)	↑1 ↓6	↑2 ↓3	↑2 ↓3	↑1 ↓2	↑3 ↓2	↑3 ↓0	↑5 ↓1	↑3 ↓1	↑20 ↓18
T_6	(7)	↑1 ↓6	↑1 ↓4	↑1 ↓4	↑2 ↓5	↑2 ↓2	↑6 ↓0	↑6 ↓0	↑6 ↓1	↑25 ↓22
All	(54)	↑8 ↓39	↑23 ↓21	↑20 ↓21	↑17 ↓29	↑17 ↓23	↑32 ↓9	↑38 ↓12	↑36 ↓8	↑191 ↓162
Set.	Max	100 Dimensions								
		MPB								
C_s 1	(2)	↑0 ↓2	↑1 ↓1	↑1 ↓1	↑0 ↓1	↑1 ↓1	↑0 ↓1	↑0 ↓1	↑1 ↓1	↑4 ↓9
5	(2)	↑0 ↓2	↑1 ↓1	↑1 ↓1	↑0 ↓1	↑0 ↓2	↑0 ↓2	↑0 ↓2	↑0 ↓1	↑2 ↓12
10	(2)	↑0 ↓2	↑1 ↓1	↑1 ↓1	↑0 ↓2	↑0 ↓2	↑0 ↓2	↑0 ↓2	↑0 ↓2	↑2 ↓14
20	(2)	↑0 ↓1	↑1 ↓1	↑1 ↓1	↑0 ↓2	↑0 ↓2	↑0 ↓2	↑0 ↓2	↑0 ↓2	↑2 ↓13
40	(2)	↑0 ↓2	↑1 ↓1	↑1 ↓1	↑0 ↓1	↑0 ↓2	↑0 ↓2	↑0 ↓2	↑0 ↓2	↑2 ↓13
80	(2)	↑0 ↓2	↑1 ↓1	↑1 ↓0	↑1 ↓1	↑1 ↓1	↑0 ↓1	↑0 ↓2	↑0 ↓2	↑4 ↓10
C	(6)	↑0 ↓5	↑6 ↓0	↑6 ↓0	↑1 ↓2	↑2 ↓4	↑0 ↓4	↑0 ↓5	↑1 ↓4	↑16 ↓24
S	(6)	↑0 ↓6	↑0 ↓6	↑0 ↓5	↑0 ↓6	↑0 ↓6	↑0 ↓6	↑0 ↓6	↑0 ↓6	↑0 ↓47
		GDBG								
F_{1a}	(6)	↑0 ↓5	↑0 ↓5	↑0 ↓6	↑0 ↓5	↑0 ↓6	↑5 ↓0	↑5 ↓0	↑6 ↓0	↑16 ↓27
F_{1b}	(6)	↑0 ↓5	↑0 ↓6	↑0 ↓6	↑0 ↓6	↑0 ↓5	↑5 ↓0	↑6 ↓0	↑6 ↓0	↑17 ↓28
F_2	(6)	↑0 ↓6	↑0 ↓6	↑0 ↓6	↑1 ↓4	↑0 ↓4	↑2 ↓3	↑5 ↓0	↑5 ↓0	↑13 ↓29
F_3	(6)	↑0 ↓6	↑3 ↓0	↑0 ↓5	↑0 ↓6	↑0 ↓3	↑1 ↓3	↑3 ↓0	↑4 ↓0	↑11 ↓23
F_4	(6)	↑0 ↓6	↑0 ↓6	↑0 ↓5	↑1 ↓4	↑0 ↓4	↑2 ↓3	↑4 ↓0	↑5 ↓0	↑12 ↓28
F_5	(6)	↑6 ↓0	↑6 ↓0	↑6 ↓0	↑6 ↓0	↑5 ↓0	↑5 ↓0	↑5 ↓1	↑4 ↓2	↑43 ↓3
F_6	(6)	↑0 ↓6	↑3 ↓2	↑3 ↓2	↑2 ↓0	↑4 ↓0	↑6 ↓0	↑4 ↓0	↑4 ↓0	↑26 ↓10
T_1	(7)	↑1 ↓5	↑3 ↓4	↑2 ↓5	↑1 ↓5	↑1 ↓4	↑6 ↓0	↑7 ↓0	↑7 ↓0	↑28 ↓23
T_2	(7)	↑1 ↓6	↑2 ↓4	↑1 ↓5	↑2 ↓4	↑1 ↓5	↑3 ↓1	↑5 ↓1	↑5 ↓1	↑20 ↓27
T_3	(7)	↑1 ↓5	↑1 ↓4	↑1 ↓6	↑1 ↓3	↑1 ↓2	↑2 ↓3	↑3 ↓0	↑6 ↓0	↑16 ↓23
T_4	(7)	↑1 ↓6	↑2 ↓4	↑2 ↓5	↑2 ↓5	↑2 ↓5	↑6 ↓1	↑6 ↓0	↑5 ↓1	↑26 ↓27
T_5	(7)	↑1 ↓6	↑3 ↓4	↑2 ↓3	↑3 ↓3	↑2 ↓2	↑5 ↓2	↑5 ↓0	↑5 ↓0	↑26 ↓20
T_6	(7)	↑1 ↓6	↑1 ↓5	↑1 ↓6	↑1 ↓5	↑2 ↓4	↑4 ↓2	↑6 ↓0	↑6 ↓0	↑22 ↓28
All	(54)	↑6 ↓45	↑18 ↓31	↑15 ↓35	↑11 ↓33	↑11 ↓32	↑26 ↓19	↑32 ↓12	↑35 ↓12	↑154 ↓219
Set.	Max	All Dimensions								
		MPB								
C_s 1	(10)	↑5 ↓3	↑8 ↓1	↑8 ↓1	↑6 ↓2	↑5 ↓1	↑4 ↓2	↑6 ↓1	↑7 ↓1	↑49 ↓12
5	(10)	↑5 ↓3	↑9 ↓1	↑9 ↓1	↑4 ↓1	↑4 ↓4	↑4 ↓4	↑4 ↓2	↑4 ↓1	↑43 ↓17
10	(10)	↑5 ↓3	↑9 ↓1	↑9 ↓1	↑6 ↓4	↑5 ↓4	↑5 ↓4	↑4 ↓3	↑4 ↓2	↑47 ↓22
20	(10)	↑6 ↓2	↑9 ↓1	↑9 ↓1	↑6 ↓2	↑6 ↓4	↑6 ↓4	↑5 ↓3	↑5 ↓2	↑52 ↓19
40	(10)	↑5 ↓2	↑9 ↓1	↑9 ↓1	↑8 ↓1	↑7 ↓2	↑6 ↓3	↑6 ↓3	↑6 ↓2	↑56 ↓15
80	(10)	↑3 ↓6	↑9 ↓1	↑9 ↓0	↑9 ↓1	↑9 ↓1	↑7 ↓1	↑7 ↓3	↑8 ↓2	↑61 ↓15
C	(30)	↑11 ↓11	↑29 ↓0	↑29 ↓0	↑15 ↓5	↑12 ↓10	↑8 ↓12	↑8 ↓9	↑10 ↓4	↑122 ↓51
S	(30)	↑18 ↓8	↑24 ↓6	↑24 ↓5	↑24 ↓6	↑24 ↓6	↑24 ↓6	↑24 ↓6	↑24 ↓6	↑186 ↓49
		GDBG								
F_{1a}	(30)	↑2 ↓14	↑2 ↓18	↑1 ↓21	↑6 ↓15	↑16 ↓7	↑26 ↓0	↑28 ↓0	↑30 ↓0	↑111 ↓75
F_{1b}	(30)	↑3 ↓20	↑1 ↓20	↑2 ↓23	↑6 ↓14	↑14 ↓7	↑28 ↓0	↑30 ↓0	↑30 ↓0	↑114 ↓84
F_2	(30)	↑0 ↓21	↑2 ↓19	↑1 ↓21	↑3 ↓23	↑8 ↓12	↑24 ↓3	↑28 ↓0	↑28 ↓0	↑94 ↓99
F_3	(30)	↑1 ↓21	↑22 ↓0	↑10 ↓11	↑16 ↓11	↑17 ↓6	↑18 ↓3	↑22 ↓2	↑21 ↓2	↑127 ↓56
F_4	(30)	↑0 ↓22	↑2 ↓16	↑0 ↓18	↑2 ↓20	↑4 ↓16	↑22 ↓3	↑28 ↓0	↑28 ↓0	↑86 ↓95
F_5	(30)	↑20 ↓8	↑16 ↓14	↑15 ↓15	↑9 ↓21	↑6 ↓20	↑9 ↓19	↑9 ↓20	↑8 ↓19	↑92 ↓136
F_6	(30)	↑3 ↓17	↑13 ↓4	↑12 ↓9	↑17 ↓4	↑20 ↓1	↑28 ↓2	↑26 ↓2	↑25 ↓2	↑144 ↓41
T_1	(35)	↑3 ↓18	↑9 ↓25	↑6 ↓27	↑6 ↓27	↑10 ↓14	↑31 ↓3	↑32 ↓3	↑32 ↓2	↑129 ↓119
T_2	(35)	↑6 ↓18	↑11 ↓11	↑6 ↓22	↑7 ↓23	↑10 ↓16	↑25 ↓6	↑27 ↓6	↑27 ↓5	↑119 ↓107
T_3	(35)	↑5 ↓17	↑11 ↓9	↑7 ↓13	↑10 ↓14	↑10 ↓9	↑17 ↓7	↑24 ↓5	↑28 ↓5	↑112 ↓79
T_4	(35)	↑3 ↓29	↑7 ↓21	↑5 ↓26	↑9 ↓19	↑17 ↓13	↑30 ↓4	↑30 ↓4	↑29 ↓4	↑130 ↓120
T_5	(35)	↑3 ↓23	↑10 ↓12	↑10 ↓13	↑15 ↓11	↑20 ↓8	↑25 ↓5	↑28 ↓4	↑25 ↓4	↑136 ↓80
T_6	(35)	↑9 ↓18	↑10 ↓13	↑7 ↓17	↑12 ↓14	↑18 ↓9	↑27 ↓5	↑30 ↓2	↑29 ↓3	↑142 ↓81
All	(270)	↑58 ↓142	↑111 ↓97	↑94 ↓123	↑98 ↓119	↑121 ↓85	↑187 ↓48	↑203 ↓39	↑204 ↓33	↑1076 ↓686

7. CONVERGENCE PROFILE

This section performs a deeper analysis of the functioning ABrCDE in terms of its convergence profile in comparison with CDE. The algorithms are compared in terms of offline and current errors, and the diversity of the algorithms is compared in terms of overall diversity and average diversity per sub-population. Diversity was calculated as the mean Euclidean distance of each individual to the average location of all individuals, scaled by the longest diagonal in the search space. All the figures in this section present results averaged over 30 repeats of each experiment.

Figure 1 gives the offline and current errors of CDE and ABrCDE during the first 10 changes in the environment on the Scenario 2 settings of the MPB. The current error of ABrCDE decreased at a faster rate, and reached a lower value than that of CDE during the period before the first change in the environment. The fast initial decrease in current error resulted in considerably lower initial offline errors for ABrCDE. ABrCDE is thus more effective at initially discovering optima in the environment. The performance difference between the algorithms became less noticeable (but still present) later in the optimisation process, as neither of the algorithms clearly performed better than the other (in terms of current error) after the fifth change in the environment.

A problem with the CDE algorithm is that, due to its greedy approach to finding a good optimum, the global optimum is sometimes not found. This yields a convergence profile for the current error that decreases sharply initially but then flattens out without reaching an error of zero. ABrCDE did not suffer from this problem, as can be seen in Figure 2, which gives the same information as Figure 1, but with a change period of 100 000 function evaluations. The ABrCDE generally reached lower current errors than CDE. This explains the trend where ABrCDE performed better than CDE at high change periods, which was found in Section 6.2.

Figure 3 gives the diversity and average sub-population diversity of CDE and ABrCDE during the first 10 changes in the environment on the Scenario 2 settings of the MPB. ABrCDE's diversity profile shows clear reactions to the changes in the environment. The average sub-population diversity of ABrCDE increased dramatically after a change in the environment, and was mirrored by a smaller increase in overall diversity. This increase in diversity is caused by resetting the value from which the Brownian radius is selected, when a change in the environment occurs. The Brownian individuals which are created using a large Brownian radius are typically located at a large Euclidean distance from the best individuals in the sub-populations, which results in high diversity. The average sub-population diversity of ABrCDE dropped sharply after a change in the environment, but always maintained a higher value than that of CDE. ABrCDE thus succeeds in its goal of providing high diversity when changes in the environment occurs, thereby improving exploration, and less diversity later to improve exploitation.

The following section compares ABrCDE to established algorithms, using several change detection strategies on variations of the MPB Scenario 2 which are commonly used by researchers to evaluate their algorithms.

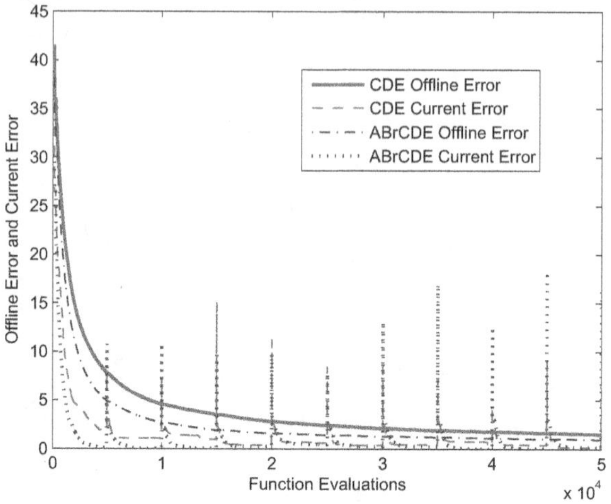

Figure 1: Offline and current errors of CDE and ABrCDE on the MPB with the Scenario 2 settings.

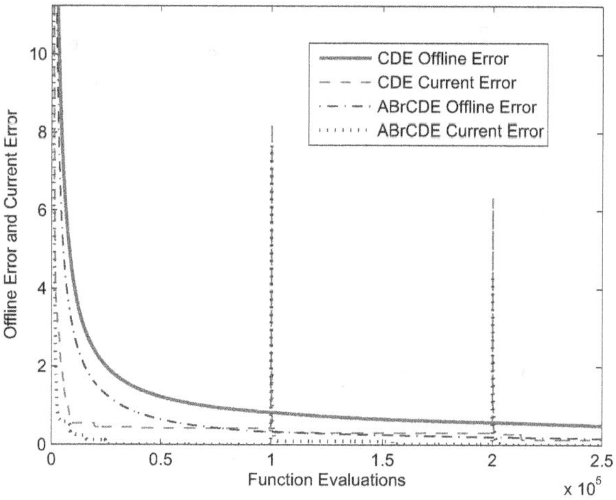

Figure 2: Offline and current errors of CDE and ABrCDE on the MPB using the Scenario 2 settings with a change period of 100 000.

8. ABRCDE COMPARED TO OTHER ALGORITHMS

An important factor to consider when comparing two algorithms is the chosen change detection strategy. Care must be taken to ensure that the compared algorithms employ the same change detection strategy so as to not bias result towards one of the algorithms. Four detection strategies were selected for incorporation into ABrCDE. The first, Det_{best}, re-evaluates the best individual over all sub-populations, after each generation. Det_{best} thus uses a single function evaluation per generation. The second change detection strategy, Det_{local}, re-evaluates the best individual in each sub-population after each generation. Det_{local} thus uses n_k function evaluations per generation, where n_k is the number of sub-populations.

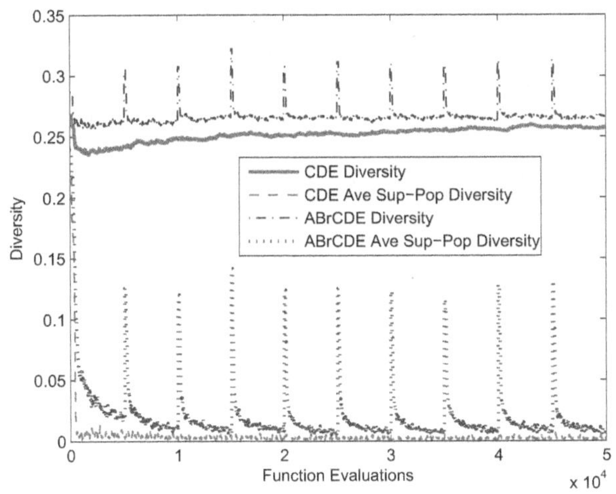

Figure 3: Diversity profiles of CDE and ABrCDE on the MPB with the Scenario 2 settings.

The Det_{best} and Det_{local} change detection strategies function differently on ABrCDE than on standard multi-population algorithms (like DynDE) where all sub-populations are evolved per generation. The third and fourth change detection strategies are variations of Det_{best} and Det_{local} where the detection is not performed in each generation, but once every n_k generations. These strategies are denoted by Det_{n_k-best} and $Det_{n_k-local}$. Detecting changes once every n_k generations ensures that the number of function evaluations used by these strategies in ABrCDE would, respectively, be similar to the number of function evaluations used by Det_{best} and Det_{local} in standard multi-population algorithms.

Table 7 lists the offline errors of ABrCDE using an automatic detection strategy (which uses no function evaluations and always works perfectly), the Det_{best} strategy, the Det_{local} strategy, the Det_{n_k-best} strategy, and the $Det_{n_k-local}$ strategy. Cases where ABrCDE performed statistically significantly worse when using a detection strategy are printed in italics. The Det_{local} detection strategy caused ABrCDE to perform worse in several instances, but the results from the other detection strategies differed from the automatic detection strategy in a minority of cases.

Table 8 lists the published results of 14 of the algorithms that were discussed in Section 2 on the variations of the MPB Scenario 2. The 95% confidence intervals were calculated from the reported standard errors or standard deviations in cases where the confidence interval was not reported. Each result was compared to the relevant ABrCDE result to determine which is better. Results were considered to be similar if the confidence intervals overlapped, i.e. neither algorithm was considered better than the other. Offline errors that are higher than ABrCDE's (i.e. ABrCDE performed better) are printed in boldface in shaded cells. Offline errors that are lower than the corresponding ABrCDE results are printed in italics.

The comparison of ABrCDE with each of the tabulated algorithms is briefly discussed below:

MMEO: [37] MMEO algorithm detects changes in the fitness landscape by re-evaluating all the best solutions and is thus comparable to the Det_{local} and $Det_{n_k-local}$ detection strategies. MMEO yielded a lower offline error than ABrCDE on experiments with change severity of 1, but confidence intervals of the two algorithms overlap (when comparing with $Det_{n_k-local}$). Therefore, MMEO cannot conclusively be considered superior to ABrCDE. Change severities of 2, 4 and 6 yielded MMEO results that are clearly superior to ABrCDE's results. ABrCDE performed worse than MMEO on experiments with various numbers of peaks, with the exception of the experiment using one peak, where the confidence intervals overlapped. The same comparative performace was observed for **HJEO** [35] and **LSEO** [36].

CESO: [31] CESO detects changes by re-evaluating the best individual in the DE population and is thus comparable to the Det_{best} detection strategy. ABrCDE performed better than CESO on experiments with a change severity of 1 and 2, but CESO performed better than ABrCDE on experiments with change severities of 4, and 6. CESO performed better than ABrCDE on all settings of number of peaks, except 10.

ESCA: [32] ABrCDE performed better than ESCA on a change severity of 1, but worse on change severities of 4 and 6. Overlapping confidence intervals were found for a change severity of 2. ESCA performed better than ABrCDE on all settings of number of peaks, except 10.

MPSO: [6] MPSO uses the Det_{local} detection strategy, and is consequently comparable to ABrCDE using the $Det_{n_k-local}$ detection strategy. ABrCDE performed better than MPSO on all change severity experiments. ABrCDE performed better than MPSO when one peak was used, but worse in experiments with 50, 100 and 200 peaks. Overlapping confidence intervals were found when using 5, 20, 30 and 40 peaks.

SPSO: [30] SPSO detects changes by re-evaluating the five best particles, and is thus comparable to ABrCDE using the $Det_{n_k-local}$ strategy. Overlapping confidence intervals were found when five peaks were used, but ABrCDE performed better than SPSO in all other reported cases.

CPSO: [52] CPSO detects changes using the Det_{best} detection strategy and is thus roughly comparable to ABrCDE using the Det_{n_k-best} strategy. ABrCDE performed better than CPSO on a change severity of 1. CPSO performed better than ABrCDE with change severities of 2, 4 and 6. ABrCDE performed better than CPSO when a change period of 10 000 was used, but as [52] did not report the confidence interval for this experiment, ABrCDE's superiority cannot be confirmed for this experiment. CPSO performed better than ABrCDE on all settings of number of peaks, except 10.

MPSOD: [39] MPSOD is compared to ABrCDE using the $Det_{n_k-local}$ detection strategy. Overlapping confidence intervals were found for a change severity of 1 and 2. MPSOD performed better than ABrCDE when using a change period of 1000.

HMSO: [25] HMSO uses the Det_{best} change detection strategy, and, as not all sub-populations are evolved per generation, it can be compared to ABrCDE using Det_{best}. ABr-

Table 7: ABrCDE using various detection strategies

Settings	Automatic	Det_{best}	p-val	Det_{local}	p-val	Det_{n_k-best}	p-val	$Det_{n_k-local}$	p-val
Cs 1	0.91 ± 0.06	0.97 ± 0.08	0.343	*1.19 ± 0.07*	0.000	0.89 ± 0.05	0.866	1.00 ± 0.08	0.187
Cs 2	1.49 ± 0.09	1.58 ± 0.09	0.182	*2.07 ± 0.12*	0.000	1.67 ± 0.15	0.164	1.48 ± 0.13	0.542
Cs 4	2.63 ± 0.17	2.57 ± 0.15	0.878	*3.45 ± 0.23*	0.000	2.58 ± 0.14	0.843	2.56 ± 0.16	0.775
Cs 6	3.27 ± 0.20	*3.63 ± 0.25*	0.017	*4.57 ± 0.30*	0.000	*3.57 ± 0.18*	0.003	*3.61 ± 0.26*	0.031
Cp 500	7.13 ± 0.31	6.91 ± 0.34	0.423	*8.21 ± 0.41*	0.000	6.97 ± 0.28	0.406	*7.66 ± 0.34*	0.040
Cp 1000	3.87 ± 0.12	3.92 ± 0.13	0.562	*4.88 ± 0.20*	0.000	*4.26 ± 0.19*	0.002	*4.09 ± 0.14*	0.023
Cp 2500	1.70 ± 0.08	*1.85 ± 0.08*	0.013	*2.46 ± 0.13*	0.000	1.79 ± 0.12	0.260	*1.89 ± 0.08*	0.002
Cp 10000	0.48 ± 0.05	0.53 ± 0.11	0.832	*0.64 ± 0.06*	0.000	0.50 ± 0.07	0.924	0.56 ± 0.12	0.797
n_p 1	4.23 ± 0.45	4.04 ± 0.52	0.552	*5.31 ± 0.65*	0.014	3.91 ± 0.52	0.279	4.21 ± 0.50	0.936
n_p 5	2.04 ± 0.13	2.08 ± 0.12	0.686	*2.66 ± 0.19*	0.000	2.07 ± 0.13	0.612	2.00 ± 0.14	0.764
n_p 20	2.34 ± 0.26	2.28 ± 0.19	0.741	2.48 ± 0.21	0.182	2.53 ± 0.19	0.070	2.27 ± 0.20	0.971
n_p 30	2.78 ± 0.20	2.58 ± 0.20	0.159	2.86 ± 0.18	0.532	2.78 ± 0.18	0.889	2.60 ± 0.20	0.177
n_p 40	2.67 ± 0.18	2.69 ± 0.12	0.775	2.96 ± 0.21	0.077	2.92 ± 0.21	0.106	2.90 ± 0.21	0.177
n_p 50	2.93 ± 0.22	2.98 ± 0.18	0.708	3.15 ± 0.17	0.085	2.72 ± 0.17	0.177	2.92 ± 0.16	0.820
n_p 100	2.79 ± 0.11	2.89 ± 0.11	0.224	*3.16 ± 0.17*	0.002	2.83 ± 0.09	0.562	2.86 ± 0.16	0.866
n_p 200	2.58 ± 0.14	2.60 ± 0.11	0.866	*2.80 ± 0.13*	0.034	2.62 ± 0.11	0.562	2.62 ± 0.11	0.592

Table 8: Reported offline errors of various algorithms on variations of Scenario 2 of the MPB

	MMEO	HJEO	LSEO	CESO	ESCA	MPSO	SPSO
Cs 1	0.66 ± 0.39	*0.25 ± 0.20*	*0.25 ± 0.16*	**1.38 ± 0.04**	**1.53 ± 0.02**	**1.75 ± 0.12**	N/A
Cs 2	*0.86 ± 0.41*	*0.52 ± 0.27*	*0.47 ± 0.24*	**1.78 ± 0.04**	1.57 ± 0.02	**2.4 ± 0.12**	N/A
Cs 4	*0.97 ± 0.41*	*0.64 ± 0.31*	*0.53 ± 0.25*	*2.23 ± 0.10*	1.72 ± 0.06	**3.59 ± 0.20**	N/A
Cs 6	*1.09 ± 0.43*	*0.9 ± 0.33*	*0.77 ± 0.47*	*2.74 ± 0.20*	1.79 ± 0.06	**4.79 ± 0.20**	N/A
n_p 1	11.30 ± 6.98	7.08 ± 3.90	7.47 ± 3.88	*1.04 ± 0.00*	*0.98 ± 0.00*	**5.07 ± 0.33**	N/A
n_p 5	N/A	N/A	N/A	N/A	N/A	1.81 ± 0.14	1.98 ± 0.05
n_p 20	*0.90 ± 0.31*	*0.39 ± 0.20*	*0.40 ± 0.22*	*1.72 ± 0.04*	*1.89 ± 0.08*	2.42 ± 0.14	N/A
n_p 30	*1.06 ± 0.27*	*0.49 ± 0.18*	*0.49 ± 0.20*	*1.24 ± 0.02*	*1.52 ± 0.04*	2.48 ± 0.14	N/A
n_p 40	*1.18 ± 0.31*	*0.56 ± 0.18*	*0.56 ± 0.18*	*1.30 ± 0.04*	*1.61 ± 0.04*	2.55 ± 0.14	N/A
n_p 50	*1.23 ± 0.22*	*0.58 ± 0.18*	*0.59 ± 0.20*	*1.45 ± 0.02*	*1.67 ± 0.04*	*2.50 ± 0.12*	**3.47 ± 0.06**
n_p 100	*1.38 ± 0.18*	*0.66 ± 0.14*	*0.66 ± 0.14*	*1.28 ± 0.04*	*1.61 ± 0.06*	*2.36 ± 0.08*	**3.60 ± 0.07**
n_p 200	N/A	N/A	N/A	N/A	N/A	*2.26 ± 0.06*	**3.47 ± 0.04**

	CPSO	MSOD	HMSO	MSO	Cellular DE	Cellular PSO	MPSO2
Cs 1	**1.06 ± 0.07**	1.06 ± 0.03	**1.42 ± 0.04**	**1.51 ± 0.04**	**1.64 ± 0.03**	1.14 ± 0.13	N/A
Cs 2	*1.17 ± 0.06*	1.51 ± 0.04	N/A	N/A	N/A	N/A	N/A
Cs 4	*1.38 ± 0.08*	N/A	N/A	N/A	N/A	N/A	N/A
Cs 6	*1.53 ± 0.08*	N/A	N/A	N/A	N/A	N/A	N/A
Cp 500	N/A	N/A	**7.56 ± 0.27**	*5.95 ± 0.09*	N/A	*1.44 ± 0.13*	N/A
Cp 1000	N/A	*3.58 ± 0.05*	**4.61 ± 0.07**	3.94 ± 0.08	3.98 ± 0.03	*1.33 ± 0.11*	N/A
Cp 2500	N/A	N/A	**2.39 ± 0.16**	N/A	**2.42 ± 0.02**	*1.08 ± 0.09*	N/A
Cp 10000	0.625 ± N/A	N/A	**0.94 ± 0.09**	**0.97 ± 0.04**	N/A	**1.1 ± 0.18**	N/A
n_p 1	*0.14 ± 0.03*	N/A	*0.87 ± 0.05*	*0.56 ± 0.04*	*1.53 ± 0.07*	**5.23 ± 0.47**	N/A
n_p 5	*0.72 ± 0.08*	N/A	*1.18 ± 0.04*	*1.06 ± 0.06*	*1.50 ± 0.04*	*1.09 ± 0.22*	*1.77 ± 0.05*
n_p 20	*1.59 ± 0.06*	N/A	*1.50 ± 0.06*	*1.89 ± 0.04*	2.46 ± 0.05	2.20 ± 0.12	N/A
n_p 30	*1.58 ± 0.05*	N/A	*1.65 ± 0.04*	*2.03 ± 0.06*	2.62 ± 0.05	2.67 ± 0.13	N/A
n_p 40	*1.51 ± 0.03*	N/A	*1.65 ± 0.05*	*2.04 ± 0.06*	2.76 ± 0.05	2.70 ± 0.13	N/A
n_p 50	*1.54 ± 0.03*	N/A	*1.66 ± 0.02*	*2.08 ± 0.02*	2.75 ± 0.05	2.77 ± 0.13	N/A
n_p 100	*1.41 ± 0.02*	N/A	*1.68 ± 0.03*	*2.14 ± 0.02*	2.73 ± 0.03	2.91 ± 0.14	N/A
n_p 200	*1.24 ± 0.02*	N/A	*1.71 ± 0.02*	*2.11 ± 0.03*	2.61 ± 0.02	**3.14 ± 0.12**	*2.37 ± 0.03*

CDE performed better than HMSO on all variations of change period. HMSO performed better than ABrCDE on all settings of number of peaks, except 10.

MSO: [26] [26] do not specify the change detection strategy that is used in MSO, but it is assumed that the Det_{best} strategy that was used in HMSO (which was developed by the same authors) is also used in MSO. ABrCDE performed better than MSO when a change severity of 1 was used, and overlapping confidence intervals were found when a change period of 1 000 was used. ABrCDE performed better than MSO when a change period of 10 000 was used. MSO performed better than ABrCDE in all other reported cases.

Cellular DE: [38] Cellular DE employs the Det_{local} change detecting strategy and is thus comparable to ABrCDE using the $Det_{n_k-local}$ strategy. ABrCDE performed better than Cellular DE when a change period of 2 500 and 5 000 were used, and similar when 1 000 was used. Cellular DE performed better than ABrCDE in two of the number of peaks experiments (1 and 5 peaks), confidence intervals overlapped for other values.

Cellular PSO: [21] Cellular PSO uses the Det_{local} change detecting strategy and is thus comparable to ABrCDE using the $Det_{n_k-local}$ strategy. Cellular PSO performed better than ABrCDE when using change periods of 500, 1 000 and 2 500, but overlapping confidence intervals were found when using a change period of 5 000. ABrCDE performed better than Cellular PSO when using a change period of 10 000. ABrCDE performed better than Cellular PSO when a single peak was present, but worse than Cellular PSO when 5 peaks were present. Overlapping confidence intervals were found for all other settings for the number of peaks, except when 200 peaks were present, where ABrCDE performed better than Cellular PSO.

MPSO2: [4] MPSO2 detects changes using the Det_{local} strategy, which makes it comparable to ABrCDE using the $Det_{n_k-local}$ strategy. ABrCDE performed worse than MPSO2 in both the reported environments.

The analysis in this section found that ABrCDE performed similar to, or better than the majority of the algorithms on at least one environment. The only exception to this statement is MPSO2, but it should be considered that the algorithms were compared on only two environments. The performance of ABrCDE indicates that it is an effective algorithm which compares favourably to the state-of-the-art algorithms aimed at DOPs.

9. CONCLUSIONS

This paper presented a novel algorithm to self-adapt the Brownian radius in an algorithm aimed at DOPs. The use of different random distributions and resetting the radius when changes occur, was investigated. An experimental comparison of these approaches found that the most effective approach uses a normal distribution to select the Brownian radius, and resets the radius to initial values when changes occur. The new approach has the benefit of reducing the number of parameters to the algorithm. Furthermore, an extensive experimental evaluation found that the results achieved by the base algorithm is improved by the self-adaptive component. A comparison to the reported results of other algorithms in the literature demonstrated that the new algorithm compares favourably to current algorithms.

10. REFERENCES

[1] P. J. Angeline, D. B. Fogel, and L. J. Fogel. A comparison of self-adaptation methods for finite state machines in dynamic environments. In *Proceedings of the Conference on Evolutionary Programming*, pages 441–449. Springer, 1996.

[2] D. V. Arnold and H.-G. Beyer. Random Dynamics Optimum Tracking with Evolution Strategies. In *Parallel Problem Solving from Nature*, pages 3–12. Springer, 2002.

[3] T. Bäck. On the behavior of evolutionary algorithms in dynamic environments. In *Proceedings of the IEEE International Conference on Evolutionary Computation*, pages 446–451. IEEE, 1998.

[4] T. Blackwell. Particle swarm optimization in dynamic environments. In *Evolutionary Computation in Dynamic and Uncertain Environments*, pages 29–49. Springer, 2007.

[5] T. Blackwell and J. Branke. Multiswarm optimization in dynamic environments. *Applications of Evolutionary Computing*, 3005:489–500, 2004.

[6] T. Blackwell and J. Branke. Multiswarms, exclusion, and anti-convergence in dynamic environments. *IEEE Transactions on Evolutionary Computation*, 10(4):459–472, 2006.

[7] T. Blackwell, J. Branke, and X. Li. Particle swarms for dynamic optimization problems. In *Swarm Intelligence*, Natural Computing Series, pages 193–217. Springer, 2008.

[8] T. M. Blackwell and P. J. Bentley. Dynamic search with charged swarms. In *Proceedings of the Genetic and Evolutionary Computation Conference*, pages 19–26. Morgan Kaufmann, 2002.

[9] S. Boettcher and A. G. Percus. Extremal optimization: Methods derived from co-evolution. In *Proceedings of the Genetic and Evolutionary Computation Conference*, pages 825–832, Orlando, Florida, USA, 1999. Morgan Kaufmann.

[10] J. Branke. *Evolutionary Optimization in Dynamic Environments.* Kluwer Academic Publishers, 2002.

[11] J. Branke. *The moving peaks benchmark.* http://www.aifb.uni-karlsruhe.de/ ~jbr/MovPeaks/, Accessed February 2007.

[12] J. Branke, T. Kaußler, C. Schmidt, and H. Schmeck. A multi-population approach to dynamic optimization problems. In *Adaptive Computing in Design and Manufacturing*, pages 299–308. Springer, 2000.

[13] J. Branke and H. Schmeck. Designing evolutionary algorithms for dynamic optimization problems. In *Advances in evolutionary computing: theory and applications*, pages 239–262. Springer, 2003.

[14] J. Brest, S. Greiner, B. Boškovic, M. Mernik, and V. Žumer. Self-adapting control parameters in differential evolution: A comparative study on numerical benchmark problems. *IEEE Transactions on Evolutionary Computation*, 10(6):646–657, 2006.

[15] J. Brest, A. Zamuda, B. Boškovic, M. S. Maučec, and V. Žumer. Dynamic optimization using self-adaptive differential evolution. In *Proceedings of the IEEE Congress on Evolutionary Computation*, pages 415–422. IEEE, 2009.

[16] H. G. Cobb. *An investigation into the use of hypermutation as an adaptive operator in genetic algorithms having continuous, time-dependent nonstationary environments.* Navy Center for Applied Research in Artificial Intelligence, Technical Report AIC-90-001, 1990.

[17] I. G. del Amo, D. A. Pelta, and J. R. González. Using heuristic rules to enhance a multiswarm PSO for dynamic environments. In *Proceedings of the IEEE Congress on Evolutionary Computation*, pages 1–8. IEEE, 2010.

[18] M. du Plessis and A. Engelbrecht. Improved differential evolution for dynamic optimization problems. *Proceedings of the IEEE Congress on Evolutionary Computation*, pages 229–234, 2008.

[19] M. du Plessis and A. Engelbrecht. Using competitive population evaluation in a differential evolution algorithm for dynamic environments. *European Journal of Operational Research*, 218(1):7–20, 2012.

[20] J. J. Grefenstette. Evolvability in dynamic fitness landscapes: A genetic algorithm approach. In *Proceedings of the IEEE Congress on Evolutionary Computation*, volume 3, pages 2031–2038. IEEE, 1999.

[21] A. Hashemi and M. Meybodi. Cellular PSO: A PSO for Dynamic Environments. In *Advances in Computation and Intelligence*, Lecture Notes in Computer Science, pages 422–433. Springer, 2009.

[22] A. Hashemi and M. Meybodi. A multi-role cellular PSO for dynamic environments. In *CSI Computer Conference*, pages 412–417, 2009.

[23] R. Hooke and T. A. Jeeves. " Direct Search" solution of numerical and statistical problems. *Journal of the ACM*, 8(2):212–229, 1961.

[24] X. Hu and R. Eberhart. Adaptive particle swarm optimisation: detection and response to dynamic systems. In *Proceedings of the IEEE Congress on Evolutionary Computation*, pages 1666–1670. IEEE, 2002.

[25] M. Kamosi, A. B. Hashemi, and M. R. Meybodi. A hibernating multi-swarm optimization algorithm for dynamic environments. In *Proceedings of the World Congress on Nature & Biologically Inspired Computing*, pages 363–369. IEEE, 2010.

[26] M. Kamosi, A. B. Hashemi, and M. R. Meybodi. A

new particle swarm optimization algorithm for dynamic environments. In *Proceedings of the Swarm, Evolutionary, and Memetic Computing Conference*, Lecture Notes in Computer Science, pages 129–138. Springer, 2010.

[27] C. Li and S. Yang. A generalized approach to construct benchmark problems for dynamic optimization. In *Proceedings of the International Conference on Simulated Evolution and Learning*, pages 391–400. Springer, 2008.

[28] C. Li, S. Yang, T. T. Nguyen, E. L. Yu, X. Yao, Y. Jin, H. g. Beyer, and P. N. Suganthan. *Benchmark Generator for CECŠ2009 Competition on Dynamic Optimization*. University of Leicester, University of Birmingham, Nanyang Technological University, Technical Report, 2008.

[29] C. Li, S. Yang, and D. A. Pelta. *Benchmark Generator for the IEEE WCCI-2012 Competition on Evolutionary Computation for Dynamic Optimization Problems*. http://www.ieee-wcci2012.org/ieee-wcci2012/, 2011.

[30] X. Li, J. Branke, and T. Blackwell. Particle swarm with speciation and adaptation in a dynamic environment. In *Proceedings of the Conference on Genetic and Evolutionary Computation*, pages 51–58. ACM, 2006.

[31] R. Lung and D. Dumitrescu. A new collaborative evolutionary-swarm optimization technique. In *Proceedings of the Conference on Genetic and evolutionary computation*, pages 2817–2820. ACM, 2007.

[32] R. Lung and D. Dumitrescu. Evolutionary swarm cooperative optimization in dynamic environments. *Natural Computing: an international journal*, 9(1):83–94, 2010.

[33] R. Mendes and A. Mohais. DynDE: a differential evolution for dynamic optimization problems. In *Proceedings of the IEEE Congress on Evolutionary Computation*, pages 2808–2815. IEEE, 2005.

[34] R. Morrison. *Designing Evolutionary Algorithms for Dynamic Environments*. Springer, 2004.

[35] I. Moser. Hooke-jeeves revisited. In *Proceedings IEEE Congress on Evolutionary Computation*, pages 2670–2676. IEEE, 2009.

[36] I. Moser and R. Chiong. Dynamic function optimisation with hybridised extremal dynamics. *Memetic Computing*, 2(2):137–148, 2010.

[37] I. Moser and T. Hendtlass. A simple and efficient multi-component algorithm for solving dynamic function optimisation problems. In *IEEE Congress on Evolutionary Computation*, pages 252–259. IEEE, 2007.

[38] V. Noroozi, A. Hashemi, and M. R. Meybodi. CellularDE: a cellular based differential evolution for dynamic optimization problems. In *Proceedings of International conference on Adaptive and natural computing algorithms - Volume Part I*, pages 340–349. Springer, 2011.

[39] P. Novoa-Hernández, C. Corona, and D. Pelta. Efficient multi-swarm PSO algorithms for dynamic environments. *Memetic Computing*, 3:163–174, 2011.

[40] F. Oppacher and M. Wineberg. The shifting balance genetic algorithm: Improving the ga in a dynamic environment. In *Proceedings of the Genetic and Evolutionary Computation Conference*, pages 504 – 510. Morgan Kaufmann, 1999.

[41] D. Parrott and X. Li. A particle swarm model for tracking multiple peaks in a dynamic environment using speciation. In *Proceedings of the IEEE Congress on Evolutionary Computation*, pages 98–103. IEEE, 2004.

[42] K. Price, R. Storn, and J. Lampinen. *Differential evolution - A practical approach to global optimization*. Springer, 2005.

[43] C. L. Ramsey and J. J. Grefenstette. Case-based initialization of genetic algorithms. In *International Conference on Genetic Algorithms*, pages 84–91. Morgan Kaufmann, 1993.

[44] A. Simões and E. Costa. The influence of population and memory sizes on the evolutionary algorithm's performance for dynamic environments. In *Applications of Evolutionary Computing*, Lecture Notes in Computer Science, pages 705–714. Springer, 2009.

[45] R. Storn and K. Price. Differential evolution - a simple and efficient heuristic for global optimization over continuous spaces. *Journal of Global Optimization*, 11:341–359, 1997.

[46] R. Thomsen. Multimodal optimization using crowding-based differential evolution. In *Proceedings of the IEEE Congress on Evolutionary Computation*, pages 382–1389. IEEE, 2004.

[47] R. K. Ursem. Multinational GA optimization techniques in dynamic environments. In *Proceedings of the Genetic and Evolutionary Computation Conference*, pages 19–26. Morgan Kaufmann, 2000.

[48] F. Vavak, K. Jukes, and T. C. Fogarty. Adaptive combustion balancing in multiple burner boiler using a genetic algorithm with variable range of local search. In T. Bäck, editor, *Proceedings of the International Conference on Genetic Algorithms*, pages 719–726. Morgan Kaufmann, 1997.

[49] K. Weicker. Performance measures for dynamic environments. In *Proceedings of the International Conference on Parallel Problem Solving from Nature*, pages 64–73. Springer, 2002.

[50] K. Weicker and N. Weicker. On evolution strategy optimization in dynamic environments. In *Proceedings of the IEEE Congress on Evolutionary Computation*, pages 2039–2046. IEEE, 1999.

[51] S. Yang. Memory-based immigrants for genetic algorithms in dynamic environments. In *Proceedings of the Conference on Genetic and evolutionary computation*, pages 1115–1122. ACM, 2005.

[52] S. Yang and C. Li. A clustering particle swarm optimizer for locating and tracking multiple optima in dynamic environments. *IEEE Transactions on Evolutionary Computation*, 14(6):959 –974, 2010.

[53] T. Zhu, W. Luo, and Z. Li. An adaptive strategy for updating the memory in evolutionary algorithms for dynamic optimization. In *Proceedings of the IEEE Symposium on Computational Intelligence in Dynamic and Uncertain Environments*, pages 8–15. IEEE, 2011.

A More Efficient Rank-one Covariance Matrix Update for Evolution Strategies

Oswin Krause
Department of Computer Science
University of Copenhagen
2100 Copenhagen, Denmark
oswin.krause@di.ku.dk

Christian Igel
Department of Computer Science
University of Copenhagen
2100 Copenhagen, Denmark
igel@di.ku.dk

ABSTRACT

Learning covariance matrices of Gaussian distributions is at the heart of most variable-metric randomized algorithms for continuous optimization. If the search space dimensionality is high, updating the covariance or its factorization is computationally expensive. Therefore, we adopt an algorithm from numerical mathematics for rank-one updates of Cholesky factors. Our methods results in a quadratic time covariance matrix update scheme with minimal memory requirements. The numerically stable algorithm leads to triangular Cholesky factors. Systems of linear equations where the linear transformation is defined by a triangular matrix can be solved in quadratic time. This can be exploited to avoid the additional iterative update of the inverse Cholesky factor required in some covariance matrix adaptation algorithms proposed in the literature. When used together with the (1+1)-CMA-ES and the multi-objective CMA-ES, the new method leads to a memory reduction by a factor of almost four and a faster covariance matrix update. The numerical stability and runtime improvements are demonstrated on a set of benchmark functions.

Keywords

CMA-ES, covariance matrix adaptation, rank-one update, Cholesky factorization

1. INTRODUCTION

Adapting the covariance matrix of additive variation operators is a key concept in evolution strategies (ES, [3]) and estimation of distribution algorithms [11]. In many applications, the time needed for the covariance matrix update can be neglected, because the algorithm's computation time is dominated by the objective function evaluations. However, for high dimensional problems and/or objective functions that can be evaluated quickly, the covariance matrix update may become a bottleneck. For example, in the covariance matrix adaptation ES (CMA-ES, [7, 6]), the number of objective function evaluations per iteration typically increases sub-linearly with the search space dimensionality n (e.g., $\lambda = 3 + \lfloor 3 \ln n \rfloor$, see [6]), while the cost of updating the full $n \times n$ covariance matrix Σ of the search distribution (or a factorization of Σ) is $\Omega(n^2)$. Most often the update further requires a decomposition of Σ in cubic time.

For large n, also the memory requirements can become relevant, in particular in the multi-objective CMA-ES (MO-CMA-ES, [8, 17]), where an individual covariance matrix is stored for each individual.

Against this background, several ways to reduce the complexity of the covariance matrix adaptation have been proposed. The most basic strategy to reduce the time complexity is to update the covariance matrix only every $o(n)$ iterations [7, 6]. However, this implies that the algorithm does not optimally exploit the gathered information. And indeed, postponing updates can lead to an increase in the number of objective function evaluations needed to achieve a desired objective function value [16].

Another approach is to impose restrictions on the covariance matrices (e.g., [13, 14, 15, 1, 12]), that is, on the dependencies (i.e., representations or encodings [5]), that can be learnt. This way, linear time and space complexity can be achieved. For example, Ros and Hansen present a CMA-ES variant restricting the covariance matrices to be diagonal [14], which works fine on separable objective functions. The recent variant proposed in [1] additionally adapts one principle component, which results in $2n$ parameters for representing Σ. Recently, Loshchilov proposed a different method [12], which stores a subset of vectors that keep track of previous successful steps and adapts the matrix to make big steps in these directions. These approaches restrict the generality of the CMA-ES and can lead to a significant decrease in performance if the objective function does not match the imposed restrictions (e.g., if there are many strong dependencies between the variables).

To speed up the general covariance update, Igel et al. [10] proposed a fast rank-one update of a non-triangular Cholesky factor L of Σ (i.e., $\Sigma = LL^T$) when the update vector is a previously sampled point from a normal distribution with covariance Σ. The result was generalized in [16] to handle arbitrary directions, which is necessary because it has been proven to be beneficial to consider updates that do not just depend on the last step in the search space (e.g., to use the concept of an *evolution path*), by simultaneously updating the inverse factor. Arnold and Hansen [2] extended the results to the case of the rank-one *downdate*, which can be used to penalize certain search directions. The computation time for the update of Σ with this type of algorithms is asymptot-

FOGA'15, January 17–20, 2015, Aberystwyth, UK.

ACM 978-1-4503-3434-1/15/01 ...$15.00.
http://dx.doi.org/10.1145/2725494.2725496.

ically optimal and a rank m update requires $O(mn^2)$ computation time. These Cholesky-update based methods considerably speed up the (1+1)-CMA-ES [10, 2] and in particular the MO-CMA-ES [8, 17], which can be viewed as running several (1+1)-CMA-ESs at the same time. However, they have two obvious drawbacks. First, instead of Σ they maintain the not necessarily triangular Cholesky factor L. The methods allowing for general updates additionally store the inverse factor L^{-1}. That is, instead of $n(n+1)/2$ parameters, $2n^2$ values have to be kept in memory. Second, L and L^{-1} are updated independently of each other. This is not elegant and bears the risk that the stored matrices L and L^{-1} diverge in the sense that one is not the inverse of the other due to numerical problems. However, the latter has not been observed to cause problems in practice, see [16].

Both issues do not occur if L is triangular. First, then L has only $n(n+1)/2$ parameters. Second, instead of storing and iteratively updating L^{-1}, which is only needed in the update to compute $\boldsymbol{w} = L^{-1}\boldsymbol{v}$, one can now solve $L\boldsymbol{w} = \boldsymbol{v}$ for $\boldsymbol{w}$ in quadratic time. Furthermore, the above-mentioned divergence problem cannot occur.

It turns out that the problem of a fast and efficient rank-one update of triangular Cholesky factors is a classical question in numerical mathematics. It has been solved in 1974 by Gill et al. [4]. In their work, the authors present various $O(n^2)$ updates resulting in triangular Cholesky factors. Versions of the algorithms have been implemented in most major software-libraries manipulating matrices, including Matlab, LAPACK and the Eigen C++ library.

This paper shows how to adopt Gill et al.'s algorithms for time and memory efficient as well as numerically stable covariance matrix up- and downdates. We will introduce the notation and recall the covariance matrix update currently used in the (1+1)-CMA-ES in section 2. In section 3, one variant of the triangular Cholesky update is described. The next section shows how to use this update as part of the (1+1)-CMA-ES. Section 4 presents timing experiments, and we conclude in section 5.

2. COVARIANCE MATRIX UPDATES AND THE CHOLESKY FACTOR

In the following, we will denote vectors by lower-case bold italics (e.g., $\boldsymbol{v} \in \mathbb{R}^N$), scalar values by lower-case italics (e.g., $v \in \mathbb{R}$), and matrices by captal letters (e.g., $V \in \mathbb{R}^{n\times n}$). Sampling from an n-dimensional multi-variate normal distribution $\mathcal{N}(\boldsymbol{m}, \Sigma)$, $\boldsymbol{m} \in \mathbb{R}^n$,$\Sigma \in \mathbb{R}^{n\times n}$ is usually done using a decomposition of the covariance matrix Σ. This could be the square root of the matrix $\Sigma = HH \in \mathbb{R}^{n\times n}$ or some arbitrary (triangular or non-triangular) Cholesky factorization $\Sigma = LL^T$, which is related to the square root by $L = HE$ where E is an orthogonal matrix. We can sample a point $\boldsymbol{z}$ from $\mathcal{N}(\boldsymbol{m}, \Sigma)$ using a sample $\boldsymbol{z} \sim \mathcal{N}(\boldsymbol{0}, I)$ by

$$\boldsymbol{x} = L\boldsymbol{z} + \boldsymbol{m} = HE\boldsymbol{z} + \boldsymbol{m} = H\boldsymbol{y} + \boldsymbol{m} \ ,$$

where we set $\boldsymbol{y} = E\boldsymbol{z}$. This holds as $\boldsymbol{y} \sim \mathcal{N}(\boldsymbol{0}, I)$ since E is orthogonal. Thus, as long as we are only interested in the value of $\boldsymbol{x}$ and do not need $\boldsymbol{y}$, we can sample using the Cholesky factor instead of the matrix square root.

Adaptation of the covariance matrix is an important building block of evolutionary strategies. For example, the (1+1)-CMA-ES creates a sequence of covariance matrices $\Sigma_k \in \mathbb{R}^{n\times n}$, $k = 1, \ldots, T$, which are related by a rank-one-update

$$\Sigma_{k+1} = \alpha_k \Sigma_k + \beta_k \boldsymbol{v}_k \boldsymbol{v}_k^T \ ,$$

where $\alpha_k, \beta_k \in \mathbb{R}$ and $\boldsymbol{v}_k \in \mathbb{R}^n$, $k = 1, \ldots, T$. As we are not interested in Σ_k itself but only in acquiring samples from the normal distribution $\mathcal{N}(\boldsymbol{0}, \Sigma_k)$, our goal is to find a simple update to H_k or L_k such that $\Sigma_{k+1} = H_{k+1}H_{k+1} = L_{k+1}L_{k+1}^T$ under the constraint of $O(n^2)$ time and memory requirement. It turns out that there exists a fast update for the Cholesky factor L_k but to date no formula for H_k is known. The update of L_k is known from numerical mathematics

$$L_{k+1} = \sqrt{\alpha_k} L_k \left(I + \gamma_k \frac{\boldsymbol{w}_k \boldsymbol{w}_k^T}{||\boldsymbol{w}_k||^2} \right) \ ,$$

where $\boldsymbol{w}_k = L_k^{-1}\boldsymbol{v}_k$, I is the $n \times n$ identity matrix and $\gamma_k = \sqrt{1 + \frac{\beta_k}{\alpha_k}||\boldsymbol{w}_k||^2} - 1$, and has been applied in the context of the (1+1)-CMA-ES in [10].

If the update direction $\boldsymbol{v_k}$ corresponds to a sample $L_k\boldsymbol{z}$, $\boldsymbol{z} \sim \mathcal{N}(\boldsymbol{0}, I)$, then we get $\boldsymbol{w} = \boldsymbol{z}$ for free. However, this is in general not the case, in particular when an evolution path is used. The evolution path is a weighted average of successful steps, and the potential sample that could have created this step has to be found and we have to compute $\boldsymbol{w} = L_k^{-1}\boldsymbol{v}_k$.

The update above has the disadvantage that the Cholesky factor L_{k+1} is not triangular, even if L_k was. Thus, L_{k+1}^{-1} has to be updated and stored separately for being able to calculate $\boldsymbol{w}$ in $O(n^2)$ time [16]:

$$L_{k+1}^{-1} = \left(I - \frac{\gamma_k}{\gamma_k + 1} \frac{\boldsymbol{w}_k \boldsymbol{w}_k^T}{||\boldsymbol{w}_k||^2} \right) \frac{1}{\sqrt{\alpha_k}} L_k^{-1} \qquad (2.1)$$

3. A MORE EFFICIENT, TRIANGULAR UPDATE

Even though the $\Theta(n^2)$ time and space complexity of the update rule described above is asymptotically optimal, it is not fully satisfactory. Maintaining two non symmetric $\mathbb{R}^{n\times n}$ matrices for updating the $n(n+1)/2$ parameters of Σ is inefficient.

Thus, we propose to replace this strategy by an update rule that ensures that the Cholesky factors are triangular. Then one has just to store the $n(n+1)/2$ parameters of the Cholesky factor L_k, because it is possible to solve systems of equations of the form $L_k\boldsymbol{w} = \boldsymbol{v}$ using backwards substitution efficiently in quadratic time.

Gill et al. [4] found solutions to the problem of updating triangular Cholesky factors in 1974. The authors offer a number of algorithms for update and downdate realizing different trade-offs between speed and numerical accuracy. Interestingly, one of the algorithms can already be derived by applying the standard decomposition algorithm. Other updates using Gibbs or Householder transformations can be developed as well, giving more numeric accuracy or having faster implementations. We derive the triangular Cholesky update using the Cholesky factorisation algorithm as a simple example in the following Lemma 1. Without loss of generality, we will now assume $\alpha = 1$.

LEMMA 1. *Let $A = LL^T \in \mathbb{R}^{n\times n}$ be symmetric positive definite and L be a lower triangular matrix. Define a partition of A and L into blocks*

$$A = \begin{pmatrix} a_{11} & \boldsymbol{a}_{21}^T \\ \boldsymbol{a}_{21} & A_{22} \end{pmatrix} = \begin{pmatrix} l_{11} & 0 \\ \boldsymbol{l}_{21} & L_{22} \end{pmatrix} \begin{pmatrix} l_{11} & \boldsymbol{l}_{21}^T \\ 0 & L_{22}^T \end{pmatrix} \ ,$$

with $a_{11}, l_{11} \in \mathbb{R}$, $\boldsymbol{a}_{21}, \boldsymbol{l}_{21} \in \mathbb{R}^{n-1}$ *and* $A_{22}, L_{22} \in \mathbb{R}^{n-1 \times n-1}$. *Let*

$$A' = A + \beta \boldsymbol{v}\boldsymbol{v}^T \in \mathbb{R}^{n \times n}$$

with $\beta \in \mathbb{R}$ *and* $\boldsymbol{v} = (v_1, \boldsymbol{v}_2) \in \mathbb{R}^n$, $v_1 \in \mathbb{R}$, $\boldsymbol{v}_2 \in \mathbb{R}^{n-1}$. *There exists a lower triangular matrix* $L' \in \mathbb{R}^{n \times n}$ *such that* $A' = L'L'^T$. *Let* A' *and* L' *have the same block structure as* A *and* L, *respectively. It holds for* L':

$$l'_{11} = \sqrt{l_{11}^2 + \beta v_1^2}$$

$$\boldsymbol{l'}_{21} = \frac{l_{11}\boldsymbol{l}_{21} + \beta v_1 \boldsymbol{v}_2}{l'_{11}}$$

$$L'_{22}L'^T_{22} = L_{22}L_{22}^T + \beta \frac{l_{11}^2}{l'^2_{11}} \left(\boldsymbol{v}_2 - \frac{v_1}{l_{11}}\boldsymbol{l}_{21}\right)\left(\boldsymbol{v}_2 - \frac{v_1}{l_{11}}\boldsymbol{l}_{21}\right)^T$$

PROOF. Using the block definition of A' the product $L'L'^T$ reads:

$$A' = \begin{pmatrix} l'^2_{11} & l'_{11}\boldsymbol{l'}^T_{21} \\ l'_{11}\boldsymbol{l'}_{21} & L'_{22}L'^T_{22} + \boldsymbol{l'}_{21}\boldsymbol{l'}^T_{21} \end{pmatrix} .$$

Using this we can now determine l'_{11} from a'_{11}, $\boldsymbol{l'}_{21}$ from A'_{21} and L'_{22} from A'_{22}. For l'_{11} holds

$$l'_{11} = \sqrt{a'_{11}} = \sqrt{a_{11} + \beta v_1^2} = \sqrt{l_{11}^2 + \beta v_1^2}$$

and for $\boldsymbol{l'}_{21}$ holds

$$\boldsymbol{l'}_{21} = \frac{A'_{21}}{l'_{11}} = \frac{\boldsymbol{a}_{21} + \beta v_1 \boldsymbol{v}_2}{l'_{11}} = \frac{l_{11}\boldsymbol{l}_{21} + \beta v_1 \boldsymbol{v}_2}{l'_{11}} .$$

Applying the above formulas to $L'_{22}L'^T_{22}$ leads to:

$$\begin{aligned} L'_{22}L'^T_{22} &= A'_{22} - \boldsymbol{l'}_{21}\boldsymbol{l'}^T_{21} \\ &= L_{22}L_{22}^T + \boldsymbol{l}_{21}\boldsymbol{l}_{21}^T + \beta \boldsymbol{v}_2\boldsymbol{v}_2^T \\ &\quad - \frac{l_{11}\boldsymbol{l}_{21} + \beta v_1 \boldsymbol{v}_2}{l'_{11}} \left(\frac{l_{11}\boldsymbol{l}_{21} + \beta v_1 \boldsymbol{v}_2}{l'_{11}}\right)^T \\ &= L_{22}L_{22}^T + \beta\left(1 - \frac{\beta v_1^2}{l'^2_{11}}\right)\boldsymbol{v}_2\boldsymbol{v}_2^T + \left(1 - \frac{l_{11}^2}{l'^2_{11}}\right)\boldsymbol{l}_{21}\boldsymbol{l}_{21}^T \\ &\quad - \frac{\beta v_1 l_{11}}{l'^2_{11}}\left(\boldsymbol{l}_{21}\boldsymbol{v}_2^T + \boldsymbol{v}_2\boldsymbol{l}_{21}^T\right) \\ &= L_{22}L_{22}^T + \frac{\beta l_{11}^2}{l'^2_{11}}\boldsymbol{v}_2\boldsymbol{v}_2^T + \frac{\beta v_1^2}{l'^2_{11}}\boldsymbol{l}_{21}\boldsymbol{l}_{21}^T \\ &\quad - \frac{\beta v_1 l_{11}}{l'^2_{11}}\left(\boldsymbol{l}_{21}\boldsymbol{v}_2^T + \boldsymbol{v}_2\boldsymbol{l}_{21}^T\right) \\ &= L_{22}L_{22}^T + \beta\frac{l_{11}^2}{l'^2_{11}}\left(\boldsymbol{v}_2 - \frac{v_1}{l_{11}}\boldsymbol{l}_{21}\right)\left(\boldsymbol{v}_2 - \frac{v_1}{l_{11}}\boldsymbol{l}_{21}\right)^T \end{aligned}$$

□

Thus, considering a rank-1 update of an $n \times n$ matrix A, we can update one row and one column of a triangular Cholesky decomposition of A in linear time. The remaining entries can be computed by a rank-1 update of an $(n-1) \times (n-1)$ matrix. Thus, if we apply this idea iteratively, we get the full update in quadratic time:

COROLLARY 1. *Let* $A = LL^T \in \mathbb{R}^{n \times n}$ *and* $A' = L'L'^T \in \mathbb{R}^{n \times n}$ *as in Lemma 1. Let* $j \in \{1, \ldots, n\}$ *and define a partition of* L *and* L' *into blocks*

$$L = \begin{pmatrix} B_{j,j} & 0 \\ B_{n-j,j} & B_{n-j,n-j} \end{pmatrix}, L' = \begin{pmatrix} B'_{j,j} & 0 \\ B'_{n-j,j} & B'_{n-j,n-j} \end{pmatrix}$$

where $B_{j,j}, B'_{j,j} \in \mathbb{R}^{j \times j}$, $B_{n-j,j}, B'_{n-j,j} \in \mathbb{R}^{n-j \times j}$ *and* $B_{n-j,n-j}, B'_{n-j,n-j} \in \mathbb{R}^{n-j \times n-j}$. *There exists* $\beta_{j+1} \in \mathbb{R}$ *and* $\boldsymbol{w}_{j+1} \in \mathbb{R}^{n-j}$ *such that*

$$B'_{n-j,n-j}B'^T_{n-j,n-j} = B_{n-j,n-j}B^T_{n-j,n-j} + \beta_{j+1}\boldsymbol{\omega}_{j+1}\boldsymbol{\omega}^T_{j+1}$$

PROOF. In the following, we sketch a proof by induction. Setting $j = 1$ we can apply Lemma 1 directly, by setting $l'_{11} = B'_{j,j}$, $\boldsymbol{l'}_{21} = B'_{n-j,j}$ and $L'_{22} = B'_{n-j,n-j}$. We see from Lemma 1 that $L'_{22}L'^T_{22}$ is again a rank-1 update to the submatrix $L_{22}L^T_{22}$ of A by setting $\beta_2 = \beta\frac{l_{11}^2}{l'^2_{11}}$ and $\boldsymbol{\omega}_2 = \boldsymbol{v}_2 - \frac{v_1}{l_{11}}\boldsymbol{l}_{21}$. We can thus apply Lemma 1 iteratively on the block $B'_{n-j,n-j}$, which prooves the result. □

From the lemma above it follows that L' can be computed in a column-wise fashion, as for example by Algorithm 3.1.

Algorithm 3.1: Triangular rank-one update used in our experiments

input : triangular Cholesky factor $L \in \mathbb{R}^{n \times n}$ of matrix Σ, $\alpha, \beta \in \mathbb{R}$, $\boldsymbol{v} \in \mathbb{R}^n$;
output: updated triangular Cholesky factor L' of $\alpha\Sigma + \beta\boldsymbol{v}\boldsymbol{v}^T$

1 $\boldsymbol{\omega} \leftarrow \boldsymbol{v}$;
2 $b \leftarrow 1$;
3 **for** $j = 1, \ldots, n$ **do**
4 $\quad l'_{jj} \leftarrow \sqrt{\alpha l_{jj}^2 + \frac{\beta}{b}\omega_j^2}$;
5 $\quad \gamma \leftarrow \alpha l_{jj}^2 b + \beta\omega_j^2$;
6 $\quad$ **for** $k = j+1, \ldots, n$ **do**
7 $\quad\quad \omega_k \leftarrow \omega_k - \frac{\omega_j}{l_{jj}}\sqrt{\alpha}l_{kj}$;
8 $\quad\quad l'_{kj} = \sqrt{\alpha}\frac{l'_{jj}}{l_{jj}}l_{kj} + \frac{l'_{jj}\beta\omega_j}{\gamma}\omega_k$;
9 $\quad$ **end**
10 $\quad b \leftarrow b + \beta\frac{\omega_j^2}{\alpha l_{jj}^2}$;
11 **end**

LEMMA 2. *Algorithm 3.1 computes* L' *from* L *as defined in Lemma 1.*

PROOF. For simplicity, we will again assume $\alpha = 1$. We will denote the value of b in the jth iteration before update as b_j. It is easy to see that the update of ω in line 7 is the same as ω_{j+1} in Corollary 1. Therefore, it remains to show that the updates of b, l'_{kj} and l'_{jj} are the same. For $\frac{\beta}{b_{j+1}}$ it holds by the update rule in line 10

$$\frac{\beta}{b_{j+1}} = \frac{\beta}{b_j + \beta\frac{\omega_j^2}{\alpha l_{jj}^2}} = \frac{\beta}{b_j}\frac{l_{jj}^2}{l_{jj}^2 + \frac{\beta}{b_j}\omega_j^2} = \frac{\beta}{b_j}\frac{l_{jj}^2}{l'^2_{jj}} .$$

Thus, as $b_1 = 1$ it follows by induction that the l'_{jj} have the correct value and $\frac{\beta}{b_{j+1}} = \beta_{j+1}$. This leaves to show that the update of l'_{kj} is correct. Note that $\gamma = bl'^2_{jj}$ and thus

$$\begin{aligned} l'_{kj} &= \frac{l'_{jj}}{l_{jj}} l_{kj} + \frac{\beta \omega_j}{b_j l'_{jj}} \left(w_k - \frac{\omega_j}{l_{jj}} l_{kj} \right) \\ &= \left(\frac{l'_{jj}}{l_{jj}} - \frac{\beta \omega_j^2}{b_j l'_{jj} l_{jj}} \right) l_{kj} + \frac{\beta \omega_j}{b_j l'_{jj}} w_k \\ &= \frac{l_{jj}}{l'_{jj}} \left(\frac{l'^2_{jj} - \frac{\beta}{b_j} \omega_j^2}{l^2_{jj}} \right) l_{kj} + \frac{\beta \omega_j}{b_j l'_{jj}} w_k \\ &= \frac{l_{jj}}{l'_{jj}} l_{kj} + \frac{\beta \omega_j}{b_j l'_{jj}} w_k \ , \end{aligned}$$

which is identical to the update of the off-diagonal elements in Lemma 1. □

Variants of this algorithm are implemented for example in Matlab as `cholUpdate` or in the Eigen C++ library as `LLT::rankUpdate`. The pseudocode in Algorithm 3.1 corresponds to the `choleskyUpdate` routine in the Shark library [9] which is based on the Eigen implementation. All implementations are in a form that can directly be used in methods such as the (1+1)-CMA-ES (see Section 4.1) or the MO-CMA-ES. It is interesting to note that this update does not even require to solve a system of equations $L_k \boldsymbol{w} = \boldsymbol{v}$.

Note that the update rule proposed by Lemma 1 is numerically very unstable for $\beta < 0$. Algorithm 3.1, however, is more stable. To understand this, note that the initially proposed update rule relies on the fraction $\frac{l_{11}}{l'_{11}}$. As we perform the update $l'_{11} = \sqrt{l_{11}^2 + \beta v_1^2}$, in finite precision arithmetic, the computed value of l'_{11}, $\tilde{l}'_{11}$ will differ from the true value, that is, $|\tilde{l}'_{11} - l'_{11}| < \epsilon$ for some $\epsilon > 0$. The error of the computation of $\frac{l_{11}}{l'_{11}}$ is then bounded by

$$\left| \frac{l_{11}}{l'_{11}} - \frac{l_{11}}{\tilde{l}'_{11}} \right| < \left| \frac{l_{11}}{l'_{11}} \right| \left| \frac{\epsilon}{\tilde{l}'_{11}} \right| < \left| \frac{l_{11}}{l'_{11}} \right| \left| \frac{1}{\frac{l'_{11}}{\epsilon} - 1} \right| \ .$$

This error can become large in finite precision as with $l_{11}^2 + \beta v_1^2 \approx 0$ the problem of *catastrophic cancellation* leads to greatly reduced precision when $l_{11} \gg l'_{11}$ and thus ϵ becomes large in relation to l'_{11}. This problem becomes more severe as the updated β' is also computed based on this fraction, which allows the error to accumulate over several iterations leading to significant errors.

Algorithm 3.1 instead relies on $\frac{l'_{11}}{l_{11}}$. In this case, the error is bounded by

$$\left| \frac{l'_{11}}{l_{11}} - \frac{\tilde{l}'_{11}}{l_{11}} \right| < \left| \frac{\epsilon}{l_{11}} \right| \ ,$$

which remains small even in the presence of catastrophic cancellation. In the case of ill-conditioned matrices, the update scheme may lead to round-off errors, still, there exist update schemes that guarantee positive definiteness for $\beta > 0$ [4].

As all operations in Algorithm 3.1 are in $O(n)$ time in every iteration of the outer loop, the whole update is $O(n^2)$, where $3/2n^2 + O(n)$ multiplications need to be computed, which are split in $n^2/2$ multiplications to update ω_k and n^2 multiplications to update L_{kj}. In comparison, the original (1+1)-CMA-ES update [16, 2] takes $2n^2 + O(n)$ multiplications for updating L_{k+1}, where the operations are evenly split between the computation of $\boldsymbol{w}_k$ and the outer product of L_{k+1}. Moreover, the original (1+1)-CMA-ES additionally needs to update the inverse L_{k+1} which costs $2n^2 + O(n)$ multiplications, leading to a total cost of $4n^2 + O(n)$ multiplications, which makes the new update less expensive.

This suggests that one can expect a speed-up of the covariance matrix update by a factor of $4/(3/2) = 8/3 \approx 2.667$. This is only to be expected for small matrices which reside fully in CPU-cache, because for large matrices the costs of reading and writing to memory will dominate. As the new algorithm requires less storage, it is also expected to reduce the running time of the algorithm in the regime of large matrices.

4. EXPERIMENTS & RESULTS

The new update rule is obviously more memory efficient than the original (1+1)-CMA-ES update. To verify that it is also faster in practice – as counting the basic operations suggests – we experimentally compared efficient implementations of both update rules. We considered the (1+1)-CMA-ES as an example. Next, we outline how the new update rule can be applied within the (1+1)-CMA-ES with active covariance matrix update. Then the experiments are described and the results are presented.

4.1 (1+1)-CMA-ES with triangular Cholesky update

For a detailed description of the (1+1)-CMA-ES we refer to [16, 2]. The new (1+1)-CMA-ES using the triangular Cholesky update is given in Algorithm 4.1, the values of the constants are the same as suggested in [2] and are listed in Table 4.1 for completeness.

In the kth iteration, an offspring individual $\boldsymbol{x}_{\text{offspring}}$ is sampled from the current parent position $\boldsymbol{x}_k$ using the current Cholesky factor L_k from the covariance matrix Σ_k. If the newly sampled individual has a better fitness than the old, it is accepted and the expected success probability $\overline{p}_{\text{succ},k}$ is updated accordingly. Based on the current success rate, the step size σ_k is updated in an exponential fashion. The remainder of the algorithm is devoted to the update of the covariance matrix, which has three cases:

- if $\overline{p}_{\text{succ}} \geq p_{\text{thresh}}$, it is assumed that some directions of the covariance matrix are too small, so that offspring are not sampled exploratory enough around the current point. To compensate this, the evolution path $\boldsymbol{p}_{c,k}$ is shrunk and the covariance matrix C_k is updated to get overall a rounder shape.

- Otherwise, if the new offspring was successful, the evolution path is updated to reflect the move in the direction of $\boldsymbol{x}_{k+1} - \boldsymbol{x}_k$ and a rank-one update in the direction of the evolution path is performed.

- In the case that the individual is particularly unsuccessful, an active update takes place, which updates C_k with a negative update weight to make far steps in that direction unlikely.

  We regard an individual to be unsuccessful when it is worse than its 5th order ancestor, that is the x_k that is five *successful* steps in the past, not counting any unsuccessful offspring.

  Care has to be taken to ensure that C_k remains positive definite, which is the case when $1 - \frac{c_{\text{cov}}^-}{1+c_{\text{cov}}^-} ||L_k \boldsymbol{z}_k||^2 > 0$,

Algorithm 4.1: (1+1)-CMA-ES with active covariance matrix update

external parameters: initial $\boldsymbol{x}_0$, σ_0, L_0

$\overline{p}_{\text{succ},0} \leftarrow p_{\text{succ}}^{\text{target}}$, $\boldsymbol{p}_{c,k} \leftarrow \boldsymbol{0}$, $k \leftarrow 0$,
$c_L \leftarrow 1 - c_{\text{cov}} + c_{\text{cov}} c_c (2 - c_c)$;
repeat
  $\boldsymbol{z}_k \sim \mathcal{N}(\boldsymbol{0}, I)$;
  $\boldsymbol{x}_{\text{offspring}} \leftarrow \boldsymbol{m}_k + \sigma_k L_k \boldsymbol{z}_k$;
  if $f(\boldsymbol{x}_{\text{offspring}}) \leq f(\boldsymbol{m}_k)$ **then**
    $\boldsymbol{m}_{k+1} \leftarrow \boldsymbol{x}_{\text{offspring}}$;
    $\overline{p}_{\text{succ},k+1} \leftarrow (1 - c_p)\,\overline{p}_{\text{succ},k} + c_p$;
  end
  else
    $\overline{p}_{\text{succ},k+1} \leftarrow (1 - c_p)\,\overline{p}_{\text{succ},k}$;
  end
  $\sigma_{k+1} \leftarrow \sigma_k \cdot \exp\left(\frac{1}{d} \frac{\overline{p}_{\text{succ},k+1} - p_{\text{succ}}^{\text{target}}}{1 - p_{\text{succ}}^{\text{target}}}\right)$;
  if $\overline{p}_{\text{succ},k+1} \geq p_{thresh}$ **then**
    $\boldsymbol{p}_{c,k+1} \leftarrow (1 - c_c)\boldsymbol{p}_{c,k}$;
    $L_{k+1} \leftarrow$ `choleskyUpdate`$(L_k, c_L, c_{\text{cov}}, \boldsymbol{p}_{c,k+1})$;
  end
  else if $f(\boldsymbol{x}_{\text{offspring}}) \leq f(\boldsymbol{x})$ **then**
    $\boldsymbol{p}_{c,k+1} \leftarrow (1 - c_c)\boldsymbol{p}_{c,k} + \sqrt{c_c(2 - c_c)}\, L_k \boldsymbol{z}_k$;
    $L_{k+1} \leftarrow$ `choleskyUpdate`$(L_k, 1 - c_{\text{cov}}, c_{\text{cov}}, \boldsymbol{p}_{c,k+1})$;
  end
  else if $\boldsymbol{x}_{\text{offspring}}$ *is unsuccessful* **then**
    $c_{\text{cov}}^{-} = \min\{c_{\text{cov}}^{-,\max}, \frac{1}{2\|\boldsymbol{z}_k\|^2 - 1}\}$
    $L_{k+1} \leftarrow$ `choleskyUpdate`$(L_k, 1 + c_{\text{cov}}^{-}, -c_{\text{cov}}^{-}, L_k \boldsymbol{z}_k)$;
  end
  $t \leftarrow k + 1$;
until *stopping criterion is met*;

$p_{\text{succ}}^{\text{target}} = \frac{1}{5 + \frac{1}{2}}$	$c_p = \frac{p_{\text{succ}}^{\text{target}}}{2 + p_{\text{succ}}^{\text{target}}}$
$d = 1 + \frac{n}{2}$	$c_c = \frac{2}{2+n}$
$c_{\text{cov}} = \frac{2}{n^2 + 6}$	$c_{\text{cov}}^{-,\max} = \frac{0.4}{n^{1.6} + 1}$
$\sigma_0 = \frac{1}{\sqrt{n}}$	$\overline{p}_{\text{succ},0} = p_{\text{succ}}^{\text{target}}$

Table 4.1: Constants used for the (1+1)-CMA-ES

as otherwise γ_k is undefined. To prevent numerical instabilities, we choose $c_{\text{cov}}^{-} = \min\left\{c_{\text{cov}}^{-,\max}, \frac{1}{2\|\boldsymbol{z}_k\|^2 - 1}\right\}$.

The function `updateCovariance`$(L, \alpha, \beta, \boldsymbol{v})$ implements the rank-one update algorithm for L to replace an update of the form $\alpha\Sigma + \beta\boldsymbol{v}\boldsymbol{v}^T$. In the experiments presented in the next section, we used the variant described in Algorithm 3.1. Again, note that the inverse of the Cholesky factor does not occur in the algorithm in contrast to the variants presented in [10, 16, 2].

4.2 Experimental setup

First, we conducted an experiment on the run-time of the algorithm itself. We performed 100000 covariance matrix update using the old formula and the new formula, respectively, with varying dimensionality $n \in \{100, 200, 400, 800\}$ and measured the running time of both algorithms.

Second, we conducted experiments on 5 different randomly rotated benchmark functions as well as their unrotated counterpart: Rosenbrock, Cigar, Discus, Ellipsoid and DiffPowers as defined in Table 4.3. For each function, we ran the (1+1)-CMA-ES with active updates [2] for 10000 iterations and 100 trials with both update rules. We measured the total time summed up over all trials. We repeated every experiment using different dimensionalities of the benchmark functions varying $n \in \{100, 200, 400, 800\}$. In the experiments we used the fact that the new algorithm produces triangular matrices to speed up the sampling of the vectors by using a matrix-vector product implementation, which takes the triangular structure into account. However, to keep both algorithms as comparable as possible, we maintained in both cases the full Cholesky factor matrix with n^2 entries.

We used Algorithm 4.1 as briefly described in Section 4.1. and the Cholesky update algorithm given in Algorithm 3.1. Our implementation is part of the open-source machine learning library Shark [9] and the code to run the experiments is available in the suplementary material.

4.3 Results

The results for the first experiment are given in Table 4.2. we see that the new algorithm always ran faster than the old one. To measure the speed-up, we calculated the quotient of the running time of the old algorithm and the new one. For $n = 100$ the speed-up is almost exactly the value 8/3 suggested by the analysis of the running time. When n increases, the differences become even larger with a factor of 5.39 with $n = 800$. This is because accessing the RAM takes a lot longer than accessing the CPU-Cache and with growing dimensionality the matrix size exceeds the size of the cache, in which case memory accesses become the bottleneck of the algorithm. As the new algorithm only accesses 1/4th the memory of the old algorithm, this is measureable in running-time.

The results are given in Table 4.4 and the speed-up factors are given in Table 4.5. When comparing the results of the unrotated to the more expensive rotated functions, it can be seen that the impact of the new algorithm becomes less pronounced as the function evaluations become more expensive, as is to be expected. We can see again that the new update rule has a growing impact with increasing n which leads to a cummulated speed-up factor of 2 for the unrotated functions. The impact is not as strong as was suggested by the stand-alone experiment as with growing n less offspring are successful and thus less covariance matrix updates are performed.

Both algorithms produced similar learning curves, which can be seen from the median and the 25 and 75 percentiles of the function values over the 100 trials as plotted in Figure 4.1.

n	original update	new update	speed-up factor
100	3.11	1.16	2.68
200	12.18	3.88	3.14
400	51.36	13.75	3.74
800	284.19	52.69	5.39

Table 4.2: Results of the timing Experiments of 100000 updates of the cholesky factor L in seconds. Speed-up is calculated as $\text{time}_{\text{orig}}/\text{time}_{\text{new}}$.

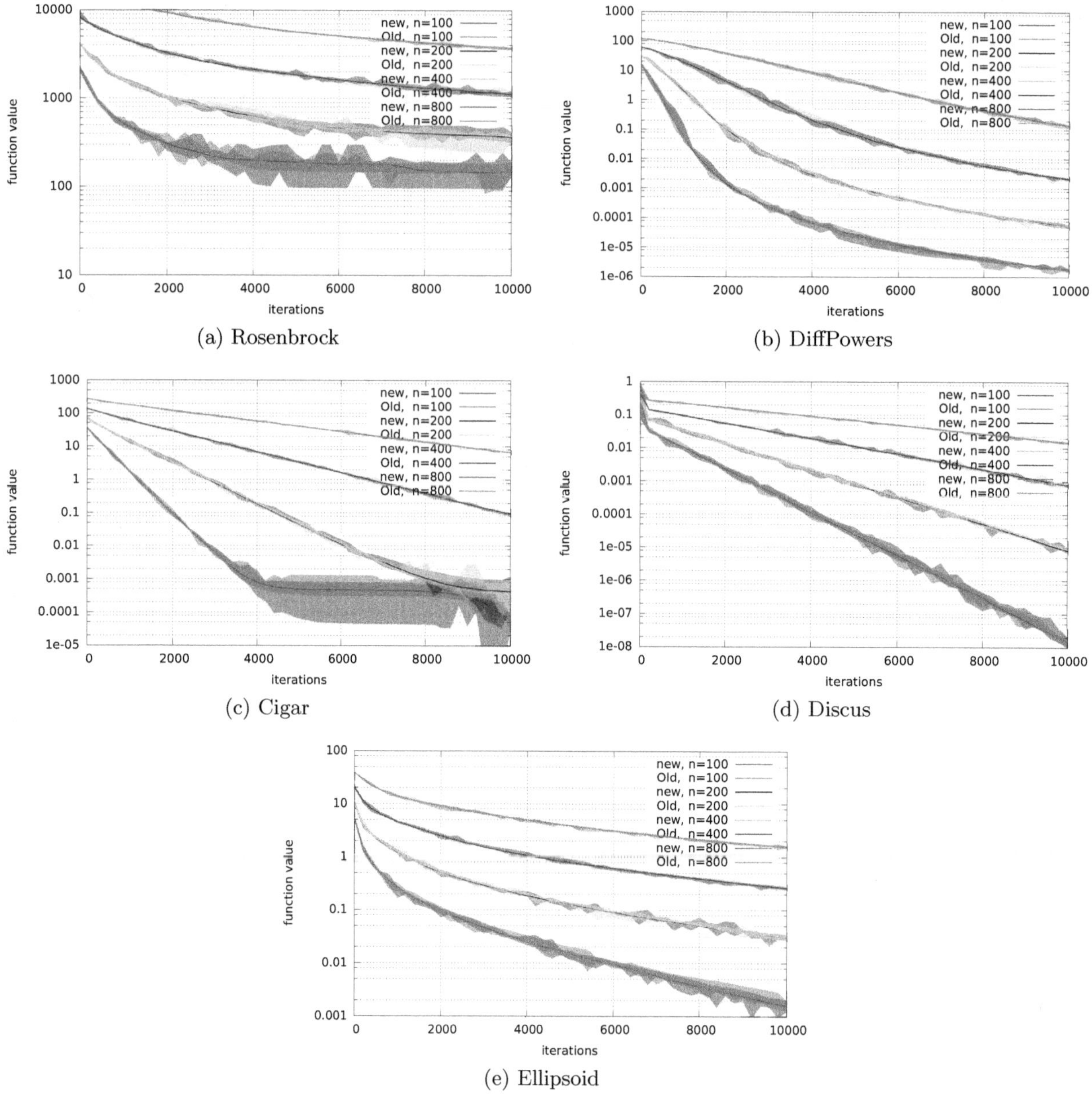

(a) Rosenbrock

(b) DiffPowers

(c) Cigar

(d) Discus

(e) Ellipsoid

Figure 4.1: Median of the function values for the old and new update rule applied to the five test functions with different dimensionalities n. The shaded areas indicate the 25 and 75 percentiles. Note that the graphs of the medians are largely overlapping

n	original update Rosenbrock	Discus	Cigar	Ellipsoid	DiffPowers	new update Rosenbrock	Discus	Cigar	Ellipsoid	DiffPowers
unrotated										
100	18.91	18.75	19.38	27.06	27.50	16.32	16.43	16.60	25.15	25.31
200	55.70	54.13	51.87	73.45	73.83	42.28	41.56	40.96	59.33	60.21
400	168.4	154.8	151.5	195.2	192.1	119.2	119.3	117.5	154.2	163.2
800	623.1	650.5	650.5	686.4	687.9	290.7	302.5	298.7	352.3	359.3
rotated										
100	21.98	22.44	23.19	31.8	32.87	19.19	19.04	18.99	27.01	27.76
200	70.47	68.49	66.18	87.19	90.5	55.68	55.97	55.21	74.19	75.90
400	213.0	200.0	196.4	232.6	227.9	176.8	188.4	182.3	215.7	227.2
800	1036	1049	1052	1087	1098	712.4	720.1	721.6	776.3	798.8

Table 4.4: Results of the timing experiments in seconds with varying number of dimensionality n. Left: the original update rule, Right: the new update rule. Experiments where run on the rotated as well as the unrotated functions.

n	Rosenbrock	Discus	Cigar	Ellipsoid	DiffPowers
unrotated					
100	1.16	1.14	1.17	1.08	1.09
200	1.32	1.30	1.27	1.28	1.23
400	1.41	1.30	1.29	1.27	1.18
800	2.14	2.15	2.18	1.95	1.91
rotated					
100	1.15	1.18	1.22	1.18	1.18
200	1.27	1.22	1.20	1.18	1.19
400	1.20	1.06	1.08	1.08	1.00
800	1.45	1.46	1.46	1.40	1.37

Table 4.5: Speed-up timing experiments in seconds with varying number of dimensionality n. Speed-up is calculated as $\text{time}_{\text{orig}}/\text{time}_{\text{new}}$ using the results from table 4.4. Experiments where run on the rotated as well as the unrotated functions.

name	formula
Rosenbrock	$f(\boldsymbol{x}) = \sum_{i=1}^{n} 100(x_{i+1} - x_i^2)^2 + (1 - x_i)^2$
Cigar	$f_\alpha(\boldsymbol{x}) = \alpha x_1^2 + \sum_{i=2}^{n} x_i^2$
Discus	$f_\alpha(\boldsymbol{x}) = x_1^2 + \alpha \sum_{i=2}^{n} x_i^2$
Ellipsoid	$f_\alpha(\boldsymbol{x}) = \sum_{i=1}^{n} \alpha^{\frac{i}{n}} x_i^2$
DiffPowers	$f(\boldsymbol{x}) = \sum_{i=1}^{n} \lvert x_i \rvert^{2+10\frac{i-1}{n}}$

Table 4.3: The formulas for the unrotated benchmark functions, where in all experiments $\alpha = 10^{-3}$. The rotated functions have the form $g(\boldsymbol{x}) = f(R\boldsymbol{x})$, where $R \in \mathbb{R}^{n \times n}$ is a random rotation matrix.

5. CONCLUSION

We presented a result on updating Cholesky factors while retaining a triangular shape and adopted it for covariance matrix adaption in randomized search and optimization. When employed within the (1+1)-CMA-ES and the the MO-CMA-ES, it decreases the memory usage by almost a factor of 4 and reduces computation time. The first is a direct result of storing only a triangular matrix instead of two full square matrices, while the latter was confirmed by numerical experiments. The new update is easy to implement and already part of major numeric libraries. Additionally it also allows for less expensive sampling of points, because of the triangular shape of the Cholesky factor. In summary, we see no reason for preferring the original Cholesky factor update rules (e.g., [10, 16, 2]) over the proposed type of methods.

Acknowledgements

We gratefully acknowledge support from the Danish National Advanced Technology Foundation through project "Personalized breast cancer screening".

6. REFERENCES

[1] Y. Akimoto, A. Auger, and N. Hansen. Comparison-based natural gradient optimization in high dimension. In *Proceedings of the 16th Annual Genetic and Evolutionary Computation Conference (GECCO)*, pages 373–380. ACM, 2014.

[2] D. V. Arnold and N. Hansen. Active covariance matrix adaptation for the (1+1)-CMA-ES. In *Proceedings of the 12th Annual Genetic and Evolutionary Computation Conference (GECCO)*, pages 385–392. ACM, 2010.

[3] H.-G. Beyer and H.-P. Schwefel. Evolution strategies–A comprehensive introduction. *Natural Computing*, 1(1):3–52, 2002.

[4] P. E. Gill, G. H. Golub, W. Murray, and M. A. Saunders. Methods for modifying matrix factorizations. *Mathematics of Computation*, 28(126):505–535, 1974.

[5] N. Hansen. Adaptive encoding: How to render search coordinate system invariant. In G. Rudolph et al., editors, *Proceedings of the 10th International Conference on Parallel Problem Solving from Nature (PPSN X)*, LNCS, pages 205–214, 2008.

[6] N. Hansen. The CMA evolution strategy: A tutorial, 2011.

[7] N. Hansen and A. Ostermeier. Completely derandomized self-adaptation in evolution strategies. *Evolutionary Computation*, 9(2):159–195, 2001.

[8] C. Igel, N. Hansen, and S. Roth. Covariance matrix adaptation for multi-objective optimization. *Evolutionary Computation*, 15(1):1–28, 2007.

[9] C. Igel, V. Heidrich-Meisner, and T. Glasmachers. Shark. *Journal of Machine Learning Research*, 9:993–996, 2008.

[10] C. Igel, T. Suttorp, and N. Hansen. A computational efficient covariance matrix update and a (1+1)-CMA for evolution strategies. In *Proceedings of the 8th Annual Genetic and Evolutionary Computation Conference (GECCO)*, pages 453–460. ACM, 2006.

[11] P. Larrañaga. A review on estimation of distribution algorithms. In P. Larrañaga and J. Lozano, editors, *Estimation of distribution algorithms*, pages 57–100. Springer, 2002.

[12] I. Loshchilov. A computationally efficient limited memory CMA-ES for large scale optimization. In *Proceedings of the 16th Annual Genetic and Evolutionary Computation Conference (GECCO)*, pages 397–404. ACM, 2014.

[13] J. Poland and A. Zell. Main vector adaptation: A CMA variant with linear time and space complexity. In *Proceedings of the 10th Annual Genetic and Evolutionary Computation Conference (GECCO)*, pages 1050–1055. Morgan Kaufmann Publishers, 2001.

[14] R. Ros and N. Hansen. A simple modification in CMA-ES achieving linear time and space complexity. In G. Rudolph et al., editors, *Proceedings of the 10th International Conference on Parallel Problem Solving from Nature (PPSN X)*, LNCS, pages 296–305. Springer, 2008.

[15] Y. Sun, T. Schaul, F. Gomez, and J. Schmidhuber. A linear time natural evolution strategy for non-separable functions. In *15th Annual Conference on Genetic and Evolutionary Computation Conference Companion*, pages 61–62. ACM, 2013.

[16] T. Suttorp, N. Hansen, and C. Igel. Efficient covariance matrix update for variable metric evolution strategies. *Machine Learning*, 75(2):167–197, 2009.

[17] T. Voß, H. Hansen, and C. Igel. Improved step size adaptation for the MO-CMA-ES. In *Proceedings of the 12th Annual Genetic and Evolutionary Computation Conference (GECCO)*, pages 487–494. ACM Press, 2010.

Partition Crossover for Pseudo-Boolean Optimization

Renato Tinós
Department of Computing and Mathematics
University of São Paulo
Ribeirão Preto, SP, Brazil
rtinos@ffclrp.usp.br

Darrell Whitley
Department of Computer Science
Colorado State University
Fort Collins, CO, USA
whitley@cs.colostate.edu

Francisco Chicano
Department of Lenguajes y Ciencias de la Computación
University of Málaga
Málaga, Spain
chicano@lcc.uma.es

ABSTRACT

A partition crossover operator is introduced for use with NK landscapes, MAX-kSAT and for all k-bounded pseudo-Boolean functions. By definition, these problems use a bit representation. Under partition crossover, the evaluation of offspring can be directly obtained from partial evaluations of substrings found in the parents. Partition crossover explores the *variable interaction graph* of the pseudo-Boolean functions in order to partition the variables of the solution vector. Proofs are presented showing that if the differing variable assignments found in the two parents can be partitioned into q non-interacting sets, partition crossover can be used to find the best of 2^q possible offspring. Proofs are presented which show that parents that are locally optimal will always generate offspring that are locally optimal with respect to a (more restricted) hyperplane subspace. Empirical experiments show that parents that are locally optimal generate offspring that are locally optimal in the full search space more than 80 percent of the time. Experimental results also show the effectiveness of the proposed crossover when used in combination with a hybrid genetic algorithm.

Categories and Subject Descriptors

I.2.8 [**Artificial Intelligence**]: [Problem Solving, Control Methods, and Search]

General Terms

Algorithms, Theory

Keywords

Pseudo-Boolean optimization; NK Landscape; Recombination Operator; Partition Crossover; Evolutionary Combinatorial Optimization

FOGA'15, January 17–20, 2015, Aberystwyth, UK.

http://dx.doi.org/10.1145/2725494.2725497

1. INTRODUCTION

A **partition crossover** operator is introduced for recombining solutions to k-bounded pseudo-Boolean functions. The set of k-bounded pseudo-Boolean functions includes MAX-kSAT problems, NK Landscapes and generalized spin glass problems. These problems are all NP Hard. All of these problems use a bit representation; the output can be any real valued number. Thus, a pseudo-Boolean function has the form: $f : \mathbb{B}^n \to \mathbb{R}$. If the function f is also k-bounded, f can be decomposed into m subfunctions, where each subfunction takes at most k bits as input. For example, in an NK Landscape, there are N variables and N subfunctions that take as input $K+1$ bits; thus, $m = N$ and $k = (K + 1)$. (Note that we will use small n when refering to problem size in general, and use capital N, where $N = n$, when specifically discussing NK Landscapes.) Heckendorn [11] has referred to the class of k-bounded pseudo-Boolean functions as *embedded landscapes.* We could also generalize Kauffman's [16] concept of NK Landscapes and use the term "Mk Landscapes" to refer to all pseudo-Boolean functions which are a linear combination of m subfunctions, where each subfunction takes at most k bits as input.

The limitation to k bounded functions is not as restrictive as it might seem. Every search problem that uses a bit representation and which has an algebraic evaluation function can be converted into a k-bounded pseudo-Boolean function in polynomial time [2]. For example, one can construct examples where it is feasible to take an NK Landscape where $n = 5,000$ and $k = K + 1 = 6$ and to convert it into another NK Landscape where $n = 10,000$ and $k = 3$, where both problems have the same global optimum (or global optima). Of course, in such cases the actual search spaces that are induced will be different. The reduction of a general pseudo-Boolean optimization problem to a k-bounded problem is analogous to the reduction of a general SAT problem to a MAX-kSAT problem [5]. A reduction to CNF-SAT that is k-bounded is routine when solving SAT instances [7] [15].

Partition crossover decomposes the evaluation function as well as the set of variables during recombination. This decomposition can be done in such a way as to make it possible to evaluate offspring using partial evaluations obtained from the parents. For k bounded pseudo-Boolean functions, the set of bits with different assignments in two parent solutions can be partitioned into q non-overlapping subsets and the objective function can be written as a sum of q subfunctions; this is done in a manner such that each variable is included in only one of the new subfunctions. Because offspring are evaluated using the sum of the q partial evaluations of the parents, the best subsolution for each set of variables in the partition can be selected in a greedy fashion. Thus partition crossover deterministically returns the best of 2^q offspring. The parents are included in the set of possible offspring. If no offspring is better than the best parent, partition crossover returns the best parent.

Previous forms of partition crossover have been developed for the symmetric *Traveling Salesman Problem* (TSP) [31] [8] and the asymmetric TSP [29]; these operators have been shown to be highly effective and to yield state of the art results when combined with a powerful local search algorithm such as Lin-Kernighan-Helsgaun Local Search [13]. Each improvement to partition crossover (and generalized partition crossover) has increased the number of "recombining components" by producing a more fine grain decomposition of the parent solutions.

The Lin-Kernighan-Helsgaun implementation [13] already includes a recombination operator in the form of "Iterated Partial Transcription" [19]. Forms of partition crossover that cut more than two common edges for the TSP finds opportunities for recombination that are missed by Iterated Partial Transcription; during recombination Iterated Partial Transcription requires that "two subchains must have the same intial and final cities" (see [19]). Also, as far as we know, there are also no published cost complexity guarantees for Iterated Partial Transcription; in the worst case, this method appears to have $O(n^2)$ cost per recombination.

The TSP recombination operator proposed in [31], denoted *partition crossover* (PX), recombines partial solutions that are not shared in common between two parents. First, a union graph $G_u = G_x \cup G_y$ is created, where G_x and G_y are two graphs representing the two parent TSP solutions. Note that G_x and G_y represent Hamiltonian circuits over the set of vertices. The shared edges of G_u are removed and the connected components are identified using Breadth First Search (BFS). All the connected components separated from the rest of the graph by exactly two common edges and with more than one node are identified as *recombining components*. The remainder of the graph is also considered a recombining component. Partition crossover considers all recombinations between the recombining components to generate the offspring. In the TSP, the cost of evaluating one solution is $O(n)$. In the existing implementations of partition crossover operators, the partial evaluation of each one of the q recombining components are computed independently; this makes it possible to greedily select the best subsolution for each component. Therefore, existing partition crossover operators finds the best of 2^q possible offspring at cost $O(n)$. There can potentially exist forms of partition crossover with finer grained partitions and more recombining components, but finding such a partition could also have greater than $O(n)$ cost.

In the current paper the term *partition crossover* is used in a general sense to include both the original PX and the generalized PX operators (GPX and GAPX) for the TSP as well as a (generalized) partition crossover operator for pseudo-Boolean optimization problems. The original partition crossover (PX) for TSP used a single crossover point [31]; all subsequent versions of partition crossover uses multiple crossover points [8] [29].

We have already noted that partition crossover for the TSP has strong similarities to the "Iterated Partial Transcription" operator proposed by Möbius et al. [19]. Those authors also note that this idea could be applied in principle to spin glass problems by "flipping clusters" of a spin glass.

In this paper, the use of partition crossover for k-bounded pseudo-Boolean optimization problems is illustrated using NK landscapes. The NK landscape model [16] is widely used in different areas of research, such as theoretical biology, optimization, and physics. The number of local optima in an NK landscape is a product of the degree of epistasis K [20]. In the NK model, $k = (K + 1)$ different loci influence each one of the N subfunctions that compose the evaluation function. The evaluation function of the NK model is $f(x) \in \mathbb{R}$ where the binary vector x is epistatically bounded by a positive integer k.

Random NK Landscapes are considered to be difficult optimization problems for *genetic algorithms* (GAs) with standard recombination and mutation operators [12] [18] [1]. One problem is that crossover operators generally do not explore the linkage between the loci in the NK model. Therefore, the offspring is generally worse than the parents because recombination is disruptive.

One operator that considers linkage is network crossover [9]. Network crossover constructs a mask based on the epistasis matrix of the NK model. To build the crossover mask, a random bit of the solution vector is chosen as the starting point for randomized Breadth First Search. When the i-th bit of the solution vector is visited, the i-th bit of the mask is assigned 1, indicating that the i-th bit of the offspring is inherited from the first parent. When a desired number of bits are visited, the search is stopped. If the search is ended before the desired number of bits is reached, a new random starting point is chosen. Unlike network crossover, partition crossover uses the parents to partition the variable interaction graph in order to create a crossover mask.

The main contribution of the current paper is to prove the feasibility of partition crossover for k-bound pseudo-Boolean optimization problems, from both a theoretical and empirical point of view. We prove that partition crossover can be implemented as a deterministic and greedy crossover operator: it returns the best possible offspring given a particular decomposition of the parents. Partition crossover also returns an offspring which is provably locally optimal in a hyperplane subspace created by fixing the bits that are shared by the parents. The offspring is not guaranteed to be locally optimal in the original search space corresponding to the objective function f under the bit-flip neighborhood. However, empirical results indicate that offspring produced by partition crossover are often also locally optimal with respect to the original objective function f and the bit-flip neighborhood.

In our empirical experiments, offspring are locally optimal more than 80 percent of the time. This means that partition crossover is capable of "tunneling" from two parents that are local optima to a new offspring that is a new and distinct local optimum in a basin of attraction different from the basins containing the parents.

The decomposability of fitness functions by recombination is discussed in Section 2. The proposed crossover is presented and analyzed in Section 3. Experimental results in Section 4 show the efficiency of the proposed crossover when applied in combination with a hybrid GA. We discuss in Section 5 the "tunneling" capabilities of the new crossover operator and outline the conclusions and future work in Section 6.

2. DECOMPOSING THE EVALUATION FUNCTION

Let us first clarify the notation used for binary strings. We write here $\mathbb{B}^n$ as a synonym of $\mathbb{Z}_2^n$: $\mathbb{Z}_2^n = \mathbb{B}^n$. This set forms an Abelian group with the component-wise sum in $\mathbb{Z}_2$ (exclusive OR), denoted with $\oplus$. Given an element $z \in \mathbb{B}^n$, we will denote with $|z|$ the number of ones of z and with $\overline{z}$ the complement of the string (all bits inverted). We will denote with $\vee$ the bitwise OR operator between two binary strings and with $\wedge$ the bitwise AND. We will assume that the $\wedge$ operator has precedence over $\vee$. However, we will use parentheses to clarify the precedence. In order to simplify the notation, we will also use binary strings to represent sets of variables. In this case a binary string represents the set of variables having 1 in the string. For example, if the set of variables is $V = \{v_1, v_2, v_3, v_4\}$, the binary string 1010 can also be interpreted as the set $\{v_1, v_3\}$.

Assume that the objective function, f, is a k-bounded pseudo-Boolean function that is made up of m subfunctions. Let $\mathbb{B}^n$ represent the domain of function f: bit strings of length n. The objective function can be decomposed as follows:

$$f(x) = \sum_{i=1}^{m} f^i(x|_{mask_i}), \tag{1}$$

where f^i is a subfunction of f and $mask_i \in \mathbb{B}^n$ is used to denote the subset of variables needed to evaluate f^i. The notation $x|_{mask_i}$ is used to represent the restriction of x to the variables in $mask_i$; this way, with $f^i(x|_{mask_i})$ we are expressing the fact that function f^i only depends on the variables where $mask_i$ is 1. If the function is k-bounded, then each subfunction f^i accepts at most k bits as inputs, and $|mask_i| \leq k$.

Any discrete function $f : \mathbb{B}^n \rightarrow \mathbb{R}$ can be represented in the following polynomial form:

$$f(x) = \sum_{i \in \mathbb{B}^n} w_i \psi_i(x), \tag{2}$$

where w_i is a Walsh coefficient and $\psi_i(x) = (-1)^{i^T x}$ generates a sign. A discrete Fourier transform, also known as the Walsh transform, can be applied to f as follows:

$$w = \mathbf{W} f, \qquad f = \mathbf{W}^{-1} w,$$

where in the general case $\mathbf{W}$ is the $2^n \times 2^n$ matrix

$$\mathbf{W}_{ij} = \psi_i(j) = (-1)^{i^T j}.$$

If the function f is a linear combination of k-bounded subfunctions, then each subfunction f^i depends on k variables. Thus, for subfunction f^i the corresponding Walsh matrix is a $2^k \times 2^k$ matrix that transforms each subfunction into a Walsh polynomial. Thus each subfunction f^i contributes at most 2^k nonzero Walsh coefficients to the Walsh polynomial of $f(x)$ [10, 11].

First, the Walsh transform is applied to each subfunction over k bits:

$$w^i = \mathbf{W} f^i,$$

where w^i denotes the Walsh transform of f^i. Then, for any k-bounded pseudo-Boolean function we can generate the Walsh polynomial for the function f by linearly combining the coefficients obtained from each subfunction f^i as follows:

$$w = \sum_{i=1}^{m} w^i.$$

The vectors w^i are summed in the normal way, by adding coefficients with the same indices. If there are m subfunctions, the number of nonzero Walsh coefficients for f is at most $m\ 2^k$. If m is of size $O(n)$, the number of nonzero Walsh coefficients is also $O(n)$.

For example, for any NK Landscape, there are at most 2^{K+1} Walsh coefficients in each subfunction, $k = K + 1$ of which are linear, and one of which is a constant offset (w_0). Thus there are at most $N * (2^{K+1} - K - 2)$ nonlinear interactions. Thus, for fixed K there are $O(n)$ nonlinear interactions. For a MAX-3SAT problems when $m = 4n$, there are at most $2^3 - 4$ nonlinear Walsh coefficients per clause. Thus there are at most $4m = 16n$ nonlinear interactions. For any fixed k, as long as $m = O(n)$ there are at most $O(n)$ nonlinear interactions.

We should note there is nothing special about the use of Walsh coefficients. But the Walsh coefficients represent a precise way of identifying the nonlinear interaction between variables. We can also express k-bounded pseudo-Boolean functions as multilinear functions; a multilinear function would also uniquely identify nonlinear interactions between variables [2].

DEFINITION 1 (VARIABLE INTERACTION). *Given a pseudo-Boolean function $f : \mathbb{B}^n \rightarrow \mathbb{R}$ whose Walsh decomposition is given by Eq. (2), we say that variables v_j and v_k of f* interact, *if there exists a nonzero Walsh coefficient w_i in the Walsh decomposition of f such that $v_j, v_k \in i$. The* variable interaction *relationship is symmetric.*

The definition of *variable interaction* is completely general and does not depend on the form of the objective function. If the objective function can be written as a sum of k-bounded subfunctions, like in Eq. (1), then two variables that interact will necessarily appear together as arguments of one of the subfunctions. For this reason, it is sometimes more convenient to say that two variables interact when they appear together in one of the subfunctions (see [4] for example). Often these two ways of defining interactions are exactly the same. However, the two concepts of interaction can differ, in the sense that two variables that interact according to the "subfunctions criterion" might not interact according to the "Walsh criterion." For example, assume a function includes two subfunctions f^l and f^r and that $f^l(x) = -f^r(x)$ and thus $f^l(x) + f^r(x) = 0$. Variables common to f^l and f^r interact under the "subfunction criterion" but not under the more precise "Walsh criterion" (unless the variables also appear together in other subfunctions). Unless otherwise stated, in this paper we will use the concept of variable interaction given in Definition 1 using the Walsh decomposition.

DEFINITION 2 (VARIABLE INTERACTION GRAPH). *Given a pseudo-Boolean function $f : \mathbb{B}^n \rightarrow \mathbb{R}$, we define the* Variable Interaction Graph *(VIG) of f as the graph $G = (V, E)$, where V is the set of variables of f and the edge set E contains all the pairs of variables (v_j, v_k) that interact.*

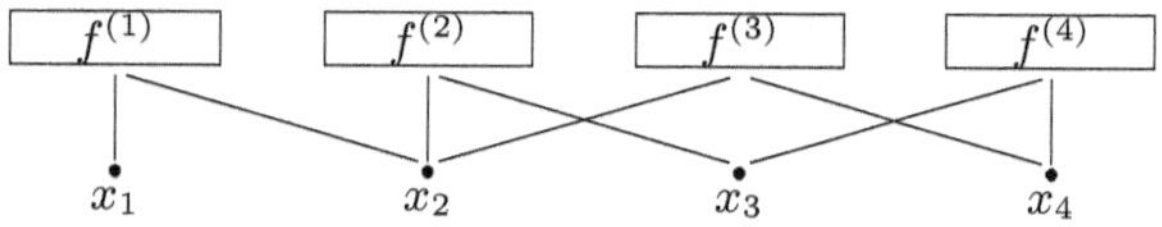

(a) Function

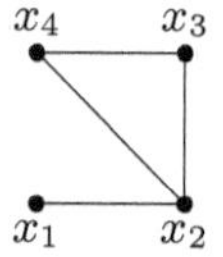

(b) Variable Interaction Graph

Figure 1: A function with $k = 2$ bounded epistasis, $n = 4$ variables and $m = 4$ subfunctions (top) and its corresponding Variable Interaction Graph (bottom). We assume here that none of the corresponding Walsh coefficients are zero.

In Figure 1 we show a function with k-bounded epistasis and its corresponding VIG.

PROPOSITION 3. *The maximum number of edges in the Variable Interaction Graph of a k-bounded pseudo-Boolean function f that can be written as a sum of m subfunctions is at most $mk(k-1)/2$.*

PROOF. Each subfunction depends on k variables and it can contribute at most $k(k-1)/2$ edges to the VIG. Since there are m subfunctions, the result follows. □

Let us now introduce some notation related to graphs. Given a graph $G(V, E)$ and a set of vertices $v \subseteq V$ of the graph, we define the *adjacency* of v, $adj_G(v)$, as the set of vertices that are adjacent in the graph to a vertex in v, that is:

$$adj_G(v) = \{w \in V | (\{w\} \times v) \cap E \neq \emptyset\}.$$

We define the *extended adjacency* of v as

$$adj^*_G(v) = adj_G(v) \cup v.$$

We will denote with $G[v]$ the *vertex-induced subgraph* of G containing only the vertices in v and the edges with both ends in v.

PROPOSITION 4. *Let $f : \mathbb{B}^n \rightarrow \mathbb{R}$ be a pseudo-Boolean function with VIG G, V the set of variables of f and v a subset of V. It is possible to additively decompose f as a sum of two functions g^1 and g^2, the first one depending on the variables in v and the second one not depending on the variables in v:*

$$f(x) = g^1(x|_{mask_1}) + g^2(x|_{mask_2}), \quad (3)$$

where $v \subseteq mask_1$ and $v \cap mask_2 = \emptyset$. The minimal set of variables a function g^1 must depend on is $adj^*_G(v)$.

PROOF. Let us define g^1 as the sum of the terms in the Walsh decomposition of f containing Walsh coefficients that include variables in v in their index:

$$g^1(x) = \sum_{\substack{i \in \mathbb{B}^n \\ i \cap v \neq \emptyset}} w_i \psi_i(x), \quad (4)$$

and g^2 is simply the sum of the other terms: $g^2(x) = f(x) - g^1(x)$. By the definition of g^2 the sum (3) holds. By the definition of g^1 we have that all terms depending on variables in v are included in g^1, so we have $v \subseteq mask_1$ and $v \cap mask_2 = \emptyset$.

A variable v' is in $adj_G(v)$ if there exists a nonzero Walsh coefficient (and term) with index including v' and a variable in v. However, we included all these Walsh terms in g^1, so it depends on all the variables in $adj^*_G(v)$. We can also notice that only the variables in $adj^*_G(v)$ are arguments of g^1.

Finally, we must prove that we need g^1 to depend on all the variables in $adj^*_G(v)$ if we want to additively decompose f in two functions with $v \subseteq mask_1$ and $v \cap mask_2 = \emptyset$. All the Walsh terms of f must be in one of the two functions, g^1 or g^2. In order to reduce the variables that g^1 depends on, we have to move one Walsh term from g^1 to g^2. But, by the definition of g^1, the moved term depends on a variable in v, and g^2 would depend on that variable. This is a contradiction, so $adj^*_G(v)$ is the minimal set g^1 must depend on. □

Given a subset of variables v of f, we would like to find a partition π of v such that f can be additively decomposed into $|\pi|$ subfunctions g^i for $i = 1$ to $|\pi|$, where each g^i depends on the variables in the subset π_i but does not depend on the variables in $v - \pi_i$. This kind of decomposition allows the variables in each subset π_i to be optimized independently from the variables in another subset. In particular, it will be used in partition crossover to select the parent providing the value for these variables. The next proposition provides the most fine grain partition on v.

PROPOSITION 5. *Let $f : \mathbb{B}^n \rightarrow \mathbb{R}$ be a pseudo-Boolean function with VIG G, V the set of variables of f and v a subset of V. The most fine grain partition π of v that additively decomposes f is the partition induced by the connected components in the subgraph $G[v]$. That partition is given by:*

$$f(x) = h(x) + \sum_{i=1}^{|\pi|} g^i(x|_{mask_i}), \quad (5)$$

where $\pi_i \subseteq mask_i$, $(v - \pi_i) \cap mask_i = \emptyset$ and h does not depend on any variable in v.

PROOF. In the following we will focus on the variables of v. The subfunctions will depend on some other variables of $V - v$ but we are not interested in these variables. Proposition 4 implies that each g^i should contain at least one connected component of $G[v]$. We can prove this by contradiction. If g^i depends on a proper subset of a connected component t, by Proposition 4, it must also depend on $adj^*_G(t)$, but since t is in a connected component of $G[v]$, $adj^*_G(t)$ contains a variable of v which is not in t and will also be an argument of another subfunction g^j. Thus, if we want the arguments of the subfunctions g to be disjoint sets of variables of v we have to include complete connected components of $G[v]$ in each π_i.

We are interested in the most fine grain partition of v which decomposes the evaluation function f. The argument of the previous paragraph implies that the most fine grain partition must be the one induced by the connected components of $G[v]$. The subfunctions g^i can be defined from the Walsh decomposition of f as follows:

$$g^i(x) = \sum_{\substack{j \in \mathbb{B}^n \\ j \cap \pi_i \neq \emptyset}} w_j \psi_j(x). \quad (6)$$

The subfunction h, which does not depend on any variable of v is:

$$h(x) = f(x) - \sum_{i=1}^{|\pi|} g^i(x). \tag{7}$$

□

Although we explicitly included a function h in the additive decomposition of f that does not depend on any variable in v, sometimes we are not interested in that function and we just assume that it is summed to any of the other g^i subfunctions. Thus, in the following we will often say that f can be written as a sum of $|\pi|$ subfunctions and not $|\pi|+1$.

3. PARTITION CROSSOVER

The main recombination operators for binary strings in the literature are *respectful* and *transmit alleles* [23] [22]: that is, all "alleles" (e.g. bits) are inherited from the parents. Partition crossover is not an exception: all the bits shared in common by the two parent solutions will be inherited by the offspring and the differing bits will be *transmitted* from one parent or the other. The key characteristic of partition crossover is that the decision as to which parent to copy for each individual bit will be based on an additive decomposition of f. This will allow the operator to select the best offspring from among an exponential number of possible offspring.

Proposition 5 defines the most fine grain way to additively decompose f when we are interested in separating the variables in a subset v. In partition crossover the set of variables v in which we are interested is the set of differing variables in the two parent solutions. Thus, instead of the VIG of the function f, it will be useful in the following to work with a reduced graph: the *recombination graph.*

DEFINITION 6 (RECOMBINATION GRAPH). *Let $f : \mathbb{B}^n \to \mathbb{R}$ be a pseudo-Boolean function with Variable Interaction Graph G and $x, y \in \mathbb{B}^n$ two solutions. We define the recombination graph of function f for solutions x and y as $G[x \oplus y]$, that is the subgraph of G composed of the variables in which x and y differ.*

In Algorithm 1, partition crossover (PX) is presented for pseudo-Boolean optimization problems. Prior to applying partition crossover it is necessary to construct the VIG, which is common to all the recombinations for the same objective function. Thus, it is provided as input in Algorithm 1.

The first step of the operator is to transfer all common bits to the offspring. This is done in line 1 of Algorithm 1. Observe that this operation can be written as the bitwise AND of the two parents. The AND of the differing bits will be zero.

Next, using the two parents x and y, determine the recombination graph and use Breadth First Search to find the connected components of the recombination graph (line 2). These connected components form a partition of the set of variables in $x \oplus y$ (the differing bits in the parent solutions).

Having determined the partition of variables in $x \oplus y$, test the two assignments from the two parents. Note that since this only includes non-shared assignments to variables, the solutions from the two parents will be complements. Proposition 5 ensures that we can write f as a linear sum of subfunctions g^i where each one depends on the variables in one component π_i and not the others (line 3). Select the assignment in each connected component that results in the best evaluation for the corresponding subfunction g^i (lines 4 to 10).

Algorithm 1 Partition Crossover (assuming maximization)

Input: f (pseudo-Boolean function)
Input: G (Variable Interaction Graph of f)
Input: x, y (parent solutions)
Output: z (offspring)
1: $z \leftarrow x \wedge y$ // Transfer the common bits
2: $\pi \leftarrow$ computePartition ($G[x \oplus y]$)
3: Let $f = \sum_{i=1}^{|\pi|} g^i$ according to Proposition 5.
4: **for** $i = 1$ to $|\pi|$ **do**
5:   **if** $g^i(x) > g^i(y)$ **then**
6:     $z \leftarrow z \vee (x \wedge \pi_i)$
7:   **else**
8:     $z \leftarrow z \vee (y \wedge \pi_i)$
9:   **end if**
10: **end for**

THEOREM 7. *For any k-bounded pseudo-Boolean function f, if the recombination graph of f for solutions x and y contains q connected components, then partition crossover returns the best of 2^q solutions, including the parent solutions.*

PROOF. Since partition crossover is considering the q connected component independently and there are two possible sources of bits (the two parents), it is exploring a subspace of 2^q solutions, which include the parent solutions. Since f can be written as a linear sum of subfunctions, each one depending on the variables of each connected component, the best solution in this subspace is obtained by optimizing each subfunction independently, that is, selecting the best parent for each connected component. This is what partition crossover does, so it must return a solution whose evaluation is better than or equal to the best of the 2^q solutions. □

From the previous theorem it is clear that a larger number of connected components implies the exploration of a larger set of solutions. In the experimental section we will study how many connected components can be found in some instances of NK landscapes. Despite the exponential number of solutions explored during crossover, the complexity of the operator is linear in n, as the next theorem states.

THEOREM 8. *If the number of nonzero Walsh coefficients of f is $O(n)$ and the epistasis degree k is a constant, partition crossover runs in $O(n)$ time.*

PROOF. The bitwise AND of line 1 requires $O(n)$ because n is the length of the binary strings. The BFS algorithm of line 2 requires $O(|E|)$, but $|E|$ is bounded by the number of nonzero Walsh coefficients, which is $O(n)$. Evaluating all the subfunctions g^i in lines 4 to 10 and assigning the corresponding values to z also requires $O(n)$ because the g functions are composed of disjoint sets of Walsh terms and there are only $O(n)$ nonzero of such terms. □

We will use an NK landscape to illustrate how the VIG and the recombination graph are used to find a partition that can be exploited by recombination. Assume we are given the following NK landscape, where $N = 8$ and $K = 2$ (and $k = K+1 = 3$). In the following table, $mask_i$ indicates

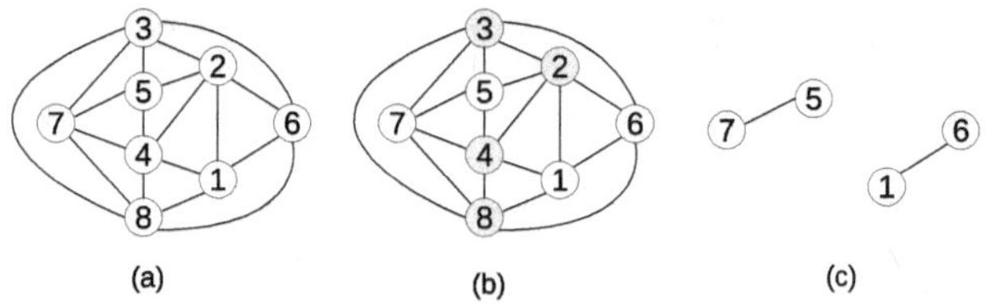

Figure 2: The VIG is shown on the lefthand side (a). When recombining the solutions 00000000 and 10001110, the vertices and edges associated with shared variables are deleted (b) to yield the "recombination graph" shown on the righthand side (c). If the recombination graph can be partitioned into q connected components, then recombination is guaranteed to return the best of 2^q possible offspring.

which bits are utilized by subfunction f^i. Bits are numbered from left to right, from 1 to 8.

$mask_1 = 8, 4, 1 = 10010001$	$mask_2 = 5, 3, 2$
$mask_3 = 6, 3, 2 = 01100100$	$mask_4 = 4, 2, 1$
$mask_5 = 7, 5, 4 = 00011010$	$mask_6 = 8, 6, 1$
$mask_7 = 7, 5, 3 = 00101010$	$mask_8 = 8, 7, 3$

The Walsh transformation of this NK landscape generates the following order-2 and order-3 Walsh coefficients (let us assume they are all nonzero):

f^1 yields $w_{1,4}, w_{1,8}, w_{4,8}, w_{1,4,8}$
f^2 yields $w_{2,5}, w_{2,3}, w_{5,3}, w_{2,3,5}$
f^3 yields $w_{3,6}, w_{3,2}, w_{6,2}, w_{2,3,6}$
f^4 yields $w_{4,2}, w_{4,1}, w_{2,1}, w_{1,2,4}$
f^5 yields $w_{5,7}, w_{5,4}, w_{7,4}, w_{4,5,7}$
f^6 yields $w_{6,8}, w_{6,1}, w_{8,1}, w_{1,6,8}$
f^7 yields $w_{7,3}, w_{7,5}, w_{3,5}, w_{3,5,7}$
f^8 yields $w_{8,7}, w_{8,3}, w_{7,3}, w_{3,7,8}$

This results in the VIG shown on the lefthand side of Figure 2.

Assume we wish to recombine two solutions 00000000 and 10001110; again, the variables are numbered from 1 to 8 from left to right. These two solutions reside in the hyperplane subspace *000***0 because these zero bits are shared in common by the parents. Because "respectful" recombination inherits all of the variable values that the two solutions share in common, recombination must generate a solution in this same subspace.

From the VIG, we will generate the recombination graph. Partition crossover first deletes those variables that share a common value assignment from the VIG. The edges connected to the variables with common values are also deleted. This yields the recombination graph. We next ask if deleting these variables and edges "partitions" the recombination graph. In our example, the variables with shared values are 2, 3, 4 and 8. The variables that have different assignments are 1, 5, 6 and 7. The recombination graph is partitioned into two independent subgraphs, as illustrated in Figure 2(c).

Since, the recombination graph partitions into two independent subgraphs, by Proposition 5 this also implies that the objective function can be partitioned into two *new subfunctions* that can be linearly combined to evaluate any and all offspring produced from the parents by partition crossover.

The following results pertain to questions about the "optimality" of offspring generated by partition crossover. We will define a function f' in relationship to a specific recombination of x and y as:

$$f'(z) = f((x \wedge y) \vee (z \wedge (x \oplus y))), \tag{8}$$

that is, if there are s common bits between x and y, f' accepts as input the $n - s$ non-common bits. Its value will be the same as f where non-common bits are taken from z and the common bits are taken from x and y. The function f' is the restriction of f to a hyperplane subspace.

3.1 Locally Optimal Parents

In practice, we will only apply partition crossover to parents that are also local optima with respect to the Hamming distance 1 neighborhood. The reason for this restriction is due to the fact that we need parents to have some degree of similarity in order for partitions to exist. For example, if we tried to recombine two random solutions, x_1 and x_2 we might expect x_1 and x_2 to share approximately one half of the bit assignments to variables. If two solutions share more than one half of the same bit assignments, then the recombination graph is more likely to partition the VIG, because more vertices are removed from the VIG when the recombination graph is constructed. Thus, partition crossover is limited to local optima because local optima are more likely to share more than one half of the same bit assignments. We could also explicitly decide which local optima to recombine by picking those that share more bits in common. This idea will be revisited in section 4 of this paper.

THEOREM 9. *Given a pseudo-Boolean function f, two solutions x and y that are local optima of f using the 1-flip neighborhood, and the function f' defined in (8), the offspring generated by partition crossover will be local optima in the function f' using the 1 flip neighborhood. However, the offspring need not always be a local optimum in f, but an improved offspring is guaranteed to be in a different neighborhood (and a new basin of attraction relative to local search) from that of its parents.*

PROOF. Because the parents are local optima, by definition there is no improving move under a bit flip in either parent that can yield an improving move. Because the offspring results from changes in the non-fixed variables in separable components (and separable subfunctions), and they share exactly the same shared variable assignments of the parents, the offspring cannot be improved by a bit flip that changes any of the variables that appear in any of the components. If such an improving move did exist, then the same improving move would exist in one of the parents, and thus one of the parents is not really locally optimal. This leads to a contradiction. Thus the offspring must be local optima in f'.

However, assume that an offspring is generated that has one variable v_a that changes in component π_i and another variable v_b changes in a different component π_j, leading to an assignment combination that did not previously exist in the parents. Such a new combination of variables assignment can lead to a potential improving move in the evaluation function f. Again assume the function is expressed in terms of the Walsh coefficients: let v_z be a variable with the same bit assignment in both parents and assume there exists a Walsh coefficient $w_{a,c,z}$ and $w_{b,d,z}$. Assume variables v_a and v_c are in π_i, and v_b and v_d are in π_j. Note that v_z must not be in the recombination graph for these variables to be in different components (otherwise there would be one single connected component containing v_a, v_b, v_c and v_d). Assume recombination generates an overall assignment to v_a, v_c, v_b and v_d that is not found in either parent, but which is better than either parent; the potential contribution of $w_{a,c,z}$ and $w_{b,d,z}$ is now different. The combination of assignments to variables v_a, v_b, v_c, v_d, v_z is at least 3 bit flips away from either parent when v_z is flipped, and thus a single bit flip (of v_z) can now potentially correspond to a new improving move.

If the new offspring is better than both parents, and the parents are local optima, then the new offspring must be in a new basin of attraction under the 1-flip neighborhood. □

This theorem makes it clear that the only bit flips that can lead to additional improving moves after partition crossover requires that local search flips a variable that had the same assignment in both parents.

In general, assume the recombination graph is partitioned into q connected components. We can, of course, always explicitly compute the Walsh coefficients, then partition the coefficients to construct q partial evaluation functions. But we can also just treat the shared bits in the subfunctions as being fixed and partition the original subfunctions. Both approaches compute the same result, and both allow a greedy method to find the best subsolution in each partition to be determined in $O(n)$ time.

THEOREM 10. *Given two locally optimal parents, at least two connected components of the recombination graph must contain more than 1 vertex for recombination to find an improving move.*

PROOF. Assume there is only one component with size greater than 1; denote this by π_L. Next assume there is one or more components of size 1. Assume the assignment from component π_L is inherited first from parent x (without loss of generality). At this point the offspring has inherited all the shared variables from parent x and all of the variables from π_L from parent x. Since all of the other components are of size 1, these moves correspond to moves in the Hamming distance 1 neighborhood. Therefore we know that the offspring must be in the same basin of attraction as parent x because all of the other components are of size 1, and the associated subfunctions g are all linear because only one variable in $x \oplus y$ contributes to each partial evaluation. Therefore, if parent x is a local optimum, all of these components with only one variable that differs from x must be disimproving or neutral moves. □

THEOREM 11. *If there are at least two "larger components" containing more than 1 vertex, and each locally optimal parent contributes improving assignments to bits in one of these "larger components," then additional components of size 1 can also contribute to improvements of the offspring.*

PROOF. Assume the offspring inherits bits m, n, o from parent x in a larger component, and bits p, q, r from parent y in another larger component; both must be improving assignments. Since both parents have contributed to the offspring, and the offspring is the best of the 2^q solutions (which includes the parents), the offspring must be better than the parents. Because the parents are local optima, the offspring must reside in a new basin of attraction. The components of size 1 still behave like Hamming distance one moves, but since the offspring is in a different basin of attraction than the parents, these Hamming distance 1 moves can correspond to new improving moves that have not already been exploited by local search. □

4. EXPERIMENTS

The proposed partition crossover (PX) operator can be applied as a recombination operator in a wide range of different search algorithms that might be used to optimize an NK landscape instance. Here, we compare partition crossover to two other crossover operators in a hybrid GA. Our goal in the current paper is not to compare to the state of the art, but rather to explore the behavior of partition crossover empirically.

4.1 Hybrid Genetic Algorithm

The hybrid GA is described in Algorithm 2. Bit-flip local search with first improvement is applied to random solutions in order to generate the initial population. Elitism is used to preserve the current best solution, while tournament selection with a pool of 5 solutions is used to select parents for crossover and mutation.

We also tested an alternative approach for selection in combination with partition crossover. The first parent is chosen by tournament selection. The second parent is the closest individual (in terms of Hamming distance) to the first parent among the solutions in the same tournament pool used to select the first parent. Only individuals that are different are selected. Therefore, the first parent is chosen based only on fitness, while the second parent is chosen based on the distance to the first parent. This increases the number of bit assignments the two parents share in common. We denote this selection mechanism as *fit/dist selection*. Our hypothesis is that we can decompose parents into more independent components by selecting parents that share more bits in common. In the limit this fails: if parents share all the bits in common, there is no partition and no components.

One of the limitations of all *respectful* and *transmitting* recombination operators is that crossover can only reach parts of the search space composed of the alleles present in the current population. Some method is needed to generate new diversity. Every 10 generations of the GA, 90% of the solutions of the current population are replaced by random solutions optimized by bit-flip local search with first improvement. The same local search is also applied to the remaining 10% of the solutions, including the best solution found in the previous generation. Flip mutation is employed with mutation rate equal to $\frac{3}{n}$. The other parameters of the GA are: population size (n_{pop}) equal to 50 individuals, number of runs equal to 50, crossover rate (p_{cross}) equal to 0.6, and the execution time for each run is $\frac{n(k-1)}{25}$ seconds.

The hybrid GAs with PX are here compared to 2 other algorithms: the same hybrid GA with *2-point crossover* [25] [6] and the same hybrid GA with *Uniform crossover* [26]. All algorithms are exactly the same, except that they use dif-

Algorithm 2 Hybrid GA
___

1: **for** $i=1$ to n_{pop} **do**
2:     $P(i)$=randomIndividual();
3:     $P(i)$=LSFI($P(i)$); // *Local Search with First Improvement*
4: **end for**
5: **while** termination condition is not satisfied **do**
6:     $Q(1)$=bestSolution(P);
7:     **for** $i=2$ to n_{pop} **do**
8:         (p_1,p_2)=selection(P);
9:         **if** $random() < p_{cross}$ **then**
10:             $Q(i)$=crossover(p_1,p_2);
11:         **else**
12:             $Q(i)$=mutation(p_1);
13:         **end if**
14:     **end for**
15:     **if** every 10 gen. **then**
16:         $Q(1)$=bestSolution(Q);
17:         **for** $i=1$ to $0.1 * n_{pop}$ **do**
18:             $Q(i)$=LSFI($Q(i)$);
19:         **end for**
20:         **for** $i=0.1*n_{pop}+1$ to n_{pop} **do**
21:             $Q(i)$=randomIndividual();
22:             $Q(i)$=LSFI($Q(i)$);
23:         **end for**
24:     **end if**
25:     P=Q;
26: **end while**
27:
28: Comments (selection):
29: i) *Both parents for GA with PX, GA with 2-point crossover, GA with Uniform crossover and first parent for GA with PX and fit/dist selection: tournament selection, i.e., the selection is based only on fitness*
30: ii) *Second parent for the GA with PX and fit/dist selection: choose the solution with the smallest Hamming distance (larger than 0) to parent 1 among the solutions in the pool used to choose parent 1, i.e., selection based on distance to parent 1.*
31: Comments (crossover and mutation):
32: iii) *The fitness of the offspring $Q(i)$ is computed after the application of mutation*
33: iv) *For GA with 2-point crossover and GA with Uniform crossover, the fitness of the offspring $Q(i)$ is computed after the application of crossover. For the GAs with PX, the fitness of the offspring $Q(i)$ is returned by the proposed method together with the solution.*
___

ferent crossover operators (and, in case of GA with PX and fit/dist selection, a different selection method for the second parent). This means that differences in the results between algorithms with 2-point crossover, Uniform crossover, and PX are only due to the effectiveness of recombination. Differences in the results of the hybrid GA with PX and the hybrid GA with PX and fit/dist selection are due to the selection operator. While the former uses standard tournament selection, the latter uses the fit/dist selection.

4.2 Results

The algorithms were applied to NK landscapes with $N = \{100, 300, 500\}$ and with $K = \{1, 2, 3\}$. The *adjacent* and *random* epistasis models were considered. In the adjacent NK model, subfunction f^i uses bit x_i and K additional bits adjacent to bit x_i. This creates a regular simple cascade of interaction that makes it possible to use exact methods to obtain the globally optimal solution for the adjacent NK model in polynomial time [32].

For the adjacent NK landscape problems, Table 1 presents the percentage of the runs that found the global optimum. The results were obtained over 50 runs. The table also presents the average difference in evaluation between the global optimum and the best solution when the global optimum is not found. The problems were posed as maximization problems. Given a solution, s' and the global optimum s^*, the percentage of difference is calculated as:

$$\%Difference(s') = 100(f(s^*) - f(s'))/f(s^*).$$

The use of partition crossover (PX) clearly improves the genetic algorithm's ability to reach the global optimum for all instances. The GA using PX found a global optimum on every run, except in the instances with $N = 300, K = 3$; $N = 500, K = 2$ and $N = 500, K = 3$. The GA using partition crossover with fit/dist selection found the global optimum 70 percent of the time in the worst case. When $N = 500, K = 3$, partition crossover used together with fit/dist selection found far more globally optimal solutions than using partition crossover and only fitness-based selection. 2-point crossover and Uniform crossover were not even close to being competitive on the adjacent NK landscape problems. Still, 2-point crossover yielded better results than Uniform crossover in terms of locating globally optimal solutions, in particular, for the smallest problems,

Table 1: Percentage over 50 runs where the global optimum was found (Found) in the experiments of the hybrid GA with the adjacent model. The average percentage difference (% Difference) with respect to the global optimum evaluation is also given.

		2-point crossover		Uniform crossover		PX		PX fit/dist selection	
N	K	Found	% Difference	Found	% Difference	Found	% Difference	Found	% Difference
100	1	100	0.000 ±0.000	88	0.011 ±0.051	100	0.000 ±0.000	100	0.0000 ±0.0000
100	2	90	0.007 ±0.029	24	0.294 ±0.347	100	0.000 ±0.000	100	0.0000 ±0.0000
100	3	62	0.086 ±0.192	4	0.657 ±0.432	100	0.000 ±0.000	100	0.0000 ±0.0000
300	1	18	0.090 ±0.087	0	0.859 ±0.262	100	0.000 ±0.000	100	0.0000 ±0.0000
300	2	0	0.611 ±0.212	0	2.157 ±0.431	100	0.000 ±0.000	100	0.0000 ±0.0000
300	3	0	1.503 ±0.402	0	3.464 ±0.506	80	0.009 ±0.023	98	0.0001 ±0.0007
500	1	0	0.364 ±0.153	0	1.371 ±0.307	100	0.000 ±0.000	100	0.0000 ±0.0000
500	2	0	1.398 ±0.327	0	3.261 ±0.377	98	0.001 ±0.004	98	0.0011 ±0.0078
500	3	0	2.791 ±0.467	0	4.851 ±0.518	40	0.029 ±0.042	70	0.0079 ±0.0183

Table 2: Mean evaluation (over 50 runs) for the hybrid GA with the random model. The evaluation functions is being *maximized.* A Wilcoxon signed rank test was used to compare the GA with PX and fit/dist selection against all of the other GAs. The symbol "=" indicates null hypothesis (the results of the algorithms are equal) cannot be rejected at the 0.05 significance level. The symbol "s" indicates the algorithm finds significantly poorer solutions compared to the hybrid GA with PX and fit/dist selection.

N	K	2-point crossover	Uniform crossover	PX	PX and fit/dist selection
100	1	0.71577 ±0.01619 (s)	0.71587 ±0.01613 (s)	0.71593 ±0.01613 (=)	0.71593 ±0.01613
100	2	0.75105 ±0.01337 (s)	0.75093 ±0.01389 (s)	0.75180 ±0.01353 (=)	0.75201 ±0.01345
100	3	0.76886 ±0.01038 (=)	0.76937 ±0.01031 (=)	0.76927 ±0.01013 (=)	0.76899 ±0.01046
300	1	0.70965 ±0.01054 (s)	0.71005 ±0.01119 (s)	0.71519 ±0.01051 (=)	0.71519 ±0.01051
300	2	0.73926 ±0.00856 (s)	0.73923 ±0.00929 (s)	0.74649 ±0.00923 (=)	0.74657 ±0.00974
300	3	0.75402 ±0.00689 (s)	0.75350 ±0.00555 (s)	0.75444 ±0.00647 (s)	0.75653 ±0.00699
500	1	0.70470 ±0.00765 (s)	0.70493 ±0.00722 (s)	0.71422 ±0.00739 (=)	0.71422 ±0.00739
500	2	0.73061 ±0.00644 (s)	0.73054 ±0.00623 (s)	0.73865 ±0.00671 (s)	0.74022 ±0.00684
500	3	0.74400 ±0.00517 (s)	0.74423 ±0.00440 (s)	0.74528 ±0.00545 (=)	0.74548 ±0.00509

where $N = 100$. This occurs because Uniform crossover is very disruptive for the NK landscapes, even for the adjacent model.

Table 2 presents the average evaluations obtained in the experiments for the random NK landscapes. A Wilcoxon signed rank test was used to compare the GA with PX and fit/dist selection against all of the other GAs. The reason why we use the signed rank test is because each of the 50 runs of the algorithms is performed on a different NK landscape instance and a different initial population. However, the i-th run of each algorithm solves the same instance and starts with the same population. That is, the samples are paired, and Wilcoxon signed rank test is appropriate. The GA with PX and fit/dist selection was significantly better than using 2-point and Uniform crossover except for the instance $N = 100, K = 3$ where Uniform crossover was best, but the differences were not significant. This probably is due to the ability of Uniform crossover to widely explore the search space, setting the stage for local search to explore different parts of the search space. For example, there could be an isolated region of the search space containing the global optimum or highly competitive local optima that are not easily reached by partition crossover. It is notable that the case where Uniform crossover was best was on a smaller problem. Again, this suggests randomness in the NK landscape instance and not a failure to scale up to larger problems (as indicated by the size of N) and greater nonlinearity (as indicated by the size of K).

Another interesting question is how many connected components can be found in the recombination graph, that is, what is the cardinality of the partitions. Recall that if there are q components, then partition crossover will return the best of 2^q distinct offspring. Table 3 shows the mean, standard deviation and the maximum number of *components* for each application of partition crossover. This table shows two interesting trends. First, as expected, the number of components is higher for adjacent NK landscapes than for random NK landscapes. Second, the number of components is higher for lower values of K. Both observations suggest that partition crossover is sensitive to problem structure, which should have a positive impact on search.

Table 4 shows the mean number of improvements that result from crossover during the first 10 generations. We limited the data to the first 10 generations because if an algorithm is able to quickly locate a good solution, that algorithm will produce fewer improvements in the later stages of search. The data in Table 4 shows that Uniform crossover very rarely results in an improved solution. This suggests that the main benefit of Uniform crossover is not in discovering improved solutions, but rather in moving the search to a new location that can be explored by other operators. Uniform crossover is strongly biased toward exploration instead of exploitation. 2-point crossover is sometimes effective at finding improving moves on adjacent NK landscapes, but appears to be no better than Uniform crossover on random NK landscapes. Partition crossover is dramatically

Table 3: Mean (and standard deviation) of the number of components for each application of crossover and the maximum number of components found by the algorithms in the experiments with the hybrid GAs.

N	K	Model	PX		PX and fit/dist selection	
			Mean numb. of comp.	Max. comp.	Mean numb. of comp.	Max. comp.
100	1	Adjacent	0.46 ±0.09	14	3.34 ±0.16	16
100	2	Adjacent	0.58 ±0.05	13	3.45 ±0.08	15
100	3	Adjacent	0.48 ±0.02	11	3.12 ±0.04	11
300	1	Adjacent	1.50 ±0.19	33	5.37 ±0.35	35
300	2	Adjacent	1.84 ±0.10	31	6.08 ±0.19	34
300	3	Adjacent	1.49 ±0.05	24	5.24 ±0.10	26
500	1	Adjacent	2.72 ±0.27	48	7.66 ±0.47	55
500	2	Adjacent	3.29 ±0.17	49	8.81 ±0.24	51
500	3	Adjacent	2.75 ±0.12	39	7.52 ±0.16	41
100	1	Random	0.40 ±0.09	13	3.22 ±0.16	15
100	2	Random	0.18 ±0.02	8	2.48 ±0.05	12
100	3	Random	0.13 ±0.00	7	2.14 ±0.02	11
300	1	Random	1.33 ±0.19	29	5.05 ±0.35	34
300	2	Random	0.33 ±0.05	12	2.77 ±0.08	16
300	3	Random	0.16 ±0.01	9	2.41 ±0.04	13
500	1	Random	2.44 ±0.27	43	6.98 ±0.47	47
500	2	Random	0.50 ±0.06	14	2.97 ±0.11	15
500	3	Random	0.18 ±0.02	10	2.46 ±0.05	13

better at finding improved offspring than Uniform and 2-point crossover. The number of improvements is higher for adjacent NK landscapes. For random NK landscapes, the number of improvements resulting from crossover decreases as K increases. This does not happen on the adjacent NK landscapes.

5. TUNNELING BETWEEN OPTIMA

Previous work on the Traveling Salesman Problem (TSP) showed that the offspring generated by *generalized partition crossover* were locally optima in the majority of cases. This means that recombination can move directly from 2 known local optima to many other local optima. We have observed on 2000 city TSP problems that one recombination can reach thousands (e.g., $q = 12$ generating 2^{12} offspring) and even millions (e.g., $q = 25$) of other local optima.

In the case of the Traveling Salesman Problem, the reason that the offspring is usually locally optimal is as follows: there can be no improving move *within* a connected tour segment after the graph unioning the two parents has been partitioned to yield the "recombination graph." Assume the local search operator is 2-opt, which reverses a single segment of the Hamiltonian circuit. There can only be improving moves using 2-opt as long the begin and end of the segment being reversed by 2-opt are not contained within a connected tour segment after the graph is partitioned.

For k-bounded pseudo-Boolean optimization problems, our theoretical results show that the offspring returned by partition crossover must be locally optimal in the hyperplane subspace in which the two parents have differing bits. The local search operator in this case is the bit-flip neighborhood, but this observation extends to any Hamming ball neighborhood of radius r in the following more restricted sense: if there is an improving move involving 1, 2, or any number of bit flips up to r bit flips that falls into the *same* connected component, that move would have already been exploited when local search was applied to the parents.

Assuming partition crossover finds an improved offspring, if the Hamming distance 1 neighborhood is used, any additional improvement in the offspring must be the result of flipping at least one variable assignment that was shared in common by the parents.

In practice, how often are the offspring produced by partition crossover locally optima? We will conduct an experiment using Algorithm 3 to explore this question empirically. In this experiment, only crossover is applied to recombine the best current solution to optimal solutions generated by local search first improvement. The population size is equal to 20 individuals, the number of runs is 50, and the number of generations is 20 (termination condition).

Algorithm 3 Recombination of Local Optima

```
while termination condition is not satisfied do
   for i=1 to maxpop do
      P(i)=randomIndividual();
      P(i)=LSFI(P(i));
   end for
   if f(bestSolution(P)) > f(x*) then
      x*=bestSolution(P);
   end if
   for i=1 to maxpop do
      Q(i)=crossover(x*,P(i));
   end for
   if f(bestSolution(Q)) > f(x*) then
      x*=LSFI(bestSolution(Q));
   end if
end while
```

Recall that parents are always locally optimal in our hybrid genetic algorithm. Also, recall that a new and different offspring is generated by partition crossover only if the offspring is better than the parents. Table 5 shows the percentage of offspring (different from the parents) that were locally optimal. Results are shown for 2-point crossover, Uniform crossover and partition crossover. As one would

Table 4: Mean number of improvements, during the first 10 generations, in the best fitness caused by crossover in the experiments with the hybrid GA.

N	K	Model	2-point crossover	Uniform crossover	PX	PX and fit/dist selection
100	1	Adjacent	6.04 ±4.23	1.26 ±1.58	26.84 ±13.48	22.78 ±11.25
100	2	Adjacent	9.90 ±4.61	0.84 ±1.35	46.94 ±15.22	38.26 ±12.33
100	3	Adjacent	7.46 ±4.60	0.56 ±0.79	55.68 ±15.61	42.76 ±12.69
300	1	Adjacent	16.04 ±6.14	0.60 ±0.88	60.50 ±11.23	57.64 ±11.11
300	2	Adjacent	16.50 ±7.07	0.46 ±0.68	87.02 ±15.64	91.12 ±13.06
300	3	Adjacent	14.60 ±5.77	0.80 ±1.12	103.40 ±15.37	104.12 ±24.72
500	1	Adjacent	16.94 ±7.53	0.66 ±0.96	75.64 ±11.64	77.74 ±10.49
500	2	Adjacent	18.64 ±7.67	0.44 ±0.50	104.92 ±15.99	110.74 ±14.23
500	3	Adjacent	15.08 ±6.16	0.36 ±0.48	126.80 ±18.35	130.86 ±17.82
100	1	Random	1.20 ±1.31	1.76 ±1.92	25.62 ±11.84	21.86 ±10.58
100	2	Random	0.52 ±1.05	0.58 ±1.07	14.68 ±10.74	9.64 ±6.01
100	3	Random	0.52 ±0.79	0.50 ±0.71	4.12 ±5.46	4.18 ±3.89
300	1	Random	0.86 ±1.09	0.78 ±1.07	59.74 ±12.75	52.00 ±12.76
300	2	Random	0.62 ±0.83	0.74 ±1.08	24.12 ±16.48	22.98 ±10.58
300	3	Random	0.40 ±0.57	0.64 ±0.98	4.00 ±4.66	4.88 ±4.62
500	1	Random	0.62 ±0.90	0.70 ±1.16	81.38 ±16.83	73.96 ±12.77
500	2	Random	0.62 ±0.75	0.60 ±0.76	31.32 ±16.81	34.14 ±15.55
500	3	Random	0.58 ±0.81	0.62 ±0.92	5.08 ±5.25	5.58 ±5.31

expect, Uniform crossover almost never produced offspring that were locally optimal.

The 2-point crossover operator is better than expected at generating offspring that are locally optimal when the problem is an adjacent NK landscape problem. The probability that 2-point crossover generates an offspring that is locally optimal decreases as K increases. For these adjacent problems, 2-point crossover has some of the properties of partition crossover, since variable interactions (like those exploited by partition crossover) are such that interacting variables are close to each other on the representation. If both crossover points used by 2-point crossover fall into regions of shared bit assignments, 2-point crossover can implicitly exploit some of the benefits and behaviors of partition crossover. Note that 2-point crossover can only isolate 2 components and *the components must be contiguous*. Also, 2-point crossover is not greedy. And so while 2-point crossover may generate offspring that are locally optimal more often than expected on adjacent NK landscape problems (where the interacting bit are contiguous), it does not generate nearly as many improving moves as partition crossover, as can be seen in Table 4.

The ability of 2-point crossover to generate offspring that are locally optimal disappears on the random NK landscape problems. When the interactions between variables is not localized, 2-point crossover cannot perform the complex decomposition that is performed by partition crossover.

Partition crossover generates offspring that are locally optimal on both adjacent NK landscapes and random NK landscapes. The probability of generating locally optimal offspring does decrease somewhat as N and K increase, but the change is not sudden or dramatic. For the adjacent NK landscapes the percentage of locally optimal offspring ranged from 93% to 100%. For the random NK landscapes the percentage of locally optimal offspring ranged from 83% to 100%. Partition crossover is surprisingly effective at "tunneling" from parents that are local optima to improved offspring that are also locally optimal.

6. CONCLUSIONS AND FUTURE WORK

A partition crossover operator is introduced that can be used for any k-bounded pseudo-Boolean optimization problem. Partition crossover breaks the set of n variables into q subsets. These q subsets of variables are made of variables that have different assignments in the two parents. The subsets of variables are partitioned such that each subset only interacts with other variables in the same subset. This makes it possible to inherit the best possible assignment of variables for each subset. Thus, given a partition of the variables into q subsets, partition crossover can return the best of 2^q offspring.

Our theoretical results show that the offspring returned by partition crossover must be locally optimal in the hyperplane subspace in which the two parents have differing bits. In practice the offspring generated by partition crossover are also usually locally optimal in the full search space as well. In the experiments presented in this paper offspring were locally optimal more than 83 percent of the time on random NK landscape problems with $N = 500$ and $K = 3$.

Empirical tests indicate that partition crossover yields significantly better results than 2-point crossover or Uniform crossover on NK landscape problems when K is relatively small.

The results presented in this paper are not intended to establish a new best known algorithm for NK landscapes or for other k-bounded pseudo-Boolean optimization problems. Pelikan et al. [21] compare evolutionary algorithms and estimation of distribution algorithms using the adjacent NK landscape model. The Linkage Tree Genetic Algorithm has also displayed good performance on adjacent NK landscape problems [27] [28]. Whitley and Chen [30] have introduced a highly efficient local search method that can identify improving moves in k-bounded pseudo-Boolean optimization problems in constant time without enumerating the neighborhood. Chen et al. [3] studies how these methods scales up as K increases for NK landscapes.

Table 5: Mean percentage of offspring different from the parents that are local optima for the experiments of recombination of local optima. Note that in the case of the PX operator, every offspring is also an improving move.

N	K	Model	2-point crossover	Uniform crossover	PX
100	1	Adjacent	74.22 ±3.99	0.39 ±0.36	100.00 ±0.00
100	2	Adjacent	47.69 ±4.56	0.01 ±0.04	95.45 ±8.36
100	3	Adjacent	30.05 ±3.87	0.00 ±0.00	97.44 ±4.47
300	1	Adjacent	77.10 ±2.81	0.00 ±0.00	97.64 ±6.66
300	2	Adjacent	50.23 ±3.29	0.00 ±0.00	95.33 ±5.86
300	3	Adjacent	30.74 ±2.87	0.00 ±0.00	94.42 ±4.36
500	1	Adjacent	78.01 ±2.36	0.00 ±0.00	97.93 ±5.02
500	2	Adjacent	50.10 ±3.24	0.00 ±0.00	93.84 ±5.91
500	3	Adjacent	31.04 ±2.53	0.00 ±0.00	93.87 ±4.03
100	1	Random	0.77 ±0.95	0.57 ±0.58	100.00 ±0.00
100	2	Random	0.05 ±0.11	0.02 ±0.07	93.16 ±10.71
100	3	Random	0.00 ±0.00	0.00 ±0.00	93.67 ±16.11
300	1	Random	0.02 ±0.06	0.00 ±0.00	97.28 ±6.38
300	2	Random	0.01 ±0.04	0.00 ±0.00	85.65 ±7.60
300	3	Random	0.01 ±0.05	0.00 ±0.00	86.46 ±17.19
500	1	Random	0.03 ±0.08	0.00 ±0.00	98.33 ±4.92
500	2	Random	0.00 ±0.00	0.00 ±0.00	84.83 ±5.64
500	3	Random	0.00 ±0.00	0.00 ±0.00	83.65 ±16.81

Chicano, Whitley and Sutton [4] show that under special conditions (e.g, the number of times that variables appear in subfunctions must be relatively uniform), a local search algorithm can be constructed to identify improving moves in radius r Hamming ball neighborhoods. Again, this is done without enumerating the neighborhood and the calculation has constant time complexity with respect to n. (The computation is sensitive to the radius r and the degree of epistasis k.) Optimal solutions have been generated for 10,000 variable adjacent NK landscape problems by looking 7 moves ahead (e.g. $r = 7$).

The results presented in this paper can potentially be combined with the results of Chicano, Whitley and Sutton [4] by combining a Hybrid Genetic Algorithm that uses some local search with smaller Hamming ball radius (e.g. $r = 3$) and partition crossover. Under these conditions, can partition crossover combined with iterated local search find the global optimum (or highly competitive solutions) using a small Hamming ball radius neighborhood?

The results in the current paper and the work of Chicano, Whitley and Sutton [4] do not deal with plateaus. The existence of plateaus is an extremely important part of the search space landscape for MAX-kSAT problems. Specialized algorithms for MAX-kSAT, such as WalkSAT [24] and other modern algorithms based on local search [14] [17] are highly effective; what makes these algorithms so effective is the strategies they employ to select moves when the search has reached a flat plateau. Future work will need to evaluate the degree to which partition crossover is affected by plateaus in the local search neighborhood.

7. ACKNOWLEDGMENTS

Renato Tinós was a visiting researcher in the Department of Computer Science at CSU. The visit of the researcher was made possible by the support provided by FAPESP (under grant 2012/22200-9), USP, and CSU. This research was sponsored by the Air Force Office of Scientific Research, Air Force Materiel Command, USAF (under grant FA9550-11-1-0088). The U.S. Government is authorized to reproduce and distribute reprints for Governmental purposes notwithstanding any copyright notation thereon. Francisco Chicano was a Fulbright Visiting Scholar at CSU supported by the Fulbright program, the Spanish Ministry of Education ("José Castillejo" mobility program), the Universidad de Málaga, Andalucía Tech, and CSU.

8. REFERENCES

[1] H. Aguirre and K. Tanaka. A study on the behavior of genetic algorithms on NK-landscapes: Effects of selection, drift, mutation, and recombination. *IEICE Transactions on Fundamentals of Electronics, Communications and Computer Sciences*, 86(9):2270–2279, 2003.

[2] E. Boros and P. Hammer. Pseudo-boolean optimization. *Discrete applied mathematics*, 123(1):155–225, 2002.

[3] W. Chen, D. Whitley, D. Hains, and A. Howe. Second order partial derivatives for nk-landscapes. In *Proceeding of the fifteenth annual conference on Genetic and evolutionary computation conference*, GECCO '13, pages 503–510, New York, NY, USA, 2013. ACM.

[4] F. Chicano, D. Whitley, and A. Sutton. Efficient identification of improving moves in a ball for pseudo-boolean problems. In *Proceedings of the 16th annual Conference on Genetic and Evolutionary Computation*, pages 437–444. ACM, 2014.

[5] T. Cormen, C. Leiserson, and R. Rivest. *Introduction to Algorithms.* McGraw Hill, New York, 1990.

[6] D. Goldberg. *Genetic Algorithms in Search, Optimization and Machine Learning.* Addison-Wesley, Reading, MA, 1989.

[7] C. Gomes, H. Kautz, A. Sabharwal, and B. Selman. Satisfiability solvers. In *Handbook of Knowledge Representation*, pages 89–134. Elsevier, 2008.

[8] D. Hains, D. Whitley, and A. Howe. Revisiting the big valley search space structure in the TSP. *Journal of the Operational Research Society*, 62(2):305–312, 2011.

[9] M. W. Hauschild and M. Pelikan. Network crossover performance on nk landscapes and deceptive problems. In *Proc. of the 12th Annual Conference on Genetic and Evolutionary Computation*, pages 713–720, 2010.

[10] R. Heckendorn and D. Whitley. A walsh analysis of NK-landscapes. In *Proceedings of the Seventh International Conference on Genetic Algorithms*, pages 41–48, 1997.

[11] R. B. Heckendorn. Embedded landscapes. *Evolutionary Computation*, 10(4):345–369, 2002.

[12] R. B. Heckendorn, S. Rana, and D. Whitley. Test function generators as embedded landscapes. *Foundations of Genetic Algorithms*, 5:183–198, 1999.

[13] K. Helsgaun. An effective implementation of the lin–kernighan traveling salesman heuristic. *European Journal of Operational Research*, 126(1):106–130, 2000.

[14] H. Hoos. An adaptive noise mechanism for WalkSAT. In *Proceedings of the National Conference on Artificial Intelligence*, pages 655–660, 2002.

[15] H. H. Hoos and T. Stützle. SATLIB: An online resource for research on SAT. In I. Gent and H. M. T. Walsh, editors, *SAT 2000*, pages 283–292, 2000.

[16] S. A. Kauffman. *The origins of order: Self-organization and selection in evolution.* Oxford university press, 1993.

[17] L. Kroc, A. Sabharwal, C. Gomes, and B. Selman. Integrating systematic and local search paradigms: A new strategy for maxsat. In *Proceedings of the 21st international jont conference on Artifical intelligence*, pages 544–551, 2009.

[18] K. E. Mathias, L. J. Eshelman, and D. Schaffer. Niches in NK-landscapes. *Foundations of Genetic Algorithms*, 6:27–46, 2001.

[19] A. Möbius, B. Freisleben, P. Merz, and M. Schreiber. Combinatorial optimization by iterative partial transcription. *Physical Review E*, 59(4):4667–4674, 1999.

[20] G. Ochoa, M. Tomassini, S. Vérel, and C. Darabos. A study of NK landscapes' basins and local optima networks. In *Proc. of the 10th Annual Conference on Genetic and Evolutionary Computation*, pages 555–562, 2008.

[21] M. Pelikan, K. Sastry, D. Goldberg, M. Butz, and M. Hauschild. Performance of evolutionary algorithms on nk landscapes with nearest neighbor interations and tunable overlap. In *Proc. of the Genetic and Evolutionary Computation Conference (GECCO)*, pages 851–858, 2009.

[22] N. Radcliffe and P. Surry. Fitness variance of formae and performance predictions. In D. Whitley and M. Vose, editors, *Foundations of Genetic Algorithms 3*, pages 51–72. Morgan Kaufmann, 1995.

[23] N. J. Radcliffe. The algebra of genetic algorithms. *Annals of Maths and Artificial Intelligence*, 10:339–384, 1994.

[24] B. Selman, H. Kautz, and B. Cohen. Noise strategies for improving local search. In *Proceedings of the National Conference on Artificial Intelligence*, pages 337–337, 1994.

[25] W. Spears and K. D. Jong. An Analysis of Multi-Point Crossover. In G. Rawlins, editor, *Foundations of Genetic Algorithms*, pages 301–315. Morgan Kaufmann, 1991.

[26] G. Syswerda. Uniform Crossover in Genetic Algorithms. In J. D. Schaffer, editor, *Proc Third International Conf on Genetic Algorithms*, pages 2–9. Morgan Kaufmann, 1989.

[27] D. Thierens. The Linkage Tree Genetic Algorithm. In *Parallel Problem Solving from Nature*, pages 264–273. Springer Lecture Notes in Computer Science, 2010.

[28] D. Thierens and P. Bosman. Evolvability Analysis of the Linkage Tree Genetic Algorithm. In *Parallel Problem Solving from Nature*, pages 286–295. Springer Lecture Notes in Computer Science, 2012.

[29] R. Tinós, D. Whitley, and G. Ochoa. Generalized asymmetric partition crossover for the traveling salesman problem. In *Proc. of the 16th Annual Conference on Genetic and Evolutionary Computation*, pages 501–508, 2014.

[30] D. Whitley and W. Chen. Constant time steepest descent local search with lookahead for NK-landscapes and MAX-kSAT. In *GECCO*, pages 1357–1364, 2012.

[31] D. Whitley, D. Hains, and A. Howe. Tunneling between optima: partition crossover for the TSP. In *Proc. of the 11th Annual Conference on Genetic and Evolutionary Computation*, pages 915–922, 2009.

[32] A. H. Wright, R. K. Thompson, and J. Zhang. The computational complexity of N-K fitness functions. *IEEE Transactions on Evolutionary Computation*, 4(4):373–379, 2000.

Information Geometry of the Gaussian Distribution in View of Stochastic Optimization

Luigi Malagò
malago@shinshu-u.ac.jp
Shinshu University & INRIA Saclay – Île-de-France
4-17-1 Wakasato, Nagano, 380-8553, Japan

Giovanni Pistone
giovanni.pistone@carloalberto.org
Collegio Carlo Alberto
Via Real Collegio, 30, 10024 Moncalieri, Italy

ABSTRACT

We study the optimization of a continuous function by its stochastic relaxation, i.e., the optimization of the expected value of the function itself with respect to a density in a statistical model. We focus on gradient descent techniques applied to models from the exponential family and in particular on the multivariate Gaussian distribution. From the theory of the exponential family, we reparametrize the Gaussian distribution using natural and expectation parameters, and we derive formulas for natural gradients in both parameterizations. We discuss some advantages of the natural parameterization for the identification of sub-models in the Gaussian distribution based on conditional independence assumptions among variables. Gaussian distributions are widely used in stochastic optimization and in particular in model-based Evolutionary Computation, as in Estimation of Distribution Algorithms and Evolutionary Strategies. By studying natural gradient flows over Gaussian distributions our analysis and results directly apply to the study of CMA-ES and NES algorithms.

Categories and Subject Descriptors

G.1.6 [**Mathematics of Computing**]: Optimization — *Stochastic programming*; G.3 [**Mathematics of Computing**]: Probabilistic algorithms (including Monte Carlo)

General Terms

Theory, Algorithms

Keywords

Stochastic Relaxation; Information Geometry; Exponential Family; Multivariate Gaussian Distribution; Stochastic Natural Gradient Descent

FOGA'15, January 17–20, 2015, Aberystwyth, UK.

ACM 978-1-4503-3434-1/15/01 ...$15.00.
http://dx.doi.org/10.1145/2725494.2725510 .

1. INTRODUCTION

In this paper we study the optimization of a continuous function by means of its Stochastic Relaxation (SR) [19], i.e., we search for the optimum of the function by optimizing the functional given by the expected value of the function itself over a statistical model. This approach is quite general and appears in many different communities, from evolutionary computation to statistical physics, going through certain techniques in mathematical programming.

By optimizing the stochastic relaxation of a function, we move from the original search space to a new search space given by a statistical model, i.e., a set of probability densities. Once we introduce a parameterization for the statistical model, the parameters of the model become the new variables of the relaxed problem. The search for an optimal density in the statistical model, i.e., a density that maximizes the probability of sampling an optimal solution for the original function can be performed in different ways, similarly, different families of statistical models can be employed in the search for the optimum. In the literature of Evolutionary Computation, we restrict our attention to model-based optimization, i.e., those algorithms where the search for the optimum is guided by a statistical model. In this context, examples of Stochastic Relaxations of continuous optimization are given by Estimation of Distribution Algorithms (EDAs) [16], see for instance EGNA and EMNA, and Evolutionary Strategies, such as CMA-ES [13], NES [32, 31] and GIGO [9].

There is a clear connection of Stochastic Relaxation with Entropy based methods in optimization. In fact, on a finite state space it is easily shown that, starting form any probability function the positive gradient flow of the entropy goes to the uniform distribution, while the negative gradient flow goes to the uniform distribution on the values that maximize the probability function itself, see e.g. [29].

We are interested in the study of the stochastic relaxation of a continuous real-valued function defined over $\mathbb{R}^n$, when the statistical model employed in the relaxation is chosen from the exponential family of probability distributions [12]. In particular we focus on multivariate Gaussian distributions, which belong to the exponential family, and are one of the most common and widely employed models in model-based continuous optimization, and, more in general, in statistics. Among the different approaches to the optimization of the expected value of the function over the statistical model, we focus on gradient descent techniques, such as the CMA-ES and NES families of algorithms.

The methods used here are actually first order optimization methods on Riemannian manifolds, see [1] for the specific case of matrix manifolds, with two major differences. First, our extrema are obtained at the border of the manifold as parameterized by the exponential family. This fact presents the issue of an optimization problem of a manifold with border which, in turn, is defined through an extension of the manifold outside the border with a suitable parameterization. Second, the actual IG structure is reacher that the simple Riemannian structure because of the presence of what Amari calls dually flat connections and some geometers call Hessian manifold. Second order optimization methods are available for the Stochastic Relaxation problem. The finite state space case has been considered in our paper [22]. Second order methods are not discussed in the present paper.

The geometry of the multivariate Gaussian distribution is a well established subject in mathematical statistics, see for instance [30]. In this paper, we follow a geometric approach based on Information Geometry [4, 7] to the study of the multivariate Gaussian distribution and more generally of the exponential family from the point of view of the stochastic relaxation of a continuous function, cf. [27]. In this work, we extend to the case of continuous sample space some of the results presented in [20, 21] for the finite sample space, using a information geometric perspective on the stochastic relaxation based on gradient descent over an exponential family. A similar framework, based on stochastic relaxation has been proposed under the name of Information Geometric Optimization (IGO) [26], where the authors consider the more general case of the relaxation of rank-preserving trasformations of the function to be optimized.

Exponential families of distributions have an intrinsic Riemannian geometry, where the Fisher information matrix plays the role of metric tensor. Moreover, the exponential family exhibits a dually flat structure, and besides the parameterization given by the natural parameters of the exponential family, there exists a dually coupled parameterization for densities in the exponential family given by the expectation parameters. Since the geometry of the exponential family is in most cases not Euclidean, gradients need to be evaluated with respect to the relevant metric tensor, which leads to the definition of the *natural gradient* [5], to distinguish it from the vector of partial derivatives, which are called as *vanilla gradient*. Such a distinction makes no sense in the Euclidean space, where the metric tensor is the identify matrix, and the gradient with respect to the metric tensor is the vector of partial derivatives.

In the following sections, besides the mean and covariance parameterization, we discuss the natural and expectation parameterizations for the multivariate Gaussian distribution based on the exponential family, and we provide formulae for transformations from one parameterization to the other. We further derive the Fisher information matrices and the vanilla and natural gradients in the different parameterizations. We prove convergence results for the Gibbs distribution and study how the landscape of the expected value of the function changes according to the choice of the Gaussian family. We introduce some toy examples which make it possible to visualize the flows associated to the gradient over the statistical model used in the relaxation.

The use of the natural parameters of the exponential family makes it possible to identify sub-families in the Gaussian distribution by setting some of the natural parameters to zero. Indeed, since the natural parameters are proportional to the elements of inverse of the covariance matrices, by setting to zero one of these parameters we have a corresponding zero in the precision matrix, i.e., we are imposing a conditional independence constraint over the variables in the Gaussian distribution. From this perspective, we can rely on an extensive literature of graphical models [17] for model selection and estimation techniques.

2. THE EXPONENTIAL FAMILY

We consider the statistical model $\mathcal{E}$ given on the measured sample space $(\mathcal{X}, \mathcal{F}, \mu)$ by the densities of the form

$$p_{\boldsymbol{\theta}}(\boldsymbol{x};\boldsymbol{\theta}) = \exp\left(\sum_{i=1}^{k} \theta_i T_i(\boldsymbol{x}) - \psi(\boldsymbol{\theta})\right) , \tag{1}$$

with $\boldsymbol{\theta} \in \vartheta$, where ϑ is an open convex set in $\mathbb{R}^k$. The real random variables $\{T_i\}$ are the sufficient statistics of the exponential family, and $\psi(\boldsymbol{\theta})$ is a normalizing term, which is equal to the log of the partition function

$$Z \colon \theta \mapsto \int \exp\left(\sum_{i=1}^{k} \theta_i T_i(\boldsymbol{x})\right) \mu(d\boldsymbol{x}) \ .$$

The entropy is

$$-\int \log p(\boldsymbol{x};\boldsymbol{\theta})\, p_{\boldsymbol{\theta}}(\boldsymbol{x};\boldsymbol{\theta})\, \mu(d\boldsymbol{x}) = \psi(\boldsymbol{\theta}) - \sum_{i=1}^{k} \theta_i \mathbb{E}_{\boldsymbol{\theta}}[T_i] \ .$$

The partition function Z is a convex function whose proper domain is a convex set. We assume that the ϑ domain is either the proper domain of the partition function, if it is open, or the interior of the proper domain. Standard reference on exponential families is [12], where an exponential family such that the proper domain of Z is open is said to be steep. Moreover we assume that the sufficient statistics are affinely independent, that is, if a linear combination is constant, then the linear combination is actually zero. Such an exponential family is called minimal in standard references.

The exponential family admits a dual parameterization to the natural parameters, given by the expectation parameters $\boldsymbol{\eta} = \mathbb{E}_{\boldsymbol{\theta}}[\boldsymbol{T}]$, see [12, Ch. 3]. The $\boldsymbol{\theta}$ and $\boldsymbol{\eta}$ parameter vectors of an exponential family are dually coupled in the sense of the Legendre transform [8], indeed, let $\boldsymbol{\theta}$ and $\boldsymbol{\eta}$ such that $p_{\boldsymbol{\theta}}(\boldsymbol{x};\boldsymbol{\theta}) = p_{\boldsymbol{\eta}}(\boldsymbol{x};\boldsymbol{\eta})$, then

$$\psi(\boldsymbol{\theta}) + \varphi(\boldsymbol{\eta}) - \langle \boldsymbol{\theta}, \boldsymbol{\eta} \rangle = 0 \ , \tag{2}$$

where $\varphi(\boldsymbol{\eta}) = \mathbb{E}_{\boldsymbol{\eta}}[\log p(\boldsymbol{x};\boldsymbol{\eta})]$ is the negative entropy of the density $p_{\boldsymbol{\eta}}(\boldsymbol{x};\boldsymbol{\eta})$, and $\langle \boldsymbol{\theta}, \boldsymbol{\eta} \rangle = \sum_{i=1}^{k} \theta_i \eta_i$ denotes the inner product between the two parameter vectors. See [28, Part III] on convex duality.

From the Legendre duality it follows that the variable trasformations between one parameterization and the other are given by

$$\boldsymbol{\eta} = \nabla_{\boldsymbol{\theta}} \psi(\boldsymbol{\theta}) = (\nabla_{\boldsymbol{\eta}} \varphi)^{-1}(\boldsymbol{\theta}) \ ,$$
$$\boldsymbol{\theta} = \nabla_{\boldsymbol{\eta}} \varphi(\boldsymbol{\eta}) = (\nabla_{\boldsymbol{\theta}} \psi)^{-1}(\boldsymbol{\eta}) \ .$$

We introduced two dual parameterizations for the same exponential family $\mathcal{E}$, the $\boldsymbol{\theta}$ and $\boldsymbol{\eta}$ parameters, so that any $p \in \mathcal{M}$ can be parametrized either with $p_{\boldsymbol{\theta}}(\boldsymbol{x};\boldsymbol{\theta})$ or with $p_{\boldsymbol{\eta}}(\boldsymbol{x};\boldsymbol{\eta})$. In the following, to simplify notation, we drop the index of p which denotes the parameterization used when the parameter appears as an argument, however notice that $p_{\boldsymbol{\theta}}$ and $p_{\boldsymbol{\eta}}$ are different functions of their parameterizations.

The Fisher information matrices in the two different parameterizations can be evaluated by taking second derivatives of $\psi(\boldsymbol{\theta})$ and $\varphi(\boldsymbol{\eta})$

$$I_{\boldsymbol{\theta}}(\boldsymbol{\theta}) = \operatorname{Hess}\psi(\boldsymbol{\theta}) \;, \tag{3}$$
$$I_{\boldsymbol{\eta}}(\boldsymbol{\eta}) = \operatorname{Hess}\varphi(\boldsymbol{\eta}) \;. \tag{4}$$

The following result shows the relationship between the Fisher information matrices expressed in the $\boldsymbol{\theta}$ and $\boldsymbol{\eta}$ parameterizations for the same distribution. The result appears in [7], see also Theorem 2.2.5 in [15].

THEOREM 1. *Consider a probability distribution in the exponential family $\mathcal{E}$, we have*

$$I_{\boldsymbol{\eta}}(\boldsymbol{\eta}) = (I_{\boldsymbol{\theta}} \circ \nabla\varphi)(\boldsymbol{\eta})^{-1}$$
$$I_{\boldsymbol{\theta}}(\boldsymbol{\theta}) = (I_{\boldsymbol{\eta}} \circ \nabla\psi)(\boldsymbol{\theta})^{-1} \;.$$

Moreover, we have

$$I_{\boldsymbol{\eta}}(\boldsymbol{\eta})^{-1} = \operatorname{Cov}_{\boldsymbol{\eta}}(\boldsymbol{T},\boldsymbol{T}) = \mathbb{E}_{\boldsymbol{\eta}}[(\boldsymbol{T}-\boldsymbol{\eta})(\boldsymbol{T}-\boldsymbol{\eta})^{\mathrm{T}}] \;.$$

2.1 The Gibbs Distribution

For each objective function $f\colon \mathcal{X} \to \mathbb{R}$, we introduce its Gibbs distribution, the one dimensional exponential family whose sufficient statistics is the function f itself. In the discrete case, it is a classical result in Statistical Physics and it is easy to show that the Gibbs distribution for $\theta \to \infty$ weakly converges to the uniform distribution over the minima of f. We refer for example to [20] for a discussion in the context of the stochastic relaxation for discrete domains. In this subsection we consider the extension of the result to the continuous case.

In the following we look for the minima of the objective function f. hence, we assume assume f to be bounded below and non constant. Given a probability measure μ, the Gibbs exponential family of f is the model $\theta \mapsto \mathrm{e}^{\theta f - \psi(\theta)} \cdot \mu$. As f is bounded below and μ is finite, the log-partition function $\psi(\theta) = \log\left(\int \mathrm{e}^{\theta f}\, d\mu\right)$ is finite on an interval containing the negative real line. We take in particular the interior of such an interval, hence ψ is defined on an open interval $J =]-\infty, \overline{\theta}[$, where $\overline{\theta} \in [0, +\infty]$. The function $\psi\colon J \to \mathbb{R}$ is strictly convex and analytic, see [12].

Define $\underline{f} = \operatorname{ess\,inf}_\mu f = \inf\{A : \mu\{f \le A\} > 0\}$, $\overline{f} = \operatorname{ess\,sup}_\mu f = \sup\{B : \mu\{B \le f\} > 0\}$, and define the *Gibbs relaxation* or *stochastic relaxation* of f to be the function

$$F(\theta) = \mathbb{E}_\theta[f] = \int f \mathrm{e}^{\theta f - \psi(\theta)}\, d\mu = \frac{d}{d\theta}\psi(\theta) \;,$$

so that $\underline{f} \le F(\theta) \le \overline{f}$.

PROPOSITION 2.

1. *The function F is increasing on its domain J.*
2. *The range of the function F is the interval $]\underline{f}, \sup F[$,*
3. *in particular, $\lim_{\theta\to-\infty} \mathbb{E}_\theta[f] = \underline{f}$.*

PROOF. 1. As ψ is strictly convex on J, then its derivative F is strictly increasing on J.

2. As F is strictly increasing and continuous on the open interval J, it follows that range $F(J)$ is the open interval $]\inf_{\theta\in J} F, \sup_{\theta\in J} F(\theta)[$, which is contained in $]\underline{f}, \overline{f}[$. We show that its left end is actually $\underline{f}$. Equivalently, we show that for each $\epsilon > 0$ and each $\eta > \underline{f} + \epsilon$, $\eta \in F(J)$, there exists θ such that $F(\theta) = \eta$. The argument is a variation of the argument to prove the existence of maximum likelihood estimators because we show the existence of a solution to the equation $F(\theta) - \eta = \frac{d}{d\theta}(\eta\theta - \psi(\theta)) = 0$ for each $\eta > \underline{f}$. Let $A = \underline{f} + \epsilon$ and take any $\theta < 0$ to show that

$$1 = \int \mathrm{e}^{\theta f(\boldsymbol{x}) - \psi(\theta)}\, \mu(d\boldsymbol{x}) \ge \int_{\{f \le A\}} \mathrm{e}^{\theta f(\boldsymbol{x}) - \psi(\theta)}\, \mu(d\boldsymbol{x}) \ge \mu\{f \le A\}\, \mathrm{e}^{\theta A - \psi(\theta)}.$$

Taking the logarithm of both sides of the inequality, we obtain, for each η

$$0 \ge \log\mu\{f \le A\} + \theta A - \psi(\theta) = \log\mu\{f \le A\} + \theta(A - \eta) + \theta\eta - \psi(\theta) \;,$$

and, reordering the terms of the inequality, that

$$\theta\eta - \psi(\theta) \le -\log\mu\{f \le A\} + \theta(\eta - A) \;.$$

If $\eta > A$, the previous inequality implies

$$\lim_{\theta\to-\infty} \theta\eta - \psi(\theta) = -\infty \;,$$

that is, the strictly concave differentiable function $\theta \mapsto \theta\eta - \psi(\theta)$ goes to $-\infty$ as $\theta \to -\infty$. Let us study what happens at the right of of the interval $F(J)$. Let $F(\theta_1) = \eta_1 > \eta$. If $\theta \to \theta_1$ increasingly, then $(\psi(\theta_1) - \psi(\theta))/(\theta_1 - \theta)$ goes to $\psi'(\theta_1) = F(\theta_1) = \eta_1$ increasingly. Hence, there exists $\theta_2 < \theta_1$ such that $(\psi(\theta_1) - \psi(\theta_2))/(\theta_1 - \theta_2) > \eta$, that is $\eta\theta_2 - \psi(\theta_2) > \eta\theta_1 - \psi(\theta_1)$. It follows that the strictly concave and differentiable function $\theta \mapsto \eta\theta - \psi(\theta)$ has a maximum $\hat{\theta} \in]-\infty, \eta_1[$, where its derivative is zero, giving $\eta = \psi'(\hat{\theta}) = F(\hat{\theta})$.

3. As F is strictly increasing, $\lim_{\theta\to-\infty} F(\theta) = \min(F(J)) = \underline{f}$.

□

REMARK 3. *Our assumption on the objective function is asymmetric as we have assumed f bounded below while we have no assumption on the big values of f. If f is bounded above, we have the symmetric result by exchanging f with $-f$ and θ with $-\theta$. If f is unbounded, then a Gibbs distribution need not to exist because of the integrability requirements of $\mathrm{e}^{\theta f}$. If the Laplace transform of f in μ is defined, then the Gibbs distribution exists, but only Item 1 of Prop. 2 applies. The result above does say only that the left limit of the relaxed function is greater or equal to $\underline{f}$. In such cases the technical condition on f called* steepness *would be relevant, see [12, Ch. 3]. We do not discuss this issue here because the problem of finding the extrema of an unbounded function is not clearly defined.*

REMARK 4. *Statistical models other that the Gibbs model can produce a relaxed objective function usable for finding the minimum. Let $p_\theta \cdot \mu$ be any one-dimensional model. Then $\lim_{\theta\to-\infty} \int f p_\theta\, d\mu = \underline{f}$ if, and only if,*

$$\lim_{\theta\to-\infty} \int f(\mathrm{e}^{\theta f - \psi(\theta)} - p_\theta)\, d\mu = 0 \;.$$

In particular, a simple sufficient condition in case of a bounded f is

$$\lim_{\theta\to-\infty}\int\left|e^{\theta f-\psi(\theta)}-p_\theta\right|\,d\mu=0.$$

In practice, it is unlikely f to be known and we look forward learning some proper approximation od the Gibbs relaxation.

The convergence of the expected value along a statistical model to the minimum of the values of the objective function f, which was obtained above, is a result weaker than what we are actually looking for, that is the convergence of the statistical model to a limit probability μ_∞ supported by the set of minima, $\{\boldsymbol{x}\in\mathcal{X}: f(\boldsymbol{x})=\underline{f}\}$, that is a probability such that $\int f(\boldsymbol{x})\,\mu(d\boldsymbol{x})=\underline{f}$. For example, if $f(x)=1/x$, $x>0$, and μ_n is the uniform distribution on $[n,n+1]$, $n=1,2,\dots$, then $\int fd\,\mu_n=\log((n+1)/n)$ goes to $0=\inf f$, but there is no minimum of f nor limit of the sequence $(\mu_n)_n$.

The following proposition says something about this issue. We need topological assumptions. Namely, we assume the sample space $\mathcal{X}$ to be a metric space and the objective function to be bounded below, lower semicontinuous, and with compact level sets $\{\boldsymbol{x}\in\mathcal{X}: f(\boldsymbol{x})\le\underline{f}+A\}$. In such a case we have the following result about weak convergence of probability measures, see [11].

PROPOSITION 5. *The family of measures $(e^{\theta f-\psi(\theta)}\cdot\mu)_{\theta\in J}$ is relatively compact as $\theta\to-\infty$ and the limits are supported by the closed set $\{\boldsymbol{x}: f(\boldsymbol{x})=\underline{f}\}$. In particular, if the minimum is unique, then the sequence converges weakly to the delta mass at the minimum.*

PROOF. The set $\{f\le\underline{f}+A\}$ is compact and we have, by Markov inequality, that

$$\limsup_{\theta\to-\infty}\int_{\{f>\underline{f}+A\}}e^{\theta f-\psi(\theta)}\,d\mu\le$$

$$A^{-1}\lim_{\theta\to-\infty}\int(f-\underline{f})e^{\theta f-\psi(\theta)}\,d\mu=0,$$

which is the tightness condition for relative compactness. If ν is a limit point along the sequence $(\theta_n)_{n\in\mathbb{N}}$, $\lim_{n\to\infty}\theta_n=-\infty$, then for all $a>0$ the set $\{f>\underline{f}+a\}$ is open and, by the Portmanteaux Theorem [11, Th. 2.1.(iv)],

$$\nu\{f>\underline{f}+a\}\le\liminf_{n\to\infty}\int_{\{f>\underline{f}+a\}}e^{\theta_n f-\psi(\theta_n)}\,d\mu=0.$$

As each of the set $\{f>\underline{f}+a\}$ has measure zero, their (uncountable) union ha s measure zero,

$$\nu\{f>\underline{f}\}=\nu\left(\cup_{a>0}\{f>\underline{f}+a\}\right)=0.$$

Finally, if $\{f=\underline{f}\}$ has a unique point, then each limit ν has to have a point support, hence has to be the Dirac delta. □

As a consequence of the previous result we can extend Th. 12 in [20] to the continuous case. Let $V=\mathrm{Span}\{T_1,\dots,T_k\}$ be the vector space generated by the affinely independent random variables T_j, $j=1,\dots,k$ and let $\mathcal{E}$ be the exponential family on the sample space $(\mathcal{X},\mu)$ with that sufficient statistics. For $f\in V$, $f=\sum_{j=1}^k\alpha_jT_j$, and $q=p_\theta\in\mathcal{E}$, consider the Gibbs family

$$p(x;t)=\frac{e^{-tf}q}{\mathbb{E}_q[e^{-tf}]},\quad t\colon t\boldsymbol{\alpha}+\boldsymbol{\theta}\in\vartheta\,. \tag{5}$$

Note that this family is actually a subfamily of $\mathcal{E}$ that moves from q in the direction $f-\mathbb{E}_q[f]$. We further assume f to be bounded below to obtain the following.

THEOREM 6. *The gradient of the function $F\colon\mathcal{E}\ni q\mapsto\mathbb{E}_q[f]$ is $\nabla F(q)=f-\mathbb{E}_q[f]$. The trajectory of the negative gradient flow through q is the exponential family in Eq. (5). The negative gradient flow is a minimizing evolution.*

PROOF. The only thing we need to verify is the fact that the velocity of the curve in Eq. (5) at $t=0$ is precisely $f-\mathbb{E}_q[f]$. The evolution is minimizing, according to the assumptions on f, because of Prop. 2 and 5. □

The previous theorem can be applied to the case when the exponential family is a Gaussian distribution. In particular it makes it possible to prove global convergence of natural gradient flows of quadratic non-constant and lower bounded functions in the Gaussian distribution. For any given initial condition, the natural gradient flow converges to the δ distribution which concentrates all the probability mass over the global optimum of f. Akimoto et. al proved in [2] an equivalent result for isotropic Gaussian distributions in the more general framework of IGO which takes into account a rank preserving trasformation of the function to be optimized based on quantiles. In this context, see also the work of Beyer [10].

3. MULTIVARIATE GAUSSIAN DISTRIBUTIONS

In this section we discuss the multivariate Gaussian distribution and discuss its geometry in the more general context of the exponential family. The geometry of the Gaussian distribution has been widely studied in the literature, see for instance [30] as an early and detailed reference on the subject.

Since the multivariate Gaussian distribution belongs to the exponential family, besides mean and covariance matrice, we can introduce two alternative parameterizations, based on natural and expectation parameters. Notice that all these parameterizations are one-to-one.

Vectors are intended as column vectors and are represented using the bold notation. Let $\boldsymbol{\xi}$ be a vector of parameters, in order to obtain compact notation, we denote the partial derivative $\partial/\partial\xi_i$ with ∂_i. When a parameter ξ_{ij} of $\boldsymbol{\xi}$ is identified by two indices, we denote the partial derivative with ∂_{ij}.

3.1 Mean and Covariance Parameters

Consider a vector $\boldsymbol{x}=(\boldsymbol{x}_1,\dots,\boldsymbol{x}_n)^{\mathrm{T}}\in\mathbb{R}^n=\Omega$. Let $\boldsymbol{\mu}\in\mathbb{R}^n$ be a mean vector and $\Sigma=[\sigma_{ij}]$ a $n\times n$ symmetric positive-definite covariance matrix, the multivariate Gaussian distribution $\mathcal{N}(\boldsymbol{\mu},\Sigma)$ can be written as

$$p(\boldsymbol{x};\boldsymbol{\mu},\Sigma)=(2\pi)^{-n/2}|\Sigma|^{-1/2}\exp\left(-\frac{1}{2}(\boldsymbol{x}-\boldsymbol{\mu})^{\mathrm{T}}\Sigma^{-1}(\boldsymbol{x}-\boldsymbol{\mu})\right). \tag{6}$$

We denote with $\Sigma^{-1}=[\sigma^{ij}]$ the inverse covariance matrix, also known as precision matrix or concentration matrix. We use upper indices in σ^{ij} to remark that they are the elements of the inverse matrix $\Sigma^{-1}=[\sigma_{ij}]^{-1}$. The precision matrix captures conditional independence between variables in $\boldsymbol{X}=(\boldsymbol{X}_1,\dots,\boldsymbol{X}_n)^{\mathrm{T}}$. Zero partial correlations, i.e., $\sigma^{ij}=0$, correspond to conditional independence assumption of X_i

and X_j given all other variables, denoted by $X_i \perp\!\!\!\perp X_j | \boldsymbol{X}_{\setminus i \setminus j}$. See [17] as a comprehensive reference on graphical models.

3.2 Natural Parameters

It is a well known result that the multivariante Gaussian distribution $\mathcal{N}(\boldsymbol{\mu}, \Sigma)$ is an exponential family for the sufficient statistics X_i, X_i^2, $2X_iX_j$, $i \leq j$. We denote with $\omega : (\boldsymbol{\mu}, \Sigma) \mapsto \boldsymbol{\theta}$ the parameter transformation from the couple mean vector and covariance matrix to the natural parameters. By comparing Eq. (1) and (6), it is easy to verify that

$$\boldsymbol{T} = \begin{pmatrix} (X_i) \\ (X_i^2) \\ (2X_iX_j)_{i<j} \end{pmatrix} = \begin{pmatrix} (T_i) \\ (T_{ii}) \\ (T_{ij})_{i<j} \end{pmatrix} , \quad (7)$$

$$\boldsymbol{\theta} = \omega(\boldsymbol{\mu}, \Sigma) = \begin{pmatrix} \Sigma^{-1}\boldsymbol{\mu} \\ (-\frac{1}{2}\sigma^{ii}) \\ (-\frac{1}{2}\sigma^{ij})_{i<j} \end{pmatrix} = \begin{pmatrix} (\theta_i) \\ (\theta_{ii}) \\ (\theta_{ij})_{i<j} \end{pmatrix} ,$$

where $k = n + n + n(n-1)/2 = n(n+3)/2$, which leads to

$$p_{\boldsymbol{\theta}}(\boldsymbol{x}; \boldsymbol{\theta}) = \exp\left(\sum_i \theta_i x_i + \sum_i \theta_i x_i^2 + \sum_{i<j} 2\theta_{ij} x_i x_j - \psi(\boldsymbol{\theta}) \right) .$$

To simplify the formulae for variable transformations and in particular the derivations in the next sections, we define

$$\theta = (\theta_i) = \Sigma^{-1}\boldsymbol{\mu} , \quad (8)$$

$$\Theta = \sum_i \theta_{ii} \boldsymbol{e}_i \boldsymbol{e}_i^{\mathrm{T}} + \sum_{i<j} \theta_{ij} (\boldsymbol{e}_i \boldsymbol{e}_j^{\mathrm{T}} + \boldsymbol{e}_j \boldsymbol{e}_i^{\mathrm{T}}) = -\frac{1}{2}\Sigma^{-1} , \quad (9)$$

and represent $\boldsymbol{\theta}$ as

$$\boldsymbol{\theta} = (\theta; \Theta) ,$$

so that

$$p_{\boldsymbol{\theta}}(\boldsymbol{x}; \boldsymbol{\theta}) = \exp\left(\theta^{\mathrm{T}} \boldsymbol{x} + \boldsymbol{x}^{\mathrm{T}} \Theta \boldsymbol{x} - \psi(\boldsymbol{\theta}) \right) .$$

Notice that since Θ is symmetric, the number of free parameters in the θ vector and its representation $(\theta; \Theta)$ is the same, and we do not have any over-parametrization.

The natural parameterization and the mean and covariance parameterization are one-to-one. The inverse trasformation from natural parameters to the mean vector and the covariance matrix is given by $w^{-1} : \boldsymbol{\theta} \mapsto (\boldsymbol{\mu}; \Sigma)$, with

$$\boldsymbol{\mu} = -\frac{1}{2}\Theta^{-1}\theta , \quad (10)$$

$$\Sigma = -\frac{1}{2}\Theta^{-1} . \quad (11)$$

From Eq. (1) and (6), the log partition function as a function of $(\boldsymbol{\mu}; \Sigma)$ reads

$$\psi \circ \omega = \frac{1}{2}\left(n \log(2\pi) + \boldsymbol{\mu}^{\mathrm{T}} \Sigma^{-1} \boldsymbol{\mu} + \log |\Sigma| \right) ,$$

so that as a function of $\boldsymbol{\theta}$ it becomes

$$\psi(\boldsymbol{\theta}) = \frac{1}{2}\left(n \log(2\pi) - \frac{1}{2}\theta^{\mathrm{T}} \Theta^{-1} \theta - \log(-2)^n |\Theta| \right) . (12)$$

Conditional independence assumptions between variables in X correspond to vanishing components in $\boldsymbol{\theta}$. As a consequence, the exponential manifold associated to the multivariate Gaussian distribution has a straightforward hierarchical structure, similar to what happens in the case of binary variables, cf [6].

Proposition 7. *The conditional independence structure of the variables in $\boldsymbol{X}$ determines a hierarchical structure for $\mathcal{N}(\boldsymbol{\theta})$ where nested submanifolds given by some $\theta_{ij} = 0$ are identified by the conditional independence assumptions of the form $X_i \perp\!\!\!\perp X_j | \boldsymbol{X}_{\setminus i \setminus j}$.*

3.3 Expectation Parameters

The expectation parameters are a dual parameterization for statistical models in the exponential family, given by $\boldsymbol{\eta} = \mathbb{E}_{\boldsymbol{\theta}}[\boldsymbol{T}]$. Let $\chi : (\boldsymbol{\mu}; \Sigma) \mapsto \boldsymbol{\eta}$, from the definition of the sufficient statistics of the exponential family in Eq. (7), since $\mathrm{Cov}(X_i, X_j) = \mathbb{E}[X_iX_j] - \mathbb{E}[X_i]\mathbb{E}[X_j]$, it follows

$$\boldsymbol{\eta} = \chi(\boldsymbol{\mu}, \Sigma) = \begin{pmatrix} (\mu_i) \\ (\sigma_{ii} + \mu_i^2) \\ (2\sigma_{ij} + 2\mu_i\mu_j)_{i<j} \end{pmatrix} = \begin{pmatrix} (\eta_i) \\ (\eta_{ii}) \\ (\eta_{ij})_{i<j} \end{pmatrix} .$$

Similarly to the natural parameters, also the relationship between the expectation parameters and the mean and covariance parameterization is one-to-one. We introduce the following notation

$$\eta = (\eta_i) = \boldsymbol{\mu} , \quad (13)$$

$$E = \sum_i \eta_{ii} \boldsymbol{e}_i \boldsymbol{e}_i^{\mathrm{T}} + \sum_{i<j} \eta_{ij} \frac{\boldsymbol{e}_i \boldsymbol{e}_j^{\mathrm{T}} + \boldsymbol{e}_j \boldsymbol{e}_i^{\mathrm{T}}}{2} = \Sigma + \boldsymbol{\mu}\boldsymbol{\mu}^{\mathrm{T}} , (14)$$

and represent $\boldsymbol{\eta}$ as

$$\boldsymbol{\eta} = (\eta; E) ,$$

so that $\chi^{-1} : \boldsymbol{\eta} \mapsto (\boldsymbol{\mu}; \Sigma)$ can be written as

$$\boldsymbol{\mu} = \eta , \quad (15)$$

$$\Sigma = E - \eta\eta^{\mathrm{T}} . \quad (16)$$

The negative entropy of the multivariate Gaussian distribution parametrized by $(\boldsymbol{\mu}; \Sigma)$ reads

$$\varphi \circ \chi = -\frac{n}{2}(\log(2\pi) + 1) - \frac{1}{2}\log |\Sigma| ,$$

so that in the expectation parameters we have

$$\varphi(\boldsymbol{\eta}) = -\frac{n}{2}(\log(2\pi) + 1) - \frac{1}{2}\log \left| E - \eta\eta^{\mathrm{T}} \right| . \quad (17)$$

Combining Eq. (6) and (17), the multivariate Gaussian distribution in the $\boldsymbol{\eta}$ parameters can be written as

$$p(\boldsymbol{x}; \boldsymbol{\eta}) = \exp\left(-\frac{1}{2}(\boldsymbol{x} - \eta)^{\mathrm{T}} \left(E - \eta\eta^{\mathrm{T}} \right)^{-1} (\boldsymbol{x} - \eta) + \right.$$

$$\left. + \varphi(\boldsymbol{\eta}) + \frac{n}{2} \right) , \quad (18)$$

which a specific case of the more general formula for the exponential family parametrized in the expectation parameters, cf. Eq.(1) in [23], that is,

$$p(\boldsymbol{x}; \boldsymbol{\eta}) = \exp\left(\sum_{i=1}^{k} (T_i - \eta_i)\partial_i \varphi(\boldsymbol{\eta}) + \varphi(\boldsymbol{\eta}) \right) . \quad (19)$$

3.4 Change of Parameterization

In this section we have introduced three different parameterizations for a multivariate Gaussian distribution, namely the mean and covariance, the natural and the expectation parameterization.

By combining the transformations between $\boldsymbol{\eta}$, $\boldsymbol{\theta}$, and $(\boldsymbol{\mu};\Sigma)$ in Eq. (8)-(11) and (13)-(16), we have

$$\boldsymbol{\eta} = (\eta; E) = \left(-\frac{1}{2}\Theta^{-1}\theta; \frac{1}{4}\Theta^{-1}\theta\theta^{\mathrm{T}}\Theta^{-1} - \frac{1}{2}\Theta^{-1}\right), \quad (20)$$

$$\boldsymbol{\theta} = (\theta;\Theta) = \left(\left(E-\eta\eta^{\mathrm{T}}\right)^{-1}\eta; -\frac{1}{2}\left(E-\eta\eta^{\mathrm{T}}\right)^{-1}\right). \quad (21)$$

Moreover, from Eq. (2), (12), and (17) we obtain

$$\begin{aligned}\langle\boldsymbol{\theta},\boldsymbol{\eta}\rangle &= \frac{1}{2}\eta^{\mathrm{T}}\left(E-\eta\eta^{\mathrm{T}}\right)^{-1}\eta - \frac{n}{2}, \quad (22)\\ &= -\frac{1}{4}\theta^{\mathrm{T}}\Theta^{-1}\theta - \frac{n}{2}.\end{aligned}$$

Finally, by Eq. (18) and (22), the multivariate Gaussian distribution can be expressed as

$$\begin{aligned}p(\boldsymbol{x};\boldsymbol{\theta},\boldsymbol{\eta}) = &\exp\left(\boldsymbol{x}^{\mathrm{T}}\left(E-\eta\eta^{\mathrm{T}}\right)^{-1}\left(\eta-\frac{1}{2}\boldsymbol{x}\right)+\right.\\ &\left. + \varphi(\boldsymbol{\eta}) - \langle\boldsymbol{\theta},\boldsymbol{\eta}\rangle\right).\end{aligned}$$

The following commutative diagram summarize the transformations between the three parameterizations for the multivariate Gaussian distribution introduced in this section.

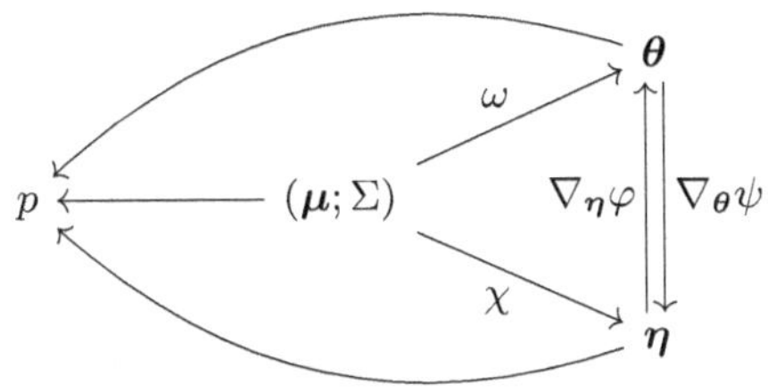

3.5 Fisher Information Matrix

In this section we introduce the formulae for the Fisher information matrix in the three different parameterizations we have introduced. The derivations have been included in the appendix.

In the general case of a statistical model parametrized by a parameter vector $\boldsymbol{\xi} = (\xi_1,\ldots,\xi_d)^{\mathrm{T}}$, the standard definition of Fisher information matrix reads

$$I_{\boldsymbol{\xi}}(\boldsymbol{\xi}) = \mathbb{E}_{\boldsymbol{\xi}}\left[\left(\partial_i \log p(\boldsymbol{x};\boldsymbol{\xi})\right)\left(\partial_j \log p(\boldsymbol{x};\boldsymbol{\xi})\right)^{\mathrm{T}}\right].$$

Under some regularity conditions, cf. Lemma 5.3 (b) in [18], and in particular when $\log p(\boldsymbol{x};\boldsymbol{\xi})$ is twice differentiable, the Fisher information matrix can be obtained by taking the negative of the expected value of the second derivative of the score, that is,

$$I_{\boldsymbol{\xi}}(\boldsymbol{\xi}) = -\mathbb{E}_{\boldsymbol{\xi}}\left[\partial_i\partial_j \log p(\boldsymbol{x};\boldsymbol{\xi})\right].$$

For the multivariate Gaussian distribution, the Fisher information matrix has a special form, and can be obtained from a formula which depends on the derivatives with respect to the parameterization of the mean vector and the covariance matrix, c.f. [25, Thm. 2.1] and [24]. Let $\boldsymbol{\mu}$ and Σ be a function of the parameter vector $\boldsymbol{\xi}$ and ∂_i be the partial derivatives with respect to ξ_i, we have

$$I_{\boldsymbol{\xi}}(\boldsymbol{\xi}) = \left[(\partial_i\boldsymbol{\mu})^{\mathrm{T}}\Sigma^{-1}(\partial_j\boldsymbol{\mu}) + \frac{1}{2}\operatorname{Tr}\left(\Sigma^{-1}(\partial_i\Sigma)\Sigma^{-1}(\partial_j\Sigma)\right)\right] \quad (23)$$

Whenever we choose a parameterization for the Fisher information matrix for which the mean vector and the covariance matrix depend on two different vector parameters, Eq. (23) takes a special form and becomes block diagonal with $I_{\boldsymbol{\xi}}(\boldsymbol{\xi}) = \operatorname{diag}(I_{\boldsymbol{\mu}}, I_{\Sigma})$, cf. [24]. The mean and covariance parameterization clearly satisfies this hypothesis, and by taking partial derivaties we obtain

$$I_{\boldsymbol{\mu},\Sigma}(\boldsymbol{\mu};\Sigma) = \begin{array}{c} \\ j \\ mn \end{array}\left[\begin{array}{c|c} \overset{i}{\Sigma^{-1}} & \overset{kl}{0} \\ \hline 0 & \alpha_{klmn}\end{array}\right], \quad (24)$$

with

$$\alpha_{klmn} = \begin{cases}\frac{1}{2}(\sigma^{kk})^2, & \text{if } k=l=m=n,\\ \sigma^{km}\sigma^{ln}, & \text{if } k=l \veebar m=n,\\ \sigma^{km}\sigma^{ln}+\sigma^{lm}\sigma^{kn}, & \text{otherwise.}\end{cases} \quad (25)$$

In the following we derive $I_{\boldsymbol{\theta}}(\boldsymbol{\theta})$ and $I_{\boldsymbol{\eta}}(\boldsymbol{\eta})$ as the Hessian of $\psi(\boldsymbol{\theta})$ and $\psi(\boldsymbol{\eta})$, respectively, as in Eq. (3) and (4). Clearly, the derivations lead to the same formulae that would be obtained from Eq. (23). For the Fisher information matrix in the natural parameters we have

$$I_{\boldsymbol{\theta}}(\boldsymbol{\theta}) = \frac{1}{2}\times \begin{array}{c} \\ j \\ mn \end{array}\left[\begin{array}{c|c} \overset{i}{-\Theta^{-1}} & \overset{kl}{\Lambda_{kl}\theta} \\ \hline \theta^{\mathrm{T}}\Lambda_{mn} & \lambda_{klmn}-\theta^{\mathrm{T}}\Lambda_{klmn}\theta\end{array}\right] \quad (26)$$

with

$$\begin{aligned}\Lambda_{kl} &= \begin{cases}[\Theta^{-1}]_{\cdot k}[\Theta^{-1}]_{k\cdot}, & \text{if } k=l,\\ [\Theta^{-1}]_{\cdot k}[\Theta^{-1}]_{l\cdot}+ \\ \quad +[\Theta^{-1}]_{\cdot l}[\Theta^{-1}]_{k\cdot}, & \text{otherwise,}\end{cases} \quad (27)\\ &= \begin{cases}4\Sigma_{\cdot k}\Sigma_{l\cdot}, & \text{if } k=l,\\ 4\left(\Sigma_{\cdot k}\Sigma_{l\cdot}+\Sigma_{\cdot l}\Sigma_{k\cdot}\right), & \text{otherwise,}\end{cases} \quad (28)\end{aligned}$$

$$\lambda_{klmn} = \begin{cases}[\Theta^{-1}]_{kk}[\Theta^{-1}]_{kk}, & \text{if } k=l=m=n,\\ [\Theta^{-1}]_{km}[\Theta^{-1}]_{ln}+ \\ \quad +[\Theta^{-1}]_{lm}[\Theta^{-1}]_{kn}, & \text{if } k=l \veebar m=n,\\ 2\left([\Theta^{-1}]_{km}[\Theta^{-1}]_{ln}+\right. \\ \quad \left.+[\Theta^{-1}]_{lm}[\Theta^{-1}]_{kn}\right), & \text{otherwise,}\end{cases} \quad (29)$$

$$= \begin{cases}4(\sigma_{kk}\sigma_{kk}), & \text{if } k=l=m=n,\\ 4(\sigma_{km}\sigma_{ln}+\sigma_{lm}\sigma_{kn}), & \text{if } k=l \veebar m=n,\\ 8(\sigma_{km}\sigma_{ln}+\sigma_{lm}\sigma_{kn}), & \text{otherwise,}\end{cases} \quad (30)$$

$$\Lambda_{klmn} = \begin{cases}[\Lambda_{kk}]_{\cdot m}[\Theta^{-1}]_{n\cdot}, & \text{if } k=l,\\ [\Lambda_{kl}]_{\cdot m}[\Theta^{-1}]_{n\cdot}+ \\ \quad +[\Lambda_{kl}]_{\cdot n}[\Theta^{-1}]_{m\cdot}, & \text{otherwise,}\end{cases} \quad (31)$$

$$= \begin{cases}-8\Sigma_{\cdot k}\sigma_{kk}\Sigma_{k\cdot}, & \text{if } k=l=m=n,\\ -8\left(\Sigma_{\cdot k}\sigma_{km}\Sigma_{n\cdot}+\right. \\ \quad \left.+\Sigma_{\cdot k}\sigma_{kn}\Sigma_{m\cdot}\right), & \text{if } k=l \wedge m\neq n,\\ -8\left(\Sigma_{\cdot k}\sigma_{lm}\Sigma_{m\cdot}+\right. \\ \quad \left.+\Sigma_{\cdot l}\sigma_{lm}\Sigma_{m\cdot}\right), & \text{if } k\neq l \wedge m=n,\\ -8\left(\Sigma_{\cdot k}\sigma_{lm}\Sigma_{n\cdot}+\right. \\ \quad +\Sigma_{\cdot k}\sigma_{ln}\Sigma_{m\cdot}+ \\ \quad +\Sigma_{\cdot l}\sigma_{km}\Sigma_{n\cdot}+ \\ \quad \left.+\Sigma_{\cdot l}\sigma_{kn}\Sigma_{m\cdot}\right), & \text{otherwise.}\end{cases} \quad (32)$$

Where Λ_{kl} a matrix which depends on the indices k and l, and $\Lambda_{kl}\theta$ is a column vector. Notice that in case of $\boldsymbol{\mu} = 0$, $I_{\boldsymbol{\theta}}(\boldsymbol{\theta})$ becomes block diagonal.

For models in the exponential family, we have a general formula based on covariances

$$I(\boldsymbol{\theta}) = \mathrm{Cov}_{\boldsymbol{\theta}}(T_i, T_j) \ . \tag{33}$$

By using Eq. (33), we can also derive the Fisher information matrix in the natural parameterization using covariances.

$$I_{\boldsymbol{\theta}}(\boldsymbol{\mu}, \Sigma) = \begin{array}{c} \\ j \\ mn \end{array} \left[\begin{array}{c|c} i & kl \\ \Sigma & a_{kl}(\mu_k \sigma_{lj} + \mu_l \sigma_{kj}) \\ \hline a_{mn}(\mu_m \sigma_{ni} + \mu_n \sigma_{mi}) & a_{klmn} \gamma_{klmn} \end{array} \right] , \tag{34}$$

with

$$a_{kl} = \begin{cases} 1 \ , & \text{if } k = l \ , \\ 2 \ , & \text{otherwise.} \end{cases} \tag{35}$$

$$a_{klmn} = \begin{cases} 1 \ , & \text{if } k = l = m = n \ , \\ 2 \ , & \text{if } k = l \veebar m = n \ , \\ 4 \ , & \text{otherwise.} \end{cases} \tag{36}$$

$$\gamma_{klmn} = \mu_n \mu_l \sigma_{km} + \mu_k \mu_m \sigma_{ln} + \mu_m \mu_l \sigma_{kn} + \mu_n \mu_k \sigma_{lm} + \\ + \sigma_{km}\sigma_{ln} + \sigma_{lm}\sigma_{kn} \ . \tag{37}$$

Finally, in the $\boldsymbol{\eta}$ parameters the Fisher information matrix becomes

$$I_{\boldsymbol{\eta}}(\boldsymbol{\eta}) = \begin{array}{c} \\ j \\ mn \end{array} \left[\begin{array}{c|c} i & kl \\ \Gamma & -K_{kl}\eta \\ \hline -\eta^{\mathrm{T}} K_{mn} & \kappa_{klmn} \end{array} \right] , \tag{38}$$

with

$$\Gamma = (E - \eta\eta^{\mathrm{T}})^{-1} + (E - \eta\eta^{\mathrm{T}})^{-1}\eta^{\mathrm{T}}(E - \eta\eta^{\mathrm{T}})^{-1}\eta + \\ + (E - \eta\eta^{\mathrm{T}})^{-1}\eta\eta^{\mathrm{T}}(E - \eta\eta^{\mathrm{T}})^{-1} \tag{39}$$

$$= \Sigma^{-1} + \Sigma^{-1}\boldsymbol{\mu}^{\mathrm{T}}\Sigma^{-1}\boldsymbol{\mu} + \Sigma^{-1}\boldsymbol{\mu}\boldsymbol{\mu}^{\mathrm{T}}\Sigma^{-1} \tag{40}$$

$$K_{kl} = \begin{cases} [(E - \eta\eta^{\mathrm{T}})^{-1}]_{\cdot k}[(E - \eta\eta^{\mathrm{T}})^{-1}]_{k \cdot} \ , & \text{if } k = l \ , \\ \frac{1}{2}\left([(E - \eta\eta^{\mathrm{T}})^{-1}]_{\cdot k}[(E - \eta\eta^{\mathrm{T}})^{-1}]_{l \cdot} + \right. \\ \left. + [(E - \eta\eta^{\mathrm{T}})^{-1}]_{\cdot l}[(E - \eta\eta^{\mathrm{T}})^{-1}]_{k \cdot}\right) \ , & \text{otherwise.} \end{cases} \tag{41}$$

$$= \begin{cases} [\Sigma^{-1}]_{\cdot k}[\Sigma^{-1}]_{k \cdot} \ , & \text{if } k = l \ , \\ \frac{1}{2}\left([\Sigma^{-1}]_{\cdot k}[\Sigma^{-1}]_{l \cdot} + [\Sigma^{-1}]_{\cdot l}[\Sigma^{-1}]_{k \cdot}\right) \ , & \text{otherwise.} \end{cases} \tag{42}$$

$$\kappa_{klmn} = \begin{cases} \frac{1}{2}[(E - \eta\eta^{\mathrm{T}})^{-1}]_{kk} \times \\ \quad \times [(E - \eta\eta^{\mathrm{T}})^{-1}]_{kk} \ , & \text{if } k = l = m = n \ , \\ \frac{1}{2}[(E - \eta\eta^{\mathrm{T}})^{-1}]_{km} \times \\ \quad \times [(E - \eta\eta^{\mathrm{T}})^{-1}]_{ln} \ , & \text{if } k = l \veebar m = n \ , \\ \frac{1}{4}\left([(E - \eta\eta^{\mathrm{T}})^{-1}]_{km} \times \right. \\ \quad \times [(E - \eta\eta^{\mathrm{T}})^{-1}]_{ln} + \\ \quad + [(E - \eta\eta^{\mathrm{T}})^{-1}]_{lm} \times \\ \quad \left. \times [(E - \eta\eta^{\mathrm{T}})^{-1}]_{kn}\right) \ , & \text{otherwise.} \end{cases} \tag{43}$$

$$= \begin{cases} \frac{1}{2}(\sigma^{kk})^2 \ , & \text{if } k = l = m = n \ , \\ \frac{1}{2}\sigma^{km}\sigma^{ln} \ , & \text{if } k = l \veebar m = n \ , \\ \frac{1}{4}\left(\sigma^{km}\sigma^{ln} + \sigma^{lm}\sigma^{kn}\right) \ , & \text{otherwise.} \end{cases} \tag{44}$$

4. NATURAL GRADIENT

We are interested in optimizing a real-valued function f defined over $\mathbb{R}^n$, that is

$$(\mathrm{P}) \qquad \min_{\boldsymbol{x} \in \mathbb{R}^n} f(\boldsymbol{x}) \ .$$

We replace the original optimization problem (P) with the stochastic relaxation F of f, i.e., the minimization of the expected value of f evaluated with respect to a density p which belongs to the multivariate Gaussian distribution, i.e.,

$$(\mathrm{SR}) \qquad \min_{\boldsymbol{\xi} \in \Xi} F(\boldsymbol{\xi}) = \min_{\boldsymbol{\xi} \in \Xi} \mathbb{E}_{\boldsymbol{\xi}}[f(\boldsymbol{x})] \ .$$

Given a parametrization $\boldsymbol{\xi}$ for p, the natural gradient of $F(\boldsymbol{\xi})$ can be evaluated as

$$\widetilde{\nabla}_{\boldsymbol{\xi}} F(\boldsymbol{\xi}) = I(\boldsymbol{\xi})^{-1} \nabla_{\boldsymbol{\xi}} F(\boldsymbol{\xi}) \ ,$$

where $F(\boldsymbol{\xi})$ is the vector or partial derivatives, often called vanilla gradient.

Notice that for models in the exponential family, and thus for the Gaussian distribution, the vanilla gradient of $F(\boldsymbol{\xi})$ can be evaluated as the expected value of $f \nabla_{\boldsymbol{\xi}} \log p(\boldsymbol{x}; \boldsymbol{\xi})$, indeed

$$\partial_i F(\boldsymbol{\xi}) = \partial_i \mathbb{E}_{\boldsymbol{\xi}}[f] = \mathbb{E}_0[f \partial_i p(\boldsymbol{x}; \boldsymbol{\xi})] = \mathbb{E}_{\boldsymbol{\xi}}[f \partial_i \log p(\boldsymbol{x}; \boldsymbol{\xi})] \ .$$

In the mean and covariance parameterization, the vanilla gradient is given by

see for instance [3].

In the following, we provide formulae for $\nabla F(\boldsymbol{\theta})$ and $\nabla F(\boldsymbol{\eta})$, in the natural and expectation parameterizations. In the natural parameters we have

$$\partial_i \log p(\boldsymbol{x}; \boldsymbol{\theta}) = T_i(\boldsymbol{x}) - \partial_i \psi(\boldsymbol{\theta}) = T_i(\boldsymbol{x}) - \eta_i \ .$$

In the expectation parameters, by deriving the log of Eq. (19) we obtain

$$\partial_i \log p(\boldsymbol{x}; \boldsymbol{\eta}) = (T_i(\boldsymbol{x}) - \eta_i)\partial_i \partial_j \varphi(\boldsymbol{\eta}) \ .$$

So that

$$\nabla F(\boldsymbol{\theta}) = \mathbb{E}_{\boldsymbol{\theta}}[f(T - \boldsymbol{\eta})] = \mathrm{Cov}_{\boldsymbol{\theta}}(f, \boldsymbol{T}) \ ,$$
$$\nabla F(\boldsymbol{\eta}) = \mathrm{Hess}\, \varphi(\boldsymbol{\eta}) \mathbb{E}_{\boldsymbol{\eta}}[f(T - \boldsymbol{\eta})]$$
$$= I_{\boldsymbol{\eta}}(\boldsymbol{\eta}) \, \mathrm{Cov}_{\boldsymbol{\eta}}(f, \boldsymbol{T}) \ .$$

A common approach to solve the (SR) is given by natural gradient descent, when the parameters of a density are updated iteratively in the direction given by the natural gradient of F, i.e.,

$$\boldsymbol{\xi}^{t+1} = \boldsymbol{\xi}^t - \lambda \widetilde{\nabla}_{\boldsymbol{\xi}} F(\boldsymbol{\xi}) \ ,$$

where the parameter $\lambda > 0$ controls the step size.

5. EXAMPLES

In this section we introduce and discuss some toy examples, for which it is possible to represent the gradient flows and the landscape of the stochastic relaxation. In particular we evaluate the gradient flows, i.e., the solutions of the differential equations

$$\dot{\boldsymbol{\xi}} = -\widetilde{\nabla}_{\boldsymbol{\xi}} F(\boldsymbol{\xi}).$$

Such flows correspond to the trajectories associated to infinite step size, when the gradient can be computed exactly.

5.1 Polynomial Optimization in $\mathbb{R}$

In this section we study some simple examples of polynomial optimization in $\mathbb{R}$. Let f be a real-valued polynomial function, we choose a monomial basis $\{x^k\}$, $k > 0$, so that any polynomial can be written in compact form as

$$f_k = \sum_{i=0}^{k} c_i x^i \ . \tag{45}$$

We consider the case of quadratic functions, where $k = 2$ in Eq. (45), so that $f_2 = c_0 + c_1 x + c_2 x^2$. In order for quadratic functions to be lower bounded and this admit a minimum, we need to impose $c_2 > 0$. We consider the one dimensional Gaussian $\mathcal{N}(\mu, \sigma)$ distribution parametrized by μ, σ, and denote by $F(\mu, \sigma)$ the stochastic relaxation of f with respect to $\mathcal{N}$. Represented as an exponential family, $\mathcal{N}(\mu, \sigma)$ is a two-dimensional exponential family, with sufficient statistics $\boldsymbol{T}$ given by X and X^2.

Let $\boldsymbol{c} = (c_1, c_2)^{\mathrm{T}}$, in the $\boldsymbol{\eta}$ parameters the vanilla and natural gradient read

$$\nabla_{\boldsymbol{\eta}} F(\boldsymbol{\eta}) = \nabla_{\boldsymbol{\eta}} \sum_{i=1}^{2} c_i \mathbb{E}_{\boldsymbol{\eta}}[X^i] = \nabla_{\boldsymbol{\eta}} (c_1 \mu_1, c_2 E_{11})^{\mathrm{T}} = \boldsymbol{c} \ ,$$

$$\widetilde{\nabla}_{\boldsymbol{\eta}} F(\boldsymbol{\eta}) = I_{\boldsymbol{\eta}}(\boldsymbol{\eta})^{-1} \nabla_{\boldsymbol{\eta}} F(\theta) \ .$$

The vanilla and natural gradients in $\boldsymbol{\theta}$ are

$$\nabla_{\boldsymbol{\theta}} F(\boldsymbol{\theta}) = \mathrm{Cov}_{\boldsymbol{\theta}}(f, \boldsymbol{T}) = \sum_{i=1}^{2} c_i \mathrm{Cov}_{\boldsymbol{\theta}}(X^i, \boldsymbol{T}) = I(\boldsymbol{\theta}) \boldsymbol{c} \ ,$$

$$\widetilde{\nabla}_{\boldsymbol{\theta}} F(\boldsymbol{\theta}) = I_{\boldsymbol{\theta}}(\boldsymbol{\theta})^{-1} \nabla_{\boldsymbol{\theta}} F(\theta) = \boldsymbol{c} \ .$$

Since f belongs to the span of the $\{T_i\}$, so that for any initial condition q in $\mathcal{N}(\mu, \sigma)$ the natural gradient flows in any parametrization weakly converge to the δ distribution over the minimum of f, given by $x^* = -\frac{c_1}{2c_2}$. Such distribution belongs to the closure of the Gaussian distribution and can be identified as the limit distribution with $\mu = -\frac{c_1}{2c_2}$ and $\sigma \to 0$. In Fig. 1 we represented an instance of this example, where $f = x - 3x^2$. Notice that the flow associated to the vanilla gradient in $\boldsymbol{\eta}$ is linear in (μ, σ) and stops at the boundary of the model, where it reaches the positivity constraint for σ. All other trajectories converge to the global minimum, and natural gradient flows defines straight paths to the optimum.

We move to the case where the polynomial f_k has higher degree. We do not consider the case when $k = 3$ since f_3 would not be lower bounded, and study the polynomial for $k = 4$, so that $f_4 = c_0 + c_1 x + c_2 x^2 + c_3 x^3 + c_4 x^4$. Notice that f_4 doest not belong anymore to the span of the sufficient statistics of the exponential family, and the function may have two local minima in $\mathbb{R}$. Similarly, the relaxation with respect to the one dimensional gaussian family $\mathcal{N}(\mu, \sigma)$ may admin two local minima associated to the δ distributions over the local minima of f.

Vanilla and natural gradient formulae can be computed in closed form, indeed in the exponential family higher order moment $\mathbb{E}[X^k]$ can be evaluated recursively as a function of $\boldsymbol{\eta}$, by expanding $\mathbb{E}[(X - \mathbb{E}[X])^k]$ using the binomial formula, and then applying Isserlis' theorem for centered moments, cf. [14].

In the $\boldsymbol{\eta}$ and $\boldsymbol{\theta}$ parameters the vanilla gradients read

$$\nabla_{\boldsymbol{\eta}} F(\boldsymbol{\eta}) = \boldsymbol{c} + \sum_{i=3}^{k} c_i \nabla_{\boldsymbol{\eta}} \mathbb{E}_{\boldsymbol{\eta}}[X^i] \ ,$$

$$\nabla_{\boldsymbol{\theta}} F(\boldsymbol{\theta}) = I(\boldsymbol{\theta}) \boldsymbol{c} + \sum_{i=3}^{k} c_i \mathrm{Cov}_{\boldsymbol{\theta}}(X^i, \boldsymbol{T}) \ ,$$

while natural gradients can be evaluated by premultiplying vanilla gradient with the inverse of the Fisher information matrix.

In Fig. 2 we plotted different trajectories for the case $f = 6x + 8x^2 - x^3 - 2x^4$. We can notice two different basins of attraction, so that the trajectories associated to the natural gradient flows converge to either one or the other local minima depending on the initial condition. As in the case of f_2 vanilla flows in $\boldsymbol{\eta}$ converge to the boundary of the model where $\sigma \to 0$, and trajectories are not straight in (μ, σ).

5.2 Polynomial Optimization in $\mathbb{R}^n$

The examples in the previous subsection can be easily generalized to the case of polynomial functions in $\mathbb{R}^n$.

In Fig. 3 we studied the case where $f = x_1 + 2x_2 - 3x_1^2 - 2x_1 x_2 - 2x_2^2$. In this example, the multivariate Gaussian distribution is a 5−dimensional exponential family, for this reason we plot the projections of the flows onto $\boldsymbol{\mu} = (\mu_1, \mu_2)$, and represent the level lines of f instead of those of $F(\mu, \Sigma)$. This explains while trajectories appear to self intersect in the projected space, which would be impossible for any gradient flow over $\mathcal{N}$. However, since f is a quadratic function, we are guaranteed that the natural gradient flows converge to the δ distribution over the unique global optimum of f for any initial condition.

6. CONCLUSIONS

This paper focuses on the study of the geometry of the multivariate Gaussian distribution, and more generally of models in the exponential family from the perspective of stochastic relaxation. We discussed two alternative parameterizations to the mean vector and covariance matrix for the multivariate Gaussian distribution, namely the natural and expectation parameterizations of the exponential family. We derived variable transformations between each parameterization and the formulae for the natural gradients. Since the natural gradient is invariant with respect to the choice of the parameterization, following the natural gradient in any of these parameterizations is equivalent from the point of view of the optimization.

On the other side, by exploiting the specific properties of each parameterization, and the relationship between Fisher information matrices, we can define alternative algorithms for natural gradient descent. In particular, by parametrizing the Gaussian distribution in the natural parameters we have the advantage of a meaningful representation for lower dimensional sub-models of the Gaussian distribution, together with closed formulae for the inverse of the Fisher information matrix, which allow to easily evaluate the natural gradient.

7. ACKNOWLEDGEMENTS

Giovanni Pistone is supported by de Castro Statistics, Collegio Carlo Alberto, Moncalieri, and he is a member of GNAMPA-INDAM.

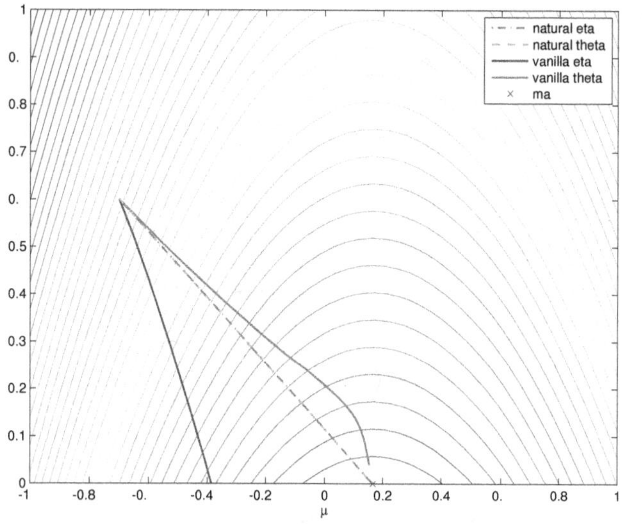

(a)

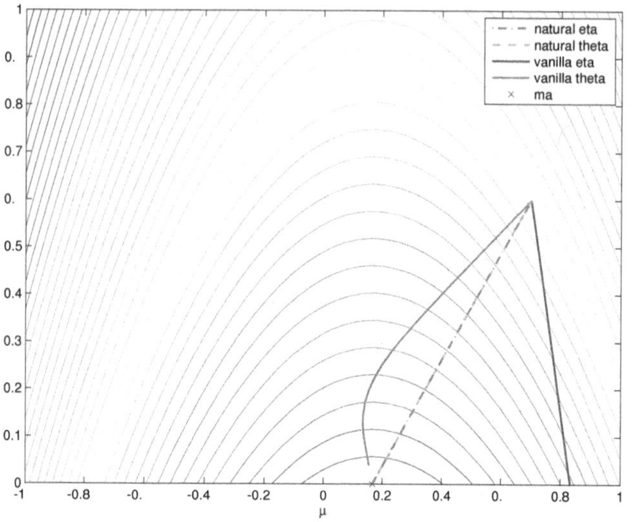

(b)

Figure 1: Vanilla vs natural gradient flows for $\mathbb{E}[f]$, with $f = x - 3x^2$, evaluated in $\boldsymbol{\eta}$ and $\boldsymbol{\theta}$ parameters and represented in the parameter space (μ, σ). Each figure represents the flows for different initial conditions. The flows are evaluated solving the differential equations numerically. The level lines are associated to $\mathbb{E}_{\mu,\sigma}[f]$.

8. REFERENCES

[1] P.-A. Absil, R. Mahony, and R. Sepulchre. *Optimization algorithms on matrix manifolds.* Princeton University Press, Princeton, NJ, 2008. With a foreword by Paul Van Dooren.

[2] Y. Akimoto, A. Auger, and N. Hansen. Convergence of the continuous time trajectories of isotropic evolution strategies on monotonic $\mathcal{C}^2$-composite functions. In C. Coello, V. Cutello, K. Deb, S. Forrest, G. Nicosia, and M. Pavone, editors, *Parallel Problem Solving from Nature - PPSN XII*, volume 7491 of *Lecture Notes in Computer Science*, pages 42–51. Springer Berlin Heidelberg, 2012.

[3] Y. Akimoto, Y. Nagata, I. Ono, and S. Kobayashi. Theoretical foundation for cma-es from information geometry perspective. *Algorithmica*, 64(4):698–716, 2012.

[4] S. Amari. *Differential-geometrical methods in statistics*, volume 28 of *Lecture Notes in Statistics.* Springer-Verlag, New York, 1985.

[5] S. Amari. Natural gradient works efficiently in learning. *Neural Computation*, 10(2):251–276, 1998.

[6] S. Amari. Information geometry on hierarchy of probability distributions. *IEEE Transactions on Information Theory*, 47(5):1701–1711, 2001.

[7] S. Amari and H. Nagaoka. *Methods of information geometry.* American Mathematical Society, Providence, RI, 2000. Translated from the 1993 Japanese original by Daishi Harada.

[8] O. E. Barndorff-Nielsen. *Information and Exponential Families in Statistical Theory.* John Wiley & Sons, New York, 1978.

[9] J. Bensadon. Black-box optimization using geodesics in statistical manifolds. *Entropy*, 17(1):304–345, 2015.

[10] H.-G. Beyer. Convergence analysis of evolutionary algorithms that are based on the paradigm of information geometry. *Evol. Comput.*, 22(4):679–709, Dec. 2014.

[11] P. Billingsley. *Convergence of probability measures.* John Wiley & Sons, Inc., New York-London-Sydney, 1968.

[12] L. D. Brown. *Fundamentals of Statistical Exponential Families with Applications in Statistical Decision Theory*, volume 9 of *Lecture Notes - Monograph Series.* Institute of Mathematical Statistics, 1986.

[13] N. Hansen and A. Ostermeier. Completely derandomized self-adaptation in evolution strategies. *Evolutionary Computation*, 9(2):159–195, 2001.

[14] L. Isserlis. On a formula for the product-moment coefficient of any order of a normal frequency distribution in any number of variables. *Biometrika*, 12(1-2):134–139, 1918.

[15] R. E. Kass and P. W. Vos. *Geometrical Foundations of Asymptotic Inference.* Wiley Series in Probability and Statistics. John Wiley, New York, 1997.

[16] P. Larrañaga and J. A. Lozano, editors. *Estimation of Distribution Algoritms. A New Tool for evolutionary Computation.* Springer, 2001.

[17] S. L. Lauritzen. *Graphical models.* The Clarendon Press Oxford University Press, New York, 1996.

[18] E. Lehmann and G. Casella. *Theory of Point Estimation.* Springer Verlag, second edition, 1998.

[19] L. Malagò, M. Matteucci, and G. Pistone. Stochastic relaxation as a unifying approach in 0/1 programming. In *NIPS 2009 Workshop on Discrete Optimization in Machine Learning: Submodularity, Sparsity & Polyhedra (DISCML)*, 2009.

[20] L. Malagò, M. Matteucci, and G. Pistone. Towards the geometry of estimation of distribution algorithms based on the exponential family. In *Proc. of FOGA '11*, pages 230–242. ACM, 2011.

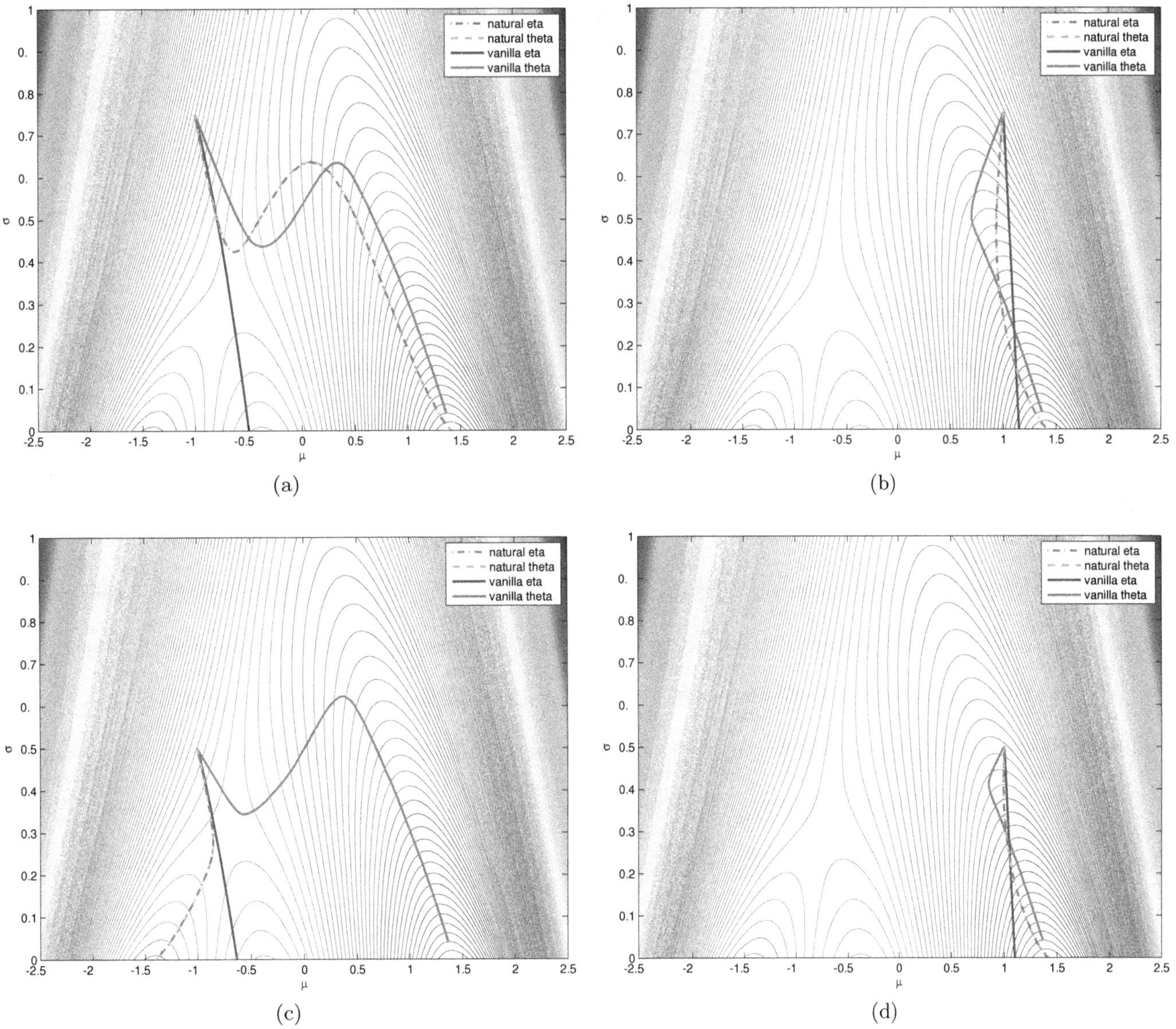

Figure 2: Vanilla vs natural gradient flows for $\mathbb{E}[f]$, with $f = 6x + 8x^2 - x^3 - 2x^4$, evaluated in $\boldsymbol{\eta}$ and $\boldsymbol{\theta}$ parameters and represented in the parameter space (μ, σ). Each figure represents the flows for different initial conditions. The flows are evaluated solving the differential equations numerically. The level lines are associated to $\mathbb{E}_{\mu,\sigma}[f]$.

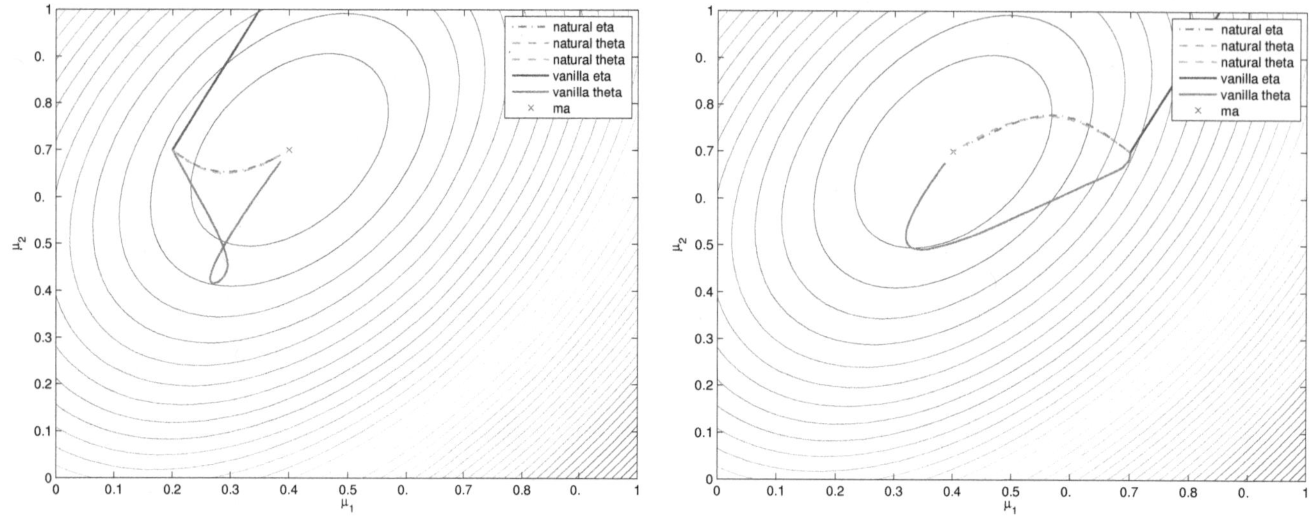

(a) (b)

Figure 3: Vanilla vs natural gradient flows for $\mathbb{E}[f]$, with $f = x_1 + 2x_2 - 3x_1^2 - 2x_1x_2 - 2x_2^2$, evaluated in $\boldsymbol{\eta}$ and $\boldsymbol{\theta}$ parameters and represented in the parameter space (μ_1, μ_2). Each figure represents the projections of the flows for different initial conditions, with $\sigma_{11} = 1, \sigma_{12} = -0.5, \sigma_{22} = 2$. The flows are evaluated solving the differential equations numerically. The level lines are associated to f.

[21] L. Malagò, M. Matteucci, and G. Pistone. Natural gradient, fitness modelling and model selection: A unifying perspective. In *Proc. of IEEE CEC 2013*, pages 486–493, 2013.

[22] L. Malagò and G. Pistone. Combinatorial optimization with information geometry: The newton method. *Entropy*, 16(8):4260–4289, 2014.

[23] L. Malagò and G. Pistone. Gradient flow of the stochastic relaxation on a generic exponential family. *AIP Conference Proceedings of MaxEnt 2014, held on September 21-26, 2014, Château du Clos Lucé, Amboise, France*, 1641:353–360, 2015.

[24] K. V. Mardia and R. J. Marshall. Maximum likelihood estimation of models for residual covariance in spatial regression. *Biometrika*, 71(1):135–146, 1984.

[25] K. S. Miller. *Complex stochastic processes: an introduction to theory and application.* Addison-Wesley Pub. Co., 1974.

[26] Y. Ollivier, L. Arnold, A. Auger, and N. Hansen. Information-geometric optimization algorithms: A unifying picture via invariance principles. arXiv:1106.3708, 2011v1; 2013v2.

[27] G. Pistone. A version of the geometry of the multivariate gaussian model, with applications. In *Proceedings of the 47th Scientific Meeting of the Italian Statistical Society, SIS 2014, Cagliari, June 11-13*, 2014.

[28] R. T. Rockafellar. *Convex analysis.* Princeton Mathematical Series, No. 28. Princeton University Press, Princeton, N.J., 1970.

[29] R. Y. Rubistein and D. P. Kroese. *The Cross-Entropy method: a unified approach to combinatorial optimization, Monte-Carlo simluation, and machine learning.* Springer, New York, 2004.

[30] L. T. Skovgaard. A Riemannian Geometry of the Multivariate Normal Model. *Scandinavian Journal of Statistics*, 11(4):211–223, 1984.

[31] D. Wierstra, T. Schaul, T. Glasmachers, Y. Sun, J. Peters, and J. Schmidhuber. Natural evolution strategies. *Journal of Machine Learning Research*, 15:949–980, 2014.

[32] D. Wierstra, T. Schaul, J. Peters, and J. Schmidhuber. Natural evolution strategies. In *Proc. of IEEE CEC 2008*, pages 3381–3387, 2008.

APPENDIX

A. COMPUTATIONS FOR THE FISHER INFORMATION MATRIX

In this appendix we included the derivations for the Fisher information matrix in the different parameterizations.

A.1 Mean and Covariance Parameters

Since $\partial_i \boldsymbol{\mu} = \boldsymbol{e}_i$, we have $I_{\boldsymbol{\mu}} = \Sigma^{-1}$. As to I_Σ, first notice that

$$\partial_{ij}\Sigma = \begin{cases} \boldsymbol{e}_i\boldsymbol{e}_i^{\mathrm{T}} \,, & \text{if } i = j \,, \\ \boldsymbol{e}_i\boldsymbol{e}_j^{\mathrm{T}} + \boldsymbol{e}_j\boldsymbol{e}_i^{\mathrm{T}} \,, & \text{otherwise,} \end{cases}$$

so that for $k \neq l \wedge m \neq n$, we obtain

$$\begin{aligned}[I_\Sigma]_{klmn} &= \frac{1}{2}\operatorname{Tr}\left(\Sigma^{-1}(\partial_{kl}\Sigma)\Sigma^{-1}(\partial_{mn}\Sigma)\right) \\ &= \frac{1}{2}\operatorname{Tr}\left(\Sigma^{-1}(e_k e_l^{\mathrm{T}} + e_l e_k^{\mathrm{T}})\Sigma^{-1}(e_m e_n^{\mathrm{T}} + e_n e_m^{\mathrm{T}})\right) \\ &= \frac{1}{2}\operatorname{Tr}\left(2e_l^{\mathrm{T}}\Sigma^{-1}e_m e_n^{\mathrm{T}}\Sigma^{-1}e_k + 2e_k^{\mathrm{T}}\Sigma^{-1}e_m e_n^{\mathrm{T}}\Sigma^{-1}e_l\right) \\ &= e_l^{\mathrm{T}}\Sigma^{-1}e_m e_n^{\mathrm{T}}\Sigma^{-1}e_k + e_k^{\mathrm{T}}\Sigma^{-1}e_m e_n^{\mathrm{T}}\Sigma^{-1}e_l \\ &= \sigma^{km}\sigma^{ln} + \sigma^{lm}\sigma^{kn} \; .\end{aligned}$$

In the remaining cases, when $k = l = m = n$ and $k = l \veebar m = n$, the computations are analogous, giving the formulae in Eq. (24) and (25).

A.2 Natural Parameters

In the following we derive the Fisher information matrix in the natural parameters by taking the Hessian of $\psi(\boldsymbol{\theta})$ in Eq. (12). We start by taking first-order derivatives, i.e.,

$$\partial_i\psi(\boldsymbol{\theta}) = -\frac{1}{2}e_i^{\mathrm{T}}\Theta^{-1}\theta \; , \tag{46}$$

$$\begin{aligned}\partial_{ij}\psi(\boldsymbol{\theta}) &= \frac{1}{4}\theta^{\mathrm{T}}\Theta^{-1}(\partial_{ij}\Theta)\Theta^{-1}\theta - \frac{1}{2}\operatorname{Tr}\left(-\frac{1}{2}\Theta^{-1}\partial_{ij}(-2\Theta)\right) \\ &= \frac{1}{4}\theta^{\mathrm{T}}\Theta^{-1}(\partial_{ij}\Theta)\Theta^{-1}\theta - \frac{1}{2}\operatorname{Tr}(\Theta^{-1}(\partial_{ij}\Theta)) \qquad (47)\end{aligned}$$

Notice that

$$\partial_{ij}\Theta = \begin{cases} e_i e_i^{\mathrm{T}} \; , & \text{if } i = j \; , \\ e_i e_j^{\mathrm{T}} + e_j e_i^{\mathrm{T}} \; , & \text{otherwise,} \end{cases}$$

so that as in Eq. (20), we have

$$\begin{aligned}\eta &= -\frac{1}{2}\Theta^{-1}\theta \; , \\ E &= \frac{1}{4}\Theta^{-1}\theta\theta^{\mathrm{T}}\Theta^{-1} - \frac{1}{2}\Theta^{-1} \; .\end{aligned}$$

Next, we take partial derivatives of Eq. (46) and (47), and since $\partial_{kl}\partial_{ij}\Theta = 0$, we get

$$\begin{aligned}\partial_i\partial_j\psi(\boldsymbol{\theta}) &= -\frac{1}{2}e_i^{\mathrm{T}}\Theta^{-1}e_j \; , \\ \partial_i\partial_{kl}\psi(\boldsymbol{\theta}) &= \frac{1}{2}e_i^{\mathrm{T}}\Theta^{-1}(\partial_{kl}\Theta)\Theta^{-1}\theta \; .\end{aligned}$$

Let $\Lambda_{kl} = \Theta^{-1}(\partial_{kl}\Theta)\Theta^{-1}$, for $k \neq l$ we have

$$\begin{aligned}\Lambda_{kl} &= \Theta^{-1}(e_k e_l^{\mathrm{T}} + e_l e_k^{\mathrm{T}})\Theta^{-1} \\ &= \Theta^{-1}e_l e_k^{\mathrm{T}}\Theta^{-1} + \Theta^{-1}e_k e_l^{\mathrm{T}}\Theta^{-1} \\ &= 4(\Sigma e_l e_k^{\mathrm{T}}\Sigma + \Sigma e_k e_l^{\mathrm{T}}\Sigma) \; .\end{aligned}$$

In the remaining case, when $k \neq l$, the computations are analogous, giving the formulae in Eq. (27), (28) and (26).

$$\begin{aligned}\partial_{kl}\partial_{mn}\psi(\boldsymbol{\theta}) &= -\frac{1}{2}\theta^{\mathrm{T}}\Theta^{-1}(\partial_{kl}\Theta)\Theta^{-1}(\partial_{mn}\Theta)\Theta^{-1}\theta + \\ &+ \frac{1}{2}\operatorname{Tr}\left(\Theta^{-1}(\partial_{kl}\Theta)\Theta^{-1}(\partial_{mn}\Theta)\right) \; .\end{aligned}$$

Let $\Lambda_{klmn} = \Theta^{-1}(\partial_{kl}\Theta)\Theta^{-1}(\partial_{mn}\Theta)\Theta^{-1}$, for $k \neq l \wedge m \neq n$

$$\begin{aligned}\Lambda_{klmn} &= \Theta^{-1}(e_k e_l^{\mathrm{T}} + e_l e_k^{\mathrm{T}})\Theta^{-1}(e_m e_n^{\mathrm{T}} + e_n e_m^{\mathrm{T}})\Theta^{-1} \\ &= \Theta^{-1}e_k e_l^{\mathrm{T}}\Theta^{-1}e_m e_n^{\mathrm{T}}\Theta^{-1} + \Theta^{-1}e_k e_l^{\mathrm{T}}\Theta^{-1}e_n e_m^{\mathrm{T}}\Theta^{-1} + \\ &\quad \Theta^{-1}e_l e_k^{\mathrm{T}}\Theta^{-1}e_m e_n^{\mathrm{T}}\Theta^{-1} + \Theta^{-1}e_l e_k^{\mathrm{T}}\Theta^{-1}e_n e_m^{\mathrm{T}}\Theta^{-1} \\ &= -8(\Sigma e_k\sigma_{lm}e_n^{\mathrm{T}}\Sigma + \Sigma e_k\sigma_{ln}e_m^{\mathrm{T}}\Sigma + \Sigma e_l\sigma_{km}e_n^{\mathrm{T}}\Sigma + \\ &\quad + \Sigma e_l\sigma_{kn}e_m^{\mathrm{T}}\Sigma) \; .\end{aligned}$$

In the remaining cases when $k = l = m = n$, $k = l \wedge m \neq n$ and $k \neq l \wedge m = n$, the computations are analogous, giving the formulae in Eq. (31), (32) and (26).

Finally, $\lambda_{klmn} = \operatorname{Tr}\left(\Theta^{-1}(\partial_{kl}\Theta)\Theta^{-1}(\partial_{mn}\Theta)\right)$, we have for $k \neq l \wedge m \neq n$

$$\begin{aligned}\lambda_{klmn} &= \operatorname{Tr}\left(\Theta^{-1}(e_k e_l^{\mathrm{T}} + e_l e_k^{\mathrm{T}})\Theta^{-1}(e_m e_n^{\mathrm{T}} + e_n e_m^{\mathrm{T}})\right) \\ &= 2e_l^{\mathrm{T}}\Theta^{-1}e_m e_n\Theta^{-1}e_k + 2e_k^{\mathrm{T}}\Theta^{-1}e_m e_n\Theta^{-1}e_l \\ &= 8e_l^{\mathrm{T}}\Sigma e_m e_n^{\mathrm{T}}\Sigma e_k + 8e_k^{\mathrm{T}}\Sigma e_m e_n^{\mathrm{T}}\Sigma e_l \; .\end{aligned}$$

In the remaining cases, when $k = l = m = n$ and $k = l \veebar m = n$, the computations are analogous, giving the formulae in Eq. (29), (30) and (26).

Next, we derive an equivalent formulation for the Fisher information matrix based on covariances. From Eq. (33), we have that the elements of the Fisher information matrix in $\boldsymbol{\theta}$ can be obtained from the covariances of sufficient statistics. Moreover, from the definition of covariance, we have

$$\begin{aligned}\operatorname{Cov}_{\boldsymbol{\mu},\Sigma}(X_i, X_j) &= \sigma_{ij} \; , \\ \operatorname{Cov}_{\boldsymbol{\mu},\Sigma}(X_i, X_k X_l) &= \mathbb{E}_{\boldsymbol{\mu},\Sigma}[X_i X_k X_l] + \\ &\quad - \mathbb{E}_{\boldsymbol{\mu},\Sigma}[X_i]\mathbb{E}_{\boldsymbol{\mu},\Sigma}[X_k X_l] \; , \\ \operatorname{Cov}_{\boldsymbol{\mu},\Sigma}(X_k X_l, X_m X_n) &= \mathbb{E}_{\boldsymbol{\mu},\Sigma}[X_k X_l X_m X_n] + \\ &\quad - \mathbb{E}_{\boldsymbol{\mu},\Sigma}[X_k X_l]\mathbb{E}_{\boldsymbol{\mu},\Sigma}[X_m X_l n] \; .\end{aligned}$$

The definition of first- and second-order moments in terms of mean vector and covariance matrix are straightforward,

$$\begin{aligned}\mathbb{E}_{\boldsymbol{\mu},\Sigma}[X_i] &= \mu_i \\ \mathbb{E}_{\boldsymbol{\mu},\Sigma}[X_i X_j] &= \sigma_{ij} + \mu_i\mu_j \; .\end{aligned}$$

In order to evaluate third- and forth-order moments we use Isserlis' theorem [14] after centering variables by replacing X_i with $X_i - \mathbb{E}_{\boldsymbol{\mu},\Sigma}[X_i]$, which gives

$$\mathbb{E}_{\boldsymbol{\mu},\Sigma}[X_i X_k X_l] = \mu_i\sigma_{kl} + \mu_k\sigma_{il} + \mu_l\sigma_{ik} + \mu_i\mu_k\mu_l \; ,$$

$$\begin{aligned}\mathbb{E}_{\boldsymbol{\mu},\Sigma}[X_k X_l X_m X_n] &= \sigma_{kn}\sigma_{lm} + \sigma_{km}\sigma_{ln} + \sigma_{kl}\sigma_{mn} + \\ &+ \sum_{\{\tau(k)\}\{\tau(l)\}\{\tau(m)\tau(n)\}} \sigma_{\tau(k)\tau(l)}\mu_{\tau(m)}\mu_{\tau(n)} + \\ &+ \mu_k\mu_l\mu_m\mu_n \; ,\end{aligned}$$

where $\{\tau(k)\}\{\tau(l)\}\{\tau(m)\tau(n)\}$ denotes the combinations of the indices k, l, m, n without repetitions, where indices have divided into three groups, $\{\tau(k)\}$, $\{\tau(l)\}$ and $\{\tau(m)\tau(n)\}$. Finally, by using the formulae for higher-order moments in terms of mean and covariance we obtain

$$\begin{aligned}\operatorname{Cov}_{\boldsymbol{\mu},\Sigma}(X_i, X_k X_l) &= \mathbb{E}_{\boldsymbol{\mu},\Sigma}[X_i X_k X_l] - \mathbb{E}_{\boldsymbol{\mu},\Sigma}[X_i]\mathbb{E}_{\boldsymbol{\mu},\Sigma}[X_k X_l] \\ &= \mu_k\sigma_{il} + \mu_l\sigma_{ik} \; ,\end{aligned}$$

and

$$\begin{aligned}
\mathrm{Cov}_{\boldsymbol{\mu},\Sigma}(X_k X_l, X_m X_n) &= \mathbb{E}_{\boldsymbol{\mu},\Sigma}[X_k X_l X_m X_n] + \\
&\quad - \mathbb{E}_{\boldsymbol{\mu},\Sigma}[X_k X_l]\mathbb{E}_{\boldsymbol{\mu},\Sigma}[X_m X_n] \\
&= \mu_n \mu_l \sigma_{km} + \mu_k \mu_m \sigma_{ln} + \mu_m \mu_l \sigma_{kn} + \mu_n \mu_k \sigma_{lm} + \\
&\quad + \sigma_{km}\sigma_{ln} + \sigma_{lm}\sigma_{kn} \ .
\end{aligned}$$

The results are summarized in Eq. (35), (36), (37) and (34). Notice that for $k \neq l$, $T_{kl} = 2X_k X_l$, and thus $\mathrm{Cov}_{\boldsymbol{\mu},\Sigma}(T_i, T_{kl}) = 2\,\mathrm{Cov}_{\boldsymbol{\mu},\Sigma}(X_i, X_k X_l)$, we introduced the coefficients a_{kl} and a_{klmn} to compensate for the constant.

A.3 Expectation Parameters

In the following we derive the Fisher information matrix in the expectation parameters by taking the Hessian of $\varphi(\boldsymbol{\eta})$ in Eq. (17). We start by taking first-order derivatives, i.e.,

$$\partial_i \varphi(\boldsymbol{\eta}) = \frac{1}{2}\,\mathrm{Tr}\left((E - \eta\eta^{\mathrm{T}})^{-1}\partial_i(\eta\eta^{\mathrm{T}})\right) \quad (48)$$

$$\partial_{ij} \varphi(\boldsymbol{\eta}) = -\frac{1}{2}\,\mathrm{Tr}\left((E - \eta\eta^{\mathrm{T}})^{-1}(\partial_{ij}E)\right) \quad (49)$$

Notice that

$$\partial_{ij}E = \begin{cases} \boldsymbol{e}_i\boldsymbol{e}_i^{\mathrm{T}} \ , & \text{if } i = j \ , \\ \frac{1}{2}\left(\boldsymbol{e}_i\boldsymbol{e}_j^{\mathrm{T}} + \boldsymbol{e}_j\boldsymbol{e}_i^{\mathrm{T}}\right) \ , & \text{otherwise,} \end{cases}$$

so that, as in Eq. (21), we have

$$\begin{aligned}
\theta &= \frac{1}{2}\left[\mathrm{Tr}\left((E - \eta\eta^{\mathrm{T}})^{-1}(\boldsymbol{e}_i\eta^{\mathrm{T}} + \eta\boldsymbol{e}_i^{\mathrm{T}})\right)\right]_i \\
&= \left(E - \eta\eta^{\mathrm{T}}\right)^{-1}\eta \ , \\
\Theta &= -\frac{1}{2}\left[\mathrm{Tr}\left((E - \eta\eta^{\mathrm{T}})^{-1}(\boldsymbol{e}_i\boldsymbol{e}_j^{\mathrm{T}} + \boldsymbol{e}_j\boldsymbol{e}_i^{\mathrm{T}})\right)\right]_{ij} \\
&= -\frac{1}{2}\left(E - \eta\eta^{\mathrm{T}}\right)^{-1} \ .
\end{aligned}$$

Next, we take partial derivatives of Eq. (48) and (49). Since $\partial_{kl}\partial_{ij}E = 0$ and $\partial_i\partial_j(\eta\eta^{\mathrm{T}}) = \boldsymbol{e}_i\boldsymbol{e}_j^{\mathrm{T}} + \boldsymbol{e}_j\boldsymbol{e}_i^{\mathrm{T}}$, we have

$$\begin{aligned}
\partial_i\partial_j\varphi(\boldsymbol{\eta}) &= \frac{1}{2}\,\mathrm{Tr}\Big((E - \eta\eta^{\mathrm{T}})^{-1}\partial_i\partial_j(\eta\eta^{\mathrm{T}}) + \\
&\quad + (E - \eta\eta^{\mathrm{T}})^{-1}\partial_i(\eta\eta^{\mathrm{T}})(E - \eta\eta^{\mathrm{T}})^{-1}\partial_j(\eta\eta^{\mathrm{T}})\Big) \\
&= \frac{1}{2}\,\mathrm{Tr}\Big((E - \eta\eta^{\mathrm{T}})^{-1}(\boldsymbol{e}_i\boldsymbol{e}_j^{\mathrm{T}} + \boldsymbol{e}_j\boldsymbol{e}_i^{\mathrm{T}}) + \\
&\quad + (E - \eta\eta^{\mathrm{T}})^{-1}(\boldsymbol{e}_i\eta^{\mathrm{T}} + \eta\boldsymbol{e}_i^{\mathrm{T}})(E - \eta\eta^{\mathrm{T}})^{-1}(\boldsymbol{e}_j\eta^{\mathrm{T}} + \eta\boldsymbol{e}_j^{\mathrm{T}})\Big) \\
&= \boldsymbol{e}_i^{\mathrm{T}}(E - \eta\eta^{\mathrm{T}})^{-1}\boldsymbol{e}_j + (E - \eta\eta^{\mathrm{T}})^{-1}\eta\eta^{\mathrm{T}}(E - \eta\eta^{\mathrm{T}})^{-1} + \\
&\quad + (E - \eta\eta^{\mathrm{T}})^{-1}\eta^{\mathrm{T}}(E - \eta\eta^{\mathrm{T}})^{-1}\eta \ ,
\end{aligned}$$

which gives the definition of Γ in Eq. (39), (40) and (38).

For $k \neq l$ we have

$$\begin{aligned}
\partial_i\partial_{kl}\varphi(\boldsymbol{\eta}) &= -\frac{1}{2}\,\mathrm{Tr}\left((E - \eta\eta^{\mathrm{T}})^{-1}\partial_i(\eta\eta^{\mathrm{T}})(E - \eta\eta^{\mathrm{T}})^{-1}(\partial_{kl}E)\right) \\
&= -\frac{1}{2}\,\mathrm{Tr}\Big((E - \eta\eta^{\mathrm{T}})^{-1}(\boldsymbol{e}_i\eta^{\mathrm{T}} + \eta\boldsymbol{e}_i^{\mathrm{T}}) \times \\
&\quad \times (E - \eta\eta^{\mathrm{T}})^{-1}(\boldsymbol{e}_k\boldsymbol{e}_l^{\mathrm{T}} + \boldsymbol{e}_l\boldsymbol{e}_k^{\mathrm{T}})\Big) \\
&= -\boldsymbol{e}_i^{\mathrm{T}}(E - \eta\eta^{\mathrm{T}})^{-1}\boldsymbol{e}_k\boldsymbol{e}_l^{\mathrm{T}}(E - \eta\eta^{\mathrm{T}})^{-1}\eta \\
&\quad - \boldsymbol{e}_i^{\mathrm{T}}(E - \eta\eta^{\mathrm{T}})^{-1}\boldsymbol{e}_l\boldsymbol{e}_k^{\mathrm{T}}(E - \eta\eta^{\mathrm{T}})^{-1}\eta + \\
&= -\boldsymbol{e}_i^{\mathrm{T}}\Sigma^{-1}\boldsymbol{e}_k\boldsymbol{e}_l^{\mathrm{T}}\Sigma^{-1}\eta - \boldsymbol{e}_i^{\mathrm{T}}\Sigma^{-1}\boldsymbol{e}_l\boldsymbol{e}_k^{\mathrm{T}}\Sigma^{-1}\eta \ ,
\end{aligned}$$

while for $k = l$

$$\begin{aligned}
\partial_i\partial_{kk}\varphi(\boldsymbol{\eta}) &= -\boldsymbol{e}_i^{\mathrm{T}}(E - \eta\eta^{\mathrm{T}})^{-1}\boldsymbol{e}_k\boldsymbol{e}_k^{\mathrm{T}}(E - \eta\eta^{\mathrm{T}})^{-1}\eta \\
&= -\boldsymbol{e}_i^{\mathrm{T}}\Sigma^{-1}\boldsymbol{e}_k\boldsymbol{e}_k^{\mathrm{T}}\Sigma^{-1}\eta \ ,
\end{aligned}$$

which gives the definition of K_{kl} in Eq. (41), (42) and (38).

Finally, for $k \neq l \wedge m \neq n$ we have

$$\begin{aligned}
\partial_{kl}\partial_{mn}\varphi(\boldsymbol{\eta}) &= \frac{1}{2}\,\mathrm{Tr}\left((E - \eta\eta^{\mathrm{T}})^{-1}(\partial_{kl}E)(E - \eta\eta^{\mathrm{T}})^{-1}(\partial_{mn}E)\right) \\
&= \frac{1}{2}\,\mathrm{Tr}\Big((E - \eta\eta^{\mathrm{T}})^{-1}(\boldsymbol{e}_k\boldsymbol{e}_l^{\mathrm{T}} + \boldsymbol{e}_l\boldsymbol{e}_k^{\mathrm{T}}) \times \\
&\quad \times (E - \eta\eta^{\mathrm{T}})^{-1}(\boldsymbol{e}_m\boldsymbol{e}_n^{\mathrm{T}} + \boldsymbol{e}_n\boldsymbol{e}_m^{\mathrm{T}})\Big) \\
&= \boldsymbol{e}_n^{\mathrm{T}}(E - \eta\eta^{\mathrm{T}})^{-1}\boldsymbol{e}_k\boldsymbol{e}_l^{\mathrm{T}}(E - \eta\eta^{\mathrm{T}})^{-1}\boldsymbol{e}_m \\
&\quad + \boldsymbol{e}_m^{\mathrm{T}}(E - \eta\eta^{\mathrm{T}})^{-1}\boldsymbol{e}_k\boldsymbol{e}_l^{\mathrm{T}}(E - \eta\eta^{\mathrm{T}})^{-1}\boldsymbol{e}_m \\
&= \boldsymbol{e}_n^{\mathrm{T}}\Sigma^{-1}\boldsymbol{e}_k\boldsymbol{e}_l^{\mathrm{T}}\Sigma^{-1}\boldsymbol{e}_m + \boldsymbol{e}_m^{\mathrm{T}}\Sigma^{-1}\boldsymbol{e}_k\boldsymbol{e}_l^{\mathrm{T}}\Sigma^{-1}\boldsymbol{e}_m \ .
\end{aligned}$$

In the remaining cases the computations are analogous, giving the definition of κ_{klmn} in Eq. (43), (44) and (38).

Hypomixability Elimination In Evolutionary Systems

Keki M. Burjorjee
Pandora Media Inc.
Oakland, CA
kburjorjee@pandora.com

ABSTRACT

Hypomixability Elimination is an intriguing form of computation thought to underlie general-purpose, non-local, noise-tolerant adaptation in recombinative evolutionary systems. We demonstrate that hypomixability elimination in recombinative evolutionary systems can be efficient by using it to obtain optimal bounds on the time and queries required to solve a subclass ($k = 7, \eta = 1/5$) of a familiar computational learning problem: PAC-learning parities with noisy membership queries; where k is the number of relevant attributes and η is the oracle's noise rate. Specifically, we show that a simple genetic algorithm with uniform crossover (free recombination) that treats the noisy membership query oracle as a fitness function can be rigged to PAC-learn the relevant variables in $O(\log(n/\delta))$ queries and $O(n\log(n/\delta))$ time, where n is the total number of attributes and δ is the probability of error. To the best of our knowledge, this is the first time optimally efficient computation has been shown to occur in an evolutionary algorithm on a non-trivial problem.

The optimality result and indeed the implicit implementation of hypomixability elimination by a simple genetic algorithm depends crucially on recombination. This dependence yields a fresh, unified explanation for sex, adaptation, speciation, and the emergence of modularity in evolutionary systems. Compared to other explanations, Hypomixability Theory is exceedingly parsimonious. For example, it does not assume deleterious mutation, a changing fitness landscape, or the existence of building blocks.

Categories and Subject Descriptors

F.2.m [**Theory of Computation**]: Analysis of Algorithms and Problem Complexity—*Miscellaneous*; I.2.m [**Computing Methodologies**]: Artificial Intelligence—*Miscellaneous*

Keywords

Evolution, sex, adaptation, speciation, hypomixability, learning parities, juntas, genetic algorithms, recombination.

FOGA '15 January 17 - 20 2015, Aberystwyth, Wales, United Kingdom

ACM 978-1-4503-3434-1/15/01 ...$15.00.
http://dx.doi.org/10.1145/2578726.2578744

1. INTRODUCTION

In recent years, theoretical computer scientists have become increasingly perturbed by the problem posed by evolution. The subject of consternation is a system thought to have computed the encoding of every biological form to have lived, that, as luck would have it, represents information the way a Turing Machine might—digitally; in strings drawn from a quaternary alphabet—and manipulates information in ways that are well understood (e.g. meiosis) or amenable to abstraction (e.g. natural selection). Contemplating what this computational system has achieved given the resources at its disposal leaves one awestruck. Yet, theoretical computer science, for all its success in other areas, has not identified anything particularly *efficient*[1] or arresting about evolution.[2]

We have on our hands what might be called a *computational origins problem*—while our physical origins have been worked out, our *computational* origins remain a mystery. Referring to this problem, Valiant speculates that future generations will wonder why it was not regarded with a greater sense of urgency [31].

If the computational origins problem is cause for reflection within Theoretical Computer Science, it is doubly so for Evolutionary Computation theorists. The promise of Evolutionary Computation was twofold: 1) That the computational efficiencies at play in natural evolution would be identified and 2) That these efficiencies would be harnessed, via biomimicry, and used to efficiently procure solutions to human problems. One might expect these outcomes to be realized in order or simultaneously. In a curious twist, however, the field has for years made good on the second part of its promise, but has not delivered on the first. This twist

[1] For the purposes of this paper, an efficient algorithm is one whose upper bounds (on, say, time and queries) match or approach the best known lower bounds for the problem at hand. For example, comparison sorting n numbers in $O(n \log n)$ time is clearly efficient. An algorithm that solves the problem in $O(n \log^2 n)$ time is relatively efficient, whereas one that does it in $O(n^2)$ time can be considered inefficient. Given this "definition", the line between efficient and inefficient computation is of course fuzzy. For our purposes, however, fuzzy lines of this kind are more revealing than the objective one that, regardless of the problem at hand, deems an algorithm efficient if and only if its complexity is polynomially bounded.

[2] The *Computational Theories of Evolution Workshop* held at the Simons Institute, Berkeley, CA from March 17 – March 21, 2014 brought together researchers from multiple disciplines to discuss the issue. Presentations available at `http://simons.berkeley.edu/workshops/abstracts/326`

makes evolutionary algorithms rather interesting from a theoretical standpoint. Find something efficient about one of the more bioplausible ones, and a piece of the computational origins puzzle may fall into place.

A big piece of the puzzle, and the subject of an ongoing debate amongst evolutionary biologists, is the part played by sex (i.e. mixing). Sex seems downright contradictory given the prevalence of widespread epistasis in biological genomes. If interaction between genes (epistasis) is the norm, not the exception [29], what sense does it make to break up groups of alleles that *collectively* confer an advantage [2]? Compared to previous answers, the one we provide—Hypomixability Elimination—is very parsimonious, relying only on the following two assumptions:

Hypomixability: There exists a small collection of loci, not necessarily adjacent to each other, whose alleles in the population of parents confer a *disadvantage* on average when mixed.

Generative Elimination: The adaptive elimination of hypomixability in some collection of loci with respect to the parent population engenders hypomixability elsewhere.

The second assumption is necessary to ensure that the advantage conferred by sex is ongoing, i.e. is not exhausted by the one-time elimination of hypomixability. We emphasize that our theory does not rely on any of the following:

1. The existence of so called *building blocks*—single genes or tightly linked sets of genes that confer an advantage regardless of the context in which they occur [13, 10, 32].
2. A changing fitness landscape, whether due to parasitism or changes in the external environment [12, 19].
3. Deleterious mutation [25, 18].

The following section introduces the idea of hypomixability elimination. In subsequent sections we demonstrate that the implicit implementation of hypomixability elimination by sexual evolution can be computationally efficient by analyzing a simple genetic algorithm with uniform crossover and deriving optimal bounds on the time and queries required to PAC-learn a subclass ($k = 7, \eta = 1/5$) of a non-trivial computational problem: learning parities with noisy membership queries [30, 9], where k is the number of relevant attributes, and η is the probability that the membership query (MQ) oracle misclassifies a query (i.e. returns a 1 instead of a 0, or vice versa). To the best of our knowledge, this is the first time efficient, not to mention *optimally* efficient, non-trivial computation is shown to occur in a evolutionary algorithm. The result hinges on a straightforward symmetry argument and an empirically reached conclusion with a p-value less than 10^{-900}.

2. HYPOMIXABILITY THEORY

We begin with a primer on schemata and schema partitions[3] [10, 23]. For any positive integer k, let $[k]$ denote the set $\{1, \ldots, k\}$. For any positive integer n, a schema (plural, schemata) of the set of genotypes $\{0,1\}^n$ is a subset of $\{0,1\}^n$ that is traditionally represented by a *schema template*. A schema template is a string in $\{0,1,*\}^n$. As will become clear from the formal definition below, the symbol $*$ stands for 'wildcard' at the positions at which it occurs. Given a schema template $\mathcal{X} \in \{0,1,*\}^n$, let $[\![\mathcal{X}]\!]$ denote the schema represented by $\mathcal{X}$. Then,

$$[\![\mathcal{X}]\!] = \{x \in \{0,1\}^n \mid \forall i \in [n], \mathcal{X}_i \neq x_i \Rightarrow \mathcal{X}_i = *\}$$

Let $\mathcal{I} \subseteq \{1, \ldots, n\}$ be some set of integers, and let $\langle \mathcal{I} \rangle_n$ denote the set of strings $\{\mathcal{X} \in \{0,1,*\}^n \mid \mathcal{X}_i \neq * \Leftrightarrow i \in \mathcal{I}\}$ Then $\mathcal{I}$ represents a partition of $\{0,1\}^n$ into a set of $2^{|\mathcal{I}|}$ schemata, denoted $[\![\mathcal{I}]\!]_n$, whose templates are given by $\langle \mathcal{I} \rangle_n$. The elements of $\mathcal{I}$ are said to be the *defining loci* of the schema partition. We shorten the mouthful *schema partition* to *spartition.*

The *order* of some spartition $[\![\mathcal{I}]\!]_n$ is simply cardinality of $\mathcal{I}$. It is easily seen that spartitions of lower order are coarser than spartitions of higher order; more specifically, that a spartition of order k is comprised of 2^k schemata.

00*0*	00*1*	01*0*	01*1*	10*0*	10*1*	11*0*	11*1*
00000	00010	01000	01010	01000	10010	11000	11010
00001	00011	01001	01011	01001	10011	11001	11011
00100	00110	01100	01110	01100	10110	11100	11110
00101	00111	01101	01111	01101	10111	11101	11111

Figure 1: A tabular depiction of the spartition $[\![\{1,2,4\}]\!]_5$ of order three. The table headings give the templates of the schemata comprising the partition. The elements of each schema in the partition appear in the column below its template.

EXAMPLE 1. *The index set $\{1,2,4\}$ induces an order three spartition of $\{0,1\}^5$ into eight schemata as shown in Figure 1.*

For any distribution $\mathcal{D}$ over $\{0,1\}^n$ and any spartition $[\![\mathcal{I}]\!]_n$, the *projection of $\mathcal{D}$ onto $\langle \mathcal{I} \rangle_n$*, denoted $\Xi_{\mathcal{I}}[\mathcal{D}]$, is a distribution over $\langle \mathcal{I} \rangle_n$ defined as follows: For any $\mathcal{X} \in \langle \mathcal{I} \rangle_n$,

$$\Xi_{\mathcal{I}}[\mathcal{D}](\mathcal{X}) = \sum_{x \in [\![\mathcal{X}]\!]} \mathcal{D}(x)$$

For any $i \in [n]$, let $\mathcal{D}_i$ denote the ith univariate marginal distribution (over {0,1}) of $\mathcal{D}$. Unless otherwise specified, the range of a *fitness* function is $\mathbb{R}_0^+$.

2.1 Mixability

We assume that mixing occurs via uniform crossover (i.e. free recombination), in other words, that loci are unlinked. The following definition introduces the concept of the mixed fitness of a schema, i.e. the expected fitness of a schema with respect to the product of marginals of some distribution over the undefined loci.

DEFINITION 2 (MIXED FITNESS OF A SCHEMA). *Let $\mathcal{D}$ and ϕ be some distribution and fitness function over $\{0,1\}^n$ respectively. For any $\mathcal{I} \subseteq [n]$, let $\mathcal{X} \in \langle \mathcal{I} \rangle_n$ be a random variable drawn from the distribution $\Xi_{\mathcal{I}}[\mathcal{D}]$, and let $X \in [\![\mathcal{X}]\!]$ be a random variable defined as follows: for any $i \in [n]$, if $i \in \mathcal{I}$, then $X_i = \mathcal{X}_i$, otherwise $X_i \sim \mathcal{D}_i$. Then the mixed fitness of $\mathcal{X}$ with respect to $\mathcal{D}$ and ϕ, denoted $\Phi(\mathcal{X}; \mathcal{D})$, is defined as follows:*

$$\Phi(\mathcal{X}; \mathcal{D}) = \mathbf{E}[\phi(X)]$$

[3]We rely only on the mathematical tools, not the conclusions, of Schema Theory [13].

The following example shows how the operator Φ can be used to express the expected fitness of a genotype drawn from the product of marginals of some distribution $\mathcal{D}$.

EXAMPLE 3. *For any fitness function ϕ and distribution $\mathcal{D}$ over $\{0,1\}^n$, the expected fitness of a genotype drawn from the product of marginals distribution of $\mathcal{D}$ is given by $\Phi(*^n;\mathcal{D})$.*

DEFINITION 4 (MIXABILITY OF A SPARTITION). *For any fitness function ϕ and distribution $\mathcal{D}$ over $\{0,1\}^n$, and any $\mathcal{I} \subseteq [n]$, let $\mathfrak{X} \in \langle \mathcal{I} \rangle_n$ be a random variable drawn from the distribution $\Xi_{\mathcal{I}}[\mathcal{D}]$. The mixability of $\mathcal{I}$ with respect to $\mathcal{D}$ and ϕ, denoted $M(\mathcal{I};\mathcal{D})$, is defined as follows:*

$$M(\mathcal{I};\mathcal{D}) = \frac{\Phi(*^n;\mathcal{D})}{\mathbf{E}[\Phi(\mathfrak{X};\mathcal{D})]}$$

As defined above, mixability is a property of some set of loci. As sets of loci are one-to-one with spartitions, the mixability of a spartition $[\![\mathcal{I}]\!]_n$ is simply defined to be the mixability of $\mathcal{I}$. Observe that knowledge of the full joint distribution $\mathcal{D}$ is not required to calculate the mixability of $[\![\mathcal{I}]\!]_n$; knowledge of $\Xi_{\mathcal{I}}[\mathcal{D}]$, and the univariate marginal distributions $\mathcal{D}_i$ for all $i \in [n] \backslash \mathcal{I}$ suffices. Mixability less than, greater than, and equal to 1 is called *hypomixability*, *hypermixability*, and *unit mixability* respectively.[4]

In evolutionary systems, it is *parents*, not individuals in the the general population, that get mixed. Thus, when we speak of the mixability of a spartition in some generation it is always with respect to the *parent distribution*. To be clear, the parent distribution in some generation is simply the distribution from which parents are sampled. Consider the following example:

EXAMPLE 5. *For any fitness function ϕ and distribution $\mathcal{D}$ over $\{0,1\}^n$ such that $\mathcal{D}$ represents a general population with at least one individual with positive fitness. If selection is fitness proportional, then the parent distribution of $\mathcal{D}$, denoted $\mathcal{S}_\phi[\mathcal{D}]$, is as defined follows: For any $x \in \{0,1\}^n$,*

$$\mathcal{S}_\phi[\mathcal{D}](x) = \frac{\phi(x)\mathcal{D}(x)}{\sum\limits_{y \in \{0,1\}^n} \phi(y)\mathcal{D}(y)}$$

As the following example shows, mixability with respect to the general population can be very different from mixability with respect to the parent population.

EXAMPLE 6. *Let $\mathcal{I} = \{1,2\}$ and let $\phi : \{0,1\}^3 \to \{0,1\}$ be a fitness function that returns the exclusive-or (XOR) of the first two of its inputs. Let $\mathcal{D}$ be the uniform distribution over $\{0,1\}^3$. Then $M(\mathcal{I};\mathcal{D}) = 1$, whereas $M(\mathcal{I};\mathcal{S}_\phi[\mathcal{D}]) = 1/2$.*

[4]Comparing the definitions above to the ones provided by Livnat et al. [20], who also use the term *mixability*, one can spot similarities and differences. Beginning with the similarities, $\Phi(*^n;\mathcal{D})$ as defined here is similar (if not identical) to the mixability measure M_1 defined by Livnat et al. [20]. On the other hand, the mixability measures $M_2, \ldots M_n$ defined by Livnat et al. have no equivalent in our formulation. These measures are defined, not with respect to some *particular* set of loci $\mathcal{I}$ as in our formulation, but with respect to *all* pairs of loci, *all* triples, *all* sets of four loci, and so on. By defining mixability with respect to a *particular* set of loci, our formulation gains crucial expressive power. Another difference is that we focus on mixability with respect to parent distributions, not general populations.

For any boolean expression b, let $[b]$ denote 1 if b is true and 0 otherwise. For any distribution $\mathfrak{D}$ over a set of schema templates $\langle \mathcal{I} \rangle_n$ and any $i \in [n]$, let $\mathfrak{D}_i$ denote the ith univariate marginal distribution (over $\{0,1,*\}$) of $\mathfrak{D}$. Thus, for any $x \in \{0,1,*\}$ and any $i \notin \mathcal{I}$, $\mathfrak{D}_i(x) = [x = *]$.

For any distribution D over $\{0,1\}^n$ or $\{0,1,*\}^n$, let $\Pi[D]$ denote the product of marginals distribution of D. For example, if $\mathfrak{D}$ is a distribution over $\{0,1,*\}^n$, then for any x in $\{0,1,*\}$,

$$\Pi[\mathfrak{D}](x) = \prod_{i \in [n]} \mathfrak{D}_i(x_i)$$

DEFINITION 7 (SPECIAL PRODUCT OF MARGINALS). *Let $\mathcal{D}$ be a distribution over $\{0,1\}^n$, let $\mathcal{I} \subseteq [n]$ be some index set, and let $\mathfrak{D}$ be some distribution over $\langle \mathcal{I} \rangle_n$. The special product of marginals $\Pi[\mathcal{I},\mathfrak{D};\mathcal{D}]$ is a distribution over $\{0,1\}^n$ defined as follows: for any $x \in \{0,1\}^n$,*

$$\Pi[\mathcal{I},\mathfrak{D};\mathcal{D}](x) = \sum_{\mathfrak{X} \in \langle \mathcal{I} \rangle_n} [x \in \mathfrak{X}]\, \mathfrak{D}(\mathfrak{X}) \prod_{i \in [n] \backslash \mathcal{I}} \mathcal{D}_i(x_i)$$

The following definition provides a sufficient, but non-necessary way to determine if a set of loci has unit mixability with respect to some distribution and fitness function.

DEFINITION 8 (MIXED EFFECT). *Let $\phi : \{0,1\}^n \to \mathbb{R}_0^+$ be some fitness function, let $\mathcal{D}$ be some distribution over $\{0,1\}^n$. For any spartition $\mathcal{I} \subseteq [n]$, the mixed effect of $[\![\mathcal{I}]\!]_n$ with respect to $\mathcal{D}$ and ϕ, denoted $\xi(\mathcal{I};\mathcal{D})$, is defined as follows:*

$$\xi(\mathcal{I};\mathcal{D}) = \frac{1}{2^k} \sum_{\mathfrak{X} \in \langle \mathcal{I} \rangle_n} \left(\Phi(\mathfrak{X};\mathcal{D}) - \frac{1}{2^k} \sum_{\mathfrak{Y} \in \langle \mathcal{I} \rangle_n} \Phi(\mathfrak{Y};\mathcal{D}) \right)^2$$

Non-unit mixability is of particular interest to us. The following theorem, explains why. Briefly, when some set of loci $\mathcal{I}$ has non-unit mixability, it is a signal that there exists a way to change the multivariate marginal distribution of the parent distribution over $\mathcal{I}$ in a way that eliminates the non-unit mixability and raises the expected fitness of the (general) population in the next generation.

THEOREM 9 (NON-UNIT MIXABILITY $\Rightarrow$ OPPORTUNITY). *For any distribution $\mathcal{D}$ and fitness function ϕ over $\{0,1\}^n$, if $[\![\mathcal{I}]\!]_n$ is a spartition with non-unit mixability, then there exists a distribution $\mathfrak{D}^*$ over $\langle \mathcal{I} \rangle_n$ such that $[\![\mathcal{I}]\!]_n$ has unit mixability with respect to $\Pi[\mathcal{I};\mathfrak{D}^*;\mathcal{D}]$, and for any independent random variables $X \sim \Pi[\mathcal{D}]$, and $Y \sim \Pi[\,\Pi[\mathcal{I},\mathfrak{D}^*;\mathcal{D}]\,]$, we have that $\mathbf{E}[\phi(X)] < \mathbf{E}[\phi(Y)]$.*

PROOF SKETCH. Observe that $\xi(\mathcal{I};\mathcal{D}) = 0 \Rightarrow M(\mathcal{I};\mathcal{D}) = 1$. The contrapositive gives us $M(\mathcal{I};\mathcal{D}) \neq 1 \Rightarrow \xi(\mathcal{I};\mathcal{D}) \neq 0$. Using this result and the premise of non-unit mixability, we get that there exists $\mathfrak{X}^* = \operatorname{argmax}_{\mathfrak{X} \in \langle \mathcal{I} \rangle_n} \Phi(\mathfrak{X};\mathcal{D})$ such that:

$$\Phi(\mathfrak{X}^*;\mathcal{D}) > \sum_{\mathfrak{X} \in \langle \mathcal{I} \rangle_n} \Phi(\mathfrak{X};\mathcal{D})\,.\,\Pi[\Xi_{\mathcal{I}}[\mathcal{D}]](\mathfrak{X}) \qquad (1)$$

Let $\mathfrak{D}^*$ be defined as follows: for any $\mathfrak{X} \in \langle \mathcal{I} \rangle_n$, $\mathfrak{D}^*(\mathfrak{X}) = [\mathfrak{X} = \mathfrak{X}^*]$. Observe that $[\![\mathcal{I}]\!]_n$ must have unit mixability with respect to $\Pi[\mathcal{I},\mathfrak{D}^*;\mathcal{D}]$, because the probability mass of $\mathfrak{D}^*$ is concentrated on just one schema template in $\langle \mathcal{I} \rangle_n$.

The right hand side of (1) is $\mathbf{E}[\phi(X)]$. The observation that $\Pi[\Pi[\mathcal{I},\mathfrak{D}^*;\mathcal{D}]] = \Pi[\mathcal{I},\Pi[\mathfrak{D}^*];\mathcal{D}] = \Pi[\mathcal{I},\mathfrak{D}^*;\mathcal{D}]$ gives us that the left hand side of (1) is $\mathbf{E}[\phi(Y)]$ □

Theorem 9 shows that if the multivariate marginal distribution over the variables indexed by $\mathcal{I}$ is all one has control over, it is always possible to eliminate non-unit mixability in a way that is *adaptive*. Choosing $\mathfrak{D}^*$ such that the entropy $H(\mathfrak{D}^*) = 0$ as we did in the proof of Theorem 9 minimizes $H(\Pi[\mathcal{I},\Pi[\mathfrak{D}^*];\mathcal{D}]) = H(\mathfrak{D}^*) + \sum_{i\notin\mathcal{I}} H(\mathcal{D}_i)$, the entropy of the special product of marginals distribution. Is it possible to adaptively eliminate non-unit mixability with less of a toll on the entropy of the special product of marginals distribution? The answer depends on ϕ. For example, if ϕ is the boolean function XOR over only the loci in $\mathcal{I}$ (an XOR $|\mathcal{I}|$-junta), the answer is no. If ϕ is the boolean function OR over only the loci in $\mathcal{I}$ (an OR $|\mathcal{I}|$-junta), the answer is yes. One could, for example, set the values of *all but one* loci in $\mathcal{I}$ to 1. Of course, one could do even better and simply *maximize* the entropy. Indeed, given only the constraint that $\mathfrak{D}^*$ eliminates unit mixability, the principle of maximum entropy obliges one to pick $\mathfrak{D}^*$ such that $H(\mathfrak{D}^*)$ is maximized, i.e. $\text{argmax}_{\mathfrak{D}^*} \sum_{i\in\mathcal{I}} H(\mathfrak{D}^*_i)$. We shall have more to say about adaptive, entropy maximizing, non-unit mixability elimination in Section 2.3.

2.2 Sampling Mixability

First we turn to the practical feasibility of identifying a set of loci with non-unit mixability. Considering the size of typical search spaces, the precise mixability of a spartition $[\![\mathcal{I}]\!]_n$ with respect to a parent distribution $\mathcal{D}$ and fitness function ϕ is, of course, unknowable. However, given some number of parents sampled from the parent distribution, the mixability can be estimated. For any $p \in [0,1]$, let $B(p)$ denote the Bernoulli distribution with parameter p. A simple estimator for the mixability of a set of loci is given below.

EXAMPLE 10 (SIMPLE SAMPLING MIXABILITY). *Let $X^1,\ldots,X^m \in \{0,1\}^n$ be the set of parents in some generation t. For any $\mathcal{I} \in [n]$, let $Y^1,\ldots,Y^m \in \{0,1\}^n$ and $Z^1,\ldots,Z^m \in \{0,1\}^n$ be conditionally independent random variables defined as follows: for all $i \in [n]$, and all $j \in [m]$, $Z^j_i = X^m_i$ if $i \in \mathcal{I}$, otherwise $Z^j_i \sim B(\frac{1}{m}\sum_{k\in[m]} X^k_i)$, and for all $i \in [n]$ and all $j \in [m]$, $Y^j_i \sim B(\frac{1}{m}\sum_{k\in[r]} X^k_i)$, then the canonical sampling mixability of $\mathcal{I}$ in generation t with respect to some fitness function ϕ, denoted $\widehat{M}_s(\mathcal{I})$, is an estimator defined as follows:*

$$\widehat{M}_s(\mathcal{I}) = \frac{\widehat{a}}{\widehat{b}(\mathcal{I})}$$

where $\widehat{a} = \sum_{j\in[r]} \phi(Y^j)$ is an estimator for the numerator in Definition 4, and $\widehat{b}(\mathcal{I}) = \sum_{j\in[r]} \phi(Z^j)$ is an estimator for the denominator.

2.2.1 Spartition Coarseness & Statistical Significance

Like all estimators, the simple sampling mixability estimator $\widehat{M}_s(\mathcal{I})$ is just a random variable, and, as such, has an expected value $\mathbf{E}[\widehat{M}_s(\mathcal{I})]$ and a variance $\mathbf{Var}[\widehat{M}_s(\mathcal{I})]$. Let us informally examine how $\mathbf{Var}[\widehat{M}(\mathcal{I})]$ changes as we remove elements from $\mathcal{I}$, i.e. as we coarsen the spartition $[\![\mathcal{I}]\!]_n$. As elements are removed, the variance of $\widehat{a}$ stays the same, whereas it is reasonable to expect that the variance of $\widehat{b}(\mathcal{I})$ decreases because one is putting "more wood behind fewer arrows". Thus, it is reasonable to conjecture that for any $\mathcal{I}'$ such that $\mathcal{I}' \subset \mathcal{I}$ we have that $\mathbf{Var}[\widehat{M}_s(\mathcal{I}')] \leq \mathbf{Var}[\widehat{M}_s(\mathcal{I})]$. Indeed, it is reasonable to expect any "well behaved" estimator of $\widehat{M}$ to have this property. Coarsening schema partitions, in other words, shortens confidence intervals around mixability estimates.

2.3 The Unit Mixability Principle

The *Principle of Unit Mixability* states that under free recombination (i.e. uniform crossover), evolution adaptively eliminates statistically significant non-unit mixability whenever it occurs in some coarse spartition $[\![\mathcal{I}]\!]_n$; furthermore, that the multivariate marginal over $\mathcal{I}$ of the parent population transitions, over one or more generations, to a distribution with maximal entropy given the unit-mixability constraint.

We submit that big, *positive* deviations from unit mixability with respect to parent distributions are rare in the real world. One needs to begin with a rather pathological distribution $\mathcal{D}$ to obtain a parent distribution ($\mathcal{S}_\phi[\mathcal{D}]$ in the event that selection is fitness proportional) such that there exists some set of loci with sizable hypermixability. Thus, for all practical purposes, the Principle of Unit Mixability predicts the adaptive, maximum entropy elimination of statistically significant *hypo*mixability if it occurs in a coarse spartition.

2.4 Parallelism in Evolutionary Systems

Observe that a naive (i.e. non-evolutionary) enforcement of the unit mixability principle by some algorithm that scans for coarse schema partitions with non-unit mixability scales poorly with n. There are $\binom{n}{k}$ spartitions of order k. When $n = 10^6$, say, the number of spartitions of order $k = 1\ldots 7$ are on the order of $10^6, 10^{11}, 10^{17}, 10^{22}, 10^{27}, 10^{33}$, and 10^{38} respectively. Is evolution capable of performing hypomixability elimination as described above within timeframes that are not equally astronomical?

Support for an affirmative answer appears in a previous paper [7], where it is shown that for any spartition $[\![\mathcal{I}]\!]_n$, infinite population evolution over $\{0,1\}^n$ using fitness proportional selection, homologous recombination, and standard bit mutation implicitly induces infinite population evolution over the set of schemata in $[\![\mathcal{I}]\!]_n$.

More formally, let the operators $\mathcal{S}$ and Ξ be as defined in the previous section. For any transmission function T and distribution $\mathcal{D}$ over $\{0,1\}^n$, let $\mathcal{V}_T[\mathcal{D}]$ be a distribution over $\{0,1\}^n$ defined as follows: For any $z \in \{0,1\}$,

$$\mathcal{V}_T[\mathcal{D}](z) = \sum_{x\in\{0,1\}^n} \sum_{y\in\{0,1\}^n} T(z\,|\,x,y)\mathcal{D}(x)\mathcal{D}(y)$$

Then, for any spartition $[\![\mathcal{I}]\!]_n$, distribution $\mathcal{P}$ over $\{0,1\}^n$, fitness function $\phi : \{0,1\}^n \to \mathbb{R}^+$, and transmission function T over $\{0,1\}^n$ that models homologous recombination followed by canonical bit mutation, there exist probability distributions $\mathcal{Q}$ and $\mathcal{R}$ over $\{0,1\}^n$, probability distributions $\mathcal{P}', \mathcal{Q}', \mathcal{R}'$ over $\langle\mathcal{I}\rangle_n$, fitness function $\phi' : [\![\mathcal{I}]\!]_n \to \mathbb{R}^+$, and transmission function T' over $[\![\mathcal{I}]\!]_n$ such that the following diagram commutes[5]:

[5]This diagram was mistakenly called a *coarse-graining* by Burjorjee and Pollack [7]. The mistake was corrected in a later paper [4], where the idea of coarse-graining was explained in detail. (It is important to point out this error to avoid confusion when we refer to coarse-graining in Section

$$\begin{array}{ccccc} \mathcal{P} & \xrightarrow{\mathcal{S}_\phi} & \mathcal{Q} & \xrightarrow{\mathcal{V}_T} & \mathcal{R} \\ \downarrow{\scriptstyle \Xi_\mathcal{I}} & & \downarrow{\scriptstyle \Xi_\mathcal{I}} & & \downarrow{\scriptstyle \Xi_\mathcal{I}} \\ \mathcal{P}' & \xrightarrow[\mathcal{S}_{\phi'}]{} & \mathcal{Q}' & \xrightarrow[\mathcal{V}_{T'}]{} & \mathcal{R}' \end{array}$$

The proof of the above is constructive. That is, ϕ' and T' are precisely specified. Crucially, there is no restriction on the index set $\mathcal{I}$. In other words, the above holds true *simultaneously* for *all* spartitions of $\{0,1\}^n$.

2.5 A Need for Science, Practiced With Rigor

Formal proof for the occurrence of hypomixability elimination beyond that referenced in the previous section—specifically formal proof pertaining to evolutionary algorithms with finite populations—is difficult to provide, not least because the analysis of evolutionary algorithms with finite populations is notoriously unwieldy. We have argued previously that resorting to the scientific method [28] is a necessary and appropriate response to this hurdle [6].

2.5.1 *Parsimony and Unification*

For a science to be viable, it must be parsimonious (i.e. based on weak assumptions). Hypomixability theory assumes the existence of one or more coarse schema partitions that are statistically significantly hypomixable with respect to the parent population. It assumes, further, that the adaptive elimination of such hypomixability engenders statistically significant hypomixability in other coarse schema partitions (the need for this assumption is explained in Section 8). These assumptions are exceedingly weak, especially when compared to the strong assumptions that have previously been made in Evolutionary Computation and Evolutionary Biology [5, Chapter 2]. Curiously, hypomixability theory *does more with less*. It is not necessary, for example, to have a theory of sex [19] that is separate from a theory of adaptation, which in turn is separate from a theory of speciation, each theory with its attendant (possibly conflicting) assumptions. All three phenomena as well as the emergence of modularity [20, 22] can be explained by one, unified, parsimonious theory.

2.5.2 *Testable Predictions*

A hallmark of rigorous science is the ongoing making and testing of predictions. Predictions found to be true lend credence to the hypotheses that entail them. The more unexpected a prediction, the greater the credence owed the hypothesis if the prediction is borne out [28, 27].

The work that follows validates a prediction entailed by hypomixability theory. As we explain in the next section, hypomixability theory predicts that a genetic algorithm with uniform crossover (UGA) can be used to construct an algorithm that efficiently solves the problem of learning parities with a noisy MQ oracle for small but non-trivial values of k, the number of relevant attributes, and $\eta \in (0, 1/2)$, the probability that the oracle makes a classification error (returns a 1 instead of a 0, or vice versa) on a given query. Such a result is unexpected because of the absence of modules/building blocks under a uniform distribution over the search space. To the best of our knowledge, the only theory in a position to predict a result similar to the one we obtain is the theory of sex proposed by Livnat et al. [20]. We have more to say about this theory in Section 9.

6 of this paper.) As ϕ' in the commutative diagram is not invariant to $\mathcal{P}$, no coarse-graining of evolutionary dynamics was previously shown. What was actually shown is arguably more interesting—implicit parallel computation.

3. PAC-LEARNING PARITIES WITH MQs

The problem of learning parities is a refinement of the learning juntas problem [24], so we approach the former problem by way of the latter. For any boolean function f over n variables, a variable i is said to be *relevant* if there exist binary strings $x, y \in \{0,1\}^n$ that differ only in their *ith* coordinate such that $f(x) \neq f(y)$. Variables that are not relevant are said to be *irrelevant*. For any non-negative integer n and any integer $k \leq n$, a k-junta is a function $f : \{0,1\}^n \to \{0,1\}$ such that for any integer $j \leq k$ only j of the n inputs to f are relevant. These j relevant variables are said to be the juntas of f. The function f is completely specified by its juntas (characterizable by the set $J \subseteq [n]$ of junta indices) and by a *hidden boolean function* h over the j juntas. The output of f is just the output of h on the values of the j relevant variables (the values of the irrelevant variables are ignored). The problem of identifying the relevant variables of any k-junta f and the truth table of its hidden boolean function is called the *learning k-juntas problem.*

The *learning k-parities problem* is a refinement of the learning k-juntas problem where it is additionally specified that $j = k$, and the hidden function h is the parity (i.e. xor) function over k inputs. In this case, the function f is completely specified by its juntas.

An algorithm $\mathcal{A}$ is said to solve the learning k-parities problem if for any k-parity function $f : \{0,1\}^n \to \{0,1\}$ whose juntas are given by the set $J \subseteq [n]$ and any $\delta \in (0, 1/2)$, $\mathcal{A}(n, k, \delta)$ outputs a set $S \subseteq [n]$ such that $\mathbf{Pr}(S \neq J) \leq \delta$.

A noisy MQ oracle ϕ behaves as follows. For any string $x \in \{0,1\}^n$, ϕ returns $\neg f(x)$ with probability $\eta \in (0, 1/2)$ and $f(x)$ with probability $1 - \eta$. The parameter η is called the noise rate. Bounds derived for the time and query complexity of $\mathcal{A}^\phi$ with respect to n and δ speak to the efficiency with which $\mathcal{A}^\phi$ solves the problem. The algorithmic learning described here is Probably Approximately Correct learning [17] with the inaccuracy tolerance ϵ set to zero: Probably Correct (PC) learning, if you will.

3.1 The Noise Model

Blum and Langley [3] give a simple binary search based method that learns a single relevant variable of any k-junta in $O(n \log n)$ time and $O(\log n)$ queries with noise free membership queries. As explained in Section 3.1 of a paper by Mossel and O'Donnell [24], once a single relevant variable is found, the method can be recursively repeated at most $k2^k$ times to find the remaining relevant variables. In an MQ setting, the introduction of noise does not complicate the situation much if the corruption of a given answer is independent of the corruption of previous answers. In this case, noise can be eliminated to an arbitrary level simply by sampling the MQ oracle $p(\frac{1}{1-2\eta})$ times, where $p(\cdot)$ is some polynomial, and taking the majority value.

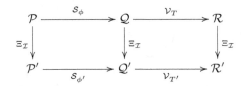

An appropriate departure from independent noise is the random *persistent* classification noise model due to Goldman, Kearns, and Schapire [11] wherein on any query x, the oracle operates as follows: If the oracle has been queried on x before, it returns its previous answer to x; otherwise, it returns the correct answer with probability $1 - \eta$. Stating matters colorfully, the noise "freezes" on genesis. We refer to it, therefore, as *freezing noise*. An oracle with freezing noise appears deterministic from the outside, so clearly the corruption caused by this kind of noise cannot be undone by querying the oracle multiple times and taking the majority value.

While the freezing noise model is appropriate for a membership query oracle, this form of noise tends to make analysis difficult. Fortunately, if it is extremely unlikely that an algorithm $\mathcal{A}$ will query the oracle twice or more with the same value, then $\mathcal{A}$ can be treated as if it is making calls to an MQ oracle with random *independent* classification noise [9]. The analysis in the following sections takes advantage of this loophole. As n gets large it becomes extremely unlikely that the membership query oracle will be queried twice or more on the same input. Therefore, the analysis treats the noise as if it were independent.

3.2 Epistasis, NK Landscapes, k-juntas with Freezing Noise, and Parsimony

Typical run-time analyses of evolutionary algorithms assume a separable fitness function (one-max, weighted linear pseudo-boolean functions, the sphere function, etc.). The assumption of separability (i.e. non-epistasis) is a strong one, and as such, limits the applicability of the results of such analyses. In contrast, k-juntas with freezing noise come with much weaker assumptions, we claim. So the results obtained are more broadly applicable.

Our claim proceeds from the observation that rampant unstructured epistasis is well modeled by freezing noise. For a case in point, observe that a 0-junta (a constant function) with freezing noise can be modeled by an NK landscape [16, 1] with $K = N - 1$. For $k > 0$, k-juntas with freezing noise cannot be modeled within Kauffman's NK framework, but can be modeled perfectly well within Altenberg's Generalized NK Maps framework [1].

A generalized NK map F is the mean of m fitness components $F_1, \ldots, F_m$ defined as follows:

$$F(x) = \frac{1}{f} \sum_{i=1}^{f} F_i(x_{j_1(i)}, x_{j_2(i)} \ldots, x_{j_{p_i}})$$

where p_i gives the number of input variables of F_i and $\{j_1(i), \ldots, j_{p_i}\} \subset [N]$ specifies the location of these variables in x.

Situating k-juntas with freezing noise within Altenberg's framework allows one to appreciate the nature of the departure from rampant unstructured epistasis when $k > 0$.

The observation that highly epistatic fitness functions with a small amount of structure are more probable than separable or near-separable (i.e low-epistasis) fitness functions completes our argument for the claim. The former class of fitness functions are more *parsimonious* i.e. less presumptive, than the latter.

3.3 Information Theoretic Lower Bound

For any positive integer k, a simple information theoretic argument shows that it is not possible to PAC-learn the relevant variables of k-juntas in less than $O(n \log n)$ time or less than $O(\log n)$ queries; not possible, in other words, to PAC-learn the relevant variables in $o(n \log n)$ time or $o(\log n)$ queries. The argument relies on Shannon's source coding theorem, part of which states that if N i.i.d. random variables each with entropy $H(X)$ are transmitted in less than $NH(X)$ bits, it is virtually certain that information will be lost [21].

Let us consider the minimum time and queries required to learn just one relevant variable. Observe that the oracle can transmit at most one bit per query and that the time required by $\mathcal{A}$ to generate each query is $\Omega(n)$. Finally recall that the entropy of a random variable X that can take an arbitrary value in $[n]$ is $\Omega(\log n)$. Thus, by Shannon's source coding theorem, the transmission of the index of a single relevant variable with an arbitrarily small possibility of error takes $\Omega(\log n)$ queries and $\Omega(n \log n)$ time.

3.4 An Initial Experiment

We ran the SGA in Algorithm 1 with uniform crossover ($asex = false$), population size $m = 1500$, bitstring length $n = 1000$, and per bit mutation rate $p_{mut} = 0.004$ for $\tau = 200$ generations using ϕ_f as the fitness function where f is a 7-parity function over $\{0,1\}^{1000}$ with juntas in $\mathcal{I} = \{45, 224, 295, 385, 696, 799, 838\}$, and ϕ is an MQ oracle with noise rate $\eta = 1/5$. The panel at the top of Figure 2 shows the frequency of the bit 1 at each locus in the initial generation and every fortieth subsequent generation. The chart at the bottom shows the simple sample mixability (see Example 10) of the juntas with respect to the parent population in each generation. As the panel on top shows, by generation 200 all the relevant loci and none of the irrelevant loci have gone to fixation. Indeed, one can simply "read off" the juntas of f by returning the index of loci in generation 200 where the frequency of the bit 1 is less than 0.05 or greater than 0.95. Note that an odd number of loci in $\mathcal{I}$ are fixed at 1. This is because the parity function chosen rewards odd parity.

Our goal, going forward, is to obtain bounds on the time and queries required to recover the juntas of *any* 7-parity function with probability of error less than δ for arbitrarily large n and arbitrarily small δ.

4. MAIN RESULT AND APPROACH

We present an evolutionary computation based algorithm that probably correctly learns 7-parities in $O(\log(n/\delta))$ queries and $O(n \log(n/\delta))$ time given access to a MQ oracle with a noise rate of 1/5. Our argument is comprised of two parts. In the first, we define a form of learning for the learning parities problem called Piecewise Probably Correct (PPC) learning and show that an algorithm that PPC-learns k-parities in $O(n)$ time and $O(1)$ queries can be used in the construction of an algorithm that PC-learns k-parities in $O(n \log(n/\delta))$ time and $O(\log(n/\delta))$ queries. In the second part we rely on a symmetry argument and a hypothesis testing based rejection of two null hypotheses at the 10^{-900} level of significance to conclude that for $\eta = 1/5$, a UGA can PPC learn 7-parities in $O(n)$ time and $O(1)$ queries.

5. PPC TO PC LEARNING

An algorithm $\mathcal{A}$ with access to some oracle ϕ is said to piecewise probably correctly (PPC) learn k-parities if for any k-parity f, whose juntas are given by $J \subseteq [n]$, $\mathcal{A}(n, k)$ outputs a set S such that for any $x \in [n]$, $\mathbf{Pr}(\neg(x \in S \Leftrightarrow$

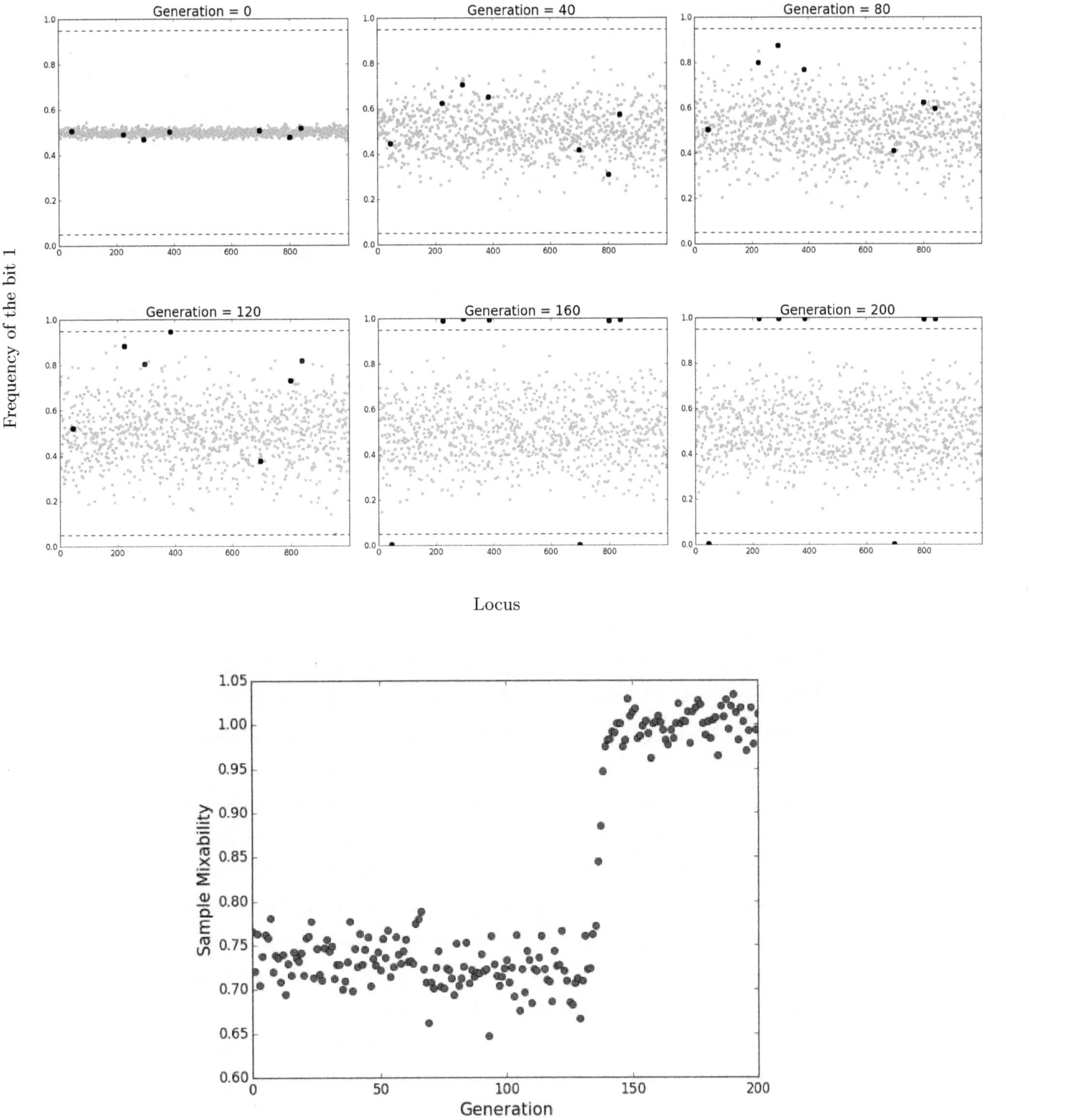

Figure 2: ***Top Panel:*** **Frequencies of the bit 1 at each locus in generations 0, 40, 80, 120, 160, and 200 when Algorithm 1 with uniform crossover ($asex = false$), $m = 1500$, $n = 1000$, $p_{mut} = 0.004$ was run with fitness function ϕ_f, where f is a 7-parity function over $\{0, 1\}$, f with juntas $\{45, 224, 295, 385, 696, 799, 838\}$, and ϕ is a membership query oracle with noise rate $\eta = 1/5$. The black dots give the location of the juntas of f. The horizontal dotted lines mark the frequencies 0.05 and 0.95.** ***Bottom Figure:*** **Simple sample mixability (see Example 10) of the juntas with respect to the parent population in each generation.**

Algorithm 1: Pseudocode for a simple genetic algorithm with uniform crossover. The population is stored in an m by n array of bits, with each row representing a single genotype. SHUFFLE($\cdot$) randomly shuffles the contents of an array in-place, RAND() returns a number drawn uniformly at random from the interval [0,1], ONES(a, b) returns an a by b array of ones, and RAND(a, b) $< c$ resolves to an a by b array of bits each of which is 1 with probability c.

```
Input: m: population size
Input: n: length of bitstrings
Input: τ: number of generations
Input: p_mut: per bit mutation probability
Input: asex: (flag) perform asexual evolution
pop ← RAND(m,n) < 0.5
for t ← 1 to τ do
    fitnessVals ← EVALUATE-FITNESS(pop)
    totalFitness ← 0
    for i ←1 to m do
        totalFitness ← totalFitness + fitnessVals[i]
    end
    cumFitnessVals[1] ← fitnessVals[1]
    for i ←2 to m do
        cumFitnessVals[i] ← cumFitnessVals[i − 1] +
                fitnessVals[i]
    end
    for i ← 1 to 2m do
        k ← RAND() * totalFitness
        ctr ← 1
        while k > cumFitnessVals[ctr] do
            ctr ← ctr + 1
        end
        parentIndices[i] ← ctr
    end
    SHUFFLE(parentIndices)
    if asex then
        crossOverMasks ← ONES(m, n)
    else
        crossOverMasks ← RAND(m, n) < 0.5
    end
    for i ← 1 to m do
        for j ← 1 to n do
            if crossMasks[i,j]= 1 then
                newPop[i, j]← pop[parentIndices[i],j]
            else
                newPop[i, j]← pop[parentIndices[i + m],j]
            end
        end
    end
    mutationMasks ← RAND(m, n) < p_mut
    for i ← 1 to m do
        for j ← 1 to n do
            newPop[i,j]← XOR(newPop[i, j], mutMasks[i, j])
        end
    end
    pop←newPop
end
```

$x \in J)) \leq 1/2$. That is, the probability that $\mathcal{A}$ misclassifies x is less than or equal to $1/2$.

Given that it takes $O(n)$ time to formulate a query, PPC-Learning in $O(n)$ time and $O(1)$ queries is clearly optimal. The following theorem shows a close relationship between PPC-learning k-parities and PC-learning k-parities

THEOREM 11. *If k-parities is PPC-learnable in $O(n)$ time and $O(1)$ queries, then for any $\delta \in (0, 1/2)$, k-parities is PC learnable in $O(n \log(n/\delta))$ time and $O(\log(n/\delta))$ queries, where δ is the probability of error*

Given the information theoretic lower bound on learning relevant variables of a parity function with respect to n, for any positive integer k, Theorem 11 states that the PPC-learnability of k-parities in $O(n)$ time and $O(1)$ queries entails that k-parities are PC-learnable with *optimal* efficiency with respect to n. The proof of the theorem relies on the two well-known bounds. The first is the additive upper Chernoff bound [17]:

THEOREM 12 (ADDITIVE UPPER CHERNOFF BOUND). *Let $X_1, \ldots, X_r$ be r independent bernoulli random variables, let $\widehat{\mu} = \frac{1}{r}(X_1 + \ldots + X_r)$ be an estimator for the mean of these variables, and let $\mu = \mathbf{E}[\widehat{\mu}]$ be the expected mean. Then, for any $\epsilon > 0$, the following inequality holds:*

$$\mathbf{Pr}(\widehat{\mu} > \mu + \epsilon) \leq e^{-2r\epsilon^2}$$

The second is the union bound [17], which is as follows:

THEOREM 13 (UNION BOUND). *For any probability space, and any two events A and B over that space,*

$$\mathbf{Pr}[A \cup B] \leq \mathbf{Pr}[A] + \mathbf{Pr}[B]$$

Crucially, the events A and B need not be independent.

PROOF OF THEOREM 11. Let $\mathcal{A}$ be an algorithm that PPC-learns k-parities in $O(n)$ time and $O(1)$ queries with a per attribute error probability $\delta' < 1/2$. For any k-parity function f over n variables whose juntas are given by J, let $S_1, \ldots, S_r$ be sets output by $\mathcal{A}$ on r independent runs, and let S be a set defined as follows

$$x \in S \iff \frac{1}{r}\sum_{i=1}^{r}[x \in S_i]\{1\} > \frac{1}{2}$$

That is $x \in S$ iff x appears in more than half the sets $S_1, \ldots, S_r$. We claim that $\mathbf{Pr}(S \neq J) \leq \delta$ if

$$r > \frac{2}{(1 - 2\delta')^2} \log\left(\frac{n}{\delta}\right)$$

Considering that it takes $O(nr)$ time to compute S given $S_1, \ldots, S_r$, Theorem 11 follows straightforwardly from the claim. For a proof of the claim observe that for each $x \in [n]$ we have exactly two cases: (i) $x \in J$ and (ii) $x \notin J$.

Case i) $[x \in J]$: Let $\widehat{\mu_x}$ be a random variable defined as follows:

$$\widehat{\mu_x} = \frac{1}{r}\sum_{i=1}^{r}[x \notin S_i]\{1\}$$

Theorem 12 entails that for any $\epsilon > 0$,

$$\mathbf{Pr}\left(\widehat{\mu_x} > \mathbf{E}[\widehat{\mu_x}] + \epsilon\right) \leq e^{-2r\epsilon^2}$$

Note that $\mathbf{E}[\widehat{\mu_x}] = \delta'$. So by the premise of Theorem 11, $\mathbf{E}[\widehat{\mu_x}] < 1/2$. Setting $\epsilon = 1/2 - \delta'$ in the expression above yields

$$\mathbf{Pr}\left(\widehat{\mu_x} > \frac{1}{2}\right) \leq e^{-\frac{1}{2}r(1-2\delta')^2}$$

Thus, $\mathbf{Pr}(x \notin S) \leq e^{-\frac{1}{2}r(1-2\delta')^2}$.

Case ii) $[x \notin J]$: An argument similar to the one above with $\widehat{\mu_x}$ defined as follows yields $\mathbf{Pr}(x \in S) \leq e^{-\frac{1}{2}r(1-2\delta')^2}$.

$$\widehat{\mu_x} = \frac{1}{r}\sum_{i=1}^{r}[x \in S_i]\{1\}$$

By combining the two cases we get that for all $x \in [n]$, $\mathbf{Pr}(\neg(x \in S \Leftrightarrow x \in J)) \leq e^{-\frac{1}{2}r(1-2\delta')^2}$. The application of the union bound yields

$$\mathbf{Pr}(\neg(1 \in S \Leftrightarrow 1 \in J) \vee \ldots \vee \neg(n \in S \Leftrightarrow n \in J)) \leq ne^{-\frac{1}{2}r(1-2\delta')^2}$$

In other words, $\mathbf{Pr}(S \neq J) \leq ne^{-\frac{1}{2}r(1-2\delta')^2}$. Finally, setting $ne^{-\frac{1}{2}r(1-2\delta')^2} < \delta$ and taking logarithms yields the claim. □

6. SYMMETRY ANALYSIS

For any positive integer m, let D_m denote the set $\{0, \frac{1}{m}, \frac{2}{m}, \ldots, \frac{m-1}{m}, 1\}$. Let G be a UGA with a population of size m and binary genotypes of length n. A hypothetical population is shown in Figure 3. The *1-frequency* of some locus $i \in [n]$ at some time step t is a value in D_m that gives the frequency of the bit 1 at locus i at time step t (in other words the number of ones in the population of G at locus i in generation t divided by m, the size of the population).

Let f be a k-junta over $\{0,1\}^n$ whose juntas are given by J and let h be the hidden function of f such that h is symmetric, i.e. for any permutation $\pi : [n] \to [n]$ and any element $x \in \{0,1\}^n$, $h(x_1, \ldots, x_k) = h(x_{\pi(1)}, \ldots, x_{\pi(k)})$. Consider a noisy MQ oracle ϕ_f that internally uses f. Let G be a UGA that uses ϕ_f as a fitness function, and let $\mathbf{1}_i^t$ be a random variable that gives the 1-frequency of G at time step t, then for any time step t, any loci $i, j \in J$ and any loci $i', j' \in [n]\backslash J$, an appreciation of algorithmic symmetry (the absence of the positional bias in uniform crossover and the fact that h is symmetric) yields the following conclusions:

CONCLUSION 14. $\forall\, x \in D_m$, $\mathbf{Pr}(\mathbf{1}_i^t = x) = \mathbf{Pr}(\mathbf{1}_j^t = x)$

CONCLUSION 15. $\forall\, x \in D_m$, $\mathbf{Pr}(\mathbf{1}_{i'}^t = x) = \mathbf{Pr}(\mathbf{1}_{j'}^t = x)$

Which is to say that for all $i, j \in J$, $\mathbf{1}_i^t$ and $\mathbf{1}_j^t$ are drawn from the same distribution, which we denote p_t, and for all $i', j' \in [n]\backslash J$, $\mathbf{1}_{i'}^t$ and $\mathbf{1}_{j'}^t$ are drawn from the same distribution, which we denote q_t. (It is *not* to say that $\mathbf{1}_i^t$ and $\mathbf{1}_j^t$ are independent, or that $\mathbf{1}_{i'}^t$ and $\mathbf{1}_{j'}^t$ are independent.) Appreciating that the location of the juntas of f is immaterial to the 1-frequency dynamics of the relevant and irrelevant loci yields the following conclusion:

CONCLUSION 16. *For all t, p_t and q_t are invariant to J provided that $|J|$ remains constant*

Finally, if it is known that that the per bit probability of mutation is not dependent on the length of the genotypes, then appreciating that the non-relevant loci are just "along for the ride" and can be spliced out without affecting the 1-frequency dynamics at other loci give us the following conclusion:

CONCLUSION 17. *For all t, p_t and q_t are invariant to n*

6.1 Note on our Use of Symmetry

This section is a lightly modified version of Section 3 in an earlier paper [6] . We include it here because our case for the use of symmetry arguments remains the same.

A simple genetic algorithm with a finite but non-unitary population of size m (the kind of GA used in this paper) can be modeled by a Markov Chain over a state space consisting of all possible populations of size m [26]. Such models tend to be unwieldy [14] and difficult to analyze for all but the most trivial fitness functions. Fortunately, it is possible to avoid modeling and analysis of this kind, and still obtain precise results for non-trivial fitness functions by exploiting some simple symmetries introduced through the use of uniform crossover and length independent mutation.

A homologous crossover operation between two genotypes of length n can be modeled by a vector of n random binary variables $\langle X_1, \ldots, X_n\rangle$ representing a crossover mask. Likewise, a mutation operation can be modeled by a vector of n random binary variables $\langle Y_1, \ldots, Y_n\rangle$ representing a mutation mask. Only in the case of uniform crossover are the random variables $X_1, \ldots, X_n$ independent and identically distributed. This absence of *positional bias* [8] in uniform crossover constitutes a symmetry. Essentially, permuting the bits of all genotypes using some permutation π before crossover, and permuting the bits back using π^{-1} after crossover has no effect on the overall dynamics of a UGA. If, in addition, the random variables $Y_1, \ldots, Y_n$ that model the mutation operator are identically distributed (which is typical), conditionally independent given the per bit mutation rate, and independent of the value of n, then in the event that the values of genotypes at some locus i are immaterial to the fitness evaluation, the locus i can be "spliced out" without affecting allele dynamics at other loci. In other words, the dynamics of the UGA can be exactly *coarse-grained* [4].

These conclusions flow readily from an appreciation of the symmetries induced by uniform crossover and length independent mutation. While the use of symmetry arguments is uncommon in Theoretical Computer Science, symmetry arguments form a crucial part of the foundations of Physics and Chemistry. Indeed, according to the theoretical physicist E. T. Jaynes "almost the only known exact results in atomic and nuclear structure are those which we can deduce by symmetry arguments, using the methods of group theory" [15, p331-332]. Note that the conclusions above hold true regardless of the selection scheme (fitness proportionate, tournament, truncation, etc), and any fitness scaling that may occur (sigma scaling, linear scaling etc). "The great power of symmetry arguments lies just in the fact that they are not deterred by any amount of complication in the details", writes Jaynes [15, p331]. An appeal to symmetry, in other words, allows one to cut through complications that might hobble attempts to reason within a formal axiomatic system. Of course, symmetry arguments are not without peril. However, when used sparingly and only in circumstances where the symmetries are readily apparent, they can yield significant insight at low cost.

7. STATISTICAL HYPOTHESIS TESTING

For any positive integer n, let f be a 7-parity function over $\{0,1\}^n$, and let ϕ_f be a noisy MQ oracle such that for any $x \in \{0,1\}^n$ $\mathbf{Pr}(\phi(x) = \neg f(x)) = 1/5$ and $\mathbf{Pr}(\phi(x) =$

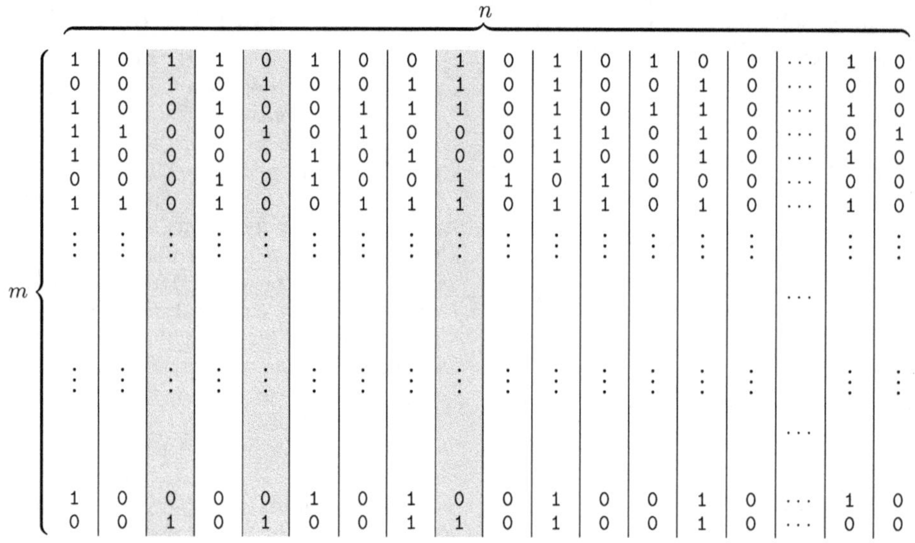

Figure 3: A hypothetical population of m genotypes, each n bits long. The 3rd, 5th, and 9th loci of the population are shown in grey.

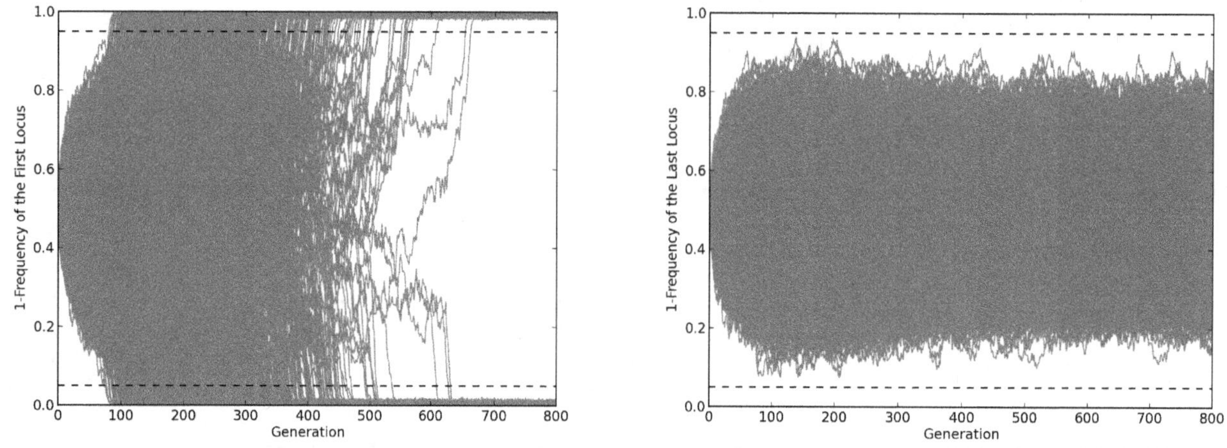

(a) (b)

Figure 4: The 1-frequency dynamics over 3000 runs of the first (*left figure*) and last (*right figure*) loci of Algorithm 1 with $m = 1500$, $n = 8$, $\tau = 800$, $p_{mut} = 0.004$, and $asex = false$ using the membership query oracle ϕ_{f^*}, described in the text, as a fitness function. The dashed lines mark the 1-frequencies 0.05 and 0.95.

$f(x)) = 4/5$. Let $G(n)$ be the simple genetic algorithm given in Algorithm 1 with genotypes of length n, population size m=1500, uniform recombination ($asex = false$), and per bit mutation probability $p_{mut} = 0.004$. Let $\mathcal{A}^{\phi}(n)$ be an algorithm that runs $G(n)$ for 800 generations using ϕ_f as the fitness function and returns a set $S \subseteq [n]$ such that $i \in S$ if and only if the 1-frequency of locus i at generation 800 exceeds 1/2.

Claim 18. *$\mathcal{A}^{\phi_f}$ PPC-solves the learning 7-parities problem in $O(n)$ time and $O(1)$ queries.*

Argument. Let D'_m be the set

$$\{x \in D_m \mid 0.05 < x < 0.95\}$$

Note that the hidden function of f is invariant to a reordering of its inputs and the per bit probability of mutation in G is constant with respect to n. Thus, Conclusions 14, 15, 16, and 10 hold. Consider the following two null hypotheses:

$$H_0^p : \sum_{x \in D'_{1500}} p_{800}(x) \geq \frac{1}{2}$$

$$H_0^q : \sum_{x \notin D'_{1500}} q_{800}(x) \geq \frac{1}{2}$$

We seek to reject $H_0^p \vee H_0^q$. Assume H_0^p is true, then for any independent random variables $X_1, \ldots, X_{3000}$ drawn from the distribution p_{800}, and any $i \in [3000]$,

$$\mathbf{Pr}(X_i \in D'_{1500}) \geq 1/2$$

which entails that

$$\mathbf{Pr}(X_i \notin D'_{1500}) < 1/2$$

The independence of the random variables entails that

$$\mathbf{Pr}(X_1 \notin D'_{1500} \wedge \ldots \wedge X_{3000} \notin D'_{1500}) < \left(\frac{1}{2}\right)^{3000}$$

Let f^* be the 7-parity function over $\{0,1\}^8$ whose juntas are given by the set $\{1, \ldots, 7\}$. Figures 4a and 4b show the 1-frequency of the first and last loci, respectively, of $G(8)$ given the fitness function ϕ_{f^*} in 3000 independent runs, each 800 generations long.[6] Thus, the chance that the 1-frequency of the first locus of $G(8)$ is in $D_{1500} \backslash D'_{1500}$ in generation 800 of all 3000 runs, as seen in Figure 4a, is less than $(1/2)^{3000}$. As $(1/2)^{3000} < 10^{-903}$, we can reject hypothesis H_0^p at the 10^{-903} level of significance.

Likewise, if H_0^q is true, then for any independent random variables $X_1, \ldots, X_{3000}$ drawn from the distribution q_{800}, and any $i \in [3000]$,

$$\mathbf{Pr}(X_i \notin D'_{1500}) \geq 1/2$$

which entails that

$$\mathbf{Pr}(X_1 \in D'_{1500} \wedge \ldots \wedge X_{3000} \in D'_{1500}) < \left(\frac{1}{2}\right)^{3000}$$

Thus, the chance that the 1-frequency of the last locus of $G(8)$ could be in D'_{1500} in generation 800 of all 3000 runs, as seen in Figure 5b, is less than $(1/2)^{3000}$. We thus reject hypothesis H_0^q at the 10^{-903} level of significance.

Each p-value is less than a Bonferroni adjusted critical value of $10^{-900}/2$, so we reject the global null hypotheses $H_0^p \vee H_0^q$ at the 10^{-900} level of significance. We are left with the following conclusions:

$$\sum_{x \in D'_{1500}} p_{800}(x) < \frac{1}{2}$$

$$\sum_{x \notin D'_{1500}} q_{800}(x) < \frac{1}{2}$$

The observation that running $G(n)$ for 800 generations takes $O(n)$ time and $O(1)$ queries completes the argument.

7.1 Other values of k and η?

The PC-learning result obtained above pertains only to $k = 7$ and $\eta = 1/5$. We expect that the proof technique used here can be used to derive identical bounds with respect to n and δ for other values of k and η as long as these values remain small. This conjecture can only be verified on a *case by case* basis with the proof technique provided. The symmetry argument used in the proof precludes the derivation of bounds with respect to k and η as is typically done in the computational learning literature. Our goal, however, is not to derive such bounds for all k and η, but to verify a prediction entailed by hypomixability theory, and in doing so to give the first proof of efficient computational learning in an evolutionary algorithm on a non-trivial learning problem. That the computational learning is *optimally* efficient is a welcome finding.

7.2 Asexual Evolution Does Not Solve Parities

As asexual evolution does not mix genotypes, it cannot be expected to capitalize on hypomixability, and hence cannot be expected to solve k-parities for any value of k. Nevertheless, for the sake of completeness, and to gain insight into the behavior of asexual evolution on ϕ_f, where f is some 7-parity function, we repeated the experiment described earlier in this section with recombination turned off. Note that the symmetry analytic conclusions 14, 15, 16, and 17 of Section 6 continue to hold. Figure 7.1 shows the 1-frequencies of the first and last loci of of Algorithm 1 over 75 runs using ϕ_{f^*} as a fitness function as before and $m = 1500$ and $n = 8$ as before. The values of τ and *asex* were changed to 10000 and *true* respectively. In other words, we greatly reduced the number of runs, greatly increased the length of each run, and disabled recombination. As the figure shows, the first locus did not go to fixation even once during the 75 runs, despite an increase in run length from 800 to 10000 generations.

8. ADAPTATION AND SPECIATION

A one-time elimination of hypomixability, even if optimally efficient, cannot explain the sustained adaptation that is observed in natural and artificial evolutionary systems. Fortunately, this problem is easily fixed by making a weak assumption. We assume that hypomixability elimination is *generative*. That is, we assume that the elimination of statistically significant hypomixability in some small collection of loci engenders statistically significant hypomixability in one or more small collections of loci elsewhere. With this assumption, adaptive hypomixability elimination can go from being a one-time occurrence to an ongoing phenomenon.

The heuristic that emerges (Generative Hypomixability Elimination) is *non-local* because it does not make use of neighborhood information. It is *noise-tolerant* because it is sensitive only to the *average* fitness values of coarse schemata, and it is *general-purpose* because it relies on very weak assumptions about the distribution of fitness over a search space. Proof of concept can be found in previous works [5, 6]. In these publications hypomixability elimination was hypothesized to be entropy *minimizing* (hence the name Generative *Fixation* [5]). The current theory that hypomixability elimination is entropy maximizing subject to the unit-mixability constraint corrects this error.[7]

The unmistakable seed of a theory of speciation lies in the observation that there are 64 different ways to adaptively

[6]To rerun the experiment and examine the results, visit `https://github.com/burjorjee/evolve-parities/tree/foga-2015` and follow instructions.

[7]For small values of k, an OR k-junta is an example of a fitness function where the evolutionary elimination of statistically significant hypomixability is not accompanied by the fixation of any juntas.

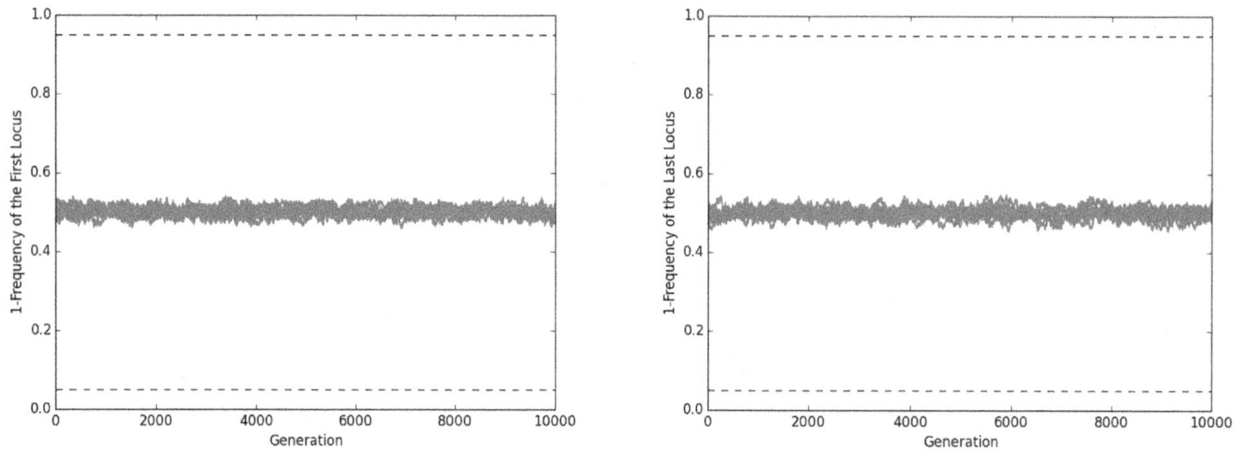

Figure 5: The 1-frequency dynamics over 75 runs of the first (*left figure*) and last (*right figure*) loci of Algorithm 1 with $m = 1500$, $n = 8$, $\tau = 10000$, $p_{mut} = 0.004$ and $asex = true$ using the membership query oracle ϕ_{f^*}, described in the text, as a fitness function. The dashed lines mark the 1-frequencies 0.05 and 0.95.

eliminate hypomixability in the 7-parity problem, no two of which are sexually compatible. While a panmictic population always pursues just one way to eliminate hypomixability in some set of loci, island/spatial models may be able to pursue two or more (sexually incompatible) ways in parallel. Each way is a branch and each branch may sprout its own branches.

9. THE EMERGENCE OF MODULARITY

It has been noted that modularity in sexual evolution can *emerge* through changes in allele frequencies under sex and selection [20, 22]. Such emergence can be readily observed in the results shown in the top panel of Figure 2. Consider locus 45, the first of the seven juntas. In generation 0, the alleles 0 and 1 at locus 45 have identical selection coefficients because the expected parity of the six remaining juntas in a genotype picked at random from the population is approximately 1/2. By generation 160, the expected parity of these six juntas in a genotype picked at random from the population is close to 1. So allele 0 at locus 45 has a higher selection coefficient than allele 1.

The emergence of modularity during sexual evolution is offered up by Livnat et al. [20] as a reason to go along with hypotheses that make an *a priori* assumption of modularity. They remark, "It is not necessary to ask, then, how mixability [i.e. emergence of modularity in their context] supports the Fisher/Muller hypothesis, the deterministic mutation hypothesis, or other hypotheses that rely on separate effects." According to Livnat et al., the support rendered to such theories by the emergence of modularity is obvious. In any event, such theories are not put on trial.

We are of a different mind. Based on the computational complexity results presented earlier in this paper, we submit that the emergence of modularity (an outcome of hypomixability elimination) is not a sideshow, but sexual evolution's *main* act; theories of evolution based on *a priori* assumptions of modularity, in effect, swoop in to explain what happens *after* the most difficult part of the show is over. What remains to be done at that point is the computational equivalent of *mopping up*. Necessary work, to be sure, but certainly not as computationally remarkable or difficult to explain.

10. CONCLUSION

The computational origins problem was introduced and for the first time, optimally efficient non-trivial computation was demonstrated in an evolutionary system. This demonstration serves as validation of a prediction entailed by hypomixability theory—a parsimonious theory that provides a unified explanation for sex, adaptation, speciation, and the emergence of modularity in evolutionary systems.

Acknowledgements

The term "frozen noise" is due to Adam Prugel-Bennett. Many thanks to Lev Reyzin for answering numerous questions about Computational Learning Theory.

11. REFERENCES

[1] Lee Altenberg. Nk fitness landscapes. *Handbook of evolutionary computation*, pages 7–2, 1997.

[2] Nicholas H Barton and Brian Charlesworth. Why sex and recombination? *Science*, 281(5385):1986–1990, 1998.

[3] Avrim L Blum and Pat Langley. Selection of relevant features and examples in machine learning. *Artificial intelligence*, 97(1):245–271, 1997.

[4] Keki M. Burjorjee. Sufficient conditions for coarse-graining evolutionary dynamics. In *Foundations of Genetic Algorithms 9 (FOGA IX)*, 2007.

[5] Keki M. Burjorjee. *Generative Fixation: A Unifed Explanation for the Adaptive Capacity of Simple Recombinative Genetic Algorithms.* PhD thesis, Brandeis University, 2009.

[6] Keki M. Burjorjee. Explaining optimization in genetic algorithms with uniform crossover. In *Proceedings of the twelfth workshop on Foundations of genetic algorithms XII*. ACM, 2013.

[7] Keki M. Burjorjee and Jordan B. Pollack. A general coarse-graining framework for studying simultaneous inter-population constraints induced by evolutionary operations. In *GECCO 2006: Proceedings of the 8th annual conference on Genetic and evolutionary computation*. ACM Press, 2006.

[8] L.J. Eshelman, R.A. Caruana, and J.D. Schaffer. Biases in the crossover landscape. *Proceedings of the third international conference on Genetic algorithms table of contents*, pages 10–19, 1989.

[9] Vitaly Feldman. Attribute-efficient and non-adaptive learning of parities and dnf expressions. *Journal of Machine Learning Research*, 8(1431-1460):101, 2007.

[10] David E. Goldberg. *Genetic Algorithms in Search, Optimization & Machine Learning*. Addison-Wesley, Reading, MA, 1989.

[11] Sally A Goldman, Michael J Kearns, and Robert E Schapire. Exact identification of read-once formulas using fixed points of amplification functions. *SIAM Journal on Computing*, 22(4):705–726, 1993.

[12] William D Hamilton, Robert Axelrod, and Reiko Tanese. Sexual reproduction as an adaptation to resist parasites (a review). *Proceedings of the National Academy of Sciences*, 87(9):3566–3573, 1990.

[13] John H. Holland. *Adaptation in Natural and Artificial Systems: An Introductory Analysis with Applications to Biology, Control, and Artificial Intelligence*. MIT Press, 1975.

[14] John H. Holland. Building blocks, cohort genetic algorithms, and hyperplane-defined functions. *Evolutionary Computation*, 8(4):373–391, 2000.

[15] E.T. Jaynes. *Probability Theory: The Logic of Science*. Cambridge University Press, 2007.

[16] S.A. Kauffman. *The Origins of Order: Self-Organization and Selection in Evolution*. Biophysical Soc, 1993.

[17] Michael J Kearns and Umesh Virkumar Vazirani. *An introduction to computational learning theory*. MIT press, 1994.

[18] Alexey S Kondrashov. Selection against harmful mutations in large sexual and asexual populations. *Genetical research*, 40(03):325–332, 1982.

[19] Adi Livnat, Christos Papadimitriou, Jonathan Dushoff, and Marcus W Feldman. A mixability theory for the role of sex in evolution. *Proceedings of the National Academy of Sciences*, 105(50):19803–19808, 2008.

[20] Adi Livnat, Christos Papadimitriou, Nicholas Pippenger, and Marcus W Feldman. Sex, mixability, and modularity. *Proceedings of the National Academy of Sciences*, 107(4):1452–1457, 2010.

[21] David JC MacKay. *Information theory, inference, and learning algorithms*, volume 7. Cambridge University Press, 2003.

[22] Dusan Misevic, Charles Ofria, and Richard E Lenski. Sexual reproduction reshapes the genetic architecture of digital organisms. *Proceedings of the Royal Society B: Biological Sciences*, 273(1585):457–464, 2006.

[23] Melanie Mitchell. *An Introduction to Genetic Algorithms*. The MIT Press, Cambridge, MA, 1996.

[24] Elchanan Mossel, Ryan O'Donnell, and Rocco P Servedio. Learning juntas. In *Proceedings of the thirty-fifth annual ACM symposium on Theory of computing*, pages 206–212. ACM, 2003.

[25] Hermann Joseph Muller. The relation of recombination to mutational advance. *Mutation Research/Fundamental and Molecular Mechanisms of Mutagenesis*, 1(1):2–9, 1964.

[26] A.E. Nix and M.D. Vose. Modeling genetic algorithms with Markov chains. *Annals of Mathematics and Artificial Intelligence*, 5(1):79–88, 1992.

[27] Karl Popper. *Conjectures and Refutations*. Routledge, 2007.

[28] Karl Popper. *The Logic Of Scientific Discovery*. Routledge, 2007.

[29] Sean H. Rice. The evolution of developmental interactions. Oxford University Press, 2000.

[30] Uehara, Tsuchida, and Wegener. Identification of partial disjunction, parity, and threshold functions. *TCS: Theoretical Computer Science*, 230, 2000.

[31] Leslie Valiant. *Probably approximately correct: nature's algorithms for learning and prospering in a complex world*. Basic Books, 2013.

[32] Richard A. Watson. *Compositional Evolution: The Impact of Sex, Symbiosis and Modularity on the Gradualist Framework of Evolution*. The MIT Press, 2006.

Convergence of Strategies in Simple Co-Adapting Games

Richard Mealing and Jonathan L. Shapiro
Machine Learning and Optimisation Group
School of Computer Science
University of Manchester
M13 9PL, UK
{mealingr,jls}@cs.man.ac.uk

ABSTRACT

Simultaneously co-adapting agents in an uncooperative setting can result in a non-stationary environment where optimisation or learning is difficult and where the agents' strategies may not converge to solutions. This work looks at simple simultaneous-move games with two or three actions and two or three players. Fictitious play is an old but popular algorithm that can converge to solutions, albeit slowly, in self-play in games like these. It models its opponents assuming that they use stationary strategies and plays a best-response strategy to these models. We propose two new variants of fictitious play that remove this assumption and explicitly assume that the opponents use dynamic strategies. The opponent's strategy is predicted using a sequence prediction method in the first variant and a change detection method in the second variant. Empirical results show that our variants converge faster than fictitious play. However, they do not always converge exactly to correct solutions. For change detection, this is a very small number of cases, but for sequence prediction there are many. The convergence of sequence prediction is improved by combining it with fictitious play. Also, unlike in fictitious play, our variants converge to solutions in the difficult Shapley's and Jordan's games.

Categories and Subject Descriptors

I.2.11 [**Artificial Intelligence**]: Distributed Artificial Intelligence—*multiagent systems*

General Terms

Algorithms, Experimentation, Performance, Theory

Keywords

Self-play convergence; opponent modelling; sequence prediction; change detection; fictitious play; Nash equilibrium; iterated normal-form games; empirical distribution

FOGA'15, January 17–20, 2015, Aberystwyth, United Kingdom.

http://dx.doi.org/10.1145/2725494.2725503.

1. INTRODUCTION

Evolutionary computation techniques, such as evolutionary algorithms, swarm intelligence methods, artificial immune systems, etc, often focus on co-adapting agents to solve a shared optimisation problem in a static environment. This is like a game where each agent shares the same reward function, which returns higher rewards for better optimisations. However, in many problems each agent has its own optimisation problem or reward function, which can depend on the other agents' strategies. In these uncooperative cases, co-adapting agents can result in a non-stationary environment making optimisation or learning difficult because the optimal strategies are changing. Examples include auction bidding agents, poker-playing agents, competing agents placing advertisements on web pages, and so forth.

A population of simultaneously co-adapting or coevolving agents in an uncooperative setting may converge or exhibit complex dynamics [37, 12, 13, 14, 38, 9, 7, 8, 2, 11, 44, 6, 23]. The goal of this work is to address the question of whether convergence is enhanced if each agent assumes that the other agents are changing their strategies over time. We study this using simultaneous-move games with two or three actions and two or three players. We compare fictitious play, which is an adaptive mechanism that assumes that the opponent uses a stationary strategy, with two new variants that remove this assumption and explicitly assume that the opponent uses a dynamic strategy. The opponent's strategy is predicted using a sequence prediction method in the first variant and a change detection method in the second variant.

Ideally, we want each agent in a multiagent system to consistently learn and change its strategy to increase its expected rewards. If an agent did this, then eventually it would learn and converge to a best-response strategy that maximises its expected rewards against the other agents' strategies. If all agents did this, then eventually they would learn and converge to a Nash equilibrium. This is why much of the literature about learning in multiagent systems searches for learning rules that will result in agents' strategies converging to a Nash equilibrium. At each step in our approach, we observe the opponent's action, predict its strategy, and play a best-response strategy to the predicted strategy.

We specifically compare the convergence in self-play of our variants and fictitious play to mixed strategy Nash equilibria. Only the empirical distributions of plays over games are considered because they almost always play pure strategies. Our convergence results are purely experimental and find that our variants converge faster than fictitious play. However, unlike in fictitious play, our variants do not always exactly converge to the Nash equilibria. For change detection, this is a very small number of cases, but for sequence prediction there are many. Combining sequence prediction with fictitious play improves its convergence, reducing these cases. Also, unlike in fictitious play, our variants converge to the mixed strategy Nash equilibria in Shapley's and Jordan's games, which are considered difficult [29].

2. CONVERGENCE TO SOLUTIONS

2.1 Solution Concepts

In an n-player finite normal-form game each player, $i \in \{1, 2, \ldots, n\}$, has a finite set of actions (or pure strategies), $A_i = \{a_1, a_2, \ldots, a_{|A_i|}\}$, and a utility function that maps tuples of actions, where each tuple contains one action per player, to rewards, $u_i : \prod_{j=1}^{n} A_j \to \mathbb{R}$. Each player i also has a strategy, $\sigma_i \in \Sigma_i \equiv \Delta(A_i)$, where $\Delta(\cdot)$ is the space of probability distributions over a set. We define the strategy profile, σ, as the tuple containing each player's strategy, $\sigma = (\sigma_1, \sigma_2, \ldots, \sigma_n) \in \Sigma = \prod_{j=1}^{n} \Sigma_j$, and σ_{-i} as the same as σ but excluding player i's strategy, $\sigma_{-i} = (\sigma_1, \sigma_2, \ldots, \sigma_{i-1}, \sigma_{i+1}, \ldots, \sigma_n) \in \Sigma_{-i} = \prod_{j=1, j\neq i}^{n} \Sigma_j$. Finally, we define player i's expected reward for the strategy profile σ as $\overline{u}_i(\sigma) \equiv \sum_{a \in \prod_{j=1}^{n} A_j} u_i(a) \prod_{k=1}^{n} \sigma_k(a(k))$, where $a(k)$ is player k's action in a. When playing, each player i simultaneously chooses an action according to their strategy σ_i producing the tuple $a \in \prod_{j=1}^{n} A_j$ and gets a reward of $u_i(a)$. Our definitions follow those by Fudenberg and Levine [22].

Typically, we want to learn a best-response strategy to maximise a player's expected rewards.

Definition 1. A best-response strategy for player i, $\sigma_i^* \in \Sigma_i$, would give it its most preferred outcome against all other players' strategies, $\sigma_{-i} \in \prod_{j=1, j\neq i}^{n} \Sigma_j$, such that

$$u_i(\sigma_i^*, \sigma_{-i}) = \max_{\sigma_i \in \Sigma_i} u_i(\sigma_i, \sigma_{-i}) \tag{1}$$

Note that for a mixed best-response strategy, all pure strategies with non-zero probabilities have equal expected rewards to each other and to the mixture. This must be true because otherwise the pure strategy with a lower (higher) expected reward than the mixture could be chosen less (more) often, creating a strategy with a higher expected reward, meaning that the original strategy was not a best-response strategy.

If all agents are playing a best-response strategy, then they are mutually playing a Nash equilibrium. A Nash equilibrium is a solution concept of a non-cooperative game with two or more players that was proposed by Nash in 1950 [33].

Definition 2. A Nash equilibrium is a strategy profile, $\sigma^* \in \Sigma$, where each player's strategy, $\sigma_i^* \in \Sigma_i$, is a best-response strategy to the other players' strategies such that

$$u_i(\sigma_i^*, \sigma_{-i}) \geq u_i(\sigma_i, \sigma_{-i}) \text{ for all } \sigma_i \in \Sigma_i \text{ and } i \in \{1, 2, \ldots, n\} \tag{2}$$

Nash proved that if players can use mixed strategies, then at least one Nash equilibrium exists for all n-player games, where each player has a finite number of pure strategies [33].

Although players may not have high expected rewards at a Nash equilibrium, each player is playing optimally given that the other players do not change their strategies. Crawford showed that it is difficult to converge to a Nash equilibrium despite highly favourable settings e.g. simple games, two-players, noiseless feedback, infinite repeats, a unique Nash equilibrium, etc. He found that if the agents adapted their strategies using gradient ascent on their expected rewards, then they would fail to converge under these settings in zero-sum normal-form games [12], general-sum normal-form games [13], and evolutionary games [14]. Thus, a lot of research in multiagent systems looks at developing learning rules that will lead to agents' strategies converging to a Nash equilibrium. In this paper, we focus on a simple, old, but also popular approach called fictitious play.

2.2 Convergence Concepts

Throughout this paper we will be interested in a very weak form of convergence, which we will call *empirical Nash convergence*. The obvious and desirable form of convergence would be one in which the agent's strategy converges to a best-response strategy against agents with stationary strategies, and to a Nash equilibrium against similar learning agents or at least in self-play. If the Nash equilibrium has mixed strategies, then the agents would converge in a statistical sense; they would play stochastically, but from distributions that are converging to stationary distributions that are the Nash equilibrium. Several gradient-based algorithms have been shown to do this in some situations, such as Dahl's algorithm [15, 11, 36], WoLF [9], experience-weighted attraction [23], etc. In other situations these algorithms fail, which is an interesting topic but not the subject of our work.

Consider the traditional version of fictitious play that we use as well as our variants. Each one of these players always plays a best-response strategy to its model. This is almost always a pure best-response strategy and is only mixed if multiple pure best-response strategies to its model exist. Thus, its strategy typically cannot converge to a mixed strategy, but its empirical distribution of plays (pure strategy choices) over games can. If, in a game, the empirical distributions of players who almost always play pure-strategies do converge to a mixed strategy profile (possibly a Nash equilibrium), then this often results in their joint strategy cycling around that profile. We define an empirical distribution, and its convergence to another distribution, as follows. Given a finite set, $\mathcal{A} = \{\alpha_1, \alpha_2, \ldots, \alpha_k\}$, and an infinite sequence of elements from $\mathcal{A}$, $S = (\alpha^1, \alpha^2, \ldots)$, $\alpha^j \in \mathcal{A}$,

Definition 3. The empirical distribution of S at time t is

$$P_S^t(\alpha_i \in \mathcal{A}) = \frac{1}{t} \sum_{j=1}^{t} [\![\alpha_i = \alpha^j]\!] \tag{3}$$

$$= \left(1 - \frac{1}{t}\right) P_S^{t-1}(\alpha_i \in \mathcal{A}) + \left(\frac{1}{t}\right) [\![\alpha_i = \alpha^t]\!], \tag{4}$$

where $[\![\cdot]\!]$ is the Iverson bracket such that $[\![\phi]\!] = 1$ if the predicate ϕ is true, otherwise $[\![\phi]\!] = 0$. Given a probability distribution over $\mathcal{A}$, $P(\alpha_i \in \mathcal{A})$,

Definition 4. The empirical distribution of S converges to P if for any $\epsilon > 0$, and for any divergence measure $D(\cdot||\cdot)$ between distributions, there exists a time t_ϵ such that $D(P_S^t||P) < \epsilon$ for all times $t > t_\epsilon$.

Finally, given a Nash equilibrium, we define empirical Nash convergence as each player's empirical distribution of plays converging to their strategy in this Nash equilibrium.

2.3 Measuring Nash Equilibrium Convergence

To measure the convergence of a tuple of strategies to a Nash equilibrium, we need to be able to measure the difference between each player's strategy in that tuple and and its corresponding Nash equilibrium strategy. In a normal-form game, each of these strategies can be represented as a discrete probability distribution. Thus, we want to be able to measure the difference between two discrete probability distributions P and Q. To do this, we use the Jensen-Shannon divergence metric because it is a true metric, meaning it is non-negative, zero if P and Q are equal, symmetric, and satisfies the triangle inequality. It is calculated using the Jensen-Shannon divergence, and is based on the Kullback-Leibler divergence. In particular, for each player, we calculate the Jensen-Shannon divergence metric between its empirical distribution of plays and its Nash equilibrium strategy, and we take the average of these values to give an average Jensen-Shannon divergence metric i.e.

$$\overline{D_{JSM}} = \frac{1}{n}\sum_{i=1}^{n} D_{JSM}(\sigma_i||\sigma_i^*), \tag{5}$$

where n is the number of players, σ_i is player i's empirical distribution of plays, and σ_i^* is player i's Nash equilibrium strategy. Here we are assuming that σ_i and σ_i^* can each be represented by a discrete probability distribution, which is the case for a mixed strategy in a normal-form game.

The *Kullback-Leibler divergence* between P and Q, $D_{KL}(P||Q)$, is defined as

$$D_{KL}(P||Q) = \sum_i P(i)\ln\frac{P(i)}{Q(i)}, \tag{6}$$

where $D_{KL}(P||Q) \geq 0$. This only holds if $P(i) = 0$ whenever $Q(i) = 0$. Also, if $P(i) = Q(i) = 0$, then it is assumed that $0 \ln 0 = 0$. If Q is a uniform distribution, then $D_{KL}(P||Q) = -H(P)$ (i.e. negative Shannon entropy, see Equation (12)).

The *Jensen-Shannon divergence* between P and Q, $D_{JS}(P||Q)$, is defined as

$$D_{JS}(P||Q) = \frac{D_{KL}(P||M) + D_{KL}(Q||M)}{2}, \tag{7}$$
$$\text{where } M(i) = \frac{P(i)+Q(i)}{2},$$

and $0 \leq D_{JS}(P||Q) \leq \ln(2)$ if log to the base e is used, or $0 \leq D_{JS}(P||Q) \leq 1$ if log to the base 2 is used.

The *Jensen-Shannon divergence Metric* between P and Q, $D_{JSM}(P||Q)$, is defined as

$$D_{JSM}(P||Q) = \sqrt{D_{JS}(P||Q)}, \tag{8}$$

where $0 \leq D_{JSM}(P||Q) \leq \ln(2)$ if log to the base e is used, or $0 \leq D_{JSM}(P||Q) \leq 1$ if log to the base 2 is used.

3. FICTITIOUS PLAY

3.1 Description

Fictitious play is an algorithm that was originally proposed by Brown in 1951 to explain Nash equilibrium play [10]. It assumes that its opponent is playing a stationary, possibly mixed, strategy and estimates this strategy using a frequentist approach. It then plays a best-response strategy to its estimate i.e. a best-response strategy to its opponent's empirical distribution of plays. If its opponent's strategy is stationary, then as more games are played its estimate becomes more accurate and in turn its best-response strategy becomes more accurate. In an iterated normal-form game, fictitious play would update its estimate of the opponent's strategy using Equation (4), where P_S^t is its estimate of the opponent's strategy at time t, $P_S^t = \tilde{\sigma}_{\text{opp}}^t \in \Sigma_{\text{opp}}$, $\mathcal{A}$ is the opponent's set of actions, $\mathcal{A} = A_{\text{opp}}$, and S is the sequence of opponent actions observed in the games. The factor $1/t$ in Equation (4) is like a learning rate and variants could change this (e.g. geometric fictitious play replaces $1/t$ with a constant $z \in [0, 1]$). Thus, at each iteration t, fictitious play predicts that the opponent will play $\tilde{\sigma}_{\text{opp}}^t$ and therefore plays a best-response strategy to $\tilde{\sigma}_{\text{opp}}^t$, i.e. a strategy $\sigma_{\text{FP}}^* \in \Sigma_{\text{FP}}$ where $u_{\text{FP}}(\sigma_{\text{FP}}^*) = \max_{\sigma_{\text{FP}} \in \Sigma_{\text{FP}}} u_{\text{FP}}(\sigma_{\text{FP}}, \tilde{\sigma}_{\text{opp}}^t)$.

3.2 Convergence of Fictitious Play

Fudenberg and Levine showed that for fictitious play in self-play, *strict* Nash equilibria are absorbing states [20]. This means that in an iterated game, if a strict Nash equilibrium is played at some point, then it will also be played at all subsequent points. For a strict Nash equilibrium, the inequalities in Equation (2) are strict, and so it is always a pure strategy Nash equilibrium. For a weak Nash equilibrium, the inequalities in Equation (2) are equalities, and so it is either a pure or a mixed strategy Nash equilibrium. Thus, if in self-play fictitious play converges to a pure strategy profile, then it must be a Nash equilibrium, and if its empirical distributions of plays converge to some (mixed) strategy profile, then that strategy profile must also be a Nash equilibrium. Finally, the empirical distributions of plays of two fictitious players have been shown to converge to Nash equilibria in self-play in: two-player, zero-sum games [35], two-player, two-action games [31], games with an interior evolutionary stable strategy [25], potential games [32], and certain classes of supermodular games [30, 28, 24].

However, for fictitious players in self-play, their empirical distributions of plays do not always converge to a Nash equilibrium. This has been shown in Shapley's game, a general-sum version of rock-paper-scissors, and Jordan's game, a three-player version of matching pennies, despite it not being true in rock-paper-scissors and two-player matching pennies [37, 27]. Fudenberg and Kreps also showed with their persistent miscoordination example that even if its empirical distribution of plays converges, its expected rewards may differ from the expected rewards of the strategy after convergence [20]. Finally, if multiple Nash equilibria exist and fictitious play converges to one in self-play, then it may not be the "best" Nash equilibrium. In fact, it may be objectively worse than another Nash equilibrium, where some players would be strictly better off. In summary, fictitious players usually cannot converge to mixed strategy profiles (e.g. Nash equilibria) as they almost always play pure strategies, but their empirical distributions of plays can. If these distributions converge to a Nash equilibrium, and they are independent from one another, then their expected rewards will also converge to those at that Nash equilibrium. This last point captures the convergence notion we consider.

3.3 Fictitious Play Example

In this example, we play two fictitious players, in self-play in an iterated game of matching pennies. The row player wins if it matches the action of the column player; otherwise the column player wins. A (loss) win is worth $(-)1$. This is shown in Table 1. Let heads be represented by 1, tails be represented by -1, x be the mean of the row player's actions, and y be the mean of the column player's actions. So, for example, $x = 0$ would mean that the row player has played equal numbers of heads and tails. The row player updates y after observing each of the column player's actions, and will play its sign. The column player updates x after observing each of the row player's actions, and will play *minus* its sign. The dynamics in expectation, of x and y, obey

$$x(t) = \left(1 - \frac{1}{t}\right) x(t-1) + \left(\frac{1}{t}\right) \operatorname{sign}(y(t-1)), \tag{9}$$

$$y(t) = \left(1 - \frac{1}{t}\right) y(t-1) - \left(\frac{1}{t}\right) \operatorname{sign}(x(t-1)), \tag{10}$$

where $\operatorname{sign}(z) = 1$ if $z > 0$, 0 if $z = 0$, and -1 if $z < 0$. If a player has played equal numbers of heads and tails, then under fictitious play dynamics, its opponent would play a (usually uniform) random action. Thus, the expectation of its opponent's play in this situation is zero. This is why these are the expected dynamics. The players' actions will never converge, because the signs of x and y will never stop changing. However, the means *do* converge, albeit slowly. To illustrate these expected dynamics, we ran 10000 iterations of recurrence relations (9) and (10). The initial values of x and y were each randomly set to either -1 or 1 with equal probability. The results are shown in figures 1a, 1b, 1c, and 1d. Note that many two-player, two-action, zero-sum, normal-form game with a mixed strategy Nash equilibrium will be similar, with x and y measuring the difference of the strategy distribution from the equilibrium strategy.

We view this as a dynamical system. We can say the following about recurrence relations (9) and (10):

1. The origin (Nash) point ($x = 0, y = 0$) is a fixed point.
2. The system cycles towards the origin, by switching strategies, as seen in figures 1a and 1b.
3. The period of a cycle grows linearly with time (see Corollary 1).
4. The amount the system moves towards the origin per cycle decreases inversely with time (see Corollary 2).
5. As a consequence of 3 and 4, the convergence rate is $\Theta(1/\sqrt{t})$, where t is time (iteration) (see Corollary 3).

Point 1 is obvious, Appendix A shows points 2, 3, 4, and 5 through its corollaries to Theorem 1, which postulates the first cycle period and the origin distance after it.

The fact that fictitious play undergoes empirical Nash convergence here, but very slowly, as shown empirically in figures 1a, 1b, 1c, and 1d, as well as theoretically in Appendix A, is part of the motivation of this work. Convergence is very slow because each agent takes an increasingly long time to respond to the change in its opponent's strategy. If an agent could identify its opponent's strategy switches more quickly, then it might converge faster, perhaps optimally like $1/t$ (proven in Appendix B), as well as in more situations. This is the idea that we set out to investigate.

4. RELATED WORK

4.1 Fictitious Play Extensions

In this paper, we only consider the traditional fictitious play algorithm as described in Section 3.1. However, to help put this work into context, we will briefly describe some extensions to it. These extensions can allow fictitious play to model changing opponent strategies, to use mixed strategies, and can improve its convergence to solution concepts. Two popular extensions, by Fudenberg and Levine, are geometric fictitious play and stochastic fictitious play [22].

Geometric fictitious play can model changing opponent strategies. It works by giving bigger weights to more recent opponent actions when updating opponent action probabilities. In comparison to the traditional update, equivalent to Equation (4), the only change is that the factor $1/t$, where t is the iteration, is replaced by a constant $z \in [0, 1]$. The constant z is a "forgetting factor", with higher values placing less weight on past opponent actions.

Stochastic fictitious play can play mixed strategies and has exploration. It does this by smoothing the best-response function i.e. instead of selecting a strategy with the maximum expected reward, strategies are selected with probabilities proportional to their expected rewards. A common approach is for player i to play strategy σ_i with probability

$$\Pr(\sigma_i) = \frac{e^{u_i(\sigma_i, \sigma_{-i})\lambda^{-1}}}{\sum_{\sigma'_i \in \Sigma_i} e^{u_i(\sigma'_i, \sigma_{-i})\lambda^{-1}}}, \tag{11}$$

where λ is a randomisation parameter. As λ approaches zero, this becomes a regular best-response. A similar approach is the κ-exponential fictitious play algorithm [21].

Various extensions are examined by Ny in [34], who looks at traditional (discrete-time) fictitious play, stochastic (smooth) fictitious play, continuous-time fictitious play, and dynamic fictitious play. Two more extensions are proposed by Smyrnakis and Leslie [39, 40], which can model a changing opponent strategy based on recent observations. The first uses a particle filter algorithm, whilst the second uses a heuristic rule to adaptively update the weights of opponent actions.

4.2 Reinforcement Learning

In this paper, we consider convergence to solution concepts, which reinforcement learning can also achieve. An agent using reinforcement learning adapts its strategy based on its rewards. In a game, this implicitly models opponents since rewards are usually determined by them. One group of reinforcement learning methods include gradient ascent, value or policy iteration, and temporal-difference learning. Singh et al. studied agents using gradient ascent on their expected rewards, specifically an Infinitesimal Gradient Ascent (IGA) algorithm, in two-player, two-action, general-sum, iterated normal-form games [38]. They proved that although the agents' strategies may not always converge, their asymptotic average rewards always do converge to the expected rewards of some Nash equilibrium. Dahl proposed the lagging anchor learning model, which draws a player's strategy towards a weighted average of its earlier strategies to improve this convergence [15]. Bowling and Veloso proposed the Win or Learn Fast (WoLF) principle for varying the learning rate, or step-size in the case of gradient ascent, to improve this convergence [9]. The idea is to learn quickly (larger steps) when losing, and slowly (smaller steps) when winning. They proved that WoLF can cause not just the expected rewards, but also the strategies of the gradient ascent agents to converge to those at a Nash equilibrium in two-player, two-action, iterated general-sum games. Several algorithms have been proposed that are based on WoLF including: WoLF-IGA [9], WoLF-PHC (Policy Hill Climb-

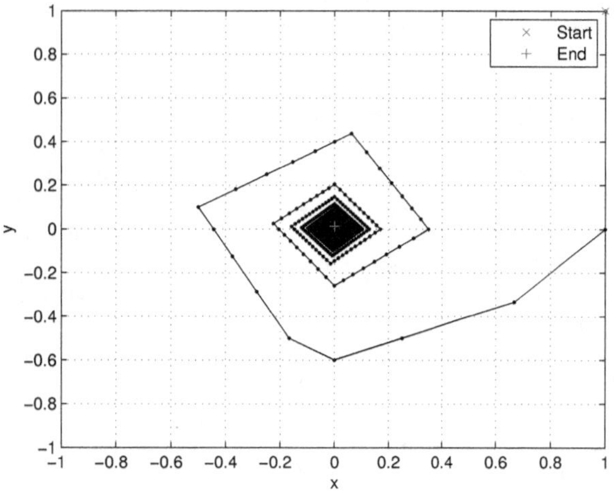

(a) At the start, $x(1) = 1$, $y(1) = 1$, and at the end, $x(10000) = 0.000080$, $y(10000) = 0.014$. They are converging to the Nash equilibrium at the centre, but more slowly as time goes on as the distance between points is decreasing.

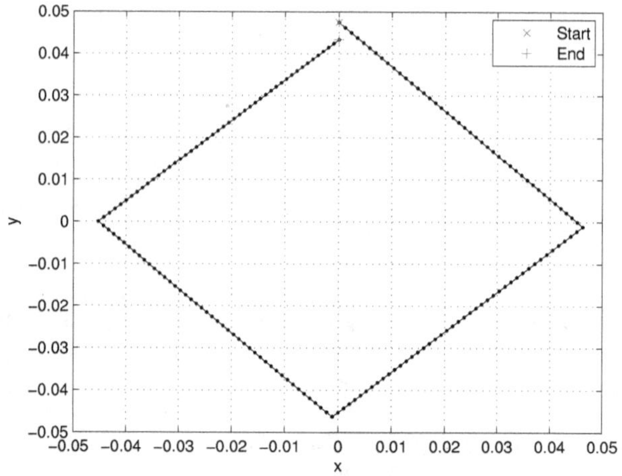

(b) One cycle between iterations 866 and 1040. At the start, $x(866) \approx 0$ but positive, $y(866) = 0.047$, and at the end, $x(1040) \approx 0$ but positive, $y(1040) = 0.043$. Note that at iterations 866 and 1040, x has just switched signs i.e. at iterations 865 and 1039 $x \approx 0$ but negative.

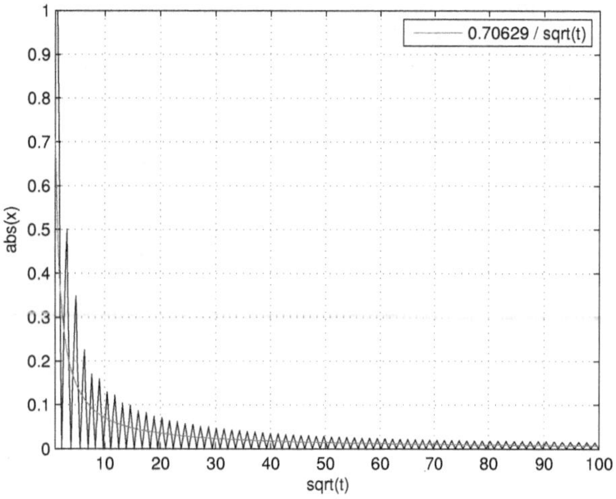

(c) The abs(x) is converging towards 0.

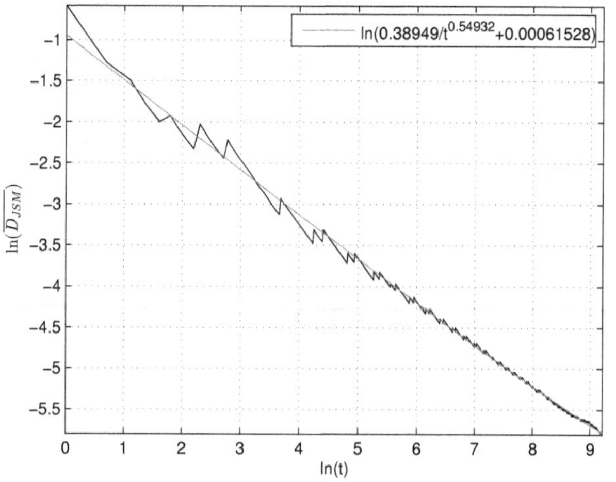

(d) The average Jensen-Shannon divergence metric is converging towards 0. See Section 2.3 for a definition of the average Jensen-Shannon divergence metric.

Figure 1: Expected dynamics of fictitious play in self-play in matching pennies over 10000 iterations. The parameters of the best-fit lines were calculated using MATLAB's Trust-Region-Reflective Least Squares algorithm [1].

ing) [9], (Policy Dynamics based WoLF) PDWoLF-PHC [7], and (Generalised IGA) GIGA-WoLF [8].

Abdallah and Lesser proposed a slightly different approach to WoLF, to speed up learning when the gradient changes direction, and to slow down learning when the gradient has the same direction [2]. They proposed an algorithm called Weighted Policy Learner (WPL) based on this idea, and found that it converges faster to a Nash equilibrium and is less sensitive to parameter tuning compared to WoLF-PHC, PDWoLF-PHC and GIGA-WoLF. Zhang and Lesser proposed augmenting IGA with policy prediction (IGA-PP) by using gradients for anticipated strategies [44]. They proposed a practical version of this algorithm called Policy Gradient Ascent with Approximate Policy Prediction (PGA-APP), and found that it converges to a Nash equilibrium more quickly and in more situations than WoLF-PHC, WPL, and GIGA-WoLF. A shared feature between WoLF-PHC, GIGA-WoLF, PDWoLF-PHC, WPL, and PGA-APP is that they use Q-Learning [42] to estimate their rewards. More recently, Awheda and Schwartz have proposed using the Exponential Moving Average (EMA) mechanism to update a Q-Learning agent's policy, and have empirically shown that it converges to a Nash equilibrium in more situations than WoLF-PHC, GIGA-WoLF, WPL, and PGA-APP [6].

Adversarial bandits are a second group of reinforcement learning methods that learn using regrets, which are based on rewards. In an adversarial multi-armed bandit problem, at each time step, an adversary sets a reward for each one of k arms, the player selects an arm, and gets its reward. The player's goal is to maximise its rewards over all time steps. This problem is like learning to play in an iterated normal-form game but without prior knowledge of your utility function and against an opponent who knows their utility function as well as your strategy at each iteration. Auer et al. proved that, in this adversarial setting, for T plays the best rate that the per-round reward of an algorithm can approach that of the best-arm is $O(1/\sqrt{T})$ [5]. Many algorithms have been proposed to tackle this problem. A popular example is by Auer et al. who proposed the Exploration-Exploitation with Exponential weights (Exp3) algorithm [5]. It selects actions according to a mixture between a uniform distribution (exploration) and a Gibbs distribution based on the empirical importance-weighted rewards of the arms (exploitation). Another example is by Audibert and Bubeck who proposed the Implicitly Normalised Forecaster (INF) algorithm [4]. It assigns a probability to each action as a function of its estimated regret. Different parameters allow it to be reduced to Exp3, or to give an improved regret upper bound compared to Exp3. The adversarial bandit problem uses pessimistic assumptions and although the algorithms that tackle it have bounded regret, and thus guarantees on their rewards, other algorithms not based on these assumptions may get higher rewards. In particular, if we accurately modelled the opponents and played a best-response strategy to these models at each time step, then we would get higher rewards.

Population-based coevolutionary algorithms are a third group of reinforcement learning methods that learn by aggregating outcomes from interactions between evolving entities. They are stochastic search methods that can find or approximate solutions in interactive domains like games. In biology, coevolution is co-adaptation between distinct populations, but in evolutionary computation it is also co-adaptation within a population. An example is the Nash memory mechanism of Ficici and Pollack [19], which like our sequence prediction method, relies on a memory to learn. It can learn a mixed strategy that monotonically approaches a Nash equilibrium strategy. It works by maintaining two sets of pure strategies. The first set has unbounded size and is the support set for a mixed strategy that is secure against its support set (i.e. its expected payoff is zero or positive against each strategy in its support set). The goal is for the mixed strategy to be secure against strategies that an external search heuristic finds. The second set has finite size and acts as a memory containing strategies that may be useful.

5. OUR FICTITIOUS PLAY VARIANTS

We compare fictitious play with two new variants, which do not assume that the opponent uses a stationary strategy. The opponent's strategy is predicted by the first variant using a sequence prediction method, and by the second variant using a change detection method.

5.1 Sequence Prediction

One approach to opponent modelling is to use a Markov model. A Markov model is a stochastic model that assumes that the Markov property holds. This property holds if the probability of the future depends only on the immediate past i.e. $\Pr(b^{t+1}|b^1, b^2, \ldots, b^t) = \Pr(b^{t+1}|b^t)$. When applied to opponent modelling, the assumption is that the probability of an opponent's action, a^{t+1}_{opp}, only depends on information from the previous iteration. This can be expressed as $\Pr(a^{t+1}_{\text{opp}}|I^1, I^2, \ldots, I^t) = \Pr(a^{t+1}_{\text{opp}}|I^t)$, where I^t is the information available to the agent at time t.

A sequence prediction method uses a model that does not assume that the Markov property holds. Instead, it assumes that the probability of the future can, in general, depend on any subset of the past i.e. $\Pr(b^{t+1}|b^1, b^2, \ldots, b^t) = \Pr(b^{t+1}|H)$ where $H \subseteq \{b^1, b^2, \ldots, b^t\}$. When applied to opponent modelling, the assumption is that the probability of an opponent's action, a^{t+1}_{opp}, can depend, in general, on any subset of information from past iterations. This can be expressed as $\Pr(a^{t+1}_{\text{opp}}|H)$ where $H \subseteq \{I^1, I^2, \ldots, I^t\}$.

Sequence prediction methods usually have two components, a short-term memory, and a long-term memory. The short-term memory, S, is an ordered sequence of the previous $k \in \mathbb{Z}$ observations i.e. $S = (b^{t-k+1}, b^{t-k+2}, \ldots, b^t)$ where b^t is the observation at time t. The long-term memory, L, is a map from sequences of observations and observations to counts i.e. $L : (b_1, b_2, \ldots, b_i) \times B \to \mathbb{Z}$, where b_i is the i-th symbol in the sequence, $0 \le i \le k$, and B is the set of values an observation can take. These mappings can be used to form conditional probability distributions such that the probability of an observation, b, given a sequence of observations, S', is the count of that observation given that sequence, $L(S', b)$, divided by the sum of the counts of any observation given that sequence i.e. $\Pr(b|S') = L(S', b)/\sum_{b' \in B} L(S', b')$.

5.1.1 *Entropy Learned Pruned Hypothesis space*

We use the Entropy Learned Pruned Hypothesis space sequence prediction method proposed by Jensen et al. [26]. It works as shown in Algorithm 1.

Here, the Shannon entropy of P, $H(P)$, is defined as

$$H(P) = -\sum_i P(i) \ln P(i). \quad (12)$$

Algorithm 1 Entropy Learned Pruned Hypothesis Space

Require: Short-term memory size $k \in \mathbb{Z}$, entropy threshold
$(0 \leq H_l \leq 1) \in \mathbb{R}$, and a set of possible observations B

1: Initialise short and long term memories $S \leftarrow (), L \leftarrow \{\}$
2: **function** OBSERVE(an observation b)
3:     Get set of all subsequences of S, $\mathcal{P}(S) \leftarrow \{(),$
$(S(1)), \ldots, (S(|S|)), (S(1), S(2)), \ldots, (S(1), S(|S|)),$
$\ldots, (S(1), S(2), \ldots, S(|S|))\}$
4:     **for all** $S' \in \mathcal{P}(S)$ **do**
5:         **if** $(S', b) \notin L$ **then**
6:             Initialise b count for S', $L(S', b) \leftarrow 0$
7:         **end if**
8:         Increment b count for S', $L(S', b) \leftarrow L(S', b) + 1$
9:     **end for**
10:    **if** $\overline{H(L(S'))} > H_l$ **then**   ▷ High entropy
11:        Remove counts for S', $L \setminus (S', b')$ for all $b' \in B$
12:    **end if**
13:    Add b to end of S, $S \leftarrow (S, b)$
14:    **if** $|S| > k$ **then**
15:        Remove start of S, $S \leftarrow (S(2), \ldots, S(k+1))$
16:    **end if**
17: **end function**
18: **function** PREDICT
19:    Get set of all subsequences of S, $\mathcal{P}(S)$
20:    $S'' \leftarrow \arg\min_{S' \in \mathcal{P}(S)} \overline{H_{\mathrm{rel}}}(L(S'))$ ▷ Low entropy
21:    **return** $\Pr(b|S'') = \frac{L(S'', b)}{\sum_{b' \in B} L(S'', b')}$ for all $b \in B$
22: **end function**

The reliable Shannon entropy of P is calculated by altering the underlying counts that P is assumed to be based on. Given $P(i) = \frac{c(i)}{\sum_i c(i)}$, where $c(i)$ is the count of i, a single count is added for an unknown and new category. The reliable Shannon entropy of P, $H_{\mathrm{rel}}(P)$, is then defined as

$$H_{\mathrm{rel}}(P) = - \frac{1}{\sum_i c(i) + 1} \ln \frac{1}{\sum_i c(i) + 1}$$
$$- \sum_i \frac{c(i)}{\sum_j c(j) + 1} \ln \frac{c(i)}{\sum_j c(j) + 1}. \quad (13)$$

The (reliable) Shannon entropy of P has a minimum value of 0 and a maximum value of $\ln(m)$, where m is the number of categories in P. Thus, it can be normalised, the normalised (reliable) Shannon entropy, $\overline{H_{[\mathrm{rel}]}}(P)$, is defined as

$$\overline{H_{[\mathrm{rel}]}}(P) = \frac{1}{\ln(m)} H_{[\mathrm{rel}]}(P). \quad (14)$$

5.2 Change Detection

A change detection method observes a sequence of observations and attempts to identify abrupt changes in the parameters of the underlying probability distribution describing those observations. It may consider if a single change has occurred, or if several changes have occurred, and may try to identify when any change(s) occurred. Any change detection method must trade-off between three metrics: false positive rate, false negative rate, and detection delay. When applied to opponent modelling, the assumption is that the underlying probability distributions describing the opponent's strategy are changing abruptly. The change detection method would then infer when the most recent changes have occurred. Observations prior to the times of these inferred

changes can then be given lower weights or discarded when predicting the new distributions.

5.2.1 Bayesian Online Changepoint Detection

We use the Bayesian online changepoint detection method proposed by Fearnhead and Liu [17] as well as by Adams and MacKay [3]. This method allows you to specify a model for the distribution and so we model the opponent's strategy as a categorical distribution using a Dirichlet conjugate prior. It works by calculating a posterior distribution over the runlength, where the runlength is the number of steps since the distribution last changed, and then using it to estimate the sample distribution [17, 3]. It assumes that the sample distribution, conditioned on a particular runlength, can be computed. This allows the marginal sample distribution to be calculated by integrating over its posterior distribution conditioned on the current runlength as follows

$$\Pr(x_{t+1}|x_{1:t}) = \sum_{r_t} \Pr(x_{t+1}|r_t, x_{1:t}) \Pr(r_t|x_{1:t}). \quad (15)$$

Here, r_t is the runlength at time t, x_t is the sample at time t, and $x_{i:j}$ are the samples from time i to time j inclusive. To predict the last changepoint optimally, this method considers all possible runlengths and weights them by their probabilities given the samples. The authors show that exact inference on the runlength can be done using a message passing algorithm. The inference procedure is as follows

$$\Pr(r_t|x_{1:t}) = \frac{\Pr(r_t, x_{1:t})}{\Pr(x_{1:t})} = \frac{\sum_{r_{t-1}} \Pr(r_t, r_{t-1}, x_{1:t})}{\Pr(x_{1:t})}$$
$$= \frac{\sum_{r_{t-1}} \Pr(r_t, x_t|r_{t-1}, x_{1:t-1}) \Pr(r_{t-1}, x_{1:t-1})}{\Pr(x_{1:t})}$$
$$= \frac{\sum_{r_{t-1}} \Pr(r_t|r_{t-1}) \Pr(x_t|r_{t-1}, x_{1:t-1}) \Pr(r_{t-1}, x_{1:t-1})}{\Pr(x_{1:t})}.$$

Note that the sample distribution, $\Pr(x_t|r_{t-1}, x_{1:t-1})$, is determined by the most recent data. The derivation just applies the laws or rules of probability (conditional probability and joint probability). The last line assumes that the runlength is independent of the previous samples and only depends on the previous runlength i.e. $\Pr(r_t|r_{t-1}, x_{1:t-1}) = \Pr(r_t|r_{t-1})$. This is a message passing algorithm as r_t can only take values based on r_{t-1}. Specifically, either $r_t = 0$ if a change occurs, or $r_t = r_{t-1} + 1$ if a change does not occur.

The probability $\Pr(r_t|r_{t-1})$ is given by a switching rate or "hazard" function $h(t)$ for both values. A simple approach is to assume that the hazard function returns a constant probability for a change $\Pr(r_t = 0|r_{t-1}) = h(0) = \gamma$. The probability of no change would then be one minus this i.e. $\Pr(r_t = r_{t-1} + 1|r_{t-1}) = h(r_{t-1} + 1) = 1 - \gamma$. The hazard function would return zero for all other values of t. Setting its value is a trade-off; high values decrease the detection delay, but increase the number of false positives/negatives. Conversely, low values increase detection delay, but decrease the number of false positives/negatives. Methods have been proposed by Wilson et al. [43] as well as by Turner et al. [41] to learn the hazard function from the data. The former can learn a hazard function that is piecewise constant using a hierarchical generative model, whilst the latter can learn any parametric hazard function via gradient descent.

The space complexity grows linearly with the number of samples because there is a possible runlength for each sample. The time complexity also grows linearly because each possible runlength requires an update. To place an upper limit on the number of possible runlengths, and in turn the memory requirements, a particle filter is used as suggested by Fearnhead and Liu [17], which maintains a finite sample of the runlength distribution. A particle filter is a Monte-Carlo method that estimates a sequential Bayesian model. Each particle represents a point in the distribution with its weight being its approximate probability. If the number of particles grows too large, then resampling takes place where some particles are thrown away and the weights of the remaining particles are updated. The resampling scheme used is called Stratified Optimal Resampling (SOR). Under this scheme the reweighting ensures that the expected values of the new weights are equal to the original weights. It is optimal in that the expected squared difference between the original and the new weights is minimised. The SOR procedure is shown in Section 3.2 of Fearnhead and Liu [17].

6. RESULTS

In the following experiments, we compare the convergence in self-play of fictitious play to our variants of it. Specifically, since each of the algorithms play pure strategies, we look at the convergence of their empirical distributions of plays (i.e. their empirical Nash convergence). For each game, we measure the distances of their empirical distributions of plays from the unique mixed strategy Nash equilibrium. Distances are measured using the Jensen-Shannon divergence metric as defined in Section 2.3. From these distances, we calculate estimates of their empirical Nash convergence speeds.

The first experiment looks again at matching pennies. The second experiment looks at various two-player, two-action, normal-form games derived from generalised matching pennies. The third experiment looks at Shapley's game. Finally, the fourth experiment looks at Jordan's game. In all of the experiments, the sequence prediction method we use is Entropy Learned Pruned Hypothesis Space (ELPH) by Jensen et al. [26] with a short-term memory size of $k = 1$ and an entropy threshold of $H_l = 1$, whilst the change detection method we use is Bayesian online change detection using a categorical model (BayesCPD-C) with a switching rate or hazard function of $h(0) = 1 \times 10^{-4}$ and 100 particles for Stratified Optimal Resampling (SOR).

In the second, third, and fourth experiments we also test a simple hybrid algorithm that combines sequence prediction with fictitious play to try to improve its empirical Nash convergence. It works by playing a best-response strategy to the distribution predicted by sequence prediction if a category in that distribution has a probability greater than some threshold, P_l, where in these experiments $P_l = 0.95$, otherwise it plays a best-response strategy to the distribution predicted by fictitious play.

6.1 Normal-form Games

6.1.1 Matching Pennies

Matching pennies is a two-player, two-action, zero-sum, normal-form game. Each player's actions are heads or tails. Player one wants to match the coin face of player two, and player two wants to mismatch the coin face of player one. There is a unique mixed strategy Nash equilibrium, which is for each player to play each of its actions with equal probability of 1/2. Table 1 shows its rewards.

Table 1: Matching pennies rewards.

	H	T
H	1,-1	-1,1
T	-1,1	1,-1

6.1.2 Generalised Matching Pennies

We create a variety of two-player, two-action, normal-form games derived from generalised matching pennies. Most are general-sum, and some are zero-sum. In these games, a player's strategy has one parameter, which is the probability of it playing its first action. Let these probabilities be p and q for the row and column players respectively. For each of these games, the rewards are set to those shown in Table 2. This creates a game with a single mixed strategy Nash equilibrium at $(p = p*, q = q*)$, where we can choose $p*$ and $q*$. This is proven in Appendix C. If we set $p* = q*$, then the game is zero-sum, otherwise it is general-sum.

Table 2: Rewards for a two-player, two-action, normal-form game with a Nash equilibrium at $(p*, q*)$, where $p*$ and $q*$ are the row player's and the column player's Nash equilibrium probabilities of playing their first actions respectively.

	C_1	C_2
R_1	$\frac{2}{q*}$ - 3,-$\frac{2}{p*} + 3$	-1,1
R_2	-1,1	1,-1

6.1.3 Shapley's Game

Shapley's game [37] is a two-player, three-action, general-sum, normal-form game. It is the same as rock-paper-scissors, which is a zero-sum game, but negative rewards are replaced with zero rewards, which turns it into a general-sum game. The unique mixed strategy Nash equilibrium is the same as in rock-paper-scissors, i.e. for each player to play each of its actions with equal probability of 1/3. Shapley showed it as an example of where the empirical distributions of plays of two fictitious players' fail to converge to the Nash equilibrium in self-play [37]. Table 3 shows its rewards.

Table 3: Shapley's game rewards.

	R	P	S
R	0,0	0,1	1,0
P	1,0	0,0	0,1
S	0,1	1,0	0,0

6.1.4 Jordan's Game

Jordan's game [27] is a three-player, two-action, general-sum, normal-form game. It extends matching pennies to include a third player. Each player can select heads or tails. Player one wants to match the coin face of player two, player two wants to match the coin face of player three, and player three wants to mismatch the coin face of player one. The unique mixed strategy Nash equilibrium is for each player to play each of its actions with equal probability of 1/2. Table 4 shows its rewards.

Table 4: Jordan's game rewards. Player 1 chooses the outer row, player 2 chooses the column, and player 3 chooses the inner row.

		H	T
H	H	1,1,-1	-1,-1,-1
	T	1,-1,1	-1,1,1
T	H	-1,1,1	1,-1,1
	T	-1,-1,-1	1,1,-1

6.2 Observations

6.2.1 Matching Pennies

The results for sequence prediction and change detection in matching pennies are shown in Figure 2. They show that the empirical Nash convergence of each method is faster compared to fictitious play in Figure 1. Specifically, comparing their average Jensen-Shannon divergence metrics, each method is converging nearly optimally like $1/t$, whereas fictitious play is converging like $1/\sqrt{t}$. Similarly to fictitious play, their agents' empirical distributions of plays cycle around the Nash equilibrium to some degree, with successive cycles getting smaller. However, the cycles of these methods get smaller more quickly. Change detection, like fictitious play, has cycles that get consistently closer to the Nash equilibrium whereas sequence prediction has more irregular cycles.

6.2.2 Generalised Matching Pennies

The results for a variety of two-player, two-action, normal-form games derived from generalised matching pennies are shown in Figure 3. They show that fictitious play has empirical Nash convergence in all of the games, which is expected theoretically. This is not the case for sequence prediction, which does not have empirical Nash convergence in most cases. In fact, the results for sequence prediction in matching pennies seem to be more of an exception rather than the rule. It seems to converge further away from a Nash equilibrium when at that Nash equilibrium at least one player has a strategy with a large magnitude. Conversely change detection has empirical Nash convergence in almost all cases. The handful of cases where it does not converge are where the Nash equilibrium is for one player to be almost indifferent between its actions, and the other player to be almost certain of its actions. The hybrid algorithm, sequence prediction and fictitious play, improves on sequence prediction by having empirical Nash convergence in more cases. The cases where it does not are where at the Nash equilibrium at least one player has a strategy with a large magnitude.

The results also show estimates for the mean empirical convergence rate, $\overline{b}$, and the mean asymptotic convergence distance from the Nash equilibria, $\overline{c}$, for each method. These estimates are calculated by fitting the equation $\overline{D_{JSM}} = a/t^b + c$ to the results of each game and finding the mean b and c parameters. For fictitious play, $\overline{b} = 0.55$, which corresponds to an empirical convergence rate like $1/\sqrt{t}$. Whereas for sequence prediction, change detection, and sequence prediction with fictitious play, $\overline{b} = 0.93$, $\overline{b} = 0.98$, and $\overline{b} = 0.95$ respectively, which corresponds to a nearly optimal empirical convergence rate like $1/t$. Also for both fictitious play and change detection, $\overline{c} = 0.00$, so they empirically converge to the Nash equilibria on average. Whereas for sequence prediction and sequence prediction with fictitious play, $\overline{c} = 0.09$ and $\overline{c} = 0.01$, so they sometimes empirically converge away from the Nash equilibria.

6.2.3 Shapley's Game

The results for Shapley's game are shown in Figure 4. They show that fictitious play does not have empirical Nash convergence. Its average Jensen-Shannon divergence metric decreases slightly but eventually oscillates around a value away from zero with constant amplitude and an ever increasing period. Change detection follows a similar pattern, except its oscillations decrease in amplitude until they eventually fade out, and its value is much closer to zero such that it essentially has empirical Nash convergence. Sequence prediction with or without fictitious play both have empirical Nash convergence at a nearly optimal rate like $1/t$.

6.2.4 Jordan's Game

The results for Jordan's game are shown in Figure 5. They show that fictitious play does not have empirical Nash convergence. Its average Jensen-Shannon divergence metric oscillates around a value away from zero with constant amplitude and an ever increasing period. But sequence prediction with or without fictitious play as well as change detection have empirical Nash convergence, each at a nearly optimal rate like $1/t$.

7. CONCLUSIONS

We have proposed two new variants of fictitious play, which assume that the opponents have dynamic strategies. The first variant uses sequence prediction to predict an opponent's strategy based on different contexts of its most recent actions and its empirical distributions of plays that have occurred after these contexts. The second variant uses change detection to infer a distribution over possible changepoints in an opponent's strategy and uses this distribution to predict its strategy. Each variant, like fictitious play, plays a pure best-response strategy to its predicted opponent strategies. We experimentally compared the convergence in self-play of the empirical distributions of plays of fictitious play and our variants to mixed strategy Nash equilibria. The results show that our variants converge faster than fictitious play. However, in generalised matching pennies games, whilst fictitious play and change detection always converge, sequence prediction does not converge in most cases. Also in these games, combining sequence prediction with fictitious play decreases the estimate of its mean convergence distance from Nash equilibria, and increases the estimate of its mean convergence speed. The results also show that, unlike in fictitious play, our variants and the hybrid algorithm converge to the Nash equilibria in Shapley's and Jordan's games, which is known to be difficult. Overall, we find that whilst sequence prediction is somewhat unstable, change detection has better self-play performance than fictitious play in these games.

Future work will investigate why our variants converge and how our ideas and results generalise beyond the examined games. We suspect that convergence mainly depends on the amount of history used, if too low, then the agent may have insufficient resolution to predict accurately. For example, using a sliding window of size one, it would always appear as if the opponent will repeat their last action. We also suspect that our ideas and results will generalise to similar normal-form games and situations where fictitious play has been successful like in limit Texas hold'em [16, 18].

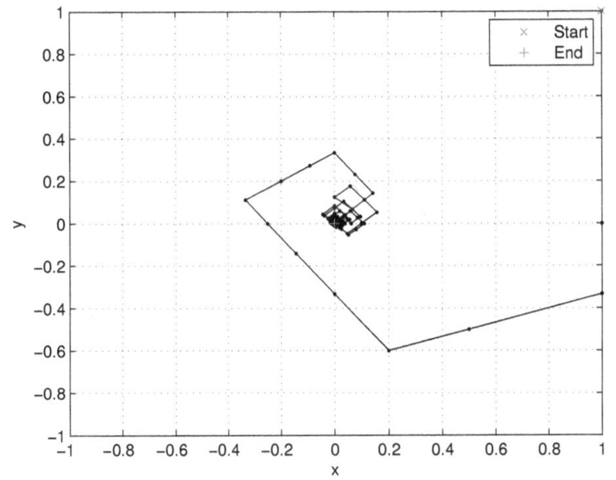

(a) Sequence prediction. At the start, $x = 1$, $y = 1$, and at the end, $x = 0$, $y = 0$. They are converging towards the Nash equilibrium at the centre.

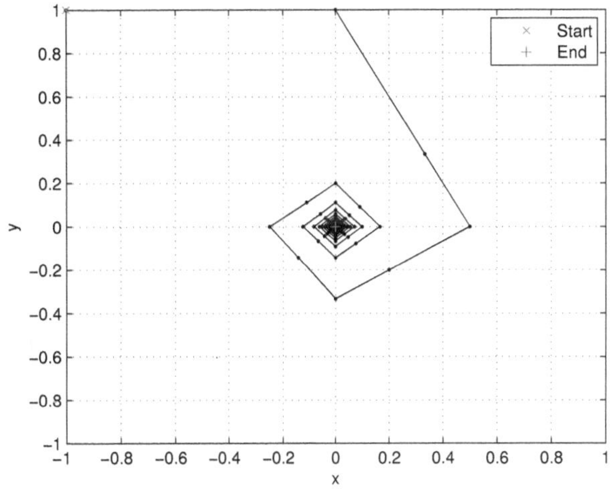

(b) Change detection. At the start, $x = -1$, $y = 1$, and at the end, $x = 0$, $y = 0$. They are converging towards the Nash equilibrium at the centre.

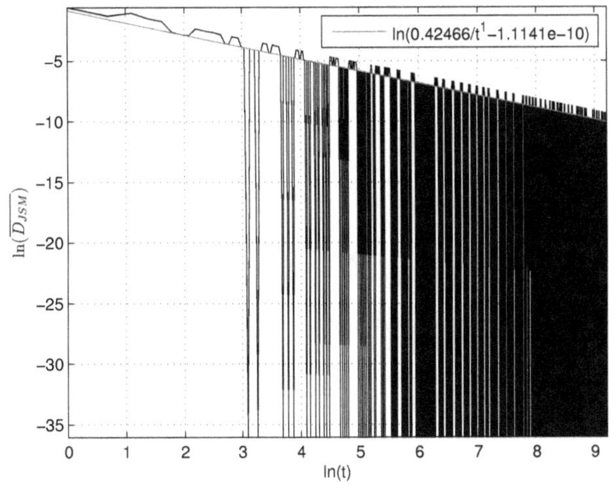

(c) Sequence prediction. The average Jensen-Shannon divergence metric is converging towards 0.

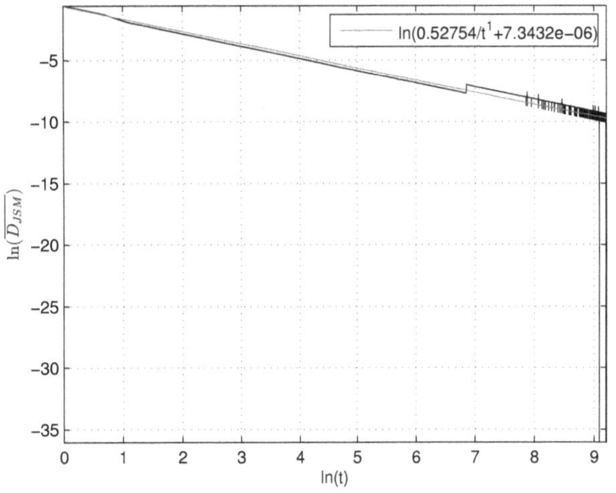

(d) Change detection. The average Jensen-Shannon divergence metric is converging towards 0.

Figure 2: Sequence prediction and change detection each in self-play in matching pennies over 10000 iterations. The parameters of the best-fit lines were calculated using MATLAB's Trust-Region-Reflective Least Squares algorithm [1].

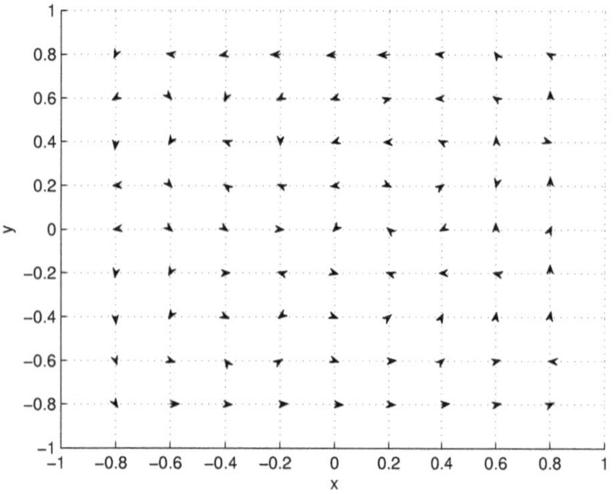

(a) Fictitious play, $\overline{b} = 0.5484$, $\overline{c} = 0.0004$. Each average Jensen-Shannon divergence metric is converging towards 0.

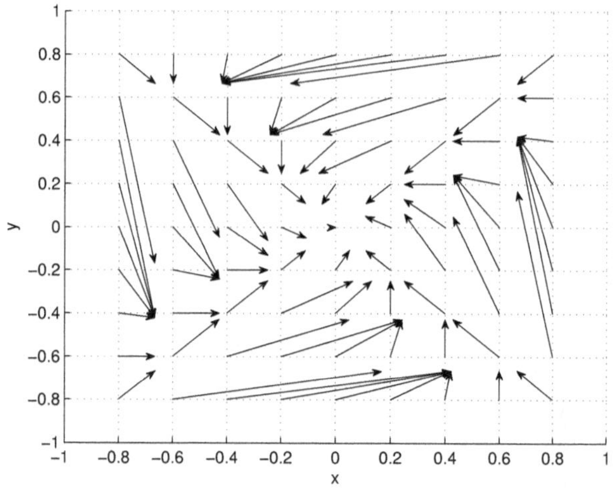

(b) Sequence prediction, $\overline{b} = 0.9307$, $\overline{c} = 0.0923$. Each average Jensen-Shannon divergence metric is converging towards $c \geq 0$, where it tends to be larger if at least one player has a Nash equilibrium strategy with a large magnitude.

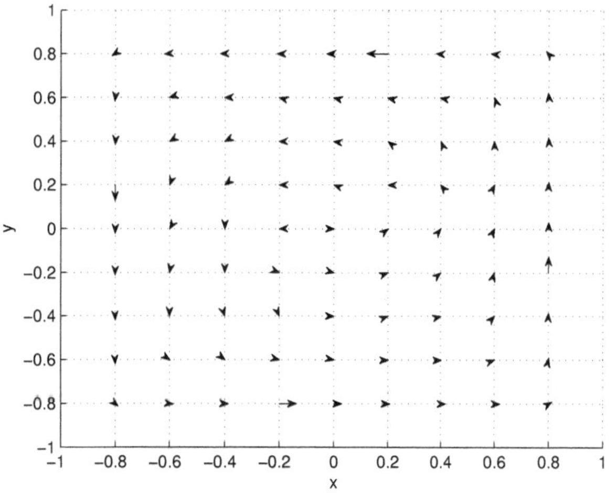

(c) Change detection, $\overline{b} = 0.9829$, $\overline{c} = 0.0010$. Almost all average Jensen-Shannon divergence metrics are converging towards 0. Only a few are converging towards $c > 0$ where one player has a Nash equilibrium strategy near 0 and the other player does not.

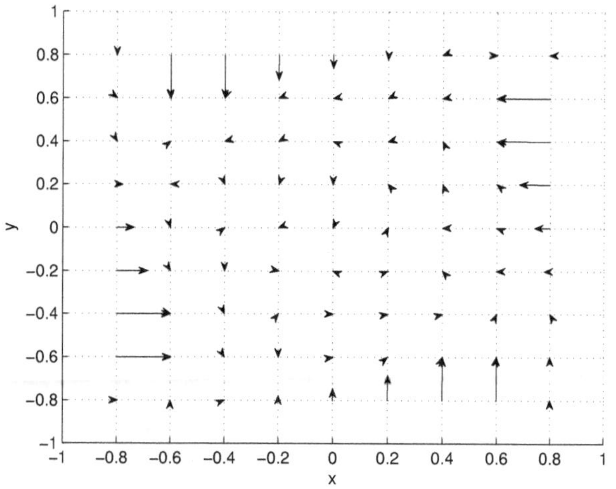

(d) Sequence prediction and fictitious play, $\overline{b} = 0.9546$, $\overline{c} = 0.0088$. Most average Jensen-Shannon divergence metrics are converging towards 0. Some are converging towards $c > 0$ where at least one player has a Nash equilibrium strategy with a large magnitude.

Figure 3: Empirical Nash convergence of various methods in self-play in two-player, two-action, normal-form games with Nash equilibria at positions $\{(x*, y*) | x* \in \{-0.8, -0.6, \dots, 0.8\}\}, y* \in \{-0.8, -0.6, \dots, 0.8\}\}$. Each arrow points from a Nash equilibrium position to the position of the method's empirical distribution of plays after 10000 iterations. An estimate for the mean empirical Nash convergence rate, $\overline{b}$, is shown for each method. This is calculated by fitting the equation $\ln(\overline{D_{JSM}}) = \ln(a/t^b + c)$ to the results of each game and taking the average of the b values. The parameters of the best-fit lines were calculated using MATLAB's Trust-Region-Reflective Least Squares algorithm [1].

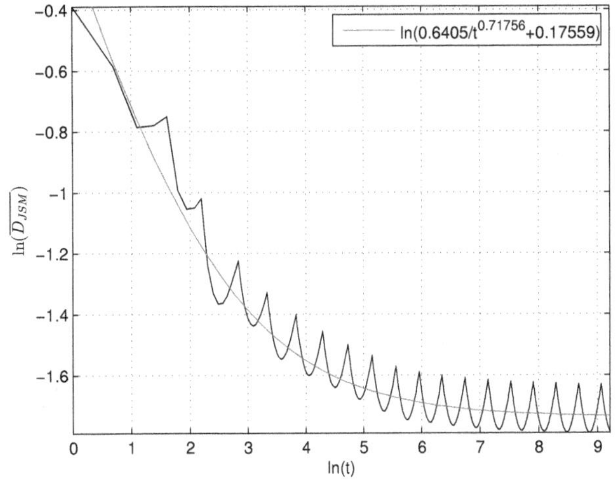

(a) Fictitious play. The average Jensen-Shannon divergence metric is oscillating around a value away from 0.

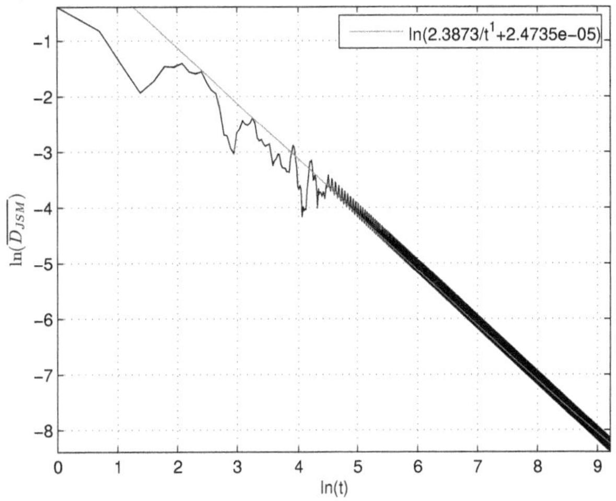

(b) Sequence prediction. The average Jensen-Shannon divergence metric is converging towards 0.

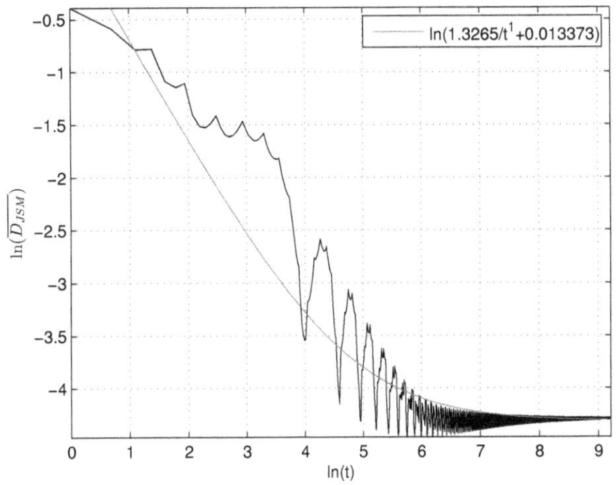

(c) Change detection. The average Jensen-Shannon divergence metric is converging towards a value near 0.

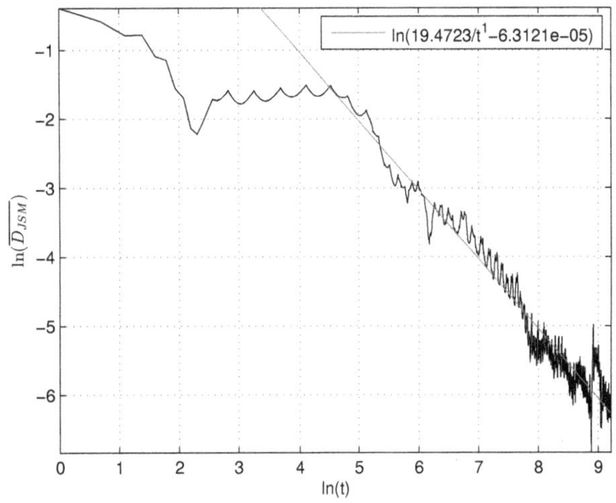

(d) Sequence prediction and fictitious play. The average Jensen-Shannon divergence metric appears to be converging towards 0.

Figure 4: Empirical Nash convergence of various methods in self-play in Shapley's game over 10000 iterations. The parameters of the best-fit lines were calculated using MATLAB's Trust-Region-Reflective Least Squares algorithm [1].

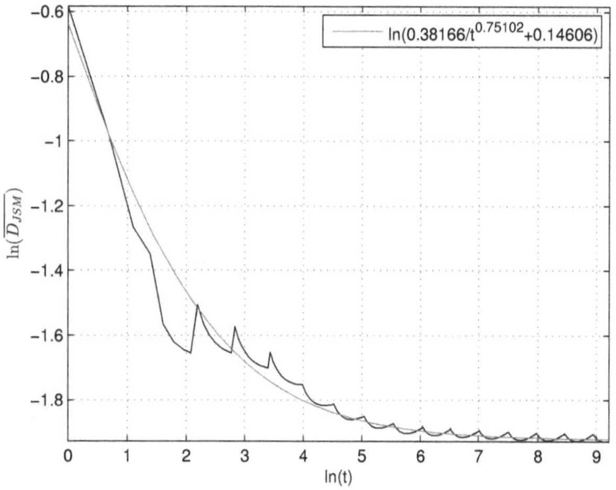

(a) Fictitious play. The average Jensen-Shannon divergence metric is oscillating around a value away from 0.

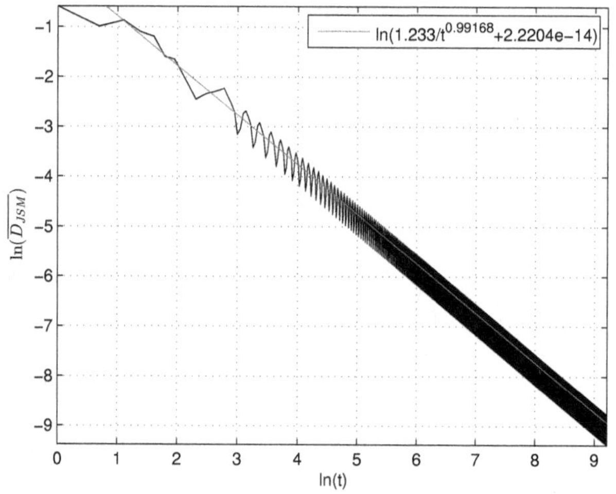

(b) Sequence prediction. The average Jensen-Shannon divergence metric is converging towards 0.

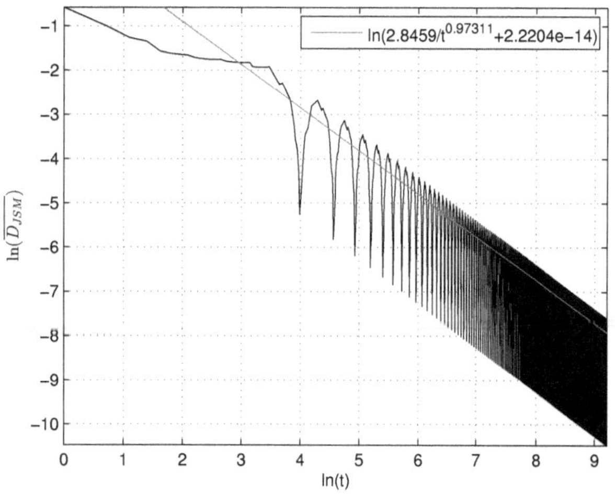

(c) Change detection. The average Jensen-Shannon divergence metric is converging towards 0.

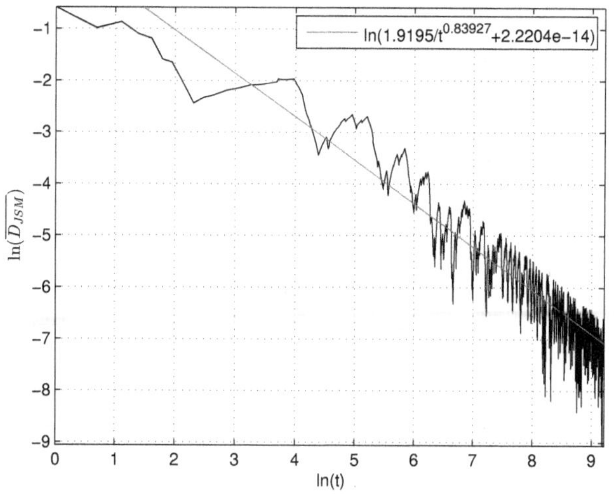

(d) Sequence prediction and fictitious play. The average Jensen-Shannon divergence metric appears to be converging towards 0.

Figure 5: Empirical Nash convergence of various methods in self-play in Jordan's game over 10000 iterations. The parameters of the best-fit lines were calculated using MATLAB's Trust-Region-Reflective Least Squares algorithm [1].

8. ACKNOWLEDGEMENTS

This work was supported by the Engineering and Physical Sciences Research Council [grant number EP/P505631/1] and the University of Manchester.

9. REFERENCES

[1] Least-squares algorithms. `http://bit.ly/1rSLrJY`. Accessed: 13/04/2014.

[2] S. Abdallah and V. R. Lesser. Non-linear dynamics in multiagent reinforcement learning algorithms. In *AAMAS 3*, pages 1321–1324, 2008.

[3] R. P. Adams and D. J. C. MacKay. Bayesian online changepoint detection, 2007.

[4] J.-Y. Audibert and S. Bubeck. Minimax policies for adversarial and stochastic bandits. In *COLT 22*, 2009.

[5] P. Auer, N. Cesa-Bianchi, Y. Freund, and R. E. Schapire. The non-stochastic multi-armed bandit problem. *SICOMP*, 32:48–77, 2002.

[6] M. Awheda and H. Schwartz. Exponential moving average q-learning algorithm. In *IEEE ADPRL*, 2013.

[7] B. Banerjee and J. Peng. Adaptive policy gradient in multiagent learning. In *AAMAS*, 2003.

[8] M. Bowling. Convergence and no-regret in multiagent learning. In *NIPS 17*, 2005.

[9] M. Bowling and M. Veloso. Multiagent learning using a variable learning rate. *AI*, 136:215–250, 2002.

[10] G. W. Brown. *Activity Analysis of Production and Allocation*, chapter Iterative Solutions of Games by Fictitious Play, pages 374–376. Wiley, 1951.

[11] J. M. Butterworth and J. L. Shapiro. Stability of learning dynamics in two-agent, imperfect information games. In *10th ACM SIGEVO workshop*. ACM, 2009.

[12] V. Crawford. Learning the optimal strategy in a zero-sum game. *Econometrica*, 42:885–891, 1974.

[13] V. Crawford. Learning behavior and mixed-strategy nash equilibria. *JEBO*, 6:69–78, 1985.

[14] V. Crawford. Learning and mixed-strategy equilibria in evolutionary games. *JTB*, 140:537–550, 1989.

[15] F. A. Dahl. The lagging anchor algorithm: Reinforcement learning in two-player zero-sum games with imperfect information. *ML*, 49:5–37, 2002.

[16] W. Dudziak. Using fictitious play to find pseudo optimal solutions for full-scale poker. In *ICAI*, 2006.

[17] P. Fearnhead and Z. Liu. On-line inference for multiple change points problems. *JRSS B*, 69:589–605, 2007.

[18] I. Fellows. Pseudo-optimal solutions to texas hold'em poker with improved chance node abstraction. 2010.

[19] S. G. Ficici and J. B. Pollack. A game-theoretic memory mechanism for coevolution. In *GECCO*, 2003.

[20] D. Fudenberg and D. M. Kreps. Learning mixed equilibria. *GEB*, 5:320–367, 1993.

[21] D. Fudenberg and D. K. Levine. Consistency and cautious fictitious play. *JEDC*, 19:1065–1089, 1995.

[22] D. Fudenberg and D. K. Levine. *The Theory of Learning in Games*. The MIT Press, 1998.

[23] T. Galla and J. Farmer. Complex dynamics in learning complicated games. *NAS*, 110(4):1232–1236, 2013.

[24] S. Hahn. The convergence of fictitious play in 3 x 3 games with strategic complementarities. *Economics Letters*, 64(1):57–60, 1999.

[25] J. Hofbauer. Stability for the best response dynamics. Preprint Vienna 1994. Revised Budapest, 1995.

[26] S. Jensen, D. Boley, M. Gini, and P. Schrater. Non-stationary policy learning in 2-player zero sum games. In *AAAI 20*, 2005.

[27] J. S. Jordan. Three problems in learning mixed-strategy nash equilibria. *GEB*, 5:368–386, 1993.

[28] V. Krishna. Learning in games with strategic complementarities. HBS Working Paper 92-073, 1992.

[29] D. S. Leslie. Convergent multiple-timescales reinforcement learning algorithms in normal form games. *AAP*, 13:1231–1251, 2003.

[30] P. Milgrom and J. Roberts. Rationalizability, learning, and equilibrium in games with strategic complementarities. *Econometrica*, 58:1255–1277, 1990.

[31] K. Miyasawa. On the convergence of the learning process in a 2 x 2 non-zero-sum two-person game. Technical report, Princeton University ERP, 1961.

[32] D. Monderer and L. S. Shapley. Fictitious play property for games with identical interests. *JET*, 68(1):258–265, 1996.

[33] J. F. Nash. Equilibrium points in n-person games. In *NAS*, 1950.

[34] J. L. Ny. On some extensions of fictitious play. 2006.

[35] J. Robinson. An iterative method of solving a game. *AOM*, 54:296–301, 1951.

[36] J. B. Sanders, T. Galla, and J. L. Shapiro. Effects of noise on convergent game-learning dynamics. *J. Phys. A*, 45(10):105001, 2012.

[37] L. Shapley. Some topics in two-person games. *Advances in Game Theory*, 3:1–28, 1963.

[38] S. Singh, M. Kearns, and Y. Mansour. Nash convergence of gradient dynamics in general-sum games. In *UAI 16*, 2000.

[39] M. Smyrnakis and D. S. Leslie. Dynamic opponent modelling in fictitious play. *CJ*, 53:1344–1359, 2010.

[40] M. Smyrnakis and D. S. Leslie. Adaptive forgetting factor fictitious play. *CoRR*, abs/1112.2315:1–23, 2011.

[41] R. Turner, Y. Saatci, and C. E. Rasmussen. Adaptive sequential bayesian change point detection. In *NIPS Temporal Segmentation Workshop*, 2009.

[42] C. J. C. H. Watkins. *Learning from delayed rewards*. PhD thesis, Cambridge, 1989.

[43] R. C. Wilson, M. R. Nassar, and J. I. Gold. Bayesian online learning of the hazard rate in change-point problems. *NC*, 22:2452–2476, 2010.

[44] C. Zhang and V. Lesser. Multi-agent learning with policy prediction. In *AAAI 24*, 2010.

APPENDIX

A. FICTITIOUS PLAY EXAMPLE DETAILS

We solve the system for one cycle (e.g. Figure 1b). Each arm of the diamond is a period of time when one agent is playing the correct strategy and the other is playing the incorrect one. At the end of the cycle the system is closer to the origin. The calculation works as follows. One calculates the time to traverse each of the diamond's four arms, and its vertex locations. The calculation is slightly complicated by the first step of each arm, where one strategy is updated by 0 instead of ± 1. The next theorem shows the calculation.

THEOREM 1. *Starting the dynamical system at time t_0 with $y(t_0) = y_0$ and $x(t_0) = 0$, and assuming that $y(t_0)$ is the time average of a series of ± 1 values (so that when it changes sign, it will go through the value 0 exactly), the time taken to traverse the first cycle is*

$$T_1 = 4t_0y_0 + 10, \tag{16}$$

and the value of y at the end of the first cycle is,

$$y(t_0 + T_1) = \frac{t_0y_0 + 4}{t_0(1 + 4y_0) + 10}. \tag{17}$$

PROOF. *A solution to recurrence relations (9) and (10) will take the form,*

$$a_i(t+\tau) = \frac{ta_i(t)}{t+\tau} \pm \begin{cases} \frac{\tau-1}{t+\tau} & \text{if opponent } a_{-i}(t) = 0, \\ \frac{\tau}{t+\tau} & \text{otherwise.} \end{cases} \tag{18}$$

Here a_i is either x or y, a_{-i} is the alternative, and the sign is positive if a_i is increasing or negative if a_i is decreasing. The time period, τ, is between changes of strategy. Traversing an arm of the cycle (or a quarter cycle), starts with $a_i = 0$ and finishes when $a_{-i} = 0$. The time taken, and values of a_i and a_{-i} after this time will be

$$\tau = ta_i + 1, \ (19) \quad a_{-i} = \pm\frac{ta_i + 1}{t + ta_i + 1} \ (20) \quad a_i = 0. \ (21)$$

Here t is the time at the start of the traversal of this arm. To get the properties of the cycle, we just have to iterate this four times starting at time t_0, with $x(t_0) = 0$ and $y(t_0)$ positive, and alternate the roles of x and y. First, subtracting from y and adding to x until $y = 0$ (arm 1), then subtracting from y and x until $x = 0$ (arm 2), then adding to y and subtracting from x until $y = 0$ (arm 3), then adding to y and x until $x = 0$ which completes the cycle. Iterating Equations (19) and (20) four times gives the result. □

To verify the claims in Section 3.3, we use the following.

COROLLARY 1. *The period of the ith cycle is proportional to i, and the time after the ith cycle is $O(i^2)$.*

PROOF. *Define T_i as the period of the ith cycle, t_i as the time after the ith cycle, and y_i as the value of y after the ith cycle. The recurrence relations implied by Equations (16) and (17) are,*

$$T_i = 4t_{i-1}y_{i-1} + 10, \tag{22}$$

$$y(t_{i-1} + T_i) = y_i = \frac{t_{i-1}y_{i-1} + 4}{t_{i-1}(1 + 4y_{i-1}) + 10} \tag{23}$$

Using $t_{i-1} = t_{i-2} + T_{i-1}$ and the value for y_{i-1} from Equation (23) yields the recursion relation

$$T_i = 4(t_{i-2}(1+4y_{i-2})+10)\frac{t_{i-2}y_{i-2} + 4}{t_{i-2}(1 + 4y_{i-2} + 10} = T_{i-1}+16. \tag{24}$$

This is solved as $T_i = T_{i-1} + 16(i-1)$. From an asymptotic perspective, this proves the result. The time after i cycles is

$$t_i = t_0 + \sum_{j=1}^{i} T_j = t_0 + iT_1 + 16\sum_{j=1}^{i-1} j = t_0 + iT_1 + 16\frac{i(i-1)}{2}$$

$$= t_0 + i(T_1 - 8) + 8i^2 \text{ which is } O(i^2). \tag{25}$$

A starting point consistent with our assumptions is $t_0 = 1$, $y_0 = 1$, and $x_0 = 0$. Thus $T_1 = 4t_0y_0 + 10 = 14$, and

$$t_i = t_0 + i(T_1 - 8) + 8i^2 = 1 + 6i + 8i^2. \tag{26}$$

So, the cycle period grows like i, and the time between cycles grows like i^2. □

COROLLARY 2. *The system converges to 0 in inverse proportion to the number of cycles.*

PROOF. *The task is to show that y decreases like $1/i$. We need to solve recursion relation (23). It is helpful to see that t_i from Equation (26) (where $t_0 = 1$, $y_0 = 1$, and $x_0 = 0$) can be factorised as $(1 + 2i)(1 + 4i)$. We solve recursion relation (23) by ansatz, guessing that $y_i = 1/(1 + 2i)$. Due to the factorisation, $y_it_i = 1 + 4i$, which gives*

$$y_{i+1} = \frac{4i + 5}{(1 + 2i)(1 + 4i) + 4(1 + 4i) + 10} = \frac{4i + 5}{8i^2 + 22i + 15}$$
$$= \frac{1}{2i + 3} = \frac{1}{1 + 2(i + 1)} \tag{27}$$

So the ansatz works, and y shrinks per cycle like $\Theta(1/i)$. □

COROLLARY 3. *The system defined by recurrence relations (9) and (10) converges like inverse square-root of time.*

PROOF. *According to Corollary 2, the system gets closer to the fixed point inversely with the number of cycles, and due to Corollary 2, the time to complete i cycles scales like i^2. Thus, in time t^2 the system gets closer to the fixed point by $1/t$, so in time t it gets closer to the fixed point by $1/\sqrt{t}$.* □

B. MAXIMUM CONVERGENCE RATE OF AN EMPIRICAL PROBABILITY

We claim Equation (4) cannot converge faster than $1/t$.

PROOF.

1. For any $\alpha \in \mathcal{A}$, its empirical probability in Equation (4), $\sum_{i=1}^{t}[\![\alpha_i = \alpha]\!]/t$, cannot converge to any probability, $0 \leq p \leq 1$, faster than $S(t) = \text{nint}(tp)/t$ where nint is the nearest integer (or round) function.
2. If $f(t) = D(S(t)||p)$ where D is the divergence, then
   (a) $f(t) \leq 0.5/t$, and
   (b) $f(t) > c/t$ infinitely often where $0 < c < 0.5$.

From point 2a it follows that $f(t) = O(1/t)$, and from point 2b it follows that $\nexists g(t) : g(t) = o(1/t), f(t) = O(g(t))$. □

C. PROOF OF NASH EQUILIBRIUM IN GENERALISED MATCHING PENNIES

We claim that the game in Table 2 has one mixed strategy Nash equilibrium at $(p = p*, q = q*)$.

PROOF. The expected reward to player 1 is $V_1 = pq\left(\frac{2}{q*} - 3\right) - p(1-q) - (1-p)q + (1-p)(1-q)$. The gradient of V_1 with respect to p is $\frac{\partial V_1}{\partial p} = q\left(\frac{2}{q*}\right) - 2$. Thus, if $q = q*$, then $\frac{\partial V_1}{\partial p} = 0$. The expected reward to player 2 is $V_2 = pq\left(-\frac{2}{p*} + 3\right) + p(1-q) + (1-p)q - (1-p)(1-q)$. The gradient of V_2 with respect to q is $\frac{\partial V_2}{\partial q} = p\left(-\frac{2}{p*}\right) + 2$. Thus, if $p = p*$, then $\frac{\partial V_2}{\partial q} = 0$. □

Author Index

www.ingramcontent.com/pod-product-compliance
Lightning Source LLC
LaVergne TN
LVHW060140070326
832902LV00018B/2883